PROFESSIONAL PRACTICE FOR

Interior

Designers

SECOND EDITION

Christine M. Piotrowski, ASID, IBD, IDEC

JOHN WILEY & SONS, INC.

New York   Chichester   Weinheim   Brisbane   Singapore   Toronto

The contents of this book does not constitute legal advice. The information provided is designed to offer information only. By publishing this book, the author and publisher are in no way rendering legal, accounting, or other professional business services and assume no legal responsibility for the purchaser's use of the contents. You are urged to seek the advice of legal counsel, or an accountant when you need legal, tax, or accounting services.

This book is printed on acid-free paper. ⊗

This publication is designed to provide accurate and authoritative information in regard to the subject matter covered. It is sold with the understanding that the publisher is not engaged in rendering professional services. If professional advice or other expert assistance is required, the services of a competent professional person should be sought.

Library of Congress Cataloging-in-Publication Data:

Piotrowski, Christine M., 1947–
     Professional practice for interior designers / Christine M.
Piotrowski. —
         p.   cm.
     Includes bibliographical references and index.
     ISBN 0-471-28597-8
     1. Interior decoration—Practice—United States—Management.
     2. Design services—United States—Marketing.   I. Title.
NK2116.2.P57   1994
729'.068—dc20   94-12116
                                                                          CIP

Printed in the United States of America

10 9 8 7 6 5 4 3 2

For my parents, Martha and Casmer:
I am sorry you are not here to share this with me.

Contents

Preface

The interior design profession has gone through tremendous changes since the first edition of this book was published in 1989. New legal requirements for accessibility affect almost every aspect of interior design. Trade showrooms have opened up to the general public. Licensing and certification have influenced the practice of designers in several states. Profit margins have eroded. Rigorous new questions in the NCIDQ exam challenge designers. Recessionary economics has touched all design firms, forcing them to find more effective management, marketing, and resource planning methods. And, of course, discussions surrounding the unification of the professional organizations have come to fruition in 1994, affecting all designers in one way or another. All of these challenges and changes as well as others have touched students and professionals alike.

Operating any business in the 1900's is a risky venture with the chances of failure very high. Design practices do not fail because the individuals involved are bad designers. They fail because of the owners' lack of business knowledge and skills to maintain the business. Educational preparation continues to focus on concepts, techniques, and the terminology of interior design. Unfortunately, even today, few schools require more than one class in interior design business practices to acquaint students with important business concepts.

I feel it is essential for all students and professionals to have a thorough working knowledge of business practices. Students must have a basic understanding of business practices in order to be more effective professionals in the future. Students need to have an appreciation for business concepts in order to understand why the boss is fretting over such things as the wasting office supplies, trying to find new clients, the awful profit margins on sales, a potential lawsuit over an incorrect furniture order, or employee problems. Professionals must constantly search for ways to become more efficient and effective in the profession. They need to understand what constitutes a contract, their legal responsibilities to the client and the boss, how to better market themselves and their services, and the importance of financial issues. Firm owners and/or managers must be sensitive to all of these issues, but especially accounting and financial management, business planning, employee management, and efficient operational concepts.

The First Edition of this book began after several years of research into design office management and general business practices. That early research revealed a lack of information concerning the complete range of business practices specifically for the professional interior designer. Consequently, I decided to prepare a reference that would be of assistance to the student and the professional in understanding the range of concerns in the establishment and management of an interior design practice. The success of the First Edition has been overwhelming. *Professional Practice for Interior Designers* received the ASID/Fixtures Furniture Joel Polsky Prize in 1990 and has been adopted as a text throughout the country.

Because of the changes and challenges mentioned at the beginning of this preface, the decision was made to revise this book. The review process began by soliciting comments from several educators who had adopted the text. Other comments came from professionals who had used the book as a reference in their business practices. The questions, comments, and discussions I had with my students during twelve years of teaching professional practice were also incorporated. All these suggestions were used a a basis for the revision of the text and figures. Each chapter has been thoroughly reviewed and updated. Numerous new figures and forms have been included to help clarify important points. Changes were made with the goal of creating a comprehensive text concerning interior design business practices for students and professionals.

This book can help provide important insights into and information on interior design professional practice for the student, and practicing professional, or the owner. Students will find that the text is easy to read, full of definitions and examples. Professionals and owners will find a thorough discussion of every aspect of planning and organizing a new practice as well as maintaining an existing small practice. Experienced professionals may find the information about business planning, employee management, marketing, and career choices useful.

You will discover that this book explores many areas that heretofore have been ignored or given cursory attention in references on interior design professional practice. Among these are legal responsibilities, personnel management, employee issues, legal requirements of contracts, business law related to the sale of merchandise, general accounting, financial management, marketing, presentation techniques, and the search for employment. Principles common to the understanding of professional practices such as history of the profession, general project management, fee methods, design contracts, an overview of the professional associations and responsibilities, and licensing have also been retained.

I would like to highlight some of the many additions to the Second Edition. Chapter 1 has been completely updated and includes a review of the Unified Voice efforts, information about the new merged organization, and a section on continuing education classes. New material on the advantages and disadvantages of business ownership, a discussion of financing a business, insurance coverage, employment discrimination, and sexual harassment have all been added to the chapters in Part 2. Additional examples of accounting records and systems, financial ratios, the role of the designer/specifier in pricing products, and sections on seller's and buyer's rights have been included in Part 3. A section on defining the target market, material about how to overcome objections, negotiating, and a new chapter dealing with how to conduct design presentations for both the student and professional have been added to Part 4 of the text.

The chapters in Part 5 on project management and Part 6 on careers have many new sections. These include an overview of the project management process, several new figures dealing with project management, an overview of the changes in trade showroom access, material concerning specification organization, a section covering contract administration, and the addition of a section on post-occupancy evaluations in Part 5. The discussion of career options has been updated and modified with additional material included on how employers review resumes and cover letters. New figures have also been added to Part 6.

There are also numerous additions to the glossary, appendix, and references. There are nearly 300 terms concerning interior design business practices defined in the glossary. An enlarged list of interior design professional associations, allied professional and trade associations, and organizations that can be of help to business owners have been added to the Appendix. Updated references have been moved to the end of each chapter, making it easier for the reader to seek out additional material on specific topics.

The Second Edition of *Professional Practice for Interior Designers* unravels, in a clear, simple manner, some of the complexities of owning, working in, and managing an interior design practice. I hope you will find the information helpful, applicable to your business practice, and thought-provoking.

Acknowledgments

A project of this scope can never be accomplished truly alone. I would like to acknowledge the many people who played important roles in the completion of the manuscript.

I would like gratefully to acknowledge the following individuals for reviewing portions of the manuscript and providing many, excellent suggestions: Jean Wilder; Ken Walters; Kristen Swanson; Lori Cutler, ASID, IBD; David Petroff, IBD; Judith C. Everett; John W. Schabow; Dr. John Durham; and Marena Bennett.

Sincere thanks to the individuals and business organizations that provided much information and the use of their documents: Office Designs; Larry Sneed, Walsh Bros. Office Equipment; Murray Goodman and Barbara Schneider, Goodmans Design-Interiors; Fred Messner, IBD, Phoenix Design One; Betty Upton, Cunninghams Interiors; Jain Malkin, Jain Malkin, Inc.; Tom Williams, AIA, and Karen Payne, Howard Needles Tammen and Bergendoff; Jack Gabus, IBD, Environetics International, Inc.; Elizabeth J. Schroeder and Melanie A. Matus, Perkins and Will; Jan Wynn, ASID, Ball Stalker Co.; Tina Swan, Ambiance; Nancy Green, Herman Miller, Inc.; Robert Bauler, Steelcase, Inc.; and James Chisholm, Transcon Lines.

I would also like to thank the Institute of Business Designers, the American Society of Interior Designers, the National Council for Interior Design Qualification, the American Institute of Architects, and the many publishers who granted permission to reprint information and documents.

Thank you to Christopher C. Everett and Eugene Balzer for photography, Clayton E. Peterson for drawings, and Peter Stephens for production assistance.

Special thanks to Judith C. Everett, Kristen Swanson, Erin Dean, and Dale Hoskins for being able to work willingly under pressure.

Jan Hancock of Knoll International not only went above and beyond the call of duty to obtain important illustrations, but also gave continued encouragement throughout the completion of the manuscript.

To my good friend Barbara Munson for adding her special touch early in the development of the final manuscript—a special thank you.

And finally special thanks for their help to the staff at Van Nostrand Reinhold: Lilly Kaufman, editor; Cynthia A. Zigmund, associate editor; Joy Aquilino, editorial supervisor; and to Kate Scheinman of the Total Book.

It is important to me to acknowledge several people who helped in many different ways with the Second Edition. First, thank you to the educators and professionals who offered suggestions, many of which were incorporated in the text. Thanks to Jack Schabow for once again reviewing the material on taxes and accounting; to the American Society of Interior Designers, Institute of Business Designers, National Council for Interior Design Qualification, Interior Design Educators Council, Construction Specifications Institute, American Institute of Architects, and other professional associations for supplying important information to update Chapter 1; Ken Walters for helping to create new forms; Miles Treaster, Inc., Office Designs, and Interior Associates, Inc. for providing additional working forms.

A special thanks goes out to Dr. Michael Kroelinger, FIBD, for discussing with me in great detail the unification of the professional associations. I also want to thank Amanda Miller, my former editor for getting me started on this revision. And thanks again to everyone at Van Nostrand Reinhold, especially Wendy Lockner and Anthony Calcara.

Finally, I would like to thank all my students over the years at Northern Arizona University. Your suggestions, patience, and encouragement have meant a lot to me through the development of the first and second editions of this book.

PART I

An Introduction to the Profession of Interior Design

Chapter 1

The Profession

To discuss the broad range of topics involved in the professional practice of interior design without discussing the profession itself would be an injustice. But first, we should ask what is a profession? Sociologists define a profession as existing when a specific set of characteristics can be associated with it. According to Abercrombie, they are the following:

1. The use of skills based on theoretical knowledge

2. Education and training in these skills

3. The competence of professionals ensured by examinations

4. A code of conduct to ensure professional integrity

5. Performance of a service that is for the public good

6. A professional association that organizes members[1]

The profession of interior design, as we know it today, is guided by all of these points. But the profession itself, and the professionals associated with it, did not evolve overnight. In fact, it is still evolving.

A professional does not emerge merely as a consequence of learning the technical principles needed in the profession. To become a professional also requires an attitude of dedicated commitment to the work one does and the advancement of the profession. In addition he or she must have some understanding of the history of the profession and the issues important to maintaining the vitality of the profession. Understanding what it takes to organize and maintain an interior design practice follows understanding the roots and contemporary concerns of the profession.

To this end, Chapter 1 will present a short history of the profession. Educational standards, which have become increasingly stringent over the years, are important especially for those readers who are just now considering a career in interior design. A brief discussion of

---

[1] *The Penguin Dictionary of Sociology,* by Nicholas Abercrombie, Stephen Hill, and Bryan S. Turner (Penguin Books, 1984), copyright © Nicholas Abercrombie, Stephen Hill, and Bryan S. Turner, 1984, 168. Reproduced by permission of Penguin Books Ltd.

the major professional associations will help the reader appreciate the breadth of design specialties within the profession. The chapter will also review the qualifying examination established as the benchmark for professional membership and licensing. Finally, the chapter will examine licensing and title registration issues and professional ethics. It must be noted that each of these topics in itself could constitute a book. However, the purpose here is to briefly introduce these topics as a reference about the growth and changes of the interior design profession itself.

History

Interior design is a young profession. The use of the term *interior design* did not appear in general usage until after World War II. Prior to that, the profession was known as *interior decoration*, and even that term was not used in relation to a profession until the turn of the 20th century.

Before the 20th century, interior decoration was the responsibility of architects and artisans such as the Adam brothers, Antonio Gaudi, William Morris, and Michelangelo. No matter what their "profession" in the arts, they clearly served the function of interior decorators. These architects, painters, sculptors, and other artisans were considered artists or craftsmen. Those who designed and produced the fabrics, carpets, and furniture items were considered shopkeepers. Called *ensembliers* or *ateliers* in Europe, the shopkeepers and shops also did not deal with interior decoration as a profession but as suppliers.

It was Elsie deWolfe (1865–1950) who brought the concept of professionalism to interior decoration. Born in New York City and a member of the upper class, deWolfe began her career as a professional interior decorator in 1904, when she was 39. Her first commission, in 1905, was for the design of the Colony Club in New York City. Her use of white and pastels was a decided change from the dark colors popular in the Victorian period. Among deWolfe's clients were such notable figures as Henry C. Frick and Anne Pierpont Morgan. Because of their often wealthy clientele, the term *society decorator* was often associated with the early decorators. DeWolfe also wrote one of the first true books about interior decoration. *The House in Good Taste* (1913) related her philosophy of decoration for homes.

DeWolfe's success inspired other women to enter the profession. It was, after all, one of the few acceptable professions for women at the turn of the century. Formal training was difficult for them to obtain. It was not until 1904 that courses in interior decoration became available. The New York School of Applied and Fine Arts—now known as Parsons School of Design—in New York City was one of the first to offer such courses. Those who could not afford or were unable to avail themselves of formal courses would learn from magazines of the time such as *House Beautiful* or *House and Garden*.

After World War I, postwar prosperity began to trickle down to the middle classes, allowing an increased interest in and employment of the interior decoration professional. Department stores, with their displays of home furnishings, flourished as women had more time to shop. Furniture manufacturing centers grew in such places as Grand Rapids, Michigan, and High Point, North Carolina. At first, most of these manufacturers produced inexpensive imitations of period pieces that remained popular in the United States at that time. By the 1920s, furniture manufacturers were producing finer quality furniture. However, the society decorators were still traveling to Europe to purchase antiques.

In the 1920s, the Art Deco style had an important impact on the interior design of houses and offices. Department stores such as Macy's, Wanamaker's, and Marshall Fields constructed vignettes[2] to display the new style. These efforts did much to popularize the Art

---

[2] *Vignette*, as used in the interior design profession, means a display of furniture and furnishings that is done to simulate an actual room.

Deco style in the United States. Art Deco also revolutionized the interior and exterior design of office buildings and other commercial structures. Most interior design in commercial structures was done by men. Dorothy Draper (1889–1969) is credited as being the first woman interior decorator who specialized in commercial interiors.[3]

By the late 1920s, many local Decorators' Clubs had been started in various parts of the country. Design education strengthened with an increasing number of formal college courses and programs in interior decoration. The profession was becoming more formalized and began to change its image from that of the untrained decorator to that of the trained professional.

It was the economic depression of the 1930s that spurred the formation of the first nationwide professional organization for interior decoration. The Great Depression had a disastrous effect on the ability of the middle class to purchase furniture produced in the United States and Europe. Many furniture manufacturing centers were on the brink of closing. The leading society decorators remained relatively unaffected by the depression since their wealthy clients could still purchase goods. However, most of these decorators were still purchasing from Europe rather than using American-made goods. The leaders of the Grand Rapids manufacturing center conceived an idea to bring the decorators to Grand Rapids. With William R. Moore of Chicago, they put together a conference to organize a national professional organization. The conference was held during July 1931, in Grand Rapids, and speakers such as Frank Lloyd Wright were scheduled in order to entice the decorators to the conference. The manufacturers provided the money—and furnishings—for the decorators to design model room displays. And, of course, the decorators were invited to the various manufacturing plants to see the furniture firsthand.

By the end of the conference, the American Institute of Interior Decorators (AIID) had been founded, with William R. Moore as its first national president. In 1936, the organization moved its headquarters from Chicago to New York and changed its name to the American Institute of Decorators (AID). The early organization established membership requirements based on education and work experience. Over the years, these requirements changed and became more stringent. However, there was still no formal testing for competency.

From the 1930 on, the modernism of the Bauhaus had a great effect on the design of buildings and interiors in the United States. The industrialism of post-World War II also led to new manufacturing techniques that changed furniture and design styles. For example, molded plywood and molded fiberglass designs, such as those by Charles Eames, revolutionized seating design. After World War II, nonresidential design became increasingly important aspect of the profession. Curtain-wall construction, suspended ceilings, changes in construction to allow for vast, open interior spaces in office buildings, the evolution of the giant corporations—all impacted on the role of the designer. The role of the decorator, as established prior to World War II, was especially challenged by those involved in commercial design. More stringent educational opportunities meant the decorators of the post-World War II era would rely on educational preparation rather than just having "good taste" in order to obtain jobs and commissions.

The furniture and furnishings industry, inexorably tied to the interior design profession, forced further changes in the profession. Trade shows, first held at the manufacturing centers and later in the major metropolitan areas at market centers like the Merchandise Mart in Chicago, became a popular way for manufacturers to present their new products to decorators, designers, and other tradespeople.

Changes in the philosophy of the work place created new furniture concepts such as that of the office landscape. Office landscape was first introduced in Germany in the early 1950s by the Quickborner Team. Office landscape, as practiced in Germany, produced offices laid out without walls, utilizing plants, bookcases, and file cabinets as "screens" while creating

---

[3]Tate and Smith 1986, 322.

wide-open floor plans. As companies embraced this planning philosophy, new specialists in space planning, lighting design, acoustics, and so forth, became part of the profession. These new design concepts created tension and arguments over admission and educational requirements for interior designers. A debate even ensued over the terms *decorator* versus *designer*.

In 1957, a group belonging to the New York branch of AID broke off and formed the National Society for Interior Designers (NSID). For many years, deep-seated disagreements over qualifications, testing, and terminology had continued between the two organizations. In 1961, the American Institute of Decorators became the American Institute of Interior Designers (AID). Finally, in 1975, the American Institute of Interior Designers and the National Society for Interior Designers overcame their differences and merged into one national organization, the American Society of Interior Designers (ASID). Today, there are over 20,000 members of ASID.

All through the 1960s, there existed discussions regarding educational training and a testing procedure for qualification. NSID likewise favored licensing to restrict practice to qualified professionals. According to Gueft, the Southern California chapter of AID was fighting for licensing as early as 1951 whereas some chapters of NSID were lobbying for licensing in the 1960s. AID favored creation of a qualifying examination. An examination was devised, and in the 1960s and early 1970s, prospective members of AID had to pass the examination for membership. Because of philosophical differences, NSID designed and utilized its own qualifying exam. It was not until 1974 that the National Council for Interior Design Qualification (NCIDQ) was formed to develop a common examination.

As interest in the profession grew, the numbers of programs in colleges, universities, and professional schools increased, as did the number of faculty involved in education. Since most of these educators considered academics as their full-time occupation, many limited their practice of interior design. Needing an organization to keep abreast of the profession as well as of advances in educational goals, the Interior Design Educators Council (IDEC) was formed in 1968. Today, IDEC publishes the only scholarly journal of the profession, the *Journal of Interior Design Education and Research*.

As concerns about educational programs evolved, AID, NSID, and IDEC worked together to encourage the creation of the Foundation for Interior Design Education Research (FIDER) in 1971 to deal with the accreditation of educational programs. Today FIDER is the agency charged with evaluating interior design education programs and determining those that meet the standards established for formal accreditation. This organization yearly publishes a list of the schools providing accredited undergraduate and graduate Interior Design programs in the United States.

In the late 1960s, a new professional organization, the Institute of Business Designers (IBD) was incorporated to meet the needs of the commercial/contract designer. IBD was conceived in 1963 by members of the National Office Furnishings Association (NOFA) who were concerned about the importance of the interior design service in office furnishings dealerships. Later in 1963, NOFA-d (NOFA designers) was formed as a branch of NOFA. Membership was open to interior designers working for office furnishings dealers, although membership was basically limited to those designers working in Chicago and New York. In 1967, NOFA was renamed NOPA (the National Office Products Association) after merging with stationery and office supply dealers. Meetings began at this time concerning the status of NOPA-d. After discussions and a pledge of assistance from NOPA, NOPA-d became an independent organization in 1969 and was renamed the Institute of Business Designers (IBD). Charles Gelber was elected the first president in 1970. Today, there are over 5000 members of IBD nationwide. The membership remains open to those who work primarily in commercial design.

Many special-interest professional associations such as the International Society of Interior Designers (ISID), and the Institute of Store Planners (ISP) were established in recent decades. Those designers who work in specialized areas such as for the federal government, engage in store planning, work in retail furniture and furnishings merchandising, facility planning, and lighting design, may also find it advantageous to join a specialized association. Several of these professional associations are discussed in a later section of this chapter.

The 1970s and 1980s saw a proliferation of new pressures and responsibilities imposed on the interior design profession. After several tragic fires in public buildings, stringent fire codes were passed to make commercial facilities safer. Today, interior designers must deal with many fire safety issues in the design of commercial interiors. The energy crisis and increased cost of electricity forced designers and suppliers to find new ways to provide satisfactory lighting at low cost. Rapid increases in the size of many businesses as well as the energy crisis created a need for new space-efficient furniture products and space-planning solutions. The mid- to late 1970s saw an explosion of products for open office design. Efforts to license individuals working as interior designers became a reality. In 1982, Alabama passed the first legislation for title registration of interior design. Designers and manufacturers, increasingly concerned with interior environmental and health factors, began the "greening" of interiors whereby environmentally safe or protected products were specified over products designed and manufactured from unhealthy or endangered natural materials. The word "explosion" barely meets the requirement of explaining the emergence of the personal computer in the office and most commercial interiors. While the computer has helped small and big business alike, it also has brought new problems for the designer—glare from overhead lighting, carpel tunnel syndrome from improper equipment placement and seating specification, and a recognition of health problems from poorly designed or specified seating. The passage in 1992 of the Americans with Disabilities Act (ADA) is yet another obligation upon the professional. The recession of the 1990s created pressures from other professions as everyone—suppliers, architects, interior designers, and even the tradespeople with whom designers deal—scrambled to obtain clients and produce revenues. The efforts of several professional associations to consolidate into one unified association came to a conclusion in 1994. The unification process (discussed in a later section) will have a profound affect on the profession of interior design, regardless of the reader's personal opinion of unification.

This section by no means attempts to be a definitive history of the interior design profession. The author leaves that task to other capable authors. Rather, this overview of the history of the profession and influences on the growth of the profession is meant to give readers an appreciation for the roots of the profession called *interior design*. Figure 1–1 summarizes its chronological development.

Interior design has seen many changes in its brief history and will continue to see changes as efforts such as licensing and certification increase and as outside influences continue to affect professional practice. In an earlier 1931 statement, AIID prepared the following definition of a decorator: "A decorator is one who, by training and experience, is qualified to plan, design, and execute interiors and their furnishings and to supervise the various arts and crafts essential to their completion."[4]

Today, ASID and the other major professional associations in the United States and Canada endorse the definition of a professional interior designer prepared by NCIDQ. The official definition has also been endorsed by the International Federation of Interior Architects/Interior Designers (IFI), by the FIDER, and those states in the United States and provinces in Canada with licensing or certification statutes. It has been reproduced in its entirety in the Appendix.

Today's interior design professionals and students are faced with continuing changes in the profession. As members work on projects restricted by legal constraints, licensing issues, educational and qualification concerns, public opinion, and better business practice, the profession will continue to grow and evolve.

---

[4]Gueft, 1980, 8. Reprinted with permission, ASID, copyright © 1988, American Society of Interior Designers.

Chronology	
1904	First real use of term "interior decoration."
	First courses in interior decoration offered at the New York School of Applied and Fine Arts.
1905	Elsie deWolfe obtains her first commission as an interior decorator. She is credited as being the first interior decorator.
1913	Elsie deWolfe publishes the first true book on interior decoration, *The House in Good Taste.*
1920's	Larger marketing effort of home furnishings by department stores.
	Manufacturing centers of home furnishings begin to develop.
	Art Deco period creates greater interest in interior decoration of homes and offices.
	Dorothy Draper credited as being the first woman interior decorator to specialize in commercial interiors.
	Decorator clubs begin forming in larger cities.
	Design education strengthened in many parts of the country.
1931	Grand Rapids furniture show. Meeting to create a national professional organization.
	July. American Institute of Interior Decorators (AIID) founded.
	William R. Moore elected first national President.
1936	AIID name changed to American Institute of Decorators (AID).
1940s	Post- World War II industrialism encouraged new technologies in furniture manufacturing.
	Industrialism produced increased need and importance of nonresidential interior design.
1950s	Development of the Open Landscape planning concept in Germany by the Quickborner Team.
1951	First time a state considers legislation to license interior design.
1957	National Society for Interior Designers (NSID) founded from a splinter group of the New York AID chapter.
1961	AID changed its name to the American Institute of Interior Designers (AID).
1963	National Office Furnishings Association (NOFA) creates NOFA-d (NOFA-designers) a professional group for interior designers working for office furnishings dealers.

Figure 1–1 A chronology of the interior design profession.

Divisions of the Profession

An in-depth discussion of the divisions of the profession and the many career choices within it is presented in Chapter 26. At this time, it would be beneficial to point out that there are two universally accepted divisions of the profession: residential interior design and commercial interior design. *Residential interior design* is concerned with the planning and/or specify-

1967	NOFA and NOFA-d changed to NOPA and NOPA-d, respectively, when NOFA merged with stationary and supplies dealers to form National Office Products Association.
1968	Interior Design Educators Council (IDEC) founded to advance the needs of educators of interior design.
	Introduction of "Action Office," designed by Robert Probst for Herman Miller, Inc. The first true open office furniture product.
1969	Institute of Business Designers (IBD) incorporated. NOPA-d was parent organization.
1970	Charles Gelber elected first national President of IBD.
1973	Foundation for Interior Design Education Research (FIDER) founded. Responsible for reviewing and accrediting undergraduate and graduate interior design programs.
1974	National Council for Interior Design Qualification (NCIDQ) incorporated. Charged with the development and administration of a common qualification examination.
1975	American Society of Interior Designers (ASID) formed from the merger of AID and NSID.
1982	Alabama becomes the first state with title registration legislation for interior design.
1988	First major discussion of the 1995 Hypotheses, the document that began discussion of the unification of the interior design professional associations.
1992	Passage of the Americans With Disabilities Act (ADA) providing accessibility standards for all public buildings.
1994	July. Target date for the emergence of the unified professional organization consisting of members from IBD, ISID, ISP, CFID, and IDEC.

Figure 1–1 Continued

ing of interior materials and products used in private residences. A private residence could be a free-standing home, a condominium, townhouse, mobile home, or apartment. *Commercial interior design*, sometimes called contract interior design because of the predominant use of a contract for services, is concerned with the planning and specifying of interior materials and products used in public and private spaces such as offices, stores, hotels, restaurants, schools, airports, and hospitals.

Educational Preparation

Formal educational preparation in interior design[5] was not available until approximately 1904. Voluntary accreditation of interior design programs was not available until the creation of the Foundation for Interior Design Education Research (FIDER), established in 1971. FIDER is a nonprofit organization recognized by the Council on Post-Secondary Accreditation, the International Federation of Interior Designers, and the U. S. Department of Education for the purpose of establishing and administering voluntary accreditation of postsecondary interior design education in North America.

---

[5]The profession was referred to as *interior decoration* until after World War II.

The traditional roots of interior design education are in the fine arts, home economics (or human ecology as it is often called today), and architecture. Current interior design programs at universities, colleges, community colleges, and professional schools assign interior design academic programs within one of these three areas. In addition, interior design programs are interdisciplinary, drawing from these three academic areas as well as from the supporting areas of business and the liberal arts. Depending on the location of the program, the professional/technical course work will have a slightly different focus.

With the organization of FIDER, educational standards and guidelines were developed to establish the common body of knowledge in interior design. Research studies conducted in the 1980s revealed distinct differences in educational programs throughout the United States and Canada. Programs ranged from two years to as much as seven years. Two-year programs essentially prepare students to enter merchandising and design assistant positions, while longer programs prepare students for entry-level professional positions in interior design businesses and design departments of architectural offices. The common body of knowledge, according to FIDER, is indicated in Figure 1–2.

Currently, there are three program levels for FIDER-accredited interior design education: Preprofessional Assistant Level, First Professional Degree Level, and Postprofessional Master's Level. These degree levels were introduced in 1989 after the revision of FIDER standards.

The Preprofessional Assistant Level of preparation must contain a minimum of 60 semester credit hours including a minimum of 15 hours of liberal arts, sciences, and humanities. This two-year preparation results in an associates degree for those interested in working in interior merchandising as design assistants, estimators, delineators, or the like. Generally, this preparation is insufficient for becoming entry-level professional interior designers.

The First Professional Degree Level of preparation must contain a minimum of 120 semester credit hours including a minimum of 30 hours of liberal arts, sciences, and humanities. The program most commonly results in a bachelor's degree although 3 year programs also exist. The total number of credit hours and their emphasis is up to the institution granting the degree. These programs provide curriculum preparation for professional-level interior designers and is also the common preparation for those seeking a master's degree in interior design.

The Postprofessional Master's Degree Level of preparation is for those designers seeking advanced studies or research work in interior design. Master's degree work commonly requires a minimum of 30 semester credit hours, with actual degree requirements up to the institution. A graduate student's work culminates in a graphic or written thesis, depending on his or her academic focus and the requirements of the institution. FIDER-accredited master's programs generally require the course work of the preprofessional level degree for entry into the graduate program.

Interior design programs may be housed in many different academic areas. Each program has a different emphasis because of the mission of the institution, department, and focus of the faculty. FIDER-accredited programs indicate to the student that the program meets educational guidelines accepted and supported by the profession of interior design. Many other programs exist that are not FIDER-accredited. It is up to the individual student and his or her family to carefully investigate the academic programs of all the institutions (accredited or not) in which the student has an interest. Prospective students should talk to academic advisors, alumni of the program, and design businesses in the area who may have knowledge of the preparation given at a particular school. Students should understand the differences in focus of a program housed in fine arts versus architecture or human ecology. Professional educational training in interior design must provide the student with the theory and skills of the profession as well as provide the general education required in the 21st century. The focus of that training must also meet the interests, abilities, and career goals of the student.

Each interior designer may have unique qualities and possess highly specialized abilities in certain areas but will, in common, hold knowledge of:

* the basic elements of design and composition that form the foundation for creative design, and an awareness of the various media in the visual arts that assist in the understanding of the universality of these fundamentals;

* theories of design, color, proxemics, behavior, visual perception, and spatial composition which lead to an understanding of the interrelationship between beings and the built environment;

* the design process, i.e. programming, conceptualization, problem solving, and evaluation, firmly grounded on a base of anthropometrics, ergonomics, and other human factors;

* space planning, furniture planning and selection, developed in relationship to application to projects including all types of habitation, whether for work or leisure, new or old; for a variety of populations, young and old, disabled, low or high income;

* design attributes of materials, lighting, furniture, textiles, color, etc., viewed in conjunction with physical, sociological, and psychological factors to reflect concern for the aesthetic qualities of the various parts of the built environment;

* the technical aspects of structure and construction, building systems, i.e.. HVAC, lighting, electrical, plumbing, and acoustics, sufficient to enable discourse and cooperation with related disciplines;

* technical aspects of surface and structural materials, soft goods, textiles and detailing of furniture, cabinetry, and interiors;

* the application of laws, building codes, regulations and standards that affect design solutions in order to protect the health, safety, and welfare of the public;

* communication skills, oral, written, and visual for the presentation of design concepts, the production of working drawings, and the conduct of business;

* the history and organization of the profession; the methods and practices of the business of interior design,; and an appreciation of a code of ethics;

* styles of architecture, furniture, textiles, art, and accessories in relation to the economic, social, and religious influences on previous cultures;

* methods necessary to conduct research and analyze the data in order to develop design concepts and solutions on a sound basis.

Foundation for Interior Design Education Reserch. *FIDER Fact Kit,* The Common Body of Knowledge. Document "Common Body of Knowledge" developed collaboratively by professional associations.

Figure 1–2 The FIDER common body of knowledge in interior design.

Professional Associations

At the time this book was being completed, members of the interior design professional associations making up the Unification Task Force—IBD, ISID, ISP, IDEC, and Council of Federal Interior Designers (CFID)—were voting to unify their associations into one new organization (a full discussion of the unification of the professional associations follows this section on professional associations). The April 1994 vote results showed that the vast majority of IBD members voted in favor of unification. Members of ISID and CFID also approved the merger by very high margins. The vote of IDEC was very close, missing the required two-thirds majority by a very small margin. The member vote of ISP was negative, with a very small percentage in favor of unification.

In June 1994, the presidents of IBD, ISID, and CFID signed the final agreement to unify the three organizations into one. Unfortunately, the name of the new organization had not been finalized at the time this book went to press. The author apologizes.

The discussions of the professional associations have been retained to provide the student and the professional a perspective on the organizations that will have likely merged by the time this book becomes reality. An overview of the new organization's structure is presented in the section on the Unification.

An important part of being a professional is to become an active member of a professional association. Interior design professional associations provide members with many tangible and intangible benefits. Some feel the greatest tangible benefit of professional association membership is the privilege to place ASID, IBD, ISID, or other association appellations after a member's name. It is not the primary reason; it is only a part of membership.

- *There is pride in accomplishment.* Pride in having achieved the educational, experience, and testing milestones that indicate the highest level of achievement in one's profession.

- *There is recognition.* Consumers and allied professionals recognize the dedication and credentials of the interior designer affiliated with professional associations. Peer recognition as a member of an association is gratifying to many others.

- *There is interaction with colleagues in design.* Interior design is both a large and a small profession. There are thousands of individuals who are affiliated with the associations, and yet the profession is small enough for many professionals to meet and become friends with colleagues across the country—or across the globe.

- *There are educational opportunities.* It is vital in this age of technology and regulations that designers continually update skills and knowledge in their field. Professional associations help in many ways through chapter meetings, seminars, and workshops, national conferences, and lively discussions of issues and concerns.

- *There are important friendships to be made.* Professional colleagues are competitors at times, but many consider each other as great friends as well. Through association, designers get to know their competitors not only as great designers or good business people but simply as people. Designers are proud of the professional and personal friendships that have been made through association activities.

These are just some of the intangible benefits of membership. The reader may think of others that are just as important to him or her.

Professional associations also provide tangible benefits for members. Some of these have already been mentioned—chapter meetings, educational updating, and national conference activities. There are many others.

- *Association leadership.* Membership offers opportunities to be involved in the growth of the profession by chapter and national office positions.

- *Mailings.* Associations provide mailings to members to keep them informed of the associations' activities as well as of external influences on the profession. Mailings might take the form of member magazines, supplemental newsletters and news bulletins, chapter newsletters, and conference reports.

- *Practice aids.* A number of associations provide sample contracts, business forms, marketing tools, reference books, and other useful aids for members to use in their practice in order to become better professionals.

- *Group insurance.* It is possible for members to take advantage of low group insurance rates for a variety of personal and business insurance needs.

- *Business services.* Discounts and special pricing are available from some associations for car rentals, telephone service, express shipping, and other similar business services.

- *Design competitions.* Professional prestige can be achieved through juried national competitions for projects, research, and writing.

- *Industry liaison.* Members receive technical information from industry suppliers.

Many other tangible benefits might be thought of by the reader.

There is no lack of reasons to become affiliated with an association appropriate to the interior designer interests and needs. The remainder of this section briefly describes the major professional associations. The reader will want to contact the national offices (listed in the Appendix) for membership applications or more specific details about the association.

American Society of Interior Designers (ASID)

The largest of the interior design professional associations is ASID. Its members are engaged in both residential and commercial interior design. The mission of ASID is to "encourage excellence in the practice of interior design, assist its members to professionally serve the public, demonstrate the value of the profession, and work for a favorable environment for the practice of interior design."[6] The ASID provides many membership benefits, including chapter meetings and activities at the local level, a national conference with numerous continuing education classes and seminars, a membership magazine called The *ASID Report,* legislative support for states seeking licensing, and many other programs and activities for the support of the association, its members, and the profession.

There are four membership categories within ASID: professional, allied, industry foundation, and student.

The highest level of membership is *professional.* These members have satisfied rigorous standards of education, work experience, and testing in order to qualify as professional level members. The minimal requirements for professional level membership are: (1) graduation from a recognized four- or five-year design school or college with a major in interior design or a related field, (2) a minimum of two years full-time employment in interior design, and (3) successful completion of the NCIDQ examination or possession of a valid state-issued interior design license. Only professional members may vote in association elections and use the appellation *ASID* after their names and in advertising.

The second level of membership is *allied.* Allied members are most commonly practicing designers, but they may also be educators and allied professionals such as architects and facility planners. Allied members meet the same general membership requirements as for professional membership, but have not as yet satisfactorily completed the NCIDQ exam or possess a state-issued interior design license. Allied members are able to use the appellation *Allied Member ASID* after their names.

Industry foundation (IF) members are those who work for suppliers to the interior design industry. Many representatives of the manufacturers and suppliers, trade showrooms, and market centers become IF members in order to interact with the membership. Industry foundation members have also generously provided financial backing to the profession through

---

[6]ASID, 1993, *Professional Closeup.*

sponsorship of seminars, continuing education classes, chapter activities, and design competitions.

Students enrolled in interior design programs may become *student* members of a chapter at their school or *student corresponding* members if their institution does not have an ASID student chapter. Students receive mailings from the national office as well as many announcements from local professional chapters. Students who are in good standing through graduation may apply for allied membership immediately upon graduation. Student members may use the membership appellation *Student Member, ASID.*

Institute of Business Designers (IBD)

The IBD represents interior designers who specialize in commercial and institutional design. The mission of the Institute of Business Designers is "to unite and advance the profession of commercial interior design. Through Advocacy of ethical standards and through legislative and regulatory activities, the expansion of the influence of our members. Through Education, the leadership and professional development of our members, and the protection of the health, safety, and welfare of the public. Through Networking, a common meeting ground for the exchange of ideas and the development of professional relationships. Through Public Relations, the enhancement of the public's understanding of the value and scope of our members' expertise."[7] The Institute provides many membership benefits, including local chapter meetings and activities, a national conference held in conjunction with the Neocon trade market, a national news magazine called *Perspective*, educational programs, industry liaison, design competitions, and many other programs and activities.

There are five membership categories in IBD: professional, affiliate, allied individual, corporate, and student.

Professional membership is the highest category of membership in IBD. It is reserved for those members whose work experience, educational background, and successful completion of the NCIDQ examination permits them to apply for this membership category. To obtain professional membership level, the member must meet one of these three standards: (1) a minimum of four years of design education plus two years of experience actively engaged full-time in nonresidential interior design; (2) three years of design education plus three years of experience in nonresidential interior design; or (3) active work in the profession of nonresidential design for a minimum of six years plus evidence of knowledge and professionalism in interior design. In addition, professional members must have successfully completed the NCIDQ exam or been certified by the Governing Board for Contract Interior Design Standards. Only professional members hold voting privileges and may use the appellation *IBD* after their names. Starting in 1994, professional members are required to obtain 1.0 continuing education units (CEUs) every two years. CEUs will be discussed in detail later in this chapter.

The second level of membership in IBD is called *affiliate* membership. Affiliate members meet similar requirements to professional members. However, affiliate members have not completed the NCIDQ exam and are required to achieve that success within five years of eligibility for the exam.

The third membership category is called *allied individual* members. These members are individuals who are interested in commercial interior design but do not qualify for professional membership. Allied professionals in architecture and graphic design, and educators who do not qualify as professional members, would fit into this category.

Corporate members are industry members who are interested and supportive of commercial interior design but are not practicing designers. These members include manufacturers, representatives, design centers, and schools.

---

[7]Institute of Business Designers, 1993, *Mission and Goals.*

Student memberships at a national level are available to students enrolled in a recognized design school or college program. Student members of IBD frequently become members of the local chapter in addition to the national student organization. Students who maintain their student membership in good standing through graduation may apply for allied membership immediately upon graduation.

International Society of Interior Designers (ISID)

The International Society of Interior Designers was established in 1979 and has chapters throughout the United States, the United Kingdom, Japan, and Mexico. "ISID takes a leadership role in the development of international design ideas and products for both the interior design industry and the public. ISID believes that excellence in design is the professional responsibility of both the practitioners and the diverse companies who contribute products and services to the interior design industry."[8] This professional association provides many member benefits including newsletters, lectures, seminars, chapter activities, award programs, and many other programs and activities.

There are several membership categories dependent upon the applicant's educational or professional background. *Professional* is the highest category and is for any individual who is engaged in interior design as a profession. Professional members must meet educational and work experience standards similar to those of the ASID and IBD. Specifically, the requirements are for a minimum of six years of education and work experience or eight years of consecutive full-time practical experience in interior design. Professional members are also required to pass the NCIDQ examination. Outside the United States, where the NCIDQ exam is not given, members are exempted from this requirement. Only professional members may vote and only professional members may use the appellation *ISID*. *Associate* members must meet educational and work experience requirements similar to those for professional members, but the associate member would not have completed the NCIDQ exam. Associate members advance to the professional membership level upon completion of the NCIDQ examination. Associate members must use the appellation *Associate ISID* and cannot vote. Professional and associate members must complete 0.5 CEU credit per year to maintain their membership standing.

There are other membership categories: practicing interior designers who have not completed all the requirements of either professional or affiliated memberships; designers who have recently graduated from an interior design program; student memberships; affiliate memberships for those in related professions; educators; and industry resource members.

Interior Design Educators Council (IDEC)

The IDEC is a professional association whose members are individuals actively engaged in the teaching of interior design programs. Many IDEC members are also professional or educator members of AISD, IBD, ISID, and other associations. The purpose of IDEC is "to the advancement of education and research in Interior Design. IDEC fosters exchange of information, improvement of educational standards, and development of the body of knowledge relative to the quality of life and human performance in the interior environment. IDEC concentrates on the establishment and strengthening of lines of communication among educators, practitioners, educational institutions, and other organizations concerned with interior design education."[9] The council provides many member benefits, including an annual conference and regional meetings where speakers, seminars, and workshops are pro-

---

[8]International Society of Interior Designers, 1992, *Membership Information.*
[9]Interior Design Educators Council, 1992, *Membership Brochure.*

vided for the presentation of research and exchange of ideas; publication of the *Journal of Interior Design Education and Research,* a refereed journal, as well as the *IDEC RECORD*—a member newsletter; and many other programs, reference materials, and activities offered to assist members in improving the teaching of interior design.

Full-time interior design educators who also have received appropriate interior design education and have professional work experience may be *Corporate* members, the highest membership level. If a corporate member also practices professionally in interior design, he or she would have to have completed the NCIDQ examination or be a professional member of an association. Members who teach interior design courses but do not qualify for Corporate membership may join as an *Associate* member. Associate members may advance to Corporate membership when they meet the qualifications. Other membership categories exist for individuals who are interested in supporting interior design education and research, but are not qualified to meet the preceding membership criteria. Graduate student membership is available for those enrolled in post-graduate degree programs.

Other Professional Organizations

A few words should be said about other professional organizations with which the interior designer may wish to affiliate.

Interior designers who specialize in the design of retail stores and shopping centers may wish to affiliate with the Institute of Store Planners (ISP). This professional association is a member organization of NCIDQ and requires its members to pass the examination in order to obtain professional membership status.

The Council of Federal Interior Designers (CFID) are designers who work for the federal government. Members design government facilities throughout the United States and overseas. CFID is also a member organization of NCIDQ and requires its members to pass the examination in order to obtain professional membership status.

In Canada, the Interior Designers of Canada (IDC) is the national interior design professional association. There is only one level of membership—professional. IDC requires that members hold professional membership in the provincial association of the province in which the member works and that the member pass the NCIDQ examination.

Some interior designers may be eligible for affiliated membership in the American Institute of Architects (AIA). The AIA is, of course, the professional organization for the professional architect. Interior designers may not be professional members of the AIA unless they meet the qualifications as architects.

International Facility Management Association (IFMA) is a professional association for those actively engaged in corporate facility management and facility planning. There are several membership categories depending on the applicant's actual work experiences in facility management and planning.

There are several other smaller or more specialized professional associations for interior designers or those affiliated with the interior design profession. Complete information regarding qualification and application procedures can be obtained from the national offices listed in the Appendix. The addresses of the national offices of the professional organizations mentioned in this chapter are also listed in the Appendix.

Unification

Unification is a concept of uniting the professional associations into one new association with a unified voice for the interior design profession. Although early discussions began in 1988 no formal meetings occurred until 1989. Since that time, representatives from the ASID, IBD, ISID, ISP, IDC, and IDEC have met to discuss creating one umbrella professional association that could address the needs of all aspects of the interior design profession. This group of organization leaders originally met to discuss the "1995 Hypothesis." The 1995 Hypothesis was first presented in 1984 by Ron Veitch, then president of IDEC, at a meeting of the leaders of the various design associations. The main points of the hypothesis are presented in Figure 1–3. Other groups, namely CFID, FIDER, NCIDQ, and the Governing Board for Contract Interior Design Standards, have also been involved in the unification discussions. CFID formally became involved with the original six groups in the Unified Voice Task Force (UVTF). It should be noted that all seven professional associations in the UVTF require the NCIDQ examination as part of professional membership qualifications.

By 1990, there was strong support among these professional associations for the development of a single organization to represent the profession of interior design. In April of 1990, a consultant, Dr. Larry Anderson of Anderson & Associates International, Inc., was selected to facilitate the meetings and future discussions. An implementation strategy and a timetable were then developed by the consultant and were introduced and discussed in 1992. The strategy and timetable were done after a membership survey showed that approximately 90 percent of the membership of the seven organizations were in favor of the concept of a unified organization.

The organizational plan, developed in 1992, was ready for membership review and voting in 1993. Members of the seven professional associations received information about the unification plan as well as requests for input through surveys and chapter meeting discussions. In early 1993, the president of the Interior Designers of Canada reported to the task force that IDC would withdraw from the Unified Voice group. Although it strongly supported the unification concept and process, the IDC board felt it would be in the best interests of IDC to withdraw from the talks. This was based on legal considerations and the differing structures of the provincial associations in Canada. In September of 1993, the ASID board voted to withdraw from the unification discussions. According to a press release from ASID,[10] the board voted against continuing discussions based on a membership response

---

The three original hypotheses are:

1. By 1995, FIDER may accredit first professional degree level education programs.

2. By 1995, NCIDQ may require, for eligibility to take its examination, a degree from a FIDER-accredited program plus work experience.

3. By 1995, a professional organization may require for membership a degree from a FIDER-accredited program, work experience, passage of the NCIDQ examination and maintenance of continuing education credits.

To these three original hypotheses, later leaders' groups added three more:

4. By 1995, 30 states may have passed a professional title registration act.

5. By 1995, there may be ONE single umbrella professional organization in the US.

6. By 1995, more interior design courses will be incorporated into architecture curricula as well as more architecture courses admitted into interior design.

Reprinted from October, 1988. *Interior Design*. News: Leaders Meet., P. 58 +.

Figure 1–3 The 1995 Hypothesis. These principles first set out the unification discussion. Courtesy of *Interior Design* magazine.

---

[10]ASID press release, September 1993.

that was not in favor of unification. However, the organization was in favor of supporting joint-venture programs with the member design organizations.

The remaining five professional association members of the Unified Voice Task Force—IBD, ISID, ISP, CFID, and IDEC—continued to move forward on unification. Organizational and implementation plan efforts continued with a target of July 1994 for the creation date of the new organization.[11] It should be noted that the interior design specialties represented by these five groups are: commercial, education, health care, hospitality, government, residential, and retail interior design planning. As was stated earlier in this chapter, the membership and boards of IBD, ISID, and CFID voted in favor of unifying. These groups moved forward with the election of officers at the international and chapter levels in June and July of 1994. The Executive Committee for the new organization is represented by members from all three of the organizations.

But why would it be necessary to have one organization rather than the existing group of organizations? The mission and benefits of the Unified Voice concept are presented in Figure 1–4. Let's look at a few of these benefits.

Mission of the Unification Task Force (UTF)

- Act as the single representative voice of the interior design specialties.

- Advance the profession and its interior design specialties through public recognition and provide leadership and services to our members programs, communication, education and research.

- Benefit public health, safety, and welfare, contribute to the enhancement of the environment, and increase the perception, appreciation, and value of design in the community.

Benefits of Unification

- Funds available for re-investment into the membership and profession.

- One consistent voice for specialties.

- Fewer appellations will reduce confusion.

- Flexible structure will allow rapid change--shape of marketplace.

- Specialty forums and special interest programs allow members to grow and change with the times.

- More organized opportunities for networking.

- Consolidated research and education.

- Opportunities to lead in new ways.

Reprinted with permission by Michael D. Kroelinger, FIBD.

Figure 1–4 Mission and benefits of the unification of several professional associations into one umbrella organization. (Reproduced with permission, Michael Kroelinger, FIBD)

---

[11]Unified Voice Task Force, September 1993, press release.

Probably the most important issue would be the opportunity to have one voice to speak for and represent the interior design profession. The strength of one voice could be critical to the future growth and true acceptance of interior design as a profession in the eyes of the public and those who continue to try, even today, to diminish if not eliminate interior design as a separate profession.

Another important issue concerns raising the standards of the profession to a common level. Bringing about consistent standards for education and qualifications for entry into the profession has been a goal of professional associations for decades. This is one of the original concepts of the 1995 Hypothesis. Even with FIDER, there remain many programs that offer interior design education without meeting the standards developed by the profession. And while the member groups have similar qualifications for membership, there are other interior design professional associations whose membership qualifications vary widely.

An important financial issue has been the significant duplication of efforts and funding by the existence of numerous associations. Each group has a national office with staffs and expenses that are supported by dues. Each group offers member benefits that are essentially the same, though naturally focused on the individual interests of the groups—benefits such as newsletters, conferences, and continuing education classes, to name a few. By the creation of one professional association, there would be significant savings in expenses and operating costs.

One Voice, as the unification process has been called, will also help with licensing discussions in those states that currently do not have legislation. There are few differences in the licensing requirements of architects and engineers, yet many differences in the way the legislatures look at what interior designers do. In fact, there are even differences in the way interior designers see their own needs for licensing because of the different views of the many professional associations. A single voice will strengthen the interests of the profession and its membership in the continued fight for legal recognition.

In addition, it is likely that the membership of the new organization would grow beyond the members of the merged groups. It is quite possible that IDEC would ask for a new vote of its membership in 1995. Since the original vote was so close, it is expected that IDEC would eventually merge. It is also anticipated that, as the new organization develops, individuals who are currently members of nonmerging organizations may also elect to become members of the new group rather then waiting for their organizations to perhaps eventually join the new group.

But what will this new unified professional organization be like? Unfortunately, at this writing, the name of the group was still being determined. However, some facts about the new professional organization are known. The new organization will be truly international in scope. Members will come not only from the United States, but Canada and several European countries as well. This is due largely to the fact that many members of ISID were from outside the United States.

There will be five membership categories: professional, associate, affiliate, student, and honorary. The professional level will be made up of practitioners and educators. Associate level membership will be for those pre-professionals who have not yet completed the NCIDQ examination. Affiliate members will be those in allied areas such as architecture, those in industry, and a category called Friends. The new group will also have a national student structure. And finally, there will be membership categories of special status for those retired from active practice, fellows, those in the media, and other very specialized and honorary situations. Members of the merging organizations will automatically become members of the new organization at the highest level for which the person qualifies. In other words, a professional member of IBD, ISID, or CFID would become a professional member of the new organization, and so on.

The minimum qualifications for membership is similar to that of current membership in any of the merged organizations. The single most important criteria for professional membership is satisfactorily passing of the NCIDQ examination. In countries where the NCIDQ is not available, the current ISID criteria for International membership will be applied. Professional members are also required to complete 0.5 CEU credits annually. Associate members of the new organization will have 5 years to complete the NCIDQ exam. If they do not do so, they may remain associate members indefinitely, but will have to pay dues at the professional level.

The structure of the organization will be made up of the International level which substitutes for the current national level officers and boards; Regional levels consisting of smaller groupings of chapters; local chapters, much like current chapters; and a new group called City Center that will be like current chapters but focused in large, densely populated cities. At the international and chapter levels, specialty Forums (defined as program units in the areas of Commercial, Education/Research, Government, Healthcare, Hospitality, Residential, and Retail interior design) will be created to assists members with specialized interests to develop programs, public relations efforts, networking, or other activities surrounding professional practice. Members will have the opportunity to participate as a member of a chapter and one or two forums. Members may pay additional fees to participate in other forums if they so choose.

The author acknowledges that the information provided on the new organization is rather skeletal in nature, but good old "Murphy's Law" prevailed. When this work is published, more details will be available as the election of international level officers, the board of directors, and chapter leadership will have been accomplished as well as the beginning of the transition of the new organizational structure. If the reader has not already received detailed information about the new organization, you are urged to contact the Unified Voice at 341 Merchandise Mart, Chicago, IL 60654, (312)467–1950.

NCIDQ Examination

The National Council for Interior Design Qualification (NCIDQ), is the recognized qualifying examination for professional membership in ASID, the unified organization ISP, IDEC, and IDC. The NCIDQ examination is also the primary examination, when one is required, in those U.S. states and Canadian provinces that have licensing, certification, or other registration statutes. Successful completion of the examination is also required for those designers who seek professional certification from the Governing Board for Contract Interior Design Standards. Contract certification will be discussed in the next section of this chapter.

The NCIDQ is an independent corporation formed in 1971 concerned with maintaining standards of practice through the testing of members of the profession and assisting in the establishment of requirements for legal qualification for licensing and title registration. Ongoing research is conducted to evaluate and analyze candidate performance, education and professional practice skill and knowledge requirements, and methods to promote public awareness of the interior design profession.

The NCIDQ examination is given twice during the year, usually in April and October, at examination centers throughout the country. When the membership committee of one of the professional associations feels that a candidate is qualified to sit for the examination, his or her name is submitted to NCIDQ. The council then contacts the member to advise him or her of the next available examination date. Of course, individuals who are not affiliated with one of the professional associations may contact the council directly to apply to sit for the examination.

Eligibility requirements consist of a minimum of six years of combined educational and practical experience. A candidate may sit for the examination if he or she (1) has a four- or five-year degree in interior design, or equivalent educational credit, plus two years of professional experience; (2) a three-year certificate in interior design, or equivalent credits, plus three years of professional experience; or (3) a two-year certificate, or equivalent credits, plus four years of professional experience. All candidates must have a minimum of two years of professional work experience and two years of academic training in interior design. Recommendations and academic transcripts are also required of all candidates. Candidates who do not meet the basic education and work experience requirements may make special application to the council for authority to take the examination.

The examination is divided into six sections given over two consecutive days—usually Friday and Saturday. A candidate may take all six sections of the exam at one time or elect to take individual sections or combinations of sections at different times. Only sections of the examination that are not passed must be taken again. Unless a professional association or state statute has different requirements, all sections of the examination must be completed within a five-year period.

The six sections of the examination are divided into three multiple-choice computer-graded tests and three practicum sections. A brief description of the six sections follows:

1. *Identification and Application.* This is a multiple-choice test in two parts. Each part is approximately 70 questions in length and testing time is one and one-half hours per part.

2. *Building and Barrier-Free Codes.* This is also a multiple-choice test lasting one and one-half hours. The questions are generic in nature rather than specific to any local jurisdiction. The questions may be based on written or graphic information.

3. *Problem Solving.* The last of the multiple-choice tests, the problem-solving section consists of questions based on written information or graphic material in relation to interior design drawings. This portion of the examination is also one and one-half hours in length.

4. *Practicum: Programming.* The programming section evaluates the candidate's ability to interpret information that is commonly part of a design program. The first part simulates a client interview. The second part requires interpretation of information and presentation of that information in a graphic format. The time limit for this section is two hours. This section, as well as all practicum sections of the exam, is juried by interior design professionals or interior design educators.

5. *Practicum: Three-Dimensional Exercises.* This section of the practicum requires the candidate to read and interpret a written problem and demonstrate ability to communicate his or her interpretation and concepts of interior space in graphic form. Completing a floor plan, a reflected ceiling plan, and elevations or axonometric drawings are required. The candidate has one and one-half hours to complete this portion of the examination.

6. *Practicum: Scenario.* The last portion of the examination requires the candidate to interpret and evaluate a written program and prepare a space plan, a furniture plan, and a reflected ceiling plan. This portion of the exam lasts two and one-half hours. When applying to sit for the scenario section of the examination, the candidate may select one of five project types. These are: corporate (generally corporate offices, professional offices, banks, or financial facilities); residential (such as single-family, multi-family, special housing for the handicapped, or elderly); retail (malls, department stores, showrooms, or specialty shops); institutional (generally doctors' offices, hospitals, or educational or governmental facilities); or hospitality (commonly hotels, restaurants, recreation facilities, and conference centers). These choices give candidates the opportunity to work with areas with which they are familiar. However, the knowledge tested is the same regardless of the type of facility. Once an election of type of facility is selected, the candidate cannot change to a different type. The examples of types of facilities within each category as previously described are not inclusive of the actual testing situation.

An examination guide is available from NCIDQ (current cost is $35). This guide provides the candidate with an overview of the six sections of the examination along with a bibliography of source information. It is not, however, an actual study guide. It does provide valuable general information about the examination, the rules for the exam, the schedule, and other important information. At the time of this writing, the only known actual study guide for the NCIDQ examination is by David K. Ballast. (See reference of this chapter for complete information.)

The STEP Program

The ASID has devised special study programs to help candidates prepare for the NCIDQ. Though sponsored by ASID, any candidate for the NCIDQ exam may participate. This Self-Testing Exercises for Pre-Professionals (STEP) program assists applicants with study and design skills needed to pass the exams. STEP program leaders point out that the program is not a crash course in design. Rather, it is a means to help preprofessionals learn to study.

The STEP workshop, conducted by specially trained educators and professionals, provides exercises covering the practicum portions of the NCIDQ. Workshop activities take candidates through various exercises that help them assess where they need additional work prior to taking the exam. Practice tests covering the multiple-choice sections of the exam are administered and evaluated as well.

The STEP workshop is conducted over a two and one-half day period and lasts a total of 20 hours. Registration fees, paid in advance, are slightly higher for non-ASID members. Registration information can be obtained from either local ASID chapter offices or by calling the ASID National Headquarters.

Governing Board for Contract Interior Design Standards

The IBD worked for many years to develop a system of certifying professional contract interior designers. In 1987, the organization approved the recommendations of the IBD Certification Action Committee, which recommended that a private corporation—separate from any state agencies—be formed to administer the certification program. The name of the corporation responsible for nationwide certification of professional contract designers is the Governing Board for Contract Interior Design Standards.

Advanced certification in contract interior design is a voluntary program. It is not required of any professional association or licensing authority. The mission of the Governing Board is: "(1) To promote the highest standards of professional practice in contract interior design for the benefit of consumers through certification, research, and education of competence standards. (2) To promote continuing education of contract interior designers and to promote on-going committment to the profession."[12] The purpose of contract interior design certification is to recognize individuals who have demonstrated a high level of competency in contract interior design and to provide a national measurement of advanced knowledge and skills in the profession.

The certification process results in a professional credential that demonstrates to clients, peers, and allied professionals that an individual has attained a high professional proficiency as a senior-level designer. The Governing Board for Contract Interior Design Standards is solely responsible for evaluating candidates applications.

The certification program has definable standards and is based on 39 core competencies. Educational requirements mirror those of FIDER and the National Council of Architectural Registration Boards (NCARB). A minimum of six years of full-time professional experience in commercial design is also required. In addition, the candidate must have successfully passed the NCIDQ or NCARB examination or the Canadian equivalent. He or she should show continued commitment to his or her own professional growth and the growth of the

---

[12]Reprinted with permission from the Governing Board for Contract Interior Design Standards, 1993.

profession by active participation in one of the professional organizations. Finally, the certification credential requires recertification every three years. Recertification, in part, would be based on professional development as marked by obtaining approved continuing education units (CEUs) or university credits related to the field.

Application for certification as a professional contract designer is in two parts. Part 1 requires the candidate to provide complete education and work experience history. A portion of the application requires the candidate to provide detailed verification of core competencies identified by the Governing Board. If the candidate's qualifications meet the minimum standards, the candidate is sent Part 2 of the application. This material consists of four essay questions related to 12 key competencies. This second part of the application has been likened by some to writing a thesis. The responses are evaluated by independent readers and recommendations are made as to granting certification. The number of those seeking certification is growing, with many designers obtaining this new status.

The Governing Board is considering similar certification procedures for designers who specialize in residential, healthcare or institutional, retail store planning, and hospitality interior design. Information on voluntary contract certification is available from the Governing Board whose address is listed in the Appendix.

Licensing and Title Acts

Licensing, title acts, legal recognition, certification—all are topics important to the interior design professional and student. Licensing efforts have been a part of the profession's activities since 1951, when the Southern California chapter of AID attempted to get a bill passed in the state legislature. They failed. Today, the national and chapter organizations continue to fight for licensing. The professional associations seek licensing and/or title registration on a state-by-state basis.

Licensing and title acts are related because both require legislation and state control. Title acts are, in fact, a type of licensing. *Title acts* are concerned with limiting the use of certain titles to individuals who meet agreed-on qualifications and who have registered with a state board. Licensing, or *practice acts*, establish guidelines as to what one can or cannot do in the practice of a profession. Individuals who wish to engage in a profession guided by a licensing or practice act must also register with a state board.

Some states have used the term *certification* rather than title registration or licensing to legally acknowledge the profession. Certification is a different way of saying that the individual practitioner meets certain stated qualifications and holds the authority from the state to sign or stamp drawings and specifications as well as use the title *Certified Interior Designer* within his or her state.

Licensing, title acts, and certification, to differing degrees, serve to limit who can practice the profession. A title act does very little to limit who can practice the activities of interior design, while the practice acts do a great deal. Certification also limits who may practice as certified interior designers, since only those designers who hold the qualifications and the stamp may use the title of Certified Interior Designer. The intent of legislation however, is to indicate to the consumer which individuals meet the specific criteria related to education and work experience indicating professional competence in the field.

Title acts only restrict the use of the title *interior designer* to those who meet the qualifications of the state title act. Interior designers who meet these qualifications must also register with a state agency or board. An individual who does not meet the qualifications of the title act may not use the title of interior designer in any of his or her business dealings. With title registration, the title of interior designer connotes to the public that the individual meets the highest standards of the profession and can thereby provide the most competent service to the consumer. These standards are related to education, experience, abiding by a code of conduct, and passing a qualifying examination.

Practice acts are commonly legislated for those professions that deal with the health and safety of the public employing those professions. Lawyers, doctors, architects, and engineers have had to meet state practice act regulations for many years. Practice acts definitely limit who may practice the profession since they usually require very stringent qualification criteria. When a person enters into a contractual relationship with an unlicensed professional, the contract may or may not be enforceable, depending on the statutes in the individual states.

In the 1980s, some of the emphasis on licensing had been the result of increasing pressure to limit the practice of interior design. Architects, building contractors, and taxing authorities have, in various states, sought to limit the interior design practice by trying to legislate certain activities common to the interior designer to other more "traditional" professions.[13] In several states, there remain legislative efforts—either in effect or under consideration—aimed at limiting what the interior designer can do.

An argument used by legislators opposed to licensing and title acts for interior designers is the belief that, since this legislation would limit who may practice the profession, competition would be limited. Such limiting of competition might have a direct effect on the size of fees that can be charged. And, of course, high fees not only limit who can afford the service, but can, in time, affect the practice of the profession itself.

In 1984, IBD and ASID conferees were able to agree that four basic criteria must be a part of any title act, licensing, or certification proposal and agreed to support only those licensing and title act efforts that at least initially included these four elements. Those four criteria are:

Minimum requirements for education and experience

An examination of minimum competency qualifications

A Code of Practice Guidelines (Code of Ethics)

A requirement for continuing education[14]

The organizations also agreed that NCIDQ be responsible for monitoring minimum requirements for education and experience through its testing program.

In 1985, ASID modified its requirements of minimal standards within title act legislation by adopting the following:

First, all bills must contain the NCIDQ definition of interior design. Second, they must require qualifications to take the state exam that are equal to those required to take the NCIDQ exam. Third, the "NCIDQ exam or equal" must be specified as the qualifying exam. Fourth, the bill must include a grandfather clause that states as a minimum: "If one has used the title interior designer for the one year immediately preceding the effective date of the act and meets all the education and/or experience required to take the NCIDQ examination, the exam will be waived, and a license issued if application is received within one year of enactment." Finally, there must be a reciprocity clause permitting designers in other licensed states to secure a license.[15]

Those who have been actively engaged in bringing licensing legislation to their states would all agree that it has not been an easy task. Nor will it be in the future. Despite the frustration of many years of struggling with legislators, and those who would rather interior

---

[13]ASID, March 1985.

[14]*Perspective,* Fall 1984, p. 1. Reprinted with permission from the Institute of Business Designers.

[15]*Report,* Jan.–March 1985, p. 4. Reprinted with permission, ASID, copyright 1988, American Society of Interior Designers.

design not be licensed, many states have obtained some type of interior design legislation. In 1982, Alabama became the first state to pass a title registration act. As of November, 1993, there are 18 jurisdictions with licensing legislation: Alabama, Arkansas, California, Connecticut, Florida, Georgia, Illinois, Louisiana, Maine, Maryland, Minnesota, New Mexico, New York, Puerto Rico, Tennessee, Texas, Virginia, and Washington, D.C. There are also eight jurisdictions in Canada that have passed similar title registration acts. Washington, D.C., and Puerto Rico remain the only jurisdictions with a practice act for interior design. Many other states are working on legislation for either title registration or practice acts.

Readers may wish to contact the National Legislative Coalition for Interior Design (NLCID), the Government and Public Affairs Department (ASID), Legislative Issues Committee (IBD), or the national offices of other professional associations for information on legislation within the reader's jurisdiction. (See Appendix for the address for the NLCID.)

Whether one works toward licensing through title registration or practice acts, interior design professionals and students must be prepared to accept the legal and ethical responsibilities such recognition brings. The next section discusses the codes of conduct of both major professional organizations; later chapters cover the legal responsibilities one must face.

Ethics

One of the characteristics of a true profession is that an organization's members are guided by a set of *ethical standards*. These ethical standards define what is right and wrong in relation to the professional behavior of the members and even the practice of the profession. While a code of ethics does provide definable and enforceable standards, it cannot, by itself, produce ethical behavior. Ethical behavior must come from within the individual designer in his or her daily dealings with clients, peers, the public, and allied professionals.

The codes of ethics of the professional associations deal with enforceable ethical standards of practice and provide philosophical comments concerning the professional conduct of members. The ASID Code of Ethics, revised in 1989, contains standards related to four areas of responsibility: (1) to the public, (2) to the client, (3) to other interior designers and colleagues, and (4) to the profession. The IBD Code of Ethics, was adopted in 1989. It consists of five sections: (1) the designer's responsibility to the community; (2) the designer's responsibility to his client; (3) the designer's responsibility to other designers; (4) designer's remuneration; and (5) publicity. Of course, the other associations also have their own version of codes of ethics or conduct. Readers interested in the codes of ethics from other associations should contact them directly. (The documents from ASID and IBD have been provided in the Appendix since these two organizations represent the majority of professional association memberships in interior design.)

These rules of conduct exist for members of the organization and address their dealing with other designers, whether or not the other designers are members of one of the organizations. The reader is urged to become familiar with both codes of conduct before completing this chapter. The following list summarizes important issues of the codes:

The designer must not knowingly misrepresent himself or herself or allow other members of the firm to misrepresent themselves or the firm to clients and others.

He or she must fully inform the client as to the means of compensation to the designers.

The codes prohibit the designer from requesting or accepting any kind of fee or other compensation from suppliers for goods specified.

Members are also prohibited from disclosing any confidential information about the client without the permission of the client.

The designer may not make any comments about another designer that may result in damaging the reputation of that designer.

A member of either professional organization may not interfere with the contractual relationship that is in existence between a client and another designer.

Judicial councils and ethics committees that review ethical charges brought against members. ASID publishes, in the *ASID Report*, the names of those members whose membership have been revoked by the national ethics committee. Although this may be personally embarrassing to the member whose name appears in print, it also serves to advise all members that the Code of Ethics will be enforced by the organization.

The 1980 version of the IBD Code of Ethics provides a fitting conclusion to this brief discussion. "To be a professional involves the acceptance of responsibility to the public. . . . Ethical conduct is more than merely abiding by the letter of explicit prohibitions. Rather, it requires unswerving commitment to honorable behavior, even at the sacrifice of personal advantage."[16]

Continuing Education

Like all other professionals, interior designers seek seminars, workshops, lectures, and intensive professional studies in their field. Many designers seek postgraduate education in interior design, architecture, and business, to name just a few broad areas. Sometimes, additional education is obtained to increase the designer's technical skills and allow him or her to advance within the firm he or she works. Sometimes, it is sought to retrain for a new area of expertise such as lighting design or CAD or to move into management. Not all professionals have the time to seek college credit, however. And many professionals do not really desire the depth of information and study required by college courses.

Courses that provide continuing educational units (CEUs) furnish short-term course work in a variety of areas. Continuing education courses last anywhere from a few hours to a few days, with the most common time limit being a full-day session. The course length and level of difficulty are primary factors in determining the number of CEU credits available for the class. Most CEU classes are under 1.0 credits. CEU classes provide a means for professional interior designers to remain current in the practice. Courses are available in almost every topic and area of the profession: basic theory and practice, such as seminars on color and light and rendering techniques: special issues of design, such as the Americans with Disabilities Act, kitchen design, or lighting design; improving personal and professional effectiveness with seminars on presentation techniques; and numerous areas of business practices, such as business planning, marketing, and personnel management.

Each association provides a number of CEU classes each year, most often sponsored at the local chapter level or as part of national conferences. For example, many chapters are diligently trying to offer two or more CEU classes through the year for their members. In addition, in 1993, there were over 50 CEU classes of various credit amounts offered at the ASID national conference alone. CEU classes have become a part of all association national meetings and major market shows.

It is important to note that reciprocity exists between many of the professional associations. It is often possible for an ASID member, for example, to take a class sponsored by IBD, AIA, ISID, IFMA, or other associations. The member should check with his or her association to determine if a course offered by a different professional association will be applicable to

---

[16]"Code of Ethics," 1980, 3. Reprinted with permission from the Institute of Business Designers, 1980.

his or her association. In some cases, the member may need to send a formal request to the association to determine if the course will count.

Members also need to clearly understand that it is up to the individual member to keep track of his or her CEU credits. To receive CEU credit, members must be sure they complete the course credit application and provide a CEU fee that is generally in addition to the course fee. The individual member's CEU file is maintained by the American College Testing (ACT) Registry located in Iowa City, Iowa (see Appendix for address). If the reader's association requires CEU credits to maintain membership, the member must request transcripts be sent to the association offices. The ACT does not automatically inform the professional associations of a professional's CEU course work each year.

Continuing education is also very important because several states that have passed licensing or title registration acts require continued education as a part of maintaining registration. The exact requirements are the responsibility of the licensing board in each state. As of 1993, Florida, Georgia, Louisiana, Maryland, New Mexico, and Washington, D.C., require continuing education for renewal of an interior design license. Arkansas, Minnesota, and Texas are still determining exact requirements for continuing education. It is the individual's responsibility to inform state boards of CEU activity.

Today's technological, litigious society makes it incumbent upon interior design professionals to keep current in the many technical, legal, and business skills and concepts of the profession. Changes in the ways design services are offered, changes in the products we specify, changes in the legal influences with which the designer must deal, all make continuing education an important part of being a professional interior designer.

Summary

In this chapter we have looked at the issues surrounding the profession of interior design: education, professional associations, qualification, licensing, and ethics. Having an understanding of what the roots and issues of a profession are is an important part of being a member of that profession. Knowing what it is all about is crucial to making the time spent in the career a meaningful commitment of time and effort rather than an ordinary "job." Society tends to grant professionals higher status, money, and respect. Yet these do not come only with accomplishing the educational criteria of the profession. They come to the individual who has the attitude of service, commitment, and knowledge expected of the professional.

Being a professional means commitment to one's colleagues, clients, allied professionals, and students. Being a professional means being involved in an appropriate association, not just becoming a member. Being a professional means having sufficient pride in one's profession to fight for the profession. All these concepts and more demonstrate what a professional interior designer should be.

References

Abercrombie, Nicholas, Stephen Hill, and Bryan S. Turner. 1984. *The Penguin Dictionary of Sociology.* New York: Allen Lane Publications (Penguin).

Abercrombie, Stanley. October 1987. "News: Leaders Meet." *Interior Design.*

Anscombe, Isabelle. 1984. *A Woman's Touch.* New York: Elisabeth Sifton Books (Viking).

American Society of Interior Designers. 1992. *Professional Closeup.* (brochure).

_____. September, 1993. "ASID Board Votes to Withdraw from Unification Talks: Pledges Cooperation with Unified Organization." (press release).

_____. 1992. *Membership Information.*

_____. 1992. *Ethics and Professional Conduct.* (brochure).

_____. 1986. "First Interior Design Practice Act Passed in Nation." *Report.*

_____. September 1993. *Interior Design Registration Laws.* (brochure).

Ball, Victoria. 1982. *Opportunities in Interior Design.* Skokie, Ill.: VGM Career Horizons.

Ballast, David K. 1992. *Interior Design Reference Manual.* Belmont, Calif.: Professional Publications, Inc.

Castlelman, Betty. June, 1987. "How Will Licensing Affect Me?" *Designers West.*

Chewning, Richard C. 1984. *Business Ethics in a Changing Culture.* Reston, Va.: Reston Publishing.

Collier's Encyclopedia. 1984. "Interior design and decoration," vol. 13. New York: Macmillan.

Council of Interior Designers. June, 1994. "Three Leading Interior Design Associations to Unify July 1, 1994." (press release)

deWolfe, Elsie. [1913] 1975. *The House in Good Taste.* Reprint. New York: Arno.

Ebstein, Barbara. January–March, 1985. "Licensing: The Design Concern for the Eighties." American Society of Interior Designers. *Report.*

Foundation for Interior Design Education Research. February, 1993. *FIDER Fact Kit.* Grand Rapids, Mich.: FIDER.

Friedmann, Arnold, John F. Pile, and Forrest Wilson. 1982. *Interior Design—An Introduction to Architectural Interiors.* 3d ed. New York: Elsevier Science Publishing.

Governing Board for Contract Interior Design Standards. 1989. *Pursuing Your Personal Best: Professional Certification for the Contract Interior Designer.* (brochure).

Gueft, Olga. 1980. "The Past as Prologue: The First 50 Years. 1931–1981: An Overview." *American Society of Interior Designers Annual Report 1980.* New York: American Society of Interior Designers.

Hughes, Nina. June, 1987. "*Interiors* Platform." *Interiors.*

Interior Design Educators Council. 1992. *Membership Brochure.*

_____. May 1994. "Members of Interior Design Organizations Vote on Unification." Press Release.

Interior Design. October 1988. "News: Leaders."

_____. February 1992. "More Trouble on the Certification Front."

Institute of Business Designers. 1993. *Membership Information.*

_____. Fall 1984. *Perspective.*

_____. 1989. *Code of Professional Conduct.* (brochure).

_____. 1992. *History of IBD.* (unpublished manuscript).

_____. February 1993. *CEUs and You. A Guide to Developing a Self-Directed Learning Path for the Professional Member.* (brochure).

International Society of Interior Designers. 1992. *Membership Information.* (brochure).

Kettler, Kerwin. May 1985. "Is There More to Licensing Than a License?" *Designer Specifier.*

Klein, Judy Graf. 1982. *The Office Book.* New York: Facts on File, Inc.

Kroelinger, Michael D. Spring, 1992. "Unified Voice Update." *Perspective*. Institute of Business Designers.

_____. Spring 1994. "Unified Voice Update." Perspective. Institute of Business Designers.

_____. 1993. *Mission and Benefits of Unification.* (unpublished material).

Massey, Anne. 1980. *Interior Design of the 20th Century.* London, England: Thames and Hudson.

Polites, Nicholas. July 1993. "Arkansas Enacts Tiered Licensing System: Interior Designers Weigh Consequences." *Interior Design.*

Rayle, Martha G. April 1992. *Unified Voice Task Force (UVTF) Update.* (Newsletter published by American Society of Interior Designers).

Russell, Beverly. March 1985. "Interiors Business: New Moves Toward Interior Design Licensing." *Interiors.*

_____. Fall 1992. "Into The Ninth Decade: A Historic View of Interior Design Through the Contribution of Women." *IBD Perspective.*

Stein, Harry. 1982. *Ethics (and Other Liabilities).* New York: St. Martin's Press.

Sweet, Justin. 1985. *Legal Aspects of Architecture, Engineering, and the Construction Process.* 3d ed. St. Paul, Minn.: West Publishing.

Tate, Allen and C. Ray Smith. 1986. *Interior Design in the 20th Century.* New York: Harper and Row.

Thompson, Jo Anne Asher (editor). 1992. *ASID Professional Practice Manual.* New York: Watson-Guptill.

Unified Voice Task Force. September, 1993. *Interior Design Organizations Target July 1994 for Unification.* (press release).

_____. April 1994. Newsletter sent to IBD members.

_____. April 1994. Newsletter sent to IDEC members.

Veitch, Ronald M., Dianne R. Jackman, and Mary K. Dixon. 1990. *Professional Practice.* Winnipeg, Canada: Peguis Publishers.

Note: There are dozens of additional articles, brochures, newsletters, and mailings on these topics. It is not possible to list all of these in this bibliography.

Chapter 2

Personal Goal Setting

Opening a studio is the dream of almost everyone who has entered the career of interior design. If not one's own studio, then professional involvement as a design director for a major design office. Perhaps the career dream is to work for a major manufacturer. Maybe it is having a project published or to be a chapter or national officer in one of the professional organizations. It may, of course, be one of any number of other career and professional titles and achievements. Yet for many, these goals are never reached.

Family, friends, children—all of these obligations and others can enter the picture and hold one back from reaching personal goals. But in most cases, the inability to achieve a goal or a dream is not due to other individuals or job responsibilities. Rather, it is more a case of a lack of planning, a lack of goals. Or maybe, setting the wrong goals.

Although businesses spend a lot of time and energy determining and setting goals for the coming year, individuals often ignore their own needs for the future. In this chapter, we will look at personal goal setting.

Goals

If You Don't Know Where You're Going, You'll Probably End Up Somewhere Else[1] is the title of a wonderful book by David Campbell, Ph.D. To know where you are going can sometimes be very difficult. But without some kind of direction, your personal and professional life can be frustrating and unfulfilling.

Several years ago, I was visiting a friend in San Diego. Because she had not lived there for long, I admired her intuitive ability to find her way around a strange city. We never checked a map. Her intuition was uncanny. Many people approach all aspects of their lives in the same way. Flying by the seat of their pants purely on intuition, they seek out educational preparation, make career decisions, move to other cities, invest in stocks—experiencing life with little planning. For a few lucky people, that method works fine. Unfortunately, for the

---

[1]Campbell 1974.

majority, living life by intuition leaves us like the Campbell book title mentioned above—somewhere other than where we thought we wanted to be.

There is nothing wrong with using your intuition. There is also nothing wrong with just experiencing life—letting it happen. However, a far greater number of individuals who are viewed by their peers as successful people achieved that success with planning and goal setting. The Pyramids, St. Peter's Basilica, and your most recent design project were not accomplished without some kind of plan. Whatever your concept of success, it also will be far easier to achieve if you have a plan for reaching it.

Most people have dreams but many have no goals. Dreams are imaginary hopes whereas, to many, goals are concrete ideas representing some kind of end that a person tries to achieve. Philosophically, goals are brief stops along the way of life that mark achievement in an individual's personal and professional life. Finally owning your own studio one day is not an end in itself, even though it may have been the goal. Now you must be ready to create new goals related to the success and growth of the studio. Goals are concrete ideas requiring effort and commitment for their achievement. Desiring to be a published designer is also not an end, since the goal of becoming published must be preceded by other goals that help you to achieve that end result.

Whether the reader is a professional actively practicing in interior design for several years or a student still negotiating his or her way through design classes, personal and professional goal setting is important. The professional who may feel unfulfilled or recently out of a job even after several years of work needs to take stock of what he or she has accomplished and the skills he or she possesses. With tighter job markets in many cities, students must have a clearer idea of the type of design job they are interested in pursuing while remaining flexible to any reasonable opportunity.

Even though you may have some general idea about what you want out of your personal and professional life, without some kind of concrete plan you will find yourself reacting to what happens to you rather than having some control over events in your life. The most successful people are those who develop a vision of their career and personal life. They establish goals and strategies that help accomplish that vision. And they continually evaluate possibilities that are presented to them to determine how these new possibilities positively or negatively affect their career and personal life.

Risks in Goal Setting

Many people have difficulty setting goals or do not consciously bother to continue to do so, once they have achieved some immediate goal such as getting a job in the interior design field. To set a goal requires commitment of time, energy, and mental processes. Some people do not wish to really make a commitment of any kind much beyond their immediate physiological needs. Setting goals also runs the risk of failure—that is, not achieving the goal. But not achieving the goal does not automatically mean failure. The goal may have been unattainable at the present time for one reason or another.

Because there are risks in setting goals, goals must be set with certain considerations in mind. First, set goals that satisfy *you*—not a spouse, a boyfriend or girlfriend, parents, or peers. If you are setting a goal to please someone else, then you will probably never achieve it. And should it be achieved, it may never bring you satisfaction.

Second, some goals are unattainable without proper experience. To become a design director at a major interior design or architectural firm does not happen overnight. It takes time to gain the experience to have these opportunities. Professionals and students alike must understand that certain goals will take time. For a professional to set a goal of increasing his or her income by 50 percent in one year or a student just ready to be graduated from college to set a goal of being a design director in two years would be goals that invite disappointment. The attainment of such goals would happen in only the most extraordinary situations.

Third, do not be afraid to change goals or change directions. Life is not perfect, and reality usually does not match fantasy. Be flexible in goal setting. Whatever first brought you into the interior design profession will probably change somewhat as your exposure, opportunities, and experience change. All of your career and life challenges will affect your potential ability to accomplish goals set in college or after a few years of working in design. The author remembers a student who accomplished commercial projects far faster than anyone else in class. When asked how she managed to do so, her response was, "I hate doing commercial design so much, I just want to get the projects finished." Her goal was to work in residential design and she obtained that kind of job right after graduation. About two years later she was around the campus again and asked, "Do you know of anyone hiring in commercial design? I hate what I am doing in residential!" Unexpected circumstances and lack of understanding about career requirements are just a few things that can affect reaching many goals.

There is one indisputable fact about life. Life will change. For most, change means growth. So don't be afraid to grow. Being open to a change of plans may offer you opportunities for personal and professional growth you have not even seriously considered in the past. For example, Mary had a goal to be a design director with a major dealer. One day she was offered a two-year position as a designer in Hawaii. Not looking at the possibilities that opportunity would provide in the future, she refused the position and stayed working in a medium-sized city in the northwest. Several years later, still not in a position to be a design director, she looks back longingly at that lost opportunity. Do not be afraid to consider or even embark upon different paths of opportunity when they arise.

Setting Goals

The best way to set goals is to try to look at yourself in the future. An instructor the author had in college had the class write their own obituaries—a rather jarring thought at age 21. But the idea was to focus on long-range goal setting. We all need to occasionally look at what each of us wants to be remembered for. What we hope we will be able to accomplish by the time we pass away some time in the future.

Understandably, writing your own obituary is difficult to do. It may be easier to start thinking of what you want to accomplish by the time you are 30 and 40 and 50 and at retirement age. And if you find *that* too hard to do, try to figure out where you want to be in your professional and personal life during the next five years.

If you are unsure of what you want to accomplish, it might help to use Figures 2–1 and 2–2 to get you started. Find a quiet place where you can think undisturbed. And be brutally honest with yourself in your answers to these questions.

Once you have some idea where you want to be, you can start looking at that goal or goals in terms of the concrete things that need to be accomplished in order to get there. "I want to own my own studio by the time I am 35." What kinds of work experience will be needed to meet that goal? Where do you want that studio to be located? Where will you get the finances to open the doors? Do you want to work alone or with someone else? Being your own boss sounds good, but are you going to be willing to sacrifice family and personal time to keep the studio in operation? These are some of the questions related to that goal.

Some of the mini-goals related to achieving the preceding goal might be:

- Work with a residential firm for five years to gain experience in residential practice.

- Work with a commercial firm for five years to gain experience with general commercial clients.

- Become a senior designer or design manager with either a residential or commercial firm in order to gain business and management experience.

- If necessary, take additional business classes at a community college or an MBA program to gain the business knowledge to own your own studio.

GOALS

The purpose of this exercise is to analyze skills, interests, and abilities in relation to the kind of job opportunities you will be seeking in interior design. Completing this exercise will make you more aware of what you have to offer your present or future employers as well as discover some goals to work on in the next year or so. Answer the following questions in as many or as few words as necessary.

1. What kind of skills in interior design do you have?
2. What special skill(s) do you have to offer your present employer or another employer?
3. If you were going to a job interview tomorrow, what specific career goal would you share with the interviewer?
4. List three of your biggest successes.
5. List three of your biggest "failures."
6. List five goals you wish to accomplish during the next calendar year.
7. List three goals you hope to accomplish by the time you are thirty.
8. List three goals you hope to accomplish by the time you are fifty.
9. Assuming it were possible for you to achieve any goal in interior design, what would it be?
10. List ten mini-goals needed to support that ultimate goal.

Figure 2-1 Personal goals exercise.

These questions ask you to look at a variety of issues concerning your professional and personal life. Combined with the exercise in Figure 2-1, these questions provided you an opportunity to look at some additional issues that can help clarify your professional and personal goals.

1. List at least three things that drew you into a career path in interior design. Write several comments about each of those items.

2. List any three people you most admire. Write down a few words or sentences that explains why you admire them.

3. If you had the means to do so, what would you most like to do--personally and professionally. Remember, no restrictions.

4. What do you think needs to be changed to make you happier in your professional and personal life?

5. What frustrates you most about your professional and personal life?

6. What do you like most about work in interior design? What do you like least?

7. When are you at your best and most secure (professionally and personally)?

8. Do you prefer to work independently or with a group?

9. Write a paragraph that would sum up what you most want to be remembered for in your professional (and/or personal) life.

10. On a sheet of paper, make two columns. On the top of one column, write the word "problem," and the other "solution." Then write in the "problem" column those things that you feel are holding you back or are problems in your professional and/or personal life. In the "solution" column, write down potential solutions to each problem. In some cases you may find that you are really writing down just thoughts than true solutions, but those thoughts will help you find a solution to the problems.

Figure 2-2 Professional goals questionnaire.

These are all concrete mini-goals needed to accomplish the larger goal of owning your own studio. Once the opportunity of opening that studio occurs, new goals must be decided related to the business and the next "stop" on the road.

Summary

It is important for all of us to set goals in order to provide direction to our lives. Setting goals is risky and they take commitment, but if the goals we set are goals that interest us, they are likely to be fulfilled.

Achieving a goal may or may not be within our control. It must be remembered that some goals take a certain kind of expertise or maybe a credential like an MBA. Without the expertise or credential, accomplishment of the goal may be unlikely. Goals take time. Just as Rome was not built in a day, obtaining the credentials to teach in a university, work for a major manufacturer, or create designs that are purchased by custom furniture manufacturers do not come overnight. Always keep in mind that life changes either by actions we take ourselves or by actions that have an effect upon us. Do not be afraid of those changes and do not be afraid of making changes if new opportunities look interesting.

Bibliography

Bliss, Edwin. 1983. *Doing It Now*. New York: Bantam Books.

Bolles, Richard Nelson. 1987. *What Color Is Your Parachute?* Berkeley, Calif.: Ten Speed Press.

Brothers, Dr. Joyce. 1978. *How to Get Whatever You Want Out of Life*. New York: Ballantine Books.

Buscagila, Dr. Leo. 1982. *Living, Loving, and Learning*. New York: Charles B. Slack.

Campbell, David. 1974. *If You Don't Know Where You're Going, You'll Probably End Up Somewhere Else*. Niles, Ill.: Argus Communications.

Covey, Stephen R. 1989. *The 7 Habits of Highly Effective People*. N.Y.: Fireside Books (Simon and Schuster).

Freudenberger, Herbert J. 1980. *Burn Out*. Garden City, N.Y.: Anchor Press (Doubleday and Co.).

Friedman, Martha. 1980. *Overcoming the Fear of Success*. New York: Warner.

Harragan, Betty Lehan. 1977. *Games Mother Never Taught You*. New York: Warner.

LeBoeuf, Michael. 1979. *Working Smart*. New York: Warner.

Ponder, Catherine. 1973. *The Prosperity Secret of the Ages*, rev. ed. Engelwood Cliffs, N.J.: Prentice-Hall.

Roger, John and Peter McWilliams. 1991. *Life 101: Everything We Wish We Had Learned About Life In School—But Didn't*. Los Angeles: Prelude Press (Bantam-Prelude).

Sher, Barbara with Annie Gottlieb. 1979. *Wishcraft—How to Get What You Really Want*. New York: Ballantine.

Viscott, David. 1985. *Taking Care of Business. A Psychiatrists's Guide for True Career Success*. New York: William Morrow.

Waitley, Denis. 1983. *Seeds of Greatness: The Ten Best-kept Secrets of Total Success*. New York: Pocket Books (Simon and Schuster).

_____. 1984. *The Psychology of Winning*. New York: Berkley Books.

PART II

How to Establish an Interior Design Practice

Chapter 3

Planning a New Practice

A great number of interior designers reach a decision one day to start their own design business. Many of these ventures succeed and go on to flourish. Many others fail. As an example, approximately 9 percent of businesses that opened in 1990 failed within one year.[1] Although there are numerous reasons for the failure of a business, many are related to not having a clearly defined plan before opening the doors. For example, a plan helps the budding business owner determine which design services will be offered and how many customers might potentially be interested in those services. Businesses may fail because the services a business owner wishes to provide are unwanted or have too few potential customers.

Anyone who might consider starting his or her own design practice needs to do serious research, thinking, and planning. The potential business owner needs to research his or her own business skills and experience. In addition, the potential business owner must also evaluate his or her motivation for starting a design practice. Planning formalizes the decisions and ideas surrounding the creation of a new business. It helps the potential business owner see if the idea is feasible and what will be required to make it work. It provides an operational tool for the owner to handle with thought, rather than pure gut reaction, many of the problems that will occur.

The first sections of this chapter summarizes information about the numerous decisions that must be made. The remainder of this chapter will look at the business plan—or business planning—with the latter considerations more in mind. Just as we saw in Chapter 2 that personal goal setting helps the individual know where he or she is going, business planning helps the firm know where it is going.

What is an Entrepreneur?

An *entrepreneur* is someone who starts and manages his or her own business. An entrepreneur might work alone or may add employees to the growing business. Entrepreneurs generally

---

[1]Small Business Administration, *State of Small Business: A Report of the President,* 1991.

try to do things differently. Often, the reason they have started a business is that they feel they have a better way to provide design services, manage an office, or sell products. Today, entrepreneurial small businesses are the leading type of business being created. In addition, small businesses account for the creation of the greatest number of new jobs.[2]

Numerous books and articles about entrepreneurs define the traits and characteristics of these individuals. However, do not become trapped into thinking that only those persons that "fit" these characteristics can be successful business owners. Charles Banfe, in *Entrepreneur,* feels that entrepreneurs come in all shapes, sizes, ages, experience levels, educational backgrounds—that there really is no typical entrepreneur.

The main characteristic that will help sustain a potential business owner through all the decisions and all the crises in starting and owning a business will be *drive.* Willingness to work and work hard. Owners of businesses do not punch in at 8:00 A.M. and out at 5:00 P.M. They commonly put in 12-hour days—often, even longer. Work is commonly taken home as well—if not in terms of actual paperwork or design work, in terms of thinking about existing problems that must be resolved. Owners seek out advice from books, consultants, friends—any source that will help them do a better job of managing and sustaining their business. And while many design office owners have said occasionally, "If someone would offer to buy my studio, I'd sell in a minute!" they haven't yet and probably won't because, deep down, the challenge of ownership is too exciting to leave.

However, successful design business owners do have some common characteristics. They have technical design expertise gained through education and work experience. It is difficult to offer design services without knowing how to properly perform those services. Most have worked for someone else, either in design or some type of business situation. Working in design provides an opportunity to experience and perhaps help manage a business. These people are highly self-motivated. Self-motivated individuals do not wait for the boss to assign them work. Designers who need to be prodded into working will find it difficult to put in the time and effort necessary to operate a business. Once again, they must have fire and the drive to succeed.

Being the boss is fun. It is also risky and a lot of hard work. Those who may be considering having their own business have already met the first prerequisite for ownership—they have the dream of ownership. Get the skills and background in design and business that will make it easier to achieve that success. And do not forget to get advice from specialists who are available to help the potential business owner. Finally, good luck!

Advantages and Disadvantages of Business Ownership

As with any risk, there are good things and bad things about owning a business. Designers see the boss leaving for long lunches, going home early, maybe driving an expensive car. Employees rarely consider the disadvantages. Part of the decision-making process is to look at both advantages and disadvantages, especially the disadvantages, to be sure the individual is prepared to accept these constraints. Some of these characteristics appear below.

Advantages

• Not having to report to a boss. As the boss, the owner makes the decisions.

• Personal satisfaction in achieving success.

---

[2]Small Business Administration. *The Facts About Small Business,* 1992.

- Having the opportunity to perform the kind of design work the individual most enjoys.

- Potentially higher income. Ownership means potential gains from the profits of the company as well as the income one draws from the business.

- Potential long-term job security. The job exists as long as the business succeeds and the owner wishes to remain in business.

- The chance to develop a creative style—an opportunity not often possible working for someone else. Designers working for others often must design in the style of the design firm.

- More contact with clients, suppliers, and other industry members. The owner makes more client contacts, deals directly with suppliers, and has the opportunity to meet others in many aspects of the design industry.

Disadvantages

- Large financial risk. Depending on business formation, the business owner might also be risking personal assets.

- Greater legal liability. Owners are liable for actions of employees as well as themselves.

- Longer hours. Typically, owners work 12-hour days, even 7 days a week with little time off for vacations or personal time. This is especially true in the first few years of the life of the business.

- Greater stress. The owner is concerned about bringing in enough business to meet all the bills, prevent any kind of bad publicity, or poor customer service. He or she must also worry that the employees are all doing their jobs properly and legally and must worry about many other problems and constraints that affect the business.

- Income often minimal in early months—even for the entire first year. Profits for a new business are traditionally low and are often plowed back into the business, either to pay expenses or expand the business.

- Long hours meaning less time for personal and social life.

- Less design input. As the business grows, the design owner often finds he or she is spending less time on design and more time on managing the business.

- Need to satisfy customer. Even though a business owner is the boss, he or she is now controlled by the wishes of the customer.

- Loss of flexibility. It is not easy to quit if the business owner finds he or she does not enjoy ownership or otherwise no longer wishes to remain in business. A financial loss might result from just closing down. It may be difficult to find someone to buy the business.

- Market changes. Changing buying motivations of potential customers (deep discounting expectations in commercial design and opening of trade showrooms in residential design) may drain away business.

It is not entirely by accident that the disadvantages of business ownership in the preceding lists outnumber the advantages. Many business owners would agree with that result. The intention in pointing out more disadvantages to advantages is not to discourage anyone from starting his or her own business. On the contrary. The intention is to be sure that the potential business owner realizes the risks involved and contemplates the business venture thoroughly before starting the new practice.

Starting a New Business

The decision to start a business must involve careful evaluation of personal motivation; consideration of the financial, physiological, and legal risks; and a commitment to doing the research and making the numerous decisions that will be required. In the past, too many designers began an interior design practice without carefully thinking through the business concept and its numerous decisions, let alone the risks involved. With two out of three businesses failing within five years,[3] the decision to start a business cannot be taken lightly.

Figures 3–1 to 3–3 have been included to provide the potential practice owner with a summary of the key decisions that must be carefully made. The questionnaires take the designer thorough many of the choices and decisions essential to starting an interior design practice. Figure 3–1 asks questions about personal motivation and attitudes about business ownership. Figure 3–2 appraises the fundamental business idea. Finally, Figure 3–3 asks

---

The following provides a sample of questions you should use to evaluate your motivation and attitudes toward starting your own business. If you are seriously thinking of starting your own business in the near future, use these questions only as a starting point in determining your interest and sincerity.

1. Why do you want to own your own business?

2. Are you dissatisfied with your present job? Why?

3. Are you prepared for the sacrifices of your personal time and energy?

4. How do your present skills and abilities prepare you for business ownership?

5. Do you have finances available to commit to the business venture or must you obtain outside start-up funding?

6. Do you have clients that will switch to your business should you leave your current employer?

7. Are you a self-starter or must you be directed in your present work situation?

8. What skills and abilities do you have that you can offer your potential clients?

9. Have you done any evaluation of potential competitors?

10. What kinds of business skills or experiences do you have to operate a business?

11. Are you a good organizer?

12. Do you have a lot of self-confidence?

Figure 3–1 Personal attitudes about business ownership.

---

[3]McCarroll, *Time,* January 6, 1992, 62.

Carefully answer these questions in order to help you define your over-all business idea. Remember to be as specific as possible in your responses. The information developed from this questionnaire can be used to develop your business plan.

Have you clarified your design and business skills? If you will have partners, do this for those other individuals as well.
What experience do you have in interior design, architecture, and/or construction?
What experience do you have in sales and marketing?
What experience do you have in managing other individuals?
What business experience or knowledge do you have?

Define your business.
What services (exactly) will you offer initially?
Will you sell products?
Will products be from inventory or special order only?
How will you price your services (fee methods)?
How will you price the products you sell?
How will you receive and deliver goods to clients?
Have you considered what language will go into design contracts?

Do you know who your customers will be?
How many potential customers are in your business area?
How many of these customers do you think you can attract?
Will your customers perceive your prices as competitive?
Will your customers see the difference in your services from your competition?
What income group will your business appeal to?

What kind of finances will be required to start your business?
What business licenses will be required? Cost?
Are you going to start your business at home? Is this legally possible in your community?
If you are going to have your business in a commercial space, have you investigated rental costs?
What kind of equipment and furniture will be necessary to start your business? What is the estimated cost of purchase? What are the possibilities to lease these items?
What kind of income are you seeking for yourself for the first year? Use this (along with estimated expenses) to determine how much revenue you will be required to generate monthly. Is that possible considering your business idea, number of potential customers, and competition?

Have you researched the competition?
Who are your main competitors?
How many other firms like yours exist within two miles?
How many other firms like yours exist within your business area?
What can you do that your competition is not already doing?
Do you know how much your competition charges for their services/products?
Why would your customers buy from you rather than an existing competitor?

How will clients find out about your business?
Will you do mass mailings?
Will you use advertising? What kind and in what media?
Are you going to develop marketing tools like a brochure?
Have you considered the design of your letter head and other business stationary?

Figure 3–2 A questionnaire to help the potential business owner define his or her business idea.

Select the name of the business.
    Use your own name?
    Use a fictitious name? (requires a legal filing. See Chapter 6).

Where will the business be located? (See Chapter 3 and 6)
    In a residence (will this violate zoning laws?)
    In a commercial site?
    Will customers easily be able to find the business location?
    Can the business location (home or commercial site) easily be modified to meet your needs?
    Will you rent or lease space?

Select a legal structure (see Chapter 5)
    Sole proprietorship
    Partnership
    Corporation
    Other forms

Are any licenses required? (see Chapter 6)
    Interior design registration?
    Contractors license?
    Business licenses?
    Transaction privilege tax license?

Will the business have employees other than the owner(s)? (see Chapters 6, 9, and 10)
    Are you aware of federal /state filings required?
    What type of benefits will be provided to employees?
    What kind of equipment will be provided for employees to do their jobs?
    How will you recruit employees?

How will business records be maintained? (see Chapters 11 and 12)
    What accounting bases will be used?
    Who will do the daily bookkeeping?
    Who will do payroll and tax records?
    Who will prepare any formal accounting records that are required?

How will the business be financed for the first year? (see Chapter 4)
    Personal investment by owner(s)?
    Investments by friends or relatives?
    Loans?
    Have you prepared an estimated cash flow statement and pro forma income statement or the
        first year?
    Have you estimated your personal living expenses for the first year?
    Have you estimated start-up costs and expenses for the first year?

Have you investigated insurance requirements? (see Chaper 4)
    What kinds of insurance are needed initially?

Will your business require inventory?
    How will you decide what the initial inventory will consist of?
    How will you finance the purchase of initial inventory?
    Where will you store any back-up inventory?
    How will you deliver goods to clients?
    Have you compared your inventory ideas with near-by competitors?

Figure 3–3 Key points to examine and explain for a business start-up.

questions about the proposed organizational structure of the new practice. The remaining chapters in Part 2 give details of many of the points raised in the questionnaires.

The Business Plan

"Fundamentally, a business plan (also referred to as a proposal, a prospectus, or a brochure) is the primary vehicle for giving credibility to an idea."[4] For an interior design practice that will resell goods, the business plan may well be the key to obtaining the funding from banks or venture capitalists necessary to purchase needed inventory. However, an interior design practice that expects to obtain revenue from selling services requires less initial funding. In this case, the business plan is prepared more to provide substantive thought as to what the business is all about and how it is going to operate.

There is no surefire way to prepare a business plan. One should not look for a perfect plan—a "template" that requires the prospective owner to only fill in the blanks. Nor should one look to his or her attorney, accountant, or banker to provide all the answers. The business plan is a personal expression of what the owner feels the firm is all about and how he or she hopes it will grow. Although preparing a business plan will not guarantee success, the process of thinking the business through will help the prospective owner face the realities of starting the business. A plan, if thoroughly done, also provides the opportunity to anticipate problems and avoid them, if possible—or at least to know how to cope with them as they arise.

The business plan is not something that can be done overnight. If a designer is anticipating opening a practice, the prospective owner should allow time to develop the business plan. It may take weeks or even months for it to be prepared, depending on how much time can be devoted to the research and writing of the plan. At times, outside consultants may be required, especially if a formal plan is being prepared to obtain substantial financial backing.

If the owner finds himself or herself preparing the plan after opening for business, an even greater amount of time may be required since the owner must simultaneously keep the business going. In this case, an outside business consultant familiar with the interior design profession may be helpful.

The plan, once completed, helps the prospective owner in many ways toward the goal of having his or her own practice. The plan helps the designer to see if the idea is realistic and feasible. Financial backing will be easier with a well-prepared plan. The business plan also sets initial goals and objectives of the firm, which can be measured by the firm's performance. Later, if performance does not meet these initial objectives, the plan and the ongoing analysis of the plan help the owner determine what to do to get back on track—assuming the plan was feasible in the first place.

Business Plan Research

An important ingredient of all business plans is research. A very thorough period of research should be undertaken before the business plan is written. Certain kinds of information are always expected to appear in the plan. It will be necessary to complete research in areas of skills and abilities, the marketplace, and operational considerations such as pricing, expected capital required, and projected financial planning. For all prospective interior design practices, items 1 through 7 in the following list must be thoroughly investigated and considered. Depending on the actual business idea and use of the plan, the items in 8–10

---

[4]Dible, Donald M., *Up Your Own Organization!* Reprinted by permission of the publisher, Reston Publishing Company, Prentice-Hall, Inc., 1974, p. 118.

and more research may also be necessary. The final step, in all instances, is to produce the actual plan.

The following steps outline the kind of research that the owner of an interior design practice must develop in order to prepare the business plan. The outline presented is in the suggested sequence in which the research should be conducted.

1. Analyze personal abilities and interests related to owning an interior design business. If additional employees are anticipated or are already hired, analyze their abilities.

2. Analyze the potential market for the firm's services. Do not forget to analyze existing competition.

3. Prepare a marketing plan that includes the aspect of the market the firm will address. Determine pricing policies, what services the firm will offer, and considerations for advertising and/or promotional activities.

4. Determine which type of business formation will be used: a sole proprietorship, a corporation, or a partnership.

5. Determine legal responsibilities and tax obligations. Consult with an attorney concerning contracts and liabilities, an accountant concerning record keeping, and an insurance representative on insurance obligations.

6. Estimate how much capital will be required to "open the doors." Estimate the first year's expenses. Determine sources of initial capital.

7. Develop a financial plan and income projections. Include projected balance sheets, income statements, and cash flow forecasts.

8. If the firm will engage in retail selling of inventoried goods, develop an inventory plan of what will be purchased, when it will be purchased, and where it will be stored.

9. Prepare an organizational plan including projected personnel needs, job descriptions, employee benefits, and purchasing procedures.

10. Develop a concept of the firm's image: appearance of letterhead, business cards, exteriors of delivery trucks, title blocks for drawing paper, and so on.

11. Produce the business plan.

The most important parts of the research for the business plan will be steps 2 and 7. One must clearly determine if the services the interior designer wishes to provide are needed in the community and if one can obtain the capital to start and maintain the business. If the research result for either of these concerns is doubtful, the business venture should be reconsidered or possibly rejected.

Writing a Business Plan

After the research has been done, the actual writing can begin. In most cases an overview of the company should come first, with the financial material second. The books listed in the References section provide several outlines of business plans. The following outline is but one suggestion.

I. Business summary

   A. Provide name of owner or board of directors

   B. Give location of business

C. Identify type of business formation (legal structure)

D. Describe business, including types of services to be performed

E. Provide a summary of the owner's and/or manager's expertise in running the business

II. Market research

A. Describe how the information concerning the business was obtained

B. Describe the need for the firm's service in the community. Include numbers of potential clients for your service

C. Describe as much as possible about the known competition

D. Detail existing sales for this kind of firm in the community. This might be available from the chamber of commerce

E. Describe any industry or local trends that might affect the success of the projected firm

III. Marketing plan

A. Detail what portions of the market the firm will address

B. Describe what services will be offered. This may be detailed enough to explain how boards will be done

C. Determine how services and/or products will be priced

D. If a warehouse/delivery service is used, determine how these charges will be passed on to the client

E. Outline what kinds of advertising and promotional activities will support the business

F. Describe any problems concerning expected seasonal business, if this appears applicable

IV. Operational plan

A. Provide organizational structure

B. Analyze hiring of personnel and job descriptions

C. Decide on record keeping and control

D. Analyze employee benefits

E. Project dealings with suppliers, delivery people, and subcontractors

F. Frame customer relations

G. Project personnel needs

V. Financial information

A. Project initial capital and first-year estimates to keep the business operating. Detail how the money will be expended

   B. Estimate additional revenue (monthly) beyond break-even points[5]

   C. Provide month-by-month projected profit-and-loss statements

   D. Decide accounting practices to be used—especially those related to depreciation, leasing, and inventories

   E. Provide a beginning balance sheet

   F. Explain how projections were made

   G. Provide any additional information required of a corporation form of business

Remember that starting a business should involve serious thought and time, or failure may result. If the prospective owner is not willing to devote the time and effort to producing a well-written business plan, he or she may not be ready to expend the energy to keep it going either.

Control and Evaluation

Planning the design business is very important. But it is equally important to evaluate the progress of the practice. Many portions of the business plan will establish some of the control mechanisms that can be used to evaluate financial and organizational success. For example, financial projections prepared in the business plan can easily be compared to actual performance. Project pricing developed in the marketing plan section can be compared to actual performance. Additional control reports might well be suggested by the firm's accountant, attorney, or from the experience of the owner/manager. These reports should address issues of asset management, productivity, and profitability. Many of these control and evaluation reports are discussed in Chapter 12 on financial management control.

Business Location

Interior design is one of those professions that many think fits nicely into a home environment. In fact, a great number of designers begin their practice by working out of a spare bedroom or a converted garage. Although this is economically attractive, the designer should strive to locate in an office as soon as possible. The designer may be a very talented, creative person, but oftentimes, the home office is a jumble of catalogs, samples, and files—not very attractive to a prospective client. Clients are often concerned about the location and the appearance of the office. After all, if the office does not appear businesslike and successful, the client may be reluctant to award the designer with a contract.

    Cities commonly have zoning restrictions against using a residential location for commercial purposes. Neighbors may complain about traffic, parking, or even delivery trucks around the home office. The home office should be considered with caution, as a location for the interior design practice. Even if the home office does not receive deliveries, it may be necessary to apply for a zoning variance (discussed in Chapter 6) to legally operate the business from the designer's home and obtain a business license.

    A business office located in a commercially zoned part of town gives the impression of professionalism. The exact location of the business office will be determined, in part, by the

---

[5]The break-even point is the point at which revenues equal expenses. At this point, the firm is neither making nor losing money.

nature of the business. If the practice is primarily commercial and seeks the office suite and corporate client, a location in the downtown business district would be the most suitable. Should the practice be specialized for a particular kind of business, such as hotels or restaurants, a location near the main hotel district or a downtown location again might be best. Residential design studios are often located near other suppliers such as carpet, wallpaper, or lighting retail stores in suburban locations. This relationship could bring a client to the designer when he or she visits another establishment.

The interior design of the studio, office, or retail store must be of the highest quality to reflect the image the firm tries to achieve. Neat reception areas that give the client an impression that the firm and its employees are professionals is important in attracting the commercial client. Retail stores with well-displayed furniture and furnishings that are cleaned, dusted, and attractively arranged is another important part of projecting the right image to residential and commercial clients. Some owners and managers say that the studio, office, or store that has merchandise, samples, and documents spread out gives the facility the appearance of casualness. More likely it gives the impression of disorganization. Casualness and disorganization are two different things, and it is important for the owner of the studio or office to understand whether the kind of client he or she wishes to attract will be turned off by the sloppy appearance of the facility.

Considering High-Tech Office Equipment

By now, almost every designer and student has become familiar with personal computers, modems, FAX machines, laser printers, sophisticated phone systems, and the many other marvelous electronic "toys" available. Some individuals are still somewhat intimidated by all the high-tech equipment options, especially computers, and remain content using less sophisticated office equipment. Other design firms have become full electronic offices, using computers, FAX machines, phone systems, and all the rest for almost every office function. Most designers are somewhere in between, utilizing some computer or other high-tech office equipment though, perhaps, not to the fullest extent.

Everyone seems to know how the basic computer software applications can help in the design office. Word processing software is used to produce letters, marketing mailings, specifications—anything that is word-intensive. No office of more than four or five individuals should probably be without at least one word processing station. Spreadsheet software is used for accounting, numerical aspects of specifications, even "what if" analysis of pricing and specifications. Database software keeps the office in touch with its clients by creating files of information on those clients (former and potential) that can easily be accessed for specific needs. Databases can also be used to organize a lot of information in product libraries.

More specialized kinds of software applications assist in other ways in the design office. Project-scheduling and time-recording software packages allow accurate record keeping and project scheduling to be done. Many of these software items also provide charting and integration of statistical information. Such software makes it easier to bill clients accurately for design time. Some design offices utilize sophisticated desktop publishing software to produce newsletters, case studies, brochures, and many other direct mailing promotional items within the office. Modems and laptop computers let designers do vital design work and record keeping while away from the office PC. Practically any kind of document that designers are used to preparing by hand or having prepared by outsiders, can be done with in-house computer hardware and software. And we haven't even talked about graphics software yet!

Today it seems that students know more than their small business owners about computer aided design (CAD) systems. Many students are disappointed to land jobs in smaller firms and find the company has no CAD capability. And the majority of students who have become fairly proficient with CAD prefer to work in offices that have that option. However, not every owner or experienced designer has the patience or interest to learn CAD. Not every design office is ready to implement CAD. Many smaller offices cannot justify the expense. But with some software available in the $150 to $500 dollar range, more and more of the smaller design offices are considering CAD for their offices. Larger firms embrace CAD as a way to speed up some of the tedious work in preparing working drawings and office systems layouts.

Although CAD is a tool, in many ways like the drafting pencil, design firms need to let designers use CAD systems for more than the accomplishment of straight drafting. Many aspects of the design of a project can be done quickly on CAD. In addition to 2-D CAD for floor plans, 3-D programs and virtual reality programs allow the designer and the client to "walk thorough" the space before any construction is begun. How exciting for the client and the designer!

Computers and all the other technological gadgets can save time, but at an expense. The first and most obvious expense is purchase price. Even simple hardware systems (main computer with 12-inch monitor, hard drive, and low-end laser printer) with limited amounts of software (word processing and spreadsheet) can cost about $3000 and up. Sophisticated CAD work stations can cost upwards of $75,000. Design firms can often lease the hardware, and the owner needs to discuss this option with the firm's accountant. A second expense is learning time. All software applications take time to learn, even the somewhat easy Macintosh® and Windows® versions. During that learning time, work gets done more slowly and many designers in very small offices often give up and go back to the manual methods. Once the application has been learned, the time savings begin to speed up the work. Cutting, pasting, and spell checkers make creating business communications and specifications almost pleasurable.

Other kinds of electronic equipment also help the designers save time. FAX machines make receiving and sending quotations, orders, letters, parts of drawings—almost anything in black-and-white produced in the office, fast and easy. But again, at a price. Modems allow designers to place orders directly with manufacturers. Laser printers produce beautiful documents, and if the firm is willing to spend a lot of money, laser printers will produce typeset-quality documents in black and white or color. These are just a few of the most commonly used high-tech office equipment options.

Throughout this book, the text has mentioned how computers or other electronic office equipment can help in the management of the business practice. Interior design firms, large and small, need to evaluate how computers can potentially be used in the firm. All firms, regardless of size, can benefit in some way from a computer system or other electronic office equipment. Sophisticated palmtop organizers allow users an electronic calendar, notebook, drawing pad, file cabinet, access to desktop and mainframe computers, the ability to send messages on E-mail, and many other tasks on a unit approximately the same size as the pocket calculators available 15 years ago.

Design firms must look at the benefits and costs of all the specialized office equipment available today. Each firm must evaluate which, if any, automatic equipment is necessary to the operation of the design firm. For example, it used to be easy to install a phone system. The owner contacted AT&T and an installer came by with the phones. Today, design firm owners are assaulted by advertising for phone systems that solve all a business's problems. There are numerous companies providing phone service, others providing the phone equipment, others providing computer lines integrated into the phone system, and even televised phone systems. No book, magazine article, or glossy manufacture's brochure can provide "the answer" to all the questions of each design firm owner. Each business must evaluate its individual office needs and take the time to research the products that will fit those needs. The rest of this section provides some insights into the evaluation process.

Determining Equipment Needs

The selection and purchase of electronic business equipment should be looked at in relation to the overall business plan of the design firm. For example, if a small three-person studio remains sufficiently busy with minimal growth projected, the purchase of a computer system to speed up paperwork processing may not be necessary. However, if the owner's business plan calls for adding in-house installers, additional personnel, and thus more paperwork, the owner must begin to look at how to handle all this additional paper.

Associated with the overall business plan will be an evaluation of specific needs of the firm. This should begin by the owner and employees looking at the many processes performed in the office. Obviously, some processes are more project-related—drafting, specification writing, and presentation materials, for example. Other processes are general office management—accounting, general business correspondence, and marketing, for example. Some processes effectively overlap—ordering merchandise, preparation of design contracts, and other project-related correspondence. The design firm owner must look at all the specific processes in the office to determine if any of them can be improved by the addition of any specific kind of high-tech office equipment. This list of suitable functions should be developed with as much input from the various users as possible. All management levels, and consultants to the firm such as the accountant, should be involved in developing the list of desired functions. For example, a design firm may determine that the creative staff is spending a lot of time doing custom cabinet designs. The firm may determine that a special CAD package to help in the design of custom casegoods and cabinets may be in order. Purchasing the wrong system—for example, one that cannot be upgraded—will become outdated far sooner than it should. This improper choice is also an expense that many firms cannot absorb.

After determining which job functions or processes might be improved with new equipment, the next step is to research what is available. Just about every retailer from K-Mart to major department stores, office supply dealers, office supply "wholesalers," and technical supply specialists sell high-tech office equipment. Before going to any of these individuals, do some homework. Read magazines like *Modern Office Technology* and *The Office*. Review specialized magazines such as *MacUser* and *PC World* for computer hardware and software guidance. City and college libraries will carry references on office equipment. Talk to associates, friends, relatives whose businesses are using high-tech equipment to get their suggestions. Some equipment suppliers also have special arrangements with the professional organizations. Check with national or local chapter offices for any brochures which they may have. The more the designer knows before making contacts with equipment salespeople, the easier it will be to make the right choices.

Larger firms hire information systems consultants to do a lot of the research for them. This may save the design staff or owner time, but there is potentially a down side to using a consultant. Communications and information systems consultants may steer the business only toward systems that the consultant likes, rather than what might be best for the firm. Choose these kinds of consultants carefully so that the business is assured of getting unbiased advice.

The next step is to select the products dealer. Designers in bigger cities have an advantage of multiple dealer options. Pricing may not vary significantly among dealers, but service, knowledgeable staff, and track record will. The dealer should be able to handle the questions without constantly needing to "get back" to the designer. Sales staff should have training and understand completely how the equipment works and its features, benefits, and limitations. The dealer should also be able to do its own service (especially for computers), rather than sending out repairs to someone else.

Once the decision to purchase computer equipment, for example, is made, proper consideration for the time it will take for someone to learn the system and everyone else learn how to deal with the new procedures, must be planned. Frustration sets in when even one person whose work is affected by the new program insists on doing things his or her own way—the old way.

Realize that high-tech office equipment products do not solve problems in and of themselves. More often than not they create problems, especially in the early stages of ownership. A firm with a problem-racked manual-ordering system may experience greater problems if the ordering system is not changed to go along with the useful qualities of the high-tech equipment. Some employees who are intimidated by computers (or other office equipment) are really afraid that the equipment will displace or eliminate personnel. In fact, in most cases, computers add to the number of employees needed. This results from increased productivity related to the uses of the computer, thereby allowing the firm to handle more work.

How much of a high-tech system the company obtains is another consideration. Almost all references and consultants suggest that companies buy the best system the firm can possibly afford based on the requirements determined within the firm. A cheap FAX machine may seem a good idea initially, but if the use of the machine overloads the equipment's capacity to perform, it will require repairs or replacement so quickly that the more expensive machine might well have been cheaper in the long run.

It is sometimes fun to be a pioneer, but not when it comes to computers or other expensive high-tech office equipment. The author does not advocate any one company's office equipment for the interior designer. Rather, the author recognizes that there are many quality products available for the interior design practice. The firm's management team must evaluate the firm's needs before purchasing any product. It is usually wise to purchase office equipment made by a manufacturer that has a track record with that product. Care in determining needs, deciding on the proper products, and locating the right vendors will lead to a happy experience with the purchase of high-tech office equipment.

Summary

Knowing you want to open an interior design practice and having the skills and experience in interior design are not enough. It is important to establish the goals and policies of the proposed practice as well as analyze the abilities of all the individuals who may be involved in the business. Through research and analysis, the best possible decisions about the configuration, direction, and future of the practice can be made. If the prospective owner or the current owner/manager is not willing to put in the effort to develop a well-thought-out business plan, he or she may not be ready to own or operate a practice. The business plan could very well be the most important piece of "design" work the owner/manager does in his or her career.

In this chapter, we have provided an overview to the idea of business ownership. We have defined entrepreneurs and looked at some of the advantages and disadvantages of business ownership. This chapter has also summarized the decisions that must be made before starting a new design practice and discussed the need for and definition of the business plan. The chapter also describes the steps in developing the research material required to prepare a business plan and provides a general outline for the plan. The prospective owner or current owner/manager who is interested in preparing a business plan for an interior design practice should refer to one of the suggested books in the References. Other sources may be found at the public library, bookstores, or from the Small Business Administration.

References

Banfe, Charles. 1991. *Entrepreneur.* New York: Van Nostrand Reinhold.

Busse, Erwin. 1989. *The Business Plan. First Step to Success.* LaConner, Wash.: Haldon Marketing Services.

Dible, Donald M. 1974. *Up Your Own Organization!* 2d ed. Reston, Va.: Reston Publishing.

Jenkins, Michael D., and Max Perlman. 1986. *Starting and Operating a Business in Arizona.* Milpitas, Calif.: Oasis.

Loebelson, Andrew. 1983. *How to Profit in Contract Design.* New York: Interior Design Books.

Mancuso, Joseph R. 1985. *How to Write a Winning Business Plan.* Englewood Cliffs, N.J.: Prentice-Hall.

McCarroll, Thomas. January 6, 1992. "Entrepreneurs: Starting Over." *Time.*

McCaslin, Barbara S., and Patricia P. McNamara. 1980. *Be Your Own Boss.* Englewood Cliffs, N.J.: Prentice-Hall.

Piotrowski, Christine. 1992. *Interior Design Management. A Handbook for Owners and Managers.* New York: Van Nostrand Reinhold.

Silvester, James L. 1988. *How to Start, Finance and Operate Your Own Business.* Secaucus, N.J.: Lyle Stuart.

Siropolis, Nicholas C. 1990. *Small Business Management. A Guide to Entrepreneurship,* 4th ed. Boston, Mass.: Houghton Mifflin.

Chapter 4

Advice and Counsel

All business owners need certain professional advisers and counselors. Since very few people have expertise in all areas of business, the interior design practice owner should find the best advisers possible to help establish and maintain the firm.

In this chapter we will discuss the most important advisers one should consider engaging when starting or operating an interior design practice. Those advisers are: attorneys, who render assistance in many legal areas; accountants, who provide information concerning financial matters; bankers, who may help obtain the financing the firm needs to operate; insurance advisers to help obtain proper insurance protection; and technical consultants, who are the many allied professionals who help the interior designer with specialized design problems.

Attorney

Although it generally is not necessary to use an attorney to start a business, it is a good idea to obtain professional advice before signing any papers. Attorneys can assist the new owner in understanding the numerous legal questions in starting a business. Questions will arise concerning everything from under what form of business to organize to the rights of employees. Firms that organize as corporations will be required by many states to use an attorney to prepare the articles of incorporation. Attorneys also help the existing businesses deal with the many questions of liability, employee issues, contracts, and many other issues surrounding the continuation of a business.

The firm's attorney can:

- Provide specific pro and con reasons for different business formations, based on the firm's goals. He or she can also advise owners considering a change in legal formation

- Prepare legal filings required dependent on the business formation

- Review design contract formats and clauses

- Review legal clauses in leases, rental agreements, purchase agreements, purchase orders, and other business forms

- Resolve employee rights, safety, and compensation questions

- Advise on many questions related to the growth and/or change of the design firm

With the escalating number of liability suits, the attorney can provide counsel on how to avoid a potential suit. The professional designer must be aware of what kinds of actions can get him or her into legal trouble. Awareness should help the designer avoid legal consequences. An attorney will, of course, be needed to represent the design firm if any suits are brought by other parties.

Accountant

Another very important source of advice and counsel will be from the firm's accountant. The new firm will probably retain an accountant rather than hire one as an employee. A large existing firm may have one or more bookkeepers or accountants on their staff and retain an outside accounting firm to do special reports. The accountant's job is to help the business owner decide what kinds of operational reports are going to be needed, to provide guidance in how to prepare those reports, to assist the owners in interpreting these reports, and to prepare the needed financial accounting reports such as the profit and loss statement,[1] balance sheet, and income statement. The accountant or accounting firm may also be needed for other important financial reporting activities, discussed below.

Day-to-day operational accounting—commonly called bookkeeping—may be done in a small firm by the owner or an experienced bookkeeper. Larger design organizations utilize full-time bookkeeping or accounting departments. Daily bookkeeping reports are the means for the firm to keep track of income and expenses. From daily operational bookkeeping records, formal financial reports such as the balance sheet can be prepared. These records, along with any other reports suggested by advisers or required by the owners, provide the quantitative financial and managerial picture of the operation of the firm. More specific concepts of accounting are discussed in Chapters 11 and 12.

Accountants can do many things for design firms besides prepare tax returns and formal accounting reports. Depending on the size of the firm and the owner's specific needs, accountants can:

- Recommend bookkeeping/accounting systems

- Help the smaller firm owner organize office management procedures

- Help analyze financial statements to discover potential problem areas

- Provide counsel concerning financial requirements for normal business operations and future plans of the firm

- Help the owner in developing records needed to obtain loans

- Provide investment counseling

Another important business responsibility where the accountant can be of help is in advising the firm on the sales tax liabilities it will have. Sales tax is imposed by cities, states,

---

[1]A *profit and loss statement* is a clearing account that summarizes the net income or loss for the accounting period. In most cases, the profit and loss statement looks very much like a formal income statement.

and the federal government whenever tangible property is exchanged from a seller to a consumer. Even though the consumer is liable to pay the tax, the seller must actually collect and return this money to the appropriate tax agency. Each taxing authority has different regulations on what items or services must be taxed. The accountant should advise the interior designer in this important issue.

Although all accountants can provide the many services the design firm will need, few accountants are really familiar with the intricacies of interior design business. If possible, the firm should seek out an accountant who has worked with other interior design firms or related professionals.

Banker

Any new business needs to have a banker on its "team" of advisers and counselors. First of all, banking facilities that will handle the firm's account need to be located. The business will need a commercial account. Commercial accounts, especially for the sole proprietorship, show the business community that the firm is a serious business.

In addition to a location for the firm's commercial accounts, banks and bankers can help the interior design practice in many ways. The firm's banker can:

- Provide the designer with help in checking credit references of clients

- Be the first source of funds when the business needs to borrow money

- Provide information on investors who may wish to invest in or loan money to the firm

- Provide investment services

The prospective business owner should look for a bank that is interested in working with smaller businesses. Any bank that is comfortable in working with the small business owner will be able to grow with the business as the business grows. Many banks have changed names and ownership several times in the last few years. It is important to seek out a bank that is stable and without financial difficulty of its own. The practice owner should be sure that the loan officer and others with whom he or she is working are always willing to explain how things work, answer all the owner's questions about how the loan process is structured, understand what the charges are for commercial checking accounts, and are expert in other banking issues of concern to the owner. If this is not happening, ask to work with another person or go to another bank.

Financing the Firm

No matter how many initial assets come from personal sources, eventually all businesses need some outside financing. Growing businesses may need funding for purchasing additional inventory, purchasing new office equipment, or even purchasing their own office space. Although business loans are a major funding source for design practices, many firms—especially those that resell products—work to establish credit with suppliers. This section briefly discusses some basic terminology associated with business financing and describes some of the major credit-granting organizations associated with interior design practices.

Operating funds often initially come from personal assets contributed by the proprietor or partners. Stock sales provide initial operating funds for corporation formations. Operating funds also are obtained from banks and other private lending organizations, loans through the U.S. Small Business Administration (SBA), and investors such as friends and relatives.

Funds that come from creditors as loans are called *debt capital.* Funds that come from investors are called *equity capital.* Creditors expect the debt capital to be repaid plus earn interest. Investors are gambling that they will receive some kind of return on their investment and know, if the business fails, they may not even get their investment back.

Anyone who has tried to buy a car, a house, or even obtain a credit card has dealt with establishing credit. For most proprietorships and partnerships, business credit starts with personal credit histories of the individuals involved. If the business owners have had good personal credit, the business will have an easier time obtaining credit. Corporations, since they are legal entities themselves, must establish credit just like an individual.

The business plan discussed in Chapter 3 is a key document needed by any business formation to obtain credit. Business plans require careful thought in describing the business venture and the financing of the venture. This careful planning provides answers to key questions that all creditors want to know:

- How much money does the business want?

- What does the business want the money for?

- How will the business pay the money back?

- What happens if the business cannot pay the money back?

Private lenders such as commercial banks and finance companies offer *long-term* and *short-term loans.* Long-term loans are for more than one year and are usually granted for the purchase of capital items like office equipment and delivery trucks or to purchase an office location. The items being purchased with the long-term loans for inventory and are usually the security for the loans. Long-term loans for inventory and for simple daily operating expenses—like stationary—might not be available. That would depend on the exact nature of the business and its start-up cost needs.

Short-term loans last for one year or less. Also called *lines of credit,* short-term loans help cover purchasing inventory and credit purchases from suppliers. These loans satisfy temporary need for cash rather than long-term needs. In may cases, these loans are also called *unsecured loans* meaning that collateral is not required. If collateral is required as protection against nonpayment, the loan is considered a *secured loan.* Unsecured loans will be made on the basis of a business's ability to repay. As a business performs positively, it will be able to obtain larger lines of credit. New businesses and businesses with poor credit histories will have to function on a cash basis for many purchases.

When a supplier allows a designer to purchase on credit, the designer is working with the supplier's money. This is especially useful to the small business owner who often does not have the cash on hand to pay for customer orders "up front." Of course, that is why designers ask for down payments or deposits from customers. The down payment or deposit becomes the prepayment required by suppliers from whom the designer cannot order on credit.

The designer establishes credit with a suppler by first filling out a credit application provided by the supplier. This information is verified along with checks on general credit rating through such credit reporting groups as Dun and Bradstreet, The Allied Board of Trade, or Lyon Mercantile (organizations that will be discussed later in this chapter). The supplier then determines the credit limits and conditions for the designer so that he or she can order without down payments.

When the designer pays bills promptly, his or her credit rating goes up with those suppliers. With small suppliers and tradespeople, this information's sometimes shared, so a good credit history with a wallpaper hanger may help get custom cabinets built on credit.

Credit-listing agencies serve as clearinghouses on the credit soundness of businesses. Other businesses, such as manufacturers, will look for these credit listings before extending credit to the interior design firm. The design firm should strive for a credit listing with one of these agencies.

A very important general agency is Dun and Bradstreet (D & B). The D & B is a national credit agency that gathers information on thousands of businesses. It obtains information on a business's operations, legal structure, financial condition, and payment history. It will also review and make available to a requesting business information on a creditor's banking records, financial records such as income statement, the D & B credit rating, and whether legal proceedings against the business have occurred or are in process. The design firm will seek to have a good credit rating with D & B and can also use the D & B reporting service to obtain information on the credit rating of potential business clients.

The Allied Board of Trade (ABT) is a credit agency specific to the interior design industry. Designers register with ABT to show to trade sources the designer and/or design firm is a member of the design community. To obtain a listing with the ABT, designers must show proof of academic training, professional standards of practical experience, and proof of business. This procedure is usually done by reporting a sales tax number and previous trade relations with suppliers. The *Credit Green Book* references the thousands of registered designers and is used by both interior designers to find trade sources and by suppliers to clarify credit information on designers.

Another specialized agency is the Lyon Furniture Mercantile Agency. This agency is a credit agency most used by retail furniture, accessories, and other interior furnishings stores. It is also used by suppliers to obtain credit information on designers who operate retail shops. If a designer is not listed in the *Lyon Credit Reference Book* (sometimes called the Red Book), Lyon will contact the designer for credit information.

Financing the design firms operations is an ongoing activity. Few firms use profits to continually finance the daily operations of the company. Investors expect a return, and some portion of the profits is paid to investors. No matter how small or large the design firm, obtaining funds and maintaining credit with suppliers is very important.

Insurance Advisors

Insurance minimizes the financial risk of the firm in the course of the business day. In today's litigious society, few design firms can afford the risk of operating without appropriate business insurance. Of course, it is best to operate so as to avoid risk rather than depend on insurance policies and an attorney to limit liability. However, as we have witnessed recently, natural disasters, riots, employee psychological distress, accidents, and other unforeseen events create the need for insurance to protect a business and its employees.

The interior design practice, whether providing only specifications and drawings or also providing goods to clients through the resale process, will have some insurance requirements. The firm with part-time or full-time employees will also be required by law to have certain kinds of insurance for employee protection. Design studios and retail stores that display goods for sale and have inventory, will have many more insurance needs than the designer/specifier.

A qualified insurance agent who handles commercial businesses will be another advisor the firm will need. The exact combination of insurance a firm requires will depend on the actual practice. An insurance agent can assist the practice owner in determining precise insurance needs. The following briefly describes basic types of insurance coverage.

Professional liability insurance. Called malpractice insurance by many, professional liability insurance for a design professional will protect the designer in the event an action causes bodily injury or property damage as a result of the professional negligence of the designer. This is the same kind of insurance physicians obtain for malpractice. Designers will want to be sure the professional liability insurance includes errors and omissions coverage (called E & O). This insurance covers the designer in the event of errors or omissions in the preparation of documents or work that was the responsibility of the designer. The ASID sponsors a policy for professional liability insurance.

Property damage, liability, and personal injury insurance. Available to many businesses as a package, this insurance group is especially important to those who own a studio, store, or warehouse. Designers who rent space can obtain variations on this package to take care of their needs. *Property damage* insurance protects the building and its contents due to loss from fire, theft, and wind. Any business that has lost all its records on the computer when a bolt of lighting struck the building understands the importance of property damage insurance. Note that there may be exclusions for events like floods or earthquakes. Supplemental coverage can be obtained for businesses that are in areas prone to these events. *Liability insurance* protects the business should it be sued by a third party for injury or property damage due to negligence, product failure, or other claims of that kind. Note that the business can be sued for the acts of the owners, employees, agents, and suppliers. For example, if the carpet installer hired by the designer breaks a lamp at the client's home, the designer is potentially as liable as the installer. *Personal injury* insurance is part of liability coverage and provides insurance in case of slander, libel, defamation, false arrest, and other personal injury torts. These personal injury torts are discussed in Chapter 7.

Automobile coverage. Cars or other vehicle owned by the company require automobile insurance just as one needs personal automobile insurance. Policies should also cover employee use of their personal car on company business. Design firms that hire tradespeople should be sure that the tradesperson has auto insurance so that the designer is not sued if the tradesperson has an accident while on a job for the designer.

Specialty insurance. There are numerous specialty insurance coverages that may be necessary for the design firm. The insurance professional, perhaps along with the design firm's accountant, will advise the designer on whether it is necessary to have any of these special insurance coverages. *Business income* insurance pays the loss of net profit and for operating expenses in case a fire or other specific, covered event prevents the business from operating. *Crime* insurance protects the firm in case of theft of money by employees or individuals other than employees. *Accounts receivable* insurance covers the loss of accounts receivable records due to fire or other specific events. *Flood and earthquake* insurance provides repayments on property losses due to floods or earthquakes.

When the firm adds employees, additional insurance coverage may be either required or desirable. The government requires the employer to provide workers' compensation insurance to protect the employee in case of work-related injuries. The firm may also wish to provide health and possibly life insurance to employees as a benefit of working for the company.

Technical Consultants

Almost every interior design firm will require the advice and counsel of allied professionals from time to time. Architects, electrical engineers, lighting designers, other mechanical systems consultants, and contractors are some of the allied technical counselors that a firm will occasionally call on to assist with parts of a project.

Technical consultants may be used for advice or to explain how a part of the project will be accomplished. In concert with the designer, they might be hired to meet with the client and obtain the necessary information to prepare plans and specifications. Technical consultants might review drawings prepared by the designer and affix the consultant's stamp to the drawings.

These allied professionals are not necessarily full-time employees of the firm, though larger firms often have one or more allied professionals on staff. The smaller interior design firm will more likely establish a working relationship with these professionals and hire them on a per-job basis, just as a client would hire an interior designer. The interior design firm should not be afraid to admit the need of these professionals. Interior designers preparing documents without the proper license and expertise can easily be sued by the client. A listing of a few of these specialists and how they help the interior designer follows.

Architects: needed to review plans that require an architect's stamp. This is usually for residences over 3000 square feet and commercial spaces that will have more than 20 employees.[2]

Electrical engineers: assist the designer with planning questions on electrical components for floor plans. Electrical engineers also may be needed to stamp electrical plans in order for the owner to obtain a building permit.

Contractors: general and specialty contractors can provide advice on ways to build or specify interior design concepts. For example, a cabinetmaker can advise the designer on how to detail drawings for a traditional custom conference wall that might include storage, plumbing, and audiovisual equipment.

Lighting designers: can provide assistance or provide the design and planning of specialized lighting concepts.

Commercial kitchen designers: provide planning and plans for commercial kitchens in restaurants, hotel food service areas, health care food service areas, and so forth.

Acoustical engineers: needed because large open office spaces and other large open areas often have critical acoustical problems. Acoustical engineers can advise on materials and finishes for furniture and architectural surfaces and locations of acoustical treatments to solve noise problems.

Landscape architects/florists: Interior plants are excellent for the interior environment, but incorrect specification and placement can be expensive. These specialists will advise the designer on the proper selection and positioning of plants in the interior. They can also provide the owner with maintenance instructions.

Health care facility specialists: individuals who have worked in health care may be hired by designers to consult with them on the design of health care professional offices. Designers often hire nursing professionals as consultants.

Miscellaneous consultants: There are many other consultants that the business owner may wish to retain from time to time. The small business owner has a hard time managing all the issues of the firm without occasional special help. In addition to the advisors and consultants listed in the preceding, the design firm owner may wish to talk to public relations agencies, advertising and marketing agencies, employment agencies, management consultants, computer consultants, and communications consultants.

Sources of Information and Assistance

The small business owner is particularly needful of information and help in the organization of a new business and the continuation of his or her design business. Even the design firm

---

[2]Both these criteria vary with the local ordinances. Check with the building department.

considered "large" also frequently needs assistance. There are many private organizations and government agencies that provide consultation or reference materials to the business owner. Although it is not possible to list all these sources in this book, the addresses of many helpful organizations are provided in the Appendix.

Private Organizations

Professional organizations such as the American Bar Association can provide assistance to business owners seeking an attorney. Other professional organizations can help the designer select a consultant as well. Check the yellow pages for the phone number or address of professional organizations' local chapter. To find the name and address of specific trade associations, check the *Encyclopedia of Associations.* This book is available at libraries.

Universities and community colleges often have a small business development center or small business institutes in conjunction with the SBA. These groups provide seminars and one-on-one counseling to the small business owner.

Government Agencies

The SBA is a federal agency providing many kinds of assistance to the small business owner. Assistance may come in the form of informational pamphlets and books, seminars, clinics, and one-on-one counseling. In addition, the SBA may be able to provide financial assistance for qualified small businesses thorough a lending bank. The main address for the SBA is in the Appendix. Local offices may be found in the U.S. Government section of the white pages in the local phone book.

The Internal Revenue Service (IRS) has *Business Tax Kits* for different business operations. Publication 334, "Tax Guide for Small Business," is especially useful. Addresses for local IRS offices are in the U. S. Government section of the white pages.

Many cities and states have small business development centers or economic development offices. These offices can provide pamphlets, seminars, and one-on-one consulting services.

Summary

It is easy to see that there are many very important advisors with whom the interior design firm owner should consult. No one designer, or even group of design professionals, will have the educational or job experience to have all the answers. Business advisors such as attorneys, accountants, bankers, and insurance advisers will help with specialized business questions that may arise for any interior design practice. Allied professionals can offer the firm advice on technical matters that the staff of the design firm may not be familiar with or legally qualified to handle. These advisors are engaged to help the firm remain professionally competent, to stay out of legal problems, and most important, to remain a viable business.

This chapter also looked at a few issues of operating a business that must be considered when creating a new venture or to maintain a design firm. Some of the ways that businesses can obtain funding and establish credit, different kinds of business insurance, and sources of information were also discussed.

References

Anthony, Robert N., and James S. Reece. 1983. *Accounting Text and Cases,* 7th ed. Homewood, Ill.: Richard D. Irwin.

Berk, Joseph, and Susan Berk. 1991. *Managing Effectively. A Handbook for First-Time Managers.* New York: Sterling Publishing.

Dawson, George M. 1991. *Borrowing for Your Business.* Dover, N.H.: Upstart Publishing.

Dible, Donald M. 1974. *Up Your Own Organization!*, 2d ed. Reston, Va.: Reston Publishing.

Kaderlan, Norman. 1991. *Designing Your Practice.* New York: McGraw-Hill.

Loebelson, Andrew. 1983. *How to Profit in Contract Design.* New York: Interior Design Books.

Siegel, Harry, and Alan M. Siegel. 1982. *A Guide to Business Principles and Practices for Interior Designers,* rev. ed. New York: Watson-Guptill.

Stasiowski, Frank A. 1991. *Staying Small Successfully.* New York: Wiley.

Stitt, Fred A., ed. 1986. *Design Office Management Handbook.* Santa Monica, Calif.: Arts and Architecture.

Whitmyer, Claude, Salli Rasberry, and Michael Phillips. 1989. *Running a One Person Business.* Berkeley, Calif.: Ten Speed Press.

Chapter 5

Business Formations

There are several kinds of business formations for an interior design practice. All have their advantages and disadvantages for the small business owner. It is important for the designer wishing to start his or her own business to understand the differences between these formations as they relate to financial liability, taxes, personal liability, and other issues so that he or she may choose the business formation most suitable to the designer's business plan. An appreciation for the various forms is necessary for understanding of the responsibilities of the owner.

This brief discussion will not provide all the answers concerning the selection of a business formation. It does, however, emphasize how important it is for the interior designer to consult with an attorney and an accountant to be sure he or she is making the right choice. In some cases, it is absolutely necessary to consult with an attorney to help set up the necessary legal papers. Major changes in the tax laws went into effect in 1987 and 1993. The prospective business owner should be discussing the merits of the different business formations with his or her accountant as well.

We will discuss sole proprietorship, general and limited partnerships, the corporation, and some specialized forms and the advantages of each in some situations. These specialized formations are the S corporation, the professional corporation, and the joint venture. Figure 5–1 is a summary of the key characteristics of each business formation. Chapter 6 will discuss the various legal fillings of each form of business. The designer is urged to read Chapter 5 and 6 together.

Sole Proprietorship

The *sole proprietorship* is the simplest and least expensive form of business. In this form of business ownership, the company and individual owner are one and the same. Business is most commonly conducted under the owner's name, such as Mary Jane Smith, but may also be done under a company trade name, such as Creative Interior Designs. Since the owner and the company are the same, the company has no existence if the owner quits operating the business unless the business is sold to another owner.

	SOLE PROPRIETORSHIP	GENERAL PARTNERSHIP	LIMITED PARTNERSHIP	CORPORATIONS	"S" CORPORATION	PROFESSIONAL CORPORATION
BASIC REQUIREMENT	Minimal costs. Cheapest and easiest formation.	Nominal costs. Partnership agreement recommended.	Slightly higher costs than General Partnership. Agreement must be filed with state.	Several fees required. Most expensive. Articles of Incorporation filed with state.	Same as Corporation.	Same as Corporation. Not allowed in some states.
LIABILITY OF OWNERS	Unlimited personal liability.	Unlimited personal liability. Liable for partners as well.	General partners - unlimited liability. Limited partner - liable up to limit of investment.	Officers & directors have criminal liability. Other owners only to limit of amount invested.	Same as Corporation.	Similar to Corporation.
DISTRIBUTION OF PROFITS OR ASSETS	Belong to proprietor.	According to partnership agreement or by Uniform Partnership Act.	Same as General Partnership.	Amounts distributed to stockholders and/or into retained earnings based on directors & officers decisions.	Same as Corporation.	Same as Corporation.
CONTINUITY	End when Proprietor wishes. May be able to transfer or sell.	Ends upon death of a Partner. May be transferred with consent of all Partners.	Same as General Partnership. Limited partners can sell their share.	Continues unless corporation ends by decision of board or reason of law. Stock transferred without needed consent.	Same as Corporation.	As regular Corporation.
TAXATION	Taxes filed on 1040- schedule C & SE as personal income. With employees: form 940, 941, W-4, W-2, W-3, 1099s if needed.	Taxes: file on 1045, 1065, schedule K & K-1 of 1065 as personal income. With employees, same as proprietorship.	Like General or other forms, depending on exact formation. With employees, same as proprietorship.	Taxes: 1120, 1120ES quarterly. For corporation, stockholders pay taxes on dividends as personal income. With employees, same as proprietorship.	Taxes: form 1120s. Personal share of corporate profit taxed as partnership With employees, same as proprietorship.	Same as Corporation.
LEGAL FILINGS	Federal EIN# if hire employees. File "Doing Business As" if using unidentifiable company name.	EIN# required. Otherwise, same as Proprietorship.	Same as General Partnership.	EIN# Required. Specific licenses may be required depending on exact nature of corporation.	Same as Corporation.	Same as Corporation.

Figure 5–1 Chart of the key characteristics of business formations.

Advantages

- The simplest to start. In most states all that is necessary to start a sole proprietorship is to establish a location, obtain any local business licenses required, and begin operations. Depending on the exact nature of the business, the proprietor will probably want to open a bank account in the firm's name, prepare the appropriate business stationery, and begin to establish credit with trade sources.

- Great freedom in management. As there is only one owner, that individual makes all the decisions as to how to organize and operate the business.

- All profits to the proprietor. There are no other owners or investors with whom to share the profits.

- Minimal special fees and formal action to create. Fees for business licenses, resale licenses, and registering the business name are minimal. These fees may total from $50 to $300, depending on the city where the proprietorship is located (note that these are annual fees). A resale license is only required if the company plans to sell merchandise to clients. If the owner uses a name for the business other than his or her own name, a Fictitious Business Name Statement will be required (see Chapter 6 for information on both these filings).

- No required filings with federal government to begin business unless employees are hired (see Chapter 6).

- The business not required to pay unemployment tax for owners income. This tax is required for employees of the company. Reduces expenses of the business.

- Generally pays tax rate similar to corporations (since tax reform act of 1987) since profits are reported on personal income tax records. This is not true if the proprietor has significant other personal income that will increase the over-all tax burden. Business income tax reported on Schedule C of Form 1040.

Disadvantages

- Personal liability for all debts and taxes. Creditor may seek payment from the owner's personal savings or property if business assets are insufficient.

- Personal liability for legal claims due to lawsuits. If a suit results in damages that must be paid by the designer, the plaintiff can collect from the firm's assets and, if necessary, from the personal assets of the owner.

- Illness or death of owner could result in failure of business.

- The owner could experience tax problems since business and personal income are easily mixed. Joanne's Interiors was audited by the IRS. In their audit, they determined that the records of Joanne Smith (the owner) insufficiently showed a separation of business income from personal income/expenditures. She was fined for insufficient payment of taxes.

- Difficult to obtain loans to finance the business or establish credit with manufacturers and suppliers. It is difficult for a sole proprietor to obtain loans from banks unless he or she has an excellent personal credit rating or substantial personal assets. For many banks, even substantial personal assets or excellent personal credit does not, in itself, mean that the business will be successful. Many suppliers will only sell initially to sole proprietorships with substantial down payments or payments in full prior to shipping.

- Owner must pay self-employment taxes (social security and Medicare contributions).

These taxes, discussed in Chapter 6, are paid by employers. The self-employed must make these payments themselves.

- Sole ownership requires multiple management skills. Not many designers gain experience in marketing, employee management, accounting, and other management skills while working for other design firms.

- May be difficult to sell the business. Design businesses often flourish because of the personal reputation of the owner. Clients may not stick with the business if it is sold to someone else. This reduces the potential value of the firm when the original owner tries to sell.

- In states with community property laws, if a couple divorces, the proprietor may be forced to sell or close the business to divide proceeds.

Partnerships

Partnerships are created when two or more individuals agree to start a business. Although no formal written agreement is required by law, it is widely recommended that a partnership agreement be prepared. If a partnership agreement is not written, most states refer to the Uniform Partnership Act (UPA) as the terms of the partnership. Partners are co-owners unless some other agreement about the level of ownership has been agreed to. Partners also act in each other's behalf and are thus each able to bind the company to agreements. There are two types of partnerships that can be used by the interior design practice: the general partnership and the limited partnership.

General Partnership

When two or more people join for the purpose of forming a business, and these people alone share in the profits and risks of the business, a *general partnership* is formed. The name of the firm may be a trade name like Creative Interior Designs, ID Associates, or it may be the partners' names, such as Brown and Williams Associates. Two or more interior designers often start a business as a partnership because the partnership brings (1) more design talent (perhaps some skill or experience that one partner lacks) to the company, (2) the assets and credit rating of the partners, and (3) shared responsibilities of the company. General partnerships do not require a formal partnership agreement. Figure 5–2 lists the items most commonly described in a partnership agreement.

Advantages

- Relative ease of formation. Very similar to sole proprietorship.

- Benefit of two or more people involved in the affairs of the business.

- Easier (than sole proprietorship) to raise capital and establish credit because more than one person is involved in the business.

- Low tax responsibility on profits—similar to the proprietorship. Individual taxes on partnership profits are reported on Schedule E on Form 1040. This income is considered personal income and is taxed as such on each individual partner's federal and state income tax forms in the same way as the income from a sole proprietorship (see Chapter 6).

- Partners do not have to pay unemployment taxes on partner's income.

These items are among the most common decisions that must be made when developing a partnership agreement. An attorney may suggest additional items depending on the nature of the business.

Name and address of the business location.

Names and addresses of the partners.

Responsibilities of each partner.

How much capital will be contributed by each partner?

How will business profits be distributed?

How will business holdings be divided in the event of the dissolution of the partnership?

How will each partners drawings be distributed?

How will the partnership be dissolved in the event of a partner's disabling illness, death,
    retirement, or other reasons?

How can ownership be transferred to another partner?

Which partners have fiduciary responsibilities?

Figure 5–2 Common items to be defined in a partnership agreement.

Disadvantages

- Unlimited financial liability for any losses or debts of the partnership. If assets of the partnership are insufficient to satisfy debts, personal assets (up to limitations established in each state) are vulnerable.

- Disagreement between partners in how to manage the partnership may create difficult problems.

- Profits are split as determined by the partnership agreement (or equally if no written agreement has been prepared).

- Partnerships are required to file many more forms with the federal and state tax authorities than is a sole proprietorship (see Chapter 6).

- If one partner is unscrupulous, the others can lose their share of the partnership assets and possibly their personal assets as well. The firm and each partner of the firm is responsible for the actions of all the other partners. This means that any wrongdoing of one partner, or any promises made by one partner, are the responsibility and obligation of the other partners also. If John Jones, one of the partners of Jones, Smith, and Brown, contracts with Knoll International for $50,000 of Bertoia chairs, the assets of Jones, Smith, and Brown and the personal assets of Mr. Jones, Ms. Smith, and Mr. Brown might be needed to pay for the order if the company's assets are insufficient.

- Any change in the relationship of the partnership dissolves the partnership. If any of the partners wishes to withdraw from the partnership, the original partnership is usually dissolved. This includes bankruptcy of one of the partners or the partnership itself. If the remaining partners (assuming there were more than two to start) or others wish to continue the business, a new partnership must be formed. If, at some time, a new partner wishes to join the firm, the original partnership is again dissolved and a new one is formed. Should one of the partners die or become physically incapacitated so as to not be able to perform agreed-upon duties, the partnership is likewise dissolved.

Limited Partnership

A *limited partnership* is formed according to statutory requirements, with a limited partnership agreement on file with the state in which it was formed. If the limited partnership operates in other states, it may be necessary that an agreement be on file in those other states. A limited partnership is formed with at least one general partner and other partners designated as limited partners. The general partner(s) have responsibility for the management of the firm. They also assume the same kind of personal financial responsibility that is true for members of a regular partnership. The role of the limited partner(s) is limited to that of investor.

The limited partner(s) contribute assets toward the operation of the partnership and receive a portion of the profits, but they cannot make any management decisions regarding the operation of the firm. The limited partner(s) has financial responsibility for only the losses and debts of the partnership to the amount of each limited partner's investment in the design firm. The general partner(s) have the same legal responsibilities as members of a normal general partnership. Should any of the limited partner(s) become involved in the management of the design firm, he or she is no longer a limited partner but a general partner. When this happens, the former limited partner now shares in the liability of the firm as do the general partners.

A limited partnership might be a good option for designers who are looking for people to invest in their company. A disadvantage for investors would be that the profits of the limited partnership are taxed as personal income. Personal income is taxed at a higher rate than many other kinds of investment opportunities.

Corporation Form

A *corporation* is an association of individuals created by statutory requirements and, as such, is a legal entity. The corporation exists independently of its originators or any other member. It can sue and be sued by others, it can enter into contracts, and it can commit crimes and be punished. A corporation also has powers and duties distinct from any of its members, and survives even after the death of any or all of its stockholders. Simply stated, a corporation is like a person, legally and financially separate and distinct from any of its members (called stockholders or shareholders), yet legally and financially responsible, like any individual person. A stockholder's liability extends only to the ownership and value of his or her stock. Individual stockholders of a corporation cannot be sued, cannot enter into contracts, and so on.

How a Corporation Is Formed

The rules governing the right to form corporations is held by the individual states. The states establish regulations concerning chartering a corporation and its general organization and operational limitations. If a firm engages in interstate commerce, it will also be regulated by the federal government. The term *incorporate* means to create a corporation. The term *incorporation* is the act or process of forming a corporation.

Corporations that might be formed for the interior design profession are called *private corporations*. This means that the corporation has been formed for private interests. Public corporations are those formed by some government agency for the benefit of the public. The U. S. Postal Service is an example of a public corporation.

When all the shares of stock of a corporation are privately held by a few individuals, and the stock is not traded on any of the public markets, the corporation is called a *close corporation.* Other names for a close corporation are family corporations or closely held corporations. If a corporation sells its stock on one of the formal exchanges (New York Stock Exchange and American Stock Exchange, or one of the small Over-the-Counter exchanges), it is commonly called a public corporation, although, by the definition given, the term is technically misleading. In this case, the sale of the stock would be regulated by the Securities Exchange Commission.

Firms generally incorporate in the state in which they do business if they engage only in intrastate commerce. A corporation formed in one state and doing business only in that state is called a *domestic corporation.* Domestic corporations are also corporations that have been organized within the United States. When firms engage in interstate commerce, they may find it advantageous to incorporate in some other state as well. In this case, the corporation must obtain permission to operate in the second state from the second state. A corporation formed in one state but doing business in another state is referred to by the other state as a *foreign corporation.* A foreign corporation does not have an automatic right to operate in the second state.

A corporation may be formed by one or more persons, depending on the state of origination. The organizers of the corporation must prepare a document called the Articles of Incorporation. This document must be prepared by an attorney and submitted to the proper authority in the state. Figure 5–3 shows the general outline of articles of incorporation.

When the articles of incorporation are completed, they are usually sent to the secretary of state, along with a filing fee. Generally, after approval, a certificate of incorporation is returned, along with the articles, by the secretary of state.

The first organizational meeting, the date of which is stated in the articles of incorporation, is then held. During this meeting, the board of directors is elected, the bylaws are prepared, discussions or actions concerning the sale of stock take place, and so on. When this agenda is completed, the corporation may formally begin operation.

It is possible for anyone to start his or her design business as a corporation. The many advantages of the corporate form influence interior designers to begin their business in this manner. There are also some disadvantages for the small firm owner or the designer who will be working alone while the business is getting established.

Advantages of the Corporation Form

- Limited financial liability of originators and stockholders. Financial liability of the originators (or principals) and stockholders is limited to the amount of money each invests in the corporation. The personal assets of the principals and stockholders

---

1. The name of the corporation.

2. The purpose and nature of the business in which the corporation will engage.

3. The initial capital structure.

4. The place the corporation will do business.

5. The names of the initial board of directors.

6. The names of the incorporates.

7. Other information as might be required by the state for that type of business.

Figure 5–3 Basic outline of items that comprise the Articles of Incorporation required for new corporate forms of business.

cannot be touched to pay any operational costs or to satisfy legal judgments resulting from the operations of the business or initiated by any individual employee of the business.

- Corporations generally have an easier time of deducting business expenses for such things as equipment, automobile usage, entertainment, and so on, than do partnerships and sole proprietorships. This changes as tax laws change.

- Corporations have continuity even if the originators and stockholders change or cease to be involved with the corporation. The originators may sell their interests in the firm to other stockholders or to outside parties at any time, and the corporation goes on. Stockholders may also sell their stock back to the principals or to outsiders, and the firm goes on without major change. If the principals or any of the stockholders die or otherwise withdraw from the operation of the business, the corporation still remains intact.

- The relative ease in raising capital through the sale of stock. The primary way a corporation raises capital is to sell stock. When the corporation is formed, the initial board of directors determines how many shares of stock will be issued and how much of this first issue will be sold. Later, the corporation may sell additional stock to raise more capital.

- Corporations obtain debt financing (loans) more readily than individuals. A firm may also raise capital by going to lending institutions and pledging future assets as collateral to secure loans. Although this method is open to partnerships and sole proprietorships as well, it is much easier for a corporation to obtain loans in this way than it is for these other forms of business.

- Shareholders elect board of directors. This gives shareholders a say in the management of the corporation.

- The corporation is a legal entity. This fact legally separates the business from the owners and managers.

- Nature of the corporation, even if only by legal appearance, may make it easier to attract employees.

Disadvantages of Corporation Form

- Most complicated and highest cost of initialization. Initial costs of incorporation include lawyer's fees and filing fees for the articles of incorporation (although some states allow for businesses to incorporate without an attorney).

- A great deal of paperwork is necessary to continue the corporation. City, state, and federal regulations will involve the filing of numerous reports. These will include unemployment insurance, taxes, funds for the employer's share of social security, and payment of city and/or state sales taxes on merchandise sold to clients. Of course, many of these forms must also be filed by other business formations, especially if the business has employees.

- The officers and directors of the corporation are liable for any criminal actions they or their representatives perpetrate in the name of the corporation.

- Stockholders have little to say about how the corporation is managed other than the election of the board of directors and officers. Their only opportunity to influence management or have a say in how the firm is managed is at the annual stockholders' meeting.

- Annual stockholders' meetings must be held. Corporate officers are required to inform the stockholders of the financial condition of the corporation and conduct other such business as might be dictated by the board of directors or stockholders. An annual financial report must be prepared by an accounting firm and provided to the stockholders.

- Double taxation. The corporation must pay taxes on its profits. In addition, stockholders pay taxes on dividend income. With recent changes in the tax laws the maximum tax rate is higher than on the same amount of income if it were reported as personal income. Corporation officers also pay employment taxes, social security and Medicare contributions, and unemployment taxes. Corporations must pay all these same taxes on all employees of the corporation.

- Corporations are more heavily regulated by state and federal agencies.

- Corporation must qualify and register to do business in other states.

S Corporations

S corporations (formally called subchapter S corporations) enjoy all of the advantages of the corporation except that they pay taxes as a partnership. Many interior designers use the S corporation form when they begin their practice in order to have the liability protection of the corporation. Designers may also wish to elect S corporation status in the early years of the business when the firm is most likely to experience business losses. These losses are absorbed by the shareholders rather than by the business itself. It is necessary to change to the corporate form when the firm no longer meets the eligibility requirements of an S corporation.

A design business choosing to qualify as an S corporation must apply to the Internal Revenue Service. The eligibility requirements include: (1) that the firm be a domestic corporation (incorporated within the United States), (2) that shareholders can only be individuals—not other corporations, (3) that there cannot be more than 35 shareholders, (4) that all shareholders be American citizens, (5) that the corporation has only one class of stock, and (6) that the firm obtains no more than 25 percent of its revenues from investments. Because of these requirements, it is common for smaller, family, or closely held corporations to elect to be treated as S corporations.

The S corporation does not pay taxes on its income as a corporation, though the corporation must file special tax reports with the government (see Chapter 6). Corporate earnings and losses are paid or deducted by the shareholders on their personal federal and state income tax forms, in proportion to the share of stock they hold in the corporation. The S corporation can choose to use the lowest tax bracket of its shareholders whether or not income is distributed.[1]

Since the advantages and disadvantages are very similar to those of a corporation, they will not be repeated here. Business owners considering the S corporation election should carefully discuss this issue with their accountant.

Professional Corporations

A relatively new form of business—a *professional corporation* (referred to as professional associations in some states)—is a corporation formed by persons in professions such as law, medicine, dentistry, accounting, and architecture. In many states, only professional services that

---

[1]Jentz 1987.

are licensed or have other legal authorization by the state may register as professional corporations. The letters *P.C.* (professional corporation), *P.A.* (professional association), or *S.C.* (service corporation) follow the name of the firm to identify it as a professional corporation.

The rules governing the right to form this kind of corporation are held by the individual states. All states and the District of Columbia allow professions to utilize this formation within the guidelines of state statute; some have very limiting restrictions related to the professional corporation. One important consideration about a professional corporation is that all shareholders must be licensed to practice the service being provided. This kind of business is formed in the same manner as an ordinary corporation. Tax benefits are the same as for any other corporation. And in most instances, the professional corporation must act like a normal corporation in order to receive those tax benefits.

Liability of the members is a little different from the normal corporation. If one of the members commits an act that is malpractice, the other members are generally not liable. Yet some courts governed by statutory regulations may rule that all members of the corporations are liable for the actions of the others.[2] Shareholders would not be liable for torts unrelated to malpractice. For example, if a delivery person working for the professional corporation had an accident while on the way to a client's home, the corporation and the delivery person would be liable, but the stockholders of the corporation would not be personally liable. As in corporations, any shareholder of a professional corporation who is guilty of a negligent act is personally liable for the injury and damages.

Strict laws enacted in 1981 have limited the formation of professional service corporations. These were passed because many felt that professional service businesses were taking too great a tax advantage from this business form. The newer rules do not allow many of the tax loopholes formerly permitted. The restrictive requirements for the professional corporation do not make this business formation especially attractive to many in the design field. And generally, only those corporations operating in states where licensing is required even have the option of professional corporation status.

Joint Venture

A *joint venture* is a temporary contractual association of two or more persons or firms that agree to share in the responsibilities, losses, and profits of a particular project or business venture. The key to the joint venture is its temporary status. It is treated much like a partnership, but it is for a limited time period or a certain activity. Not being a legal entity, it cannot be sued, but the individual members of the joint venture can be sued. The profits and losses of the venture are usually taxed as they would be for a partnership.

The firms agreeing to enter into a joint venture should prepare a formal agreement clearly explaining the responsibilities of each party, the conditions of the arrangement, the manner in which the profits and losses will be divided, the method for paying employees, and so on. Because a joint venture is like beginning a brand-new business, joint venture companies often select a new name for the temporary partnership for the duration of the project. When this happens, neither firm loses its original identity, and both generally go on with other projects that are separate from the joint venture project. When the project is completed, the temporary partnership ends, and each firm goes back to working on a completely individual basis.

This kind of business relationship is most often entered into by architectural offices for very large projects, but it is something that can also be used by interior design firms. Architectural and interior design firms enter into joint ventures for several reasons. The most common reason is that a project is so large that no single firm would have the time and

---

[2]Clarkson 1983.

support team to do it alone. Devoting the entire work force to one project, especially commercial projects that often take a substantial amount of time, would leave any design firm without a steady source of income. Depending on the income from that one project might leave the design firm in financial straits until the project is completed.

Joint ventures also give firms an opportunity to gain experience in a kind of project for which they have little or no experience. One firm may have the staff to do the drafting and documentation needed for a hospital project but no experience with the interview and design development stages of hospital design. A second firm may not have enough draftspersons to handle the increased workload but has the interview and design development experience to plan the hospital. If these two firms create a joint venture, both will gain from the project.

The joint venture also provides a very strong design team for the client. Using the expertise from two firms can mean better design and follow-through for the client than when only one firm, which may not have the support staff or expertise to complete the project in a timely fashion, is employed.

Combining the staffs of two or more firms increases the speed inherent in a large staff. If one firm were to obtain the contract, it might be necessary to hire additional designers, either to work on the new project or other existing projects. This learning-time cost can be a problem in completing any of the projects the firm has under contract and could be too costly for the design firm even to undertake. The temporary partnership brings the staffs of both firms into use and may negate any further need to hire additional employees on a short-term basis.

Through the joint venture, both firms continue with their own individual identities and with projects other than the joint venture project. If the firms did not create a temporary partnership in this way, but wished to join together, one firm would have to merge with the other. This, of course, means that one firm would no longer exist.

Finally, a joint venture gives the two firms an opportunity to learn from each other in areas other than design. The relationship of the two firms may bring about exchanges of information on how to make presentations, ideas on general business practices, marketing strategies, and so on. Although competing firms do not willingly give away their design and business secrets, some ideas and concepts can be shared while respecting the integrity of both firms.

Summary

Determining which business formation to use is one of the many important decisions that must be made as an interior designer plans for his or her own business. It is important to understand the many differences in the formations so as to appreciate the obligations of the owner.

This chapter has briefly outlined the advantages and disadvantages of the many legal forms of business that can be used by the interior design practice. We have covered the advantages and disadvantages of the sole proprietorship, partnership, corporation, S corporation, professional corporation, and joint venture. In our next chapter, we will discuss the legal filings necessary to form a business using one of the major forms.

References

Anthony, Robert, and James S. Reece. 1983. *Accounting Text and Cases*, 7th ed. Homewood, Ill.: Richard D. Irwin.

Barnes, A. James. 1981. *A Guide to Business Law*. Homewood, Ill.: Learning Systems.

Clarkson, Kenneth W., Roger LeRoy Miller, and Gaylord A. Jentz. 1983. *West's Business Law, Text and Cases,* 2d ed. St. Paul, Minn.: West Publishing.

Cushman, Roger F., and James C. Dobbs, eds. 1991. *Design Professional's Handbook of Business and Law.* New York: Wiley.

Jentz, Gaylord A., Kenneth W. Clarkson, and Roger LeRoy Miller. 1987. *West's Business Law—Alternate UCC Comprehensive Edition,* 3d ed. St. Paul, Minn.: West Publishing.

Loebelson, Andrew. 1983. *How to Profit in Contract Design.* New York: Interior Design Books.

McKenzie, Ronald A., and Bruce H. Schoumacher. 1992. *Successful Business Plans for Architects.* New York: McGraw Hill.

Piotrowski, Christine M. 1992. *Interior Design Management.* New York: Van Nostrand Reinhold.

Prentice-Hall. 1987. *1987 Federal Tax Handbook.* Paramus, N.J.: Prentice-Hall.

Research Institute of America. 1987. *Federal Tax Coordinator,* 2d. ed., vol. 6. New York: Research Institute of America.

Siegel, Harry, and Alan M. Siegel. 1982. *A Guide to Business Principles and Practices for Interior Designers,* rev. ed. New York: Watson-Guptill.

Siropolis, Nicholas C. 1990. *Small Business Management. A Guide to Entrepreneurship,* 4th ed. Boston, Mass.: Houghton Mifflin.

Sweet, Justin. 1985. *Legal Aspects of Architecture, Engineering, and the Construction Process,* 3rd. ed. St. Paul, Minn.: West Publishing.

Veitch, Ronald M., Dianne R. Jackman, and Mary K. Dixon. 1990. *Professional Practice. A Handbook for Interior Designers.* Winnipeg, Canada: Peguis Publishers.

Chapter 6

Legal Filings

Depending on the exact nature of the practice, even without employees, some legal forms are required to begin most types of businesses. This chapter discusses some of the various legal papers or applications—other than partnership agreements and articles of incorporation—that must be processed in order to start an interior design business. Some of the filings are only necessary once employees are hired. And a few specialized filings that do not necessarily relate to starting a practice but that may be required or needed are also covered in this chapter. Such filings include title registration and copyright protection.

A caution about legal filings. Changes are made annually in many of the requirements for business filings, especially those applied to tax laws. The documents discussed in this chapter are broad guidelines of what is required of each form of business. The business owner or prospective business owner must consult with his or her accountant and attorney to be sure the correct forms are filed each year.

Federal Forms

The federal government requires one form to be completed by any business formation. That form is the Application for Employer Identification Number. Additional forms are required of all businesses that have employees. And, of course, different income tax forms are required depending on the form of business. This section will briefly describe the different federal forms required to begin and maintain a business.

SS-4: Application for Employer Identification Number

The employer identification number (EIN), issued by the Internal Revenue Service (IRS), identifies the interior design firm to the federal government as a business. It is required of all businesses that have been formed as corporations or partnerships or any formation with employees. A sole proprietorship formation with no employees would not be required to apply for an EIN. In that case, the proprietor can use his or her social security number. However, since the EIN is required on the Schedule C, obtaining an EIN is recommended for the sole proprietorship form. Partnerships are required to obtain an EIN.

Remember, when the practice has been formed as a corporation, anyone working for a corporation is an employee. This means that even if only one individual actually *generates income* for the corporation and this one individual is one of the board of directors/stockholders for the corporation, that individual is an employee.

An S corporation must file a Form 2553 within 75 days of the date that operations of the corporation commence. This form must be signed by all the shareholders electing to be taxed as an S corporation.

Formations with Employees

When the firm has employees, additional federal forms must be completed.

Form 940: Employer's Annual Unemployment Tax Return

Form 940 is used to report and pay the Federal Unemployment Compensation Tax. It must be filed and paid on an annual basis in January. The liability is calculated quarterly and must be deposited when it reaches or exceeds $100.

Form 941: Employer's Quarterly Federal Tax Return

Form 941 reports the amount of income tax and social security withheld from all the employees' wages. It also reports the amount of social security and Medicare tax matched by the employer for all employees. The amount of social security and Medicare tax must be calculated on a monthly basis and paid to the depository bank by the date found in IRS circular E.

Form W-4: Employee's Withholding Allowance Certificate

Each employee is required by law to fill out a Form W-4. The employer is required to keep this form on file and must send a copy of the W-4 to the IRS if the employee claims ten or more exemptions or claims an exemption from withholding. This form indicates the number of deductions to which the employee is entitled, which determines how much income tax is withheld from wages. With the 1987 Tax Reform Act, it is even more important for employees to fill out this form correctly as they may face penalties if too much or too little tax is withheld. Employees who paid no income tax in the previous year and expect not to have any tax liability in the coming year may file the W-4 on an "exempt" status. Employers and employees should consult with an accountant to be sure they are fulfilling their legal responsibilities related to Form W-4.

Form W-2: Employer's Wage and Tax Statement

By January 31 of each calendar year, the employer must give each employee two copies of the Wage and Tax Statement. States with a state income tax require three copies so that a copy is available for filing with the state tax return. Form W-2 shows all wages paid; federal, state, and city taxes withheld; and social security taxes (shown as FICA) withheld. Other information may also be reported on this form depending on the structure of benefits and wages for the interior design firm.

Form W-3: Transmittal of Income and Tax Statements

Copy A of all W-2s and a completed Form W-3 are filed with the Social Security Administration by the employer. Form W-3 totals all the information on the W-2 and provides income information to the Social Security Administration.

Unemployment Taxes and Worker's Compensation Insurance

Few design businesses with employees will be exempted from paying federal and state unemployment taxes and workers' compensation insurance. Generally speaking, unemployment taxes provide funds to eligible employees in the event they are laid off from their job. Workers' compensation insurance is an insurance program to provide funds to cover the expenses of work-related injuries. Federal financial requirements for unemployment tax responsibility are set at a low threshold and almost all businesses with employees, even only one employee, will pay unemployment tax. State laws generally require most businesses, regardless of size, to provide workers' compensation insurance.

Forms 1099: Information Returns

In certain circumstances, the employer will have to file one or more copies of Form 1099. There are many different 1099s to report specific information. These forms report taxable income that does not fall under the normal wages category. Some special types of income include dividends on stock and nonemployee compensation, such as compensation paid to contract labor. Other 1099s may have to be filed, depending on the exact nature of the business and its benefits program.

Federal Income Tax Forms

Each business formation must file federal income tax forms. The exact form differs for each business formation. The following is a brief description of the most common federal tax forms filed for each business formation.

Sole Proprietorship

Schedule C Form 1040 or C-EZ Form 1040 and Schedule SE Form 1040

The proprietorship, as such, does not pay income taxes. Taxes are the responsibility of the sole proprietor. Income and deductions from this business form are filed on Schedule C Form 1040 or Schedule C-EZ Form 1040 if the design firm had gross receipts of $25,000 or less and business expenses of $2,000 or less. A self-employment tax is required of any net earnings totaling at least $400 in the taxable year. The self-employment tax is figured and reported on the Schedule SE Form 1040. The self-employment tax is the equivalent of the social security tax paid by employees. The government acts as an agent to collect this tax for the Social Security Administration. Both schedules are filed with the standard form 1040 and are due at the same time as the 1040. Sole proprietors may have to pay estimated taxes if the estimated tax and self-employment tax will exceed the withholding and credits amount by $500 or more.

Partnership

The partnership as an entity does not pay income taxes. Each partner, however, is responsible for paying income taxes on his or her share of the earnings of the partnership as part of his or her own personal income tax. The partnership must prepare and file a Form 1065. This is an informational return that must be signed by one of the partners. The estimated tax payment requirement for a partnership is like that of the sole proprietorship.

Schedule K Form 1065 and Schedule K-1 Form 1065

Schedule K and Schedule K-1 of Form 1065 are used to show each partner's share of income, deductions, credits, and so on.

Schedule E, Form 1040

Each partner's share of the income or loss is reported on Schedule E of Form 1040. This schedule is filed along with the remainder of the individual Form 1040 filed by each partner.

A limited partnership, depending on the partnership agreement, may require federal tax forms other than those listed. If the interior design practice has been formed as a limited partnership, the partners should consult with an accountant to be sure they are filing the correct forms.

Partners also must report and pay their self-employment tax. They will use the 1040-SE schedule to report that tax.

Corporation

Interior design practices formed as corporations are entities in and of themselves and, as such, the business entity must file income tax forms. In addition, each employee and stockholder of the corporation must provide appropriate information on his or her individual Form 1040.

Corporations pay taxes based on graduated rates. For the most part, the corporation determines the gross income and taxable income of the firm in a fashion similar to that of an individual. However, the corporation has certain limitations as to exclusions of income and certain advantages as to deductions from income. Exactly what factors constitute income and what factors constitute allowable deductions for a corporation should be determined in consultation with an accountant. All corporations that expect to have a tax liability of $500 or more must make estimated tax payments. Depending on one's actual status in relationship to the corporation, some employees of the corporation may have to pay a self-employment tax.

Form 1120

Form 1120 calculates and reports the total actual income tax for the previous year. Smaller firms whose gross receipts, total assets, and total income are under $500,000 may be able to use the Form 1120-A short form. It is due by March 15 if the corporation is on a calendar year accounting basis. The filing time for corporations on a fiscal year accounting basis would be different. Each quarter (April 15, June 15, September 15, and December 15), the corporation must prepare an estimated income tax for the current year using a Form 1120 ES and deposit the quarterly amount with a Federal Tax Deposit (FTD) Coupon Form. The deposit must be made in a Federal Reserve or an authorized commercial bank.

Depending on the exact nature of the corporation, its sources of revenue and expenses, and general business dealings, other forms may have to be filed. The firm's accountant can provide guidance on which other (if any) forms are required.

S Corporations

The S corporation basically pays no income tax as a corporation, although it may have to pay income tax on such items as capital gains, and it may have to pay the minimum tax. Net income (or loss) of the S corporation is passed on to the shareholders. The shareholders are responsible for paying taxes on their share of the income. The S corporation retains its privilege not to pay federal taxes as long as the S corporation does not lose its eligibility to be an S corporation. A business must file Form 2553 to indicate that it has elected S corporation status for tax purposes.

Form 1120S

The subchapter S corporation must file a copy of Form 1120 S each tax year. This is a calendar year report that informs the IRS of gross income and allowable deductions, distributions to stockholders, and information on the stockholders as related to the stockholders' percentage of income and loss.

Professional (Private) Corporations

The professional (also called private) corporation, in order to receive the tax benefits of this formation, must behave as a standard corporation. Therefore, it must file the same tax forms with the federal government that the standard corporation must file. Employees of the private corporation will be subject to self-employment tax.

Joint Ventures

Since joint ventures are special forms of partnerships as far as the federal government is concerned, the joint venture must file annual partnership returns. Each member of the joint venture must also report his or her share of the gains and losses of the venture on his or her personal income tax return. This is done until the joint venture is terminated.

State Forms

It is not possible in the space allotted to discuss fully all the specific requirements of the various states. The following is a rather general discussion of the legal filings that would be common to all the states. In some cases, a firm located in one state and doing business in another state may also need to file specific forms or obtain licenses to operate in that other state. The interior design practice owner must check with the proper counsel to be sure he or she is fulfilling the requirements of each state in which the firm will be located.

Employer's Identification Number

Many states will require that the business obtain a state employer's identification number in addition to the federal identification number. This number, issued by the state revenue service, helps to determine the rate of tax the business must pay. It also helps to determine the withholding and unemployment taxes for which the business may be responsible. In the states where an employer's identification number is required, it is most often required whether or not the business has employees.

State Transaction Privilege (Sales) Tax License

Most states will require all businesses to obtain the Transaction Privilege Tax License whether or not the business will be selling goods. It is imperative for businesses that intend to resell goods to the end user. The sales tax license allows the interior designer to pass on the state sales tax to the consumer. It must be remembered that if the business fails to collect and pay this tax to the state and/or city, the taxing authority will hold the business responsible for the tax moneys. Generally, the amount collected must be reported and paid on a quarterly basis. Sales taxes are discussed further in Chapter 13.

Use Tax Registration Certificate

If the business will be purchasing goods from out of state, and these goods are taxable in the state in which the interior design firm is doing business, the business will be required to obtain a Use Tax Certificate. This insures that sales taxes or use taxes are collected either by the state selling the goods to the interior design firm or by the firm to the state where the goods become the end users.

Corporation Identification Numbers

Since the privilege of operating a corporation rests with the states, the states require that all businesses formed as corporations be registered by the state before operations begin. In most cases, corporation identification numbers are obtained from the state department of revenue. In many states, the corporation may also be regulated by either the state attorney general's office or some other state office.

Employee Withholding Reporting

For businesses with employees, the firm must file income tax withholding, unemployment, and workers' compensation reports with the state revenue department. The manner in which these are collected, their amounts, and the reporting methods vary from state to state. The interior design firm must check with the proper agency to be sure it meets the legal obligations of its particular state.

Personal Property

In states where personal property of the business is taxed, a report of the value of the personal property of the business will have to be reported. In most cases, this information will be given to the county attorney or county assessor of the county in which the business is located rather than to the state revenue department.

Income Taxes

All forms of business will have to report income and losses of the business on a yearly basis. Since most states model their income tax reporting on the federal laws, the reporting methods will be similar. Forms and actual reporting methods are, of course, different for each state.

There are some additional similarities between federal and state income tax filing requirements. Most business formation may have to pay estimated taxes based on profitability. The tax period for the state is the same as businesses use for federal taxes.

There are no special filings for sole proprietorships in order to organize. Only limited partnerships and corporations must file specialized forms (as discussed in the previous chapter) to start the business. Proprietorships and partnerships must file a Fictitious Business Name Statement (discussed below) if the name of the business does not reflect the ownership of the firm. Corporations must file their articles of incorporation with the secretary of state and may have to file additionally in other states in which the business operates. As with federal regulations, businesses with employees are required to file and pay many similar employee forms to state revenue agencies.

Other Forms

Doing Business under a Fictitious Name

If the business is operating under a name other than that of the owner(s), the state will require the business to file a Fictitious Business Name Statement. Many business people refer to this as a DBA statement. The acronym means *Doing Business As*. This filing will be required of all forms of business except corporations and is usually filed with the county clerk. Its purpose is to identify to the state and the general public the owner(s) responsible for any business formed within the state. In some states, it may also be necessary for the new business to publish a statement of ownership. It is relatively common for corporations to print a copy of the corporation papers in the business section of the local newspaper.

Local Forms

Each city and county may also have particular licenses, property taxes, or tax requirements that the business must obtain and file. The interior design business owner should be checking with local city and county authorities to be sure that these requirements are satisfied.

City Transaction Privilege (Sales) Tax License

Many cities also require transaction privilege (sales) tax licenses. In some states, it is possible to obtain this form at the same time the business applies for the state license. If it is not available from the state, it can be obtained from the offices of the city in which the business is residing. The city license serves the same function as the state license.

Zoning Restrictions

Cities have certain zoning restrictions as to where businesses may operate. Many interior design businesses begin operation out of a private home. If the interior design firm is selling merchandise to clients, this business may very well be operating illegally. Should neighbors complain to the city that the designer is operating a business in a residentially zoned area, the designer may be liable for a fine.

It is best to check with the local zoning office before applying for a city business license. If the business does not have employees, does not have deliveries arriving at the residence, keeps visits of clients to a minimum, or conducts direct sales, it may be legal for the interior designer to operate a business out of his or her home even if the area is residentially zoned. In some cases, it may be necessary to apply for a zoning variance. The zoning variance allows the business to operate legally in the residentially zoned area. A request for a zoning variance usually requires notification of neighbors and a hearing before the zoning commission.

Specialized Filings

Interior Design Title Registration or Licensure

Interior designers working in states where title registration or licensing requirements have been passed must meet certain regulations so as to maintain their practice under the title of *interior designer*.

Title registration/licensing regulations vary among each of the regulated states. Students and professionals must keep abreast of how these laws are becoming formulated in their state and be prepared to meet the specific requirements of the statutes. Refer to Chapter 1 for a detailed discussion of interior design title registration or licensure.

Contractor's Licenses

In many states, the supervision of construction work and the installation of architectural finishes that an interior designer might specify for a client need to be done by a licensed contractor. Such items as structural work, carpet laying, wall-covering installation, and other items that are attachments to the building may often be done only by a licensed contractor. Although it is rare that interior designers be required to obtain a general or one of the several specialized contractor's licenses, some firms obtain these documents as a means to expand the potential of the practice. More frequently, the interior designer hires contractors and subcontractors who hold these licenses to do the work.

The requirements related to the use of licensed contractors for construction work and installation of architectural interior finishes or attachments vary from state to state. Most states require that work done for private residences be performed only by licensed contractors. Some states do not have restrictions on who may work on commercial facilities. If the designer hires unlicensed contractors to perform work when a licensed contractor is required, the client may not have any legal obligation to pay the designer. It may also be a criminal offense for the interior designer to use the unlicensed contractor.

States will have various provisions regarding the definition of a contractor as it is being discussed here. The owner of the interior design firm should be familiar with the statutes of the state in which the firm is located, and of *any* state in which it may be doing business. Questions should be directed to the state registrar of contractors or other appropriate authority.

Work Authorization Verification

With the passage of the Immigration Reform and Control Act of 1986, it is now unlawful for individuals and businesses to hire aliens who do not have proper authorization to work. Since it is also unlawful for the company to discriminate in its hiring practices, companies are required to have all applicants hired after November 6, 1986, submit acceptable identification and work authorization information.

Not only must the applicant be asked to provide acceptable documents, but the individual or business doing the hiring must keep a record of the request and verification on file. Figure 6–1 shows Form I-9 available from the U.S. Department of Justice, Immigration and Naturalization Service.

Copyrights, Trademarks, and Patents

The work of the interior designer usually results in a great deal of intangible design work in the creation of floor plans, sketches, and sample boards. Often, it is hoped, these intangible items result in a completed interior, or possibly a custom-designed product. There will be some instances when the designer will wish to legally protect these design ideas so that they cannot be duplicated or copied without permission and fair compensation. In some cases, the client may also wish that these designs not be duplicated.

The method of legally protecting written and graphic designs is by *copyright*. A *trademark* protects words and/or symbols specific to a person or business. This trademark must be affixed to the goods the person or business produces to identify its goods from those made by some other person or business. The design firm's logo could be considered a trademark if it is distinctive and not used by any other business. The legal protection of custom product design that results in a tangible object is by a *patent*. This section will focus on copyright protection since most of what an interior designer creates may be copyrighted.

In a very broad sense, the Federal Copyright Act of 1976 protects works of authorship and pictorial or graphic works. Design specifications would fall within the authorship category, whereas drawings and plans would fall within the latter category. The design idea itself is not copyrightable or patentable. But a drawing of a custom-designed product would be copyrightable. And the object itself, if it is substantially different from any other cabinet design, must be patented to receive legal protection from unauthorized duplication. Any written or graphic work created after January 1, 1978, is protected by copyright for the life of the author/designer plus 50 years.

It has been upheld in court that work commissioned by a client and done by the designer still belongs to the designer even when there are no clauses in the design contract giving ownership to the designer. This protection is afforded only when the work contains the proper notification and meets registration and publication requirements.

The copyright begins at the moment the interior designer begins the act to complete the work. This means that the moment the interior designer begins the working drawings, sketch, or specifications the right to legally protect the work begins. However, the work must bear a copyright notification prior to its being "published" in order to receive full legal protection.

Publication occurs when the creator has somehow distributed the work to others for review without restriction of use. It is not limited to mean that the work is printed and published by a publishing house. For example, if the interior designer gives a floor plan to the

EMPLOYMENT ELIGIBILITY VERIFICATION (Form I-9)

1 | **EMPLOYEE INFORMATION AND VERIFICATION:** (To be completed and signed by employee.)

Name: (Print or Type) Last	First	Middle	Birth Name

Address: Street Name and Number	City	State	ZIP Code

Date of Birth (Month/Day/Year)	Social Security Number

I attest, under penalty of perjury, that I am (check a box):

☐ 1. A citizen or national of the United States.

☐ 2. An alien lawfully admitted for permanent residence (Alien Number A _____).

☐ 3. An alien authorized by the Immigration and Naturalization Service to work in the United States (Alien Number A _____ ,

or Admission Number _____ , expiration of employment authorization, if any _____) .

I attest, under penalty of perjury, the documents that I have presented as evidence of identity and employment eligibility are genuine and relate to me. I am aware that federal law provides for imprisonment and/or fine for any false statements or use of false documents in connection with this certificate.

Signature	Date (Month/Day/Year)

PREPARER/TRANSLATOR CERTIFICATION (To be completed if prepared by person other than the employee). I attest, under penalty of perjury, that the above was prepared by me at the request of the named individual and is based on all information of which I have any knowledge.

Signature	Name (Print or Type)		
Address (Street Name and Number)	City	State	Zip Code

2 | **EMPLOYER REVIEW AND VERIFICATION:** (To be completed and signed by employer.)

Instructions:

Examine one document from List A and check the appropriate box, **OR** examine one document from List B **and** one from List C and check the appropriate boxes. Provide the **Document Identification Number** and **Expiration Date** for the document checked.

List A Documents that Establish Identity and Employment Eligibility	List B Documents that Establish Identity	**and**	List C Documents that Establish Employment Eligibility
☐ 1. United States Passport	☐ 1. A State-issued driver's license or a State-issued I.D. card with a photograph, or information, including name, sex, date of birth, height, weight, and color of eyes. (Specify State)_____)		☐ 1. Original Social Security Number Card (other than a card stating it is not valid for employment)
☐ 2. Certificate of United States Citizenship			☐ 2. A birth certificate issued by State, county, or municipal authority bearing a seal or other certification
☐ 3. Certificate of Naturalization	☐ 2. U.S. Military Card		
☐ 4. Unexpired foreign passport with attached Employment Authorization	☐ 3. Other (Specify document and issuing authority) _____		☐ 3. Unexpired INS Employment Authorization Specify form # _____
☐ 5. Alien Registration Card with photograph			
Document Identification # _____	**Document Identification** # _____		**Document Identification** # _____
Expiration Date (if any) _____	**Expiration Date (if any)** _____		**Expiration Date (if any)** _____

CERTIFICATION: I attest, under penalty of perjury, that I have examined the documents presented by the above individual, that they appear to be genuine and to relate to the individual named, and that the individual, to the best of my knowledge, is eligible to work in the United States.

Signature	Name (Print or Type)	Title
Employer Name	Address	Date

Form I-9 (05/07/87)
OMB No. 1115-0136

U.S. Department of Justice
Immigration and Naturalization Service

Figure 6–1 Employment eligibility verification. (U. S. Department of Justice, Immigration and Naturalization Service)

client for his or her review, the plan has been published. Providing to the client or to others copies of the work for the purpose of display constitutes publication.

Copyright notification must contain the following elements:

1. The word *Copyright,* the abbreviation *Copr,* or the copyright symbol ©.
2. Year of publication.
3. The name of the copyright claimant for the copyright.

Notice of the above three elements does not begin the copyright. Notice serves to protect what the claimant publishes. Copyright begins at the moment of creation.

Copyright notification itself, however, does not provide complete legal protection. The proposed copyrighted materials must be *registered* with the federal government in order for the interior designer to file suit in federal district court for infringement. In order to register a copyrightable item, the creator must obtain the proper forms from the copyright office. The V-A form is used for graphic works and the T-X form is used for books, articles, and other general written works. As of this writing, these forms may be obtained by calling the copyright hotline at (202) 287–9100. After dialing this number, the caller will hear a recording telling him or her that the only messages acted upon will be for the ordering of forms. Any other message will be ignored. The recording will provide a second number that the caller may use to obtain general information regarding copyrighting. As of this writing, that number is (202) 479–4700. If preferred, the designer may write to the copyright office for information. The address is in the Appendix.

An original form, not a photocopy of the form, must be accompanied by one copy of the work if the work is unpublished and two copies of the work if it has already been published. The copy of the work must be a "best edition" copy. Since originals cannot be readily submitted, properly prepared photocopies, photographs of the work, or diazo prints of floor plans may suffice. What constitutes a best edition copy, however, is up to the copyright office. A fee to process the copyright will also be required.

It is not necessary to send each project under a separate copyright form. A bulk of work, called a collection, may be submitted at one time. A collection can constitute any work created within the same year as long as all the work is of the same basic type and falls under the same form.

Registration, in order for full statutory and actual damages to be awarded, must occur either prior to the work being published or under specific circumstances. If the work is registered within three months of first publication, the copyright holder would still be able to claim statutory and actual damages. If the work is registered up to five years of first publication, there is a presumption of a valid copyright. After five years, the claimant will have to prove that he or she is the original author. In both of these cases, the copyright claimant may receive actual damages but not statutory damages or attorney's fees and costs.

Statutory damages refer to set amounts determined by the court for each infringement. *Actual damages* relate to damages the copyright holder suffers as a result of the infringement. Actual damages may mean payment of design fees, profits the designer might have lost, and profits the infringer may have made by the infringement.

Infringement is any unauthorized use of copyrighted materials. This can best be explained with a few examples. Assume that the designs have been properly copyrighted. The designer prepares the custom design of a cabinet, and the cabinetmaker not only produces the cabinet for the client, but begins to produce the design for other clients of his or her own. Since the plans were provided to the cabinetmaker for the exclusive use of producing one set of the cabinets, the cabinetmaker has infringed on the designer's copyright by producing additional copies of the cabinet. In a second example, the designer has prepared a set of working drawings for the interior of a small fast-food restaurant in a specific location. If the owner of the fast-food restaurant later duplicates the plans in another location, the restaurant owner has infringed on the copyright.

Copyrights of any design work created by individuals who are employees of an interior design firm belong to the employer, not the employee. This is true as long as the work was done as part of the normal responsibility of the employee. However, an independent contractor (contract laborer) performing interior design work for a firm owns the copyright, not the firm hiring the individual.

Although it may not always be necessary for the interior designer to be concerned with the copyrighting of design documents, there may be certain projects or parts of projects that require this protection. Knowing how to prepare the documents for legal protection is very important. Including a clause in the design contract related to "design ownership" or "copyright permission" would also aid in legally protecting the designer.

Summary

An individual or group of designers may have the skill, experience, and finances to open a design practice. Once the proprietorship's business plan, the partnership agreement, or the articles of incorporation have been prepared, there are several other legal filings required by the federal, state, and local governments. This chapter has attempted to briefly describe those legal forms and documents.

Some states require specialized filings or documents. Those discussed here are interior design title registration or licensure and contractor's licenses. One or more of these specialized filings affect almost all interior design practices in some way. This chapter has also reviewed provisions of copyright law as might apply to interior design practice.

The reader, whether a professional considering opening his or her own practice or a student, should now be able to see that there is much work involved beyond design skill and ability in establishing a practice. The next four chapters will conclude the topics related to organizing and establishing a practice. Chapters 7 and 8 will provide an overview of the legal responsibilities of the designer, and Chapters 9 and 10 will explore office organization and personnel concerns.

References

Barrientos, Lawless J. 1983. *Arizona Business Kit for Starting and Existing Businesses.* New York: Simon and Schuster. (Materials for other states available.)

Blue, Martha. 1990. *By the Book. Legal ABCs for the Printed Word.* Flagstaff, Ariz.: Northland Publishing.

Davidson, Marion, and Martha Blue. 1979. *Making It Legal.* New York: McGraw-Hill.

Federal Tax Coordinator. 1987. 2d. ed., vol. 6. New York: Research Institute of America.

1987 Federal Tax Handbook. 1987. Paramus, N.J.: Prentice-Hall.

Jenkins, Michael D. (and the Entrepreneurial Services Group of Ernst and Young.) 1992. *Starting and Operating a Business in Arizona.* Grants Pass, Or.: Oasis. (Material for all 50 states and the District of Columbia is available).

Jentz, Gaylord A., Kenneth W. Clarkson, and Roger LeRoy Miller. 1987. *West's Business Law— Alternate UCC Comprehensive Edition,* 3d ed. St. Paul, Minn.: West Publishing.

Patterson, L. Ray, and Stanley W. Lindberg. 1991. *The Nature of Copyright. A Law of User's Rights.* University of Georgia Press, Athens, Ga.

Strong, William S. 1984. *The Copyright Book: A Practical Guide,* 2d ed. Cambridge, Mass.: MIT Press.

Sweet, Justin. 1985. *Legal Aspects of Architecture Engineering and the Construction Process,* 3d ed. St. Paul, Minn.: West Publishing.

Tax Guide for Small Business. 1992. Publication 334. Department of the Treasury, Internal Revenue Service.

Chapter 7

Legal Responsibilities

As professional licensing and increased recognition continue to become a reality, interior designers must face their increasing legal responsibilities. Interior designers are legally liable for the work they or members of their staff do and as such can be sued. This exposure includes the planning, specification, and execution of the design and design documents. Even the smallest design project involves activities and responsibilities that can lead to potential legal actions against the designer. And the more complex projects of both residential and commercial designers create an even greater number of potential legal actions. Commercial designers have added responsibilities toward fire and barrier-free codes.

These ominous statements are not made to demoralize the designer. Rather, to bring awareness. With growth in stature as professionals in a profession that is gaining stature, also goes responsibility. Interior designers must be aware of how the law can negatively affect their practice for such activities as malpractice and negligence even as it can also help protect them. It is the responsibility of the professional designer to be aware of the legal responsibilities that affect his or her practice. It is necessary not to become lawyers, but to understand all the ramifications of engaging in a professional practice so as to avoid legal consequences.

This chapter will briefly introduce the differences between criminal and tort law and discuss issues of tort law that are important to the designer. The next chapter will cover warranties and product liability. Legal issues of employment are explained in Chapter 10. Legal responsibilities concerning contracts for services are covered in Chapter 15. Chapter 16 will cover legal responsibilities related to the selling practices of designers as defined by the Uniform Commercial Code (UCC). These chapters do not constitute legal advice. Please do not use the information provided to substitute for discussions with an attorney.

Criminal versus Tort Law

When a person (or business, in the case of a corporation) perpetrates a wrong against society, a crime has been committed. If the alleged wrongdoer commits an offense that is regulated by statute—which is considered an offense against all people in society—the offense is a criminal offense. The punishment for the criminal act is imprisonment and/or a fine.

Although most people think of a crime as an offense against another person, there are some crimes affecting business. Embezzlement, or the fraudulent taking of another person's property or money by the one entrusted with it, is a well-known crime affecting business. Falsifying public records or altering legal documents are forms of forgery. These are but a few of the areas where crimes are committed against businesses or even by businesses. If a corporation is involved, the corporation officers can be held responsible for their acts or neglectful acts of employees on behalf of the corporation.

Most legal problems interior designers experience do not involve criminal acts but rather they involve torts. A _tort_ is "alleged wrongful conduct by one person that causes injury to another."[1] This injury may be to the person or to the person's property. When one person causes injury to another person or his or her property, the injured person may seek various remedies for the damages caused. Since the act is against one person by another, a tort is a civil action where the person harmed sues, in a civil court, the person who has done the harm. Some torts, such as assault and battery, are also criminal acts if there are statutes that describe them as such.

By far the most common kinds of tort cases that might involve interior designers are related to negligence and breach of contract. Negligence liability, often referred to as professional negligence, legally means that the designer failed to use due care in the carrying out of his or her design responsibilities. Breach of contract liability refers to the failure to complete the requirements of a contract. Other torts that can affect the interior practice, although these are less likely to occur, are torts for false imprisonment, defamation, and misrepresentation. Strict liability, a tort related to product liability, is another tort liability that can entangle the design practice. Strict liability is discussed in the next chapter.

Negligence

One of the kinds of torts most commonly involving interior design practice is _negligence._ "Negligence is the failure to use due care to avoid foreseeable injury which might be caused to another person or property as a result of the failure to exercise due care."[2] The person accused of negligence created a risk. This risk must be such that a reasonable person could anticipate it and prevent it. If there is no creation of risk, there cannot be negligence. Because of this factor, it is rather a way of committing a tort than a kind of tort.

Negligence is also considered an unintentional tort. Negligence is unintentional because the designer did not believe any wrongful consequences of an act would occur or even wanted them to occur. But the conduct created a risk and that risk of harm creates the environment for the tort of negligence.

To prove negligence, the harmed party must prove several things. First, that the defendant owed a duty—most commonly "reasonable care"—to the plaintiff; second, that there was a breach of that duty either intentionally or unintentionally; third, that the act caused damages—that the act caused the harm; and fourth, that there were damages or harm to persons or property. Inadvertently switching numbers on a purchase order that results in the wrong wallpaper being hung at the client's home is negligence. Selling and installing a carpet that the designer knows does not meet fire codes is negligence.

Professional negligence indicates that the designer in some way was negligent in relationship to his or her conduct in executing a project. All the elements of negligence apply to professional negligence. Some examples of professional negligence, pointed out in Justin Sweet's _Legal Aspects of Architecture Engineering and the Construction Process,_ are worth repeating here.

---

[1]Clarkson 1983, 35. Copyright West Publishing Co.
[2]Barnes, A. James, _A Guide to Business Law,_ Richard Irwin, 1981, p. 11.

Specifying material that did not comply with building codes

Failing to inform client of potential risks of using certain materials

Drafting ambiguous sketches causing extra work

Designing closets not large enough for the clothing to be contained in them

Designing a project that greatly exceeded the client's budget

Failing to engage and check with a consultant[3]

Duty of Care

Interior designers owe a duty of care to their clients in many ways. This duty relates to the care in selection of materials and products that are proper and adequate to meet the functional and legal (if codes are binding) needs of the project. Specifying residential grade carpet in most commercial interiors would give inadequate performance and would be negligent. A designer owes a duty to the client to not allow defective work to be done on the job site. A designer visiting a job site sees that the carpet installer is using a nonquick-release glue to affix carpet tiles when a quick-release glue was specified; the designer has a duty to the client to stop the work and have it corrected. The designer also has a duty not to expose others to risks created by defective designs. The designer must be sure that the structure of the building will support any wall-hung units that are specified.

Breach of Duty

A breach of the duty of reasonable care results when the designer fails to act in a way that is considered reasonable for the professional designer. The breach may be an act such as knowingly specifying the wrong carpet for the client (intentional) or an omission such as not stopping the work when the designer sees that the carpet being installed is incorrect (carelessness).

Causation

A person may have a duty to another, and he or she may in some way breach that duty, but the act (the breach of duty) must cause some injury or harm for a tort to have been committed. If the injury occurs exclusively because of the designer's act, then there is a causation in fact. An example will help to explain this. A designer knows that the manufacturer requires 5/8-inch drywall to support its wall strips and knows that the client has already installed 1/2-inch drywall; if the designer has the wall strips hung anyway, there is a causation in fact. Often, the "but for" test is used to determine causation in fact—"But for the wrongful act, the injury would not have occurred."

How far a person's responsibility goes in performance of a wrongful act is covered by proximate cause. "The question is whether the connection between an act and an injury is strong enough to justify imposing liability."[4] If the consequences of the act that does harm are unforeseeable, there is no proximate cause. For example, if the wall strips pull out from the wall and the falling books hit a lamp, which shatters and starts a fire that burns down the house, there would probably be proximate cause if it were reasonable that the lamp would

---

[3]Sweet 1985, 329–330. Copyright West Publishing Co.
[4]Clarkson 1983, 53. Copyright West Publishing Co.

create a fire when broken in such a manner. How foreseeable one act is on another is determined by the courts and is not easy to establish.

Injury

A tort of negligence has not occurred unless there has been some legally recognizable loss, harm, wrong, or invasion to a plaintiff. Injury must occur in order for the plaintiff to recover compensation. There does not have to be an injury to a person for this element to exist. The delay in delivery of sufficient furniture for a business to operate can be considered an injury if the delay was the fault of the designer. Remember, plaintiffs in tort cases seek compensation for damages from the defendant; they usually do not seek punishment. Courts more often find in favor of the plaintiff when personal injury—rather than property or economic damage—occurs.

Principal Defenses for Negligence

The principal defenses for negligence are assumption of risk and contributory negligence. In assumption of risk, the plaintiff who knowingly and willingly enters into a risky situation will not be able to recover damages if injury occurs. If a client agrees to purchase a residential grade carpet, knowing it will not provide the wear required in his or her commercial installation, the designer would be absolved of the negligence.

In using contributory negligence as a defense, it must be shown that both sides were negligent and that injury resulted. This comes from the idea that everyone should look out for his or her own interests and safety. Where contributory negligence is successfully used as a defense, the plaintiff will not be able to recover damages no matter how great the injury or how slight the contributory negligence.

Intentional Torts against the Person

Intentional torts against the person must show intent; that is, the person consciously performed the act knowing or substantially certain that the act would harm another. Assault, battery, false imprisonment, defamation, invasion of privacy, and misrepresentation are some of the torts included in this area.

Assault occurs when a person intentionally performs an act so that another has a feeling of apprehension or fear of harm or physical injury. Actual contact or physical harm is not necessary for an assault to occur; causing another to be apprehensive is enough. A *battery* occurs when there is intentional touching or other physical contact by one upon another without consent or justification.

False imprisonment (or false arrest) is the intentional confinement of a person for an appreciable duration of time. This is of particular importance to designers who are engaged in retail selling. A business owner must be reasonably certain that someone has shoplifted in order to detain the customer, or the customer can sue for false imprisonment. In many jurisdictions, shoplifting has not occurred until the person has walked out the door of the business with goods not properly paid for.

Defamation is the wrongful harming of a person's good reputation. If the defamation is in writing it is called *libel;* if it is oral, it is *slander.* To be defamatory, statements must be made to or read or heard by a third party. It is not necessary for the defamed party to hear or read the defamation. It is for this reason that interior designers must be careful about what they say or write concerning their competitors or competitor's products. Telling a client that Jones Interiors "did a lousy job" on their last three residential commissions would be defamation by slander. Jones Interiors could sue the offending designer.

Invasion of privacy is a tort against a person's right to freedom from others' prying eyes.

For this reason it is important to obtain written permission to photograph an installation (and any people who may be seen in the photograph) if it is used for publication. Care must also be taken in obtaining information concerning a person's or business's affairs—such as obtaining credit information without permission.

To misrepresent is to alter facts to deceive or use fraud in order to receive personal gain. *Misrepresentation* would begin by a misstatement of facts—not opinions, unless the person expressing the opinion is considered an expert in the subject matter—that the speaker knows to be false. These "untrue facts" must be made with the intent that the client will rely on them. The deceived party must have justifiably relied upon the information, and the reliance must have caused damages to occur.

Sellers' talk or "puffing" is not usually considered misrepresentation unless the seller represents as fact something that he or she knows is not true. To say that your design firm is the "best interior design office in town" is not misrepresentation or fraud since the word *best* is subjective, not objective. To say "we are the only firm in town that can do this work" when it is not true would be misrepresentation.

Intentional Torts against Property

The three torts against property are trespass to land and personal property, conversion, and nuisance. Although each may be a problem to the interior designer, the torts of trespass to personal property and conversion are potentially the most damaging.

Trespass to land means entering land that does not belong to us. *Trespass to personal property* occurs when a defendant either injures the personal property of another or interferes with the owner's right to exclusive possession or use of the personal property. The most common form of trespass of personal property is conversion.

Conversion occurs when the rightful property of one person is taken by another. In criminal law this is commonly called stealing or theft. When an employee takes merchandise or supplies that belong to the employer and uses those items for his or her own use rather than for company-related use, conversion has occurred. Although most employers do not prosecute or sue (remember, both are valid here) when employees take home pens and paper paid for by the employer, they have a legal right to do so. Another instance of the tort of trespass to personal property is illustrated in the following example: Jane is at the client's office to measure for new draperies. While she is measuring the window, she knocks over a lamp and breaks it. Jane has trespassed upon the personal property of her client and is liable to replace the lamp—even if it no longer worked prior to Jane's breaking it.

A suit for *nuisance* can also be brought against an interior designer. "A nuisance is an improper activity that interferes with another's enjoyment or use of his or her property."[5] For the designer this could mean that the designer and the client can be sued by a neighbor because the noise and dust from a remodeling project has interfered with the neighbor's enjoyment of his or her home.

Code Compliance

An area of professional responsibility that is very important—especially to the commercial interior designer—is compliance with various codes. *Codes* are systematic bodies of law created by federal, state, and local jurisdictions to insure safety. Codes are written by many different independent agencies and adopted and modified by federal, state, and local jurisdic-

---

[5]Jentz 1987, 55. Copyright West Publishing Co.

tions. During the course of a project, the interior designer's work may need to be judged against building codes, life safety or fire codes, and barrier-free (handicapped-access) codes. Other codes the project may have to meet include electrical codes, health department codes, and zoning laws.

Interior designers must be sure they understand which codes apply in the locations where they are designing. Code compliance is not an option—it is a legal necessity. Information can be obtained from local fire marshals, planning and building departments, and state and federal agencies responsible for specific types of structures. It is usually possible to purchase the necessary code books from the local planning and building department. Noncompliance with codes can result in work being stopped, torn out, and/or redone—generally at the expense of the interior designer.

Building Codes

Building codes primarily regulate structural and mechanical features of buildings. They define minimum standards for the design, construction, and quality of materials based on the use, type, and occupancy of the building. There are three model codes used in the United States:

1. *Uniform Building Code* (UBC). Written by the International Conference of Building Officials (ICOB), the UBC has been adopted by most states west of the Mississippi River.

2. *Basic/National Building Code* (NBC). Written by the Building Officials Code Administrators International (BOAC), the NBC is used primarily by states east of the Mississippi River.

3. *Standard Building Code* (SBC). Written by the Southern Building Code Congress International (SBCI), the SBC is also used by states east of the Mississippi River.

The model building codes are revised every two to three years. Although it is a good idea to obtain each new addition of the applicable building code, the designer should be aware that not all jurisdictions change to the new code each time it is revised. In addition, local building conditions may require additional code requirements. Designers who work in metropolitan areas or who design work in several different cities also need to be sure they are using the right version of the building code for each jurisdiction. Two cities next to each other in an urban area may have slightly different requirements. The local planning or building department can advise the designer on the applicable code.

Fire Safety Codes

Fire safety or *life safety* codes and regulations exist to provide a reasonable measure of safety in a building from fire, explosions, or other comparable emergencies. The model code used by most jurisdictions is the Life Safety Code written by the National Fire Protection Association. Covering many of the same concerns with design, construction, and materials as in the building codes, the Life Safety Code attempts to lessen the danger to life from fire, smoke, and hazardous fumes and gases. The intent of these codes is to prevent a fire whenever possible. However, since all fires cannot be prevented, the codes also focus on fire control. Fire prevention is facilitated by the regulation of hazards and such things as controls on the kinds of materials—both construction and furnishings—that can be used in buildings. Fire control is facilitated by the requirement of fire sprinklers, fire doors, and the like.

Fire codes focus on such matters as egress (corridors, halls, doors, etc.), interior architectural finishes, and fire protection equipment such as sprinklers and smoke detectors. Fire regulations related to furniture construction and fabrics or finishes are more a matter of federal, state, and local regulations. Codes developed by the New York Port Authority, Boston Fire Department, and California State Fire Marshall's Office (to name a few), have been adopted by many of the states to regulate these furniture construction and the fabrics or finishes of furniture. The designer is again cautioned to check with local or appropriate fire marshals or building departments to clarify which fire safety standards are applicable in the firm's working area.

Barrier-Free Regulations

Building codes have worked to make public buildings more accessible to the handicapped and thus *barrier-free.* However, as most handicapped individuals will say, there is still a long way to go before true accessibility is a reality. In January of 1992 the Americans with Disabilities Act (ADA) opened the door, literally and figuratively, to making all buildings—public and private—accessible to the handicapped. The ADA itself is civil rights legislation, not a building code. Until a state or local jurisdiction creates statutes of enforcement or incorporates the ADA regulations into its building code, a complaintant would have to file a civil rights action in federal court.

The ADA legislation deals with four distinct areas: employment, public service and transportation, public accommodations, and telecommunications. This means the legislation is a comprehensive package of requirements that denies discrimination against disabled individuals in many areas of their life. Applicable to our discussion in this section are a few items concerning Title III, Public Accommodations.

The intent of Title III is to provide access for a disabled person equal to that of the general public. New construction must be designed and built to meet the new design criteria called for in Title III. Existing buildings may have to make what are called "readily achievable" accommodations and changes to meet the criteria. If an existing building is going to be remodeled, it will have to include all reasonable design changes. If an existing building is not undergoing any remodeling, the owners will have to make the readily achievable changes if it is economically feasible to do so. Of course, if an individual files a civil rights suit against the building owner, the end result of that suit may also be a requirement to make changes even in an old building. For example, for a new restaurant, seating must be provided that is as accessible for the disabled as the general public. Public restrooms must also be designed to meet the new standards. In an existing restaurant, the owners may be required to make seating as accessible to the disabled as the general public since that is readily achievable. Modifying undersized restrooms might not be required unless an individual wins a civil rights suit against the restaurant.

The ADA affects every public and private building and type of business with few exceptions. Private residences are excluded as are commercial facilities. Commercial facilities are defined in the ADA as nonresidential buildings used by a private entity and where only employees of the entity are given access.[6] A designer's warehouse and the offices of a private corporation (as long as the general public is denied access) are examples of a commercial facility. The designer's studio or office is not considered a commercial facility as far as the ADA is concerned, assuming that the designer's clients are given access to the studio or office. There are special application requirements for restaurants and cafeterias, medical care facilities, business and mercantile buildings, libraries, transient lodging, and transportation facilities.

This author, having had a disabled parent for nearly 30 years, understands and appreciates the importance of this landmark legislation. It is hoped that designers will not view the ADA—or any code or regulation for that matter—as infringement upon design creativity, but as part of making all interior environments enjoyable to all individuals. Unfortunately, it is beyond the scope of this book to go in depth into all the design criteria and regulations of

---

[6]Commercial facilities may have to make reasonable, readily achievable accommodations for employees, based on Title I of the ADA law.

the ADA. Numerous reference guides have been published recently to assist the designer in complying with the law. A few are listed in the References.

Plan Review Boards

All jurisdictions have *plan review boards* (PRB) or *design review boards* (DRB) whose responsibility it is to review construction drawings prior to issuance of building permits. Depending on the contract responsibility, the owner, architect, or interior designer will submit copies of plans and specifications to the plan review board. The plans are first reviewed by a member of the building department. This individual will be looking for any omission or discrepancy in design as regulated by building, mechanical, fire, and accessibility codes and regulations as well as compliance with all other local building and construction standards. Plans get "red lined" or "red marked" to show where problems exist. If too many red marks occur, the plans are rejected and must be redrawn and perhaps—if necessary—redesigned. If only a few red marks end up on the plans, these are usually worked out among the owner, architect, designer, contractor, and the building department prior to or during the construction. Many projects also are reviewed by the fire department, engineering department, planning and zoning department, state health department, or other groups looking for specific compliance with regulations and codes within their jurisdictions.

Since meetings of the plan review board are subject to open meeting laws, anyone can sit in on the meeting. Designers who have never been "under the fire" of a PRD meeting, should sit in on a meeting sometime. If nothing else, it will make the designer more careful about the production of plans and specifications for all future projects!

Summary

As interior designers seek professional recognition, they must also accept professional responsibilities and liabilities. Students beginning their pursuit of a career, as well as those already actively engaged in the profession, must realize that their design efforts—whether in residential or commercial design, whether in the specification of products or the drafting of floor plans—place them in a position of responsibility to their clients that goes beyond designing an aesthetic environment.

This chapter briefly discusses the differences between criminal and tort law. It also discusses many of the common tort classifications that can result in a civil suit against the interior designer. Chief among these are negligence and the concept of professional negligence.

The designer is responsible for being familiar if not thoroughly cognizant of the many regulations and legislation that affect the interior design and related professions. Building codes, earthquake protection, fire safety codes, barrier-free regulations, performance testing for flammability, and quality standards are just a few of these regulations.

Designers must gain awareness of their legal responsibilities in designing interiors as well as in everyday professional practice. Today's interior designer is held accountable for his or her activities in design. The information in this chapter is provided to help the designer gain some understanding of that accountability so as to avoid legal problems. The reader may also wish to review items in the References, obtain copies of the applicable regulations, or take CEU classes for familiarization.

References

Barnes, A. James. 1981. *A Guide to Business Law.* Homewood, Ill.: Learning Systems.

Building Owners and Managers Association. 1991. *ADA Compliance Guidebook. A Checklist for Your Building.* Washington, D.C.: BOMA.

Clarkson, Kenneth W., Roger LeRoy Miller, Gaylord A. Jentz. 1983. *West's Business Law, Text and Cases,* 2d ed. St. Paul, Minn.: West Publishing.

Cushman, Robert F., and James C. Dobbs, eds. 1991. *Design Professionals Handbook of Business Law.* New York: Wiley.

Federal Register, vol. 56, no. 144. *Nondiscrimination on the Basis of Disability by Public Accommodations and in Commercial Facilities; Final Rule.* 1991. Washington D.C.: Department of Justice.

Hopf, Peter S., and John A. Raeber. 1984. *Access for the Handicapped.* New York: Van Nostrand Reinhold.

Jentz, Gaylord A., Kenneth W. Clarkson, and Roger LeRoy Miller. 1987. *West's Business Law— Alternate UCC Comprehensive Edition,* 3d ed. St. Paul, Minn.: West Publishing.

Sweet, Justin. 1985. *Legal Aspects of Architecture, Engineering, and the Construction Process,* 3d ed. St. Paul, Minn.: West Publishing.

Chapter 8

Warranties and Product Liability

Today's litigious society means that interior designers must fully understand the implications of warranties and product liability. Specifying and selling furniture and other goods to clients creates legal responsibility. Whether the designer sells architectural finishes in a small residential studio, or specifies the full range of products in larger residential and commercial projects, the expectation that the client is receiving properly specified goods is high.

Designers are liable for the performance of the products that are specified in any project. Products must meet the expectations of reasonable use and fitness in the situation where they will be installed. The designer is also responsible that the products are specified and installed in such a way as not to cause injury to the people who use the spaces or injury to the spaces themselves. These requirements are expected of all individuals who call themselves or are licensed as professional interior designers.

This chapter will review basic concepts of warranties on products and legal concepts of product liability. This information goes hand in hand with the discussion on negligence in the previous chapter.

Warranties

The days when the phrase "buyer beware" was standard for consumers has long since past. Consumers are protected by a large number of regulations and laws to place much of the burden on the marketplace to provide safe products rather than on the buyer be wary. Other regulations and laws help to satisfy the customer so that what he or she purchases meets correct standards of design, manufacturing, and use. Warranties are one way that the buyer is protected.

Warranties place a burden on the seller that the goods he or she sells meet certain standards. Four important kinds of warranties are governed by the Uniform Commercial Code (UCC)[1]:

---

[1]The UCC is a body of law that regulates commercial transactions. Section 2 of the UCC sets out laws related to the sale of goods, warranties, and products liability. The law that regulates contracts for the sale of goods is discussed in Chapter 16.

1. Warranty of title (section 2–312)
2. Express warranty (section 2–313)
3. Implied warranty of merchantability (section 2–314)
4. Implied warranty of fitness for a particular purpose (section 2–315)

When the designer or design firm offers a warranty on the product he or she sells, failure to honor that warranty is a breach of contract duty and gives the client the right to sue. The seller's breach also allows the customer to cancel the order.

Warranty of Title

The first aspect of warranty of title[2] is that the seller has title to the goods and can legally sell them to others. Basically this means that the seller,[3] knowingly or not, is not selling stolen goods or goods he or she does not have authorization to sell. If an interior design firm does not have authority to buy and sell Steelcase systems from Steelcase, because of a lack of a dealership agreement, it would not be able to imply to the client that it could purchase the goods from Steelcase and sell the products to the client. Since the designer cannot take title to the goods from Steelcase, he or she cannot pass title to the client.

A second part of warranty of title is that the buyer would be protected from loss if he or she unknowingly buy goods with a lien attached. A *lien* means that someone other than the person who has ownership or possession of the goods has a security interest in the goods. If the buyer buys the goods knowing that there is a lien, he or she will not be able to collect from the seller.

A third part is warranty concerning infringement. This means that the goods do not have any patent, copyright, or trademark claim by anyone. For example, a designer created a logo whose copyright was registered by the design firm. However, the client was not shown the design at that time. Six months later, the designer started a design practice and contacted the former client about possible work. The client hired the designer to produce a logo and was shown the logo the designer had designed for the previous employer. The client bought that design and incorporated it into all the letterhead of the firm. The original design firm can sue both the client and designer for infringement.

Express Warranties

Promises, claims, descriptions, or affirmations made about a product's performance, quality, or condition that form the "basis of the bargain" form *express warranties*. In effect, the *basis of the bargain* means that the information provided was what primarily influenced the decision of the buyer. Interior designers and salespeople, in the course of their discussions with clients about a product's viability, often make statements about what the product can or cannot do. When are these statements covered under express warranty and when are they not?

The seller does not need to use words such as "warranty" or "guarantee" in the sales presentation nor does he or she even need to intend to make such a warranty. How precise these statements have to be and how strongly they are worded is not clear in the UCC.

When statements made by the seller are only the seller's opinion or relate only to the worth of the product, no express warranty is made. For example, Jim Jones says to a client,

---

[2] *Title* signifies ownership of the goods.
[3] A seller is anyone who sells something. A merchant is someone in the business of selling a certain type of goods. Anyone can be a seller; people in business are merchants.

"This is the best open office system on the market." It is an expression of opinion, not based on statements of fact. This kind of salesmanship, called *puffing*, is characterized by statements of opinion, not fact. On the other hand, a statement from Jim Jones such as, "This wood flooring is care-free," is a promise that could be interpreted by the customer as meaning he or she would not have to wax the floor. In this situation, an express warranty was made by Jones.

If the salesperson is believed to be an expert concerning the goods being sold, the statements of opinion are likely to be express warranties. Although the opinions about a manufacturers' product by an interior designer who specifies but does not sell products will probably be considered puffing, the statements of a manufacturer's representative who has worked for that company for many years could be considered warranties. Since the code does not make it clear as to what is puffing and what is an expression of warranty, it is important to be careful in making statements about quality and performance of a product. If the statement is reasonable, and a reasonable person believes the statement, a warranty may be created.

Implied Warranty of Merchantability

Implied warranties exist as operations of law and as such do not require that a contractual relationship between the parties be established. The *implied warranty of merchantability* affects sales made by merchants. In its simplest form, the code says that the goods must be "fit for the ordinary purposes for which such goods are used."[4] As long as the merchant is a merchant of the kind of goods in consideration, he or she is liable.

Under this section of the code, goods sold must be of fair to average quality and be comparable in quality to other similar goods. They must be fit for the normal purpose of the good. They must be packaged and labeled adequately and must conform to the statements made on the packaging or labels. For example, strippable wallpaper must be strippable; fire-retardant fabric must not ignite or burn within the limits stated on the binder; a solid brass headboard must be solid brass.

This section of the code makes an implied warranty of merchantability applicable to every sale by a merchant. Liability does not disappear even if the merchant is unaware of any defect in the product. The interior designer will likely be liable along with the manufacturer when a product fails or causes some injury to person or property.

Implied Warranty: Fitness for a Particular Purpose

Implied warranty of fitness for a particular purpose affects the goods any seller—merchant or not—sells to another. When the seller knows the intended purpose for the goods and the buyer must rely on the seller's knowledge to select or recommend goods for the purpose, an implied warranty of fitness for a particular purpose would exist.

The seller does not need to know the exact purpose of the purchase. However, if he or she has a general idea of the purpose, and if the buyer has relied on the seller's knowledge or skill in selecting the goods, an implied fitness warranty would also be created.

For example, Mrs. Damon hires John Simmons to redecorate her home. As part of the services offered, Simmons sells to Damon the wall coverings for the kitchen and bathrooms. Damon made it clear to Simmons that the wallpaper in the bathroom would have to withstand a lot of steam and dampness since her husband takes long, hot showers. A few weeks after installation, the wallpaper begins to peel away. Since Simmons knew the purpose of the

---

[4]Quinn 1978, 2–143. Reprinted by permission from *Uniform Commercial Code Commentary and Law Digest* (1978), Copyright 1978 Warren, Gorham and Lamont, Inc. 210 South Street, Boston, Mass. All rights reserved.

goods and Damon relied on the professional knowledge of Simmons, a breach of an implied warranty of fitness existed. Of course, the paperhanger, if he or she also knew the purpose of the purchase, would also be liable for breach.

Magnuson-Moss Warranty Act

The Federal Trade Commission enforces the Magnuson-Moss Warranty Act. This legislation was enacted to help make it easier for the consumer to understand what was being warrantied in any product sold to end-users. Warranties between merchants are regulated by the UCC rules.

The act does not require sellers to provide a written warranty for goods sold to consumers. "But if a seller chooses to make an express written warranty, and the cost of the consumer goods is more than $10, the warranty must be labeled as 'full' or 'limited.' In addition, if the cost of the goods is more than $15 (FTC regulation), the warrantor is required to make certain disclosures fully and conspicuously in a single document in 'readily understood language.'"[5] In this case, who warrants the goods, what is covered, limitations, the legal rights of the consumer, and how enforcement is made must all be spelled out.

Full warranties require repair or replacement at no charge to the buyer should goods be defective. There cannot be a time limit on the replacement. If there is, it is not a full warranty but a limited warranty. Should it not be possible to repair the goods in a reasonable time, the customer has the right to a refund or a replacement.[6] Limited warranties must be clearly stated as to what is warrantied and the time limit of the warranty.

Disclaimers of Warranty

An express warranty can be disclaimed if the manufacturer or seller does not make any express promises or statements of fact relating to or describing the goods. This would be true whether the statements were written or verbal. Saying, "We guarantee that this fabric will not show wear for five years," constitutes an express warranty. A disclaimer to that statement might be, "We provide no warranty beyond that of the manufacturer, and their tests under normal use in a home indicate the fabric will show no significant wear for five years."

An implied warranty-of-fitness disclaimer must be in writing. For example, a designer sold a client a kitchen stool with a cane seat for use at the kitchen counter. The confirmation said something like "ABS Designs provides no warranty of fitness beyond that of the manufacturer's for normal, reasonable use." A few weeks after purchase, the client uses the stool to stand on and the cane breaks, resulting in injury to the client. The designer would have no liability since the client was using the stool in a manner that was not normal and reasonable for the product; the manufacturer did not design the chair to be used as a ladder.

Disclaimers of fitness are also written with such words as is. It is common to see retailers label used furniture "as is" to protect themselves against claims on used or damaged goods. Even new merchandise, however, is sold "as is" to imply no warranty other than what the manufacturer has provided.

An implied warranty of merchantability can be verbal, but it must be specific as to disclaiming merchantability. For example, Cobb Designs sells Mr. Smith a budget-priced guest chair to be used as a desk chair based on the needs described by Smith. Cobb verbally informs Smith that he does not warrant merchantability of the chair since it is not fit for use as a desk chair. The chair does not hold up, and Smith wants Cobb to replace it. Since it was

---

[5]Jentz 1987, 314 and 316. Copyright West Publishing Company.
[6]Jentz 1987, 316.

disclaimed as to merchantability, Cobb would not be liable to replace the chair on those grounds.

Goods that the seller asks the buyer to inspect before the buyer accepts the goods and that the buyer refuses to inspect would have no implied warranty concerning defects. If the seller does not ask the buyer to inspect the goods, and the goods are damaged or defective, the seller would be liable.

Products Liability

When a buyer purchases some goods from a seller, the buyer has a right, under common law and sales law, to expect those goods to meet certain minimal standards of materials, workmanship, and design for its intended use. If the goods fail, certain express or implied warranties may have been breached. Manufacturers and sellers of goods may be liable to end-users, bystanders, and other merchants if individuals are physically harmed or if property damage occurs. This is called *products liability*. Products liability includes the areas of tort law related to negligence and strict liability and contract law related to warranty.

Products Liability and Negligence

Chapter 7 defined negligence as a failure to use care that is expected of a reasonable person and that this failure to use care results in injury to another person or his or her property. Manufacturers of products must use this same care in the design, materials selection, production, and testing of their products so that they will be safe when used as intended.

The plaintiff must show that the manufacturer did not use due care and that the defective product caused the injury. The plaintiff must also show that he or she used the product as designed and knew the risk of using the product incorrectly. For example, Mrs. Williams purchased numerous cane-seat chairs for use in a small resort facility. The chairs were placed in guest suites and rooms for use as dining chairs. A few months after installation, a guest used the chair as a "ladder." The caned seat gave way under the guest's weight, his leg fell through the seat and he fell, breaking his arm. The guest attempted to sue the resort, the manufacturer, and the designer. His products liability suit would likely fail since the guest was using the chair for other than its intended purpose.

Designers must take time to be sure they are specifying products suitable for the client's use and that the client is carefully warned if the designer feels the client is demanding a product that is unsuitable for the client's use. Written disclaimers indicating that warnings were given and that the designer accepts no responsibility for misuse should be given to the client, with a copy kept on file. These may not eliminate all liability, but would show the court a conscientious effort to warn the client.

Strict Liability

Strict liability means that "people are liable for the results of their acts regardless of their intentions or their exercise of reasonable care."[7] Strict liability, as it applies to product liability, must be a concern of interior designers. The interior designer specifies a product and if the product fails, causing injury, the designer is almost always named in the suit along with the manufacturer. It should be remembered that product liability will usually be concerned

---

[7]Clarkson 1983, 393. Copyright West Publishing Company.

only with reasonable, normal use of the product. If the client uses a product in a way for which it was not designed, the interior designer would not be responsible.

Strict liability is sometimes called liability without fault. Generally considered a negligence tort, liability without fault involves some act that has departed from the use of reasonable care. For the designer, this may result from incorrect information in drawings, documents, and/or specifications that causes injury. For example, if the designer incorrectly labels a material in a construction drawing and the structure later fails, causing injury, the designer would be responsible based on this premise.

It is also important to note that under strict liability people are responsible for their acts regardless of their intent or use of reasonable care. For example, a painter hired to paint the exterior of a home uses reasonable care when using spray painting equipment. However, the next-door neighbor goes out to inspect his house and finds overspray of the blue paint on the side of his white house. The painter would be liable under strict liability.

Strict liability doctrine can be applied to manufactured products when the purchaser can show that "(1) the product was defective, (2) that the defect made the product unreasonably dangerous and (3) that the defect was the proximate cause of the injury."[8]

For strict liability to be applied to a products liability case, the injured party (plaintiff) must prove several things.

1. The goods were defective when purchased.

2. The defective goods are unreasonably dangerous to any user.

3. Physical injury has occurred to himself or herself or to his or her property.

4. At the time of the injury, the goods were substantially in the same condition as when purchased.

For example, Mr. Shasta of Shasta Commercial Interiors, orders from a textile company fabric described as fire retardant for use on restaurant booths. A few months after installation, a dropped cigarette smolders and ignites the fabric causing extensive damage to the restaurant. A strict liability case would be brought against the textile company and probably the designer if it can be shown that the goods were defective at the time of purchase. Further, it would have to be shown that injury was caused to the premises, that the untreated fabric was dangerous in its use, and that the fabric was in a basically unchanged condition since purchase. Although most of the liability in this case would rest on the manufacturer of goods, there is nothing in tort law or the UCC to prevent the unknowing designer from also being liable.

Liability without Fault for Design Defects

Interior designers create many design elements and custom products. Designers also specify and sell products primarily designed and manufactured by someone else. In both cases, the designer may be liable if the design of the specified product causes injury due to defective design.

Mary Nixon designed and produced the drawings for a custom table-desk. The desk was manufactured according to the specifications and drawings provided by Mary. Three months after delivery, the client was propped on the front edge of the table desk (but he was not literally sitting on the desk). The desk leg nearest where the client was propped split at the joint causing the client to fall on his left side and break his left arm. It appears that there was a design defect in the way the joint between the top of the table leg and the desk top was

---

[8]Clarkson 1983, 393.

designed. This is because the specifications and drawings provided by Mary were inadequate to safely use the desk for its intended purpose. Had the client been actually sitting on the desk, Mary would less likely have been liable since a desk is generally not designed to be sat on.

Interior designers must be careful that the custom treatments and products that they design are properly designed and meet performance standards relating to the structural integrity of the design. Those unfamiliar with product design should either refrain from creating custom designs themselves or retain the services of product designers, craftspeople, or other appropriate experts to help in the design of custom goods. Designers also need to be constantly vigilant that the goods that are specified from manufacturers are designed safely and have no history of liability from design defects.

Warranty Law and Products Liability

Warranty law and products liability is the only portion of products liability related to the UCC. Warranty responsibility and product liability are based on the areas of warranties discussed in the previous sections. They are mentioned here in relation to an injury to a third party.

In contract law, the only parties that have regress for injuries are the parties to the contract. However, much of what is governed by the UCC easily affects third parties not a part of the original contract. The Code provides regulations that make the manufacturers and/or sellers liable to injuries to parties not a part of the original contract. For example, Mrs. Johnson hires an interior design company to redecorate her home. Through this company, she has some wall-hung shelves installed in the living room. One day, a bracket pulls out of the wall so that a shelf strikes a guest of Johnson. The guest sustains a head injury. If it were not for UCC section 2–318, the guest would not be able to sue the installer for an implied warranty of merchantability—only Mrs. Johnson could.

However, the Code is not clear on how responsible sellers and manufacturers are. It has been written with three alternatives giving different amounts of responsibility. Alternative "A" is limited to household members and their guests who use or are injured by the goods. Alternative "B" is broader, not limiting injury to family members or guests, and alternative "C" is the broadest, protecting anyone who is injured by the defective product.

Summary

These last two chapters have looked at many legal responsibilities expected of the professional interior designer. The public and the profession expect anyone engaged in the practice of interior design to accept the legal responsibility of his or her practice activities. In a legal sense, it matters very little whether an interior designer primarily does residential spaces or commercial spaces. The legal responsibilities described in these two chapters remain in force. Of course, the size and complexity of many commercial projects makes the commercial interior designer more exposed to liability, especially as concerns warranties and products liability.

All designers, regardless of their experience in the field, need to remain mindful of the legal consequences of their actions. Constant care is very important today. The designer should not get involved in design projects that may be out of his or her area of expertise. He or she must become familiar and comply with applicable codes and regulations and maintain accurate records to limit his or her liability.

References

Cushman, Robert F., and James C. Dobbs, eds. 1991. *Design Professional's Handbook of Business and Law.* New York: Wiley.

Jentz, Gaylord A., Kenneth W. Clarkson, and Roger LeRoy Miller. 1987. *West's Business Law Alternate UCC Comprehensive Edition,* 3d. ed. St. Paul, Minn.: West Publishing.

Quinn, Thomas M. 1979. *Uniform Commercial Code Commentary and Law Digest.* Boston, Mass: Warren, Gorham and Lamont.

_____. 1991. *Quinn's Uniform Commercial Code Commentary and Law Digest,* 2d. ed., vol. 1. Boston, Mass: Warren, Gorham and Lamont.

Reznikoff, S. C. 1989. *Specifications for Commercial Interiors,* rev. ed. New York: Watson-Guptill.

Sweet, Justin. 1985. *Legal Aspects of Architecture, Engineering and the Construction Process,* 3d ed. St. Paul, Minn.: West Publishing.

Chapter 9

Business Organization and Personnel Management

The business organization of a small interior design practice is not very complicated, nor should it be. However, once the firm begins to grow in finances, number of clients, and employees, organizational structure becomes necessary. The purpose of this organizational structure is to aid all employees to understand the various activities of the firm and to show who is responsible for those activities. The larger the firm grows, the more complex the organizational structure will become. As long as the firm continues to plan for changes in the organization rather than reacting to them, the firm will continue to grow and prosper.

Personnel issues are important to the business organization. Articles in trade magazines report high turnover rates and basically low salaries. How much of this situation is due to the lack of good personnel management is difficult to say. But the articles do indicate that job satisfaction is an important issue for interior designers. The areas of personnel management discussed in this chapter will be job classifications, job descriptions, performance evaluation, the employee handbook, compensation, and fringe benefits. Other legal considerations of personnel management including the concept of employment at will and employee contracts will be discussed in Chapter 10.

Office Organization

Many interior design practices begin as one-person studios, located in the owner's home. In this smallest of situations, the owner is the president, business manager, marketing director, designer, salesperson, draftsperson, order entry clerk, expediter, complaint department, bookkeeper, secretary, librarian, installer, and any other title required to get the job done. Eventually, the practice becomes prosperous enough to add one or two support people.

It is possible that another designer may join the practice as an employee, but more frequently the single designer practice finds a compatible partner, and the practice changes to a partnership or corporation. Now decisions must be made as to which of the two partners (for simplicity) will be responsible for which business functions: marketing, financial management, operational management, and employee supervision. It must be decided if employees will be hired and given responsibility for certain activities such as office management, bookkeeping, and day-to-day accounting, or if one of the partners will take on these responsibilities. Decisions must also be made as to what the business card will look like, what the boards will look like, as well as all the specific issues of operating the practice. The partners need to sit down and honestly evaluate their strengths and weaknesses in order to determine who will do what. A business plan, discussed in Chapter 3, is a must when the business changes legal formation. Egos must be put aside. The failure of the partner in charge of marketing to be really able to market can very well mean the failure of the business.

In the early stages of the smaller practice, the emphasis is on obtaining clients and earning sustainable revenues. A client base must be established along with the development of a good design reputation and excellent customer service. Owners of these smaller businesses rarely put much emphasis on management issues and few have management experience. The main concern is survival and the focus of all tasks, whether for a single practitioner or a small group of employees, is producing the work that will result in revenue.

As the firm grows, the focus changes somewhat. Expanding the client base continues to be important and the firm may even seek new types of clients. The owner must consider whether he or she will spend his or her time on design projects, marketing, or managing the firm. Owners quickly find that management and organizational issues become increasingly important as the business grows.

As the firm approaches ten or more employees, the small, personal, "family" business of the early days may get into communications trouble. The open door to the owners' offices never seem to close; thus these important senior members have trouble getting their work done. New secretaries go with their complaints to the owners rather than to senior secretaries who are supervising them. Delivery personnel come straight to the owners' office rather than to the warehouse supervisor. As is often the case in many fast-growing companies, good yearly planning has not been going on. As a result, it frequently seems that everyone is spending more time "stamping out fires" than getting really productive work done. The *chain of command*[1] becomes increasingly important. It is time for some organizational planning.

Everyone knows that the designers are one group of workers, that the secretaries and clerks constitute another work group, and bookkeepers and warehouse and delivery people form others. So the start of organizational planning is obvious. Authority must be delegated within these work groups in order to manage each staff group. If the group is large enough, the staff will require titles that differentiate seniority and responsibility. If decisions as to who will manage each work group have not already been established, the owners will need to evaluate each of the existing employees to see if any of them can take on the management responsibility. If not, the owners will need to determine what to do until external individuals can be interviewed and hired.

Job descriptions need to be worked out for each distinctly different job or job level in the work groups. An employee handbook describing specific personnel policies also needs to be prepared. In addition, policies regarding work activities for each group needs to be established. And on the assumption that this was not done in the past, a procedure for developing yearly marketing plans, financial plans, budgets, and the annual business plan will have to be prepared—overwhelming tasks for many business owners. Yet these are things that must be done to assist the practice in continuing to achieve healthy, profitable growth.

How projects are managed administratively is an important part of the firm's organization. When the single owner obtained a client, it was very obvious who was responsible for all the design activities. When a partner joined the firm, each partner was most likely responsible for his or her own design project work. As design employees were added as assistants, some project responsibility was delegated to these less experienced individuals. But what starts to happen when the company grows to about six or eight designer-salespeople plus the owners? Who brings in the new work? What happens to it once the client signs the contract? Who is responsible for all the design work? Who writes the specifications?

---

[1]Chain of command refers to the formal reporting links from one level of employee to another.

Business Organizations

The following covers the primary business organizations that are found in the interior design profession. The purpose is to describe the different ways that a practice can be organized. Of course, these brief descriptions are very generalized and should not be considered the only way to organize an interior design business.

Residential Retail Stores

Retail stores involved in interior design furniture sales and services often have one group of individuals who are strictly floor salespeople. These individuals remain in the store and sell merchandise to clients who do not really need an interior designer's services. These clients are often just looking for one or two items to supplement or replace something in their homes or offices. If the company is large enough, these "in-house" salespeople may specialize in areas such as furniture, wall coverings, and floor treatments. In-house salespeople may or may not be trained interior designers.

A second group in the retail store would be the interior designers. When clients require the services of an interior designer, they are referred to one of the people in this group. The interior designer is responsible for finding out what the client needs in the way of products and services, discusses contracts (if the company charges a fee for design service), and is responsible for all the design work needing to be done. In some situations, the designer may have an assistant (an entry-level interior designer) to help him or her gather information, find appropriate products, and prepare necessary documents. However, the experienced interior designer is the primary person dealing with the client.

Office Furnishings Dealers

Office furniture dealers, generally considered retail establishments, will have outside salespeople and a group of designers. The salespeople are responsible for selling products, but their efforts also often bring in a major portion of the interior design work done by the company. When they find a client who also needs interior design services, they will alert the appropriate department.

In smaller dealers, interior designers work out of the "interiors department." In this situation, it is common that any one of the designers, with the time and experience to handle a client, will meet with the client and be responsible for the project. In larger companies, there might be an interiors department or even a separate, affiliated interior design company. In either of these cases, the interiors group is headed by a manager and the salesperson would contact the design director concerning the project. The design director would either visit with the client face-to-face or assign one of the senior designers to that task. Whoever then meets with the client must get the complete picture of the project, determine if and what amount of fees will be charged, and determine who would be responsible for preparing all the design work.

In a small firm, a contract would be prepared by the designer who visited with the client. In larger firms, the contract is likely to be prepared by the design director or, with approval of the design director, by the project designer who interviewed the client.

Independent Interior Design Firms

Independent interior design practices may or may not sell furnishings or have a retail showroom. Client contact, contract development, design responsibility, and project management responsibility in a small firm are all part of what each designer in the firm would be expected to do. Most probably, the owner will also be doing a lot of project work in addition to management duties.

The larger firms will have various management and staff levels. Client contact is usually the responsibility of the owner, the senior designers, or possibly a design marketing manager. Senior designers are primarily responsible for managing projects and they often supervise a team of designers and support personnel in the completion of the project. In some firms, there will also be individuals with many specialized job functions, such as specification writers and renderers who free the project designers from such activities.

Job Classifications

Organization and project responsibility becomes more critical when the design department has several interior designers with varying amounts of experience and expertise. In these situations a more formally organized structure becomes essential.

The chain of command or, more formally, the organizational structure, helps everyone in the organization understand what are the formal communication patterns. The organizational chart is a graphic representation of the chain of command. Even though it is commonly found that the "real chain of command" does not exactly reflect the organizational chart, larger organizations find it useful to chart the company in order to show the formal flows of official communication. Figure 9–1 shows an organizational chart that defines the job classifications to be reviewed. This discussion of typical job classifications does not include the owner, since that job has many unique activities based on the organization and size of the firm. The descending order of responsibility reflects no specific organization and merely describes the most common levels.

Design Director

At the top of the organizational chart is the manager. The job title might be design director, vice president-design, design manager, or perhaps some other title indicating leadership. This person can have many different job responsibilities depending on the actual size

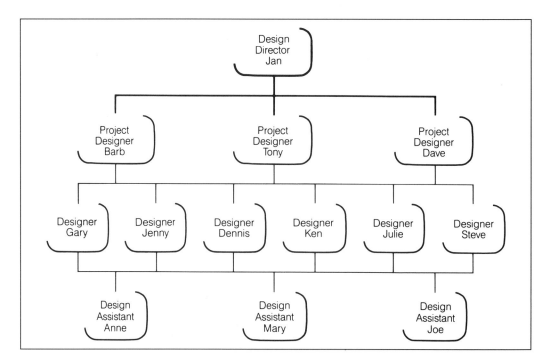

Figure 9–1 Design office organizational chart.

of the firm, but usually the job responsibilities will include (1) administration, (2) marketing, and (3) design.

Administrative duties include all the management functions. Planning, hiring and firing, assignment of work, and preparing contracts are some of these. In addition, the design director is responsible for preparing various management control reports, establishing policies, and attending management meetings. The training and development of the design staff is an important part of the design director's responsibilities.

The most important marketing duties of the design director are making contacts and subsequent presentations to prospective clients. Design managers are often involved in the development of marketing tools such as brochures. In many firms the director is also the company's public liaison for design activities. And, of course, he or she is involved in planning and participating in the development of marketing plans.

Design responsibility of the manager may be minimal in large, very active design firms, or it may be an important part of the manager's responsibility in a small firm. By design responsibility, we mean that the manager is in charge of design projects when he or she plays the role of the project designer. In this situation, the design director is making client contacts, preparing design documents (or supervising others in their preparation), preparing and reviewing purchase orders, and making himself or herself available for installation supervision.

In addition, the design director sets the minimum standards for all design work that leaves the office by reviewing projects during their progress and before they are presented to clients. In this second role, the design director remains involved with project activities without actually doing them.

In very large design firms, the design department leadership may be broken down into two or more areas. The design administration and marketing group would be responsible for all administrative functions such as hiring and all marketing activities of the interior design department. The design production division would be responsible for ensuring the quality of project execution. It would be common for these two groups to be headed by different individuals who report to a design department head, such as VP, Interior Design.

Project Manager

The second common level in larger firms come under such titles as project manager, senior designer, and senior project designer. In large firms where the design director is primarily involved in administration, this position becomes the key design and client contact level. Project managers commonly have five or more years of professional experience and have substantially developed the technical design skills needed by the hiring firm. Often, they are also required to have good communication skills in dealing with clients and other designers.

The project manager is the lead designer and may supervise other designers. As the lead designer, he or she meets with clients to determine needs, substantially designs the interior, prepares or directs others in the completion of design documents, and is responsible for order entry supervision and installation supervision. In some firms, the project manager is required to market the firm's design services to obtain new projects and may even be required to negotiate the design contract.

Staff Designer

The next level of designers are given titles such as staff designer or designer. Staff designers commonly are required to have one or more years of professional experience and well-developed technical design skills as needed by the particular firm. On large projects, these individuals would work under the supervision of the project designers. They may be involved with client interviewing and information gathering conducted by the project designer; they may be asked to prepare preliminary drafting and other documentation and preliminary product specification, in addition to other tasks assigned by the project designers. On smaller projects, they may be responsible for all phases of the project from obtaining needed information from the client to being responsible for installation supervision. Administrative responsibility is limited to personal time and record keeping.

Design Assistant

The entry-level position for most firms is commonly called design assistant,[2] or junior designer. *Entry-level* means that these individuals have little professional experience other than an internship. They work under the direction of a more experienced designer for one or more years. The kinds of work performed are most commonly drafting, preparation of sample boards, preparation of specifications lists for furniture and furnishings, perhaps installation supervision, maintenance of the library, and other tasks assigned by the design director or project designer. After several months, it is not uncommon for the design assistant to be given full responsibility for small-size projects. As in the case of the designer, administrative responsibility for the design assistant would only require time and record keeping for his or her individual efforts.

Other Job Classifications

Depending on the actual interior design practice and size of the firm, there may be some additional specialized job classifications. In large office-furnishings dealers, commercial interior design firms, and architectural firms, a job classification called *space planner* might exist. Space planners are responsible for the overall space plan or for tenant improvement work, but not the specification of furniture and furnishings. The documents they prepare are working drawings and the needed specifications for construction.

Another specialized job classification would be *specification writer* or estimator. As the title implies, these individuals are responsible only for the preparation of finished specification documents. This job classification is most commonly found in very large interiors firms or architectural firms.

A job classification that can be a specialization or an expected responsibility of any designer is a *renderer* or *graphics designer*. Renderers and graphics designers have as their major responsibility the production of perspectives and colored renderings of the interiors designed by the interiors staff. Graphics designers are also responsible for the design of graphics, such as business cards and brochures, presentations and presentation graphics for clients, as well as similar graphics for the interior design firm. Only the larger firms might have specialized renderers and graphics designers.

Another specialist in the design office is the *computer-aided design (CAD) operator*. A CAD operator has experience in the use of some kind of computer-aided design equipment and software. Depending on how this job is used in the firm, the workers may have been trained interior designers or computer operators. They may serve as a separate function of the firm or they may be a part of the interiors department.

Job Descriptions

The *job description* communicates the qualifications, skills, and responsibilities of each job classification within the firm. Many design firms with five or fewer employees rarely have job descriptions. In fact, many larger design firms, especially those that have experienced rapid

---

[2]Note that FIDER defines a design assistant differently than the context used here. Refer to Chapter 1 for the FIDER definition of design assistant.

growth, often are without job descriptions as well. However, as the firm grows, job descriptions help to organize and control growth as well as organizing the work in the office and keeping work efforts on track. Job descriptions should be provided to individuals at the point that they are seriously being considered for a position or upon hiring. Job descriptions should also be available to existing employees so that they may see what qualifications and skills are required of higher-level positions.

Job descriptions do not need to be elaborate. The small firm may find a simple structure such as Figure 9–2 satisfactory. Larger firms may find detailed job descriptions of greater value (see Figure 9–3). It is common to prepare job descriptions in outline form. They should contain statements that are specific enough to differentiate among individuals yet broad enough to allow the manager some flexibility in hiring. The content of the job description must be kept current and complete. It also must accurately reflect the desired skills required to perform the responsibilities of the position. As much as possible, the descriptions of responsibilities should be stated in measurable terms to aid in performance evaluation.

Job descriptions should contain statements related to qualifications, skills required, and responsibilities, and they may contain statements related to the job. The qualifications section will outline the minimal educational requirements. This section would also specify the minimum amount of work experience in years. Statements such as "graduation from at least a four-year college or university with a major in interior design" would set one of the minimum criteria for an interior design position.

In the section concerning skills required, statements related to any specific technical

---

Interior Design Consultant
Smith, Jones Interiors

Responsibilities:

Assist clients.
Evaluate and specify products to meet client needs.
Prepare layouts, plans, and other documents as required.
Prepare color boards.
Obtain signed sales orders.
Prepare cost estimates for all work required of the project.
Complete all required purchase orders.
Coordinate installation and delivery.
Share in housekeeping chores in the office/studio/warehouse.

Qualifications:

Bachelor Degree in Interior Design. Associate degree in interior design with work
    experience in interior design or sales of interior furnishings would substitute for a college
    degree.

Work Experience:

Minimum of two years actual sales/interior design experience required.

Skills:

Portfolio should show training in color coordination, product coordination, drafting, and the
    ability to space plan.
Knowledge of residential products and how to specify those products.
Proven sales record.

Figure 9–2 An example of a basic job description. This example might be most useful to a small residential firm.

SENIOR DESIGNER

Principal Responsibilities
1. Responsible for seeking out prospective clients; determine the scope of the project; the work to be done; select the appropriate design contract from our Master Contract; present the contract; get credit approval, signature, and deposit *before* work begins.
2. Responsible for entire project which may include layout drawings, color coordination, furniture selection, design concept, merchandising, installation, and sign-off. Function as the Project Designer on assigned projects.
3. Compile comprehensive schedules of equipment and colors; coordinate color schemes for the offices and entire building when applicable.
4. Collaborate with the Associate Director in establishing schedule of production effort, design reviews, presentation meetings, and/or periodic progress checks as dictated by the nature and scope of the project. Responsible for coordinating the work load of Staff Designers with Associate Director.
5. Responsible for dealer/client conferences and presentations regarding design project.
6. Recommend type of equipment required to facilitate the job function of each of the customer's areas and occupants; review work and communication flow for client; recommend work flow improvements.
7. Suggest methods of control for acoustics; suggest lighting improvements; direct clients to proper source of supply for their accessories required to furnish office when applicable.
8. Participate in periodic project reviews to evaluate standard of design and the appropriateness to client needs, requests, and exception. Develop a "team effort" on each project.
9. Develop and maintain client work file containing records of all written correspondence, notes on all pertinent verbal discussions, design sketches, schedules, contracts; develop a diary of job from inception to completion.
10. Allocate time in design contract to give on-site consultation or supervision of installation.
11. Provide technical supervision for Staff Designers in performing their assigned tasks.
12. Maintain client confidence and good relations. Develop effective communications and keep client informed of project status.
13. Approve all staff design work before it leaves Office Design. Make certain Staff Designers are *not* sent out on *initial* design projects alone. They should *always* be accompanied by a Senior Designer, Interior Architect, or Project Coordinator. (EXCEPTION—smaller projects and after Associate Director's approval.)
14. Responsible for the successful completion of project so that we can collect our total design contract fee.
15. Keep a ledger sheet on each job with a breakdown of hours billed and time (dollars) remaining on contracts and coordinate status with Staff Designers.
16. Review Staff Designers' time sheets to better evaluate the time needed by different Staff Designers to do different types of contract jobs.
17. Assist sales personnel, through design, in securing profitable project sales.
18. Perform any of the following job functions to support sales representatives as directed.
    (a) Information gathering.
    (b) Space planning and layout.
    (c) Selection of style, type, and color of furniture, upholstery, wallcoverings, finishes, carpet, and accessories.
19. Merchandise products necessary to create proper environment.
20. Inform Associate Director of any prospective design contracts.
21. Assist in developing goals and objectives of Office Designs.
22. Coordinate work load of Staff Designers with Associate Director and other Senior Designers.
23. Help each Staff Designer evolve into a Senior Designer with continuing responsibility for their professional development.
24. Attend weekly sales meeting for product and company knowledge.

Figure 9–3 Job description for a senior designer. (Reproduced with permission, Walsh Bros. Office Equipment, Phoenix, AZ.)

25. Attend Office Design meetings and participate in Office Design projects when requested.

26. Continue personal education through seminars, professional organizations, and other training experiences.

27. Report competitive practices or products for evaluation by management or design staff.

28. Participate in growth of firm as a cooperative member of the team and accept other responsibilities assigned by supervisors.

Special Responsibilities

1. Aid in layout and product selection for floor display, when requested.

2. Aid in layout and design of department within the company as requested by management.

Position Qualifications

Education: College degree in interior architecture or design, or associate degree with actual experience and knowledge may substitute in some cases—desired.

Experience: Four to six years experience with actual design firm in a sales support role or design contract marketing—desired.

Figure 9–3 (Continued)

abilities along with any skills or abilities of a general nature would be outlined. Although this section often comes second in a job description, it is often easier to finish writing this section after the responsibilities section is completed. In any case, it is important for the skills required to correlate with the responsibilities expected and the qualifications demanded. These skills and general abilities should be listed in the order of importance to the job. For a firm involved in commercial interior design, drafting skill may be of primary importance for an entry-level design assistant, and therefore should be listed first. For a residential firm, color coordination may be primary for an entry-level person.

The responsibilities section must be detailed enough so that the individual in the position knows what is expected of him or her. Large corporations, which have a great deal of experience in the preparation of job descriptions, often have very detailed outlines of responsibilities. Interior design firms, which have limited experience in this area, often have vague, unclear descriptions (if they have them at all).

A reference as to whom the person reports, either as a separate section or within the responsibilities section, should be noted. This helps clarify the chain of command and also aids new employees in knowing who will be his or her supervisor. Since people leave positions, reference is best made by job title rather than by name.

Performance Evaluations

For almost every owner or manager of a design firm, preparation of *performance evaluations* of employees is an unpleasant task. In part, the evaluation is difficult for design managers since few have training or experience with the performance evaluation process. In far too many practices the performance evaluation is an informal mental review of each employee's work contribution. This informal review is almost always based on the manager's subjective opinions rather than any objective evaluation of work performance based on the responsibilities of the job. In addition, far too often performance reviews are used solely to determine compensation increases of employees rather than to assist in their development and training.

Managers also dislike evaluation because preparing them can take so much time. Even with an informal review process, it is not uncommon for the manager to spend many hours during the year considering each employee's past performance and discussing these impressions with the employee. To many managers, a formal process will mean even more time spent on this activity.

Employees also find the review process an anxiety-producing, negative time period. Far too many employers conduct performance evaluations as a time for negative criticism rather than an evaluation of progress and direction toward development of the employees. It is no wonder that employees dislike the evaluation process.

In this section, we will discuss the performance evaluation and suggest some ways to make it more useful to the employee and the employer, and perhaps less difficult for the employer.

Purpose

The purpose of the performance evaluation is to appraise the positive and negative work efforts of an employee. Its primary goal should be the development of the employee for the future, not the punishment of the employee for past performance (see Figure 9–4). These evaluations must be based on the responsibilities that the employee understands to be within his or her control during the period of the evaluation. Evaluations must primarily be made objectively and based, as much as possible, on measurable criteria related back to responsibilities (See Figure 9–5).

Performance evaluation should be designed to

1. *Encourage the development of employees.* Companies that continually hire designers straight out of college, train them for a year or two, and then see them leave for a job with more responsibility at another company apparently enjoy being part of the educational processes of the interior design profession. However, this kind of hire/train/gone/rehire circle costs the firm more in the long run than the savings obtained by continually hiring inexperienced designers at low salaries. The training, development, and keeping of quality employees costs the company less and helps the company grow by showing clients that the firm is stable.

2. *Aid the employer-employee supervisory relationship.* Individuals in management positions in interior design offices should have as clearly defined aspects of their job the supervision and training of design staff employees. Even though the design director is often expected to "wear many hats" in the office, the management of design personnel should not be the least important. Managers must take the time to observe the design staff as to how they do the work assigned. When necessary, they must be ready to train employees in aspects of the firm's design processes. And they must be ready to recognize when employees are in need of training from outside sources.

3. *Determine compensation increases, promotions, and dismissals.* Too many companies and employees view the performance evaluation as a means to the end for an increase in salary or a promotion. When this is the primary goal, individuals who do not get the expected increase or promotion often become frustrated and leave the design firm. This occurs most often when the reason for not receiving the increase or promotion is never clarified or when the employee suddenly finds out that he or she was not doing what was expected in order to receive the adjustment. However, a well-thought-out review process can be counted on as a means to determine these adjustments as well as to help in the motivation of employees toward agreed-on responsibilities and work performance.

4. *Aid human resource planning.* The evaluation process helps determine which areas of expertise existing employees have and which areas of expertise are needed either through training or the hiring of new employees. For instance, if the design firm decides to pursue health care facilities planning, performance evaluations will help the manager decide whether or not someone within the firm can do the work. Understanding this, the manager

---

SUBJECT: YOUR PERFORMANCE REVIEW

Date: _____

To: _____

From: _____

The firm has implemented a Performance Review Program for all employees. The main purpose of the program is to provide the opportunity for regular, two-way communication between employee and supervisor, which should result in improved job performance and productivity. Please be reminded that your performance review does not directly affect your compensation review, and we ask that you respond to this review as openly as possible.

Your Performance Review meeting is scheduled on _____ at __ A.M./P.M. Please allow at least one hour for this meeting. You will need a copy of your current job description for this review and copies of each of these attached forms: Employee Performance Review Summary and Employee Performance Review Worksheets.

Since each employee is to share the responsibility of the review with his or her supervisor, you are asked to do a self-review prior to our meeting. Please use your job description, which lists your major responsibilities, and the attached Review Worksheet, which will review the level of performance for each of the responsibilities. Number each item to correspond with the numbering on your job description. Write in any comments you care to make.

Also please complete the Performance Review Summary, and spend a few minutes thinking about item 4—your goals for the next performance review.

As your supervisor, I will also prepare for your review in the same way. Then at our scheduled meeting, we will review both Worksheets and the Summary, and reach agreement on the level of performance expected.

Again, the main purpose of this program is to improve communications, thus resulting in improved job performance and productivity. This is not just an exercise in filling out forms! Our goal is to *talk* about and *improve* performance. Think of the program as an ongoing "process," and not a one-time "grade." Remember that your comments and suggestions about your job performance are welcome, and you are encouraged to play an active role in this process.

This performance review program will be a continuous process, and I will provide you regular feedback on an ongoing basis as to your performance throughout the year.

Thank you for your cooperation in this very important program!

_____

Figure 9–4 Sample notice of the employee's performance review. (Reproduced with permission, Office Designs, Phoenix, AZ.)

can then recruit someone experienced in health care work or someone to take over the current staff member's ongoing responsibility as he or she shifts to the new area.

For the employee, the performance appraisal must tell each how he or she is doing. It should also tell the employee where he or she can likely progress in the future and how to advance there. For new employees, this means that the manager must indicate clearly what the responsibilities of the position are and what kind of performance level will be expected. A well-written job description will define responsibilities. If, however, the individual's actual job responsibilities deviate from the job description in some way, these should be written down and clearly understood by both parties. Performance levels also need to be discussed and agreed on. Interim evaluations should focus on the achievement of goals and, where

---

EMPLOYEE PERFORMANCE REVIEW SUMMARY

Name _____ Position _____
Dept./Div. _____ Supervisor _____

1. What is the basic purpose or objective of this position?
   _____
   _____

2. How well have the basic objectives been accomplished?
   _____
   _____
   _____

3. What changes in approach to the job would help improve the overall job performance?
   _____
   _____
   _____

4. List specific goals for the next performance review and when they should be completed.

GOAL	TARGET DATE
_____	_____
_____	_____
_____	_____
_____	_____
_____	_____

5. How well have the goals from the past performance review been accomplished?
   _____
   _____
   _____

6. Additional comments:
   _____

(use reverse side for additional comments)

Supervisor's Signature _____ Date _____
Employee's Signature _____ Date _____

Figure 9–5 A performance review summary sheet. (Reproduced with permission, Walsh Bros. Office Equipment, Phoenix, AZ.)

satisfactory progress does not exist, constructive criticism and direction toward the development of success should be addressed.

For the continuing employee, the evaluation must be based on responsibilities and performance levels agreed to at the last review. Since the performance evaluation is for development of the individual, deficiencies must be in terms of correction and future achievement, not punishment. Discussion should also occur regarding new goals and how current and expected responsibilities and performance levels fit into these goals. This becomes the performance criteria for the next review.

Timing

Although informal evaluation situations may occur at any time for any level of employee, most companies find that a formal evaluation should take place yearly. It is a very good idea, however, for new employees to be evaluated more frequently during the first year. A common schedule has the first evaluation take place at the end of the probationary period, which is usually 90 days. Many firms find it advantageous to have reviews at 30-, 60-, and possibly 75-day intervals for new employees during the 90-day probationary period. Subsequent evaluations would occur after the first six months and then after one year. The one-year date can be either at the anniversary date of hiring or on a day set for all evaluations.

New employees, especially those just out of college, are going to be looking for more constant evaluations of their progress. This is due in part to the uncertainty of being in a new situation as well as to the familiar constant evaluations received in college. However, if employees know what their responsibilities are and what level of performance is expected, constant evaluation and "pats on the back" will not be necessary or expected.

The Evaluator

The performance evaluation is most commonly performed by the employee's immediate supervisor. In design offices where people often work in teams to complete projects, individuals who are not truly an employee's supervisor may be asked to evaluate an employee's performance. If this occurs, the employee should be made aware of who is making the evaluations and why he or she is involved if that person is not, in fact, the employee's supervisor.

Often individual evaluations are supplemented by self- or peer evaluations. Self-evaluations can be helpful, but it is not uncommon for employees to either be too hard or too easy on themselves as compared to a superior's evaluation. Peer evaluations, where employees rate coworkers, only seem to work when employees trust each other, when they are truly in a position to be very familiar with each other's work, and when they are not competing with each other for raises or promotions. Experience has shown that peers will either be too easy on each other so as not to get coworkers angry or too hard on individuals they do not like.

The Instrument and Evaluation

For the performance evaluation process to be effective and meaningful, the instrument used must produce reliable and valid measurements of the criteria. An instrument is reliable if it produces consistent data. This would mean that if two different supervisors were to evaluate the same individual, the results should be the same. For the instrument to be valid, it must deal with only those factors that are relevant to an individual's performance. For example, a design assistant may be told that drafting is a primary responsibility of the position. If the quantity of work produced is not relevant, but the quality of work is, then only the quality of work should be evaluated. Projects themselves cannot be easily evaluated under the constraints of validity. What can be evaluated more easily is how things were done; such as error-free drafting and specification writing, proper completion of necessary correspondence, the meeting of schedules with clients and others, and so on.

The rating scale must be as objective as possible. Dealing with specific skills and skill levels as they relate to job responsibilities is one way to maintain objectivity. Being sure the rating instrument does not contain a lot of questions related to either the personality, attitude, or appearance of the employee also maintains objectivity. The instrument should also not evaluate based solely on the employer's personal opinion—especially if that personal opinion has not been satisfactorily communicated to the employees. The right kind of evaluation method will help obtain the objectivity in the evaluation that is necessary to make it fair for all employees.

The most commonly used evaluation method is the rating scale (see Figure 9–6). Rating scales consist of four or five valuations such as outstanding, very good, satisfactory, fair, and poor. If valuations such as these are used, then each is given some kind of numeric scale also. The evaluator is asked to assign one of these values to a series of job traits. These traits may be stated as questions or as short statements of one or more words.

These ratings are then "totaled." If certain traits are to receive more value than others, then the traits or grouping of traits have to be weighted. Then a total is given. In the simplest

EMPLOYEE PERFORMANCE REVIEW WORKSHEET

Name _____   Position _____

Date of Review _____   Date of Job Description _____

CODE: PR—Principal Responsibilities   DR—Department Responsibilities
             GR—General Responsibilities   CR—Company Responsibilities
             SR—Special Responsibilities

CODE	JOB DESC. LINE #	BRIEF DESCRIPTION OF THE TASK	COMMENTS REGARDING PERFORMANCE OF TASK	LEVEL OF PERFORMANCE				
		Both the employee and supervisor are to fill out as many worksheets as needed.	Please use the back of this sheet for any additional comments.	EXCELLENT	STANDARD ABOVE	STANDARD	IMPROVEMENT NEEDED	UNACCEPTABLE

Figure 9–6 Sample performance rating sheet. (Reproduced with permission, Walsh Bros. Office Equipment, Phoenix, AZ.)

form, the person with the highest ranking gets the highest salary increase (or first shot at promotion, and so on). This does not mean that the person with the lowest ranking gets fired, but it does mean that he or she definitely requires the most counseling for improvement. In almost all cases, employers should be required to provide a written sentence or two related to each trait evaluation. Some firms, however, only require comments when very high or very low ratings are given.

Since rating scales are prone to subjective judgment, the ratings are also affected by such things as the evaluator's being overly strict or overly lenient. The ratings can also be affected by central tendency mistakes and halo effects. Sometimes managers, in a mistaken belief that employees will do better work when coerced, will have exceedingly harsh standards of performance. They feel that negative motivation will somehow inspire the employee to work harder. On the other side is the employer who tries too hard to give the employee a good rating, thereby never giving an honest assessment. Being too harsh will frustrate employees, whereas being too lenient will allow less than satisfactory work to be considered acceptable. Lenient evaluations eventually catch up with employees, surprising them with the knowledge that their work is below par and their services are no longer required. Other employees, seeing someone "getting away with it" will wonder why they are working so hard.

Central tendency mistakes refer to a manager's ratings of all employees in the average or satisfactory range. In this case, no one is judged as being outstanding, or poor, or even above average or below average. When no distinction is made, there is no motivation for the outstanding employee to continue to work hard and no motivation for the poor employee to improve. In fact, very little motivation exists for anyone when this occurs.

The *halo effect* appears when the evaluation of one set of traits colors the other traits. If someone is given low ratings on traits related to the quality of the work he or she does, that person may also be given low ratings on other traits, such as initiative, even if he or she really has high levels of initiative.

To overcome these problems, evaluators could use a method of forced distribution. *Forced distribution* is like grading on a curve in school. The evaluator is forced to place a certain percentage of employees in each of the categories. Knowing that only certain percentages of individuals will be ranked in the highest category encourages the evaluator to make a more conscientious effort at objective evaluations. However, there are some problems with forced distributions. First, some individuals do not make it into the highest categories because one aspect of their performance always holds them back. This is akin to the student who never seems to be able to study for multiple-choice tests and always does poorly in classes with exams, but is outstanding in studio classes. Another problem with forced distribution is that with everyone knowing that only a few individuals will be ranked very high, the average employee might not see any reason to try to improve. Finally, the wrong kind of competitive atmosphere may be created in the office where people believe it necessary to undermine coworkers in order to advance.

There are some other methods of evaluation that can be used. One is a checklist where the evaluator checks off the items that best (or least) describe the employee's performance. The items on the checklist are very specific statements related to job behavior.

Another method is a comparison of one employee to another. One way of doing this is by the paired comparison method. Employees are first paired. "In a four-person department, for example, employee A would be compared with B, A with C, A with D, B with C, and so on. Then for each trait, analyze who is the most effective employee of the pair. After all the traits are compared, add up the number of times the employee was rated highest. The employee chosen most often for traits of equal value receives the highest rating."[3] Other methods of

---

[3]Block, Judy R., *Performance Appraisal on the Job: Making It Work*. Reprinted by permission of the publisher, Executive Enterprises Publications Co., Inc., New York, N.Y., 1981, pp. 35–36.

ranking can be found in some of the listings in the References and in other books on performance appraisal.

Interview

The interview should be scheduled sufficiently in advance for the manager and employee to be adequately prepared to discuss the employee's past performance with respect to previously agreed-on goals. Notice to the employee should also indicate what will occur during the interview. The interview should be private and only the employee and manager should be present.

Sufficient time must be scheduled so that the interview can progress uninterrupted by telephone calls, clients, or anything else. A minimum of one hour is generally required if the interview does not include a discussion of next year's goals, but two or more hours may be needed to fully discuss both issues. The employer should allow approximately half the time for his or her comments and the other half for the employee's comments.

It is important for the employer to put the employee at ease at the beginning of the interview and to explain to the employee how the interview will proceed. The employer must also be clear that the purpose of the evaluation is for the continued development of the employee as well as a review of current performance. The employer and employee should understand that the review is not a disciplinary session.

The employer should start his or her review comments with a positive statement. This helps put the employee at ease and keeps him or her from being immediately on the defensive. Criticism should be constructive in nature. It often helps to place comments on negative performance between positive comments. The employer should seek to be as descriptive as possible in positive and negative comments, and these comments should be based on performance criteria, not personal feelings. This attitude helps the employee understand more precisely what he or she is doing right or wrong.

The employee should be asked to evaluate his or her own progress for the year. Some evaluators start with the employee's comments so that the employee does not become unnecessarily defensive about the negative comments of the employer. It is necessary for the employee to comment about his or her own performance to allow the employer to understand how the employee views his or her own work role.

The interview should focus on strong points if the evaluation received a high mark. This reinforces positive future activity and motivates the employee to make further progress. If the evaluation received particularly low marks, the employer must be prepared before the interview for potential hostility and disbelief, and should have a course of action in mind if the employee gives no indication that improvement may be possible.

The last portion of the interview should focus on the future, with discussions concerning what the employee can do to resolve performance deficiencies. Discussion and negotiation must occur so that the course of action becomes an agreed-on plan, not one dictated by the employer. Most successes come from focusing on two or three of the more important negative areas rather than a longer list. This is a more satisfactory method since it is difficult for people to try to improve on many things and at the same time maintain positive aspects. A realistic timetable for the improvement should also be agreed to as an aid in future evaluation.

The interview should be concluded with a summary of the satisfactory and unsatisfactory areas as well as the action plan for the resolution of agreed-on unsatisfactory areas. The interview should end on a positive note with the employee clearly understanding how his or her performance is viewed by the employer and what the future will bring for that employee.

After the interview, the employer should prepare some notes related to what occurred during the interview. This is also a good idea for the employee. The agreed-on goals and timetable should be prepared as soon as possible. Whoever is responsible for preparing this must quickly provide a copy to the other party. It should then be reviewed individually and any discrepancies should be discussed and agreed on immediately.

The employer should follow up the evaluation through observations and other monitoring of the employee's progress toward the goals. Some areas may need special monitoring, and the manager must be ready to spend the time training or working with the individual. Remember that performance evaluations fail when the employer only considers evaluation and development as important issues during the formal evaluation time period.

The Employee Handbook

The purpose of an *employee handbook* is to provide managers and employees a concise reference to company policies. In small design firms, the employee handbook might include both general operating policies, such as the policies related to special ordering merchandise for clients, as well as personnel policies. In larger firms, it is likely that there is one handbook for personnel issues and one or more additional handbooks to explain operational policies by department. As with job descriptions, many design firms do not have an employee handbook.

A well-designed handbook will help to clarify policies in order to prevent complaints, grievances, and morale problems before they occur. The policy handbook will also help the company prevent complaints or lawsuits related to equal employment opportunity laws. These well-defined policies also assist managers and owners in the decision-making and control process by providing consistent treatment of the defined issues. In recent years, some legal issues have surfaced concerning employee handbooks. Chapter 10 will briefly discuss the concept of "implied contracts" as applied to employee handbooks. Anyone considering writing a handbook should read that section as part of his or her research.

How to Prepare a Handbook

It is important that the individual charged with preparing the handbook be given full authority and responsibility—and time—to accomplish the task. In relatively small firms, the owner will most likely attempt to prepare the handbook himself or herself. In departmentalized firms, managers may be asked to submit policies related to their areas. Then either through committee meetings or through the efforts of one manager, a composite handbook would be produced.

Many policies may already be in writing or are well known even though they are not written down. These become the starting point for the handbook. Some information may have to be obtained from company records. For example, paid holidays may have varied over the years. Company records will show which holidays were considered paid each year. Vacation and sick-time allowance history may also only be obtained from company records.

Many companies have "unwritten rules" that have sprung up over the years, but which have dubious authority. These unwritten rules should be discovered and decisions made as to their current validity. An example of an unwritten rule might be that "no employee may make client appointments outside the office from 8:00 to 9:00 A.M." This unwritten rule may have addressed an earlier need to be sure someone was in the studio to answer the phone until the bookkeeper came in at 9:00. Now that there is a secretary who comes in at 8:00, the unwritten policy probably has no validity.

The organization and contents should be logical, clear, and concise. For example, the firm may wish to use a format that mirrors the logical sequence of events of an organization. In this case, issues related to hiring would be first, perhaps followed by hours of work, absenteeism, and such employee benefits in the middle, and termination at the end.

As much as possible, clear and concise wording is important. Terminology that everyone understands or is in common usage should be adopted. Instead of "The studio, workrooms, warehouse, and bookkeeping areas will be open and maintained by appropriate personnel on a daily basis, Monday through Friday from 8:30 A.M. to 5:30 P.M.," use "Scheduled work hours all departments: Monday–Friday, 8:30 A.M. to 5:30 P.M."

Remember that the employee handbook and the included policy statements are to inform, not to impress with flowery prose. Also remember that some employees are not interior designers, and may not be familiar with some of the jargon of the interior design profession.

The new handbook, when completed and approved by management and owners, should not just be handed to employees. Especially when a design firm has never had a handbook, it is important for upper management and the department managers to meet with employees to explain why the handbook was prepared, to define the purpose of the handbook, and to go over the contents. Even if employees have not been a part of the process, at least they will feel less threatened by a new set of rules if they are explained before the rules are put into effect.

What to Include

Precisely what depth of information should go into a policy handbook is up to the interior design firm. The complexity of written policies should match the management style and philosophy of the owners or managers while providing the policies needed to aid management in control and decision making. Many people begin a career in interior design because they seek freedom of expression and a certain freedom of time. A studio composed of primarily self-motivated, self-directed individuals will rebel or even quit if a great number of strictly enforced "rules" are suddenly thrust upon them. Figure 9–7 summarizes the common parts of employee handbooks.

A. Overview

B. Introduction
   Provides an overview of the company.

C. Organization
   Provides a description of the responsibility areas and organizational structure.

D. Employment and hiring policies
   Details hiring procedures, if performance evaluations are performed, and promotion policies.

E. Compensation
   Details compensation policies for all levels of employees. This section commonly defines pay periods, bonuses, and fringe benefits (if any).

F. Time-off
   Details company paid holidays (if any), vacation policies, sick leave, and other paid or nonpaid days off.

G. Training
   Provides information about any company training or reimbursement for training for educational purposes.

H. General rules and policies
   Details work week, overtime, tardiness, and such things as use of company phone and mail for personal business, dress code and other general work conditions.

I. Leaving the company
   Will include information on termination policies, expected notice, severance pay (if any), and policies on references.

Figure 9–7 Common parts of an employee handbook.

FOREWORD

The purpose of the Burns Interiors Employee Handbook is to provide each employee with a complete source of the policies and procedures of the firm. Our experience has shown that providing each employee with a handbook of this information helps to promote consistency in the operations of the firm. This consistency results in a more efficient, productive and, therefore, more profitable association for the employees and the firm.

As you flip through the pages, you will see that the handbook is broken down into four parts: Introduction, Personnel Policies, Operating Policies, and Department Policies and Procedures. The Introduction provides you with the philosophy and mission statement of Burns Interiors, a brief history of the firm, and a presentation on the organizational structure of the firm. In the section on Personnel Policies, there is an explanation of hiring, performance evaluation, termination policies, and employee benefits. Section three on Operating Policies explains general business policies such as the business hours, holidays and sick leave, overtime, and so forth. The final section contains policies and procedures specific to your department. The material in this section may be supplemented by additional information provided to you by your supervisor. These, of course, should be inserted in this section.

The policies and procedures of this firm have evolved over many years. As the firm changes, so may some of its policies. As policies and/or procedures change, these will be completely presented and discussed with employees.

We are happy to have you as an employee at Burns Interiors and look forward to working with you for many years. The management wishes you great success as you grow with us.

MaryLee Burns, President

Figure 9–8 Example of an opening statement for an employee handbook.

A new handbook should begin with a statement related to the purpose of the manual and the reason for its development and implementation. Figure 9–8 gives an example of a short introductory statement. All the policy statements for each category within the handbook will follow. Figure 9–9 provides an example of policies related to hours of work.

After the handbook is prepared, it must be remembered that it is not ever really finished. Contents should be reviewed periodically by management and owners to keep it as up to date as possible. As the business continues to change, policies need to be reviewed and possibly modified.

Whatever the size of the firm or the type of practice, written policies related to operational and personnel issues aid the owners and management of the firm in running the interior design practice in a professional manner. Written policies also help clarify how things are done and where employees stand in their relationship with the firm. Policies that are clear and functional for the type of practice will be adhered to by all employees. Those that are counter to what is happening in the firm or seem to be constantly ignored by some in the firm cannot be enforced and also tend to undermine the management.

Compensation and Fringe Benefits

What the salary for working at an interior design office is and how it is arrived at are very important considerations for both the employee and the employer. There is more than one way for interior design employees to be compensated. *Compensation* is any kind of payment for the performance of basic work responsibilities. It most commonly is in the form of the weekly or biweekly paycheck. *Fringe benefits* are other kinds of payments to the employee that are optional or may not even be provided by an employer. Fringe benefits, such as paid vacations and health insurance, also make a significant contribution to the total compensa-

5. Hours of Work

A. Business Hours

Monday through Friday, 8:30 a.m. to 5:30 p.m.

Both hourly and salaried employees are expected to be at work during normal business hours.

B. The Work Week

The normal work week for hourly and salaried employees is forty (40) hours.

C. Lunch Hours

Hourly employees are entitled to one hour for lunch. It must be taken between 11:30 a.m. and 2:00 p.m. Salaried employees are expected to take one hour for lunch. It should be taken between 11:30 a.m. and 2:00 p.m.

D. Breaks

Hourly employees are entitled to two 15-minute breaks. One should be taken in the morning and one in the afternoon.

E. Overtime

Hourly employees must have the approval of their supervisor to work overtime. Overtime pay begins after a minimum of forty (40) hours of work in a normal work week. The pay rate for overtime will be 1½ times the normal hourly rate.

Hourly employees may taken compensatory time in place of overtime pay. One hour of compensatory time may be taken in place of the 1½ times overtime pay rate. Approval and arrangements must be made with the employee's supervisor.

Salaried employees are not entitled to overtime pay.

F. Absences

You must keep your supervisor informed of absences you know of in advance.

If you must be unexpectedly absent for illness or some other reason, you must telephone your supervisor as soon as possible. If you must be absent for more than one day, telephone your supervisor daily.

G. Lateness

You should contact your supervisor if you find that you will be unavoidably late.

Figure 9–9 A page of policies from an employee handbook.

tion package. The most common methods of compensation will be briefly discussed in this section.

Compensation

The most common methods of compensating design employees are: hourly wage, straight salary, and commission. Bonus plans, technically called incentive compensation, are sometimes tied to any of these.

In the *hourly wage,* the interior designer is paid some rate for every hour he or she works. The weekly salary would then be computed by figuring the average work day (e.g., 8 hours) and the average work week (e.g., 40 hours). If a design assistant is paid $6.00 an hour, his or her weekly gross salary would be $240 per week for a forty-hour week. Some firms, however, have slightly shorter work weeks. It is possible for a company's work week to be 35 or 37 hours. It is up to the individual company to determine the length of its normal work week. Since the federal wage and hour laws apply to interior design firms, the firm has to pay hourly wage employees overtime for any hours worked beyond the normal work week. This amounts to time-and-a-half for weekday overtime work and double time for Sundays and holidays.

Gross salary, as anyone who has held some kind of a job realizes, is the compensation amount before any deductions. The employer must withhold (deduct) amounts for federal income tax, social security[4] and Medicare contributions, possibly state income taxes, and possibly voluntary contributions for such things as health insurance. The amount of compensation left after these deductions is called *net pay* or "take-home" pay. It is common for the basic withholding deductions for taxes and social security to amount to 20 to 35 percent of gross pay.

From an employee's standpoint, an hourly wage is a good compensation method since it pays employees for every hour (and portion of an hour) they work. The employee, however, will have to show the manager that he or she is being very productive during the workday to be sure that overtime worked is really necessary. Overtime hourly wages for interior designers can be very costly to the firm if the overtime is not expected when estimating design fees or when it occurs because employees have not been productive during the workday.

Because of the nature of interior design work, the hourly wage is used less often as a method of compensation, except where the monitoring of the employee's productivity and work responsibilities are relatively easy. It is more commonly used to compensate entry-level employees and "production" employees such as secretaries, bookkeepers, and delivery people.

The *straight salary* method of compensation provides a fixed amount of salary to the employee no matter how many hours in the week he or she works. Of course, the firm still requires the employee on salary to work a normal work week of 35 to 40 hours. The employee's weekly pay would be determined by dividing the yearly salary by 52 weeks.

An employee compensated on a straight salary method would not be eligible for any overtime pay. When overtime is worked, the employee usually is expected to, at some convenient time, utilize compensatory time. *Compensatory time* is time off during the normal work week to make up for the overtime hours worked. In all cases, the utilization of compensatory time must be approved by the manager so that the absence of the employee will not be detrimental to the regular office work. Firms generally have an additional policy that compensatory time cannot be "saved up" for an extended period nor added at the beginning or end of a vacation period.

Interior designers whose work responsibilities are more involved with the selling of products or services rather than in design work may be paid a *commission*. When commission is used as the compensation method, the designer is paid some percentage of the gross, net sale, or gross margin of the merchandise sold or the amount of the contract.

Commission on the gross sale means that the commission percentage is paid on the amount for which the client is billed. For example, if the designer is paid 10 percent of the gross sale, and the client was billed $5000, the commission to be paid would be $500.

When commission is based on the net sale, the percentage is calculated after certain items are deducted. Deductions could include discounts, freight charges, delivery charges, and returns. For example, assume a gross sale of $5000 has a commission on the net sale of 10 percent, and a $250 deduction for delivery and freight charges. The commission paid to the designer would be $475.

In the gross margin method of paying commission, the commission percentage is paid

---

[4]Social security shows up on the check stub as FICA. FICA stands for Federal Insurance Contributions Act. Social security is the more common name for FICA.

based on the gross margin of the sale. *Gross margin* (also called *gross profit*) is the difference between the selling price and the cost price of the goods or services being sold. Designers are motivated to sell merchandise and services for the highest gross margin possible in order to receive the most commission possible. In the preceding example of a $5000 sale, with a 10 percent commission, assume the cost price of the sale $2500. The amount of commission to be paid in this case would be $250.

Some firms utilizing the gross margin commission method also often incorporate a sliding scale of commission. In this situation, different percentages are paid depending on the amount of the gross margin percentage. For instance, if the gross margin was 90 percent (nearly retail price) the commission percentage might be 50 percent. If the gross margin was only 5 percent (nearly cost price) the commission percentage might only be 2 percent.

Incentive compensation is payment over and above regular compensation. The two common types of incentive compensation are merit pay and bonus plans. *Merit pay* is an amount added to an individual's basic annual compensation amount, often for the reward of quality work done in the past. It is commonly referred to as a "raise" or salary increase. Another kind of compensation increase added to the basic annual compensation is a cost-of-living increase. A *cost-of-living increase* is generally across-the-board. Generally, all employees may receive a cost-of-living increase to help offset increases in inflation. Merit pay is an increase that could go to all employees, but probably will only go to some individuals due to their high level of performance during the past year. Incentive compensation is primarily awarded to hourly and salaried employees. Those on commission rarely receive incentive compensation.

Bonus plans are methods of paying extra compensation based on the employee's producing more than a specific personal quota. Bonuses are most commonly paid to design employees who sell merchandise. If they meet or exceed their sales quotas, the employees would be paid some kind of bonus. Since designers responsible for creative and "on the boards" design work cannot easily establish a quota of design work, bonuses are less often paid to these individuals. However, some interior design firms do have a bonus method that rewards the "on the boards" designers. These are usually based on meeting or exceeding the amount of contracts budgeted or for exceeding a budgeted amount of specifications on a certain kind of furniture or furnishings.

Fringe Benefits

Compensation only represents part of the payments from the employer to the employee. Approximately 20 to 60 percent of payments to the individual is from fringe benefits. These fringe benefits represent approximately 32.5 percent of the overall payroll.[5]

Fringe benefits take many forms and will not be offered consistently from one interior design firm to another (see Figure 9–10). The most common fringe benefits given or paid directly to the employee are group health insurance, paid vacations, paid holidays, and employee discounts on purchases. Other benefits offered to the employee might include group life insurance, supplemental health insurance such as dental programs, paid sick leave, profit-sharing plans, and professional-growth benefits. Professional-growth benefits would include such things as paid educational benefits, partial or full payment of professional association dues, and partial or full payment of NCIDQ testing fees.

Other benefits that would not directly be paid to the employee but must be paid by the employer include social security tax contributions, worker's compensation taxes, and unemployment compensation taxes. These are benefits that the employee may or may not draw from for some time. Social security would not be payable until the employee retires (or is physically disabled and can no longer work). Workmen's compensation covers on-the-job

---

[5]Beam 1985, 5.

Health insurance.

Life insurance.

Supplemental insurance such as dental, disability, and vision care.

Retirement plans such as profit sharing.

Paid holidays, vacations, and sick leave.

Employee purchase discounts.

Payments for employee professional association dues.

Payments for NCIDQ or other testing and licensing fees.

Reimbursements for employee use of personal automobile.

Payments for employee educational enhancements.

Figure 9–10 The most common voluntary fringe benefits provided by businesses.

injuries, unemployment compensation would only be paid, under certain circumstances, when the employee is laid off from the design firm.

When an individual is applying for a job, considering a promotion, or weighing the merits of staying with the present employer, the complete benefits package must be looked at carefully. A position with one firm with a slightly lower salary but a good employer-paid health insurance program may be better than another position where the salary is a bit higher, but there is no health insurance program available to employees.

Summary

As interiors firms grow, it becomes increasingly important for the owners and managers to review and define the organizational structure. Job responsibilities become more specialized and roles must be defined. The development and utilization of job classifications and job descriptions assist owners in the employee management of growing design firms.

To keep good employees, research has shown that more must be done for employees than occasional raises. Performance evaluations keyed to job descriptions help employees understand how they are doing. These also show employees where they can advance in the firm. Employee handbooks clarify work rules and operational procedures. Fair compensation and fringe benefits are also needed to keep turnover low.

All these issues are of critical importance to the practice owner and managers. Design firms are really individuals who must be managed and motivated to achieve the business goals of the company. Without effective office organization and employee management, the smooth operation of the firm becomes difficult if not impossible. The next chapter will cover legal issues of employment, such as the agency relationship and employment contracts.

References

Beam, Burton T., Jr., and John J. McFadden. 1985. *Employee Benefits.* Homewood, Ill.: Richard D. Irwin.

Berk, Joseph, and Susan Berk. 1991. *Managing Effectively. A Handbook for First-Time Managers.* New York: Sterling Publishing.

Block, Judy R. 1981. *Performance Appraisal on the Job*. New York: Executive Enterprises Publications.

Charnov, Bruce H. 1985. *Appraising Employee Performance*. Westbury, N.Y.: Caddylak Publishing.

Coxe, Weld. 1980. *Managing Architectural and Engineering Practice*. New York: Wiley.

Finter, Andrea. July 1984. "Designer Salary Poll Links Job Tenure and Compensation." *Contract*.

——————. June 1985. "Senior Designers' Average Pay: $37,300." *Contract*.

Getz, Lowell. 1986. *Business Management in the Smaller Design Firm*. Newton, Mass.: Practice Management Associates.

Gibson, Woody. October 1980. "Design Wages Depend on Function." *Contract*.

Lawson, J. W, II. 1970. *How to Develop a Company Personnel Policy Manual*, 5th ed. Chicago: The Dartnell Corp.

Shapero, Albert. 1985. *Managing Professional People*. New York: The Free Press.

Slavin, Maeve. September 1983. "Jobs Are Not What They Used To Be." *Interiors*.

Stern, Natalie. November, 1982. "Top Contract Furniture Sales People Can Boost Earnings 33% with Timed Move." *Contract*.

Stitt, Fred A., ed. 1986. *Design Office Management Handbook*. Santa Monica, Calif.: Arts and Architecture Press.

Tobias, Sheila, and Alma Lantz. November 1985. "Performance Appraisal." *Working Woman*.

Wagner, Michael. September 1985. "Interiors Business. Salaries and Bonuses Are Up for Designers." *Interiors*.

Whitmyer, Claude, Salli Rasberry, and Michael Phillips. 1989. *Running a One-Person Business*. Berkeley, Calif.: Ten Speed Press.

Woodward, Cynthia A. 1990. *Human Resources Management for Design Professionals*. Washington, D.C.: AIA Press.

Chapter 10

Legal Issues of Employment

"It is becoming much harder to be an employer than to be an employee!" commented a design director one day. Interpretations of older laws and the enactment of new laws to protect the employee have made it difficult for the employer to hire or fire individuals when they do not perform as expected. Many new strategies are being used to protect the employer. Many employers are finding it necessary to protect themselves with employment contracts. Firms never before finding it necessary to have job descriptions and performance evaluations are busy developing these important documents to clarify the responsibilities of the employees. Even small design studios with just a few employees are looking into the development of employee handbooks to explain how things are to be done within the studio.

Employees generally do not want to sue their employers over personnel issues, and most do not. However, more and more employees are utilizing the courts to satisfy their grievances. In the interior design profession, suits might occur as a result of misunderstandings about work requirements, company policies, or layoffs for which there is seemingly little reason. As women claim their right to be treated fairly and equally in the work place, sexual harassment and discrimination complaints are increasing. Although employers in larger firms are quickly learning their rights and obligations, far too many interior design employees only find out about legal rights and obligations after some unpleasant experience.

In this chapter we will look at many issues related to legal regulation of employment and issues that are related to legal regulation. We will briefly discuss federal laws regulating employment, the agency relationship, the concept of employment at will, and employment contracts. This chapter will define the difference between employees and independent contractors and define illegal sexual harassment. Legal issues concerning interviewing for a position are detailed in Chapter 27.

Federal Laws Regulating Employment

Many of the laws written to protect employees have more impact on firms that are unionized. Since it is almost unheard-of for an interior design firm to be unionized, there will be no attempt to discuss those laws. However, several federal laws do affect employment in the nonunion professional office.

Employment Discrimination

Whether in a large or a small firm, employment discrimination is a key concern for employers. Several laws exist to protect employees from job discrimination. Title VII of the Civil Rights Act of 1964 along with the Equal Employment Opportunity Act of 1972 and the Civil Rights Act of 1991 prohibit the employer from discriminating on the basis of sex, race, color, religion, or national origin. These laws and their subsequent amendments reinforce these prohibitions as well as prohibitions related to educational opportunity and other public issues of discrimination. Although these laws apply to firms with 15 or more employees, all design firms should abide by their intent. Title VII complaints are reviewed by the Equal Employment Opportunity Commission (EEOC). Should the EEOC determine there is sufficient cause, it will file a civil lawsuit against the employer.

Equal employment laws make it illegal for employers to ask verbally or on a job application such things as (1) age, (2) date of birth, (3) maiden name, (4) marital status, (5) gender, or (6) any other directly stated question related to age, gender, religion, national origin, race, or marital status. Discrimination laws do not stop at the hiring process. They apply throughout all the stages of employment. For example, Jane had repeatedly asked for flexibility in her work hours to take a class at the community college. Without being given a reason, she was refused the request each time. Harvey had been granted the same request the first time he asked. On the face of the facts presented, it appears that Jane has grounds for a discrimination complaint to the EEOC.

It is possible for the employer to obtain information in less direct ways if the information has significance as to whether the interviewee is capable of performing the job responsibilities. For example, it is legal for the employer to ask something like, "Are you between the ages of 23 and 50?" or "Are you a citizen of this country?" The key, of course, is whether the questions and the way they are asked are used to discriminate against potential employees. Additional sample illegal questions in the hiring situation are given in Chapter 27.

Chapter 7 described the Americans with Disabilities Act (ADA) in relation to design compliance. Title I of the act affects the hiring and promotion of employees. This portion of the ADA restrains employers from discriminating against any handicapped person who is otherwise qualified for a job. Employers with 25 or more employees were required to comply with the law beginning in July 1992. Employers with 15 or more employees must begin complying by July 1994. Furthermore, the employer is required to make "reasonable accommodation" in the structuring of the job and/or modification of the work as needed to do the job. For example, a paraplegic designer who has the qualifications and skills required for a design position must be given equal consideration as a nonhandicapped person. When the handicapped person is hired, the employer must attempt to make reasonable changes in the work areas. The drafting station, for instance, could be reconfigured using modular furniture that is more flexible and accommodating to a person's specific needs.

Interior design practices involved in work with the federal government would need to comply with some additional federal laws. Executive Order 11246 requires firms that do more than $10,000 of business with the federal government to have nondiscrimination clauses in their contracts. If an interior design firm does more than $2500 of work for the federal government, the Rehabilitation Act of 1973 and 1974 would require the design firm to be sure that handicapped employees are accommodated. Other requirements may be enforceable depending on the exact nature of the design firm's work with the federal government.

Other Issues

The Equal Pay Act of 1963 requires employers to pay all employees with the same basic work responsibilities and work experience the same amount of salary or wages. In this case, if two employees with the same job title and job responsibilities were hired at the same time and started with approximately the same work experience, each must be paid the same starting wage. If future proven performance or responsibility issues became different for the two individuals, then each could be paid a different amount.

The Occupational Safety and Health Act (OSHA) of 1970 requires all employees to be given a safe place to work. OSHA inspectors, although primarily found in production facilities, do make inspections in the office environment. In the interior design studio, an OSHA inspector may look for properly located and functioning fire extinguishers, first-aid kits, and the proper reporting of employee injuries.

The National Labor Relations Act protects the employee from being fired or otherwise discriminated against as a result of the employee's filing any kind of charges or giving testimony against the employer. An example might be an employee who is fired after filing a complaint related to a wage discrimination claim with the Federal Wage and Hour Board. Depending, of course, on the exact nature of the complaint and the manner in which the firing took place, the employer would be liable for illegally firing this employee.

State legislatures have also passed many laws that affect legal issues of employment. Design employers are urged to speak to an attorney to be sure that their business is in compliance with employment laws. Prevention is cheaper than having to deal with employees through the court system. Employees should speak to an attorney or contact the EEOC when the employee feels that he or she may have experienced any kind of employment discrimination.

The Agency Relationship

In common law, an *agency relationship* occurs when one person or entity agrees to represent or do business for another person or entity. The first person is called the agent and the second the principal. The agency relationship also gives the principal the right to control the conduct of the agent in the matters entrusted to the agent. In today's law, the employer-employee relationship is another type of agency relationship. The principal in the interior design office is the owner (or controlling board member), whereas the agents are all the employees, whether they are in management positions or staff positions.

"An employee is defined as one whose physical conduct is controlled, or subject to control, by the employer."[1] In many ways, employees are also agents since, they also represent the owner. However, an employee is a legal agent of the firm only when he or she has the authority to act in place of the owner. For example, Roger, Phyllis, and Kelley work for Marjorie. All four designers are expected to call on clients, obtain the information to prepare a design contract, and prepare the required design activities to complete the project. Only Marjorie, as the owner, is allowed to sign the design contracts. If Roger, Phyllis, or Kelley sign a design contract, the contract would not be binding on the firm.

The agency relationship, in some manner, will spell out the specific extent of the relationship between the employer and employee. Unlike most contractual relationships, the conditions of the agency relationship do not have to be in writing. There does have to be affirmative agreement to the effect that the employee is willing to be an agent for the employer. Accepting a position and knowing what the responsibilities of the position cover

---

[1]Clarkson 1989, 594. Copyright West Publishing Company.

would imply agreement and creates an implied contract. Since all positions in the firm have different responsibilities and different levels of trust within the employer-employee relationship, it is important for employees to fully understand their responsibilities. For example, not all employees will have the right to sign purchase orders to buy supplies for the office. Carefully prepared job descriptions, as discussed in Chapter 9, explain most of these responsibilities.

Because of the agency relationship, each party is obligated to certain duties with respect to the other party. Each party has a primary duty to the other to act in good faith toward the other party. There are specific legal duties of each party in an agency relationship. Let us look first at the duties of the employer to the employee.

Employer to Employee

The employer is obligated to provide the employee with a reasonable amount or kind of compensation for the completion of the agreed-on services. What this reasonable amount would be is not defined by law except that it must conform to what would be customary compensation for the services performed.

The employer also has a duty to assist and/or cooperate with the employee so that he or she may be able to perform the agreed-on services. It could be construed as a violation of the employer-employee agreement if the employer prevents or inhibits the employee from performing his or her duties. For example, if it is understood that the employer provides all the necessary tools and materials for the employee to do drafting work, and later requires the employee to pay for those tools, the employer is inhibiting the employee from performing his or her duties.

Common law, as well as federal and state regulations, requires the employer to provide safe working conditions for employees. Should an employee feel that his or her working environment was unsafe, the employer cannot dismiss the employee for reporting unsafe conditions.

The preceding relate to general duties of the employer to the employee. Other duties may also be required of the employer, depending on the exact nature of the agreement.

Employee to Employer

The employee has several basic duties to the employer and may have additional ones as outlined by any formal agreement or written contract. The employee has an obligation to perform his or her duties with reasonable diligence and skill. At what level the diligence and skill must be is related to what would be considered common for the services required and experience level expected. For example, if an employee is hired as a renderer on the basis of a high quality portfolio, the employer has a right to expect that all the rendering work performed would be of that same quality.

A second duty of the employee is of loyalty. An employee is expected to act in the interests of the employer, not for the benefit of any outside party or even of the employee. This means, for example, that a designer preparing the design work for a major company cannot be hired by the client to design an additional area of the company "on the side." Should the designer engage in moonlighting[2] this way, the employer would have the right to terminate the employee for breach of the agency relationship.

---

[2] *Moonlighting* is when an individual holds or engages in work outside his or her main job.

Another fundamental duty of the employee to the employer is a duty to keep the employer informed of anything related to the relationship. "What the agent actually tells the principal is not relevant; what the agent *should have told* the principal is crucial."[3] The following provides an example: One day Mary Anne mentions to her boss that company A appears to be ready to order 100 chairs from a certain manufacturer. The boss, thinking that it is a good opportunity to order an additional amount of the same chair for inventory, orders another 100. After the order is placed, Mary Anne learns, but neglects to tell her boss, that the client has changed his mind and will not order that chair after all. The furniture store, now responsible for paying for all the chairs, could consider Mary Anne in breach of the agency relationship.

A fourth duty of the employee is that of obedience. By this it is meant that the employee is required to follow all legal and clearly stated instructions or policies of the employer. Only certain emergency situations allow the employee to deviate from these obligations. For example, if the company has a policy that warehouse workers may not use the company vehicle for personal business, it would be a violation of this duty of obedience if one of the drivers used a company truck on the weekend without getting permission from the proper supervisor.

Finally, for the employee who has access to company funds or property, the employee has a duty to keep a proper accounting of the inflows and outflows of funds or use of property. A designer who has authorization to sign purchase orders for supplies would be breaching this duty if he or she used one of the purchase orders to obtain supplies for his or her own needs. In this case, the breach is also a criminal act, and the employer could press charges.

Shop-Right

A doctrine part of the employee-employer relationship is the doctrine of shop-right. The *shop-right* doctrine says that any creation or invention of tangible or intangible products that are not the result of the employee's normal working duties, belong to the employer not the employee. If an employee creates or invents something on company time, the employer has a shop-right interest in the invention, but the employee has ownership rights. For example, if the employee has not been hired to write articles on design theory but uses company time to write articles, the employer has a shop-right to use the articles without paying the employee any kind of royalty.

This distinction is important because it differs from the notion of copyright ownership. Remember from the discussion on copyright in Chapter 6 that any creative works, tangible or intangible, produced on the job and as part of normal work responsibilities belongs to the employer, not the employee. A custom-designed coffee table prepared for a client belongs to the employer if it is reasonable for the design of custom furniture to be a regular part of the employee's duties.

Employment at Will

The concept of *employment at will* relates to the doctrine that an employee, who is not bound by a written contract and who has no written terms of his or her employment spelled out, can be fired by the employer at any time with no explanation. Traditionally, the courts have

---

[3]Jentz 1987, 479. Copyright West Publishing Company.

ruled, since the employee may quit at any time without reason, the employer has the right to fire the employee at any time without reason, as long as the firing does not violate any federal or state employment laws.

The vast majority of employees in the interior design profession are subject to the employment-at-will doctrine. Most design employees are put to work and continue in specified duties without ever signing an employment contract. Since there is no contract, the employer is not bound by law to give the employee any reason for termination. Likewise, the employee has the right to give notice and leave the firm at any time without any reason.

There are some restrictions on the employer's right to terminate an employee under the employment-at-will doctrine. An employee cannot be fired merely because of his or her sex, race, religion, age, or handicap. An employer cannot fire an employee because of malice, retaliation, or bad faith.

Employees under employment-at-will have also been fired unfairly for reasons other than those concerning discrimination. If an employee believes he or she was fired unfairly, or not in accordance with his or her written or implied contract, the employee may have grounds for a wrongful discharge suit. Wrongful discharge basically means the employee was fired without good cause. Wrongful discharge litigation stems from judges who have felt that the employment legislation passed by federal and state governments have not always gone far enough to protect employees. Common-law wrongful discharge is based on legal precedent rather than statutes. Under the concept of wrongful discharge, workers cannot be fired for performing "public obligations" such as jury duty or voting. Employees also cannot be fired because he or she reported company violations of health or safety laws (called *whistle-blowing*).

Another aspect of wrongful discharge affecting employment at will terminations involves *implied contracts*. Many courts have ruled that verbal agreements to working conditions constitute an implied contract between employer and employee. This is especially true when the company has an employee handbook. Numerous states have determined that implied contracts exist as represented by statements and promises in employee handbooks. In the case of terminations without reason, if the handbook describes the procedure for dismissal, an employee cannot be terminated unless the firm has followed that procedure. For example, if a company named Business Office Furniture had the statement "no employee will be dismissed without good cause" in its handbook, an employee could not be fired unless the employee was told what that "good cause" reason was.

To be protected from charges of firing for discrimination or wrongful discharge, the designer must be able to prove in court that the firing was as a result of one of these illegal reasons. This can be very difficult for the employee to prove. The designer can protect himself or herself by requesting written information regarding expectations and performance evaluations on a regular basis. It is also important for the designer to document any events that might relate to the reasons listed for possible termination. The designer should also maintain copies of performance evaluations signed by the supervisor as well as notes about meetings concerning job performance.

Large firms have attempted to protect themselves from potential charges by changing management practices. Regular performance evaluations of all employees hired "at will" is one way to insure that a terminated employee has been fired for inadequate work performance. Documented meetings during which the manager discusses and warns employees not meeting expectations is another method the employer can use to protect his or her right to fire noncontract employees. Adding disclaimer statements to employee handbooks also affords the employer protection against lawsuits.

Although it is harder for an employer to fire an employee for little or no reason, the courts still support the idea that the employer must retain the right to fire employees who are incompetent, unqualified, unwilling, and so on. However, as more and more court cases related to improper termination occur, it is important that both employers and employees take the hiring, evaluation, and termination sequence more seriously.

Both employers and employees should be aware of each other's rights in terms of employment and termination. Employers may no longer terminate an employee capriciously if the employee is fulfilling his or her duties in accordance to satisfactory levels of performance. And employees have the right to retain employment without fear of retaliation, sexual harassment, and discrimination.

Employment Contracts

Employment contracts are becoming a part of the interior design profession although not yet a widespread practice. Employment contracts are more prevalent for various sales and management positions. Traditional "on the boards" design positions are more often considered employment at will.

An employment contract does not have to be in writing. As was explained in the preceding sections, an oral employment contract technically would be formed when the employer and employee have agreed to such things as responsibilities, compensation, and terms of employment. Written contracts are prepared to clarify more complex issues that may be of interest to the employer or the employee. An interior designer responsible for sale of goods may want a written contract to spell out commission structure, sales quotas, bonuses, seasonal layoffs, and so on. Many employers seek written contracts to limit the employee from taking clients to competing firms if the employee quits. Figure 10–1 is a sample employment contract.

In general, the written employment contract should cover

1. *Compensation.* Will the employee be paid hourly, on salary, or by commission? If commission will be paid, the method of payment should also be spelled out.

2. *Employment responsibilities.* This should indicate, in sufficient detail, what the employee has been hired to do. Many companies refer to and attach a copy of the appropriate job description.

3. *Termination.* Even with an employment contract, termination must be allowed by either party. Statements to that effect and the manner in which either party must give notice should be in the contract. For the protection of the employee, statements should also outline how any outstanding commission (if commission is part of the compensation method) is to be paid.

4. *Termination for cause.* Such a clause protects the employee from being terminated for some capricious reason. Reasons for termination for cause include negligence, incompetence, dishonesty, disloyalty, and nonadherence to company policies.

5. *Territory rights.* Sales personnel especially are limited to working with clients only in certain territories. This territory might be only certain cities, or states, or even certain clients. If the employee is limited to his or her territory, this fact should be defined in the contract.

There may be other clauses in the contract to protect one or the other party. A clause regarding return of company property may be in the contract. Although most employment contracts in the interior design profession would not have an ending date, the employer or the employee may wish to have a duration clause that specifies a fixed date when the contract would expire. It is generally understood that the contract remains in force as long as both parties agree to continued employment.

Some employers put *restrictive covenants* in employment contracts. "Restrictive covenants are provisions in contracts that do not allow the [salesperson] to directly compete or work

Business Designers Group, Inc..
87 N. Spokane Avenue, Suite 345
Anywhere, Washington

October 199x

Ms. Denise Wilson
123 S. Washington Avenue
Anywhere, Washington

Dear Denise:

The following constitutes the employment contract between Business Designers Group, Inc. employer, and Denise Wilson, employee.

Employment

You shall devote your full time and best efforts to interior design activities and perform these activities to the best of your ability. You are not allowed to work for clients or other design firms outside the employ of Business Designers Group, Inc.

The starting job classification for your employment is **Designer.** The duties and responsibilities of a Designer include: project design and specification, working with senior designers, job site supervision or coordination, and maintenance of the design library. The attached job description completely details your responsibilities.

Compensation

Designers are compensated on a salary basis. Your starting salary will be _____ annually. This salary will be paid on the basis of 26 equal pay periods.

You are eligible for the bonus program after you have worked full-time for a period of six (6) consecutive months. Bonuses are determined based on a percentage of income. The details of the bonus calculations are outlined in the attachment, "Business Designers Group, Inc. Bonus Policies." This attachment is considered part of this employment contract.

Designers are entitled to a ____ percent commission on all accessory specifications. Payment is made only after receipt of payment from the client.

Merit and cost-of-living increases are only awarded at the beginning of the calendar year. Merit raises are determined on the basis of performance reviews. Any salary increase thus earned will begin at the next regular pay period after the completion of performance reviews. Performance reviews are conducted for all employees during November and December. Cost-of-living increases are at the discretion of the owners, not the design department manager.

Benefits

All benefits are described in detail in the company handbook. There is a company profit-sharing plan. Eligibility and details are available from the Personnel Manager.

Termination

Your employment may be terminated by either party upon written notice. This notice must specify the date of termination and be hand-delivered or delivered by certified mail.

   A. Within thirty (30) days of termination, you will be paid outstanding commission on sales made prior to your termination where all the merchandise has been delivered and accepted to the customer.

   B. Commissions due on sales begun prior to your termination but not delivered prior to your termination will be paid within 30 days of receipt of payment by the customer.

Figure 10–1 An example of an employment contract for an interior design position.

C. Bonus payments will be prorated on the number of calendar days you worked between the last date of the previous bonus payment and the date of termination notice.

Noncompetition Provision

The employee may not go to work for a competitor of Business Designers Group Inc. for a period of 30 days from the date of termination of employment with Business Designer Group Inc.

The employee will not make available to a subsequent employer any confidential information concerning the operations and client of Business Design Group.

Return of Company Property

Upon termination of employment, the employee will surrender all handbooks, files, equipment, price lists, catalogs, customer information, and other company records or property.

Modifications to the Contract

No changes, modifications, additions, or deletions shall be made to this contract unless those changes, modifications, additions, or deletions are in writing, and are signed by both parties.

The above constitutes the total legal agreement between the parties named. Signatures below signify agreement to the terms of the employment contract. One copy shall be placed in your employment file. The second copy should be retained by the employee.

_____   _____
Denise Wilson, Employee   Date

Business Designers Group, Inc.

_____   _____
Jonathan Tate, President   Date

Attachments:
Job description, Designer
Business Designers Group Inc. Bonus Policies

Figure 10–1 (Continued)

for a competitor after leaving [his or her] old company."[4] These restrictive covenants can effectively prevent the employee from working for a competitor of the employer, starting his or her own business, and limit the territory in which the employee may seek new employment. Restrictive covenants in employment contracts are enforceable by the courts as long as they do not last for an unreasonable length of time or unfairly restrict the individual from

[4]Sack 1981, 46.

making a living in the same location as the former employer. What that length of time is and what area is considered reasonable would be up to the courts in the area.

Employment contracts can protect both the employee and the employer. If the employer requests that a written contract be signed, the prospective employee should be certain that he or she understands all the terms of the contract. If an oral agreement is made, the same advice is suggested. In fact, many authors on employee rights suggest the employee prepare a letter that summarizes the oral agreements to employment and send this letter to the employer. It is far more pleasant for both the employer and employee to be in agreement concerning the terms of employment, compensation, and other conditions of the employment relationship rather than at odds about those conditions in court.

Independent Contractors

Thus far, this chapter has discussed issues of employment when a designer works for an employer. The employment scenario is going through many changes, at the time of this writing. One of those changes involves the use by design firms (and all businesses) of independent contractors.

The use of independent contractors is not a new concept in business or in interior design. A designer who hires a wallpaper hanger is hiring an independent contractor. However, with the sluggish economy of the early 1990s, design firms also began to hire design personnel as independent contractors. An *independent contractor* is someone who works for himself or herself and though he or she may be subject to the direction of an employer, is not subject to the control of an employer. The independent contractor usually has a specific

---

For an individual to be considered an independent contractor, the following factors will be considered:

* The person hiring the independent contractor has no control over <u>how</u> the contractor does the work for which he or she was hired. This is a very key issue in determining the status of an independent contractor.

* The independent contractor provides his or her own equipment and supplies to perform the job duties required.

* The independent contractor is usually hired for a short-time with no expectation of permanent employment. Often the independent contractor is hired "for the job," which means only for a specifically defined task.

* Payment for services is commonly at the end of the job or by use of one or more partial payments (depending on the length of the job).

* The independent contractor must engage in professional work distinctly different from that of the person hiring the contractor. Interior designers hired by interior design firms to do interior design work might not be considered independent contractors, especially if the other conditions mentioned in the preceding are not met.

Figure 10–2 Guidelines for defining an independent contractor.

short-term work relationship with the firm and is often paid at the completion of the work, though progress payments are possible.

Wallpaper hangers, floor covering installers, contractors, and subcontractors are all examples of independent contractors as long as the work that they do and the equipment that they use to do the work are not controlled and provided by the designer. Designers who hire architects to review drawings produced by the designer have hired an independent contractor. Design firms who hire consultants are hiring independent contractors. Designers and others who work free-lance are generally independent contractors.

Independent contractors are not employees of the design firm and have no rights to benefits that employees enjoy. Employers are not required to withhold deductions for income tax, and generally are not required to pay or withhold social security, Medicare, or pay for worker's compensation insurance. Also, employers are not liable for the negligent acts of independent contractors in the performance of his or her contractual work responsibility. There are strict guidelines for defining independent contractors. Figure 10–2 summarizes these guidelines.

Sexual Harassment

Unfortunately, sexual harassment can be a problem in the office. Women and men in all sizes and types of offices have been exposed to or recipients of sexual harassment. According to Sack, *sexual harassment* includes "unwelcome sexual advances, requests for sexual favors, and verbal or physical conduct of a sexual nature when . . . (1) The person must submit to such activity in order to be hired, (2) The person's consent or refusal is used in making an employment decision, (3) Such conduct unreasonably interferes with the person's work performance or creates an intimidating, hostile, or offensive working environment."[5] Sexual harassment is illegal as it is in violation of Title VII of the 1964 Civil Rights Act and the Civil Rights Act of 1991. Employees should know that Title VII applies to businesses with 15 or more employees. However, sexual harassment should not be tolerated in any size organization.

Most cases of sexual harassment occur between employers and employees, but some peer harassment is also considered illegal sexual harassment.[6] In some cases, the employer might be liable for sexual harassment of an employee by a customer, especially if the employer has been informed of the situation and does nothing about it. Of course, the customer might also be liable.

As seen by widely publicized cases in the media, sexual harassment is not easy to prove. The first thing someone should do who feels that he or she has been sexually harassed is inform the person exhibiting the unwanted behavior to stop. If a designer feels that he or she is being harassed by a supervisor, he or she should document for his or her files any details about the episode. These notes would be needed to prove that harassment rather than work deficiencies was the reason for termination, should that occur. The individual should file a written complaint with the proper supervisor or person in authority. If the individual is working in a small office and the harassment is coming from the owner, the designer should submit the letter to the owner. In larger offices, check with other employees to determine if the harassment is widespread. Of course, if nothing positive results from the written complaint, the designer will want to speak to an attorney or the EEOC. Delays in contacting the

[5]From: *The Employee Rights Handbook* by Steven Mitchell Sack. Copyright © 1991 by Steven Mitchell Sack. Reprinted with permission by Facts On File, Inc., New York.
[6]Peer harassment is not illegal under Title VII.

proper authority may be interpreted as acceptance of the behavior and could result in jeopardizing a claim if one is filed later.

Sexual harassment is unwanted sexual advances. If the individual accepts the advancements, he or she could not later claim the actions constituted harassment. Do not tolerate this kind of behavior from coworkers, bosses, even clients. Learn more about sexual harassment by reading one of the books in the References or any of the other numerous books and articles which have appeared recently.

Summary

Part of the organization and continued growth and development of interior design practices involves employees. There are many laws that apply to the interior design profession regulating the hiring and firing of employees. Employers and employees should be familiar with these laws to lessen government intervention or lawsuits. The employer-employee relationship itself also involves specific legal obligations on the part of both parties.

Employees have rights in the design office and they should become informed about those rights. Discrimination in all phases of the work situation and sexual harassment are among the most widely occurring problems in employee-employer relationships.

All these legal issues are not meant to handcuff the employer or employee. Rather, both sides must realize that hiring employees and accepting positions with companies must be done in good faith as well as within legal restraints. It is too expensive for companies to hire, train, and fire, or watch employees leave design firms. It is too emotionally draining for the employee to have to sue or even threaten to sue over employment misunderstandings or mistreatment. As the profession continues to grow and change, it must accept the responsibilities related to employees as well as it accepts responsibilities related to the client.

References

Bernardo, Stephanie. July/August 1985. Fire Me . . . and I'll Sue! *Success!*

Clarkson, Kenneth W., Roger LeRoy Miller, and Gaylord A. Jentz. 1983. *West's Business Law,* 2d ed. St. Paul, Minn.: West Publishing.

Epstein Lee. 1977. *Legal Forms for the Designer.* New York: N and E Hellman.

Eskenazi, Martin, and David Gallen. 1992. *Sexual Harassment. Know Your Rights!* New York: Carroll & Graf.

Goodale, James G. 1992. *One to One: Interviewing, Selecting, Appraising, and Counseling Employees.* Englewood Cliffs, N.J.: Prentice-Hall.

Harragan, Betty Lehan. September 1986. Career Advice. *Working Woman.*

Jentz, Gaylord, Kenneth W. Clarkson, and Roger LeRoy Miller. 1987. *West's Business Law—Alternate UCC Comprehensive Edition,* 3d ed. St. Paul, Minn.: West Publishing.

Liddle, Jeffrey L. 1981. "Malicious Terminations and Abusive Discharges: The Beginning of the End of Employment at Will." *Employee Termination Handbook.* Englewood Cliffs, N.J.: Executive Enterprises Publications Co., Inc.

McWhirter, Darien. 1989. *Your Rights at Work.* New York: Wiley.

Sack, Steven Mitchell. 1981. *The Salesperson's Legal Guide.* Englewood Cliffs, N.J.: Prentice-Hall, Inc.

_____. 1991. *Employee Rights Handbook*. New York: Facts on File.

Sweet, Justin. 1985. *Legal Aspects of Architecture, Engineering and the Construction Process,* 3d ed. St. Paul, Minn.: West Publishing.

Woodward, Cynthia A. 1990. *Human Resources Management for Design Professionals.* Washington D.C.: AIA Press.

Work In Progress/Age Analysis
As of July 1987

	Total ($)	Work In Progress ($)	Current ($)	Accounts Receivables 30 Days	60 Days	90 days	120 days and Over
				$800			
...rporation	$1,567	$767	1,500		3,500		2,0...
...te Co.	3,000	1,500	2,000				
...ess Park	8,500	3,000	2,750		3,200		
...s	10,500	7,750		4,500		700	
...ration	16,500	6,800	2,750	250	1,500		1...
...nd Trust	7,500	4,500	3,700			1,250	
...nt Co.	11,500	5,600	9,500	6,500			
...ductor Inc.	35,000	17,500	1,500	1,250		1,950	$...
...ster, P.C.	7,500	3,500					
	$101,567	$50,917	$23,700	$13,300	$8,200	$1,950	

PART III

Managing the Business Finances

Chapter 11

Financial Accounting

Financial accounting is concerned with the day-to-day and periodic measurement and reporting of a firm's monetary resources. This measurement and reporting would be of interest to external individuals such as bankers, government agencies, stockholders, and auditors. All the various accounts, journals, and ledgers that are kept by the firm and used to prepare balance sheets, income statements, and statements of cash flows are part of financial accounting. Although financial accounting is prepared for use by external individuals, the firm's members—especially its owners and management—should be familiar with the information and able to read, interpret, and analyze the results.

The material in this chapter will introduce the reader to several essential components of financial management. First will be a discussion of the different accounting methods used to record information followed by a review of the elements of the balance sheet, the income statement, and the statement of cash flow (formally the funds flow statement). These reports, often prepared by a professional accountant, show anyone inside or outside the firm the financial condition of the design firm. Other accounting documents such as the journal and ledgers are the daily bookkeeping records that must be maintained. This chapter will not cover how to actually do daily bookkeeping, but will introduce the reader to basic concepts. Finally, the last two sections of the chapter will explain cash management and financial ratios. These two areas help owners quickly examine the flow of cash through the business and analyze financial success or failure.

Accounting Methods: Accrual versus Cash Accounting

Before discussing financial accounting reports it is important to look at the accounting bases used by businesses. The two most common accounting bases are the accrual method and the cash accounting method. Central to the difference between the two methods is the time when revenue and expenses are recognized (recorded). *Revenue* is the amount of inflows from the sale of goods or the rendering of services during an accounting period. *Expenses* are outflows of resources as a consequence of the efforts made by the firm to earn revenues. Rent, monthly utility bills, salaries, and advertising costs are examples of expenses.

In *accrual accounting,* revenue and expenses are recognized at the time they are earned

	Accrual Method	*Cash Method*
Revenue	$ 5,250	$ 3,250
Expenses	(4,000)	(3,500)
Gross Income	$ 1,250	$ − 250

Figure 11–1 Comparing accrual and cash accounting methods for the realization of revenue.

(in the case of revenue) or incurred (in the case of expenses), whether the revenue has actually been collected or the expense actually paid. This means that the income and expenses for the year are recognized in the year they are incurred. For example, Jane Doe Interiors has revenues of $5250 for January. Of that, $3250 is from cash sales and $2000 from invoices to clients that have not yet been received. In the same month, expenses of $4000 were incurred for the period—$3500 has already been paid and $500 is still due. With the accrual method, there would be a $1250 profit for the month. In this case, the profit is a "paper profit" since $2000 has not been collected yet (see Figure 11–1).

In *cash accounting,* revenue and expenses are recognized in the period the firm actually receives the cash or actually pays the bills. In the preceding example, only $3250 of revenue and $3500 of expenses would be recognized for the month since that was all that was actually received or paid out. Using the cash accounting method, Jane Doe Interiors would show a $250 loss for the month.

There are some important limitations in using the cash method. The cash method cannot be used by the regular corporation form (S corporations may use the cash method). The cash method also cannot be used to calculate income (loss) for tax purposes by any form of business if that business maintains inventories or if the business uses inventories as the means of arriving at the businesses income. In these cases the Internal Revenue Service expects businesses to pay income taxes based on the accrual method. Businesses that sell products or maintain sellable inventory must also pay income taxes based on the accrual method. This means, a small design studio that orders goods for clients, even though not truly kept "in inventory" cannot use the cash method. Other than the regular corporation, the cash method can be used for daily or nontax accounting needs.

It is recommended that all firms use the accrual method for an additional reason. Even though the accrual method may require extra accounting time, it provides a more comprehensive picture of profit and loss for the firm at any period. Having a more accurate financial picture of the firm at all times helps the owner/manager make more intelligent management decisions.

This chapter discusses accounting principles based on the accrual method.

The Balance Sheet

A *balance sheet,* sometimes called a statement of financial position, shows the financial position of a firm as of a particular moment in time with a statement of its assets (resources) and equities (claims against total resources) of that moment. The balance sheet is composed of two parts that must equal each other. These two parts are called Assets and Equities. The businesses, assets are typically shown on the left side or top of the page and the equities on the right side or bottom.

There are three important formulas to keep in mind when reviewing a balance sheet.

Total Assets = Total Equities.

Total Assets = Liabilities + Owner's Equity.

Total Assets − Liabilities = Owner's Equity.

The first reflects the final outcome of all balance sheets. The total amount of asset accounts must always equal the total amount of equity accounts. The second formula shows the breakdown of the two sections that make up the equity side of the balance sheet. Liabilities are moneys the firm owes to creditors. Owner's equity represents moneys invested in the firm by the owners. The third formula shows that owner's equity claims will only remain after all liabilities are paid out of the assets. Liabilities accounts always have first claim on the assets of a firm.

Remember these formulas as we discuss the balance sheet. The reader may wish to refer to the balance sheet in Figure 11–2 during this discussion.

Balance Sheet
Arizona Interior Designs
As of January 31, 19X8

Assets

Current Assets:		
Cash	$ 5,200	
Accounts Receivable	15,350	
Inventory	5,713	
Supplies	750	
Prepaid Expenses	1,250	
Total Current Assets		$28,263
Fixed Assets:		
Plant and Equipment:		
Office Furniture at Cost	$23,500	
Less: Accumulated Depreciation	(1,200)	
Automobile at Cost	12,500	
Less: Accumulated Depreciation	(5,600)	
Net Plant and Equipment		29,200
Total Assets		$57,463

Equities

Current Liabilities:		
Accounts Payable	$ 750	
Notes Payable	1,550	
Accrued Expenses	1,010	
Deferred Revenues	2,325	
Total Current Liabilities		$ 5,635
Other Liabilities:		
Long-term Debt		17,500
Total Liabilities		$23,135

Owner's Equity

Common Stock	$25,000	
Retained Earnings	9,328	
Total Owner's Equities		34,328
Total Equities		$57,463

Figure 11–2 Typical balance sheet for a corporation form of business.

Assets

Assets are any kind of resource—tangible or intangible—that the firm owns or controls and that can be measured in monetary terms. Note that employees, though useful to the firm, are not accounting assets, since the firm cannot own the employees.

Assets are of three general kinds: current assets, which are resources the firm would normally convert to cash in less than one year; fixed assets—also called property, plant, and equipment—which are the long-lived items used by the firm; and other assets, which are such assets as patents, copyrights, and investment securities of another firm.

Current assets typically include the following accounts: Cash, Accounts Receivable, Inventory, Prepaid Expenses, Supplies, and Marketable Securities. *Cash* is the cash on hand in the firm's bank accounts, checking accounts, cash registers, or petty cash boxes. *Accounts Receivable* is the account that shows what others owe to the firm as a result of sales or billings for services. *Inventory* shows those items purchased by the firm for resale to the firm's customers. For an interior designer, a chair purchased to be sold to the firm's clients is inventory; a chair purchased and used by the bookkeeper in the office is equipment—the value of which is recorded in the Fixed Assets account. *Prepaid Expenses* are prepayments of expenses, such as insurance policies paid on the equipment the firm owns and rent that may have to be paid in advance. *Supplies* represents the value of normal office supplies. *Marketable Securities* are investments expected to be sold within the year for cash.

The *Fixed Assets* or property, plant, and equipment account include the following categories: building and equipment, which is represented by the building, if owned by the firm, and any capital equipment—furniture used by office staff, blueprint machines, copy machines, typewriters, delivery trucks, and so on. The accumulated depreciation on these items is also shown on the balance sheet. Property or land is shown as a separate entry since it is not depreciated—land does not "wear out." Note that in Figure 11–2, the company does not own its building, so it is not listed as an asset.

Depreciation results from the concept that capital equipment has a limited useful life. It is intended to express the usage of a fixed asset in the firm's pursuit of revenue. Although many think of deprecation as a way to express the "wearing out" of an object, it more accurately relates to the usage of the object, not the wear and tear. Accountants predict what will be the useful life of the equipment and determine the depreciated value of the equipment for each year the firm owns the item.

The category for Other Assets includes investments the firm has made in other firms. If the investments are to be held for more than one year, they are listed here. If they are expected to be sold within a year, they are to be listed under Current Assets. The value of copyrights, trademarks, patents, licenses, and similar intangible assets the firm might have are also listed in Other Assets. Of special interest to the design firm is the value placed on copyrighted designs or patents on furnishings the firm may have obtained. These copyrighted designs or patents solely belong to the design firm and cannot be used by others without the permission of the firm. Patents and copyrights are *amortized,* which is the practice by which the value of the patent or copyright is reduced over time to record its usage in the firm's earning activities. Amortization is essentially the same as depreciation, except that it applies to intangible assets.

Equities

Equities are claims by outsiders and/or owners against the total assets of the firm. The equities side of the balance sheet is made up of two sections, Liabilities and Owner's Equities. *Liabilities* are amounts that the firm owes to others as a result of past transactions or events. Liabilities always have first claim on the firm's assets. Should a business cease operation for any reason, all outstanding liabilities must be paid before owners or stockholders receive any funds. The two categories of liabilities are Current and Noncurrent.

Current Liabilities are obligations due within one year or less. These accounts are considered current liabilities: *Accounts Payable*—claims from suppliers for goods or services ordered (and possibly delivered) but not yet paid for, Notes Payable (short-term loans), and *Accrued Expenses* (expenses owed for the period, but not yet paid). Examples of Accrued Expenses are salaries due, rent, utility bills not yet paid, and so on. *Deferred Revenues* are revenues received for service or future sale of goods, but the service or goods have not been delivered yet. The most common source of deferred revenues for a design firm would be from retainers or down payments the client has paid to the designer.

Two other current liabilities accounts are *Taxes Payable* (sometimes called Estimated Taxes), which represent the amount of income tax or other taxes owed to government agencies but not yet paid, and *Current Portion of Long-term Debt*, which would show how much of the long-term debt, perhaps resulting from the purchase of a delivery truck by the firm, is to be paid during this next one-year period.

Other Liabilities or noncurrent liabilities are amounts owed that will not be paid during the coming one-year period. The main item listed would be the balance of principal owed on a long-term loan.

The *Owner's Equity* section shows the amount the owners have invested in the firm. For a sole proprietorship, owner's equity would be shown as "Michael Smith, Capital" and the amount Michael Smith invested to start the firm plus any additions he made to the capital of the firm. For a partnership, it is customary to indicate the amount invested by each partner as a separate line, in much the same way as for a proprietorship. A partnership and proprietorship will also show a beginning and ending balance to show any withdrawals (or drawings) made by the owners against the assets. *Drawings* are fixed amounts withdrawn by proprietors or partners as "salaries." Drawings are not truly salaries, however, and are not treated as employee's salaries during the bookkeeping process. A separate drawing account is set up for every partner. Figures 11–3 and 11–4 show owner's equity in these forms of business.

A design firm that is a corporation would show Stockholders' Equity, since the corporation is owned by stockholders. The amount of money obtained to run the corporation is listed as Capital Stock and Paid-in Capital Stock. Par value of issued and outstanding stock is reported to represent the legal minimum claim on assets associated with the stock itself. Paid-in Capital Stock is the excess of par value representing the claims on assets arising purely from the value of stock at the time of its issuance.

Another item in Stockholders' Equity would be *Retained Earnings*. This represents the claim on assets arising from the cumulative undistributed earnings of the corporation after dividends are paid to stockholders for use in the business. Retained Earnings does not refer to cash in and of itself. It may be in some other form such as a vehicle, equipment, or marketable securities. There is no retained earnings section on the balance sheet of a proprietorship or partnership. Earnings are treated as noted above for these forms of business.

Each general category is added to obtain Total Assets and Total Equities. Total assets must always equal total equities.

Owner's Equity	
Michael Smith, capital as of January 1, 19X6	$25,000
Deduct: 19— drawings	(5,500)
Michael Smith, capital as of December 31, 19X7	$19,500

Figure 11–3 Reporting format of owner's equity for a proprietorship on a balance sheet.

Owner's Equity		
Judith Jones, Capital	$10,000	
Alice Smith, Capital	10,000	
Barbara Rogers, Capital	7,000	
Total Partnership Equity		$27,000

Figure 11–4 Reporting format of owner's equity for a partnership on a balance sheet.

The Income Statement

The *income statement* formally reports all the revenues and expenses of the firm for a stated period of time. The period of time may be a month, quarter, or a year. The result shows the net income (or loss) for the firm during the period. The essence of the information reported on an income statement is shown in Figure 11–5. The income statement is also commonly called a *profit-and-loss (P & L) statement. Revenues* are the inflows of moneys to a company from the sale of goods and services. For an interior design firm, revenues may result from the fees it charges clients or from the amounts received from the sale of goods. For the sale of goods to yield revenue for the firm, the goods must be goods that "pass through" the design firm's hands. What this means is that items that are specified by the designer but sold to the end-user by someone else would not be revenue-producing for the design firm. For example, John Everett specifies tables and chairs for a new restaurant, but the restaurant owner purchases the goods directly from the manufacturer. Since the sale did not pass through Everett's books, he cannot recognize those funds as revenue. The design fee to specify those goods, however, would be revenue for Everett since those funds are billed through Everett's office.

Expenses are the outflows of assets used to generate revenue. Since assets must always equal equities, expenses are also decreased in owner's equity. Net Income (or Profit) is the eventual difference between revenues and expenses. A loss occurs when expenses are greater than revenues.

The income statement used in the following discussion (see Figure 11–6) is formatted with the consideration that the firm has instituted a cost accounting system to measure and evaluate costs of doing business against the revenues the firm has generated. In a cost accounting system, certain, if not all costs, directly related to the generation of revenue are costed or charged to the particular revenue-producing activity. For a design firm, this means that all costs related to a particular job are recorded for that job. These costs show up on the income statement under the category of Cost of Sales as either Direct Labor or Direct Expenses. The author believes it is important for a design firm to use this method in order to have an accurate view of the activities of the firm. This point will be discussed further.

The easiest way to understand the parts of an income statement is to start at the top entry

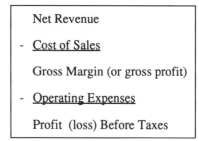

Figure 11–5 The brief format for an income statement. It shows the heart of the items reported to determine profit or loss.

and work through the various parts. The income statement in Figure 11–6 shows income generated from fees and goods sold. First note the heading. The date indicates the status of the firm prior to that date.

Gross Revenue to Net Revenue

Gross Revenue is all the revenue generated by the firm for the period. For our purposes, we will break this down into Revenue from Fees—the design fees for interior design services—and Revenue from Sale of Goods, which are revenues related to the sale of products to clients. We further break down the revenues from Sale of Goods to show (1) Product, the amount the client paid the design firm for the goods; (2) Freight-in, which is the freight charges the client paid for goods; and (3) Delivery, which represents the delivery and/or installation charges the design firm billed the client.

Total Gross Revenue is the total amount of revenue generated from all means by the firm for the period. Adjustments that are made for such things as returns and allowances, damages, or any extra discounts the designer offers to clients for prompt payment. These are subtracted from the Total Gross Revenue to obtain Net Revenue.

Cost of Sales to Gross Margin

Cost of Sales refers to the costs paid in the direct generation of revenues. In retail sales this is called Cost of Goods Sold and relates to changes in inventory. In our example Cost of Sales is broken down into two parts as was revenue—from fees and from products. Under the section of Cost of Sales from Products, there are three lines corresponding to those in revenues. The first is Cost of Goods, which shows the change in inventory and any special orders delivered during the period; (2) Freight-in showing the actual charges the firm was billed for goods delivered to the firm; and (3) Delivery and Installation, which would show the cost of delivery and/or installation of products to the company (this could include salaries paid and cost of trucks, equipment, and so on needed to deliver products to the customer).

Under Cost of Sales from Fees there are four items. The first, Direct Labor, should be the easiest to determine. *Direct Labor* is the time the designers spent directly involved in the generation of the designs under contract where fees for services were charged. The amount of direct labor can easily be determined from the time sheets kept by the design staff. This amount can be calculated against the salary paid to the various designers. Direct Labor could also include the time secretarial staff and management staff spend working on the projects under contract. Since this is often harder to keep accurate account, the time spent on projects by management and support staff are more commonly figured as overhead.

In Figure 11–6, other line items shown are for supplies, reproduction, and long distance telephone charges. These are legitimate costs against projects done under contract. They are presented to give a truer view of the "profitability" of the firm's activities. Many firms do not show these charges at all, putting them into appropriate categories of overhead expenses.

All these adjustments (costs) are totaled and subtracted from Net Revenue. The result is *Gross Margin,* which is sometimes called gross profit but which does not represent profit. "Gross margin is the difference between the revenues generated from selling products (goods or services) and the related product costs."[1] Gross margin does show the amount of revenue available to cover overhead expenses to keep the firm in business.

Overhead Expenses

Overhead Expenses, also called Selling and Administrative Expenses, are those expenses that are incurred whether the firm produces any revenues or not. They are often thought of

---

[1]Anthony, Robert N., and James S. Reece, *Accounting Texts and Cases,* 7th ed., Richard Irwin, 1983, p. 908.

Income Statement
Arizona Interior Designs
Period Ending January 31, 19X8

Gross Revenue			
From Fees		$18,400	
From Sale of Goods			
Product	$37,500		
Freight-in	2,625		
Delivery	3,250		
		43,375	
Total Gross Revenue		$61,775	
Net Revenue			$61,775
Cost of Sales			
From Products:			
Cost of Goods	$25,000		
Freight-in	2,500		
Delivery	3,000		
From Fees:			
Direct Labor	12,750		
Supplies	185		
Reproduction Expense	95		
Telephone (Long-Distance)	105		
Total Cost of Sales		43,635	
Gross Margin			$18,140
Operating Expenses			
Salaries	9,500		
Payroll Taxes	1,400		
Group Insurance	95		
Rent	850		
Heat, Power, and Light	250		
Telephone	165		
Promotion	105		
Travel Reimbursements	175		
Supplies and Postage	225		
Depreciation Expense (Furn.)	300		
Depreciation Expense (Auto)	1,000		
Insurance	200		
Dues and Subscriptions	57		
Professional Consultants	150		
Printing and Reproduction	50		
Interest Expense	200		
Total Operating Expenses			14,722
Other Revenue			
Interest			350
Net Income Before Taxes			$ 3,418
Less: Provision for Income Taxes			− 627
Net Income			$ 3,141

Figure 11–6 Income statement for a corporation form.

as those expenses needed to keep the doors open. They are reported in as much detail as is needed by the firm and anyone who would be looking at the income statement. Expenses listed in Figure 11–6 represent the many expense items that are common to an interior design firm.

A few comments about some of these items. The item "Salaries," represents the amount of expense paid out for nonrevenue-generating labor activities (or activities that cannot be easily costed to projects). This usually includes salaries for secretaries, accounting personnel, and management personnel. However, it also would include that portion of the design staff's salaries that cannot be considered direct labor. "Telephone" represents those normal telephone charges and other telephone charges that the firm cannot or chooses not to cost back to specific revenue generating activities. "Promotion" can be actual promotional expenses such as magazine advertising or the cost of placing the firm's Yellow Pages ad. It can also represent the expense of a business lunch.

As can be seen from the example, a firm can go into quite a bit of detail in order to have an accurate picture of the firm's financial standing. If an interior design firm has invested in a good computer system, the record keeping and data entry this much detail requires would be easier. Many management reports that would be helpful in the control of the design firm can then be generated. More detail on this topic will be covered in Chapter 12.

All these expenses are totaled and subtracted from Gross Margin to obtain Net Income. *Net Income* or loss represents the amount of income (or loss) that results when all remaining expenses (deductions) are subtracted from gross revenues. If the result is positive, net income represents the dollar amount of profit the firm made for the period reported. Should expenses be greater than revenues, than a loss would be reported for the period. If the design firm is a corporation, this result would be titled "Net Income Before Taxes," since it is necessary for a corporation to show its estimated income taxes on the income statement. Unless the firm has some extraordinary expenses, such as a loss from fire, the next line should show a Provision for Income Tax, which is the estimated tax for the period. This amount is subtracted to determine Net Income. Should the firm receive income from sources other than the operation of the firm, such as interest earned on checking or savings accounts, it would be added before the Net Income Before Taxes result is determined.

This is not true for proprietorships or partnerships since the income of these types of businesses is personal income and is reported along with any other income made on individual or family tax statements. These forms would not show a provision for income tax. The next line, in these cases, would be Net Income.

The Statement of Cash Flows

The *Statement of Cash Flows* reports "net cash flows from operating, investing and financing activities for a period of time."[2] This information is useful to potential investors and creditors as well as management in their various decisions concerning the firm. The information to prepare the Statement of Cash Flows comes from the balance sheet, the income statement, and, for corporations, from the retained earnings portion of the income statement. Although the report can be useful for those reviewing the financial condition of any business formation, it is primarily prepared by the corporation form of business ownership.

Prior to 1987, this type of financial information was reported as part of the Statement of Changes in Financial Position (sometimes called the Funds Flow Statement). This statement reported the sources and uses of funds during a given period. Because of an increased emphasis of reporting this information on a cash-basis format, the Financial Accounting Stan-

---

[2]Imdieke, Leroy, F., and Ralph E. Smith, *Financial Accounting,* John Wiley and Sons, Inc., 1987, p. 18.

dards Board recommended that cash flow information be recorded in the statement of cash flows format. This practice was begun in 1987.[3]

Although the Statement of Cash Flows provides information about cash receipts (inflows) and cash payments (outflows) from all areas of the firm, its primary purpose is to report inflows and outflows for a given time period. Cash, for accounting purposes, is money, checks, or items such as money orders that are accepted by banks. The Statement of Cash Flows also reports the inflows and outflows of cash equivalents. Cash equivalents are very liquid, short-term investments, such as money market funds, that can be converted to cash quickly. However, if these kinds of investments are made only for the temporary investment of excess cash, they are not to be considered a part of the data to make up the statement.

The inflows and outflows come from the three areas: operations, investments, and financing. Operations activities are those involved in the normal revenue generation activities of the firm. Operations flows would come primarily from the payments and receivables from clients and the payments the firm makes to others in the generation of revenues. Depending on the nature of the firm, operations flows might also come from interest earned, if the firm loaned money to someone, or dividend receipts from certain kinds of investments. Investments inflows and outflows result from lending money and receiving payments on those loans; purchasing or selling certain kinds of securities; and the purchase or sale of assets such as property, buildings, or equipment the firm owns. Financing inflows and outflows come from the finances invested in the company by the owners and the subsequent payments to those owners for the investment as well as payments received and returned to creditors, such as banks for mortgages.

The net cash inflows and outflows from operations, investments, and financing are reported in the statement. A firm may use either a direct or an indirect method for reporting operations flows, and can report investments and financing flows either within the body of the operations flow statement or as a separate report to that statement.

Direct Method of Operations Flows

In the direct method, all major categories of inflows and outflows are reported as line items (see Figure 11–7). Subtracting outflows from inflows gives the net cash flow from operations. In order to report this, the accountant must convert an accrual basis of accounting to a cash basis of accounting. "The main advantage of the direct method is that it shows the operating cash receipts and payments. Knowledge of where operating cash came from and how cash was used in operations in past periods may be useful in estimating future cash flows."[4]

Indirect Method of Operations Flows

To the nonaccountant, the indirect method is more difficult to understand. Net cash flows from operations are reported by making various adjustments of inflows and outflows from an accrual basis to a cash basis. Adjustments are needed for noncash expenses, revenues, and gains and losses, with further adjustments made to noncash items such as prepaid expenses (see Figure 11–8). "The main advantage of the indirect method is that it focuses attention on the differences between income and cash flow from operating activities. An understanding of the differences may be important to investors, creditors, and others who wish to use assessments of income as an intermediate step in assessing future cash flows."[5]

---

[3]Imdieke and Smith 1987, 646.
[4]Imdieke and Smith 1987, 649.
[5]Imdieke and Smith 1987, 654.

RAINBOW INTERIOR DESIGNS, INC.
Statement of Cash Flows
For the Year Ended December 31, 19X6

Cash Flows from Operating Activities:		
Cash Received from Customers (1)	$58,755	
Dividends Received	564	
Cash Provided by Operating Activities		$59,319
Less Cash Paid:		
To Suppliers for Purchases (2)	17,653	
To Suppliers for Operating Expenses (3)	27,435	
For Interest and Taxes (4)	3,576	
Cash Disbursed for Operating Activities		48,664
Net Cash Flow from Operating Activities		10,655
Cash Flows from Investing Activities:		
Purchases of Property, Plant, and Equipment (5)	−3,550	
Net Cash Flow from Investing Activities		−3,550
Cash Flows from Financing Activities:		
Net Increase from Customer Retainers	2,350	
Net Increase from Customer Deposits	1,775	
Proceeds of Long-term Debt	8,500	
Payments on Long-term Debt	−1,776	
Dividends Paid	−650	
Net Cash Provided by Financing Activities		10,199
Net Increase (Decrease) in Cash and Cash Equivalents		$17,304
Schedule of Noncash Investing and Financing Activities:		
Notes Payable Given in Exchange for Equipment		$ 3,550
(1) Accrual Basis Sales		$60,605
Add: Beginning Accounts Receivable		7,900
Less: Ending Accounts Receivable		−9,750
Cash Received from Clients		$58,755
(2) Accrual Basis Cost of Goods Sold		$18,700
Less: Beginning Inventory		−5,678
Plus: Ending Inventory		3,995
Plus: Beginning Accounts Payable		5,616
Less: Ending Accounts Payable		−4,980
Cash Paid to Suppliers for Purchases		$17,653
(3) Operating Expenses Other Than Depreciation		$27,920
Less: Beginning Prepaid Expenses		−1,275
Plus: Ending Prepaid Expenses		1,415
Plus: Beginning Accrued Expenses		3,325
Less: Ending Accrued Expenses		−3,950
Cash Paid to Suppliers for Operating Expenses		$27,435
(4) Interest Expense		$ 657
Income Tax Expense		2,919
Cash Paid for Interest and Taxes		$ 3,576
(5) Cash Paid for Computer		$ 3,550
Cash Payments for Building and Equipment		$ 3,550

Figure 11–7 Statement of cash flows (direct method).

RAINBOW INTERIOR DESIGNS, INC.
Statement of Cash Flows
For the Year Ended December 31, 19X6

Net Cash Flow from Operating Activities:		
Net Income		$10,848
Adjustments to Convert Net Income to Net Cash Flow from Operating Expenses:		
Depreciation Expense		1,125
Increase in Accounts Receivable		−1,850
Decrease in Inventory		1,683
Increase in Prepaid Expenses		−140
Decrease in Accounts Payable		−1,636
Increase in Accrued Expenses		625
Net Cash Flow from Operating Activities		10,655
Cash Flows from Investing Activities:		
Purchase of Equipment	−$3,550	
Net Cash Used by Investing Activities		−3,550
Cash Flows from Financing Activities:		
Proceeds from Customer Retainers	2,350	
Proceeds from Customer Deposits	1,775	
Proceeds of Long-term Debt	8,500	
Payments on Long-term Debt	−1,776	
Cash Dividends Paid	−650	
Net Cash Provided by Financing Activities		10,199
Net Increase in Cash		$17,304

Figure 11–8 Statement of cash flows (indirect method).

Cash Flows from Investments

Cash flows from investments are simply reported as individual line items related to whether they are inflows or outflows (see Figure 11–8). Common inflows are such items as cash generated in the sale of property, buildings or equipment, income from loans made to others, and receipts from the sale of certain securities. Outflows are just the opposite—purchasing equipment, making the loan, or buying the securities.

Cash Flows from Financing

Cash flows from financing activities are also simply reported as individual line items indicating which were inflows and outflows (see Figure 11–8). Financing inflows represent revenues from the sale of stock, contributions by partners, and loans made by the firm from short- or long-term debts like mortgages. Outflows would be the payments made by the firm to repurchase stock that others hold, stock dividends, and repayments on loans.

The indirect method of reporting cash flows from operations, which utilizes the investments and financing activities as a separate report, is similar in format to the previous cash basis statement of changes in financial condition. A decision as to which format to use should be based on the needs and uses of the statement by the design firm and the recommendation by the firm's accountant.

Noncash Basis Reporting

Some firms, mainly larger-sized corporations, may have other investments and financing activities that are of a noncash basis. This activities must also be reported, but since they affect a small number of interior design firms, they will not be discussed here.

Accounting Records and Systems

The balance sheet, income statement, and cash flows are summary reports. They are generated from the information maintained in the accounting records. These accounting records are commonly referred to as the daily bookkeeping records.

In accounting terminology, events that affect the financial aspects of a firm, either revenue-generating or expense-generating, are called *transactions*. These transactions must be recorded in an organized manner so that the firm can report or review its financial condition.

Design businesses may use either single-entry or double-entry bookkeeping systems. A single-entry system is very simple. It is set up based on the income statement and includes business income and expense accounts. Because of its simplicity, it is used by many small businesses. The double-entry bookkeeping system uses journals and ledgers (discussed below) and the accounts are based on the entries found in both the income statement and the balance sheet. In the double-entry system, transactions are first entered in the journal and then summary information is transferred to the appropriate ledger. The next section provides additional information about the double-entry system.

Accounts

Financial organization is established in accounts. *Accounts*, with different names for clarification, show additions (increases) to the account and subtractions (decreases) to the account. In its simplest form, the account record looks like the letter T, hence the name T-account (Figure 11–9).

The left-hand side of the T-account is called the *debit* side, whereas the right-hand side is the *credit* side. In these accounts, debit and credit have no other meaning in accounting than "left" and "right" respectively. They are not substitutes for the words *increase* or *decrease* since,

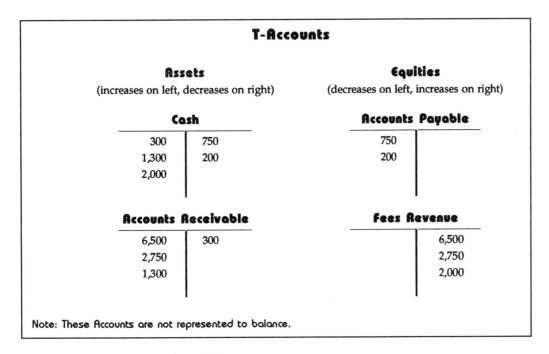

Figure 11–9 Sample format of typical T-accounts.

Assets		=	Liabilities		+	Owner's Equity	
increase	decrease	=	decrease	increase	+	decrease	increase
(+)	(-)		(-)	(+)		(-)	(+)
debit	credit		debit	credit		debit	credit

Figure 11–10 This figure clarifies that some accounts show increases as a debit while other accounts show decreases as a debit.

for some accounts, the increase side of the T-account will be on the right and the decrease on the left. Figure 11–10 shows this accounting phenomenon.

Journal, Ledger, and Chart of Accounts

Following a business transaction, entries are made in a journal. A *journal* is a chronological record of all accounting transactions for the firm (see Figure 11–11). Journal entries show the date of occurrence, the name of the account to be debited or credited, the amount of the debit or credit, and a reference to the ledger account to which the entry has been posted. Entries are posted to different ledger accounts from the journal. Posting, therefore, is the transferring of a journal entry to the correct ledger account.

The *ledger,* often called a General Ledger, is a group of accounts. Most people are familiar with the general ledger book, a bound book for all entries. But a ledger does not need to be a bound book. Such a book may work for a small firm, but larger firms will use loose-leaf pages or computers. The general ledger is often supplemented by various subsidiary ledgers. These provide detailed information to support the general ledger. For an interior design firm, an important subsidiary ledger would be the accounts receivable ledger (see Figure 11–12). This ledger would have separate accounts for each client who purchases on credit from the designer. A few other ledgers are:

Cash receipts ledger: shows all the moneys received by the firm.

Cash disbursements ledger: records moneys paid out to cover expenses.

Accounts payable ledger: records amounts the design firm owes to others.

Purchase order ledger: shows outstanding orders for goods and/or services for clients or the firm.

Payroll ledger: records payments to employees.

A *Chart of Accounts* is a list of all the accounts the firm is using. Typically, the chart of accounts is set up to have account names that mirror the items shown in the balance sheet and income statement and is based on management's (and others') desires about what needs to be accounted for. A useful starting place would be the accounts that relate to the information needed to prepare the balance sheet and income statement. Accounts would be set up for Cash, Accounts Receivables, Fixed Assets, Accounts Payable, Payroll, Telephone, Rent, Sales Revenue from Fees, and so on. The chart of accounts is a statement about how the firm will categorize the events it seeks to control. The list is numbered in some logical

19X6		Accounts	Ledger	Debit	Credit
March	6	Cash..........................	1	2,350	
		Sales........................	26		2,350
	6	Accounts Receivables..........	2	678	
		Design Fees..................	3		675
	6	Inventory	5	5,675	
		Cash........................	1		2,000
		Accounts Payable	21		3,675

Figure 11–11 Simple journal entries.

order. These code numbers are the ones used to cross-reference journal entries to posting entries. The chart of accounts should be set up so that it can increase in complexity as the firm grows, with appropriate accounts added as needed.

Trial Balance

Remember that assets must equal liabilities and debits must equal credits. This does not mean debits and credits will be equal within each account, but when all accounts are considered, they will be equal. A test to see if accounts are balanced and that lists all the account balances with the debit and credit side totaled separately is called a *trial balance.*

Mary Smith

123 Main Street

Date		Explanation	Debit		Credit		Balance	
Oct	1	Balance					150	00
	7	Sales Check # 6801	325	00			775	00
	11	Received on Account			500	00	225	00
	28	Sales Check # 7002	120	00			345	00
Nov	2	Received on account			300	00	45	00

© 1993, Christine Piotrowski

Figure 11–12 A sample page from an accounts receivable ledger.

There are two purposes of a trial balance. One is to check the accuracy of the posting entries to see if total debits equal total credits. The other is to establish summary balances in all accounts in order to prepare the balance sheet, income statement, and changes in financial condition. A trial balance can be done whenever the accounts are up to date.

Cash Management

For interior design firms to stay in business, a constant inflow of cash that equals or exceeds the outflows of cash is needed to pay the expenses for the same period. The statement of cash flows discussed earlier reports to those outside the firm the sources and uses of funds for a period. In this section, we will briefly discuss a simple cash flow statement that is easily prepared by a manager and used in cash management.

For design firms that do not sell merchandise, the cash flow cycle will be relatively short. Firms that sell merchandise have a constant cash flow problem related to receiving enough cash from some source to pay for the merchandise that is on order. Whatever the case, there must always be enough cash available to pay current bills. Employees will expect to be paid within 7 to 14 days of when work was completed. Suppliers generally have a 30-day payment period before penalties are charged. The faster the firm can collect on its receivables, the more efficient its cash flow cycle will be. However, it is not uncommon for a firm to have a significant percentage of its receivables out over 120 days.

Good basic business practices will aid in keeping cash flow operating efficiently. Many of those business practices will be discussed in later chapters as well as in this and the next section. Among these good business practices are understanding and following good pricing policies for both fees and products, obtaining credit reports on clients with whom the firm is unfamiliar, preparing design contracts to help protect the designer from possible stoppages or losses of revenue, and policies requiring substantial retainers and deposits before work is begun or products are ordered. Careful timekeeping, scheduling, and project management including constant monitoring of outstanding orders and receivables will all aid the firm in protecting narrow margins of profit. Thorough monitoring of budgeted versus actual time estimates, fee estimates, and gross profit expectations can eliminate errors from happening more than once.

The best situations in cash management require substantial retainers and deposits as well as the prompt receipt of receivables. However, as already pointed out, aged accounts (those older than 30 days) are all too common in the interior design profession. When the firm needs cash, however, the owners may go to the firm's banker for short-term loans. Keeping the banker informed of the financial situation at the design firm will aid in the loan approval process, as will a good history of prompt repayment of those loans. But going to the bank every time the firm is short of cash to pay bills is not the best solution. Good management of the firm and the firm's cash flow is the answer.

Figure 11–13 shows a simple cash flow statement. A cash flow statement begins with the current known cash balance. If the entire cash flow statement is for projected cash flow, then the beginning cash balance for each month can be estimated. In order to show how the cash flow statement works, however, the beginning cash balance is the actual balance (as determined by revenue minus expenses). The next line shows the known and projected revenues for the months being reviewed. This projected revenues combines the known work in progress amounts for each period with forecasts of additional work in each month. Adding the beginning cash balance to the projected revenue provides a projected gross revenue amount.

Operating expenses are the projected combined expenses for each month. These would include salaries, fringe benefits, rent, utilities expenses, and other costs of doing business. The next line shows each month's responsibility for a bank line of credit that was obtained in a previous month. This amount is the amount of principal and interest due each month. Note that in March the firm expects a one-time expense of $6000 for a computer. The last

Cash Flow Statement
19X7

	Actual January	Projected February	Projected March	Projected April
Beginning Cash Balance	$ 9,000	$13,600	$13,200	
Projected Revenues	22,000	18,000	23,000	26,000
Projected Gross Revenues	31,000	31,600	36,200	
Operations Expenses	17,000	18,000	20,000	23,000
Purchase of Computer			6,000	
Line of Credit Debt	400	400	400	400
Ending Cash Balance	$13,600	$13,200	$ 9,800	

Figure 11–13 Simple cash flow report. Notice how it basically repeats the format of an income statement.

line shows the ending cash balance for each month. This balance is carried up to the beginning cash balance line in the forecast months. The reader may wish to fill in April's figures to obtain the ending balance for the month (and to see how well the firm is doing)!

Financial Ratios and Percentages

Understanding the financial reports is an important step in managing the financial performance of a business. As any accountant would say, that is only part of really understanding whether a business is being financially successful or not. There are several ratios and percentages used to evaluate the numerical information contained in the balance sheet and income statement. These ratios and percentages give an even clearer message as to the overall financial success (or lack of it) of a business.

By using ratios and percentages, a designer may evaluate almost anything that can be measured in numerical terms. Ratios are quite common and are used every day by almost everyone in one way or another. In our everyday experiences, we might use ratios to determine the amount of fat in a portion of food, the miles per gallon our car gets, or how much of the time estimated to complete a project has been used. Ratios, as we remember from math class, is one number over another. With ratios, we are comparing two numbers. A ratio can become a percentage when we divide one number into another. Of course, for a ratio to become a percentage, the large number (the denominator in this case) must be divided into the small number (the numerator). For example, if we divide 75 by 100 (75/100), we will get a percentage—75 percent. When using ratios, remember that when we compare a part to the whole, the whole is always the denominator.

There are a great number of ratios that accountants and financial analysts use to evaluate a business. In this brief discussion, we will discuss but a few of the key ratios. Figure 11–14 shows several financial ratios.

One important group of ratios are profit ratios. A business can only remain viable if it sustains a profit. As a rule, profitability (or income) is affected by increases in volume and changes in price or both. One way for a design firm to increase its profitability is to increase its fee base. Another is to bill more hours of design fee. The profit margin on sales ratio tells the business how much profit was obtained from every dollar of sales. Using the information in Figure 11–6 (income statement), you can see that the firm's profit margin on sales (fees only) was 17 percent. Find the data in the income statement and use the formula in Figure 11–14 to calculate this percentage. How can the firm increase this ratio?

A second important profitability ratio is the ratio that tells the return on total assets, often expressed as ROA. This ratio measures the amount of profit generated by the use of

1. Profit margin on sales = net income / total sales

2. Return on total assets (ROA) = net income / total assets

3. Return on equity (ROE) = net income / owner's equity

4. Current ratio   = current assets / current liabilities

5. Quick ratio (or acid test) = current assets - inventory / current liabilities

6. Debt ratio = total debt / total assets

7. Working capital = current assets - current liabilities

8. Net profit = earnings before interest and taxes (EBIT) / net sales

9. Return on investment = EBIT / total assets - total liabilities

10. Average collection period = accounts receivables times 360 / total sales

11. Inventory turnover ratio = cost of goods sold / average inventory

12. Gross margin percentage = gross margin dollars / net revenue

Figure 11–14 Financial ratios useful to business owners to determine financial performance of the business.

the assets of the company. The ROA for Arizona Interior Designs is 5 percent. Is this firm using its assets effectively to achieve a reasonable profit?

Numerous efficiency ratios can be developed to review how well the business is operating. One very important efficiency ratio is the average collection period ratio. This ratio tells the business how many days, on average, it takes to collect accounts receivable. If this ratio is low, that means the business is receiving payments from clients quickly. If it is high, it means that clients are taking a long time to pay—and this can seriously affect cash flow for the business. The data for the average collection period ratio comes from the balance sheet and income statement. Note that the 360 in the denominator represents the number of days in the year.[6] Should this firm try to improve its collection policies?

For design firms that have inventory, it is important to know how long that merchandise is in stock. The longer that inventory is held in the office or warehouse, the longer dollars are tied up that can better be used in some other way. Design firms, like any business that sells from its inventory, needs to turn over that merchandise and keep what it sells fresh. The information for this ratio comes from the balance sheet and the income statement. It appears that the firm is turning over its inventory quite quickly. Is it possible that this might not actually be true?

Two other groups of ratios that are of particular importance to investors are the liquidity ratios and the debt ratios. Liquidity ratios show the design firm's ability to pay its debts. Of particular importance is the firm's ability to pay its current liabilities with available current assets. A second liquidity ratio is the working capital ratio. It measures the amount of cash that is available to operate the business on a daily basis. If a firm's working capital is less than its operating expenses, it may not be able to pay all of its current bills. Debt ratios indicate how much of the firms financing has come from debts—loans and lines of credit—rather

---

[6]Accountants generally use 360 rather than 365 days to determine the number of days in a year in this type of ratio.

than direct investment by the owners and/or stockholders. Potential new investors will be concerned about high debt ratios since it will mean that those loans will be paid off before any return is made on investing into the firm.

Ratios help determine the financial health and locate some of the potential financial or operational problems of a design firm. Ratios are of more importance to the owner or manager of the firm than to employees. However, employees should understand there is a lot of number crunching that goes on behind the scenes in operating a design practice. Awareness brings about concern and concern brings about the realization that every employee in the design firm affects the financial health of the company.

Summary

This chapter by no means fully explains financial accounting. Although interior designers rightly utilize the services of accountants to prepare the formal accounting statements needed periodically, too many leave the day-to-day bookkeeping chores to accountants or others who better understand these financial matters, never themselves bothering to have more than a cursory knowledge of the firm's financial condition.

It is important to understand the financial aspects of the interior design business and to be conversant with the terminology and concepts of financial accounting. No matter who does the daily bookkeeping in the long run, the practice owner is responsible for accurate recording of financial transactions.

In this chapter we have looked at the basic concepts and definitions and parts of the balance sheet, income statement, and statement of changes in financial condition. We have also looked briefly at the concepts related to accounting records and systems, cash management, and financial ratios.

In the next chapter we will be looking at managerial accounting and some brief concepts concerning management control systems. These concepts relate to reporting methods generated from the financial statements and created to help owners and/or management plan, organize, and control the design firm.

References

Anthony, Robert N. 1983. *Essentials of Accounting,* 3d ed. Reading, Mass.: Addison-Wesley.

Anthony, Robert N., and James S. Reece. 1983. *Accounting Texts and Cases,* 7th ed. Homewood, Ill.: Richard D. Irwin.

Donnahoe, Alan S. 1989. *What Every Manager Should Know About Financial Analysis.* New York: Simon and Schuster.

Getz, Lowell. 1986. *Business Management in the Smaller Design Firm.* Newton, Mass.: Practice Management Associates.

Getz, Lowell, and Frank Stasiowski. 1984. *Financial Management for the Design Professional.* New York: Watson-Guptill.

Head, George O., Jr., and Jan Doster Head. 1988. *Managing, Marketing, and Budgeting for the A/E Office.* New York: Van Nostrand Reinhold.

Horngren, Charles T. 1981. *Introduction to Financial Accounting.* Englewood Cliffs, N.J.: Prentice-Hall.

Imdieke, Leroy F., and Ralph E. Smith. 1987. *Financial Accounting.* New York: Wiley.

Loebelson, Andrew. 1983. *How to Profit in Contract Design.* New York: Interior Design Books.

Ragan, Robert C. 1987. *Step by Step Bookkeeping,* rev. ed. New York: Sterling Publishing.

Chapter 12

Financial Management Control

Financial management control, or managerial accounting, is concerned with the planning and analysis of all the financial aspects of the firm. The reports that are prepared are used to help individuals within the firm to manage and control the performance of the firm.

Financial management control goes beyond financial accounting. You will recall from the preceding chapter that financial accounting is concerned with the day-to-day and periodic measurement and reporting of resources that would be of interest to external individuals. A financial management control report, on the other hand, would be one that analyzes any kind of financial or numerical information that would be of interest to the owners and/or the managers of the firm. Control reports can show many things. One simple example would be a report that summarizes how much of all possible work time for each designer is billable to clients as opposed to house or nonbillable time.

Owners, business managers, and design directors—those in the firm entrusted to plan, organize, and control the organization—are responsible for financial management control. In most small firms financial management control is almost always the responsibility of the owner, who receives assistance from the firm's accountant in developing reports. In medium- and large-size firms, the reports are usually generated and analyzed by the managerial element.

As a whole, interior design businesses have been slow to accept this part of business management. However, regardless of the size of the firm, financial management control should be a part of operations. The planning and control aspects of financial management and managerial accounting can assist all sizes of firms in preparing for success and handling problems. As the interior design firm grows, this function becomes more important.

The Management Function

Because financial management control is primarily a function of owners and managers, it may be helpful briefly to describe managerial activities as they relate to financial management. Management is a very complex activity with many different meanings. For our purposes here, *management* means the effective direction of staff members and financial resources under a manager's control toward the goals and objectives that the owners of the firm have established.

There are two broad extremes of management style. One is very autocratic, in which planning and decision making come down from the manager to the staff. Very little staff input is requested or even tolerated. This autocratic style of management is often apparent in very small firms, where the owner also performs all the management functions. The other is more democratic or facilitative. In this style of management, staff input is desired and responsibility is often given to staff members to accomplish certain managerial tasks. Although this style of management is more likely to exist in larger firms, it can appear in any size firm, just as the autocratic style of management may show up in any size firm.

Managers perform four broad, generally accepted functions:

1. Planning

2. Organizing and directing

3. Decision making

4. Controlling

In *planning,* managers help chart the future direction of the firm. Planning involves research of staff capabilities and resources of the firm in its various segments. With this knowledge, managers prepare goals, objectives, and strategies. These goals, objectives, and strategies involve every aspect of the firm: operations, including personnel and production; marketing; and financial planning. The preparation of the annual business plan is an example of this function.

The *organizing and directing* function occurs as the manager determines how best to use the resources at his or her disposal to perform the work activities of the firm. For example, if the firm is large enough so that a division of the labor for completing projects is desired, the manager determines who will perform which tasks and how these tasks will interrelate.

Decision making is the activity of making reasonable choices between the alternatives available. It is a part of all the other management functions and seems to occur almost all the time in the manager's day. For example, in firms where new projects are generated through a manager, salesperson, or marketing individual, the manager must decide which designer will be responsible for completing the project.

The *control function* requires the manager to monitor the activities of the interior design department and take any necessary steps to ensure that the plans, policies, and decisions of the manager and the firm are being carried out. This is done in part by reviewing the kinds of reports that will be discussed in this chapter. It also occurs when the manager makes adjustments or develops new evaluative mechanisms to help the firm achieve its goals and objectives.

Although each of these functions are discussed separately, they are continually intermixed. Managers find themselves engaged in all these functions every day. This reality is part of the stress and excitement of the management role.

Different parts of this book discuss more specific activities of the management process. Chapters 9 and 10 looked at personnel management; Chapters 13 and 14 look at the components of determining pricing and fee structures, and Chapter 21 looks at time management and project control. Other chapters also deal with the whole picture of managing an interior design practice.

There are many fine general books on management in the libraries and bookstores. The reader may wish to review one or more of these books or even take a course in management to gain a more complete understanding of the management function.

Goals and Objectives

Establishing goals and objectives is an important aspect of financial management control. An organizations' *goals* are broad statements, without regard to any time limit, of what the firm wishes to achieve. One of the goals for an interior design firm might be "to become the premier residential design firm in the city." *Objectives* are more specific statements combined with time limits aimed toward accomplishing the firm's goals. Some objectives for the example goal might be, "During the next year, we will seek to obtain a product mix that will provide the very highest quality merchandise." Also, "In order to gain recognition as a quality residential design firm, we will seek to get at least one project per year published in one of the trade or shelter magazines."

To further ensure successful accomplishment of these goals and objectives, more specific strategies must be established. These *strategies* are highly specific actions that have definite time limits within the year of the plan. To continue with the example, a strategy might be, "During the next six months, we will negotiate to be the only design firm in this city to sell Baker Furniture products."

All the goals, objectives, and strategies of the annual business plan must relate back to the firm's mission statement. This *mission statement* is almost always a philosophical statement of what the firm sees as its role in the professional area. Figure 12–1 is an example of a company mission statement.

The Annual Business Plan

The purpose of the annual business plan is to bring together all the planning elements of the firm into one plan. This annual plan is a systematic investigation of what the firm can do, what the client base of the firm demands, and what the firm then decides to try to do for the year. Similar in many ways to the originating business plan, it is the ongoing plan for the business. The plan should contain information related to all areas of the business: administration, personnel management, marketing, facilities, and finances.

In many situations, the business plan comes down from the owner to the employees without input from the employees. This is called "top-down" planning. Employees feel that they are not part of the process or the organization when, without their input, the plan is handed down to them to accomplish. Since they have no responsibility in establishing the goals, employees feel no particular responsibility in accomplishing them, either. In this situation, it is not uncommon for the goals and objectives of the firm and the employees to be in conflict. What the firm wishes to accomplish may not be what the employees feel they are able to accomplish. Top-down planning sets the stage for potential failure of the plan.

It is important for planning to start with the employees and for their input to be considered. Planning should begin with a general discussion of what the owners and managers wish to accomplish for the coming year. Employees, within their work groups, should discuss how they see themselves and their group affecting these general goals. The work groups, with their managers, determine goals and objectives for the group. The managers further review these goals and objectives and present to the group and the owners what they feel are in the best interests of the company and the group. Management then considers all the goals and objectives of the various work groups and proposes the final annual plan.

An annual business plan should cover:

1. *Goals and objectives.* Goals and objectives should be developed in two parts: first, the overall goals and objectives with appropriate strategies of the whole firm; second, the goals and objectives of the various responsibility groups. Individual goals and objectives should not be part of the annual business plan since the plan may be shown to outside individuals.

The Business Purpose And Goals Of Goodmans

BUSINESS PURPOSE

Goodmans is a furniture-based, problem-solving company in the office products industry. Our mission is to serve our customers with services and products that create more productive, efficient and aesthetic environments. We are committed to maintaining a climate in which our people have an opportunity for personal growth and creativity while being part of a team that delivers total customer satisfaction.

GOALS

To Be More Important To The Customer

To identify from the customers' perspective, their needs and values, and to provide solutions through outstanding services, products, and follow-up.

To Be Better To Ourselves

Communicate and experience the "Goodmans' Culture" at all locations, to continually train for individual skills and provide an opportunity for personal growth and encourage everyone's participation in "The Good Plan." To achieve this in an atmosphere of freedom, excitement and comfort.

To Be Financially Strong

To financially strengthen the company in order to continue sound growth by meeting and/or exceeding our key financial and performance goals.

Figure 12–1 An example of a company mission statement. (Reproduced with permission, Goodmans Design-Interiors, Phoenix, AZ.)

2. *Administration.* The administration portion of the plan will outline support staff requirements for the projected year. This section will include the goals and objectives of such areas as management, secretarial, bookkeeping, and warehouse—in other words, areas not directly related to the generation of income.

3. *General planning and policy development.* Goals and objectives related to any changes in planning procedures, policy development, and general operational matters would be covered in this section. It may also cover how project boards are to look, what changes to expense policies may occur, and general personnel policies such as vacations and sick leave.

4. *Personnel management.* This section of the plan will deal directly with how staff members will be hired, job descriptions, salary and benefits, training, and performance evaluations.

5. *Facilities and equipment.* The facilities section will cover topics directly related to space utilization, construction, and equipment.

6. *Marketing plan.* The marketing plan must identify what the firm intends to do to generate new business. It does so by clearly identifying in which segments of the marketplace the firm is currently involved and what segments the firm may wish to enter in the coming year. The marketing plan will seek to identify who will be responsible for bringing in new business, how these new markets will be approached, and so on.

7. *Financial plan.* The financial plan outlines all the profit, revenue, and expense levels required to achieve the goals and objectives of the firm. Part of this planning will contain statements regarding such things as billable hours, expected administrative salaries and expenses, and cash flow projections. Budgets from each department will be presented and combined into a projected income statement for the year.

8. *Budgeting.* Budgeting, a function of all the parts of the business plan, will primarily involve financial information related to revenues and expenses. However, such things as time budgeting for various expected projects as well as for house and administrative activities; space utilization budgeting for the housing of offices and support spaces such as the warehouse; and other plans for the current or near future should be included.

Inherent in all of these portions of the plan will be the means of measuring performance. Having goals and objectives with no way of determining success will result in a meaningless expenditure of energy in the planning and writing process. Performance evaluation is not just part of the individual staff employees productivity results, but relates to all other planning and budgeting analysis. Such things as whether the job descriptions were actually written and were adhered to in hiring, whether the newly purchased truck was cost effective, and whether projects were obtained from the hospital market or not are all part of performance evaluation of the planning process.

The annual business plan helps a firm know where it is going for the coming year. It also aids a design firm in planning for the long range. At some point, after the firm has had a measure of success, it becomes important for the owners and managers to be looking beyond the immediate day-to-day, year-by-year goals. Long-range planning takes those firms toward greater possibilities. Instead of by accident, firms move ahead by careful planning.

What Is Pro Forma?

A major part of management is forecasting what might happen in the future. In order to help the owner or manager make decisions, accountants frequently ask their clients to project in financial terms what might happen. A frequently used device is the pro forma income statement. In business terms *pro forma* means a projection. So a pro forma income statement is one created with projected numbers in place of actual numbers. Other projections can be created using a pro forma concept. As part of her business plan for her new design studio, Jane Robertson prepared not only a pro forma income statement, but also a pro forma balance sheet and cash flow statements.

The basis of a pro forma income statement will be any known numbers such as many fixed expenses. Assumptions and "best guesses" as to what might happen in the future are factored in to produce the numbers on the statement. Generally, people will overestimate more often than underestimate projected numbers for a business. The designer utilizing a pro forma statement must have done some real homework on such things as the current and potential future economic situation, inflation, and changes in expenses (will salaries go up?).

Pro forma projections allow owners and managers the opportunity to ask questions, evaluate the alternatives, and make a decision about future projects, purchases, changes in company direction, and expansion, to name a few. The secret to producing accurate pro forma statements is careful, detailed analysis of the problem and research into the factors that may have an effect on the projections.

Budgeting

Budgeting, a part of the management planning function, involves annual managerial goals expressed in specific quantitative terms, usually monetary terms. Too often, interior design firms budget by taking figures from the previous year and adding a modest percentage of increase for the coming year. This informal method of budgeting can work satisfactorily during normal economic conditions. However, when economic conditions become slow or very volatile, the design firm has a difficult time meeting goals or perhaps even maintaining the practice.

Budgeting encourages the manager to plan for rather than react to the various events affecting the firm. It forces the manager to formally plan his or her coming efforts, and it allows for easier analysis of success and problems. Formal budgeting also permits the discovery of potential problem areas and provides the opportunity to determine a course of action prior to their occurring. In addition, budgeting focuses the efforts of the whole organization by coordinating all the various individuals' and group's efforts toward the firm's annual goals.

Although budgeting generally focuses on profits, it is important to also look at expected expenses and gross revenues. By reviewing last year's figures, managers can begin to forecast what will likely happen in the coming year. With further analysis, budgeting for what the company will actually attempt to accomplish becomes more realistic.

The simplest and most common method of budgeting in many firms is to look at last year's figures and then, by applying various percentages of increase or decrease, come up with the new budget. The common budgeting looks at what can be accomplished, based on the economic outlook and built-in prejudices and conservative forecasting of managers. As pointed out earlier, this can work fairly well in normal circumstances, but there is greater success if budgeting is done more formally and in sufficient detail to provide a more accurate picture of what the firm needs to do. The past is always a good starting point, but it should be used in conjunction with good research and planning (see Figure 12–2.)

One well-known budget concept, which received attention during the Carter Administration, is zero-based budgeting. Zero-based budgeting assumes that each year the managers of the firm start with a zero budget level and must justify all costs as if the department or activity were starting new. This means that no costs are considered as ongoing from year to year. Zero-based budgeting is rather complex for a small firm and is generally more adaptable to larger, multidimensional design firms. Very few firms utilize zero-based budgeting any more.

Reporting Performance

Two important types of reports used by management to determine if the firm's plans are being accomplished are information reports and performance reports. Information reports are generally not made up of financial or other numeric data. They are prepared in a narrative form used to provide management with information needed in the operation of the organization. A summary of an article related to general economic forecasts for the geographic area of the design firm, which also discusses how these forecasts may affect the design firm, is an example of an informational report.

The second, and more important to our discussion here, are performance reports. Performance reports consist primarily of financial or other numeric kinds of information. By sifting through financial and other numeric information, such as time records, many detailed performance reports are possible.

For a reporting system to be useful to a manager it must be credible. According to Getz and Stasiowski, a reporting system has credibility when it abides by the following guidelines.

1. It is accurate. This does not mean that the numbers must just add up, but rather that any mistakes in the system must be corrected in the next reporting cycle. . . .

Design Department Proposed Budget
Arizona Interior Designs
19X7

	19X6 *Actual*	*19X7* *Proposed*
Revenue:		
From Fees	$320,800	$401,000
Cost of Sales:		
Direct Labor	217,500	271,875
Supplies	3,580	4,475
Reproduction Expense	2,540	3,175
Telephone (Long-Distance)	1,588	1,985
Total Cost of Sales	225,208	281,510
Gross Margin	$ 95,592	$119,490
Operating Expenses: (Those Directly Costed to Design Department)		
Salaries	53,590	66,987
Payroll Taxes	15,005	18,756
Group Insurance	650	800
Promotion	1,400	1,750
Travel Reimbursements	3,500	4,375
Supplies and Postage	5,750	7,190
Professional Dues	3,500	4,000
Printing and Reproduction	6,680	8,350
Total Operating Expenses	$ 90,075	$112,208
Net Income	$ 5,517	$ 7,282
Profit to Sales	2%	2%

Figure 12–2 A simple budget report.

Expense Report ($)
April 19X6

Expense	*Actual*	*Budget*	*Variance*
Salaries	12,000	10,500	− 1,500
Payroll Taxes	1,575	1,200	− 375
Group Insurance	250	250	
Rent	1,200	1,200	
Heat, Power, and Light	450	375	− 75
Telephone	275	300	25
Promotion	350	425	75
Travel Reimbursements	657	500	− 157
Supplies and Postage	550	600	50
Depreciation Expense	900	900	
Insurance	750	750	
Dues and Subscriptions	150	50	− 100
Professional Consultants	1,000	750	− 250
Printing and Reproduction	560	350	− 210
Interest Expense	805	805	
Total Expenses	21,472	18,955	2,517

Figure 12–3 Performance report—variance analysis for the expense report.

2. The reports must be timely for them to be useful. How timely the reports are depends on how the firm is organized and how much it is willing to spend in the financial area. . . . The typical architectural or engineering firm should not have to wait longer than two weeks after the close of the accounting period to receive financial statements. . . .

3. The reports should be fair. By fair it is meant that cost allocations to the various profit centers should be made on an equitable basis. . . . Generally, direct labor is the basis for distributing overhead costs but this may not always be the best way. . . .

4. The reports should be clear, which means they must be quickly and easily understood. The reports should not require further analysis or additional calculations on the reader's part.[1]

ABC Interior Design, Ltd.
Projected Revenue by Client Type
19X6, 19X7 (Est.), 19X8 (Est.)

	19X6	*19X7*	*19X8*
Open Office Planning:			
Under 10,000 Sq. Ft.	$ 33,550	$ 45,000	$ 55,000
10,000–20,000 Sq. Ft.	22,575	36,000	40,000
Over 20,000 Sq. Ft.	10,800	17,000	25,000
Subtotal	$ 66,925	$ 98,000	$120,000
Medical Facilities:			
Physician's Suites	22,575	28,000	32,000
HMOs	15,700	25,000	35,000
Hospitals	35,600	40,000	25,000
Subtotal	$ 73,875	$ 93,000	$ 92,000
Banking Facilities:			
Branch Offices	17,550	22,500	28,000
Corporate Offices	5,500	10,000	10,000
Subtotal	$ 23,050	$ 32,500	$ 38,000
Professional Offices:			
Attorneys	8,750	12,000	15,000
Accountants	3,650	5,000	7,500
Insurance Co.	5,400	6,500	8,000
Corporate	15,900	35,000	30,000
Real Estate	4,750	7,500	10,000
Others	4,890	8,000	7,500
Subtotal	$ 43,340	$ 74,000	$ 78,000
Government Agencies:			
Federal	5,500	7,500	9,000
State	8,500	9,000	12,000
City	2,500	5,000	7,500
Subtotal	$ 16,500	$ 21,500	$ 28,500
Grand Total	$223,690	$319,000	$356,500

Figure 12–4 Performance report—projected revenue by client type.

---

[1]Getz, Lowell, and Frank Stasiowski, *Financial Management for the Design Professional,* Watson-Guptill Publications, 1984, p. 138. Copyright © 1984 Whitney Library of Design, an imprint of Watson-Guptill Publications.

Performance reports are most effective when reviewed in terms of variance analysis. *Variance analysis* looks at financial and numerical data in relation to the differences between planned (or budgeted amounts) and actual amounts (see Figure 12–3). However, a manager must not only look at the quantitative differences. For the data to be truly meaningful, he or she must also ask questions as to why the variances occur. This analysis quite often begins with informal meetings with the individuals involved. The manager's judgment is then used to make decisions related to the variances.

Variance analysis of data related to finances is looked at in terms of the variance's effect on net income. "An unfavorable variance is one whose effect is to make actual net income lower than budgeted net income."[2] In this use, the words *favorable* and *unfavorable* do not relate to positive and negative nor should they relate by themselves to managerial performance. They are only to be interpreted as algebraic impacts on the variance of net income.

It is important for firms to look at certain blocks of information to determine if goals and objectives are being met. Reports related to revenue generation, expenses, and profits are the most important (see Figures 12–3 and 12–4). To have the most use, summary reports should be prepared on a monthly basis.

Some examples of specific reports that can be useful, depending on the size and complexity of the interior design firm, are as follows. Figures 12–5 and 12–6 are examples of some of these reports.

1. Revenues from sources—fees and sales of goods

2. Work in process and aged receivables

3. Deferred income

4. Employee utilization and productivity

5. Comparisons of fees earned to budgeted estimates

JLP Design Consultants, Inc.
Work in Process/Age Analysis
As of June 1986

Client	Total	Work in Process	Current	Accounts Receivables 30 Days	60 Days	90 Days	120 Days and Over
Oceansview Real Estate	$ 1,067	$ 567		$ 500			
Lands Development Co.	3,500	1,000	$ 2,500				
A. J. Business Park	7,500	3,000	2,500		$2,000		
City Schools	9,500	5,750	3,750				
Phoenix Corporation	15,500	6,000		5,500	2,000		$2,000
Bethany Bank	8,500	5,000	3,000	500			
Meadows Development Co.	12,500	5,500	3,000			2,500	$1,500	
Technical Center Inc.	25,000	15,500	6,000	2,000			1,500
S.D.C. Associates	6,500	2,000	1,500	1,500		1,500	
TOTALS	$89,567	$44,317	$22,250	$10,000	$6,500	$3,000	$3,500

Figure 12–5 Performance report—work in process/age analysis.

---

[2]Anthony and Reece 1983, 908.

EMPLOYEE UTILIZATION REPORT
WEEK ENDING AUGUST 29, 19X6

WEEK END	# of EMP.	TOTAL HOURS	BILL-ABLE	% BILL	HOUSE	MTG/ADM.	MISC.
7/18	10	450	256	57%	95	15	27
7/25	10	476	325	68%	48	12	91
8/1	10	395	185	47%	65	15	130*
8/8	10	423	356	84%	26	13	13
8/15	11	469	278	59%	86	21	84
8/22	11	475	322	68%	55	15	83
8/29	11	455	312	69%	44	25	74

*Includes one person on paid week vacation.

Figure 12–6 Performance report—employee productivity.

6. Revenues by client type (or size of project)

7. Month-by-month profit and loss statements (with variances)

How often should reports be prepared? This would largely be determined by the firm's ability to produce the required reports. If, as is the case for many small- to medium-sized firms, the design director is preparing these reports, getting them done on a monthly basis is a laborious task. In very small firms where the owner must either prepare these reports himself or herself or pay an accountant to do them, they may appear every three to six months—if done at all. Ideally, most kinds of reports would be prepared on a monthly basis where the previous month's data would be available within the first ten days of the month.

This kind of reporting is difficult to handle if it is done manually. Computer systems that can link accounting and other numeric data to generate tabled reports would be a relatively easy solution to the problem. Software that also can automatically prepare charts and graphs from the numeric data provides an additional analysis aid for the manager. Several spreadsheet and database applications can make it easier for owners and managers to prepare performance reports.

Summary

Managerial financial reports provide important information to the owner and manager of an interior design firm. These reports help the owner and manager make decisions related to many financial, personnel, and operational issues of the practice.

Interior design firms utilizing computers for accounting and data management can quickly produce these and many other useful financial managerial reports. However, the variety and complexity of these reports must aid the managerial function—not burden it with preparation and analysis of useless reports.

Managerial reports are prepared to assist in the management of the firm—not to become the over riding issue. Companies or managers who become slaves to the numbers may miss the opportunity to involve the company in new design areas, hire designers who have a chance to grow with the firm and become loyal employees, or other issues related to the overall mission and goals of the design firm.

A key to the planning and ongoing success of the firm can be found in the annual plan. Managerial reports provide a great deal of the information necessary to prepare the annual plan. The combination of the financial managerial reports and the preparation of the annual business plan will not guarantee overwhelming success of the firm, but it will provide an important basis for proper decision-making in the present and the future.

In the next two chapters we will discuss how the firm may price the goods and services it wishes to provide. Chapter 15 will then cover what makes a legal contract and what should go into an interior design contract.

References

Anthony, Robert N., and James S. Reece. 1983. *Accounting Texts and Cases,* 7th ed. Homewood, Ill.: Richard D. Irwin.

Anthony, Robert N., John Dearden, and Norton M. Bedford. 1984. *Management Control Systems,* 5th ed. Homewood, Ill.: Richard D. Irwin.

Berk, Joseph and Susan. 1991. *Managing Effectively. A Handbook for First-Time Managers.* New York: Sterling Publishing.

DePree, Max. 1989. *Leadership Is an Art.* New York: Doubleday.

Garrison, Ray H. 1985. *Managerial Accounting,* 4th ed. Plano, Tex.: Business Publications.

Getz, Lowell. 1986. *Business Management in the Smaller Design Firm.* Newton, Mass.: Practice Management Associates.

Getz, Lowell, and Frank Stasiowski. 1984. *Financial Management for the Design Professional.* New York: Watson-Guptill.

Glueck, William F. 1980. *Management,* 2d ed. Hinsdale, Ill.: Dryden Press.

Shapero, Albert. 1985. *Managing Professional People.* New York: The Free Press.

Stitt, Fred A., ed. 1986. *Design Office Management Handbook.* Santa Monica, Calif.: Arts and Architecture Press.

Chapter 13

Product Pricing Considerations

Establishing the price for goods or product-related services sold by the design firm is critical to whether or not the firm makes a profit. The *price* is, of course, what something sells for. There are many factors involved in determining the price of a product or service. And, unfortunately for the individual new to the interior design profession, there are many different "prices" with which one has to deal.

Designers who sell merchandise to clients must be acutely aware of the selling prices they quote to clients. In many cases, this may be the only revenue generated by the design firm. Making a mistake in the calculation and quotation of product selling prices is always costly to the design firm and almost always comes out of the designer's commissions as well.

Several product pricing concepts will be discussed in this chapter. To begin, in order to understand how prices are established, it would be best to explain the different kinds of "prices." The terminology and methodology of preparing prices on the tangible goods sold to the client as a result of the interior design service will be explained. Designers frequently charge clients for the shipping of goods from the manufacturer to the designer. And, of course, there are additional expenses in the delivery and installation of goods at the client's home or commercial job site. Terminology related to shipping, delivery, and installation will be defined in this chapter.

It is also critical for designers to understand when sales and use taxes are required on the sale of goods. Forgetting to charge the customer sales tax does not remove the obligation of the payment of that tax. Designers can be fined quite heavily for the failure to collect and pay sales taxes. We will look at some of the requirements of sales tax collection by the interior design professional.

Many designers do not sell merchandise, but have the responsibility for pricing and budgeting the goods specified in the project. This chapter will briefly discuss the role of the designer/specifier in the pricing of merchandise.

Understanding product pricing terminology and the pricing practices used in interior design are critical for anyone involved in the profession. Clients are rarely nice enough to pay additional sums to the designer because he or she made a mistake. Care in pricing and budgeting merchandise is as important as determining how much design fee to charge.

Price Terms

In the interior design field, there are many terms related to price. Some are terms quoted to the client by the designer and different price terms quoted between a supplier and the designer. To add to the possible confusion, some of these price terms often mean the same thing.

There are three different terms that are used to represent the price the designer must pay to the supplier for the goods: net price, wholesale price, and cost price. *Net price* and wholesale price generally mean the same thing and represent a 50 percent reduction (or discount) from the suggested retail price (or list price). *Wholesale price* can also be defined as a special price to a designer from a supplier at a value lower than what the goods would cost the consumer. *Cost price*, however, is not always the same as net or wholesale. Not all designers will have the privilege to purchase goods at the 50 percent discount from all suppliers. Because of the lack of quantity-purchasing agreements, some designers receive a discount from the suggested retail that is less than 50 percent. Pricing from manufacturers to designers is governed by federal law. This point will be discussed at the end of this chapter.

There are four different price terms designers use to quote prices to clients. These are suggested retail price, list price, selling price, and retail price. The first two generally mean the same thing. *Suggested retail price* is the price suggested by the manufacturer for use by all sellers. The price term *list price* is generally accepted to be the same as suggested retail price. *Selling price* is a term many designers use to refer to the actual price at which they sell goods to the client. Since some designers sell goods at a discount (a price lower than suggested retail) and others may occasionally sell goods at a higher price than suggested retail, selling price is not always the same thing as the first two terms.

It should be pointed out that designers may sell merchandise to the end-user at any price they wish. They are not obligated to sell goods at suggested retail price. In fact, federal laws prohibit manufacturers from requiring merchants to sell goods to the end-user at a set price.

Retail price is a term commonly used in retailing. Retailing involves businesses that sell goods to the consumer or end-user, such as department stores and specialty stores. In retailing, retail price generally is not a price suggested by the manufacturer but rather a price determined by the retailer

In our discussions in this chapter, we will use the term *selling price* to mean the price quoted to the client and *cost price* to mean the price the designer must pay for the goods.

Catalog Pricing

When a designer requests a catalog from a supplier, the catalog will often come with a "price list." Many manufacturers send a price list for suggested retail or list prices. When this occurs, the designer must then negotiate with the manufacturer's representative for the discount percentage the design firm may expect. This may be as small as 10 percent or as much as 50 percent.[1] The manufacturer may offer variable discounts to different design firms as long as these decisions are soundly based. Such things as the amount of goods purchased over some specific time and whether or not the designer will inventory goods are two possible reasons. The cost price to the designer will result from determining the price after the discount percentage is subtracted from the suggested retail or list price.

Some manufacturers send net price lists with their catalogs. A net price list means the designer can purchase the goods at the price in the catalog. This net price list, of course, is the designer's cost price.

---

[1]For very large dollar-volume purchases, manufacturers may give the designer a larger discount than 50 percent.

It is common for suppliers to send price lists in terms of list price rather than net price since many suppliers offer varying discounts based on volume of purchases. However, enough firms utilize the net price list so that the designer must be very careful in understanding what price list he or she is reading. Most often, furniture price lists are retail or list price values whereas textiles and carpeting are net price values. A selling price determined by quoting or discounting a net price list means that the designer has sold the goods to the client for the same or lower than the price the designer has purchased the goods from the supplier. When the firm receives a price list that is not clearly marked with "suggested retail," "list," "retail," "net," or "wholesale," it should contact the representative or the factory to determine what the price list represents.

Discounts

A *discount* is a reduction, usually stated as a percentage, from the suggested retail price. A designer receives a discount from a supplier for ordering goods. Some designers give clients discounts when the client purchases goods.

The full discount price given by most manufacturers is 50 percent from the suggested retail. Remember that this is also called net price. Some manufacturers use a code word such as *keystone* to mean a 50 percent discount. Another price code used by some manufacturers is to indicate something like "your discount is *5/10.*" This code might mean that the designer will take $5.00 off the dollar portion of the quoted price and 10 cents off the cent portion of the quoted price. For example, if the retail price of the goods are $23.50, the designers price would be $18.40. These price codes are used to protect designers should clients try to directly contact suppliers to determine profit margins of the designer. However, not all designers receive the full discount of 50 percent. A manufacturer may determine that a 50 percent discount will only be given to those companies that are stocking dealers or that purchase a certain minimal quantity of goods in a given time period. *A stocking dealer* is a vendor that stocks a certain inventory level of goods at all times. A designer that does not have a retail store but has consistently purchased a similar quantity of goods, may be given the same discount as a stocking dealer.

It is simple to determine the cost amount by use of the discount percentage from the suggested retail. For example, if a design firm receives a 50 percent discount for purchases made from Sherry Jones Wallcoverings, then wallpaper with a suggested retail of $35 per yard would cost the designer $17.50 per yard.

The following formulas might help:

Discount in dollars = suggested retail times discount percentage is

$$= \$35 \times 0.50 = \$17.50$$

Cost = Suggested Retail – Discount

$$= \$35 - 17.50$$

$$= \$17.50$$

These same formulas are used whenever calculating discounts to determine cost.

Quantity Discount

A *quantity discount* is a discount greater than the normal 50 percent discount allowed because a large quantity of merchandise is purchased at one time. For example, if a designer purchases one chair, the discount would probably be 50 percent if that is the firm's normal discount. If the firm ordered 500 chairs, the manufacturer would most likely give a larger discount—perhaps 55 percent. Remember that quantity discounts given between manufacturers to designers are regulated by federal law to prevent price discrimination.

Multiple Discounts

Multiple discounts are a series of discounts from the suggested retail price. Multiple discounts are usually only given by manufacturers to designers for very large orders. Occasionally, the design firm may offer a multiple discount to the client—again, because of a very large order. The written notation for such a discount is given as 50/5 or 50/5/2. This does not mean that the designer takes 55 percent off the retail price in the first example or 57 percent off in the second. Rather, each discount is taken separately. For example, if the manufacturer offers a 50/5/2 discount on a large purchase of $500,000 of seating, the cost to the designer would be figured as

Total retail price	$500,000
Less 50 percent	−250,000
	250,000
Less 5 percent	−12,500
	237,500
Less 2 percent	−4,750
Cost	$232,750

Trade Discounts

Trade discounts are discounts given as a courtesy by some vendors to designers and others in the trade. These are usually a small percentage off retail, though they can be up to a 50 percent discount. Many retail stores that deal with specialized residential or commercial furnishings products, offer trade discounts to the local design community. For example, if Foot Candle Lighting, a retail lighting fixture store, offered designers a 15 percent discount for fixtures purchased from their store for resale, they would be offering a trade discount. To calculate what the cost price to the designer would be, use the previous formula.

$$\text{Discount in dollars} = \$150 \times 0.15$$
$$= \$22.50$$

$$\text{Cost} = \text{suggested retail} - \text{discount in dollars}$$
$$= 150 - 22.50$$
$$= \$127.50$$

Cash Discount

Another discount term familiar to design firms that sell merchandise is a cash discount. More commonly used in accounting, *cash discounts* are given by manufacturers and suppliers to those customers who pay their bills promptly. A notation like 2/10 Net 30 must appear on the invoice if a cash discount is allowed. The notation translates into an additional 2 percent deduction from the cost price if the invoice is paid within 10 days of receipt of the invoice. If it is not paid within 10 days, then the cost price is as stated and is due within 30 days. The cash discount is taken after all other discounts are taken. For example, the cost to the firm for an order of goods is $3000. The invoice offered a cash discount of 2/10 Net 30. If the firm paid the invoice within 10 days, it would only pay $2940.

$$\text{Cash discount = cost times percentage}$$

$$= \$3000 \times 0.02$$

$$= \$60$$

$$\text{Amount due} = \$3000 - 60$$

$$= \$2940$$

Deep Discounting

A discounting term that emerged in design industry terminology in the 1980s is deep discounting. A pricing strategy embraced by many manufacturers of commercial furniture, *deep discounting* represents an extremely large discount from suggested retail price for very large orders. For example, a manufacturer might offer a deep discount of 65 percent off retail for a two or three million dollar order. In many cases, these discounts are offered directly to the end-user. The designer or dealer may be totally bypassed in the transaction or might receive a small percentage for servicing the job at the local level.

Many designers have argued that deep discounting practices (sometimes called *buying the job*) have made a major negative impact on the design industry. They feel these big discounts, once enjoyed by a customer, will be expected for all purchases. They argue that deep discounts erode profit margins, hurting many firms that sell commercial goods. Other designers have stated that this pricing policy affects even those designers who sell goods but rarely do larger jobs. Those designers report they often feel like "order takers" rather than designers.

Manufacturers counter by saying that deep discounts have become a part of the competitive nature of the industry in the 1990s. They state that commercial furniture dealers have forgotten that commercial furnishings products are commodities and that deep discounting is a way of selling that commodity. The big profit margins and treatment of very large projects, especially systems projects, of the past are gone, say manufacturer's representatives. Many of these representatives feel that deep discounting is a pricing strategy that designers and sellers must understand and learn to accept.

Regardless of a designer's specialty or whether he or she sells goods or not, discounting techniques are important parts of the professional responsibility of interior designers.

Selling Prices

Most design firms operating retail showrooms sell merchandise to clients at the suggested retail price. However, since the designer can sell the merchandise at whatever price he or she determines, some firms mark up or add a dollar amount to their cost at a rate so that the resulting price is higher than suggested retail. This is a practice one might find in either residential or commercial retail sales. In commercial design, it is more acceptable to use a selling price other than retail since the client commonly purchases at a price lower than retail for all the company's other needs.

The two methods of determining a selling price other than using retail are discounting from retail and markup from cost. Both of these methods are used in commercial design. Residential designers who operate their own studios, but who do not inventory furniture, also may use one of these methods rather than the retail method.

Discount from Retail

The designer can offer to the client any discount he or she wishes. The selling price based on a discount from retail is calculated in the same way the discount is calculated to find cost. For example, the designer has prepared a specification of products with a total retail price of $4500. The designer has decided to offer the goods to the client at a 25 percent discount. The selling price would be $3375. That figure is determined in this way:

$$\text{Discount in dollars} = \text{retail price times discount percentage}$$

$$= \$4500 \times 0.25$$

$$= \$1125$$

$$\text{Selling price} = \text{retail price} - \text{discount in dollars}$$

$$= \$4500 - \$1125$$

$$= \$3375$$

Markup from Cost

Although many in the design community use the discount from retail as the way for finding the selling price, some use an approach that utilizes a markup from cost to arrive at the selling price. A *markup* is a percentage amount added to the cost of goods to get the selling price. Suggested retail is usually a 100 percent markup from net price. Selling price, however, can be any markup percentage or dollar amount added to the cost price by the designer.

When the cost of the goods is known, it is necessary to multiply the cost by the percentage of markup. For example, an end table costs the designer $100. With a 100 percent markup the selling price would be $200.

$$\text{Markup in dollars} = \text{cost price times markup percentage}$$

$$= 100 \times 1.0$$

$$= \$100$$

$$\text{Selling price} = \text{cost} + \text{markup in dollars}$$

$$= \$100 + \$100$$

$$= \$200$$

If the same table was to be sold at only a 50 percent markup, the selling price would be $150.

$$\text{Markup in dollars} = 100 \times 0.50$$

$$\text{Markup in dollars} = \$50$$

$$\text{Selling price} = \$100 + \$50$$

$$= \$150$$

There are two ways to find the markup percentage. One is to find the markup percentage based on the retail price of the product. The other is to find the markup percentage based on the cost price of the product. For example, the retail price of a table lamp is $200, the cost price is $100, and the markup in dollars is $100. To find the markup percentage based on retail price, use the following formula:

$$\text{Markup percentage based on retail} = \text{markup in dollars} \div \text{retail price}$$

$$= \$100 \div \$200$$

$$= 50\%$$

The formula for the markup percentage based on cost price is

$$\text{Markup percentage based on cost} = \text{markup in dollars} \div \text{cost price}$$

$$= \$100 \div \$100$$

$$= 100\%$$

In practice, most retailers use the markup percentage based on retail as a method of determining the markup percentage, whereas most interior designers use the markup percentage based on cost for determining markup percentage.

Gross Margin

As you will recall from Chapter 11 on financial accounting, the gross margin is the difference between revenue and cost. In relation to pricing, gross margin is the difference between selling price and cost. Many design firms use the gross margin or gross margin percentage to determine commission on sales. Since gross margin is also the amount of revenue left to pay all overhead expenses, the gross margin is important for design firms that do not charge separately for design services. Among other things, the gross margin must cover the expense of design services. In the preceding example, the gross margin is $875 if we assume a net price for the designer's cost. The gross margin percentage would be 26 percent assuming a cost of $2500.

To calculate the gross margin dollars for the example:

$$\text{Gross margin dollars} = \text{selling price} - \text{cost price}$$

$$= \$3375 - \$2500$$

$$= \$875$$

To calculate the gross margin percentage:

$$\text{Gross margin percentage} = \text{gross margin in dollars} \div \text{selling price}$$

$$= \$875 \div \$3375$$

$$= 26\%$$

Markdown from Retail

A term used in retail when discounts are taken for promotional sales of one kind or another is *markdown*. A markdown is calculated in the same way as a regular discount. Interior designers do not usually refer to the discount from suggested retail to get their cost or the discount they give to their clients as a markdown. They may, however, refer to a discount as a markdown if they markdown inventory during a clearance sale.

Pricing Review

The cost price to the interior designer could be retail, retail less a trade discount, or retail less a full discount that equals the net price or wholesale price. It can also be retail minus a less than full discount given by the supplier, a cash discount after the cost amount is determined, or an amount after quantity discounts are taken from the retail price. The selling price to the client could be retail, suggested retail, list price, retail less a discount, or cost plus a markup.

Down Payments, Deposits, and Retainers

These three terms are used by many designers interchangeably, although that should not be the case. They all have different legal definitions even though they are similar in concept.

Down payments are a portion of the total selling price paid at the time goods are ordered. It is common for designers to request clients to provide a down payment at the time the order is prepared in order to process orders. This is especially true when designers must special-order goods for the client. The down payment serves as earnest money, which is a good indication that the client is serious about the order. *Earnest money* is defined as a sum of money paid by a buyer primarily when a contract for the purchase of goods or real estate has been created. Designers often use this down payment money as the prepayment required by the supplier. Of course, depending on the designer's terms of sale and the exact ordering situation, the designer may have to return all or part of the down payment should the client cancel the order.

The term "down payment" does create a problem for designers in several states. Some states require down payments to be deposited in a separate escrow account and be used exclusively for the client from whom it has been collected. In other words, if your state requires this separation of funds, you would not be able to use the deposit from Mr. Smith to order something for ABC Electronics. Check with your tax accountant or attorney to see if your state regulates these kinds of down payments.

The term deposit has several legal definitions. For our purposes, *deposit* means money that is part of the purchase price prepaid by the buyer as security in contracts for the sale of goods or real estate. The deposit, just as is the down payment, is credited toward the full purchase price as the contract is fulfilled. And, like the down payment, the deposit would be returned in accordance with the contract should the contract not be performed to completion. Deposits generally do not create the same problems in terms of separation of funds as described in the discussion of down payments. However, the designer should check with his or her accountant to be sure that this is true in his or her state.

Retainers are payments to a professional to cover future service or advice by that professional. Retainers are not prepayments to be applied to the sale of goods, but to the contracting or retaining of design services or other professional services. It is common for people to "retain" their attorney or have an attorney "on retainer." Interior designers and other design professionals in allied areas usually require clients to pay a retainer as earnest money on a design services contract. Designers can also create an open-ended design contract in which the designer is "on retainer" with a client. This would mean that the designer is more or less on call to the client and whenever the client requires design services, the fee for those services has already been negotiated. Additional discussion about retainers as earnest money for design services contracts is located in Chapter 15.

Freight Matters and Costs

Freight, also called shipping, is the cost and process involved in the delivery of goods from the manufacturer to the interior designer. Most frequently, freight is handled by trucking companies that are working as a transportation source for the manufacturer. Many of the manufacturers have their own trucks to handle the freighting of products from the factory to the interior designer's warehouse, but many use independent companies—especially for small orders. Goods are sometimes shipped by train, but this is generally done only for very large loads or when the manufacturer sends one of their trucks "piggy-back."[2]

---

[2]*Piggy-back* means that the truck's trailer is loaded on a train flatcar and shipped by train to the general destination. Then the trailer is removed from the train and driven to the warehouse or the client's final destination.

The notation FOB is often found within the price list. *FOB*, according to the Uniform Commercial Code (UCC), means "free on board," and there is usually a second notation such as "factory" or "destination" following it. Some people are more familiar with the definition of FOB to mean "freight on board." Both interpretations mean the same thing. We will use "free on board," since that is the definition used by the UCC.

Free on board means that the manufacturer is responsible for the costs of loading the goods onto the truck or train. The costs of transporting the goods to the delivery destination are covered in the second part of the notation. This second notation is the indication as to which party is responsible for the freight charges and when ownership of the goods changes hands. If a manufacturer's catalog says *FOB Factory*, this means the buyer assumes ownership or *title* of the goods when they are loaded on the truck at the factory. In this case, the interior designer pays all transportation costs and assumes all risks during transit. If the catalog has the notation *FOB Destination*, then the manufacturer retains ownership of the goods until they reach the delivery destination. The costs of transportation would also be paid by the manufacturer in this case.

Some manufacturers, as a means of reducing their own liability and as a convenience to their customers, may want to pass ownership of the goods to the buyer as it leaves the factory loading dock, but will pay the freight charges. In this case, the notation in the catalog will read something like *FOB Factory—Freight Prepaid*. What this means is that the interior designer has ownership and responsibility for damages during transit, but the manufacturer will pay the transportation charges to the destination.

It is very important for the design firm to understand what the shipping policies are for the different manufacturers and suppliers it uses. Shipping charges can be quite costly for the interior designer if the firm is located a great distance from the manufacturer's factory.

These charges are also legitimate charges that the client should have to pay if the goods are not sent prepaid by the supplier. Most interior designers charge clients "actual freight," which means that the designer will bill the client whatever the interior design firm was billed for the transportation of the goods to the designer's warehouse. Some firms add a small service charge to the actual freight charges to cover handling the payment and the necessity of dealing with the freight companies over damages in transit.

Occasionally, firms will determine a "freight factor." This factor is obtained by finding the average and usual freight charges for all the kinds of goods and quantities of goods received FOB Destination. This factor is added to the selling or cost price (as determined by the policies of the firm) of any goods ordered for the client that are shipped to the designer's warehouse. There are a few other terms related to the freight process, but these will be discussed in Chapters 24 and 25.

Delivery and Installation Charges

A project or sale is not complete until the merchandise has been delivered or installed at the client's job site. Chapter 24 has a detailed discussion on the delivery and installation processes. Here, this section briefly covers basic information about charging for those services. For our purposes, *delivery* means taking tangible goods to the job site and placing the goods in their correct location. *Installation* requires some additional services or work along with the goods. Carpet must be *installed* to create a completed job. An area rug, however, is *delivered* to the site. It is then placed where desired by the client.

Many retail stores will not charge for delivery if the client's location is within a limited geographic area of the store's location or warehouse. Beyond that limited geographic area, most firms charge clients for the cost of delivering the merchandise. Delivery charges can be either a flat rate determined by how far away the client is from the warehouse or an hourly charge. Hourly charges are often quoted door-to-door. *Door-to-door* means that the client is charged from the time the delivery truck leaves the warehouse loading dock to the time it leaves the client's site location.

Delivery services include many activities that require the expense of adequately trained personnel as well as costs of transporting the merchandise to the client from the designers warehouse. Delivery services involve transportation of the merchandise to the client's location, uncartoning, simple assembly, and placing the merchandise in the desired location. Delivery services should also include removal of any cartoning or packaging materials and dusting or a slight cleaning of the merchandise. As Chapter 24 will further discuss, the delivery personnel or the designer should also explain to the client how to care for the merchandise.

Some items also require installation. Wallpaper, carpet, drapery, and other architectural finishes need to be installed. A roll of carpet is not finished goods. Until the carpet is installed, that item is not complete. The trades- and craftspeople who do this work will charge for their time and materials to complete the installation. As for architectural finishes, all these installation charges are the liability of the client and the design firm must remember to pass them on in the pricing of the finishes. The charges to install architectural finishes might be higher for remodeling projects than for new construction projects. The designers must charge not only for the installation of the new goods, but for the removal of the old materials, and the preparation of the surfaces for the new goods.

Some furniture items also require installation or specialized assembly. A wall-hung book-case unit in a home needs to be assembled and properly hung on the wall. Open office-systems furniture needs to be installed and assembled by a trained installer.

Exactly what constitutes installation services will depend on the products being installed. In general, the goods must be delivered to the job site and some type of preparation of the surfaces or area is required prior to installation. In addition, specialized supplies are often required such as tack strips for carpet, adhesives for wallcoverings, and wall anchors for wall-hung furniture items. When the items are installed, some will also require initial cleaning or dusting and, as with the delivery of simpler items, maintenance and care instruction should be provided by the installer or the designer.

These installation charges are required to make a finished product and should be absorbed by the client and not the design firm. The designer must be familiar with the job site so that he or she can explain what services will be required of the installer. Neglecting to tell the carpet installer that the existing carpet is a glue-down installation (which will require removal of carpet and prepping the floor) will result in an improperly quoted price on the installation of new carpet. In many offices, this error in pricing comes out of the commission of the designer.

Sales and Use Taxes

It is very important for the interior designer and the design firm to fully understand the laws relating to the charging of sales tax on the goods and services they provide. Sales taxes not collected from the client will be collected by the state or city from the interior design firm.

In order to sell merchandise to clients, the design firm must obtain *resale tax certificates* (sometimes called seller's permits) from the state sales tax agency (see Chapter 6). When cities, counties, or other similar entities also require the collection of sales tax, the business will also have to obtain similar permits from them as well. Permits will also have to be obtained if the business is located in other cities or states.[3] The resale tax certificate exempts the designer from paying the sales tax at the time he or she orders the merchandise for the client. It is then the designer's responsibility to collect the sales tax from the client.

In many states, a *use tax* is required to be paid on any goods that the business purchases for use in the operations of the business. In essence, the use tax replaces the sales tax when

---

[3]The means for obtaining this license were discussed in Chapter 6.

the business is a customer. The liability to pay the use tax amount to the state is on the buyer, not the seller. For example, ABC Interiors purchased a computer for use in the accounting office. Since ABC Interiors is a business, it will not have to pay sales tax on the computer, but it will have to pay use tax. ABC Interiors must report and pay that use tax to the state tax agency. The use tax insures that the state will still receive some tax monies on the sale of goods used by businesses.

There is much differentiation in the tax laws from state to state regarding when sales and use taxes must be collected. It is therefore very important for the firm to understand all the laws of the state in which they are doing business. What might be taxable for a design firm working out of an office in Manhattan and selling to a client in New York City might not be taxable in New Jersey.

The remainder of this section focuses on the sales tax—not use taxes—that must be charged on purchases by the designer firm's customers. Generally, the following guidelines would be applicable anywhere, but in no way are they to be construed as absolutely true for all practice areas.

As a rule, all items considered tangible personal property would be taxable. *Tangible personal property* is any property that is movable, can be touched, or has physical existence. Some examples of personal property are sofas, desks, chairs, and draperies. Some processes such as labor, installation, delivery, and freight have various kinds of interpretations as to when sales tax must be collected and when they are exempt. A case in point is draperies. In many states the labor to make the drapery and hang the finished product in the home is taxable since it is considered a vital part of completing the item. But the charges a drapery store might ask just to rehang a drapery after it was cleaned would not be taxable since the labor of hanging the drapery is now considered a service.

Items such as wall-to-wall carpet, wall coverings, and installed mirrors, although they are in essence personal property (they are moved from the factory to the job site), are legally considered fixtures or sometimes capital improvements. A *fixture* is legally defined as "a thing which was once personal property, but has become attached to real property in such a way that it takes on the characteristics of real property and becomes a part of that real property."[4] Sales tax must be charged if the installation of this product becomes part of the building or becomes permanently affixed to the structure in such a way as to make it difficult or impossible to remove without damage to the structure. Depending on the answer to this analysis and the state laws that prevail, tax may or may not have to be charged. In many instances, sales tax would be charged on the material and supplies needed to manufacture the finished goods, but not the labor. In some states, as in the drapery example, if the labor to manufacture and install the capital goods is necessary to make "finished goods," then sales tax would also be charged on the labor.

Certain circumstances (for example, if the freight and delivery charge can be considered part of making the finished goods), will require sales tax to be charged on these activities. However, in most cases, these charges are either considered a service and generally not taxable or are considered part of doing business and are calculated into the price of the goods. When freight and delivery charges are calculated into the price of the goods, sales tax might technically be calculated, but it is not paid to the state or city revenue office. It is important, as with all sales tax collection policies, for the design firm to obtain information from the firm's accountant or the state and city revenue departments as to the requirements for charging sales tax in this situation.

In general, design fees, such as hourly fees that do not relate to specific purchases of goods, are exempt from sales taxes. If, however, the design fee is added as part of the selling price of some goods, then the total price would be taxable. For example, if the designer added a 25 percent charge for design services to the selling price of $5000 worth of office

---

[4]Clarkson, 1983. p. 1203. Copyright West Publishing Co.

furniture, the taxable amount would be $6250—the $5000 of tangible goods and the $1250 of design fee. If the design fee was a separate line item, then sales tax would only be charged on the tangible goods.

The design firm is responsible for recording sales and use taxes and paying the appropriate amounts to the state tax agency. The firm must also keep complete records of items that are exempt from taxes. The burden of knowing which items are taxable and which items are not wherever the design firm does business is on the design firm. State tax auditors have the authority to seize the monies and/or property of the business should auditors discover the business has not submitted the proper amount of sales and use taxes.

The Role of the Designer/Specifier

The preceding discussion focuses on how a designer who sells goods to the client prices those goods. Many designers do not sell goods to the client at all. These designers, often called designers/specifiers, prepare the plans and specifications for residential and/or commercial projects, but do not wish to involve themselves in actual selling of merchandise. Interior designers working in architectural offices are another group of designers who infrequently involve themselves in the direct selling of merchandise to clients. Designer/specifiers, however, are responsible for many of the same activities as those who do sell products.

There are many similar responsibilities related to specifying a project whether the designer will be directly selling the merchandise or not. Of these activities, three are of special concern to the designer who does not sell merchandise to clients. These are: estimating a project budget, preparing the purchasing specifications, and assisting the client with evaluation and selection of sellers.

Estimating a Project Budget

Even though the designer/specifier is not selling merchandise to the client, the client naturally needs to have some idea of what the project will cost. However, the actual cost of the project to the client will not be known until the client either begins purchasing from suppliers or the bid process is complete. Designer/specifiers working with residential clients will most often budget or price a project based on all the retail prices of the specified goods. Since it is possible for the client to obtain some of the specified goods "on sale" or at a discount from a seller, the budgeted price will almost always be slightly higher than what the client actually pays for the completed project. Of course, if the client delays purchasing any of the items, the prices may be higher than the budgeted amounts.

When a designer/specifier works with a commercial client, the project will probably go out to competitive bidding. *Competitive bidding* is a process where several, perhaps dozens of sellers, provide prices for the project to the client. The final cost of the project to the client will not be known until the bidding process is over. This results in a more difficult budgeting situation for the designer/specifier and the client. The designer cannot guarantee a firm price since he or she is not selling the merchandise. All that can be provided is a "best guess" based on methods such as: (1) a retail basis with estimates as to potential discounts, (2) a cost price plus percentage markup, or (3) on a cost price plus a predetermined high-low negotiated markup. The first two are self-explanatory. The third budgeting option needs a bit of explanation. Occasionally, a bid will be set up so that the sellers providing prices must agree to only a specified markup on their cost. This condition is clearly indicated in the bid documents that the sellers obtain at the onset of the bid. Sellers must carefully consider if this negotiated or set markup is sufficient to justify providing a bid on the project. The budget is closer to the actual purchase price since the costs of the products are fairly well known by the designer.

Preparing Purchasing Specifications

Purchasing specifications can be as simple as what many designers call an equipment list or as complex as formal competitive bidding documents. A comprehensive equipment list will provide quantities, descriptions, manufacturers' names, and a budgeted unit price (see Figure 13–1). This equipment list would then be used by the client in his or her shopping to purchase the necessary goods. Along with the equipment list the designer will often also provide the names and addresses of recommended sellers, installers, and craftspeople who can meet the demands of the designer and the client in the completion of the project.

When a formal bid is used to purchase goods and services, the designer is responsible for preparing the specifications for all of the furniture, finishes, and equipment (FF&E). Along with these specifications, additional documentation is included which clarifies the responsibilities of the sellers, installers, and tradespeople who are awarded the bids along with many other aspects of the completion of the project by the winning bidders. An explanation of the bid process and the documentation that must be included in a formal bid is discussed in Chapter 23.

Specification list for:
Mrs. S. Jones
Job Number   921078

Quantity	Manufacturer	Prod. No.	Description	Unit price	Extend price
1	Pace	S9630	96 " Tuxedo sofa Fabric: COM Schumacher T-897 Moss	$2500	$2500
2	Pace	C3630	Club chair. Fabric: COM Schumacher S-29 Lt. Grey	750	1500
1	Herman Miller	ES670	Eames Lounge Chair Fabric: Black Leather	2200	2200
1	Herman Miller	IN50	Noguchi Table Finish: Ebony	1900	1900
2	Pace	T3030	End table. Finish: Frame--Black Top: White Marble	550	1100
2	Steifel	LTB235	Table Lamp Finish: Bright Chrome	150	300
1			Custom Entertainment Unit Built to drawings (see attached) Finish: Maple and Ebony per drawings	3500	3500
Wall treatment					
36 rolls	Blumenthal	W345	Wool charm Color: Honey Price: goods and installation		720

Total for Product		$13,720
Freight and Delivery		530
Sales Tax		823
Total		$15,073

Figure 13–1 A comprehension equipment list to be used to prepare a project specification.

Assisting the Client with Evaluation and Selection of Sellers

As mentioned in the preceding section, even when the designer prepares a simple equipment list, he or she commonly makes recommendations as to potential sellers and suppliers of the merchandise and/or installation of products. One might argue that the responsibility of assisting the client with evaluating and selecting sellers is more critical when formal bid documents are necessary. The bidding process allows any seller that feels he or she is capable of supplying the specified merchandise to provide a bid to the client. But not all sellers are really able to fulfill the coordination and requirements of bids, especially major projects. For example, although J. D. Furniture Store, which is a small retailer, may wish to bid on a project like a major hotel installation, the designer and client must determine if J. D. Furniture Store really is capable of ordering, delivering, and installing the merchandise called for in the bid.

In some bids, the exact specification of merchandise is left a little vague so that the client and the designer must evaluate alternative merchandise. Frequently, multiple sellers of office systems furniture are involved in providing bids. The designer must assist the client in determining if the products from several different manufacturers are sufficiently the same as the product named in the bid specification. Although the example is for office systems, the designer may have to provide this same assistance for every single product specified.

One of the major concerns of the designer who does not sell merchandise to the client is that the client may purchase merchandise other than what was specified. The designer is concerned about a lack of proper quality and suitability for the intended purpose when the client purchases on his or her own. To limit liability, the designer must include clauses in the design contract and the purchase specification regarding this issue. This is discussed more fully in Chapter 15.

Federal Laws and Pricing Practices

The Federal Trade Commission was established by the federal government to prevent unfair or deceptive competition or practices between businesses. One of the most important pieces of legislation that the commission enforces is the Robinson-Patman Act. This legislation makes it illegal for a merchant to charge various merchants different prices for the same goods. "If goods of similar grade and quality were sold at different prices, and these differences could not be justified by differences in production and distribution costs, the practice would violate the Robinson-Patman Act."[5] For example, if a manufacturer were selling the same quantity of product to two different design firms, it would have to offer the goods at the same price to both. However, if one firm had a record of purchasing a larger quantity of goods or stocking a quantity of goods, then the manufacturer could sell the goods at different prices to each designer. However, price discrimination only affects sales between merchants. A merchant has the legal right to sell to the consumer at any price he or she determines. If Wendy Jones Interiors decides to sell a Knoll chair to Mrs. Smith for $1000 and the same chair to Mr. Peters for $750, the designer would not be in violation of any laws as long as Mrs. Smith and Mr. Peters are the end-users.

Another important enforcement duty of the Federal Trade Commission is related to those practices by businesses that limit competition. The Sherman Act prohibits practices where businesses make agreements in restraint of trade or engage in price-fixing. An exam-

---

[5]Jentz 1987, 778. Copyright West Publishing Co.

ple of restraint of trade would be when two or more businesses have agreed not to sell in each other's territory or to each other's customers. This agreement limits the consumer's options. Price-fixing occurs when two or more businesses agree to sell the same goods to the consumer at the same price. This practice relates directly back to the concept of suggested retail. At one time, certain consumer goods were sold at the same price no matter where someone went to purchase them. These prices were dictated by the manufacturers. Some people even referred to these goods as "fair trade goods." However, enforcement of the Sherman Act negated these "fair trade" pricing polices. Today, all goods sold to the consumer are sold at whatever price any merchant that carries the goods determines, to sell them. This means that a suggested retail price by the manufacturer is just that—suggested. The designer can sell the goods at any price he or she determines, higher or lower than the suggested retail. If the manufacturer insists that the designer sell the goods to the consumer at a particular price, then the manufacturer is in violation of the Sherman Act.

There are several other pieces of legislation affecting businesses in order to prevent unlawful business practices related to such things as monopolies, mergers, and labor relations. The ones already discussed, however, have the most relevance to the interior design practice.

Summary

The competition of the marketplace and the demands of the consumer—whether residential or commercial—have forced designers to review critically their pricing policies and strategies. The days of selling every item at more than 100 percent markup are gone for all but a small number of designers. Deep discounting practices have certainly cut into personal commission and business revenues forcing many designers and design firms out of the industry.

It is very important for interior designers to understand the many ways they can price the goods and services they sell to their clients. The pricing terminology discussed in this chapter covers the more commonly used terms for the sale and cost price of the goods the designer might sell. It also covered the terminology related to down payments and deposits, and the shipping, delivery, and installation charges of getting goods to the client. In addition, a brief discussion of the applicability of sales and use taxes on the goods designers sell was provided.

After examining the information presented in Chapter 14 on determining design fees, we will be ready to look at what goes into a design contract (Chapter 15). The design contract will be the main source of information finalizing the pricing for the interior designer's services and the way in which he or she will price any goods sold to the client.

References

Black, Henry Campbell. (Joseph R. Nolan and Jacqueline M. Nolan-Haley). 1990. *Black's Law Dictionary*, 6th ed. St. Paul, Minn.: West Publishing.

Clarkson, Kenneth W., Roger LeRoy Miller, and Gaylord A. Jentz. 1983. *West's Business Law, Text and Cases*, 2d ed. St. Paul, Minn.: West Publishing.

Jentz, Gaylord A., Kenneth W. Clarkson, and Roger LeRoy Miller. 1987. *West's Business Law— Alternate UCC Comprehensive Edition*, 3d ed. St. Paul, Minn.: West Publishing.

McCarthy, E. Jerome. 1981. *Basic Marketing*, 7th ed. Homewood, Ill.: Richard D. Irwin.

Quinn, Thomas M. 1991. *Quinn's Uniform Commercial Code Commentary and Law Digest*. Boston, Mass.: Warren, Gorham and Lamont.

Siegel, Harry, with Alan M. Siegel. 1982. *A Guide to Business Principles and Practices for Interior Designers,* rev. ed. New York: Watson-Guptill.

Siropolis, Nicholas C. 1990. *Small Business Management,* 4th ed. Boston, Mass.: Houghton Mifflin.

Terry, John V. 1990. *Dictionary for Business and Finance,* 2d ed. Fayetteville, Ark.: University of Arkansas Press.

Chapter 14

Determining Design Fees

For many interior design firms, the only source of income for the firm results from the fees charged to the client for services. These fees must cover the cost of the designer's time or salary expense and overhead expenses such as electricity, cost of drafting paper, and telephone calls, and provide a margin of profit as well.

There are a number of different methods that can be used to charge for design services. Although all can be applied to either residential or commercial practice, some are more commonly used in residential and others are more appropriate in commercial practice. Exactly which method or methods should be used for a particular firm and type of practice must be carefully determined by the owner in consultation with the firm's accountant. There is no one way to satisfy all situations and all types of practice.

Although some of these methods require the sale of goods, this chapter focuses on compensation methods for providing required services. Pricing methods for the sale of goods were covered in the preceding chapter.

Billing Rates

In almost all cases, the method of charging a fee to the client is related to the billing rate of the firm. For some methods, especially the hourly, flat fee, and square footage method, the billing rate is primary to the determination of the fee. In other methods, such as cost plus or percentage off retail, it has an indirect bearing on the fee itself.

The simplest method for determining the billing rate is to multiply the *direct personnel expense (DPE)* by a factor—commonly 3.0. The DPE is a number that includes not only the salary rate of the employee, but also any costs of benefits—such as unemployment taxes, worker's compensation, medical and/or life insurance, FICA, sick leave, pension plans, and paid holidays. Figure 14–1 shows typical direct personnel expenses. The word *direct* in the DPE represents those personnel expenses related to billable time; that is, any time a designer works on a project, that time is billed in some manner to the client. Remember that it is rare for the design firm to bill 100 percent of all the designer's time on the job.

Traditionally, the most commonly used multiple is 3.0. That multiple does not always satisfy the needs of every firm so that each firm should determine its own DPE multiple. To

[handwritten margin note: Direct Personnel Expense]

1. Paid holidays
2. Paid vacations
3. Paid sick leave
4. Health insurance
5. Group life insurance
6. Pension or profit-sharing programs
7. Dental insurance
8. Employee discounts
9. Educational expense allowances
10. Professional dues reimbursements
11. Unemployment taxes
12. Social security insurance
13. Workers' compensation insurance

Figure 14-1 Typical direct personnel expense items.

determine this, consideration must be made of all employee costs for all billable employees (secretaries and bookkeepers are not billable employees). When the actual annual cost of each of the billable employees is determined, that is divided by the total revenue goal of the company to determine the DPE multiple. For example, if the total revenue goal of a firm is $250,000 and the total billable direct personnel expenses is $85,000 the DPE would be 2.9. This means that the salary rate would be multiplied by 2.9 to determine a billing rate so that a designer who is paid $17 an hour would be billed out at $49.30 or rounded to $50 per hour.

Many firms make the mistake of determining the billing rate only on the salary rate per hour of the employees. When this is done, the firm is reducing the amount of money left to provide for overhead expense coverage and for profit. On average, the cost of employee fringe benefits can add up to 60 percent to the cost of the employee. Many firms are also under the impression that the three times factor allows for a profit margin of 33 percent. In these days of very tough competition, earning a 33 percent profit margin is almost unheard of. Many new interior design firm owners have been very surprised to find a net profit of only 2 to 4 percent—if they had any net profit at all.

Billing rates can also be used to help determine if the flat fee and the percentage rate methods are sufficient. The fee divided by the billing rate multiple will give the amount of salary dollars that can be used by that project at the profit margin the firm normally maintains. This method helps determine if the amount of salary dollars available is sufficient to cover the expenses and desired profit for the project. If it is determined that the project cannot be done for that amount, then the firm can either reject the project or try a different fee method or combination of methods to assure proper compensation.

Methods of Charging

There are some differences between residential and commercial interior design that can affect the choice of fee method. In commercial practice, the projects are almost always more complicated than a residential project and, therefore, are handled over a longer time period. Because of the greater complexity and duration, there is more of a chance for something to go wrong. Because of the larger size and complexity of projects, fees for a commercial project are always larger than for residential projects. All these factors also point out the necessity for greater time management, time keeping, and scheduling.

There are also certain factors that affect the residential project that must be considered in determining a fee method. In residential projects, it is common for the client to take longer to make up his or her mind concerning the decisions that the client is asked to make.

Because of this, the designer often finds himself or herself required to do more "shopping" for the products that go into the project. Since many more custom manufactured items are specified in residences, the delivery and completion of the project can often take a considerable amount of time. The designer must sometimes be ready to go back to the client long after mentally having finished with the project. Residential clients are less inclined to pay for design services when the designer is also selling the client the products. They are used to the "free" design services offered by the retail establishments and often argue about being charged twice.

No matter what the configuration of the practice, the client's reluctance to pay a fee for service as well as pay the designer for furniture is a common problem. When the firm is a design/specify practice, the client only pays the firm for interior design services. When the firm is a retail showroom or studio, it is less common for the firm to charge a fee in addition to the cost of the merchandise. However, when the firm both charges for the interior design service and then attempts to sell the merchandise to the client, the firm often runs into difficult negotiations with the client concerning being charged twice. As competition continues to increase, more and more firms that in the past confined themselves to selling services are now also becoming suppliers to their clients. This may dramatically change the way firms charge for services in the future.

Hourly Fees

The *hourly fee* is commonly charged based on the firm's DPE, as discussed in the first section of this chapter. It is a very satisfactory way of insuring that the firm is compensated for all the work it does for the client. The hourly fee is a customary method of charging by firms that do not intend to sell merchandise to the client. And it can be used by those in residential or commercial practice.

Many clients, however, are reluctant to agree to the hourly fee since the meter is always running. The longer the designer works on the project, the greater the charges. The client is often afraid to allow the designer this much freedom in setting the time schedule. Clients are often afraid that the designer will take extra time in order to increase the fee. Many firms get around this objection by setting a "not to exceed" limit on the contract. What this means is that the designer must estimate the actual amount of time he or she will spend on the project and quote a fee that will cover all the expected work. The client cannot be charged more than that maximum. The designer must be careful in estimating time. He or she should also be sure that a clause is included in the contract to allow additional charges if the cause for delays or extra work is due to the client.

The hourly fee is often used

1. For the initial or specific consultations on small-scale projects

2. To cover travel time to the client's job site, to markets, or for other travel time

3. When the project involves a great deal of consultation time with architects, contractors, and subcontractors

4. When it is necessary to prepare working drawings and specification documents

5. When the designer perceives that the client will have difficulty in making up his or her mind

6. Whenever it is difficult to estimate the total amount of time needed to complete a job as a result of the design circumstances. An example might be a law office in which each partner wishes to have his or her office designed in a very individual manner

Firms use the hourly rate in different ways. One way is to use the rate based primarily on a professional level so that, depending on who is doing the work, a different hourly rate is charged. This means that the principal will charge a very high rate for his or her time as compared to the design assistant. A principal could charge $50 to $200 per hour. A senior or project designer might charge $45 to $175 per hour. Midlevel designers might charge $40 to $150 per hour, and design assistants and draftspeople might charge $25 to about $75 per hour. These rates would be established by first determining the DPE for each level of the creative staff. Additional dollar amounts might be added based on the reputation of the designer and the value of his or her service. Of course, local competition may prohibit a firm from adding dollars above the DPE multiple.

Other firms find averaging all the rates of the designer levels and charging one rate no matter who is doing the work to be a satisfactory solution. The danger here is that if the principal or senior designer is largely involved in the project, his or her time will not be generating adequate income. When entry-level designers are involved in the project, they often take longer than experienced designers. The averaging method can result in under-charging or overcharging the client.

A third method of charging the hourly fee is by charging by the kind of service rather than the personnel. In this case, the firm determines three or more levels of service and sets a fee amount to charge for each level of service. Three levels might be design (or creative) service (the highest level of service); documentation and drafting (those activities involved in the preparation of final drafting of floor plans and other drawings, preparation of texture boards or documents, and bid documents); and the third, and lowest level of fee, would be for supervision and/or miscellaneous (which would involve such things as travel time within the city, meetings with architects and contractors, meetings with the client, site visits, and so on). This method has the same problems as the averaging method.

The hourly fee method provides a way of charging the client for all (or almost all) the time put into the solution to the client's project. However, clients often object to the open-endedness of the fee. This method can be used successfully by many designers without the "not to exceed" clause if the client trusts the designer's ability to manage the project.

Flat Fee

The flat fee method, also called the fixed fee method, is similar to the hourly method with a not-to-exceed figure. With the flat fee method, however, the estimated fee is usually charged to the client whether the amount of time estimated is correct or not. This means, if the firm has estimated badly and the time involved exceeds the estimated fee, then the firm cannot be compensated for the extra time. If the firm has estimated too high, and the project does not require the full amount of the estimated time, the firm is not obligated to refund any of the fee to the client. The flat fee would include charges for all services and expenses other than those that the firm charges as reimbursable expenses. This fee method appeals to those clients clearly interested in the bottom line.

In order to use this method, it is important for the designer to know the salary and overhead costs of the company completely and to have a thorough understanding of the services that must be performed. He or she must also have a feeling for the decision-making ability of the client so as to predict if the client will be difficult or easy to work with and if the client understands the time element so that all phases of the project can be satisfactorily accomplished. It is also important for the designer to have job-time histories for similar projects to aid in estimating. And, of course, he or she should have a very good idea of the client's budget.

The designer must be very comfortable in his or her ability to estimate time for various kinds of projects when using the flat fee method. The firm that has built up a history of working on various kinds of projects and that has a written record of the time element of those projects is in the best position to use the flat fee method. It is rare that clients will allow the designer to charge more for work that was estimated as part of the original fee. It is, however, a fee method that can be used in both residential and commercial practice. Because of the greater amount of custom work, the more personalized service involved, greater amount of shopping for products, and generally heavier use of time, it is more difficult to use this fee method in the residential field.

The flat fee method is a satisfactory method of charging fees when

1. Goods are not being purchased from the designer. This allows the designer to utilize goods that he or she might not normally use since the designer is not selling the goods. For the client, this may mean that the goods specified are at a lower cost than those the designer would be trying to sell.

2. The amount of goods to be purchased is so small as to result in an insignificant amount in comparison to the time involved. The design firm will put the time into the project knowing that it will be fully compensated rather than depending on the profit from the small amount of goods.

3. Whenever a large amount of like items are to be purchased. This is often the case for projects such as restaurants and office complexes that standardize on products and require little additional time after the final product selections are made.

4. When it is easy to determine the time and requirements of the project.

Square Footage Method

In this method, the fee is determined by some rate per square foot times the amount of square footage of the project to be designed. Commonly used in commercial design and rarely used in residential practice, the *square footage method* can be a profitable way of determining the design fee. Whenever firms have sufficient experience in specific kinds of jobs so that they can be comfortable with a fee rate, the square footage method is an excellent compensation method.

With the square footage method, the firm must determine what will be the percentage for the various phases of the project. As mentioned in the discussion of the hourly fee method, the project could be broken down into at least three phases: design, documentation/drafting, and supervision. Each firm must determine if these phases sufficiently describe a project for themselves. If the firm normally charges a different rate for each of these phases, then the firm must determine what fee rate correlates to on a square footage fee.

For a firm that has never used a square footage fee, it might come up with an average by gathering data on several projects that are very similar to those being considered for square footage factoring. The actual design fee charged divided by the square footage of the project will provide the firm with a historical view of the square footage cost of doing design work.

Using the data from the *Interior Design* magazine 1993 "Giants"[1] article, the average fee in dollars per rentable square foot (RSF) for offices was approximately $2.75. The fee for hotel spaces was $3.18, restaurants was $6.75, and medical $5.26. It is easy to see from this variation in fee that the type of space and complexity of the project affects the amount of the square foot fee that can be charged. In addition, regional factors, the design firms' experience, and local competition may drive fees up or down. Each firm must look at its fee per square foot in relation to the national average and determine if its fee is in line with the national average and what is appropriate in the firm's geographic location. Charging a higher fee than what the local traffic will bear will bring frustration and a loss of work.

Percentage of Merchandise and Product Services

Akin to the architect's percentage of construction cost method, the design firm can determine and negotiate a percentage of the cost of the goods and installation that will be

---

[1]Lobelson, *Interior Design,* January 1993, 21.

involved in the project. This might include the furniture, wall coverings, floor coverings, ceiling and window treatments, lighting fixtures, accessories, built-in cabinets, and even general construction costs. The *percentage of merchandise and product services method* is used by the commercial design field rather exclusively.

Very similar in concept to the cost plus percentage method, the method is often utilized by firms that generally do not sell any of the merchandise to the client. The percentage rate will vary with the size or complexity of the project. The larger the project, the smaller the fee. The more complex the project, the greater the fee. For example, a large project like a hotel with a large dollar volume but potentially smaller amount of design decisions would require a smaller fee than a group of individually designed executive offices.

Since the project fee is based on cost, the client may actually save money if any extra discounts are provided for the purchasing of merchandise. The designer, however, must carefully negotiate the percentage because the firm could lose a considerable amount of money if the project is bid and won by a firm trying to "buy" a project at a very low price. Budgets must be carefully considered to ensure that the client has the project done as required along with fair compensation to the designer. This method should be used cautiously and only in combination with another method that will ensure fair compensation for design time and services.

Value-Oriented Method

The dramatic increase in competition in many markets has lead designers to consider a fee method called the *value-oriented* or value-based method. This fee method uses the concept that the design firm prices its services based on the value or quality of the services rather than the cost of doing those services.

Traditionally, most fee methods are based on time or cost rather than value. With value-oriented fees, the designer must show the client how his or her services are superior to competing designers. For most clients, all designers do the same thing and provide the same services. The designer must show how he or she differs from the competition and thus is worth the fees requested. If the client perceives that what one design firm offers has greater value than what other design firms offer, the more valued firm wins the contract. In many cases, this perceived value also means that the design firm can charge a premium for its services. Firms with a lot of experience are expected to do a better job than a new firm or designers trying to get into a new segment (for them) of the market. For example, a design firm that has specialized in restaurants for ten years will have a far greater expertise in that type of facility than a firm that has primarily done offices for the same ten years. The first firm will try to show the client that experience has value and that value should be compensated fairly.

Clients who are unfamiliar with or do not appreciate the time and subtleties involved in completing a project react favorably to the value-oriented method. The fee is based on the designers' ability and experience to do the work and to meet the expectation of the client rather than the time to do the project. When the designer can clearly differentiate his or her experiences and ability, this fee method should be considered.

Retail Method

The *retail method* is the most common method of obtaining fees when the firm actually sells merchandise to the client. In the retail method, the design firm charges the client the retail price suggested by the manufacturer or supplier. If the manufacturer does not provide a suggested retail price, then the design firm marks up the merchandise from the net or cost price. Since both the suggested retail price and the common markup percentage used is 100 percent, the retail method provides a high gross profit margin for the firm.

It is more commonly used by residential firms than those primarily involved in commercial design. And it is commonly used by firms that perceive the amount of time needed on any given project or client to be small in relation to the budget for the merchandise. If it is estimated that a great deal of planning, custom design, drafting, specification writing, or supervision work is required, the retail method would not be a suitable fee method. Should these kinds of activities be the major part of the project, then another fee method should be used, or the retail method in conjunction with another method might be used.

Discounting or Percentage Off Retail

A second common fee method directly related to the purchase of goods is *percentage off retail* or *discounting.* In order to gain a competitive edge, some firms offer merchandise at a percentage off retail and expect that the volume of merchandise purchased by the client to offset the design service costs. It is a method common for commercial firms, especially office furnishings dealers. This method is also used somewhat by residential designers who also sell large quantities of goods.

In this method, the design firm reduces the selling price of the merchandise by some percentage off the suggested retail price. Care must be taken in determining what that discount will be since the resulting difference between selling price and the net price is the gross margin needed to cover profit and overhead costs. As long as the discount still allows for the needed gross margin to cover overhead expenses and provide a profit margin, the fee method works. However, the larger the discount, the smaller the gross profit margin and the less the potential to pay off expenses and maintain profits.

Office furnishings dealers have been finding that this method does not always cover the cost of design services. This has become true because of the rash of deep discounting on systems projects that frequently occurred in the late 1980's and into the '90s. Because of these deep discounts (discussed in Chapter 13), dealers have been forced to charge design fees, such as an hourly fee, to make sure the designer's time is covered.

Cost Plus Percentage Markup

The *cost plus percentage markup* method allows the design firm to add a specific percentage to the net cost of the merchandise being purchased by the client. The percentage determined must be sufficient to cover the design firm's costs and profit margin desired if it is the only compensation method used. It is often used in commercial design and is also commonly used in the residential market. It can be the least remunerative method if a very small markup is added to the net price. It can be used as the exclusive fee method if the amount of goods to be purchased from the firm is sufficient to compensate for the time the designer must put into the project.

Many designers/specifiers who do not actually sell the merchandise to the client use this fee method. It works well for these firms and others as long as

1. The budget is not cut at the last moment.

2. The client does not use a lot of existing furniture in the new project.

3. The client does not decide to hold off purchasing any of the merchandise to a later time, thereby reducing the amount of fees the firm may collect.

Of course, these three points affect the profitability on almost all fee methods discussed in this chapter.

Another segment of the design community that uses the cost plus percentage method are those firms that are just getting started. Many new design firms offer this method of compensation as a way of competing with the larger more established firms that can operate at the full retail basis method. If a firm decides to commonly use this method of obtaining fees, it must be sure it is covering the costs of its design practice. Without careful calculation of costs, the designer may not be fully compensated for his or her design talents. Any firm considering the use of this method should use it in conjunction with some other fee method to be sure the firm receives a reasonable gross margin to cover costs and obtain a profit.

Combination Method

In many cases, using only one of the described fee methods will not provide sufficient compensation to cover all the expenses and desired profit margin for the firm. It is often necessary for almost all commercial firms and many residential firms that are not primarily retail showrooms to use more than one method of obtaining design fees.

Since projects involve a variety of activities, it is defensible for the firm to charge the client a variety of fees. For example, let us consider a project that involves a lot of time in meetings with the client, contractors, and the architect as a result of the designer's responsibility in specifying interior finish materials, but not a large dollar volume of actual materials to be purchased. The designer may find that an hourly charge for meetings, travel, and on-site supervision in combination with either a cost plus percentage or percentage discount from retail for the merchandise sold would adequately compensate the designer in this situation.

In another case, the project may require a large amount of time in drafting along with the preparation of specifications for rooms that are basically multiples, but the goods would be purchased from a vendor. This might occur for a hotel project or major office complex. Here the designer may charge an hourly fee for the drafting and a flat fee or a percentage of the selling price for the design and preparation of specifications for the areas that are basically the same. Properly considered for the project requirements, a combination of design fee methods can provide excellent compensation to the designer at a fair price to the client.

Estimating Design Fees

Regardless of which fee method is used, the key to profitability in providing design services is properly estimating the design fees. And the keys to effectively estimating the design fee are (1) understanding the scope of services to be provided and (2) carefully calculating costs to ensure that the fee method satisfactorily covers costs and provides a profit margin.

Design projects can be complex endeavors involving several people and many months or they can involve one designer for a few days. The first step must be a detailed analysis of what must be done, to what extent each design activity will be taken, and how long everything will take. Firms use estimating sheets such as the one in Figure 14–2 to assist in calculating what has to be done and how long it will take. The experience of the designer or the firm in doing similar projects sets the basis of the time estimates after determining what has to be done.

With this information in hand, the designer or manager can apply one or more fee methods to the project to determine which method provides the best potentially profitable compensation for the particular project. As previously discussed, projects requiring a lot of meetings, drafting, and specification writing would be best charged as an hourly fee. Projects that have a lot of similar design decisions (multiple spaces like hotels and hospitals) might work out better with a flat fee or a percentage of cost. Computer simulations can be set up that will compare costs and revenue generation of the fee methods a firm generally uses. These simulations would then help the design director determine which fee method has the greatest profit potential for a particular job.

Unfortunately, there is no absolute way for a designer to charge for services. Each design firm must make that determination itself. The firm must consider the kinds of clients with which it will be working, the types of design spaces, and the competition in its local region. The firm must be ready to modify its fee methods when necessary to remain competitive.

PROJECT ESTIMATE

Estimate in hours

	EST. TOTAL HOURS	D.A.	D.	P.D.	S	CADD	SUP
Programming							
Interview client							
Questionnaires							
Inventory							
Measure jobsite							
Verify jobsite conditions							
Meetings with others than client							
Feasibility/program report							
Review meeting with client							
Revisions							
In-town travel							
Other							
Design Development							
Base building plan							
Relationship diagrams							
Preliminary space plan							
Preliminary furniture plan							
Preliminary material selection							
Preliminary walls selection							
Preliminary floors selection							
Preliminary ceilings selection							
Preliminary windows treatment selection							
Preliminary furniture selection							
Preliminary other selection							
Preliminary budget							
Other sketches							
Meet with architect or others than client							
Review with client							
Revisions							
In-town travel							
Other							
Design Finalization							
Final relationship diagram							
Final space plan							
Final furniture plan							
Final materials selection							
Final presentation boards							
Perspectives/sketches							
Renderings							
Working drawings							
Final budget							
Custom design/shop drawings							
Meetings with architects & others than client							
Review with client							
Revisions							
In-town travel							
Other							

Figure 14–2 Comprehensive form that can be used to estimate design fees. (Reproduced with permission, Christine Piotrowski, *Interior Design Management,* 1992, Van Nostrand Reinhold, Inc.)

	EST. TOTAL HOURS	Estimate in hours (continued)					
		D.A.	D.	P.D.	S	CADD	SUP
Contract Documents							
Bid plans							
Bid specifications							
Bid forms							
Client meetings							
Revisions							
In-town travel							
Other							
Construction/Installation							
Job site supervision—construction							
Job site supervision—finishes							
Job site supervision—furniture installation							
Scheduling							
Procurement administration							
Meetings with architects & others than client							
Meet with client							
Change orders							
In-town travel							
Other							
Project Completion							
Punch-list/walk-thru							
Supervise completion of punch list							
Client meetings							
In-town travel							
Other							
Out of town travel							
Typing							
TOTAL							
RATE							
FEE							

© 1991, Christine M. Piotrowski

Figure 14–2 (Continued)

Indirect Job Cost Factors

In this chapter, we have looked at several common methods of determining fees for the generation of income for the interior design firm. No matter how carefully considered, it is possible for the firm to lose a certain amount of profit because of the unexpected. Although some of these indirect job cost factors can be calculated into the design fee, they more commonly happen once the project has begun as a result of the project process rather than a planned-for occurrence.

One of the most common indirect job cost factors for firms that are doing strict cost accounting would be overtime. No matter how carefully a project has been estimated, if the design firm must pay overtime salary to any of its staff, the gross margin of the project and potential profitability will decline. A career in interior design is rarely a 9:00 to 5:00 job. However, careful supervision of projects by the design director or project designers will help to hold down the amount of overtime needed for projects. Some firms control overtime costs by not paying designers on an hourly basis but rather on a salary basis, as discussed in Chapter 9. This does help on the direct salary expense, but not from the overhead expenses that are still incurred when the office is working past normal business hours. In addition, it is common practice (as pointed out in Chapter 9) to provide compensatory time for overtime worked by salaried employees. Comp time is nonrevenue generating.

A second indirect job cost factor that occurs rather often is the indecisive client. This is the person who just can't seem to make up his or her mind about any number of things—colors, furniture styles, patterns, the furniture or space arrangement, and so on. Experienced interior designers learn to recognize the indecisive client during the initial interviews. But often even the most experienced designer gets a client who just can't seem to make up his or her mind. If the fee method is the hourly method, this would have little concern on the final outcome since the designer continues to charge for all the changes and extra meetings. But when a fee method has been established that limits the amount of fee that can be charged, the designer must diplomatically find ways to get the client to make up his or her mind and move on with the project.

An added cost that occurs whenever a designer has ventured into a project that he or she has never done before is the need for technical or professional consultation that was not expected. Oftentimes designers may be asked to do projects requiring construction documents. Most cities have strict regulations as to who may prepare construction documents. Designers may suddenly discover that they must obtain an architect's or other professional consultant's stamp on drawings even though the drawings were prepared by the interior designer. This unexpected fee will reduce the expected profit margin.

Unusual job site and delivery costs can also add to the cost of a project. In open office-systems work, it is common that thermostats, light switches, air-conditioning vents, and the like always seem to end up right where the interior designer planned to hang a wall strip or attach a divider panel. In residential design, it is common for the client to have made some kind of change at the site without telling the interior designer. Sometimes a designer may specify a very large piece of furniture, which may be very difficult to deliver. The most common occurrence is the very large conference table that cannot be delivered up the elevator but must be placed on the top of the elevator cab or hoisted up on cranes from the exterior of the building.

Unless careful project management occurs, furniture may be ready for delivery to the job site, but the job site may not be ready to receive the merchandise. In situations where the design firm does not have a warehouse ready to hold merchandise, an extra cost will be involved in storing and later delivering to the job site. In many cases, this extra cost will be borne by the design firm even though the delay was not caused by the design firm, since the management of the project is all considered to be part of the normal and expected services of the firm.

All of these examples lead to extra design time that may not have been calculated for or otherwise considered in the fee and contract. The extra costs of some of these examples may be passed on to the client if the proper clauses are in the design contract. Those clauses will be discussed in the next chapter. Unfortunately, the extra costs discussed in this section are often the responsibility of the design firm.

Summary

All interior design firms are in business to make a reasonable profit while providing quality services to clients. The owners and managers of interior design firms must understand their particular firms and each one's operations and the kinds of clients that each wishes to obtain as well as the general market that the firm is in so that the firm will stay in operation.

The income the firm generates, whether from fees for services only, from the sale of goods, or a combination of both must be sufficient to cover the costs of the firm and provide a net profit to sustain the firm. In this chapter, we have looked at the different ways the firm can generate this income by several fee methods. No fee method is perfect for all circumstances for all firms. Each firm must determine for its own type of business which situations warrant a particular fee method.

Once the fee method for the particular project situation is determined, the next step is to prepare a design contract or proposal. In our next chapter, we will look at the preparation of such a contract.

References

Foote, Rosslyn F. 1978. *Running an Office for Fun and Profit.* New York: McGraw-Hill.

Getz, Lowell. 1986. *Business Management in the Smaller Design Firm.* Newton, Mass.: Practice Management Associates.

Getz, Lowell, and Frank Stasiowski. 1984. *Financial Management for the Design Professional.* New York: Watson-Guptill.

Loebelson, Andrew. 1983. *How to Profit in Contract Design.* New York: Interior Design Books.

_____. January, 1993. "Interior Design Giants." *Interior Design.*

Shenson, Howard L. 1990. *The Contract and Fee-Setting Guide for Consultants and Professionals.* New York: Wiley.

Siegel, Harry, with Alan M. Siegel. 1982. *A Guide to Business Principles and Practices for Interior Designers,* rev. ed. New York: Watson-Guptill.

Stasiowski, Frank. 1985. *Negotiating Higher Design Fees.* New York: Watson-Guptill.

_____. 1993. *Value Pricing for the Design Firm.* New York: Wiley.

Stitt, Fred A., ed. 1986. *Design Office Management Handbook.* Santa Monica, Calif.: Arts and Architecture Press.

Chapter 15

Preparing Design Contracts

Interior designers enter into contracts of one sort or another every day. The most common occurrence of a contractual relationship occurs when a designer offers to provide some service or product to a client and the client agrees to purchase that service or product. In these contractual relationships, it is the interior designer's responsibility to fulfill the agreement. In many cases, designers and clients enter into contracts and they do not know they have done so. Or they should have entered into a contract, but did not.

Designers and clients also breach or break those contracts. Sometimes this is done knowingly and willingly (hoping the other party does not sue), sometimes by accident, and sometimes by mutual consent (which is not really a breach at all). Interior designers are also sometimes faced with the threat of "I'm going to sue for breach of contract," or "I'm going to sue because we had a contract." Yet the designer may not even know he or she has breached in the first place or had a contract in the second.

In this chapter we will review the basic ingredients of a contract and contract law as it deals with a contract for services or a combination of services and goods. The formats and examples of contracts in this chapter primarily deal with contracts for design services. The next chapter will discuss the specific differences concerning contracts for the sale of goods. The counsel of an attorney is strongly recommended for a complete explanation of the legal considerations of contracts. The information in this chapter is general in nature and should not be construed as legal advice.

Definition and Basic Elements of a Contract

Basically, a *contract* is a promise or agreement between two or more parties to perform or not perform some act. The performance or lack of performance of this act can be enforced by the courts. Not all promises or agreements are legal contracts, however.

A legally enforceable contract must have certain elements or it may not be enforceable. The basic requirements of a contract are

   1. *Agreement.* This must include an offer by one of the parties and acceptance of the offer by the other party.

2. *Consideration.* This must be legally sufficient enough for a court to take it seriously.

3. *Contractual capacity.* This must exist by both parties involved in the contract.

4. *Legality.* The contract must exist only to support the performance of some legal act.

5. *Reality of Assent.* It must be shown that both parties' consent to enter into the contract was genuine.

6. *Form.* The contract must be in a legally appropriate form—which most commonly means "in writing."

Agreement

To be a valid contract, the first element that must exist is that there must be agreement to the contract by the parties involved. For this to happen, one of the parties must make an offer and the other party must agree exactly to the terms of that offer. If either of these elements is missing, there is no contract.

The contract must also include the following categories of information: (1) identification of the parties, (2) identification of the subject matter with which the contract is concerned, (3) what consideration is to be paid, and (4) duration of the contract.[1]

Offer

For an offer to be binding, there must be serious intention by the *offeror* (the party who makes the offer to the other party, who is called the *offeree*). Merely expressing an opinion is not a form of valid intention. For example, if John Doe says to his client that "the project can probably be completed in five days" his client could not sue if it actually takes him ten days, since the five days was an opinion, not a promise. Also, if Doe's client says to him, "I plan to hire your firm exclusively to design all my restaurants," Doe could not sue his client, since the client was only expressing intention, not making a promise.

Interior designers are often invited to bid on design projects or sales of goods. An *invitation to bid* or negotiate is not an offer but merely shows a willingness on the part of the client to enter into discussions with the designer about a potential contract.

An offer must also be given in terms definite enough for a court to determine if the contract was fulfilled or not. For an interior designer to put in the contract the statement, "select all finishes" could leave the firm responsible for selecting interior and exterior finishes, when the firm only considered selecting interior finishes.

The third element of a legal offer is that the offer be communicated to the offeree so that the offeree knows of the existence of the offer. Unless the client knows that out-of-town travel expenses are over and above the design fees, the client would not be expected to pay these charges.

The last element in a legal offer is the ability to terminate the offer or the acceptance of the offer. If the designer's proposal states that the price for the services is good for ten days and the client responds on the fifteenth day, the designer is not obligated to still provide the services at the stated price. It should be noted that the time period of the offer begins when the offeree receives the offer, not when it is prepared or mailed by the offeror. Should there not be a time limit stated in the offer, the time limit terminates at the end of a reasonable period of time considering the circumstances of the offer.

An offer can also be terminated if the offeror (most commonly the designer) withdraws the offer before the offeree (the client) accepts it. It is, of course, important that the offer be withdrawn prior to its being accepted. For example, if an interior designer discovers that he

---

[1]Clarkson 1983, 109. Copyright © West Publishing Co.

or she has miscalculated his or her bid to the city of Chicago but has already turned in the bid, he or she must revoke his or her offer prior to the closing date and time of acceptance of bids. If all bids are due by Friday at 5:00 P.M., and the designer discovers the error on Friday at 5:30 P.M., it is too late to revoke the bid.

Another way to terminate the offer is for the offeree to reject the offer. Should this happen, there is no obligation of either side to fulfill the contract. Should the client later wish to accept the offer, the designer can refuse, accept, or modify the original offer. This is because the client's refusal of the offer terminated the original offer. But if the client says something like, "Is this the best price you can give me on the sofa?" that does not represent a rejection of the offer.

The last method of terminating an offer is for the client to make a counteroffer. If Ms. Jones says, "Your design fee is out of the question. I am prepared to pay only $5000 for these services," the offer of $5000 is now a counteroffer to the designer which the designer is now in the position of accepting or rejecting.

Acceptance

The second part of an agreement has to be acceptance by the offeree that shows agreement to the terms of the offer. "In order to exercise the power of acceptance effectively, the offeree must accept unequivocally. If the acceptance is subject to new conditions, or if the terms of the acceptance change the original offer, the acceptance may be considered a counteroffer that implicitly rejects the original offer."[2] Should a designer have a contract with a client to design the client's home for a fee of $5000, but the terms of the contract do not ask for a retainer, the designer cannot ask the client to pay a retainer, since that was not part of the original offer.

Generally, acceptance cannot be construed if there is "silence" or no response from the client, unless it can be shown that the client, by his or her silence, has received a benefit from the goods or services the designer has provided. For example, if a designer decides to proceed with the space planning of an office for a client even though the client has not yet accepted the terms of the contract, the client would not be obligated to pay the design fee for the services provided unless the client took ownership (benefit) of the space plans somehow.

Finally, acceptance must be made within the time limit set in the terms of the offer. If no definite terms are stated, acceptance must be made within a reasonable time, considering the conditions of the offer and the subject of the offer.

Consideration

Consideration is the "price" the offeree "pays" to the offeror for the offeror's fulfilling the promise. Generally, in an interior design contract, the consideration will be the design fees that the client pays to the designer for providing the services agreed to by the client. The consideration must be adequate enough to be fair.

A promise to give consideration for something that has already occurred or that the designer is already obligated to do is not binding. If the client says, "Because you did such a great job on finishing the office installation on time, I will give you a $500 bonus," the client is not legally obligated to pay the bonus since it is consideration for something that has happened in the past. Considerations are negotiated for actions that take place in the future or in the present, not in the past. Similarly, if the design contract says the designer will provide a watercolor rendering of the living room, and later the designer tells the client that he

---

[2]Clarkson 1983, 129. Copyright © West Publishing Co.

or she must pay the designer an additional $500 for that rendering, the client is not obligated to pay since the firm is already legally obligated to supply that rendering for the consideration outlined in the contract.

Contractual Capacity

Both parties to a contract must have legal capacity to make a contract. *Contractual capacity relates to the full legal competence of the parties.* It is very important for the designer to be sure that the person agreeing to and signing a contract has the legal capacity to enter into the contract. In residential design, the interior designer would normally be dealing with a legally competent adult head-of-household or spouse. In commercial interior design, the designer often deals with people other than the actual owner of the business or the chairperson of the board of the corporation. Rarely does a minor (under the age of 18) have contractual capacity.

In a commercial project, the interior designer must be sure that the person signing the contract has the authority to bind the corporation or business to that contract. Not all employees, even with fancy job titles, have that authority.

Legality

Contracts must describe legal acts in order for the courts to have the authority to enforce them. An illegal contract would be any contract that, if performed, would constitute an act against legal statute, break tort law or in any other way be opposed to the public good. The main way the concept of legality would affect a contract into which an interior designer might enter, would be relating to contracts in restraint of trade.

Contracts in restraint of trade are made to be detrimental to the public good and generally have an effect on the potential for fair competition in a given market. If two or more interior design firms in a market area where they basically were the only sources for furniture, got together and agreed to sell merchandise at the same markup, they would be guilty of collusion and their agreement would be in restraint of trade—illegal. If one subsequently lowered prices and the other sued saying they had an agreement, the suit would be thrown out—and both firms would likely be charged with a crime.

Some contracts in restraint of trade are actually legal, however. Certain clauses in employment contracts that restrain the activities of former employees can be legal if the restrictions relating to noncompetition are reasonable.

Reality of Assent

Sometimes a contract that is made by two parties who have the full legal ability to make a valid contract, may not be enforced because the reality of assent of one or another of the parties is questioned.

This might occur because of (1) a mistake (this must relate to a mistake by one or another of the parties in the facts of the terms of the contract, not an error of judgment or quality); (2) fraudulent misrepresentation, (the terms of the agreement were presented with information intentionally incorrect in an attempt to deceive the other party); (3) undue influence, (when one party exerts so much influence on the other that the party being taken advantage of virtually does not exercise his or her own free will); and (4) duress, (this would negate a contract if the offeree was forced under certain kinds of threats to agree to the contract).

Form

In many cases, an oral contract would be binding on both parties. But a series of statutes called the *Statute of Frauds* requires that some contracts be in writing in order for them to be enforceable. The three most important considerations as they relate to the interior designer would be (1) contracts for the sale of goods that amount to more than $500, (2) contracts that cannot be completed within one year of their origination, and (3) contracts for the sale of real estate.

For Sale of Goods

Interior designers often take orders for furniture and furnishings without any written agreement from the client. "I wouldn't think of asking Mrs. Smith for a contract to order a sofa." Yet many of these same designers will find themselves owning all kinds of furniture and furnishings their clients later refuse to accept.

The Statute of Frauds as well as the Uniform Commercial Code require a written contract to be in existence for the sale of any goods of an amount over $500. This "contract" need not be any kind of formal contract, but merely a written document that states the date, quantity, description, and terms of the agreement; and it must be signed by the party or parties involved. This aspect of a contract for the sale of goods will be discussed in detail in the next chapter.

Contracts Whose Performance Will Take More Than One Year

Interior designers often are involved in contracts that will take more than one year to complete. If the terms of the contract are such that the project or requirements of the contract cannot be completed in one year, the Statute of Frauds will require the contract to be in writing for the contract to be binding. If the terms of the contract indicate that the project will be completed within one year, it would not be necessary for the contract to be in writing. The time limit begins one day after the contract is agreed to by both parties.

The Sale of Real Estate

A contract for the sale of real estate, which is any land and buildings, plants, trees, or anything else affixed to the land, must always be in writing. Any oral contract for this kind of transaction would not be binding on either party.

Developing the Design Contract

There are many things the designer needs to know to properly prepare a design contract. Designers regularly use questionnaires or other forms to help them obtain that information (see Figure 15–1). Much of this information is obtained directly from the client. Additional information may have to be obtained from other individuals involved in the project such as the architect.

At this point, the designer most needs to understand what the scope of the project will be and all the potential services that the client will need the designer to perform. Each design activity takes time. Some require expense items (like the materials to build a model). For many projects, specific activities may require more than one designer to be involved (interviewing and documentation). Missing out on understanding the full scope of the project could mean the designer provides services for no charge. Or it could be doing a part of the project improperly creating legal liability. The client interview to understand the full scope of the project cannot be taken lightly. Figure 15–2 provides just some of the questions that must be answered prior to writing a design contract.

The Form of the Contract

Whether or not it is legally required that a contract for interior design services or even the sale of goods be in writing, it is safer for the design firm to establish a policy that all sales of services and goods be accompanied by a written contract. A written contract is the strongest evidence that a designer has to show that a contract for services or goods exists between the

A. GENERAL INFORMATION

CLIENT:

CURRENT ADDRESS:	PROJECT ADDRESS:
PHONE:	PHONE:

PROJECT #

CLIENT PROJECT COORDINATOR:	NAME:
	PHONE:
SALESPERSON:	NAME:
	PHONE:
DESIGNER:	NAME:
	PHONE:
INSTALLER:	NAME:
	PHONE:
PROJECT COORDINATOR:	NAME:
	PHONE:

SITE STATUS: ☐ NEW   ☐ EXISTING   ☐ REMODELING
BID: ☐ YES   ☐ NO   SUBMIT DATE:
USED FURNITURE: ☐ YES   ☐ NO
NEW FURNITURE: ☐ YES   ☐ NO
NEED TO BE REFURBISHED: ☐ YES   ☐ NO
NEED DISPOSITION: ☐ YES   ☐ NO
RECONFIGURATION: ☐ YES   ☐ NO
ACKNOWLEDGEMENT DOUBLE CHECK: ☐ YES   ☐ NO

WORKSTATIONS QUANTITIES:
NEW: EXISTING: RECONFIGURED:
COMMENTS:

CRITICAL DATES:
CUSTOMER OCCUPANCY   DATE:
ORDER ENTRY   DATE:
INSTALLATION   START DATE: END DATE: NO. OF PHASES:

Figure 15–1 A form designers use to obtain detailed information about the design project. (Reproduced with permission, Interior Associates, Inc., Des Moines, IA).

B. SITE

GENERAL CONTRACTOR:

ELECTRICIAN:

PHONE COMPANY:

RESTRICTIONS ON SITE:

FLOOR # :

PUBLIC ELEVATORS: ☐ YES ☐ NO DIMENSIONS:

FREIGHT ELEVATORS: ☐ YES ☐ NO DIMENSIONS:

PADDING NEEDED: ☐ YES ☐ NO

RECEIVING DOCK: ☐ YES ☐ NO DIMENSIONS:

INSIDE DOOR OPENINGS: DIMENSIONS:

OUTSIDE DOOR OPENINGS: DIMENSIONS:

HALL CLEARANCE: DIMENSIONS:

STAGING AREA LOCATIONS:

SPECIAL SITE CONSIDERATIONS:
WALL OR FLOOR PROTECTION
CO—ORDINATION W/TRADES
ENTER/EXIT KEYS / TIME FRAMES

Figure 15–1 (Continued)

Who are the owners?

Is the project new construction or a remodeling project?

What is the square footage of the project?

What is the budget?

What is the targeted completion date?

Are architectural floor plans available or will the space need to be site-measured?

Have you worked with this client before?

Does the current design staff have the time and experience to do this project?

Will consultants or additional staff be required in order to do this project?

If it is a remodeling project, what legal restraints or other restraints that might be on the space?

How much demolition is expected?

How much supervision must be done on site?

Will the project go out to bid, or has a purchasing agreement already been established?

Will the project be completed all at once or done in stages?

What portions of the construction or the interiors project will be handled by the owner?

Does the client require moving services or will he or she take care of this himself or herself?

How much existing furniture will be used?

What styles of new furniture are preferred?

Are new architectural finishes to be selected?

Are custom cabinets, furniture items, or treatments expected?

Are office systems furniture (or other furniture) evaluations required prior to specifications?

Figure 15–2 Typical questions that the designer must have answered prior to preparing a design contract for services.

client and the designer. Designers whose major source of income comes from performing services rather than selling goods should never begin any design work until a written contract has been executed and signed by the client. Designers should be concerned about conducting themselves in a professional and businesslike manner regarding insistence on a written agreement prior to beginning design work. Although it is true that an occasional client's feelings may be bruised by the contractual situation, it is better to lose an occasional client than the revenue that goes uncollected.

Not all agreements have to have the same form. Just as there is no such thing as an ideal way to charge, there is no ideal contract. To protect the design firm from the potential loss of income, an appropriate variety of contracts should be developed with the assistance of the firm's attorney. These different agreements should focus on the various kinds of business in which the design firm engages.

"The Statute of Frauds and the UCC require either a written contract or a written memorandum signed by the party against whom enforcement is sought. In other words, any confirmation, invoice, sales slip, check, or telegram can constitute a writing sufficient to satisfy the Statute of Frauds."[3] The only signature required is that of the party being charged.

---

[3]Clarkson 1983, 215. Copyright © West Publishing Co.

Clearly, it is not necessary for the interior designer to have a long formal contract for every sale or service agreement. Sometimes these long agreements actually are detrimental to the negotiation. The client may be reluctant to sign a formal-looking contract for goods or services. In general, however, any memo, letter, even a telegram, or FAX can be considered a legally enforceable contract if it contains the date, identifies the parties involved, details what services are to be provided by the interior designer, what is the charge and the terms of payment, and is signed by the parties, especially the party being charged—the client. Such items as a time limit of the agreement and other terms that seem appropriate are terms up to the discretion of the designer. What must be covered in a contract for the sale of goods will be covered in the next chapter.

Interior Design Contracts: Content and Form

What the final form of a design contract will be is determined from the information obtained in the meetings with the client, the designer's knowledge and experience with similar projects, and the thorough knowledge of the abilities of the design staff of the firm. All three play an important part in what clauses go into the contract and even if a contract is prepared for the client.

Earlier we discussed the minimal form requirements for a contract to be enforceable. Whether the contract is for a residential project or a commercial project, there are certain specific items that should be in the contract to protect both the designer and client.

Before looking at these specific items, it is important to add a few brief comments about letters of agreement. Many designers prefer to use the terminology "letter of agreement" to "contract" stating that the word contract scares many clients. What the designer chooses to call the written agreement outlining design services does not matter. A letter of agreement is a contract but is generally less formal in content. It is a legal contract as long as it spells out the information concerning the offer in sufficient detail so that the courts (if necessary) can determine the nature and facts of the offer and agreement. In fact, the simple statements, "ABC Designs agrees to prepare the plans and specifications for the remodeling of the family room for Mr. James Madison. The charge for these services will be $35 per hour," if it is dated and signed by the client and the designer, constitutes a legal contract. (The author strongly cautions, however, not to use such simplistic contract language.)

Contracts in residential design projects are often short—only two or three pages—written more as a letter than filled with "legalese." Though these rarely have the length and detail of a contract for a commercial project, both kinds of contract have the same basic parts. Figure 15–3 shows a checklist of what should be in the contract. The first five items will be in almost all contracts regardless of size and type of project. The next six items generally should be covered in a residential contract and certainly in a commercial project contract. Items 12–14 are more specific to commercial projects. The last two items should be in any contract for fees. Each item shall now be thoroughly discussed as they relate to residential and commercial projects noting any differences. These items are discussed in the typical order they would appear in the contract. Refer to Figures 15–4 and 15–5 for sample contracts.

1. *Date.* Contracts must be dated with the day, month, and year.

2. *Client's name and address.* It is very important for the names of the clients obligated to the contract to be clearly stated at the beginning of the contract. In residential design, it is important for the husband's and wife's names to be on the contract and that both sign the contract. This obligates each in the event of divorce, separation, or death of either of the spouses.

In commercial design the name of the person having the authority to contract for the business should be listed, and the contract should be signed by that person. The address of the home office is usually listed here when the business has several locations.

1. Client's name and address
2. Detailed description of project areas
3. Detailed scope of services to be provided
4. Detailed purchasing arrangements
5. Method and payment of compensation
6. Reimbursements for out-of-pocket expenses
7. Charges for extra services
8. Designer responsibility disclaimer
9. Charges and responsibilities of third parties
10. Photographic and publishing rights
11. Termination of contract
12. Responsibilities of the client
13. Ownership of documents
14. Time frame of contract
15. Matters of arbitration
16. Conditions and amount of retainer
17. Signatures

Figure 15–3 Checklist of typical clauses in design contracts.

January 30, 19xx

Mr. and Mrs. John Reed
1551 W. Willow Street
Seattle, Washington

Dear Mr. and Mrs. Reed:

Thank you for meeting with me concerning the redesign of your home. This letter shall serve as a proposal of the professional services we will provide for remodeling the kitchen and family room at your residence on 1551 W. Willow Street.

We will provide the following services:
1. Plan the space, furniture and equipment based on our meeting of June 12.
2. Prepare detailed 1/4-inch scale furniture floor plans of the two rooms as they exist.
3. Prepare detailed 1/4-inch scale preliminary space and furniture floor plans for the remodeling.
4. Develop preliminary selections of materials and furniture.
5. Review the preliminary plans and selections with you.
6. After approval by you of floor plans and selections, we will prepare detailed 1/4-inch scale floor plans, working drawings, and written specifications necessary for construction of the spaces.
7. Review the revised plans and selections with you.
8. Provide counsel and guidance in the selection of necessary contractors to perform the required work.
9. Periodic inspections at your home during the construction to be sure all work is done according to professional standards and the specifications.

The fee for the services described will be _____ . Any work requested but not described in this proposal or was required after your approval has been given, will be over and above the stated fee and will be charged at _____ per hour.

Figure 15–4 Sample design contract for a residential project.

Billing for services shall be in the following manner:

10%   upon signing the contract (retainer)
20%   at the end of the preliminary review meeting
50%   at the completion of the preparation of drawings and specifications
10%   when construction and furniture orders are placed
10%   upon completion of the project

All payments are due ten days after receipt of invoice.

Three sets of drawings and specifications will be provided as part of the base charge. Should you require additional sets of the drawings and specifications, they will be provided at our cost plus 10 percent.

The above base fee does not include client-approved expenses for long-distance telephone calls, out-of-town travel to shop for resources, and special renderings. These charges, if required, will be billed separately at our actual cost plus 10 percent.

As we discussed at our June 12 meeting, we will not be providing any of the furniture or materials required.

We will perform the services described in good faith, but cannot be responsible for the performance, quality, or timely completion of work by others. Further, we shall not be responsible for any changes to the project the client or contractor(s) make without informing the designer.

You are expected to grant reasonable access to the premises for the designer and the designer's agents as well as contractors required to perform the agreed-on work. By signing this proposal, you understand that the peace and privacy of your home may be disrupted for the time required to perform the work.

This proposal may be terminated for any reason by either the client or the designer provided ten days written notice is given. In the event of termination by the client, the client will pay the designer for all work done and expenses due up to the date of termination.

It will be our pleasure to begin your project as soon as we have received a copy of this proposal signed by both of you, and a check for the retainer. We appreciate your selection of our firm for your interiors project and look forward to working with you.

Sincerely yours,

(Interiors Firm Name)

_____   _____
(Design Director)   Mr. John Reed

_____   _____
(Date)   (Date)

                                          _____
                                          Mrs. Betty Reed

                                          _____
                                          (Date)

Figure 15–4 (Continued)

May 21, 19xx

Mid-west Insurance Corp.
5555 North Avenue
Plains, Nebraska

Dear Mr. Graves:

We are pleased to submit the following proposal of professional interior design services for the space planning and interior design of your branch office in Lincoln, Nebraska at
_____ .

SCOPE OF SERVICES

A. Programming and Schematic Design
   1. Meet with you and/or selected members of your staff to determine all requirements that will affect the space planning and interior design of your project.
   2. Obtain floor plans from the architect.
   3. Inventory existing equipment that might be used in the new space plan.
   4. Determine preliminary programming and project objectives as well as budget considerations.
   5. Review all informational findings with the client.
   6. Prepare preliminary schematic layouts.
   7. Develop preliminary furniture, color and materials selections.
   8. Review schematic layouts, selections and sketches with the client.

B. Design Development
   1. Finalize space plans showing locations of walls, furniture, and built-in equipment.
   2. Finalize selections of all materials, finishes, and treatment for furniture, walls, flooring, windows, and ceilings.
   3. Finalize lighting specifications.
   4. Prepare a budget of all interior furnishings.
   5. Prepare presentation boards with representational photos and finish samples.
   6. Present plans, specifications, and presentation boards for the your approval.

C. Contract Documents Phase
   1. After final approval of all space plans, furniture layouts, and product selections, prepare appropriate working drawings and documents for the construction of the space and installation of the interiors. This will include dimensioned floor plans, furniture plans, electrical location plans, reflected ceiling plans, and cabinet shop drawings as needed.
   2. Prepare architectural specifications, as required.
   3. Prepare bid specifications for furniture and other moveable equipment.
   4. Provide information for the preparation of bid specifications for floors, walls, windows, ceilings, and lighting fixture materials or products (bid specification to be written by others).

Figure 15–5 Sample design contract for a commercial office project.

D. Contract Administration Phase
1. Assist you in obtaining competitive bids for furnishings and equipment.
2. Assist you in coordinating the schedule for delivery and installation of the work.
3. Make periodic visits to the job site to ensure that the work is progressing according to the specifications in the bid documents.
4. Supervise installation of furniture and moveable equipment covered in the bid documents.
5. Upon completion of the installation, the designer shall prepare a punch list of items needing attention by the designer or vendors. This will be reviewed with you prior to transmittal to appropriate parties.

TERMS OF COMPENSATION

For the interior design and consultation services outlined above, you will be billed an hourly fee basis of _____ per hour for Senior Designers, _____ per hour for Designers, _____ per hour for Design Assistants, _____ per hour for Draftspersons and _____ per hour for secretarial workers.

We estimate the total fee for the project as outlined will not exceed _____. You will be invoiced monthly for actual hours worked. Payment is due within ten (10) days of receipt of invoice. A late payment charge of 1-1/2 % per month (18% per annum) will be added to invoices thirty days past due.

The total fee is based on a maximum of two revisions after each client review. Work required or requested beyond the two revisions will be charged at the described hourly fees, but will be in addition to the maximum estimate.

Additional services not outlined in this proposal but requested by you or required after client approval results in changes in the project will be billed separately at an hourly rate of _____ .

Fees include provision of three sets of documents for the client's use and six (6) sets of contract documents. Additional sets of contract documents shall be provided at a cost of _____ per set.

REIMBURSABLE EXPENSES

Reimbursable expenses are in addition to the charges detailed above. Such expenses as out-of-town travel and living expenses, long distance telephone charges, special renderings, mock-ups, and reproduction costs other than those detailed shall be billed at actual cost to the designer.
Out-of-town travel in the interest of the project shall only be made with proper notification and approval of the client. At this time, it is estimated that a minimum of three site visits will be necessary during the progress of the project.

GENERAL CONDITIONS

1. The designer shall not be responsible for the quality, workmanship, or appearance of products should you purchase products other than those specified.
2. The designer is not responsible if you, architect, or contractor(s) make changes to the project without notification to the designer.
3. The designer or representatives of the designer reserves the right to photograph the project upon completion.

Figure 15–5 (Continued)

4. This proposal may be terminated by either party upon seven (7) days written notice. In the event of termination by you, you shall pay the designer for all services performed and reimbursable expenses due up to the date of termination.
5. Drawings, specifications, and sample boards, as instruments of service, are the property of the designer. The designer reserves the exclusive copyright to these items and provides them to you for your use on this project only. Any reproduction or reuse of the drawings, specifications, and sample boards without the prior written consent of the the designer is not permitted.
6. The timely completion of this project and the fees quoted is based on the signed return of this proposal to the designer within ten (10) calendar days.
7. Any controversy or claims arising out of or relating to this project or breach thereof, shall be subject to review and settled by arbitration. Arbitration shall be in accordance with the rules of the American Arbitration Association. The decisions of the arbitrator shall be final and binding on both parties.

Approval of this proposal is signified by your signature in the space below. Work will begin on your project when the designer receives a signed copy of this proposal along with a check for a retainer of _____

We would like to thank you for the opportunity to submit this proposal for professional interior design services. We look forward to a set of challenges which we pledge to meet with our best professional efforts and attention.

Sincerely,

Authorized:

West Interior Design, Inc.   _____
                                            (Company)

_____   _____
(Design Director)   (By)

_____   _____
(Date)   (Title)

                                            _____
                                            (Date)

Figure 15–5 (Continued)

3. Detailed description of project areas involved. To avoid confusion and arguments over extra charges, or threats of breach, it is important for the project areas involved to be detailed at the beginning of the contract. In a residential project, this may mean as broad as "your residence at 1234 Hummingbird Lane," which means the designer is responsible for the scope of services to be defined in the contract for the entire house. If the services relate to only the living room, the contract should say that.

A contract for a commercial project needs to be even more specific. If the address of the project is different from the main office, it should be listed. It may be necessary to list the specific area by department or room and even amount of square footage. "The main dining room, foyer, and meeting rooms, but excluding the kitchen of your restaurant at the Harbor Hotel, San Diego," is a clear definition of what rooms in what building will be done on this contract. To say, "your restaurant at the Harbor Hotel," leaves the designer open to a lot of unplanned additional design. Should the client want additional areas to be included or added, a secondary contract may be prepared to cover these areas and the services they require.

4. *Detailed scope of services to be provided.* Services required for a project vary greatly from project to project. So that there is little room for disagreements about doing or not doing something, it is important for the scope of services to be considered thoroughly and spelled out in specific detail. It is best for these services to be outlined in the general order in which they take place and, whenever possible (based on the type of project and in consideration of the fee method), in the phases in which they will take place. Figure 15–6 shows a large range of services that might be required of either a residential or commercial project. Figure 15–7 shows some additional services more common to commercial projects. Only those services that the designer understands are to be performed should be listed in the contract.

One service that should be discussed before going on is on-site supervision requirements. This one service causes considerable misunderstandings between designer and client. To the designer, on-site supervision generally means occasional trips to the job site to be sure that all furniture and furnishings are being installed properly and that all construction is going along as designed. Certain phases of the project will require the designer to be on the job site for substantial periods of time. Other phases will require a short visit once a day or every few days. The client, however, often feels that on-site supervision means that the designer will be on the site all day, every day, seeing to every detail of the construction and installation. For most projects this is, of course, impossible and impractical. How much supervision and what kind—even who in the office or representing the office is to supervise—should be clearly spelled out in the scope of services.

Designers must also be careful of using words such as "supervise" or "manage" in relation to the installation of interior finish materials. Today, some states are requiring that this work be done only by licensed contractors.

1. Interview client
2. Inventory existing furniture
3. Measure job site
4. Obtain architectural plans of job site
5. Consult with architects, contractors, engineers, or others
6. Prepare preliminary space plans
7. Prepare preliminary furniture layouts
8. Prepare preliminary color selections
9. Prepare preliminary furniture and finishes selections
10. Prepare preliminary cost estimates
11. Design custom cabinets or other custom items
12. Prepare preliminary specifications
13. Select accessories and graphics
14. Receive client's preliminary approval
15. Review final furniture layouts
16. Prepare working drawings—partitions
17. Prepare working drawings—mechanical drawings
18. Prepare working drawings—custom designs
19. Prepare texture/sample boards
20. Prepare renderings
21. Receive client approval of final documents
22. Purchase goods
23. Observe trades for construction and installation
24. Supervise furniture installation
25. Complete final walk-through and punch-out

Figure 15–6 Checklist of basic design services.

1. Prepare feasibility studies
2. Interview employees via questionnaires
3. Interview employees (one-on-one)
4. Sign design and specification
5. Prepare bid documents

Figure 15–7 Additional design services typical in commercial projects.

5. *Detailed purchasing arrangements.* This clause should inform the client of the conditions under which the design firm will be selling any products to the client. If the design service is provided by designers on staff of a retail store, the purchasing arrangements will be outlined by store policy.[4] The minimal information that should be covered in this clause is how the client will be charged for furniture and furnishings, the terms of payment, penalties for cancellation of orders, the design firm's responsibilities toward warranties of goods sold, charges for installation, freight, sales tax, delivery costs, and whether or not there is a late payment penalty on the sale of goods.

The clause should also have specific language regarding what happens if the client purchases the goods specified from someone other than the designer. In some cases, the only way the designer is receiving compensation for services is by the sale of goods. If goods are purchased from someone else, the designer would not receive compensation unless this was covered in the contract.

It is also common for all these considerations to be spelled out on the contract for the sale of goods and only a reference to these conditions made in the contract for services. Since many commercial designers and some residential designers specify products only and do not sell the goods to the client, this clause may not even be in the contract.

6. *Method and payment of compensation.* This section details how the designer will be paid for his or her services. It should begin by describing how the design fees will be charged. Remember, there are many different ways of charging. For example, "For the above services, an hourly fee of $50 per hour for project designers, $40 per hour for designers, and $30 per hour for assistants will be charged based on actual hours worked per month." This tells the client exactly how they will be charged. This section should also detail how the client will be billed and whether or not there are any penalties for late payment. Moreover, the section might continue, "You will be billed monthly, based on actual hours worked. Payment is due ten days after receipt of invoice. Late penalties of 1–1/2 percent per month on the unpaid balance will be charged for any invoices thirty days or more overdue."

7. *Reimbursements for out-of-pocket expenses.* *Reimbursable expenses* are those costs that are not part of the design contract but that are made in the interest of completing the project. The most costly reimbursable expense that might be incurred are for out-of-town travel and living expenses or per diem in connection with the project. *Per diem* is a term that means a dollar amount that is allowed to cover hotel, meals, and transportation costs. These expenses are something that the client should pay for, but they should not be part of the design fee. Other typical reimbursable expenses are long-distance telephone calls, postage, blueprinting, computer time, and overtime. Some firms include the cost of renderings, models, and mock-ups as reimbursable expenses.

Most firms charge reimbursable expenses at actual cost. Some however, add a service

---

[4]A signed authorization should be part of this policy so that nothing is ordered or given to the client without his or her signature. Confirmation proposals are discussed in detail in Chapter 22.

charge to the expense. If a service charge is added, this should be clearly stated in the contract.

Many firms only put a clause concerning reimbursable expenses in the contract when they anticipate out-of-town travel, the need for renderings or models, or inordinate amounts of the other kinds of expenses listed. Expenses such as blueprinting, telephone calls, and data processing are often considered costs of doing business and are not charged to the client.

8. *Charges for extra services.* A clause concerning charges for extra services is provided to deal with the situation where the client may request more areas to be done, or more kinds of services to be performed than were outlined in the scope of services. It protects the designer so that he or she will not be required to perform design services for free. It also informs the client as to how additional work can be added to the contract or done at the same time, and how the client will be charged.

This section would also spell out what the situation will be when changes are made by the client to the project after certain phases of work have been completed. If the designer has already received approval for certain phases of the project, and changes are then made by the client, the designer should be compensated for the additional work. For instance, after the space planning was approved by the client and the designer began final drawings, the client decided to add three more offices that had not been originally planned. The designer should be compensated at some reasonable amount for the time it will take him or her to redo the space plan and the final drawings. This kind of clause would allow that to happen.

9. *Designer responsibility disclaimer.* This section would specifically describe any portions of the project for which the designer would not claim responsibility. If the designer were not required to plan the lighting for an interior, he or she should state that the firm claimed no responsibility for the lighting in the finished interior. There are also some kinds of activities that can only be done by licensed professionals. If the law requires that exterior landscaping be planned by a licensed landscape architect, the interior designer should disclaim any responsibility for the design of the exterior landscaping.

Another factor that might be in this section would be the designer's disclaimer if the client purchases products other than those specified. This would protect the designer from potential negligence or product liability suits if the products the client does purchase are not the same as those specified.

A third situation that might be covered under this section involves the designer's not being responsible for changes made by the owner, architect, or contractor without the designers' consent. Should the client or the contractor change the length of an alcove that is to receive a custom-made piece of furniture, the designer should not be responsible for the furniture not fitting if he or she was not informed of the change.

10. *Charges and responsibilities of third parties.* After meeting with the client, the designer should have an idea of whether the project will require the consultation of any third parties such as architects, specialized consultants such as lighting designers and commercial kitchen designers, contractors, or landlords. Although it is possible to calculate these charges into the design contract when they involve short meetings, it is usually safer to make this a separate charge. When a project requires extensive architectural services, the third-party service may be better dealt with as a separate contract between the client and the third party. However, the designer should still charge for the time he or she must spend with the third-party professional. As with item 8, this section might appear in either a contract for a residential or commercial project.

11. *Photographic and publishing rights.* It is unlikely that the designer will wish to photograph or use every project in one of the firm's publications. It should be standard practice, however, to include a clause obtaining permission for all projects. Clients should know up front the designer's intention to use the projects for photography and publication. Some clients may object to having this kind of intrusion. In some commercial installations, it may be against company policy because of security. Often, when clients object to photographing

their living or working quarters, the designer may be able to get permission by not publishing the name of the client. Remember that releases must also be obtained from any recognizable people in the photographs, even if the owner of the space has given permission to photograph the interior.

12. *Termination of contract.* As a means of protection for the designer, a termination clause should be included. This clause is to ensure compensation for services rendered in the event that the project ends for some reason other than by the designer's wishes. If the client runs out of money, cannot take the space, and must end the project, it is important for the designer to be paid for design work that has been prepared. Without this kind of clause, it would be more difficult for the designer to collect. Something like, "In the event the project is terminated through no fault of the designer, the designer will be compensated for all work actually performed." Something more clearly defined, depending on the kind of fee arrangements or exact nature of the project, may be necessary.

13. *Responsibilities of the client.* In many commercial projects there are certain provisions that are important for the client to perform in order for the project to proceed successfully or to be completed with few headaches. These should be outlined in this section. Responsibilities of the client might include providing a place to receive, unpack, and stage products prior to installation on the job site; provide reasonable access to the job-site; designate an employee to be liaison between the designer and the owner; and provide approvals expeditiously. Some of these conditions, such as having access to the job site, may also be important for residential projects.

14. *Ownership of documents.* Many interior designers and other design professionals wish to protect their design ideas from being copied or imitated without fair compensation. It is necessary to put a provision in the contract that warns the client that he or she may not reuse the design ideas without compensating the designer. The designer must copyright his or her design documents as an added protection. Copyright is the legal means of protecting the drawings or plans and specifications that interior designers produce. Something to the effect of, "Documents and specifications are provided for the fair use by the client in completing the project as listed within this contract. Documents and specifications remain the property of the designer and cannot be used or reused without permission of the designer," will clarify the issue. If the designer needs or wishes to use this clause, it would serve him or her to become somewhat familiar with the copyright law so that he or she can answer the questions of the client. Refer back to Chapter 6 for more information on copyright.

15. *Time frame of the contract.* As we saw in the beginning discussion of contracts, the time frame or time limits of a contract is an important part of the offer. Many interior design projects, whether residential or commercial, must work around some time-ending date, usually the move-in date.

A second important date is the time limit that the designer can wait before he or she receives the signed contract in order to complete the project by the move-in date. An example of clause is, "In order to complete the project as specified in the scope of services, the signed contract must be received by the designer no later than June 20, 19xx." This should help the client in making up his or her mind quickly as to whether or not he or she will engage the designer.

Another time frame clause that will appear in many commercial contracts relates to renegotiation of the contract when the contract is expected to last over a long period of time. This is not for the project that extends over more than one year, since this should be taken into consideration when the contract is drawn up. Rather, it concerns those relationships between designer and client where the designer is on a retainer for an extended period of time. In this relationship, design work may be scattered over time and it may be necessary for the design firm to renegotiate a fair increase in its fee every so often.

16. *Matters of arbitration.* In any project where the possibility of disagreement might occur, a clause concerning *arbitration* should be included. This clause would spell out what

would happen in the event that there was disagreement between the parties that could not be resolved. Rather than going to court, an arbitrator (a disinterested third party) would be called in to listen to the arguments of both sides and then render an opinion of what must be done. Both client and designer must agree beforehand to abide by the decision of the arbitrator.

17. *Conditions and amount of retainer.* A *retainer* is an amount of money paid by the client to the designer for professional services work that will be done in the future. The retainer is applied by the designer to the total fee of the project as work progresses. In some ways, the retainer acts as "earnest money" from the client showing his or her good faith in proceeding with the project. The retainer provides operating funds to the designer to purchase the needed production materials and services to begin the design services portion of the project. If a retainer is expected, the amount and when it is due must be spelled out in the contract. It is a good idea also to briefly explain how it will be applied to the total fee. Typically, the retainer clause is at the end of the contract.

A *deposit* (or down payment) is a similar concept, but it is usually applied towards the purchase of furniture and furnishings. Return to Chapter 13 for additional information on down payments and deposits.

18. *Signatures.* Room should be provided for both parties to sign. To enforce the contract, the client only must sign. The client, on the other hand, will want the designer to sign as a token of the designer's good faith.

Each contract, whether for residential or commercial projects, must be developed to suit the individual project. A form or standard contract can be developed to cover almost all contingencies, and then parts can be "cut and pasted" to make the final contract. A word processor makes this very easy.

Standardized contracts can be obtained from ASID, IBD, and AIA. These organizations have prepared contracts that meet the conditions of many normal projects. Space is provided to type in standard information, such as the designer's name and address, and some can be imprinted with the design firm's name. Whatever the final form of the contract, it should be periodically reviewed by the firm's attorney to be sure that the contract meets the conditions of the firm's individual practice.

Now let us look at what constitutes legal performance and termination of a contract.

Performance

A contract terminates when both parties perform the acts or activities promised in the terms of the agreement. Sometimes there is disagreement as to whether or not the terms have been performed. This is especially true when the contract insufficiently specifies the required services. In contract law there are three types of performance: (1) complete, (2) substantial, and (3) performance far below reasonable, resulting in material breach.

For complete performance to be considered, the terms expressed in the agreement must be fully accomplished in the manner in which they are specified in the contract. If a design contract had as one of its terms the provision that "the designer provide a watercolor rendering of the lobby and dining room," the contract would not be complete if either of these renderings was not provided to the client or not done in watercolor. This would be true even if all other terms in the contract were completed. In this case, the client would have grounds to sue for breach of contract if he or she so chooses.

Since it is sometimes impossible to satisfy a party's idea of complete performance, the courts hold that performance is complete if it is done so as to be "substantially complete." Substantial completion means that the performance cannot vary greatly from what was spelled out in the contract. If, in the preceding example, the designer provides a rendering of the spaces in the contract but uses markers as the medium, the court might rule that the term was substantially performed and that the client must pay the designer for the services performed. Note that the substitution of a different medium than was called for does technically constitute a breach of contract.

Performance that is inferior to that which is called for by the terms of the agreement would cause a material breach of contract and would excuse the nonbreaching party from fulfilling his or her obligations in relation to the contract. In our example, should the designer provide only pencil or ink sketches of the areas rather than the watercolor renderings, something has been provided but it is inferior to what was agreed to, a material breach would have occurred. The nonbreaching party would not have to pay agreed-to fees and would be entitled to damages.

The phrase *breach of contract* has been used several times in this section. A breach of contract occurs when one of the parties of the contract does not perform his or her duties as spelled out in the terms of the agreement. If the breach is minor (as when the designer does the renderings in markers rather than watercolor) the client would not be excused from his or her obligation to the designer, but the client would not have to pay until the designer provided the renderings in watercolor or until some other agreement was worked out. If the breach is material (as when the designer only provides pencil sketches rather than watercolor renderings), the client is excused from their contractual agreements and may also be entitled to damages. A material breach takes place when only minor discrepancies from the terms of the contract occur allowing the remainder of the contract to be completed. A decision of a material breach terminates the agreement when major or material ones occur.

A breach of a contract can occur easily, especially if the designer has not been careful in the preparation of the terms of the agreement. And, in fact, it is generally easier for the interior designer to breach the contract than it is for the client. It is extremely important for the designer to understand the scope of the project, and what the terms of the agreement are so that the designer does not leave himself or herself open to a breach.

A type of remedy related to breach of contract is specific performance. *Specific performance* is an equitable remedy where the court requires the breaching party to perform what was required in the contract. As it relates to breach of contract, the party that breached the contract would be ordered to perform whatever was required in the contract that he or she so far has not done. The nonbreaching party would generally be satisfied with specific performance since it requires that what was bargained for actually be done. It is most likely to be applied only if the monetary damages are insufficient to satisfy the party who was breached. However, courts are reluctant to apply specific performance to service contracts since such application requires the courts to force someone to perform a specific service.[5]

Termination by Agreement

Contracts can be terminated by agreement. We saw in a preceding section, where we discussed the termination of contract clause, how the designer seeks to protect himself or herself if something occurs that is not the designer's fault. It is not necessary for there to be such a clause in the contract for the contract to be terminated by agreement.

It is possible at any time for the contract to be terminated if both sides agree to the termination. If a clause does not exist in the original contract, it would be necessary for a second contract dealing with the terms of the termination to be written as a protection to both parties. An oral agreement to terminate the contract is not advisable. All terminations by agreement, regardless of who initiated the termination, should be spelled out in writing.

---

[5]Jentz 1987, 227.

Summary

The major portion of what the interior designer does for clients can be covered by contracts of one sort or another. Too often, designers have caused themselves a loss of fees as a result of their failure to understand what constitutes a contract, to prepare one properly, or to have one at all. The professional designer must realize that in order to protect himself or herself, he or she must insist on the preparation of contracts. The designer must also get the contract signed by the client before beginning design work. Regardless of the designer's enthusiasm to do a project, today the professional designer should not undertake a design project nor order goods for clients until the appropriately prepared contract has been signed by the client.

This chapter has described in a general sense what legally constitutes a contract and a contractual relationship. It then covered the kinds of clauses commonly found in an interior design contract. The chapter may not answer all the questions or special needs; therefore, the designer should discuss the matter and form of contracts with an attorney. Although most attorneys understand contract law, few understand the interior design, architecture, and construction professions. Ideally, work with an attorney who is familiar with the design industry. More information on contracts and contract law can be found in the References. A course in business law that emphasizes contracts would also provide additional material for study.

References

Alderman, Robert L. 1982. *How to Make More Money at Interior Design.* New York: Whitney Communications Corporation.

Barnes, A. James. 1981. *A Guide to Business Law.* Homewood, Ill.: Learning Systems.

Clarkson, Kenneth W., Roger LeRoy Miller, Gaylord A. Jentz. 1983. *West's Business Law, Text and Cases,* 2d ed. St. Paul, Minn.: West Publishing.

_____. 1989. *West's Business Law, Text and Cases,* 4th ed. St. Paul, Minn.: West Publishing.

Cushman, Robert F., James C. Dobbs, eds. 1991. *Design Professional's Handbook of Business and Law.* New York: Wiley.

Davidson, Marion, and Martha Blue. 1979. *Making It Legal.* New York: McGraw-Hill.

Jentz, Gaylord A., Kenneth W. Clarkson, and Roger LeRoy Miller. 1987. *West's Business Law—Alternate UCC Comprehensive Edition,* 3d ed. St. Paul, Minn.: West Publishing.

Loebelson, Andrew. 1983. *How to Profit in Contract Design.* New York: Interior Design Books.

Neubert, Christopher, and Jack Withiam, Jr. 1980. *How to Handle Your Own Contracts,* rev. ed. New York: Greenwich House.

Shenson, Howard L. 1990. *The Contract and Fee-Setting Guide for Consultants and Professionals.* New York: Wiley.

Siegel, Harry, and Alan M. Siegel. 1982. *A Guide to Business Principles and Practices for Interior Designers,* rev. ed. New York: Watson-Guptill.

Stasiowski, Frank. 1985. *Negotiating Higher Design Fees.* New York: Watson-Guptill.

Sweet, Justin. 1985. *Legal Aspects of Architecture, Engineering, and the Construction Process,* 3d ed. St. Paul, Minn.: West Publishing.

Chapter 16

The Sale of Goods and the Uniform Commercial Code

The sale of goods involves the transfer of title for goods from one party to another. Before this transfer can take place, one party must make an offer to buy or sell the goods while another party must accept the offer to buy or sell. This transferring of ownership of goods is covered within a section of law called the law of sales. To guide the relationships between the various levels of buyers and sellers within the law of sales is the function of the Uniform Commercial Code (UCC). The law of sales, as represented by Article 2 of the UCC, governs the sale of goods (not services), real property (real estate), or intangible property (such as stocks).

For the majority of the members of the interior design profession, selling and ordering goods for clients is an everyday occurrence. In speaking to many professional designers during the research for this book, the author has found that although some may have heard of the UCC, few designers know that it is the area of law that regulates the sale of goods.

The Code is important for those new to the profession as well as to professionals who do not really understand the legal ramifications of selling merchandise. This chapter is not meant to be an in-depth discussion of the Code. The section of the Code that deals with sales is quite extensive. We will, however, attempt to provide some basic understanding regarding how the Code affects the daily work of the interior designer who engages in the sale of goods.

History

Most laws related to commercial business activity come from the individual states. During the early years of this country, this fact often resulted in confusing and conflicting laws. As the nation's commercial business activity became more complex, the problems became more acute.

In the late 1800s, the National Conference of Commissioners on Uniform State Laws was established to create uniform statutes related to business activities. These statutes, revised over the next 55 years, helped to illuminate many of the problems of commercial business. Yet there remained instances when these uniform statutes overlapped. Work was begun in

1945 to revise all the statutes into one uniform document. In 1957, after much work, the Uniform Commercial Code was completed.[1]

The purpose of the code is to help "state legal relationships of the parties in modern commercial transactions. The Code is designed to help determine the intentions of the parties to a commercial contract and to give force and effect to their agreement."[2]

The code consists of 10 articles:

1. General provisions

2. Sales

3. Commercial paper

4. Bank deposits and collections

5. Letters of credit

6. Bulk transfers

7. Documents of title

8. Investment securities

9. Secured transactions

10. Effective date and repealer

This chapter will be limited to a discussion of sections of Article 2.

The UCC has been adopted by all states except Louisiana. This state has only adopted certain sections of the Code. Since 1958, certain sections of the Code have been revised to meet current needs and to refine the statutes. The following discussion is based on the 1989 revision.

Definitions

The interpretation of the statutes stated in Article 2 vary depending on whether the buyer of goods is an end-user (customer) or a merchant. It is therefore necessary to define some common terms as they relate to the Code. Although there are many definitions in the Code, the main ones we wish to look at here are for *goods, sale, seller, merchant, buyer,* and *price.*

Goods are any item that is tangible—that is, has physical existence—and is movable. Furniture and accessories are tangible goods. The sale of tangible goods is covered by the UCC. Items such as carpet, wall coverings, and window treatments are goods because they do have physical existence, but when these items are permanently attached to a home or building, they are now generally considered real property. Or are they? The sale of the merchandise itself from the supplier to the designer and the designer to the client would be covered by the UCC since the goods do not become real property until they are "permanently" attached to the structure. If the client later wants to remove these goods from his or her home or office and sell them or even sell the building with the merchandise intact, the sale would be governed by real estate law.

A *sale* has occurred when the seller transfers title or ownership of the goods to a buyer and the buyer has provided some consideration to the seller. Whenever the designer agrees in good faith to sell a piece of furniture to a client for some amount of money, and the client

---

[1]Stone 1975, 2.
[2]Clarkson 1983, 9. Copyright © West Publishing Co.

takes delivery of the furniture and sends the designer a check for the agreed-upon price, a sale has occurred. There are, however, some special considerations with regard to when "ownership" actually occurs.

A *seller* is anyone who sells goods or agrees to sell goods. The interior designer, selling goods to clients, would be considered a seller. It should be pointed out that a manufacturer who sells goods to the interior designer could also be considered a seller. However, both the interior designer and the manufacturer are considered "merchants."

A *merchant* is anyone who is involved with the buying and/or selling of the kinds of goods with which he or she is dealing. In other words, "a person is a merchant when that person, acting in a mercantile capacity, possesses or uses an expertise specifically related to the goods being sold."[3] Thus, although the interior designer who sells a personally owned stereo to a friend is a seller, when he or she sells a chair to that same friend and that sale occurs through the business, the designer is now considered a merchant.

Many interior designers who sell goods never have a showroom, warehouse, or installation crew as employees of the firm. Any interior designer, however, who purchases goods— whether or not through a firm's inventory account—and resells them to a client so that the purchase and resale "pass through" the design firm's books, is a merchant.

A person becomes a *buyer* when he or she contracts to purchase or purchases some goods. A buyer also is someone who buys from one who is in the business of selling goods. A client purchasing a sofa from an interior designer is a buyer. Is the interior designer a buyer when he or she purchases the sofa for the client? Yes, and the designer is protected by the same rights as the end-user as long as the purchase is from a seller whose business it is to sell the sofa.

Finally, *price* can be any kind of payment from buyer to seller including money, goods, services, or real property. Therefore it is possible, for example, for a client to offer to trade his or her own professional services as the price of a sofa.

The Sales Contract

For the most part, the statutes related to the sale of goods as covered by the UCC generally follow the principles of contract law. That means that an offer to sell something must be made, an acceptance to buy the goods must occur, and proper consideration must be exchanged from buyer to seller. This section will look at how "offer," "acceptance," and "consideration" occur in sales law.

As discussed in Chapter 15 on contracts, the Statute of Frauds contains a provision that the sale of goods with a value of over $500 must be in writing to be enforceable. This provision is contained within section 2–201(1). Although a written contract for the sale of goods does not mean the designer will force the client to take the goods, it gives the designer the legal right to sue for payment if he or she so chooses.

Offer (Section 2–204, 2–205, 2–206, 2–305, 2–308, and 2–311)

Normally, a contract exists when an offer is followed by an acceptance. In sales law, however, the nature of offers and acceptances, renders the point at which a contract exists more inexact. Because offers and acceptances in sales contracts are exchanged verbally, through the mails, and by the conduct of the buyer and seller, it is more difficult to determine exactly when a contract exists. To assist with this problem, the UCC in section 2–204 states that a

---

[3]Jentz 1987, 244. Copyright © West Publishing Co.

contract exists when there is sufficient agreement to an offer to consider a contract to be formed. This agreement may be verbal, written, or by the actions of the parties.

In contract law, the terms of the offer and acceptance must be clearly stated before the contract can be effective. Because of the unusual circumstances that surround offers and acceptances in sales law, the UCC allows for the offer to be valid even if one or more terms of the agreement are not stated, provided that the parties intend to go through with the contract and the courts can agree that a contract was intended and can determine a remedy for breach.

Open Terms Provisions—An Introduction

There are provisions that allow the contract to be valid even if some of the terms of the contract are indefinite. Terms include quantity, description, part number, delivery location, payment, and price. In general, if the terms are incomplete, it is likely that the contract will still be valid as long as it can be shown that both parties intend to fulfill the contract. However, the more terms left incomplete, the more difficult it will be for the courts to determine if the contract is valid. For example, should a designer order some tables and all the terms needed in the purchase order are present except the finish of the wood, the order would still be valid. However, when the quantity is missing, the order is usually considered invalid as the courts cannot determine the full value of the contract to establish a remedy.

Open Price Term

If the price is missing, the other party can cancel the offer or determine a reasonable price. For example, should ABC Design Company agree to furnish drapery tiebacks for a client, but forget to provide a price for those tiebacks, the client can either set a reasonable price for the items or cancel the order for the tiebacks.

Open Payment Term

A third open term related to offers is an open payment term. If it has not been specified when payment for the goods will be due, the UCC stipulates that payment will be due upon delivery to the buyer or at the time of "receipt of goods." The buyer receives the goods when he or she takes physical possession of the goods. Additionally, if payment terms are not specified, the payment must be in cash, check, or agreed-upon credit.

For the client, receipt of goods takes place when the goods are delivered to his or her home or office or when the client leaves the designer's place of business with the goods. According to subsections 2–310 (b and c), receipt of goods shipped from a manufacturer to the designer occurs when the goods are placed in the hands of the carrier. This is the reason that invoices often arrive prior to the goods. However, this means that payment is due before the goods can be inspected. All buyers have the right to inspect the goods before they must make payment. These same subsections provide for that right of inspection, but the inspection must be done promptly. If the goods are not as ordered, the seller must be notified immediately for the buyer not to be bound to payment.

Open Delivery Term

If the location for the delivery has been omitted, it is customary that delivery be made at the seller's business location. This could be quite costly to the designer in the supplier/designer relationship since it would be the designers' responsibility to pick up the goods from the seller. It is unlikely that major manufacturers of goods would not call to check with the designer as to a delivery location.

Section 2–307 states that delivery and payment are due at one time for all the items being sold unless provisions in the agreement or "circumstances" allow for delivery and payment in lots. The designer should have as a term on his or her purchase order that informs the supplier whether shipment of less than the full order is acceptable. For large-sized projects involving multiple items, it is not unusual for the client to want the goods delivered as soon as they arrive. The designer would like to deliver the goods to the client promptly to keep cash flow operating smoothly. However, in order to receive payments for goods delivered in lots rather than as a whole, a term in the sales contract must be provided to notify the buyer of this fact. Without a written term in the contract, payment would not be required until the entire order is delivered even though several deliveries are made to complete one order.

The Firm Offer

Normally, in contract law, an offer to sell or buy goods has a time limit. That time limit can be set by the offerer. If the offer is not in writing, or not accompanied with payment by the offeree (buyer), the offer can be revoked by the seller at any time before the buyer can accept. However, in sales law, special provisions are made when the seller is a merchant and apply whether the buyer is a merchant or an end-user. If the merchant makes an offer in writing, whether or not consideration has been given by the buyer, or a time limit to the offer has been set, the merchant cannot revoke the offer either during the time limit or for a reasonable time. In this situation, a *firm offer* has been made. For example, Mary Smith signs a written contract to sell $30,000 of furniture to a client, but the client does not sign the agreement and does not provide any down payment. Ten days later, Mary realizes that she made an error in her calculations. If the client accepts the contract, Mary would lose $2000, since she used a net price list to discount some of the goods. Legally, Mary cannot revoke the offer since it was a "firm offer" in writing and signed by her.

The points in this discussion are important to the interior design practice. They show the value of good paperwork preparation of the specification list, the contract for the client, and purchase orders. Designer omissions can cost time and money. They could even allow for lawsuits against the designer.

Acceptance (Section 2–206 and 2–207)

In most situations, the offerer (the seller) establishes the way that acceptance can be made. If acceptance is not made in the manner specified, the acceptance can be rejected or considered a counteroffer. However, the law generally allows the acceptance to be valid if it is received within the time limit set, even if by a different method of acceptance. Usually the seller would want an oral acceptance followed by a signed acceptance of the sales proposal.

In the designer/end-user relationship, there are usually few problems or questions related to the existence of the contract. This is because, in everyday practice, the designer prepares a confirmation proposal that states who is being charged; lists the quantities, descriptions, and prices of the items being sold; lists the terms of sale such as when payment is due; and then requires the signature of the client on the confirmation. Assuming price is not an issue, rarely does the client make acceptance in any way other than by signing the confirmation. And rarely does the client propose other terms to the sale, thus making a counteroffer.

A key to the agreement between designer/client would be the time limit of the offer and whether or not the client signs the agreement. If the designer's proposal states that the offer is only good for ten days, the client must respond within that ten-day period. If he or she does not, the designer does not legally have to honor the original offer. If there is no time limit, the client has a "reasonable time" to respond. For example, a month after receiving the proposal, the client signs and returns the confirmation. However, the price of the goods to the designer increased during that time. The designer may very well be expected to sell the goods at the quoted price, thus lowering his or her profit margin. Thus, it is important that all offers to sell goods to clients have stated on the confirmation a time limit for acceptance.

The major concerns of acceptance in the UCC relate to the merchant/merchant relationship. Acceptances between merchants become more complicated since offers and acceptances can occur many ways. The most common method for offers to buy and sell merchandise occurs through the mail via the use of purchase orders and acknowledgments. Many designers still insist on telephone orders, although this is not advisable.

In contract law, a contract exists only if all the terms of the offer are exactly matched by the acceptance. Any differences constitute a counteroffer. In sales law it is not uncommon among merchants for the terms on the purchase order and the terms of the acknowledgment to have some differences. In interior design practice, the quantity, description, and price commonly match. Terms such as ship date and general terms of the sale often vary. The UCC allows for a contract to be formed when the conditions of the purchase order and acknowledgment are different, as long as the offeree's response indicates a definite acceptance to the original terms of the offer and there are no conditional terms in the offer or acceptance. For example, designer A sends a purchase order to manufacturer B for some custom-made bedspreads. The purchase order is prepared following the instructions in the catalog. The acknowledgment comes back from B with the statement "on condition that a 50 percent deposit be submitted within ten days of receipt of acknowledgment. No work will be started until deposit is received." If this term is not stated in the catalog, no contract exists unless the buyer agrees, because the seller has added a condition to the terms of the offer.

When the differences in terms are minor, and neither party objects to the differences, a contract is formed. If the offer and acceptance is made over the phone, the printed confirmation and acknowledgments are proposals to the oral contract and, again, a contract is formed as long as no objections are made and the differences are minor.

What all this means to the designer is that he or she must not only carefully prepare the terms of sale on his or her purchase order, but he or she must also be familiar with terms and conditions of sale from all the suppliers. What is ordered is usually not the problem in interior design orders. The price, ship dates, warranties, and payment terms are more often the issue. Chapter 24 contains an example of the terms and conditions on the back of a firm's sales order (see Figure 24–3).

Should the acknowledgment contain discrepancies in quantities, descriptions, and so on, it is important for the designer to make prompt written notification of the errors to the supplier. Failure to do so means acceptance of the acknowledgment, hence a contract, and the designer will "own" the merchandise even if the error is made by the supplier.

If there are material differences between the designer's purchase order terms and a supplier's acknowledgment terms, the designer may be protected by the UCC constraints against material differences. *Material differences* means substantial or essential changes to the original. However, to be protected, the designer is encouraged to object in writing to any terms different from his or her own.

Consideration

In general, the UCC does not differ with the general contract law precept that consideration must be part of the acceptance. Between designer and client that consideration is primarily a downpayment paid upon signing the agreement and the belief the client will pay full value at a later time. Between designer and supplier, consideration is generally the good-faith credit that the supplier affords to the designer knowing that the designer will pay the supplier after the goods are shipped.

There are strict rules governing consideration when the buyer or seller attempts to modify the contract. For example, after the designer sends the purchase order to the supplier and the supplier acknowledges the order to the designer, but merchandise is not yet shipped, the supplier informs the designer that the price will go up 10 percent as a result of an increase in materials price. The designer subsequently notifies the supplier that he or she accepts the increase. Later, the designer changes his or her mind and says that he or she will only pay the original price. Whether or not the designer accepts the increase orally or in writing, he or she will be bound by the new price. This is true as long as it can be shown by the supplier that the change in price was due to a reason such as a change in availability of materials to manufacture the finished goods causing an increase in price for the finished goods. If the supplier makes a mistake in his or her pricing, the modification of the contract would be invalid.

What this means is that once the terms and conditions are agreed to between the designer and supplier, later modifications agreed to are binding if they are reasonable as a result of something beyond the control of the party asking for the modifications. If the supplier later tells the designer that the price will be higher and the designer does not agree, the contract is revoked. If the original or modified contract must meet the statute of frauds or has a condition that changes must be in writing, these changes must be in writing to be valid.

Statute of Frauds

Although section 2–201 in the code is very specific about a contract for the sale of goods over $500 being in writing to be valid, there are certain exceptions as stated in subsections of 2–201.

First, between merchants, an oral agreement would be valid if one party sends the other party a signed confirmation outlining the details of the agreement. The receiving merchant has ten days to respond in writing to any conditions or content of the offer to which he or she does not agree. Failure to respond within the ten days forms a valid contract.

Second, an oral contract for the special manufacture of goods that would not be suitable for anyone else, and whose manufacture has substantially been started, forms a contract. For example, Mary Jones Designs places a telephone order to Smith's Drapery Company for the manufacture of ten different-sized arched miniblinds at a price of over $800. A month later, after production is started but not finished, the client cancels the order and Mary Jones calls to cancel the order. If it is unlikely that the blinds can be sold to another client of Smith's Drapery Company, Mary Jones Designs would be liable. It is for this reason that designers include in the terms of their confirmations, a statement that a restocking charge, say at least 25 to 50 percent, is charged for any order the client cancels.

A third case would be if one party to the contract admits in court or in legal proceedings that a contract did exist, then an oral contract would be binding for what was admitted. For example, Robert Class placed a telephone order for 50 yards of Wilton weave carpet from an English mill. The value of that carpet was $4000. The mill shipped 500 yards. Class refused the shipment, and the mill sued. Class admits in court that he ordered 50 yards of carpet. Since Class admits that an oral contract did exist, he would be liable to pay for the 50 yards of carpet.

Last, an oral agreement is enforceable up to the amount of payment made and accepted or the amount of goods delivered and accepted. For example, if a designer makes a verbal contract to order miniblinds for a client, and the client provides the designer with a deposit, the client is liable to pay for and accept the quantity of blinds the deposit covers. If the designer delivers a portion of the order for the blinds, the client is also liable for the value of the blinds that are delivered.

Far too many designers agree to sell goods to clients and/or order goods for clients without a written contract. The designer placing orders for clients without the client signing a confirmation may not have legal recourse if the client later refuses delivery. If the designer fails to send a confirming order to the manufacturer, the manufacturer may not be bound to a sale. And, the designer failing to read an acknowledgment for an oral agreement will be obliged to accept whatever was orally agreed to.

Title

When goods are bought and sold, ownership of those goods changes from seller to the buyer. In legal terms that ownership is called *title*. For a sale to take place, goods must exist and be identified in the contract. Section 4 of the UCC clarifies the law related to the title of goods.

Title passes in several ways. The most common way is at the time and place the physical delivery of the goods is performed by the seller to the buyer. When the designer buys from a manufacturer, title often passes by use of a shipment contract. In this case, title passes to the buyer at the time the seller turns over the goods to some shipper. A third way title passes is by a destination contract. A destination contract states that the manufacturer turns over the goods to a shipper but the title does not pass to buyer until the goods arrive at the buyer's destination.

Risk

It is very common between merchants that title passes either through a shipping or a destination contract. Title passes to the client when the goods are physically delivered to his or her home or business location. Since title can change at differing times, the Code must address who is liable for the risk of loss during the movement of the goods. Shipping of goods is governed by the UCC in sections 2–319 through 2–323.

FOB (free on board)[4] is a term used in conjunction with a destination to indicate where title passes and who has the risk of loss should the goods be damaged in transit. In a shipment contract (FOB factory warehouse), the risk for loss is transferred to the buyer when goods are passed to the carrier. If the goods are damaged before arriving at the buyer's location, it is the buyer's responsibility to recover damages from the carrier. In destination contracts (FOB destination) the risk for loss is transferred to the buyer at the buyer's destination. If the goods are damaged in transit, it is the seller's responsibility to recover the damages from the carrier. (Additional discussions concerning FOB can be found in Chapters 13 and 24.)

Sales on Approval

A common special-sale situation in the interior design profession is the sale on approval. Simply, the client is not sure about a product and takes it to his or her home or business location to see if it is appropriate. If the client subsequently keeps the product, he or she pays for it. If the client does not, the product is returned.

There is a normal condition to the sale on approval regulated by the UCC that is explained by the following example. Mrs. Miller finds a sofa on a showroom floor, but is just not sure it will go with her decor. She asks if she could try it "on approval." The store allows her five days to decide. If she calls and says she will keep the sofa before the five days are up, or fails to call before the five days and makes no attempt to return the sofa, the store will consider the sofa as sold and send her a bill. Should Miller damage the sofa before the five days, and before she approves of the sale, the loss would be Miller's. If it were damaged in transit or some way, but not by fault of Miller, the loss would be the seller's (section 2–326 and 2–327).

The Seller's Rights and Obligations

Sellers are always concerned that the buyer will cancel the order or want to change the order after it has been placed. Designers as sellers should protect themselves from these problems by having clauses in the sales agreement that stipulates under what conditions an order can be canceled or changed. Many designers indicate that restocking charges will be assessed if

---

[4]As noted in Chapter 13, FOB can also mean "freight on board."

the client cancels an order. This *restocking charge* is a fee to cover the paperwork costs that have already been accumulated as well as a small penalty for taking back merchandise the client may not want.

The seller has other rights when the buyer refuses to accept the goods or in some other way breaches the sales contract. One of the important rights relates to a client becoming insolvent while he or she has taken delivery but not yet paid for the goods. If this happens, the designer has the right to demand the return of the goods. This must be done quickly, however. The written demand for the return of the goods usually must be done within ten days of delivery of the goods.

Another situation involves partial deliveries to clients. For example, Mrs. Randolph ordered new dining room and living room furniture from Smyth's Interiors. Smyth's delivered the living room furniture, but the dining room items were not in. Since the goods were delivered, Smyth's billed Mrs. Randolph for the partial delivery. Mrs. Randolph refused to pay the bill. If the terms and conditions on the sales contract from Smyth's Interiors stated that partial deliveries would be billed separately, then Mrs. Randolph would be in breach of contract. Smyth's could withhold delivery of the other furniture items until Randolph paid for the previous delivery.

Another frequent problem for designers is when a client will claim that the items delivered are not those specified in the sales agreement. Most frequently, this concerns a color of fabric. Let us say that New Age Foods ordered 50 forest green upholstered chairs. When the chairs were delivered, New Age Foods claimed that the chairs were not the right color green and refused to accept and pay for the goods. If the designer can show that the fabric was substantially the correct color (barring anything greater than a dye lot variation), the buyer would be in breach of contract to refuse acceptance of the order. The designer, on written notification, would have a right to cancel the order and could sue the client as well for the breach. However, if the designer is not justified in canceling the order, the buyer can sue the designer for breach of contract.

The seller has an obligation to deliver the goods described in the sales agreement to the client within specified time periods. In most situations, any discrepancy in what was delivered versus what was ordered is the responsibility of the seller. Designers must protect themselves from the potentiality of a buyer trying to cancel an order, refuse an order, or refuse to pay for goods. This can be done by being very careful in writing up the descriptions of the goods on sales orders, getting the buyer's signature on the sales order, carefully preparing purchase orders, and checking on the progress of orders. If the delivered goods are as described, the buyer knows what was to be ordered and knows the terms and conditions of the sale, the buyer has no choice but to pay for the goods. Figure 16–1 lists some hints on how to avoid problems in selling goods.

The Buyer's Rights and Obligations

If the seller has delivered the goods that were described in the sales contract, the buyer has an obligation to pay for those goods. Because of this obligation, it is important for the designer to describe what was to be ordered on the sales agreement in sufficient detail so that the client clearly understands what he or she is purchasing. If the sales agreement stated "one 30 × 60 desk," there is a lot of room for argument on both sides as to whether the "right desk" was actually delivered. However, if the sales order stated "one Stowe-Davis, Number 3060DP, 30 × 60 double pedestal desk; finish, walnut; trim, polished chrome," there is very little disagreement as to what was to be ordered. Any modification in what was delivered versus what was described gives the buyer the right to refuse the delivery. If the delivered goods are as described in the sales agreement, they are referred to as conforming goods. If the goods are somehow different, they are nonconforming goods. *Nonconforming goods* are simply any goods that are not as described in an order.

* Fully describe on the sales agreement the goods to be ordered and sold.
* Do not process any purchase orders until the client has signed the sales agreement.
* Be sure to go over the terms and conditions on your sales agreement with each new client and whenever a client orders goods from the firm.
* Obtain credit reports on all new customers.
* Obtain client signatures or initials approving all goods that might be questioned, such as upholstered furniture items.   Request samples of current fabric dye-lots when necessary.
* Be sure that the terms and conditions concerning the client's right to cancel an order are clear and protect the design firm. Be certain the designers also explain the client's legal rights to cancel an order.
* Be sure that you work with manufacturers and suppliers who provide reputable service and goods. Understand the terms and conditions of sale from every supplier with whom the firm does business.
* Keep the client informed of the progress of all special orders.
* Inspect all merchandise at the time of delivery to the firm's warehouse. Make sure this is done prior to paying the supplier in full.
* Insist that the client signs-off on all goods delivered to the client. Take care of any discrepancies immediately so that the client has little room to argue for nonpayment.

Figure 16–1 Tips that may help the designer avoid problems when selling goods.

The buyer is also obligated to make payment for the delivered conforming goods in accordance to the terms in the sales agreement. If the terms were cash payment upon delivery, the designer will expect the client to provide cash or a check. Should the terms have been a credit purchase, the buyer will be expected to make payment within the time frame indicated in the sales agreement. C.O.D. (cash on delivery) shipments are valid only if C.O.D. shipment was agreed to in the sales contract.

The buyer also has a right to inspect the goods prior to paying. When the designer sells goods to the client, the client has the right to inspect the items to be sure that the delivered goods are those specified in the sales agreement. If they are nonconforming goods, the buyer has the right to refuse the goods (or any part of the order that is nonconforming) and not pay for the nonconforming goods. Designers purchasing goods for the client also have the right to inspect the goods prior to paying the supplier. Even though it is common for the manufacturer to send a bill for goods prior to the designer receiving the goods, the designer has a right to inspect and verify that the order was correct prior to being obligated to paying for the goods. According to the UCC, this right is absolute for all buyers except for C.O.D. orders. This is just one reason that it is very important for the designer to check all deliveries from manufacturers and suppliers.

Should the buyer reject the goods as nonconforming, the buyer must promptly notify the seller of the same. Written notification with a full description of what the problems were is the best way to provide notification. If the buyer does not provide notice and retains the goods, the seller will expect the buyer to pay for those goods. The longer the goods are in the hands of the buyer, the more likely the buyer will be obligated to pay for the goods even if they are nonconforming. If the buyer rejects some or all of the goods as nonconforming but uses the goods without prior agreement from the seller, the buyer is taking "ownership" of the goods and the seller will legally expect the buyer to pay for the goods. State laws generally allow buyers a 72-hour *right of refusal*. In some states, this is called a three-day right of cancellation. This means that, even if the goods are as ordered, the buyer has 72 hours in which to return the goods and receive full repayment. The exact conditions of the right of refusal vary by state.

Although many companies have the philosophy that "the customer is always right," according to sales law that is not necessarily true. Designers who will be buying and selling goods need to understand not only their rights as a seller, but the rights of buyers as well.

Summary

Selling goods to clients is often a profitable way of producing revenues for the interior design practice. But the buying and selling of goods also has many legal considerations and constraints. Although it is easy, in fact, to pick up the phone and order a dozen chairs or write a purchase order for those same chairs, there are many regulations that govern legally how that order can be placed, how ownership of the goods changes hands, and what responsibility the seller has to the buyer concerning defects or injury that might be caused by the goods.

In this chapter we have tried to explain the basic concepts of the law of sales, as regulated by the Uniform Commercial Code (UCC). We have defined basic terms related to sales and selling, discussed how a sales contract is made, and noted how a sales contract is different from a normal contract. We have also briefly discussed the statute of frauds, explained when title and risk passes from the seller to the buyer, and noted the responsibility of the seller and buyer in selling goods.

Although the UCC standardizes most of the laws related to the sale of goods, the designer must still check with the firms' attorney to know which part of the code is valid in his or her state and if there are any state or city regulations that supersede the UCC.

References

Clarkson, Kenneth W., Roger LeRoy Miller, and Gaylord A. Jentz. 1983. *West's Business Law, Text and Cases,* 2d ed. St. Paul, Minn.: West Publishing.

Cushman, Robert F., and James C. Dobbs, eds. 1991. *Design Professional's Handbook of Business and Law.* New York: Wiley.

Jentz, Gaylord A., Kenneth W. Clarkson, and Roger LeRoy Miller. 1987. *Wests Business Law— Alternate UCC Comprehensive Edition,* 3d ed. St. Paul, Minn.: West Publishing.

Quinn, Thomas M. 1991. *Quinn's Uniform Commercial Code Commentary and Law Digest,* 2d. ed., vol. 1. Boston, Mass.: Warren, Gorham and Lamont.

Stone, Bradford. 1975. *Uniform Commercial Code in a Nutshell.* St. Paul, Minn.: West Publishing.

Sweet, Justin. 1985. *Legal Aspects of Architecture, Engineering, and the Construction Process,* 3d ed. St. Paul, Minn.: West Publishing.

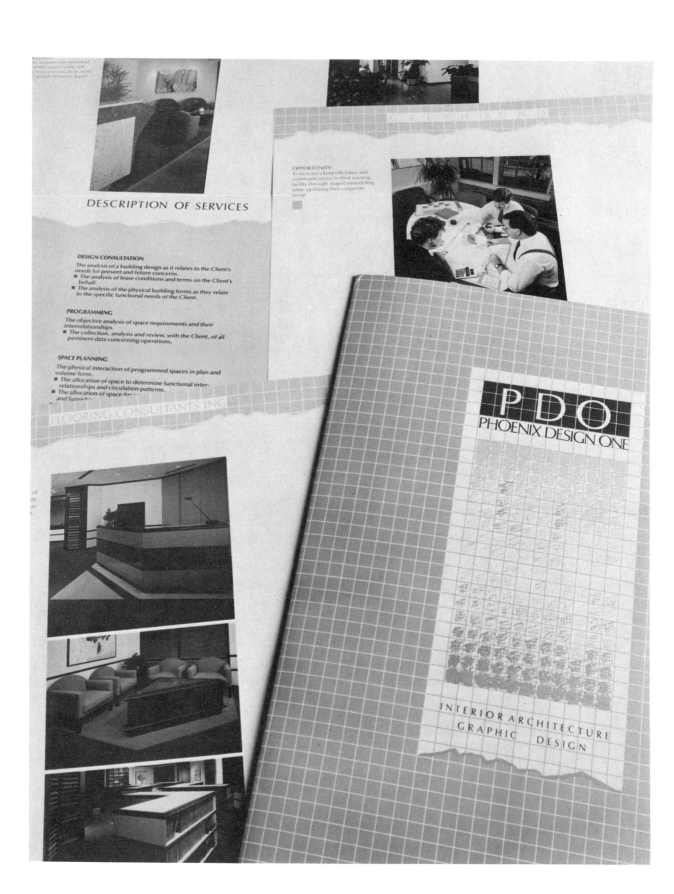

DESCRIPTION OF SERVICES

DESIGN CONSULTATION

The analysis of a building design as it relates to the Client's needs for present and future concerns.
- The analysis of lease conditions and terms on the Client's behalf.
- The analysis of the physical building forms as they relate to the specific functional needs of the Client.

PROGRAMMING

The objective analysis of space requirements and their interrelationships.
- The collection, analysis and review, with the Client, of all pertinent data concerning operations.

SPACE PLANNING

The physical interaction of programmed spaces in plan and volume form.
- The allocation of space to determine functional inter-relationships and circulation patterns.
- The allocation of space for and furnishing

OPPORTUNITY
To increase client efficiency and communications in their existing facility through staged remodeling, while updating their corporate image.

P D O
PHOENIX DESIGN ONE

INTERIOR ARCHITECTURE
GRAPHIC DESIGN

Marketing and Business Development

Marketing Interior Design Services

Although many interior designers are fortunate enough to obtain prospects or commissions from referrals and previous clients, more and more design firms are planning to market their design services. An important reason for this increasing interest in marketing design services is the expanding competition design firms now face. Many designers previously working for someone have opened new offices in new market areas. Architects and office furniture dealers have also started interior design departments or created subsidiary companies. There are also many designers moving into attractive markets, such as the southwestern states. Downturns in the economy also force many changes in how design firms market their services.

With all the increased competition for design business, firms must look beyond traditional methods of obtaining commissions. Sitting behind a desk at the studio waiting for the phone to ring is still done—by far too many designers. Design professionals committed to the expansion of their businesses, however, must always be thinking past the current project and beyond what former clients might be able to provide. This necessity is especially the case in commercial design since contacts may be promoted, change companies, transfer to other cities, retire, or lose responsibility related to the interior designer's interests. In this chapter we will look at the basic ideas of marketing analysis and the development of the marketing plan.

Definitions

Many designers do not like to think about marketing because they are too busy with other work. Others think that marketing means selling and refuse to consider themselves "salespeople." Every time he or she makes a presentation, the designer is engaging in selling. And selling is a part of marketing. But selling is not marketing, and marketing is not selling. A few definitions might help.

There are many definitions of *marketing*. Most include the concept of moving goods and services from producers to consumers. A definition that relates to how interior designers might look at marketing is "the performance of activities which seek to accomplish an organization's objectives by anticipating customer or client needs and directing a flow of need-satisfying goods and services from producer to customer or client."[1] The well-known management consultant, Peter Drucker, wrote "the aim of marketing is to know and understand the customer so well that the product or service sells itself."[2]

Selling, on the other hand, "is the personal, oral presentation of products or services to prospective customers for the purpose of making sales. . . . the salesman ideally does more than make the customer desire the product; he tries to win the customer's regard for the company which sells the product (and) tries to extend the confidence and regard of the customer to himself."[3]

Some of the many promotional activities involved in the process of marketing interior design services shall be explored in Chapter 18. The "personal selling" done by the designer to obtain a commission or finalize a project presentation is a part of the marketing process. We will look at personal selling techniques in Chapter 19. Chapter 20 shall discuss some techniques used to make presentations.

Marketing Analysis

Marketing analysis involves gathering and analyzing data about such things as the abilities and interests of the staff, potential clients, the economy, and the competition. This analysis will allow the firm to make better plans and decisions about the direction of the firm's business efforts. The goal of marketing analysis is to find out what the client wants and then provide it.

Marketing analysis can be done by consulting firms that specialize in this kind of work. Sometimes advertising agencies will do marketing analysis. Small firms and designers just beginning their practices often try to do their own marketing analysis. Although this can meet with success, it is a time-consuming and detailed process. Firms determined to do this work internally should be prepared for a revenue generating designer being away from client work.

Internal Analysis

It is important for a design firm to market to the right clients. But before the firm can begin to market to those target clients, the firm must know all about itself and what it can do.

Marketing analysis must start with understanding all about the firm. One of the techniques used by corporations is called *SWOT*, which stands for strengths, weaknesses, opportunities, and threats. SWOT analysis can be used by managers and employees to plot the perceived strengths, weaknesses, opportunities, and threats of the firm. It should be pointed out that this analysis method is sometimes criticized because responses can be either too harsh or too meaningless to have validity. However, SWOT analysis taken seriously and constructively can result in useful planning information.

SWOT analysis is done by preparing statements that relate to positive (strengths) and negative (weaknesses) conditions within the firm and conditions that affect the firm. An example of a strength might be "average monthly billable hours over 75 percent for all design staff." A weakness would be "high turnover at junior designer and designer levels."

Opportunities and threats are often harder to determine. Firms that are busy keeping up with current day-to-day practice often miss seeing potential opportunities for, or threats to, the practice. An opportunity might be a contact with the real estate brokerage company

---

[1]McCarthy 1981, 8.
[2]Drucker, Peter F. *Management: Tasks, Responsibilities, Practices*. Harper and Row Publishers, Inc., 1973, p. 64.
[3]*Colliers Encyclopedia*, 1975, vol. 15, 422. Copyright © 1975 Macmillan Educational Corporation.

helping a corporation locate housing for headquarters' personnel moving into the design firm's city. Another opportunity might be getting a design project published in a trade magazine. A definite threat would be new legislation limiting aspects of traditional interior design practice, such as requiring contractors' licenses for supervision of materials installation.

This kind of formal internal analysis helps the design firm to understand what it can do, what it wants to do, what it must work on to improve present services so that the firm will be in a position to offer additional services. It also helps define outside influences on the firm that affect the mix and ability to offer services to clients.

A part of this internal analysis involves determining what the firm's philosophy or mission is. It is not enough for management to say that the firm will provide "the best interior design service in town" unless the owner and everyone associated with the organization understand what being the best means to that particular firm. What does being the best mean? Returning phone calls promptly? Being sure service and delivery people treat the client as the designer would? Satisfying the client "no matter what it takes"?

How might the firm plan its philosophy? If a business plan was done originally, many aspects of this philosophy should already have been developed. If not, the owner needs to do some thinking about what he or she perceives the firm is all about. He or she should also talk to former clients—good and bad—about the performance of the firm and their satisfaction with the firm. Employees should be encouraged to openly provide their comments about what the firm is all about to them. From this discussion and examination, a philosophy of the firm that can be incorporated into the marketing plan as the company mission statement will emerge. The mission statement is a philosophical statement of what the firm sees as its role in the profession. It contains broad statements of what the company wishes to achieve during no specific time period. Refer to Figure 12–1 in Chapter 12 for an example of a mission statement.

SWOT analysis will help the firm know what it can do by simply reviewing the skills and interests of the owner and all the staff. A firm cannot seek open office planning projects if no one has experience in that kind of project. As part of this review, the owner/manager should ask each staff member to provide an up-to-date résumé. In addition, each person should prepare a detailed personal analysis of his or her own skills and interests. For the design staff, additional information concerning key projects done for the present employer as well as past employers might also provide important information. In such a case, the designer should discuss his or her role on the project and his or her personal evaluation of the success of the project. All this data will help define what the firm can do.

External Analysis

External analysis involves research into the marketplace, the consumer, and the competition. The purpose of this analysis is to find out what the consumer needs and wants; if any other design firm is providing for those needs and wants; if so, how they are providing those services; and how much of this kind of service is going to be needed in the future. This information, along with the previous information, helps the design firm find its place in the market and aids in the development of the marketing plan.

External analysis involves the use of primary and secondary sources of information. The easiest sources of information to obtain are from secondary sources. Secondary sources are generally those sources of information that are already in existence or produced by others. These include such things as government, trade association, and general business publications such as the *Wall Street Journal*. Local business reports in newspapers, chamber of commerce publications, and reporting services such as the McGraw-Hill Dodge Reports are other secondary sources of information.

These publications will give the design firm various forms of information from general economic trends and the announcement of new firms opening in the local area. Local glossy magazines and chamber of commerce reports present economic outlooks and forecasts, show growth of or losses in population, and provide business and demographic information. All this gives valuable hints as to potential clients for the residential and commercial interior designer.

Primary sources are sources of information that provide specifics from people who may have direct knowledge about the information sought. Some scientific research methods used to gather primary data through the use of surveys or questionnaires would be observation and interviews—either casual or structured. However, the most common method of primary data gathering used by design firms would be casual interviews—or more precisely, casual conversation.

Some means of obtaining information through the use of casual conversation include "picking the brain" of past clients, meeting with design professionals at conferences and seminars, and talking with professionals such as architects, contractors, and developers. In addition, contacts with government agency employees, manufacturers' representatives, vendors and subcontractors, and even employees of the firm will provide information that can be used in developing a marketing plan.

Another relatively easy form of primary research—observation—can be done whenever anyone working for the firm is driving around town. Everyone should keep his or her eyes open for new construction, remodeling, or work in progress related to the interior design firm's practice. This kind of observation may not bring an immediate lead, but could result in a contract at a later time.

An expensive form of primary marketing analysis is the formal questionnaire or survey. Surveys may be conducted by mail, telephone, or in person. The decision as to the exact survey to use would involve size of audience, length of survey, and immediacy of response. Although surveys can be helpful to the design firm for some specific kinds of research information, the cost and time involved usually limits its use to large practices.

The design firm must be looking for answers to such questions as

1. What are the trends in the profession, and how will these trends affect the firm's potential business?

2. Are there sufficient potential clients for the firm's services within a reasonable distance?

3. How might new technologies or legal considerations (codes, licensing) affect the business?

4. How are the services to be offered put forth in the community now? By whom? Are fees charged or not?

5. Is anyone else offering the services in the way the firm plans to? If no one else is providing the service, there may be no need for it.

6. What can the competition do that the firm cannot?

7. What can the firm do better than the competition?

8. Will the firm be able to get the products and services from suppliers and subcontractors to meet the needs of the potential clients?

The internal and external analysis should provide a body of knowledge about the firm's practice and staff, the kind and amount of clients available, general economic and legal trends or restrictions prevalent in the area, and the competition. This information will allow the design firm to set about preparing a definite plan to achieve the desired results first stated in the company mission statement.

Marketing analysis should not be a one-time endeavor. This is an activity that must be continued by the firm throughout its existence. Part of the business plan should include consideration as to how, by whom, and when market analysis is done on a continuing basis.

Defining the Target Market

By defining a firm's strengths, weaknesses, and general market interest, the firm is ready to define its target market and clarify its marketing mix. A *target market* is a group of customers to which the firm wishes to appeal. Residential designers have private residences as their target market. Healthcare designers target hospitals, medical suites, and perhaps other related health care facilities. Healthcare designers would not develop a marketing plan that would appeal to owners of private residences and residential designers would not target owners and developers of medical suites. The firm develops a marketing mix to appeal to its chosen target market. The *marketing mix* includes defining the product to be offered, the price for the product, and the development of promotional activities to inform the target market of the firm's desire to offer the product. Readers who have taken an introductory marketing class will recognize these three elements as part of the traditional *four Ps of marketing*.

The four Ps of marketing are four basic variables that create a firm's marketing mix. The first is *product*. An interior designer's product is generally considered to be professional design services rather than tangible goods. But in marketing, a product can be either a service or goods. Designers who sell goods must also establish which goods it will sell. The product that the designer offers to its target market must be something that satisfies potential customer's needs. Offering watercolor rendering services to allied professionals in a market that does not demand watercolor rendering services is a futile venture. The firm must utilize its analysis of the company and its preferred market area to determine which products are needed by potential clients.

The second P of marketing is *place*. This means that the firm must find ways of getting its product to the places where potential customers exist. The professional offering watercolor rendering may not be able to get much business in a very small community, but he or she would probably have greater success by offering these services in large cities. Business owners must recognize that the client drives the need for products, and that the products must be offered or made available where the client is. The need is not based on the designer's desire to offer products that only the designer perceives as necessary or only in a location where he or she wishes to reside.

The potential client finds out about the availability of a product through the third P, *promotion*. Promotional activities inform potential clients of the existence of the design firm and the services that the firm offers, whether or not the designer is located in the same geographic area as the client. Promotional activities, discussed in detail in Chapter 18, include personal selling, public relations, advertising, development and use of brochures, and other sales promotional materials.

The last of the four traditional Ps of marketing is *price*. Establishing the right price for the product, as was discussed in Chapters 13 and 14, is a difficult management activity. If the firm sets a price that is too high in relation to competition, the firm will not secure work with many clients. If the price is set too low, clients will suspect the firm's ability to do the work and may discount serious consideration of the design firm.

There is one other variable to be factored into the determination of a marketing mix. That variable is *perception*. Clients perceive the designer in terms of image, business professionalism, and, of course, design ability. If a design firm's image, for example, does not meet the client's perception of the image of a designer, the client is less likely to hire the designer. Perception also impacts on the client's willingness to pay the price the designer is asking. If the designer's creative reputation, quality of service, and methods of doing business have a high value to the client, the client is more willing to hire that designer and even conceivably pay a higher price for the design services. Should the client not perceive the value of a designer's service, the client will not be willing to pay the price, even if the designer is a truly creative professional.

All these variables are important factors that a firm must investigate and consider in developing a marketing plan. One variable is not really any more important than another. Each is important by itself as well as in relation to the other items. Ignoring one variable could upset the marketing mix and make it difficult, if not impossible, for the design firm to successfully market its services.

The Marketing Plan

Marketing plans should be developed for a particular length of time—usually one year. Yet consideration for short-term and long-term goals, objectives, and strategies must also be incorporated into the yearly plan. Goals, you will recall from Chapter 12, are broad statements, without regard to any time limit, of what the firm wishes to achieve. Objectives are more specific statements combined with time limits aimed toward accomplishing the firm's goals. Strategies are highly specific actions that have definite time limits within the year of the plan.

Short-term goals, objectives, and strategies would usually be those that can be accomplished in less than one year, where as long-term goals and objectives are those that are expected to take from three to five years or more to accomplish. The accomplishment of long-term goals and objectives must be based on short-term goals and objectives. A goal for a small design firm might be "to become well-known in Boston for residential restoration work." An objective to meet this goal might be "to have one or more projects published in the local press." A strategy then might be "to invite local columnists and editors to tour previous projects and keep them informed of new assignments."

Just as there is no perfect business plan, it is difficult to offer one outline for a marketing plan for all interior design firms. Some firms will want to have a very formal plan with a table of contents, references, and budgeting information. If the plan is to be used internally so that the owners, managers, and staff know what is going on, a more informal format can be presented.

Figure 17–1 shows an example of a portion of a sample marketing plan. Some of the items the plan should cover would include:

1. *An introduction.* Statements based on what information was used to prepare the plan as well as the use and purpose of the plan.

2. *Goals statement(s).* A revised statement of general business goals based on the information gathered in the analysis.

3. *Capabilities.* A discussion of the firm's abilities related to the kinds of clients who previously hired the firm.

4. *Services.* A listing of the services the firm can and is going to offer. Subsequent sections should discuss who will be responsible for these services and how will they be done.

5. *Clientele.* Quantitative information as to potential numbers, market share, and possible growth in each client category. Both existing and new client objectives should be stated.

6. *Policy decisions.* A discussion of such things as how the firm will charge services to clients, how the firm will charge for consultants, whether or not the firm will bill reimbursable expenses, whether or not the firm will sell merchandise, what policies there will be related to purchasing of products for resale.

7. *Marketing organization.* A statement of who will be responsible for ongoing marketing analysis.

8. *Marketing effort.* Answers to such questions as: In what ways will the firm accomplish

II. Client base
   A. Current year
   1. Our current client base is primarily from the Midland area. Current clients within the city limits represent 80 percent of total sales. The remaining 20 percent are from clients outside the city limits but within a 30-mile radius.
   2. The majority of current work is residential. Eighty-five percent of clients purchase merchandise and services for homes. Fifteen percent of clients purchase merchandise and services for offices or other commercial facilities.
   3. Services vs. merchandise.
      a. Of residential sales, 70 percent of all revenues are merchandise sales. Twenty percent are from design fees, and 10 percent represent other services such as repairs not needing additional merchandise.
      b. Of commercial sales, 90 percent of all revenues are merchandise sales. Design fees represent only 10 percent of revenues from commercial projects.
   4. Type of purchaser.
      a. Sixty-five percent of residential customers purchase goods or services for their existing homes.
         (1) Sixty percent of purchases are for only a few replacement items in one or two rooms.
         (2) Thirty percent of purchases are for new floor coverings, window coverings, and/or wall coverings.
         (3) Ten percent of purchases are for many items in two or more rooms.
      b. Twenty percent of residential customers purchase goods or services for a new house.
         (1) Forty-five percent of purchases are for new floor coverings, window coverings, and/or wall coverings.
         (2) Thirty-five percent of purchases are for only a few replacement items in one or two rooms.
         (3) Twenty percent of purchases are for many items in two or more rooms.
      c. Fifteen percent of residential customers purchase goods or services for a second (vacation or rental) house.
         (1) Fifty-five percent of purchases are for only a few replacement items in one or two rooms.

Figure 17–1 A page from a sample yearly marketing plan.

its goals? How will it use advertising and public relations? How will results be monitored to see whether or not they are successful? How much financially will be committed to marketing?

   9. *Evaluation.* A discussion of how the goals will be measured so as to indicate success of the marketing plan.

   10. *Forecasts.* Amount of sales, profit, number of new clients, additions to personnel. These should be stated as both quantitative and qualitative measures.

   It is wise to involve the entire staff in the analysis and the planning for the yearly marketing plan. Final decisions, of course, should be made by management. It is almost always true that when plans are passed down by management without staff input, the staff feel resentful of not being taken into the planning process. If the staff do not believe in the plan, it will not be very successful.

Summary

Many designers determine that the way to get more business is to go out and make a few more calls or run another sale on some excess inventory. Although these methods certainly bring in a small amount of business, they are not the kinds of activities that sustain a design practice. If the firm is not calling on or attracting the right clients, or running sales on the products clients might want to buy, the efforts will be wasted.

In this chapter we have discussed how the firm can develop a marketing effort by presenting the kinds of analysis that must be obtained, discussing establishing a target market, and offering a suggested outline for a marketing plan. In the next chapter we will look at the concept of promotion and many of the promotional tools that can be used to aid in the marketing effort.

References

Bachner, John Phillip, and Naresh Kumar Khosla. 1971. *Marketing and Promotion for Design Professionals.* New York: Van Nostrand Reinhold.

Berry, Leonard L., and A. Parasuraman. 1991. *Marketing Services.* New York: The Free Press.

Brannen, William H. 1981. *Practical Marketing for Your Small Retail Business.* New York: Prentice Hall.

Colliers Encyclopedia. 1975. Vol. 15, s. v. "Marketing." New York: MacMillan Educational Corporation.

Coxe, Weld. 1971. *Marketing Architectural and Engineering Services.* New York: Van Nostrand Reinhold.

Davidson, Jeffrey P. 1990. *Marketing for the Home-Based Business.* Holbrook, Mass: Bob Adams.

Drucker, Peter F. 1973. *Management: Tasks, Responsibilities, Practices.* New York: Harper and Row.

Hayes, Rick Stephan, and Gregory Brooks Elmore. 1985. *Marketing for Your Growing Business.* New York: Ronald Press.

Jones, Gerre. 1983. *How to Market Professional Design Services,* 2d ed. New York: McGraw-Hill.

McCarthy, E. Jerome. 1981. *Basic Marketing,* 7th ed. Homewood, Ill.: Richard D. Irwin.

Morgan, Jim. 1984. *Marketing for the Small Design Firm.* New York: Watson-Guptill.

Putman, Anthony O. 1990. *Marketing Your Services.* New York: Wiley.

Weitz, Barton A., and Robin Wensley. 1984. *Strategic Marketing.* Boston, Mass.: Kent Publishing.

Chapter 18

Promoting the Interior
Design Practice

Promotion is the method used to get the designer's message—even existence—before the client. To be more precise, *promotion* is "communicating information between seller and buyer—to influence attitudes and behavior."[1]

Many use the term *promotion* to mean public relations, but promotion is much more than public relations. Promotion also includes publicity, publishing, advertising, and direct selling. Today, promotional activities are important for the healthy growth of any interior design business.

Competition forces design firms to consider many promotional activities. Should the firm attempt to get a project published in one of the trade magazines? Is it proper for the firm to advertise in local magazines? Can the firm afford to publish a brochure? These questions and many more are being asked in design firms every day as a part of the continual search for new clients, new markets, and greater recognition. In this chapter, we will explore many of the ways the interior designer can get his or her message across to prospective clients.

Public Relations

Public relations refers to all the efforts of the firm to create an image in order to affect the public's opinion of the firm. Getting an article about the firm's involvement in a major project published, producing a brochure, helping coordinate an in-office product seminar for the public or other professionals, making contributions to professional organization fundraisers, and even placing an advertisement in the annual "designers" issue of a local magazine are all examples of public relations activities.

A public relations professional will review and evaluate what the design firm does. He or she will then provide suggestions as to how these services are viewed by the type of clients

---

[1]McCarthy 1981, 761.

with whom the firm deals. The firm can then direct its future promotional efforts to obtain additional clients. A public relations professional can do such things as:

- Research public opinion about the firm.

- Write newsletters, brochures, and other general mailings.

- Produce special events and programs like seminars, open houses, and the company holiday party for clients.

- Design a new company logo and graphics identity package.

- Write and place news releases in local newspapers or national trade publications.

- Produce audiovisual presentations.

Through the firm's research about itself and the public, a picture of the activities needed within public relations, publicity, and general promotional activities will emerge. The public relations professional makes suggestions as to which activities are going to lead to the most promise of success—that is, more client contacts and potential sales. He or she may suggest that a new company image be started by redesigning the company logo and graphics—or maybe by news releases about recent successes. Perhaps a brochure or newsletter mailing to former and prospective clients is appropriate. Whatever the strategy, the result is to gain positive recognition for the design firm in the public's mind. And this recognition will eventually lead to future business and greater revenues.

Publicity

A direct form of promotion is publicity. *Publicity* is "any unpaid form of nonpersonal presentation of ideas, goods, or services."[2] This is the kind of promotional communication that design firms strive to achieve as much as possible. Traditionally, this was the accepted form of promoting professional services.

Publicity takes many forms. It can be planned or accidental. Unfortunately, most accidental publicity is bad publicity. Bad publicity—such as being named in the newspapers following a personal injury suit—is not something a design firm desires. Design firms seek to create planned publicity that will help potential clients view the firm in a good light and seek them out for design contracts. An example of good publicity would be the mentioning of the interior design firm in an article about the grand opening of a new hotel or corporate center. This article is not something that the design firm pays for, but the information alone would create public awareness and potential new client leads.

A good activity resulting in publicity is charitable and community service work related to interior design. Helping the community theater with props and set designs might be an example. Volunteering services on restoration projects is another. Many chapters of ASID get members involved in designing rooms in model houses or display houses. These are often tied to a charitable group, with proceeds from public tours going to the charitable organization.

Larger firms may, with the cooperation of manufacturers, be able to put on exhibits or seminars. Renting a meeting room in a hotel and filling it with a well-designed product display, or providing a good educational seminar for the end-user and other professionals who might help the firm, are excellent forms of publicity.

---

[2]McCarthy 1981, 749.

Publication Opportunities

The most sought-after kind of planned publicity is publication of projects in trade and shelter magazines. Although this form of publicity often has a limited audience consisting of primarily professional peers, reprints can be obtained and mailed or given to prospective and former clients. ASID has prepared a pamphlet called *How To Get Design Work Published.* This publication lists general guidelines for preparing publication material for most of the trade and shelter magazines. The pamphlet also provides information concerning the type of projects and kinds of materials each of the magazines might be interested in publishing.

Many large cities have local magazines that are used for promoting the good qualities of the city or state. These magazines often have articles on residences or commercial properties, giving designers an outlet to the consuming market. Some of these magazines even have special issues focusing on the local design community.

It is also possible to submit appropriate projects to the professional publications of clients. Such magazines as *Today's Office* and *Corporate Design* run articles and photos of executive offices. *Ayer's Directory of Publications,* published by Ayer's Press, lists information on all the magazines published annually in the United States and is available at most public libraries.

Manufacturers of many kinds of products use photographs of installations with their products in paid advertising. Designers should seek to negotiate for the project designer's and the firm's name to receive a byline in the ad.

Another outlet for publicity is entering and winning one of the various trade competitions. ASID and IBD provide to its members a yearly list of major competitions. Others are announced in the trade magazines or sent to designers through mailings from the sponsoring group. Winning projects of major competitions get published in one of the trade magazines, thus providing valuable public recognition to the design firm and designer. It can also lead to feature articles in the local newspaper or other media, resulting in additional public exposure for the firm.

Press Releases

A *press release* is an effective, inexpensive way for any size of design firm to achieve increased public awareness. Almost any kind of news or announcement can be prepared as a press release. However, newspapers and magazines, having limited space, will likely only use those items they feel are about significant, newsworthy events. Examples would include announcements for a large or unusual project, sponsorship of a seminar or workshop, the winning of a design award, the opening of the firm, or the relocation of the design firm (see Figure 18–1). In most cities, announcements about promotions and new hires are relegated to a minimal statement in a business briefs column.

Public relations professionals have experience in preparing press releases; they also have many contacts with local and national print, radio, and television media. These contacts can be utilized to obtain the best coverage for the press release. If good journalistic techniques are used, however, an in-house individual can prepare a press release.

The text of the release should be prepared in concise journalistic style, using the classic five Ws and an H: who, what, when, where, why, and how. The most significant information should be presented in the first paragraph, with additional details presented in subsequent paragraphs. Text should be typed double spaced with wide side margins for editorial comments. Long releases of three or more pages are less likely to be picked up. One- or two-page press releases have the best chance of reaching the media. When the editor or news director reads a press release, he or she may have additional questions. The name, address, and telephone number of the individual responsible for writing the release should be placed at the top of the first page so that media personnel know whom they should contact.

L. Green Design Associates
Interior Design Consultants
9876 West Third Street
Phoenix, Arizona 85001

For Immediate Release

For further information contact
Joanna Hughes
Telephone: 602-555-3451

L. GREEN DESIGN ASSOCIATES AWARDED MILLS INC. DESIGN CONTRACT

L. Green Design Associates has been awarded the interior design contract for the new Mills Incorporated corporate offices.

Mills Incorporated, a research and development company in the computer industry, will be moving corporate offices consisting of 350 employees to Phoenix from the Midwest.

Linda Green, President of L. Green Design Associates, will lead a team of the firm's designers in the space planning and interior design of the new offices. "It is our intention," said Ms. Green, "that the interior design will integrate employee needs for flexibility and creativity with the company's need to show clients that Mills Incorporated is a contemporary, innovative, yet stable company that can solve the problems of the computer industry."

L. Green Design Associates specializes in the space planning and interior design of professional, corporate, and multiemployee general business offices. The firm has completed projects throughout Arizona, New Mexico, Colorado, and California.

Figure 18–1 A sample news release.

It is also necessary to indicate at the top of the release when it can be used. Often, press releases are prepared for immediate release. "Immediate release" indicates that all the information in the text is timely and ready for publication. If the information concerns an event in the near future—for example, a seminar to be held next week—the date of preferred release should be clearly indicated.

Supplemental materials, such as line drawings or photographs, provide information that the text cannot easily explain. They also may make an otherwise routine story more interesting. Magazines will prefer color transparencies rather than color photographic prints. If a black-and-white photograph is sent, it should be a glossy print. Newspapers will readily use black-and-white glossy prints, but are rarely able to use colored photographic work at all. When line drawings, such as floor plans, are submitted, these should be PMTs or high quality mylar reductions. PMT is a name for a diffusion transfer process (sometimes called a STAT) that results in a direct positive reproduction of line copy or artwork.

If people are in the pictures, names and titles and signed model releases should be provided. Not having a model release with the photograph could prevent the photograph from being published.

It should be pointed out that even providing the best-written, concise, informative press release about a truly significant event, does not guarantee that print media will pick it up. Being selective, especially at a local level, as to who receives the release may help get it noticed and published or even broadcasted. All areas of the media like to "scoop" their colleagues. Knowing that the design firm has attempted to provide that scoop just may help to get the release noticed.

Promotional Tools

Promotional tools are the many printed mechanisms that are used by the interior design firm to get its story before the public. Although there are any number of tools that can be used, we will look specifically at the company logo and the general graphic image, brochures, photo portfolios, newsletters, and the audiovisual presentation.

Public relations professionals talk about these items as indirect promotional tools. Indirect promotional tools are those printed or visual tools that are directed at nonspecific general audiences. What they are, what goes into them, and how they are delivered to the prospective client, all play a role in furthering the image desired by the firm.

The Graphic Image

By *graphic image*, we are referring to the total package of materials used by the designer to communicate written materials and presentations. This includes the company logo, business cards, letterhead and other stationery, business forms, and drawing-paper identification.

A *logo*, which is a symbolic image of the company, can be a strong identification mark for the firm. It can be used on all the written communication media mentioned as well as on many other items related to the business. If the firm has delivery trucks, the trucks should be painted the same design and colors as the logo. The logo, in essence, should be the same design and color on all materials related to the company. This consistency will help the client identify the logo with the firm and help bring about client awareness and identification (see Figures 18–2 and 18–3). The rest of the design of the business card, stationery, and so forth must be compatible with the logo.

Firms should be careful in the color selection used for stock and ink, type size, typeface, and size of finished format. Oversized or special-size cards may be very creative but will be difficult for the client to keep on file. Standard type fonts, such as Microgramma, Helvetica, and Futura make very clean, easy-to-read business cards and stationery.

Brochures

A brochure can be a helpful tool of the firm. The image the brochure relates should mirror the rest of the firm's image. A few excellent photographs of very good installations will be far superior to a lot of inferior shots and wordy copy. The graphic identification should be carried through from the other graphics. Copy must be well-written and brief, since clients do not have a lot of time to read the lengthy history and philosophy a designer may wish to express.

The brochure gives the interior design firm the opportunity to show selections of its best work and tells something about the firm (see Figures 18–4 and 18–5). The content of the brochure gives a taste of what the firm is about, but it does not tell the client everything. Thus, the brochure does what it is intended to do—get an invitation from the client for the designer to tell a more complete and personal story.

The brochure does not need to be a four-color glossy extravaganza. But it should be very well done and have high quality photography. Care must be taken that the photographs chosen do not date the brochure. Featuring photos of the design staff is a compliment to each designer, but when that person leaves, his or her photograph in the brochure can date or even negate the brochure.

Copy should be short, just enough to tell who the brochure is from, identify the photos, and tell something about the company. Clients want to get some idea of what the design firm can do for them. The copy should set the stage for further discussions.

The brochure takes expertise in graphics, composition, photography, and copywriting

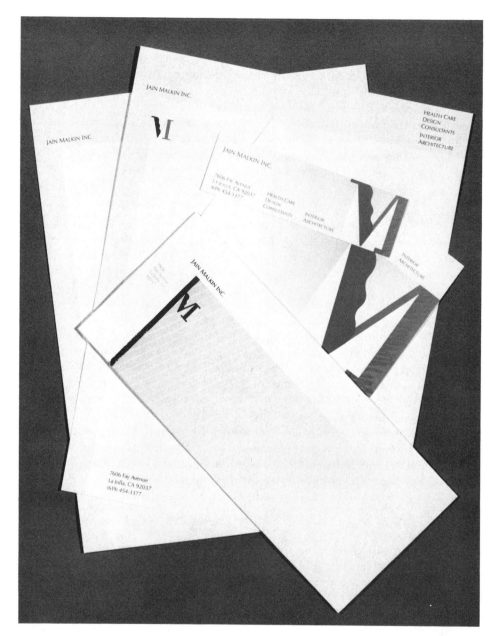

Figure 18–2 Design firm logo on letterhead and related materials. (Reproduced with permission, Jain Malkin, Inc., La Jolla, CA.; graphic designer: Miriello Grafico; photo: Eugene Balzer).

skills. Although the firm may wish to prepare the conceptual content of the brochure, it is recommended that the actual production be left to public relations professionals or professional graphic designers.

Photo Portfolio

Another useful promotional tool is the *photo portfolio*. This is a selection of project photos taken by a professional architectural photographer. If shot in transparency or negative format, these photos can be used for several purposes. This media is preferred by magazines for color reproduction. Enlargements from negatives or transparencies can be framed and hung

Figure 18–3 Design firm logo as used on the cover of a brochure. (Reproduced with permission, Goodmans Design-Interiors, Phoenix, AZ.; photo: Christopher C. Everett).

in the office or lobby as a display for the waiting client. Transparencies can be used for audiovisual presentations. A book filled with prints of installations can be shown to the client during the marketing stage of a design project.

It is important to get the permission of the client and have anyone in the photo sign a release—especially if it will be published. This is to protect the designer from being sued for invasion of privacy. It is also a good idea to have a clause in the design contract giving permission to photograph and submit for publication all work, whether the firm expects to do this or not. The photographer will have the release forms, should there be people in any of the photos.

Newsletters and Case Studies

Newsletters have long been popular with architects but rarely developed by interior designers. These are not the in-house communication of firms to tell everyone whose birthday it is; rather, they inform clients and perhaps peers of projects received or completed, new staff hired or promoted, and so on (see Figure 18–6). The newsletter can be inserted in the brochure or sent as a separate mailing.

A case study of a particularly interesting or challenging project can be a separate publication. A *case study* tells what the design program was, some unique features of the project, and may have before-and-after photographs. It can also discuss the solution and ideally has some quotes regarding the quality of the project from the client. Case studies can be developed for a variety of projects. They also can be inserted into the brochure to show a special expertise by the firm (see Figure 18–7).

Neither the newsletter nor the case study needs to be in color, but each should be well done. Both can be accomplished in one or two pages and might include black-and-white photos or line drawings.

Audiovisual Presentation

The audiovisual presentation can be an effective way for the design firm to quickly, and very visually, tell its story to the client. It is often a simple presentation prepared especially for the client from the firm's slide collection and narrated by the designer. Many professionals

Figure 18–4 Brochure covers from multiservice organization. (Reproduced with permission, Howard, Needles, Tammen and Bergendoff, Phoenix, AZ. and Kansas City, MO.; photo: Eugene Balzer)

think the simple tailor-made presentation is successful since it is tailored to the specific client and project. They also appreciate its the low cost. Today, many firms are using videotape presentations rather than multimedia slide presentations.

Who should be responsible for producing these presentations is an important question. The simple tailor-made presentation should be put together by the designer making the presentation and run through until he or she is familiar with the slides and verbal comments. References on how to prepare slide presentations are listed at the end of this chapter. The multimedia presentation and videotape presentation, on the other hand, are complex, time-

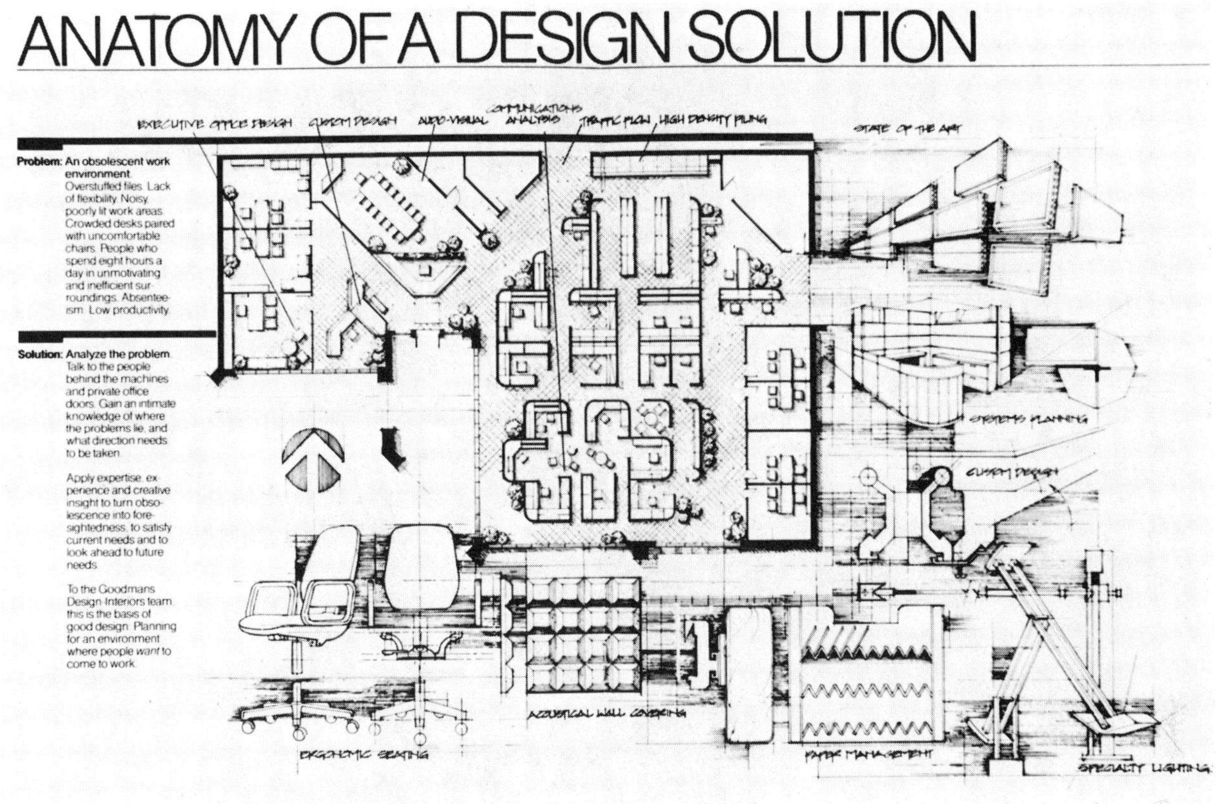

ANATOMY OF A DESIGN SOLUTION

Figure 18–5 Centerfold of the brochure used by Design-Interiors, highlights the final design solution. (Reproduced with permission of Design-Interiors, Phoenix AZ.; photo: Christopher C. Everett)

consuming events to create and produce. Their production should be left in the hands of professionals.

Direct Mailing

Direct mail can mean just about anything—from a letter to any number of the items already listed. Since printing and postage are ongoing expenses, the key is to get the mailed item to the right person. To do that, the firm must have a good mailing list. The mailing list for most designers starts with past and existing customers. Additions to the list might come from researching chamber of commerce membership lists, appropriate professional association membership lists, or even the phone book.

Many people, however, still think it is wrong or unethical to send out mailings to people the firm does not know. All of us receive "junk" mail from unsolicited sources. Most of that ends up in the wastebasket. Often, junk mail sent to businesses ends up the same way. It is best if the list includes only former clients and contacts. The firm can then develop referrals from these names. Even the best-prepared mailing may receive only a 2 to 6 percent return when mailed to previously unknown contacts.[3]

Mailings must have some impact and should be designed to catch the eye of the receiver.

---

[3]Kliment 1977, 58.

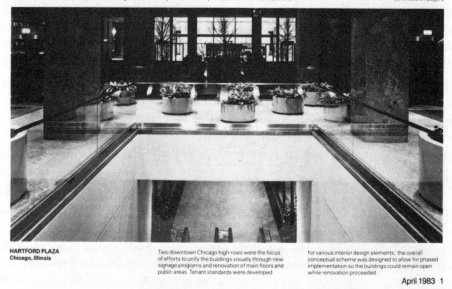

Perkins&Will   Chicago, New York, Washington
Architects, Engineers, Planners, Interior & Graphic Designers

PROGRESS

Facilities Management: Controlling Physical Assets

Reduction in demand for basic and consumer goods and services, slow receivables, lay-offs, and changing capital markets are phenomena almost all sectors of the economy have faced to some degree during the early 80's. The result has been commitment to tighter management of an organization's assets. Asset management includes people, equipment, and facilities. It is no surprise, then, that a full service architecture, engineering and interior design firm like Perkins & Will has experienced increased interest from its clientele in a specialized section of this process—Facilities Management.

In its most comprehensive sense, facilities management is the process of inventorying and evaluating the location, condition, function, and economic value of an organiza-

tion's physical assets. In other times we called this systematic effort Master Planning. While the terminology has changed, the intent has not. Whatever it is called, the objective is to make the best economic use of the real estate owned and/or occupied by an institution. The required activities fall into two categories.

- Identification in an organized and retrievable manner of all pertinent data related to real estate and property assets.

- Analysis of this data to determine the most appropriate means of using and managing the asset.

These analyses take on many different forms depending on an organization's specific objectives. They can deal with land, build-

ings, improvements, interior space, or furnishings. They can address immediate needs for space or cash, or they can position the company to respond intelligently to future conditions.

Furnishings

Beginning with the most tangible facilities, companies are looking at their furnishings, carpeting and other moveable equipment to determine whether they are functional, for how long, and what they are worth. When one real estate investment trust recently acquired two neighboring, but dissimilar office buildings, it decided to market the buildings as one unit. To achieve this, the public had to view the two buildings as related even though the architecture, bay

continued on page 2

HARTFORD PLAZA
Chicago, Illinois

Two downtown Chicago high-rises were the focus of efforts to unify the buildings visually through new signage programs and renovation of main floors and public areas. Tenant standards were developed

for various interior design elements, the overall conceptual scheme was designed to allow for phased implementation so the buildings could remain open while renovation proceeded.

April 1983 1

Figure 18–6 A newsletter providing information about projects with which the design firm has recently been involved. (Reprinted with permission, Perkins & Will, Chicago, IL; photo: Eugene Balzer)

They need to be well-designed and creatively thought out. A good graphics designer or market specialist might be the answer for the design of the mailing. Direct mailings used by interior designers are usually cover letters accompanied by a brochure or newsletter. But direct mailings might also be announcements of sales, holiday promotions, and seminar invitations. Ideally, direct mailings should be followed up by a personal call. It gives the firm a

Figure 18–7 Perkins & Will utilizes one-page case studies inserted in a folder for promotional presentations. (Reprinted with permission, Perkins & Will, Chicago, IL; photo: Eugene Balzer)

Figure 18–8 Magazine advertisement placed by a design firm. (Reproduced with permission, Office Designs, Phoenix, AZ.)

chance to see how the receiver reacted to the mailing and to make an appointment to further discuss its contents or answer questions the receiver may have.

Advertising

Advertising is defined as any kind of paid communication in media such as newspapers, magazines, television, or radio. If the firm pays the newspaper to run an announcement of some kind about the firm, it is advertising. If the newspaper runs an announcement or article about the firm and the firm does not pay for it, it is publicity (see Figure 18–8).

Advertising continues to be a rather controversial way for professionals to promote their services. It was not until 1978 that the AIA gave its approval to some forms of advertising.[4] The IBD code of ethics, approved in 1981, states "Members may purchase dignified advertisements and listings in newspapers, periodicals, directories, or other publications . . ."[5] There has always been a reluctance by the professions to engage in advertising of services. Few interior design firms that earn their revenues from service fees rather than from selling products have utilized the opportunity to advertise. However, as competition has gotten tougher, design firms have begun to advertise, just as lawyers and dentists have.

About the only form of direct advertising all designers use are yellow-page ads in the phone book. Many rely on ads in which the firm's name, address, and telephone number are printed very small. Firms that sell furniture out of retail showrooms or small studios often take out larger-size ads. The firms that make more or most of their money from sales of goods often use advertising related to product promotions or sales. Not only do they use the phone book, but many regularly run ads in magazines, newspapers—even on billboards, and buy radio or television spots.

Summary

Today's highly competitive market makes it very risky for interior designers to expect that all their business will come in on the basis of referrals. Design firms must recognize that promotional activities must be undertaken to ensure a steady supply of clients. It is important to exploit the exposure that publicity brings to a firm. It is also important to be sensitive to the possibility of using other promotional devices as mentioned in this chapter.

The promotional concepts discussed in this chapter suggest many tools the firm may utilize to promote itself to potential clients. These include publicity, news releases, and publication opportunities in trade magazines. It also discussed several mechanisms for communicating information about the design firm to the client via the firm's graphic image, brochures, newsletters, and photographic media. In the next chapter, we will discuss an additional aspect of the whole concept of promotion—that of direct, personal selling.

References

Austin, Richard L. 1984. *Report Graphics*. New York: Van Nostrand Reinhold.

Bachner, John Philip, and Naresh Kumar Khosla. 1977. *Marketing and Promotion for Design Professionals*. New York: Van Nostrand Reinhold.

[4]Jones 1983, 150.
[5]"Code of Ethics," p. 3. Reprinted with permission from the Institute of Business Designers, 1980.

Bly, Robert W. 1991. *Selling Your Services.* New York: Holt.

Coxe, Weld. 1971. *Marketing Architectural and Engineering Services.* New York: Van Nostrand Reinhold.

Hays, Rick Stephan, and Gregory Brooks Elmore. 1985. *Marketing for Your Growing Business.* New York: Ronald Press.

Institute of Business Designers. 1980. Code of Ethics (pamphlet P105). Chicago: Institute of Business Designers.

Jones, Gerre L. 1983. *How to Market Professional Design Services,* 2d ed. New York: McGraw-Hill.

_____. 1980. *Public Relations for the Design Professional.* New York: McGraw-Hill.

Kliment, Stephen A. 1977. *Creative Communications for a Successful Design Practice.* New York: Watson-Guptill.

McCarthy, E. Jerome. 1981. *Basic Marketing,* 7th ed. Homewood, Ill.: Richard D. Irwin.

McCaslin, Barbara S., and Patricia P. McNamara. 1980. *Be Your Own Boss.* Englewood Cliffs, N.J.: Prentice-Hall.

Morgan, Jim. 1984. *Marketing for the Small Design Firm.* New York: Watson-Guptill.

Putman, Anthony O. 1990. *Marketing Your Services.* New York: Wiley.

Chapter 19

Sales Techniques
for Interior Designers

The best design idea ever will not become a reality if the designer and design firm cannot convince the client to buy. Interior designers are involved in many different selling situations. In one kind of selling, the designer must make presentations to clients to obtain a design contract. Designers must also sell their design ideas—the color concepts and floor plans of the overall design concept. A third selling situation for many designers requires the selling of products. These may be products that are part of the project concept or individual items the client is looking to buy. Finally, the designer must sell himself or herself; the client must have confidence in the designer before allowing him or her to proceed with the project.

Some designers find it extremely easy to sell their concepts and products. Others feel frustrated by their inability to sell their ideas or sell products. People talk about "born salespeople" and proverbial salespeople who can sell the Brooklyn Bridge. Speaking as one who was not born to be a salesperson, selling can be learned and selling can be fun. It becomes easier with practice and experience. And it becomes easier as the designer learns products and becomes comfortable in successfully achieving design concepts.

In this chapter, we will discuss several selling techniques used by designers. Although some of these techniques seem to focus on selling products, they can and are successfully applied to selling design services. Chapter 20 will discuss the formal design-selling presentation and some techniques related to the formal presentation.

What Is Selling?

Selling, like marketing, is finding out what the client wants and providing it. But, unlike marketing, *selling* is personal, often one-on-one communications. Some people do not like selling or salespeople because they believe sales involves manipulating people to buy what they do not want. This kind of selling is practiced by many so called "salespeople." But that is not the kind of selling we wish to talk about in this chapter.

Interior design professionals, as salespeople, do their utmost to find out what the client really wants in the way of design services and products and then tries to provide those services and products. Satisfying the client and obtaining the sale makes both individuals or groups winners. It is not necessary to try to sell clients what they do not want. If fact, it is bad business to do so.

Concept Selling

Concept selling means explaining and obtaining approval from the client of the overall design idea. Concept selling is difficult since it involves selling intangibles. How the living room will really look, or how the restaurant will look, is difficult for clients to understand. Most have a hard time visualizing the colors and fabrics on the pieces being recommended. Clients also are not used to reading floor plans, making it difficult for them to visualize the interior space plans. The designer must use all of his or her technical training to explain how the space will look before it is complete. This is, of course, why floor plans, color boards, sketches, even renderings are used to communicate the design concepts in the designer's head to the client.

In concept selling, the designer must gain the client's confidence. Many designers believe that if he or she is unsure about anything related to the project, the designer will lose the client. After all, the designer is in the client's home or business learning how the client lives and works. The designer must display total confidence in what he or she suggests the client do to and purchase for his or her home or business.

In many ways, this means becoming the client's "friend," although not in a normal sense. To become too close or too personal a friend with people for whom the designer is working can create difficult situations for both sides. Slow payment, no payments, errors by the designer—all lead to tense moments when the two parties are no longer friends. Becoming friends can make conducting business more difficult. Yet the designer must show concern, thoughtfulness, and empathy for the client's interiors problems. Being totally businesslike certainly has its place, but so does having a sense of humor and knowing when it is all right to relax and be somewhat casual.

Successfully selling the design concept is the culmination of the design-selling responsibilities of the interior design professional. Obtaining agreement, and being able to proceed with the order not only brings financial success to the designer, but also personal satisfaction in seeing tangible completion of the project.

Selling Techniques

Discovering techniques to help the designer sell his or her services and products is a very personal business. What will work for one designer could lead to frustration and failure for another. Although interior designers use many techniques to help them sell, two important characteristics have always been present in the presentation methods used by successful designers. Those characteristics are enthusiasm for what they are doing and interest in the needs of the client. Successful professionals must have genuine interest in their clients and the needs of the clients.

Clients come to interior designers for help in solving the client's problems in making the home or business attractive and functional. Clients also come to designers to get help in making decisions because many have a hard time making decisions or are reluctant to do so. This is because they are afraid they will get blamed if theirs is the wrong decision. Interior designers are hired to help in both of these cases.

Probing

Probing is a technique for asking different kinds of questions in order to uncover the needs of the client. Probing is accomplished by asking questions that will either elicit a closed response, such as a "yes" or "no" answer, or a response where the client is encouraged to talk. This second kind of probing question is called an *open probe*.

Questions posed using closed probing techniques are questions geared toward finding out specific information. They are also used when the client is not particularly responsive to other kinds of questions. For example, a designer might ask this short series of questions:

DESIGNER: "Do you have a preferred color scheme?"

CLIENT: "Not really."

DESIGNER: "Do you prefer warmer colors like oranges, rusts, and yellows?"

CLIENT: "No."

DESIGNER: "Do you prefer cool colors like blue and green?"

CLIENT: "Yes."

DESIGNER: "Would a color scheme combining blues and greens together be satisfactory to you?"

CLIENT: "I think I would like that."

Questions stated as open probes, on the other hand, are attempts by the designer to get the client talking freely about some topic. They are also used to try to get the client to expand on previously mentioned information or to talk in broader concepts.

By the careful combination of open and closed probes, the designer obtains the information required to discover the actual needs of the client. Discovering the needs of the client allows the designer to use a selling technique of describing features and benefits of products and services related to those needs.

Features and Benefits

An important selling technique, whether selling products or services, is a technique of describing features and benefits. *Features* describe specific aspects or characteristics of a product or service. For example, a plastic laminate top on a desk is a feature of many desks. *Benefits* relate to features of a product or service that directly relate to a client's needs about that product or service. A benefit of the plastic laminate desktop might relate to the ease of maintenance (it will not mar as easily as a wooden top).

Once the designer knows the needs of the client, it is relatively easy for him or her to point out the various features and benefits of the services or products being discussed as they relate to those needs. If the services and products meet the needs of the client, obtaining confirmation and closing the sale is much easier and quicker.

Closing Techniques

Closing is the art of knowing when to ask for the sale. If you are lucky enough for the client to say, "I'll hire you," or "I'll take it," without having to ask first, you probably do not even need to read this chapter at all. Most designers, however, do not know how to ask for the sale, whether they are selling their services or selling the products during a presentation. Far too many designers wait for the client to conclude the sales presentation. And the client often does so—by not signing the agreement.

Closing techniques involve words and actions that the designer uses to ask for the sale. Asking for the sale assumes that agreement has been reached on the issues being discussed. The sooner the designer asks, the sooner the client signs the agreement, and the sooner the designer can move on to another job.

There are many techniques recommended by numerous how-to-sell books on the market today. Some of those books are listed in this chapter's References. The following will recount some of the techniques other professionals use with great success.

Related to the technique of using features and benefits is one of supporting needs with the features and benefits of the product and/or service and then using a trial close when at least two needs have been supported with features and benefits. Supporting needs with features and benefits shows the client that the designer is really trying to solve his or her needs and provide him or her with only what is needed—not what the designer wants to sell. Remember, trying to close the sale means that agreement has been reached on needs.

DESIGNER: "You said that you are looking for a sofa bed for the guest room that is comfortable and that will have a fabric that will be easy to maintain. Is that correct, Ms. Smith?"

SMITH: "Yes, it is."

DESIGNER: "I have already shown you that this sofa bed, made by company X, has been rated by an independent testing company to have the most comfortable mattress on the market. This nylon basket weave fabric, which you liked, will be easy to maintain. Why don't I work up the final price with this fabric and see when we can deliver it to your home?"

Assuming the price is not an issue, if the client says that will be fine, the designer is finished with the sale and only needs to finish writing up the paperwork. However, if the client says no, the designer must assume that something has not yet been agreed to and must probe to ask more questions, support needs by discussing other features and benefits, and then try again to close the sale.

Another frequently used closing technique is to close when the designer obtains client agreement to a secondary issue concerning the sale. In the preceding example, when the designer obtained agreement about the fabric choice, he or she would follow with questions related to color of the fabric. When these two issues are agreed to, then the designer is ready to ask for the sale.

Many designers use third-party testimonials or third-party stories to help in the close. "After an extensive product review, IBM accepted this chair group for the company's standard office desk chair." Recalling how a previous client was satisfied by the service or products often helps to alleviate fears of the decision-making process.

A closing technique that many designers use, though perhaps reluctantly, is related to a forthcoming event. For example, a client who may be hesitant to close the sale today, may be encouraged if he or she knew that the price on the goods was going up in a few weeks. "I can only guarantee this price for the next ten days, since we have already been informed of a price increase on January 1," the designer would say. This technique is perfectly legitimate and, when related to price increases, is actually a benefit to clients. It should, however, only be used in complete honesty. Telling a client that the price of the goods is going to go up when it will not, or telling him or her that the plant will close for two weeks when it will not, is not a professional sales technique.

Another useful, though unpopular technique, is the utilization of some kind of physical action that encourages the client to close the sale. A common physical action is to begin writing up the sales order for the client to sign. Another is to place a pen, in a position for the client to pick it up and use immediately, on top of the design contract or confirmation. If the client does not object to the activity or pull back, the designer knows that the sale is about to be closed.

Overcoming Objections

In any selling situation, the client will have some objections to what is being discussed or proposed. One of the many mysteries of becoming successful at selling services or products is to understand how to overcome these objections. An obvious part of overcoming objections is actually hearing the objection. That sounds simplistic, but it is brought up because too many designers do not listen to the client and miss the signs or even the words of the objections. It is imperative to listen carefully to everything the client is saying so that the designer will not be in the following situation:

Sally Jones, a designer, was on a call with Bill Rogers, one of the project designers. They were at the office of Mr. Anthony Smith. Mr. Smith had been responding to a question by Ms. Jones concerning color and style preferences for the remodeling of the office, and in the middle of that discourse, Mr. Smith said that he really did not like a lot of browns and tans. Bill Rogers looked up from his notebook and said, "I really think that browns would be great in your new office." Both Jones and Smith looked at Rogers and then looked at each other. Although the names have been changed to protect the guilty, it is a true story that shows that even the most experienced designers can lose attention, and potentially lose the client.

Many of the top selling "experts" feel that unless the client makes some kind of objection, it is quite possible the designer is not even making any headway. Objections sometimes occur because the client does not understand what the designer is talking about, but is embarrassed to say so. Sometimes objections are raised because the client really cannot afford what is being discussed, but cannot admit it. And sometimes objections are raised because the client is just afraid of making a mistake and would rather not buy than make a mistake.

Although there are potentially as many different objections as there are clients, we will discuss a few of the most common in this section. The first is price. It is rare that price is not a factor or not a reason for raising an objection. "Your competition charges less per hour," "I can get free design services from another studio," "The sofa is too expensive," are typical comments heard by interior designers. Depending on the exact nature of what is being discussed, it is necessary for the designer to review information already gathered about the needs of the client. It is also necessary to then ask additional questions to clarify the exact nature of the objection. Perhaps the designer can overcome this objection by restating quality characteristics of the product or discuss how his or her services are different from the competition. How much money any design firm is ready to leave on the table in order to obtain a project or sell furniture is up to the management and the designer.

A second common objection is "I need to talk this over with my spouse, " (partner, boss, etc.). This objection often comes up for two reasons: first, the client is afraid of making a mistake and will not make a decision unless someone else confirms. There is not much the designer can do at the moment unless he or she can review information about the service or product so as to help alleviate the concerns of the client. This may lead to the client making the decision without consulting with the other party. Be careful about becoming a pushy typical salesperson, which could lose the sale altogether. Second, the designer was not careful in setting up an appointment with the decision makers in the first place. In initial conversations, the designer must be sure he or she understands who is making the decision. The presentation should be arranged so that all the decision makers are at the meeting. In that way, the designer only makes one presentation. For example, Barbara and Mary had been working with the facility managers for a large corporation on a new color scheme for one of the corporate office buildings. The facility managers kept pushing a continued use of the existing colors while Barbara and Mary were trying to update the color scheme. It was finally time to present to the president and the color scheme presented was the existing colors preferred by the facility managers. The president sort of liked it, but he was not enthusiastic. For some inexplicable reason, Barbara and Mary brought loose samples of the color scheme they really wanted to present. The president thought it was great and gave his okay.

Whatever the objection is, the designer must listen to the objection and be ready to refute or answer the objection. Successful designers do not become successful by giving in to these objections without trying to understand the nature of the objection and then trying to sway the client. However, *never* argue with the client. Getting him or her angry not only means that the problem is unresolved, but the designer may lose the client.

Negotiating

Negotiating is an activity wherein the two parties are trying to reach agreement about some point of discussion. Every reader of this book has some experience at negotiating. It might have been with parents to stay out late on a Saturday night. Or with a teacher to change a grade on a test. It might have been a salary increase. Or even the fee for a design project.

Negotiating creates a "win-win" situation since both parties have reached some kind of agreement that satisfies both parties. If a negotiation reaches a "I win, you lose" situation, than it is not a successful negotiation since only one party is happy. The "I win, you lose" situation is not negotiation, but manipulation. And manipulation has no place in the bag of skills of successful interior designers.

Here are five tips that might help in future negotiations

1. *Always be truthful.* A successful negotiation depends on the trust between the two parties. If the parties to a negotiation do not trust each other, they will never be able to successfully negotiate anything.

2. *Start with a plan.* You may be great on your feet, but if you are about to negotiate an important design contract or a salary increase, do not fool yourself into thinking you can pull it off without planning what you are going to say.

3. *Only negotiate for what you are prepared to do or are able to do.* Do not put issues, design expectations, or anything on the table that you have no intention of doing or cannot pull off.

4. *Use your power.* If the other person has more "power" than you have, you must reduce that power by the use of your own power. Power is based on perception. If you think you have it, you do. Using your power means having confidence in yourself and your point of view.

5. *Have patience.* The best negotiators know that it takes patience to work toward win-win conclusion. Nobody likes being browbeaten or intimidated into making a decision. You have an advantage by taking time rather than rushing.

Success in negotiation is not just a natural gift; it can be learned. Each successful negotiation affects how you conduct future negotiations. And how you go about a negotiation session will also affect the future relationship between the individuals involved.

Summary

Throughout this book, we have seen how there is more to interior design than being able to put colors, fabrics, and furniture together into a workable floor plan. One of the most important nondesign activities of the interior designer is selling. Without being able to quickly determine what the client needs and then having the ability to convince the client that the design ideas and products the designer establishes are what is needed, the designer cannot stay in business.

In this chapter we have reviewed some of the many techniques that are used by the designer to sell services and products. All these techniques help the designer conclude the sales presentation for services or products. Waiting for the client to say "I'll take it," usually leads to frustration and low revenues. The techniques discussed in this chapter are those commonly used by many design professionals. We have defined concept selling and looked at selling techniques, techniques concerning overcoming objections, and negotiating.

References

Bly, Robert W. 1991. *Selling Your Services*. New York: Henry Holt.

Delmar, Ken. 1984. *Winning Moves—The Body Language of Selling*. New York: Warner Books.

Faria, A. J., and H. Webster Johnson. 1993. *Creative Selling*, 5th ed. Cincinnati, Ohio: South-Western Publishing.

Fast, Julius. 1970. *Body Language*. New York: Pocket Books.

Fisher, Roger, and William Ury. 1981. *Getting to Yes*. New York: Penguin Books.

Frank, Milo O. 1986. *How to Get Your Point across in 30 Seconds or Less*. New York: Simon and Schuster.

Goodman, Dr. Gary S. 1984. *Selling Skills for the Non-Salesperson*. Englewood Cliffs, N.J.: Prentice-Hall.

Hopkins, Tom. 1982. *How to Master the Art of Selling*. New York: Warner Books.

Johnson, Spencer, and Larry Wilson. 1984. *The One Minute Sales Person*. New York: William Morrow and Company.

Nierenberg, Gerard I., and Henry H. Calero. 1971. *How To Read a Person Like a Book*. New York: Pocket Books.

Nierenberg, Juliet, and Irene S. Ross. 1985. *Women and the Art of Negotiating*. New York: Simon and Schuster.

Roth, Charles B. 1970. *Secrets of Closing Sales*, 4th ed. New York: Prentice-Hall.

Stasiowski, Frank. 1985. *Negotiating Higher Design Fees*. New York: Watson-Guptill.

Ziglar, Zig. 1991. *Ziglar on Selling*. Nashville, Tenn.: Thomas Nelson.

Chapter 20

Presentations

Designers make presentations throughout the phases of the relationship between the designer and the client. Presentations are made to initiate contact between the client and the designer. Presentations are made in order to obtain the right to prepare a design contract as well as obtain the signed contract. Designers are in effect making mini-presentations each time they meet with the client during the course of the project. And, of course, the designer often makes a final presentation near the end of the project design process.

Many designers really do not like making presentations. They do not like the butterflies that swell up in their stomachs or the idea that the client may not like or will question the designer's ideas. Other designers relish this part of professional practice. Their confidence, enthusiasm, and comfort in working with clients in these situations is admired by colleagues.

This chapter will provide some basic guidelines on making presentations. The chapter begins with a discussion of prospecting presentations. It also includes a discussion of marketing presentations to generate new clients. Especially for students, some comments about making project presentations are provided. The chapter concludes with numerous general guidelines for making any kind of design presentation.

Prospecting for Clients

Interior designers can no longer depend solely on past customers and referrals for new work. Design firms of all sizes and specialties must aggressively attract new clients by the use of promotional tools and thoughtful marketing strategies. Developing and implementing any of the promotional tools discussed in Chapter 18 provide a tangible means of marketing. An aggressive form of marketing that many designers today find useful is called prospecting.

Prospecting is the process of locating new clients and obtaining appointments with them to discuss how the design firm may assist the client. *Prospects* are potential clients in the firm's business area who may require design services. They would include clients who have worked with competitors, though not those clients already under contract with competitors. The annual business plan, specifically the marketing section of that plan, is used to identify potential clients in the firm's business area (see Chapter 17).

Identifying potential prospects is only part of the process. The designer must also qualify prospects. Qualifying a prospect means that the designer has determined that there is sufficient reason to pursue a prospect. To be most effective, the designer should devote time to those potential clients who have the greatest likelihood of retaining the designer. Those clients that have the greatest likelihood of retaining the designer are those target clients identified in the marketing plan. Of course, not all potential clients in the firm's business area are really viable prospects. If the design firm specializes in restaurant design, for example, facilities that have been open for only a year or so will not need design services for some time. Restaurants that have been open for several years, however, may be looking for some kind of assistance, even if it is only a new carpet. Obviously, a design firm that is a restaurant designer/specifier is not interested in only selling carpet. This firm will want to focus on determining if clients need total design or total remodeling, not just product purchasing.

Prospecting presentations are generally done over the telephone or by stopping in on the client.[1] In many cases, these presentations are also called cold calling. *Cold calling* means that the designer is contacting potential clients that he or she has never met before. Telephone solicitations are a form of cold calling. Designers do not particularly enjoy cold calling—many feel that it is unprofessional. However, in today's market, competition has forced many designers to make greater use of cold calling techniques to obtain an initial in-depth meeting with potential clients. Although cold calling techniques such as telephone solicitations and drop-in visits are not the most effective means of marketing, they are techniques used by many in the profession as additional ways of making client contacts.

A prospecting presentation requires the development of information that explains to the client who the designer is and why the designer is contacting him or her. Since these contacts are usually short, the designer must get to the point quickly. For example, the following might be the kind of opening a designer could use to make a cold call on a potential client. "Hello, Mr. Stevens. My name is Rhonda Tower and I am the design director at Robbins and Porter Commercial Interiors. I saw in the Dodge Reports that your firm is planning to add office space at your Dallas facility. It would be our pleasure to make a presentation to you on how Robbins and Porter Commercial Interiors might be of service to your company."

The goal of the prospecting contact is to obtain an appointment with the client so that the designer may then make a marketing presentation. To make prospecting presentations, the designer must prepare carefully, just as he or she would with any kind of presentation. The designer should script what it is he or she wants to say before hand. This allows the designer to anticipate questions and objections. It is important to emphasize the benefits of the potential meeting to the client and clarify why it is of advantage to the client to listen to the designer's prospecting presentation. The details of the firm's services can be presented at the marketing presentation. Through the script, the designer must tell the client that he or she is interested in being of service to the client.

It is important for the designer to take notes as he or she talks to the potential client. The script may leave room for the notes below each question. Some designers develop contact sheets or cards to record the call. It is also important to keep track of names, titles, and key words that might give the designer a hint about the potential of the contact. Do not tape record the call. Recording a telephone conversation or a face-to-face meeting without the other person's permission can be illegal.

---

[1]No, the author is not advocating a door-to-door salesperson's approach to marketing design services. However, some individuals working in commercial design do make drop-by calls on potential commercial clients.

Marketing Presentations

Once the client has expressed an interest in the designer or firm, it is up to the project designer, design director, or marketing manager to gain enough information about the potential project to properly prepare for a formal marketing presentation. The purpose of a marketing presentation is for the designer to explain how he or she does a project and why the client should select the designer to do the pending project. Of course, only the larger design firms really think of this first in-depth meeting with the client as a "marketing presentation." Many designers simply think of this presentation as the initial interview and do not even think of it as a presentation. Whatever it is called, it is an important introduction of the designer to the potential client and should always be handled thoughtfully and professionally.

Both the designer and the client are trying to achieve specific goals in a marketing presentation. One important goal for the designer is an attempt to establish a relationship with the client that is conducive to business. Designers talk about the necessity of becoming friends with the client. Not literally, of course, but establishing empathy is important. This relationship is necessary so that the client will have confidence in the designer's ability to handle the project. The designer also wants to clarify the extent of the firm's experiences, ability, and interest in undertaking the potential project. This is generally the bulk of the marketing presentation. What many designers would consider to be the main goal of a marketing presentation is to leave with a firm commitment on the client's part for the designer to go forward with the project. Firm commitment generally means that the designer is ready to develop a design contract which will be presented a few days later. In some situations, a signed contract will already have been prepared as part of the marketing presentation. In those cases, the final goal of the presentation is to obtain the client's signature on the contract.

The client has several concerns he or she also wishes to address. Clients want to know how the designer approaches projects. Potential clients also want assurance that the designer is capable of handling the project. They do not want to find out later that the designer does not have the expertise to satisfactorily complete the project. In some situations, clients are looking for preliminary design solutions at the time of the marketing presentation. This is most often true of smaller projects than when extensive design planning and specification are required. What many clients feel are the most important bits of information the designer should provide at this time are the project costs and how long the project will take. Designers prefer to talk in generalities about design fees at this point, returning with a complete contract for design services a few days later. Except for small projects, designers also refrain from specifically quoting project costs for products and/or construction at this time. Should the client require estimates for products and construction, *feasibility studies,* which are in-depth estimates of the cost of planning and specification, can be accomplished within a few days or a few weeks. The remainder of this section provides many tips on conducting a marketing presentation.

Preparation

Major formal marketing presentations require a great deal of preparation. Few designers successfully obtain important or large projects based on presentations that are "spur of the moment" affairs. Whoever made the initial contact with the client has already obtained some valuable information about the direction and content of the presentation. The following are just a few of the questions that must be answered in order for the designer to put on the best possible marketing presentation.

1. What are the prospective project requirements?
2. To whom will the presentation be made?

3. How many people will attend the meeting?

4. Where will the presentation take place?

5. Who from the design firm should be involved in the presentation?

6. What is it about the design firm that the client will want to know?

The answers to all of these questions will have an influence on the content and format of the presentation itself.

In initial meetings, the project designer or design director has obtained enough information about the project to understand what kind of project is involved and some of the client's design goals. This information is obviously important in order for the content of the presentation to be focused on the type of project being proposed. For example, clients do not really care to hear how many doctor's offices a design firm has done if the project is a retail store. Likewise, they want to know if the designer is appropriately experienced to do the remodeling of their home, not if he or she knows everything there is to know about carpeting.

In most cases, the presentation is made to the person who will make the decisions regarding hiring the designer and approving the floor plans and specifications. In residential design, the designer rarely consults at this stage with anyone but the owner of the home and the family. In commercial design, it is not uncommon for the design firm to make initial contact with a purchasing agent, not the owner or principal of the company. In such cases, the designer may make an initial presentation to the purchasing agent and a more formal presentation to the owner at a later time. Commercial projects are often the responsibility of a group of clients. For example, a medical office building may be owned by a group of doctors. The marketing presentation would likely be made to the whole group. The level the presentation is to and the number of individuals involved will shape different planning strategies. For a few people, a photo portfolio of previous projects would work quite well. But for a larger group, it would probably be more effective to use slides or a video presentation.

Most designers prefer to conduct marketing presentations for major projects in the firm's office. This allows the designer to control the presentation environment. Distractions can be held to a minimum while the designer puts his or her best foot forward. In the case of smaller projects, the presentation or initial interview is conducted by the designer who will be responsible for the potential project. With larger projects and or in larger firms, marketing presentations are most commonly conducted by the design director. The lead or senior designer who will be responsible for the project will actively participate in the presentation.

The designer must make careful preparation of the graphic, written, and audiovisual materials that will be used. The middle of the marketing presentation is no time to discover that something is broken or missing. Visual aids for the meeting need to be organized and checked to be sure they are of a quality presentable to the client. Slides have an uncanny habit of going into the tray upside down. Boards or drawings need to be clean and neat. The proper number of brochures or other handouts must be prepared. Extra sets of hand-outs should be available in case additional members of the client's party arrive.

Part of the preparation involves determining who will participate from the design firm and what each person's role will be. For most residential projects, the designer who made the initial contact with the client will be making the presentation. In commercial firms, the presentation could be made by the designer assigned to the project, but more often it is the responsibility of the design director or project manager.[2] The designer(s) who will be re-

---

[2]In general, the larger the project, the more likely it will be for the design director to be the primary presenter.

sponsible for actually doing the project would also participate in the presentation. Be careful not to have so many representatives from the firm at the meeting as to overwhelm the client. Commercial design firms commonly intimidate clients with great groups of people with the mistaken belief that the client "wants to see the whole team." Remember that anyone from the design firm that comes to the presentation must participate in the presentation or he or she should not be there.

Content

The content of the presentation must do two things: answer questions that the client has about the designer's ability and experience to do the project and provide the designer the opportunity to tell his or her story. The client wants to know such things as how long it will take and how much it will cost to do the project. Because clients also want to know how the designer is going to solve their problem, it will be necessary to tell the client how the project will be approached.

As part of preparation, the designers involved in the presentation will have determined what will be covered and in what order. The agenda can be set up to follow this outline. The content of the presentation should take on the basic form of the old strategy in organizing any report or presentation:

1. Tell them what you are going to tell them.

2. Tell them.

3. Tell them what you told them.

4. Ask for the sale.

This four-step outline requires a bit of discussion since all but a few students and many designers consistently fail to accomplish the steps.

The first step, *tell them what you are going to tell them,* is quite simply an overview of what will be discussed at the meeting. This first step should include quickly going through the agenda, introducing other members of the design firm, and briefly describing what each will discuss. Part of the purpose of the first step is to stimulate the potential client's attention and interest. Even though the client has agreed to meet with the designer (which automatically suggests interest), the client still needs a reason to listen to the presentation. The *tell them what you are going to tell them* step provides that reason.

The second step, *tell them,* is the body or the presentation itself. It is important for the presenters to be enthusiastic, alert to the client's body language, and responsive to questions. The content of the main portion of the presentation focuses on discussing everything the firm members want the client to know about them as well as how the firm will approach the client's potential project. Answers to specific questions the client has revealed should also be handled. If the discussion digresses from the outline, the designer should go back to any item he or she feels still needs to be covered.

Step three, *tell them what you told them,* is a summary of the points that you have made during the presentation. Do not forget to remind the client of the important points he or she has heard. Remember to highlight the features and benefits of your services as they relate to the needs the client has expressed (see Chapter 19).

The last step, *ask for the sale,* amounts to requesting that the client give the go-ahead to prepare a design contract, sign the already prepared contract, or in some other way provide a positive conclusion to the presentation.

Designers often use a variety of techniques in the development of the content of a marketing presentation. The rest of this part discusses a few of them.

It is often useful to bring neat project files from previous projects similar to the one under discussion. These project files can be used to show the client how the firm organizes a project and controls all the documentation involved. Be sure to delete pricing information or other confidential information from the project file that might unduly influence the potential client.

Since clients are interested in seeing how other design problems similar to theirs have been solved, slides or photographs—especially before-and-after pictures or plans—graphically communicate how the firm handles interior design problems.

A marketing presentation must be a planned communication concerning what the client wants to know and what the designer wants to tell him or her. Winging it may make the presentation look fresh, but it also generally looks unprofessional and disorganized. A prepared presentation may sound the same to the designer since he or she has made it or heard it many times before. But it always sounds fresh to the client since he or she has never heard it before.

The biggest mistake the designer can make during the marketing presentation is to ignore that the client has goals and questions during this very early phase of a potential project. Too many designers get carried away with telling their story while forgetting to tell the client what he or she wants to know. The designer who has been careful to cover what the design firm wishes to tell about itself as well as to answer the questions of the client, will regularly conclude the presentation on a positive note.

The Presentation

It is difficult to describe a "model" or sure-fire presentation. There are far too many variables in such things as individual designer's style, customer interest, and kinds of design projects. However, it is possible to provide a few generally useful tips in conducting the presentation. Please note that while these tips are grouped in this section, they are applicable to almost any kind of design presentation.

An agenda or outline for the meeting should be prepared with the role determined for each participating member of the firm. For each individual presenter, the outline also helps make sure that what is necessary to be said will be said. Have this agenda ready to distribute to the client for the most formal of presentations. It would be optional for other situations.

A conference room at the design studio or office is preferable. The client should be positioned directly across from the designer or at right angles (see Figures 20–1 and 20–2). This allows the designer to easily see and evaluate the client's eyes and body language, which is important for evaluating whether the presentation is going well or whether the client's interest has been lost.

When it is necessary to go to the client's "territory," the designer should ask that a conference room be made available. Getting the client out of his or her office moves the presentation to a neutral area and allows for some control of the presentation situation by the designer. A presentation held in an office over the client's desk is not only an awkward situation, but it also allows the client to be distracted by phones, people dropping in, and other interruptions.

In the home, if at all possible, the presentation should be made in the dining room rather than the living room. For most families, the living room is the formal room, the room they can easily say "no" in. The dining room allows the designer to sit directly across or at right angles to the client, which is considered a more satisfactory informal situation.

During the presentation, the designer should be aware of his or her own body language and the body language of the client. If you must stand, stand relaxed, but with good posture. When sitting, lean forward showing interest in what you are saying and what the client says

Figure 20–1 This sketch shows the presentation arrangement in which the client and designer sit across the conference table from one another. (Drawing: Clayton E. Peterson)

Figure 20–2 This sketch shows the presentation arrangement in which the client and designer sit at right angles to ne another at the conference table. (Drawing: Clayton E. Peterson)

in response to your statements. If the client folds his or her arms across his or her chest, it might mean that the client does not like what is being said. Watch for the client either pushing back or leaning forward over the conference table. If he or she leans or pushes away from the table, he or she is possibly losing interest in what is being said. If he or she leans forward, this kind of body language indicates interest. There are many other body language indicators that help the designer interpret whether or not the message he or she is sending to the client is being received favorably. More information on body language can be found in some of the books listed in the References.

Use good eye contact. This does not mean staring down the client to make him or her uncomfortable. It does mean to look the client in the eye from time to time. Many perceive eye contact to mean honesty and trustworthiness. Others interpret the lack of eye contact to be related to either a lack of confidence or disinterest. Maintaining eye contact with an individual for about five seconds, looking away for awhile, and then returning to eye contact so that eye contact is maintained about 50 percent of the time is a beneficial use of the technique.

How you say what you say is also important in communicating a favorable message. Beware of using fillers like *er, well, okay, you see,* and *umm.* These words are indicators of powerless language. To the astute client, these fillers also show lack of preparation and lack of confidence in what the presenter is trying to say and sell. Instead of fillers, a controlled pause to create dramatic effect should be used. Also eliminate the use of qualifiers in your presentations. Qualifiers are words such as *but* or *however* used at the beginning of a sentence. A statement such as, "This is the best chair to use in your secretarial pool. However, there are others that have better fabrics available," dilutes the confidence the client needs in the decision making process. "Such hedges tend to be spoken with nonassertive body language (such as downcast eyes, slumped posture or a nervous smile) and in a timid, uncertain voice."[3]

Many designers and consultants believe that handouts should not be distributed until the verbal portion of the presentation is completed. When handouts are given to the client as the presentation continues, it is almost a certainty that he or she will look through the brochure, newsletters, contract, or whatever was handed out rather than listen to the presentation. The client often misses important points, and questions about what was said, which will mean lost time later. This could result in the designer's not being able to present everything he or she wanted to present because information has to be repeated. Enough time should be allowed at the end of the presentation for distributing and going over any handouts prepared for the client.

It is also commonly recommended that presentations not begin with slides, videos, or similar materials. Interest in those visuals should be built upon verbal presentations first. It is better to get the client excited and interested in what he or she will be seeing before showing visuals. When the visuals are presented, be careful not to show so many that the client falls asleep. Present a sufficient amount of visuals to make a strong impression without boring the client.

After the summary and the "ask for the sale" portion of the presentation is concluded, the designer should be sure to thank the client for his or her time. Do not forget to shake hands and use the last few minutes for small talk about continued interest in the project. Be friendly and continue to show confidence in obtaining and completing the project.

---

[3]Elsea, Janet G., *The Four-Minute Sell,* Simon and Schuster, 1984, p. 83.

Follow-Up

It is important after the presentation for the designer not to wait for the client to call. The designer should follow up on the presentation with a letter and/or a phone call. The follow-up contact should cover such things as thanking the client for his or her time, restating important points of the presentation, and emphasizing continued interest in working with the client. This courtesy may be all the client needs when deciding between two or more designers or design firms.

Any documentation, site visits, third party testimonials, or other actions that were promised during the presentation must be taken care of as promptly as possible. Delays also hurt the designer's chances of closing the sale.

Project Presentations

Project presentations may be conducted numerous times during the course of the contract. There are basically two kinds of project presentations—preliminary or ongoing presentations and final project presentations. Preliminary presentations are conducted periodically to insure that the designer is on track with his or her design decisions. The final presentation is conducted when the designer has completed all the project planning, design, and specifications required in the contract.

The goal of the designer during *preliminary presentations* is to obtain client approvals of whatever is being discussed. Obviously, approvals will not be achieved for everything at each preliminary presentation. Since this is where options are discussed, designers, especially young designers, must not let client objections frustrate them. Professional designers learn quickly that not all suggestions made by the designer are automatically approved by the client. Some designers even make certain kinds of suggestions that will guarantee being vetoed as a means of directing the client toward the solutions the designer wishes to pursue. In many cases, educating the client is a big part of the preliminary presentations. Clients sometimes want the darndest things in an interior, and part of the designer's responsibility is to explain why certain design ideas and concepts might not be appropriate for the client's situation and needs.

During preliminary presentations, designers often work more informally. They often use rough sketches and show drawings that are freehand rather than technically drawn. Many designers review floor plans and elevations on tracing paper. Product selections are shown as the pages from product catalogs and loose fabric and finish samples. This informality, as long as it is not sloppy and totally unprofessional looking, creates a comfortable atmosphere so that the client feels involved in the project. Changes at this stage do not waste a lot of the designer's time since materials are less formally prepared.

Clients should be asked to sign off on approved products and floor plan proposals. Many large firms use a form such as Figure 20–3 to detail preliminary and final product specifications. Note that the form provides a place for the client to initial or sign. Signed approvals allow the designer to move on through the project with confidence. The signed approval also provides a mechanism to charge clients for work that has to be redone because the client changes his or her mind *after* the initial approval.

Whether the preliminary and final presentations are held at the client's location or the designer's office is really dependent on the designer's style, the size of the project, and the demands of the client. The client wants to feel in control of the project and when the designer comes to him or her, the client feels in control. The larger or more complex the project, the more likely the preliminary presentations will be held at the designer's office. Having preliminary presentations at the designer's office also provides access to additional resources such as the product materials and diazo machine should it be necessary to make

Product Control Sheet

Job Name: _____   **Job #:** _____

Room/Area: _____   **Control Number:** _____

Item Specification
Manufacturer:
Catalog Number:
Case/Frame Finish:
Hardware Finish:
Size   W: D: Ht: Sh:
Other:
Special Installation Instructions:
Fabric:
Grade: Yards Required/Unit:
Repeat: Stain Repellent: Fire Retardent:
COM Supplier:

Sketch/Photograph	Fabric

Delivery Time: _____   **Shipping Location:** _____
_____
_____

Unit Price (net): _____   **Quantity:** _____

Upholstery: _____

Special Handling: _____   **Freight:** _____

Total Item Net _____   **Delivery:** _____

Client Signature: _____

© 1993, Christine Piotrowski

Figure 20–3 Typical control sheet that can be used for client sign-off on each item for which agreement has been achieved.

additional prints. Many of the design professionals that the author spoke to prefer to conduct preliminary meetings at the client's location unless the project is quite large and complex. "We have found that going to the job site or office is good psychologically for clients. They are paying us to develop design ideas, but they want to be serviced. Going to them in the early stages is one of the ways we service the client," related a design director. Residential designers often find it is helpful to make the preliminary presentation at the client's home. Many interior designers who specialize in residential report that showing the client everything in the environment in which it will be placed works very well.

The key to successful preliminary presentations is never forgetting three things: first, always give the client some choices during the presentation. Designers often use a trick of presenting three options. One option works, but really is a fairly obvious poor choice (though the designer should not admit this). The second option is an acceptable alternative—something the designer can "live" with. The third option is the one the designer is most interested in using. Making it look as though the client has no voice in the project often leads to the client feeling left out and can produce disagreement even though the client may like the design concepts presented.

Second, always involve the client in the presentation. Ask the client questions, especially questions that bring acceptance of the concepts under discussion. Getting the client involved makes it easier for the client to feel comfortable about the design concepts. Feeling comfortable about design concepts leads to a greater chance of final approval at the end of the formal presentation.

Third, keep the preliminary presentations relaxed and somewhat informal. Following this tip keeps the presentation "preliminary." Discussion and disagreement need to occur during the preliminary presentation. Formality might encourage tension while informality allows for the necessary give-and-take that must occur in early stages of the project. Of course, the preliminary presentation must still be presented using appropriate businesslike behavior. There is a time for jokes and there is a time for business.

Final project presentations are done to review the design decisions one last time. The goal of the final project presentation is to obtain the go-ahead to order product or begin the bidding process. Ideally, the designer is hoping for approval of all the design concepts and product selections. Of course, it is more common that a few changes are still made at this stage.

With very large projects, a substantial amount of time may have elapsed since the last preliminary presentation. Final presentations pull all the earlier decisions together into one package. They also are used to show the client specialized graphics such as detailed rendered floor plans, perspectives, sample boards, models, and perhaps computer simulations. All the last-minute hesitations by the client must be resolved at this time so the project can go forward. Presenting the final cost estimates (for bid situations) or actual final cost of the project is also done at this time. The designer must be ready not only to defend design decisions, but also be prepared to negotiate any questions about costs of the project. Signed approvals on product selections and plans should also be obtained. The signed documents become part of the project files, just like those obtained during the preliminary presentation.

In contrast to the preliminary presentations, most designers prefer that the final project presentation be made at the designer's office. This is especially true of larger projects. Again, it is a matter of designer and design firm style. Knowing where the final presentations will occur is important so that the designer can know how to put the documentation together. In reality, presenting a relatively simple project to one or two clients can be done successfully over a conference table, the client's desk, or even a dining room table. When the project is complex and several representatives of the client will need to be present, a different set of presentation graphics may need to be prepared.

Reviewing project materials with the client is an important professional activity. Designers need to have thought as much about how to show the drawings and other documents as about what is to be said. Involving the client in the presentation, using professional language without getting hung up on jargon or highly technical descriptions, exuding confidence in the designer's ideas, and creating excitement and enthusiasm in the design solutions are all important parts of conducting successful preliminary and final presentations.

Other Guidelines for Making Presentations

The preceding material in this chapter has discussed many tips for making specific types of design presentations. Frequently, these tips overlap and are a useful part of any kind of presentation. In fact, many of the items discussed can be applied to job interviews, asking for a raise or promotion, and even dealing with personal out-of-office relationships. This last section provides several additional presentation guidelines that students and designers alike might find useful in their professional practice.

- You only have one chance to make a first impression. Remember that the first 30 to 60 seconds create the strongest impression. Do your best to make this initial contact as professional and confidence-building as possible.

- Facial expressions should be relaxed and friendly. Do not scowl or look so tense that you appear ready to have root-canal work. If you know what you are going to say and have confidence in your ability to pull off the presentation, it will be easy to look as though you are having a good time.

- Stick to your time limit. Be sure you understand how long you have for the presentation and never exceed the time limit unless the client gives permission.

- Never be late for the presentation or begin the presentation late by your own fault.

- Final presentations must not be taken lightly. Designers need to be thinking of how they are completing the necessary presentation documents.

- If you develop standardized presentations, be sure they are tailored for each different client. Lawyers want to know about how you have handled law offices, not homes.

- Plan for breaks, if necessary. Especially long presentations such as many major, final project presentations, may take two hours or more. Plan breaks into your presentation and use the time to set up additional visuals. Since it is your presentation, arrange for refreshments as well.

- Prior to a presentation, do not consume milk products, salty foods, or alcohol. These items dehydrate most people, and most designers do not need to get "cotton mouth" in the middle of a presentation. If you are susceptible to dry mouth, be sure you have a glass of water handy.

- Do not smoke during your presentation even if your client does. The cigarette will get in your way and distract the client from what you are saying.

- Talk to the client, not the board or projector screen. Too many designers and students direct what they are saying to the board or screen rather than the audience. The client does not want to admire your back. He or she wants to see your face as you are talking. Observe how weather broadcasters gesture and communicate the weather. They are very good at communicating while keeping their face to the camera.

- Be a good listener. Really pay attention to the comments and questions of the client. Do not worry about what you are going to say in the middle of what the client is asking. You will probably miss important information.

- Do not criticize competition. If the client asks you what you think of a competitor, say something simple like "I understand he is a competent designer." Bad-mouthing the competition is unprofessional and will only come back to haunt you later.

- Do not forget to incorporate third party testimonials into your presentation. The fact that Apple Computer, for example, is using a particular product may be an important selling point to a client.

- If you make a mistake, do not make a big deal out of it. Calling attention to the problem only makes you feel worse and may totally throw you off balance. Say something like, "Let me clarify that last point," and move on.

- If a piece of equipment does not work properly or there is a problem with a sample board, for example, quickly determine if you can go on without the item. If it is critical to your presentation, one of the other members from the design firm can fix the item while you continue with other information. If that is not possible, suggest a short break so that you can fix the item without the client watching. Of course, this should not have happened if you checked out everything before the presentation began.

- Do not get into an argument with the other party. Even if you are "right," arguing sets the wrong impression. Try to move on as graciously as possible.

- If the potential project is out of the country or with foreign companies, bone up on body language and customs of the other country. This kind of homework is absolutely necessary if your firm seeks to work with clients from around the world.

- Use an outline or script. Designers who are lacking in presentation experience or are uncomfortable with making presentations need to write out what they want to say. However, it is unwise to read this script back to the client. It sounds very unnatural.

- Always define your goals. If you do not know what you want to say or accomplish in your meeting, you will almost always be dissatisfied at the end of the meeting.

- Anticipate the other person's responses and questions. Trying to determine what the other party's concerns are makes you more thorough and professional.

- Be enthusiastic. Clients cannot be excited about a project if you are not enthusiastic yourself.

- Dress appropriately. Business clients expect designers to look as though they understand business. Residential clients generally are comfortable with more trendy attire than with conservative business clothing.

- Use professional language. Part of being a professional is sounding professional. Use proper language and speak distinctly. It is okay to use technical words, but be prepared to explain any technical language incorporated into the presentation

- Use good posture. Stand and sit straight, shoulders back—just as Mother always said!

- Use gestures carefully. Gestures are helpful to emphasize important points. Hands that are constantly in motion are distracting.

- As much as possible, use consistent graphics. For example, it is more difficult to present boards when one is horizontal and the next vertical, and back again. The same can be said for slides. A consistent look indicates that you have thought about all the little details so that you will be prepared to handle the big details.

- Practice, practice, practice! The more often you run thorough a presentation, especially with a colleague there to critique, and the more often you do presentations, the easier and more effective they will become.

Summary

Designers are constantly making presentations. The focus of the presentation might be to make contact with a prospective client, conduct initial project interviews or marketing presentations, or explaining and defending design plans and specifications during the course of the project. Designers also make presentations when they interview for jobs, negotiate raises with the boss, participate in professional association meetings, and many other situations that may be business- or nonbusiness-related. Successfully navigating through the presentation builds confidence and increases the designer's professional competence.

Few educational programs strongly emphasize presentation techniques though many recommend or require students to take speech classes. A great deal of emphasis is placed on how to technically do the graphics, but less on how to make the presentation. Students and professionals generally learn how to do presentations through "on the job training." In this chapter, we have discussed many techniques and provided numerous guidelines on structuring and performing design presentations. Considering and practicing these concepts when faced with making a presentation should help students and professionals make effective design presentations.

This concludes the discussion on marketing of design services and business development. In the next part we will cover the many activities related to project management.

References

Axtell, Roger E. 1991. *Gestures.* New York: Wiley.

Bly, Robert W. 1991. *Selling Your Services.* New York: Henry Holt.

Delmar, Ken. 1984. *Winning Moves—The Body Language of Selling.* New York: Warner Books.

Elsea, Janet G. 1984. *The Four-Minute Sell.* New York: Simon and Schuster.

Faria, A. J., and H. Webster Johnson. 1993. *Creative Selling,* 5th ed. Cincinnati, Ohio: South-Western Publishing.

Hoff, Ron. 1988. *I Can See You Naked. A Fearless Guide to Making Great Presentations.* Kansas City, MO.: Andrews and McMeel Books.

Tom Hopkins. 1982. *How to Master the Art of Selling.* New York: Warner Books.

Jones, Gerre. 1983. *How to Market Professional Design Services,* 2d ed. New York: McGraw-Hill.

Kenney, Michael, for Eastman Kodak Company. 1982. *Presenting Yourself.* New York: Wiley.

King, David, and Karen Levine. 1979. *The Best Way in the World for a Woman to Make Money.* New York: Warner Books.

LaBella, Arleen, and Dolores Leach. 1983. *Personal Power.* Boulder, Col.: New View Press.

Molloy, John T. 1975. *Dress for Success.* New York: Warner Books.

————. 1977. *The Woman's Dress for Success Book.* New York: Warner Books.

————. 1981. *Molloy's Live for Success.* New York: Perigord Press–William Morrow.

Nierenberg, Gerard I., and Henry H. Calero. 1971. *How to Read a Person Like a Book.* New York: Pocket Books.

Peoples, David A. 1988. *Presentations Plus.* New York: Wiley.

Smith, Terry C. 1984. *Making Successful Presentations.* New York: Wiley.

Thompson, Jacqueline, ed. 1981. *Image Impact.* New York: A & W Publishers.

Ziglar, Zig. 1982. *Zig Ziglar's Secrets of Closing the Sale.* New York: Berkley Books.

PART V

Project Management

Chapter 21

Project Management Techniques

Interior design is a process in which the designer must obtain and assimilate information in order to convert that information into design concepts, space plans and furniture plans, and sketches and projected drawings. Furniture items and finishes must be selected and color schemes coordinated. These graphic and written forms of design documents are used to explain the design concepts to the client and show him or her how goals will be accomplished. Yet, when all that is done, only about 50 percent of the project has been completed.

In principle, it does not matter if the project is a living room or a new Las Vegas megahotel. The design process, the project phases, and project management are the same. All projects must be managed so that the required work is done quickly, correctly, and with as few problems as possible. That is not an easy task. As one senior project designer related, "My dream is to have a project go from start to finish with no problems, no extra worries, no delays. After 14 years of commercial work, it still hasn't happened."

This chapter begins the discussion of project management by providing a brief overview of the phases of a complete design project. It continues by explaining basic concepts and techniques of time management and time records. To an interior designer, one of the absolute truths is that time equals money. Whether the designer is paid by the hour or receives compensation in some other way, the efficient, productive use of time has a direct bearing on yearly income. It is therefore very important for the interior designer to make the best use of his or her time while on the job.

It is also very important for the designer to control the project instead of letting the project control the designer. The scheduling methods that help the designer and design manager keep track of activity for each project and when each phase needs to be completed are an important factor in project control. This chapter will conclude with brief discussions on project budgeting and project files or job books. Project management requires the careful use of the designer's time, recording and retention of information, the use of numerous forms and documents, and other tasks necessary to complete a design project. Few designers can be successful without careful project management.

Project Phases and Project Management

Interior design projects have several distinct phases. Though some firms may use slightly different terms for these phases, a design project generally consists of the programming phase, the schematic design phase, design development, the contract documents phase, the construction administration phase, and the project completion stage. Obviously, not all work done by all interior designers always involves the many activities that fall into each of these project phases.

Understanding what goes on in each phase as it relates to the business management of the firm is very important to professionals and students alike. This section will not attempt to fully describe how to do these phases or how to do a project. There are many other books the reader might use for that. Rather, this section will briefly describe how to manage the phases of a project. In small firms, managing these phases is the responsibility of the project designer. In larger design firms, the project designer will be relieved of some responsibility as others become involved in certain phases or activities.

For our purposes, we will assume that the information necessary to prepare a design contract has already been obtained and that the contract has been signed by the client. Refer to Chapter 15 for information about how the initial information to prepare a design contract is gathered.

Programming Phase

The *programming phase* is often thought of as the information-gathering portion of a project. The designer seeks from the client and other involved individuals as much information as possible about the interior space, functional needs, aesthetics, and expectations concerning the project. In this phase, client interviews are conducted to determine the client's goals and objectives, visits are made to the job site, and inventories and analysis of existing furnishings and equipment are conducted. In addition, interviews with employees might be conducted and designers may be required to field-measure the site or obtain floor plans. Much time must be spent and careful notes must be taken in order for the interior designer to successfully design and prepare the documents required for completing the project.

Designers are helped through this process by utilizing a variety of specialized forms. Client interview forms developed by many firms help define the client's needs related to space requirements and furnishings and equipment requirements. For large commercial office projects, designers might find employee questionnaires more time-efficient. Office systems manufacturers such as Steelcase Inc., Herman Miller Inc., and Haworth, Inc., provide detailed workstation and employee interaction questionnaires for use by designers. When the client feels he or she needs to use existing equipment, designers may use a special form to analyze and inventory the furniture and equipment the client already owns. These are just a few examples of the special forms that designers create to help obtain the information they will need about the client's requirements and the interior space to be designed.

Schematic Design Phase

The *schematic design phase* involves the execution of preliminary design decision's. Students and professionals alike realize that this phase is where written design concepts are finalized along with preliminary floor plans, design sketches, as well as the selection of preliminary materials, finishes, and equipment. From a project management point of view, the designer is working with estimating forms for the architectural finishes, furniture specifications, construction estimates from contractors, and budgets. Estimating forms such as Figure 21–1 help designers in this phase of the project.

With the review and approval of the selections and graphic documents, the designer is

WALLCOVERING

OFFICE
DESIGNS
A WALSH BROS. AFFILIATE

PROJECT _____ PROJ. # _____

BILLING ADD. _____ INST. ADD. _____

_____   _____

_____   _____

CONTACT_____ PHONE _____ - _____ - _____

☐ ROOM (NO.) (NAME) _____

☐ MANUFACTURER: _____ PHONE _____ - _____ - _____

   PATTERN _____ YDS/ROLL _____

   COLOR _____ ROLLS/BOLT _____

   WIDTH _____ REPEAT _____ PRE-TRIMMED (YES)   (NO)

   NET/ (YD) (ROLL) (BOLT) (LIN. FT.) (LIN. YD.) _____

   (* MIN YDGE REQ.) _____   FREIGHT _____

                    QTY. REQ'D _____ X _____ = [_____]

   STOCK CHECKED/DATE _____ NAME _____

   RESERVED/DATE _____ TIME _____ WITH _____ HOW LONG _____

   ORDERED (PHONE) (NORMAL)   DATE _____ TO SHIP _____ HOW _____

☐ INSTALLATION REQUIREMENTS: ☐ SEALING REQ'D   ☐ EVENING INST.

   ☐ NEW CONST.   ☐ PLATES COVERED   ☐ WEEKEND INST.

   ☐ REMOVE EXIST. MAT.   ☐ NORMAL INST.   ☐ WEEKDAY/END INST.

   ☐ FLOATING REQ'D   ☐ _____   ☐ _____

☐ ESTIMATE:

   ☐ PLAN FURNISHED   ☐ PHYSICAL MEASURE

   QUOTED BY_____ DATE _____

   INSTALLATION PRICE/ (YARD) (ROLL) (BOLT) (LF)_____ X _____ = [_____]

   SPECIAL REQ. PRICING _____ = [_____]

                              GRAND TOTAL = [_____]

                                     M.U. = _____

                                     S.P. = [_____]

1808 NORTH CENTRAL AVENUE / POST OFFICE BOX 1711 / PHOENIX, ARIZONA 85001 / (602) 252-4433

Figure 21–1 An estimating form to help establish what kind and how much wall covering will be needed for a project. (Reprinted with permission, Office Designs, Phoenix, AZ.)

ready to move on to the next phase of the project. Many designers require client signatures or at least the initialing of plans, drawings, and specification sheets prior to moving to the next phase. Obtaining client sign-offs at this stage provides assurance of proper reimbursement to the designer for any changes that the client makes while the designer is preparing finalized drawings and documents (see Figure 20–3 in the previous chapter).

Design Development Phase

The *design development phase* of a project involves the preparation of all final plans, presentation graphics, and specifications that are required to explain the design concepts to the client. Along with these graphic documents, the designer prepares a more complete project budget. The project budget is the common project management form necessary at this stage. Figure 21–2 is an example of a budget for a project that will not be put out for competitive bidding. Depending on the project and the actual design responsibilities, the client will be receiving either the actual pricing and equipment lists for furniture, finishes, and equipment, or an estimate with broader specifications pending formal bidding. Here again, it is very important for the designer to obtain signed approvals of all drawings and specifications before moving the project on to the contract documents stage.

Contract Documents Phase

The *contract documents phase* of the design project involves the final preparation of all construction or working drawings, schedules, and specifications required to build and install the design project. Much of this work will be accomplished with the use of computers in larger firms. For projects that will be procured through the competitive bid process, detailed specifications concerning the furnishings, finishes, and equipment will be prepared along with the construction specifications. A detailed discussion of specification documents and the bid process can be found in Chapter 23.

Contract Administration Phase

The *contract administration phase,* sometimes called the construction/installation phase, is the portion of the project that involves actual construction work as well as the placing of orders for all the furniture and equipment and installation of architectural finishes. The project management responsibility for interior designers in this stage centers on the ordering, receiving, and installation supervision of furniture and finishes. Several forms are an integral part of this phase. They include the purchase order, acknowledgment, invoice, and shipping forms. These documents are discussed in Chapter 24.

Along with ordering merchandise or letting construction contracts during this phase will be work supervision. Interior designers are traditionally responsible for the installation supervision of the architectural finishes and furnishings they have specified for the project. Coordination and cooperation with the architect, general contractor, and subcontractors is necessary to insure the smooth accomplishment of the overall project. As discussed in Chapter 6, interior designers must be careful that they hold the proper license to do the installation supervision, or must be willing to relinquish this responsibility to a licensed contractor.

Project Completion Phase

The last phase of the project, the *project completion phase,* primarily involves inspecting the job site to be sure that all the work and merchandise required for the project has been done properly, completely, and in accordance to the specifications. Site inspections, usually called a *walk through,* are done by the designer with the client to determine if there are any omis-

Preliminary Specifications

Client _____

Job Number _____ Date _____

Designer _____ Room/Area_____

Quantity	Manufacturer	Catalog #	Description	Unit Price	Total Price
				Total	
				Freight	
				Delivery	

Special Instructions

© 1993, Christine Piotrowski

Figure 21–2 Specification form that can be used to produce a project budget.

sions or damages. Notations are made on a form called a *punch list*. Final payment to the designer is often withheld until all items on the punch list are taken care of. Larger design firms often prepare *postoccupancy evaluations* a short time after the client has moved in. These might be just for the use of the design firm or as part of the fine-tuning process desired by the client. These activities and forms are discussed in Chapter 25.

One form used by design firms throughout the phases of the project is the *transmittal letter* (see Figure 21–3). The transmittal letter is a form letter that can be used for many purposes. It can be used to send information to the client, consulting architects and/or engineers, subcontractors, leasing agents, manufacturers, or anyone involved with the project.

The transmittal is designed to eliminate the need to write a separate letter or memo in order to transmit or ask for information. It is a handy fill-in-the-blank form that should be sent with materials of any kind. It tells the receiver what is being sent and for what purpose. It also gives instructions to the receiver for resubmittal or action the sender requires. It is an invaluable aid to speedy correspondence. Usually a two-part form, the original goes with the material being sent and the copy is placed in the job file.

Time Management

As professionals in all fields find they have more to do, theories of time management and organization have evolved. Time management theories were not developed to make the user a slave to his or her job, but rather to help him or her organize time to be as productive as possible on the job. Books discussing time management techniques abound. They all are based on similar concepts of creating to-do lists, prioritizing those lists, handling papers once, and keeping a calendar and reminder notebook handy.

Time management has to do with control, decision making, and planning. It does not suggest that a person controls his or her time so rigidly that there is no room for flexibility to meet emergencies. Nor is it so loose to prohibit getting anything of value done. In his book, *How to Get Control of Your Time and Your Life,* Alan Lakin, a renowned time management consultant, discussed the 80/20 rule. As it relates to time management, the *80/20 rule* maintains that when activities are arranged in order of importance, 80 percent of a person's time will be spent performing 20 percent of the activities. What this means is that, in a list of ten items, if a person accomplishes the two most important items, he or she achieved 80 percent of the total value of time spent. Most companies can look at sales records and see that approximately 80 percent of the sales was generated by 20 percent of the sales staff. The main thrust of the 80/20 rule is to concentrate efforts on the few items with the highest priority to generate the greatest value or return.

Determining which activity has the highest priority is done by generating a daily to-do list and prioritizing that list. Early in the morning or very near the end of the day, a person should prepare a list of what has to be done for that or the following day. Items on this list come from previous lists, calendars, schedules, memos, and so on. Decisions are made with regard to what needs to be done for the day—or at least attempted. This can be "complete the floor plan revisions for Jones's house," or "select the carpet for the Andrews' living room," and even "pick up cleaning on the way home."

Items on the list should also be planned for expected time use. How long will it take to complete the floor plan revisions, and so on? If expected time allowances are not planned, one tends to get frustrated with a neverending list that never seems to get done. Because interruptions and emergencies occur, it is wise to plan for one less hour of work per day. For example, plan for a seven-hour work day rather than a full eight-hour day. The one hour of padding allows for phone calls, drop-in visitors, emergency projects, and so forth.

The next step is to prioritize the list by categorizing each item as *A* or *B* (see Figure 21–4). *A*-items are the more important tasks needing to be done that day. Depending on the item, noncompletion of an *A*-task could damage the designer's reputation or the reputation

LETTER OF TRANSMITTAL

DATE:		JOB NO.
ATTENTION:		
RE:		

INTERIOR ASSOCIATES, INC.
DESIGN GROUP OF AHERN PERSHING
300 S.W. 5th STREET · DES MOINES, IA · 50309 · (515) 244-0193

TO: _____

ITEMS TRANSMITTED

☐ ATTACHED
☐ UNDER SEPERATE COVER

	QUAN.	DATE	DESCRIPTION
☐ COPY OF LETTER	_____	_____	_____
☐ CHANGE ORDER	_____	_____	_____
☐ ORIGINAL DRAWINGS	_____	_____	_____
☐ SEPIAS	_____	_____	_____
☐ PRINTS	_____	_____	_____
☐ SPECIFICATIONS	_____	_____	_____
☐ SAMPLES	_____	_____	_____
☐ SHOP DRAWINGS	_____	_____	_____
☐	_____	_____	_____

REASON TRANSMITTED

☐ APPROVAL
☐ REVIEW AND COMMENT
☐ FOR INFORMATION

☐ APPROVED AS NOTED
☐ CORRECT AND RESUBMIT
☐ NOT APPROVED

☐ RETURN SIGNED ORIGINAL
☐ AS REQUESTED
☐ APPROVED AS SUBMITTED
☐

REMARKS _____

COPIES _____

SIGNED _____

Figure 21–3 A typical transmittal letter. Used by design firms to accompany samples and drawings sent to other designers, vendors, or others involved in the project. (Reproduced with permission, Interior Associates, Inc., Des Moines, IA)

Activities for April 14, 1986	
① MEET WITH ROY FOR PATRICK CORP CHARGES (8:30)	45 MIN
② CALL DR CUMMINGS 555-0528	30 MIN
③ MEET WITH TOM DAVIS 7 REVIEW PLANS (10:30)	1 hr 30 MIN
⑤ WORK ON PLANS FOR SOUTHEAST CENTER	2 HRS
④ LUNCH MEETING STEELCASE (12:30)	1 HR
⑥ CALL CARPET INSTALLER — SET MEETING TO Go OVER PLANS7 DR CUMMINGS	15 MIN
⑦ WORK ON SPECS FOR ROBERTSON HOUSE	2 HRS
⑧ WORK ON FAB SELECTIONS FOR ELLIS	

Notes
PICK UP CLEANING
TENNIS LESSON   7:30 PM

Figure 21–4 A prioritized to-do list showing activities and time estimates for completion.

of the company. The completion of B-tasks is less pressing; B-tasks could be finished the next day or some other day.

Once items are all listed as A or B, they should be prioritized further by number. After this numbering has been done, the 20 percent of tasks that will gain the 80 percent of value will appear. Work on accomplishing A1 first, then move on to A2 and so on. If A2 cannot be done (for example, A2 was to call a client, but the client was not in), move on to A3 and plan to go back to A2 a little later in the day. Record that the call was made but that the client could not be reached. (Record also if a message was left for the client).

Crossing items off the list as they are completed shows accomplishment and allows for a feeling of satisfaction. Those tasks not completed are transferred to the next day's list. If an item continually shows up on the list, but never gets done, the task may need to be labeled an A1 some day! It also may point to a problem (for example, a habit of procrastinating too much on certain kinds of activities), or a need to reassess effective use of time during the day.

A key to the to-do list is to break down big projects into small segments. Any large-sized task should be broken down into manageable segments with target dates that will lead to the completion date required. This method will assure getting the project done on time.

It is important to keep the to-do list handy, along with a daily appointment calendar. There are several kinds of calendars available. One of the best calendars to purchase or develop is the "portable desk," an organization that contains a monthly calendar, a day-by-day calendar divided by hours, pages for the to-do list, and memo paper. The portable desk organizes schedules, appointments, and notes in one notebook.

A final note about time management. The suggested methods for time management do work, but it takes a certain amount of discipline to get into the habit of creating to-do lists and prioritizing them every day. New habits are difficult to generate and it is necessary to keep after this one in order to obtain results.

Time Records

Since so many designers charge for services by hourly rates, it is crucial to keep accurate time records for all professional services. Keeping time records involves documenting, as closely as possible, all time spent on projects and other office or company business.

Time records are kept for several reasons:

1. To keep accurate records for billing, particularly if charging by the hour for professional services; some clients wish to see time records before paying their bills.

2. To check on the progress of current jobs in order to determine if too much time is being used. If the project is running over the estimated time, the reasons need to be analyzed: Did the client change his or her mind too often? Is the designer being nonproductive? Was there an error in the requirements or plans? Was enough time budgeted?

3. To relate amount of profit to time spent on the project. A client who requires a lot of selling or time-use for activities like specification writing and drafting, may not be profitable unless charged by the hour.

4. To help determine budget and fees for new projects based on recorded histories. If the company has a history that 2000-square-foot residence jobs can be accomplished in X amount of hours, that information saves time and errors in writing new contracts or even determining if that kind of project should be taken again.

5. To determine how productive staff members are and give management an indication of how much time is billable (versus time devoted to nonbillable house time).

A wide variety of management control reports can be generated from time sheets. These reports were discussed more fully in Chapter 12.

Time records are only as accurate as employees keep them. How exact the records need to be will be a function of management control. Most companies only expect the designers to record time based on quarter-hours. And the designers must record the activities of a normal work day plus any overtime. It is easy for most people to keep track of a day's activities on one sheet and then transfer the time related to individual projects and nonbillable time to the appropriate sheet for that project. Records need to be kept on a daily basis and, depending on the needs of the firm, compiled on a weekly or monthly basis. The example shown in Figure 21–5 can be used for the daily report sheet or the weekly or monthly report. Each report should contain the client's name or the project's name, the designer's name, a description of the work, and the hours of work per description.

TIME RECORD

JOB NO.

CLIENT				DESIGNER	
ADDRESS				MONTH OF	19
CITY	STATE	ZIP		SALESPERSON	

DATE	DESCRIPTION OF WORK DONE	DESIGN	DRAFTING	SUPPORT
	TOTAL HOURS FOR MONTH			

COMMENTS

TOTAL _____ HRS. AT $ _____ = $ _____

MATERIALS_____ = $ _____

TOTAL CHARGE $ _____

PAGE

OF

Figure 21–5 Preprinted form that is used to record time worked on design projects. This firm uses one time sheet per customer rather than combining all client work on one sheet. (Reproduced with permission, Goodmans Design-Interiors, Phoenix, AZ.)

Project Schedules

Project schedules help the designer maintain control of the project. As mentioned earlier, breaking down a large task into manageable units helps to get the task done on time. In contract work, projects are often large, and it is vital to the designer and the client that they be done in an organized fashion.

Project schedules can take many forms, depending on who is using the information. For the designer responsible, the schedule may be day-by-day—or, at least, week-by-week—descriptions of what must be done to reach the target completion date. For the project manager or design director, a week-by-week or monthly schedule would be needed to aid in accepting, estimating, and assigning new work.

Milestone charts may be the easiest method of scheduling. Here the designer outlines the activities required by the project and establishes a target date for their completion (see Figure 21-6). Space to indicate who has responsibility for each activity may also be part of the chart. The actual date of completion should be noted, as this will aid in future estimating.

A reasonably easy, yet more graphic, method of scheduling is by use of a bar chart. Figure 21-7 provides an example. This chart can be done on a daily basis for the designers with responsibility for the project, or it can be a simple monthly chart for the design manager. The bar charts will help in future estimating of time needed for similar projects.

Bar charts consist of a description of tasks required on the left and horizontal bars showing the time in days, weeks, or months required to complete the task on the right. A disadvantage of the bar chart method is that it does not necessarily show how one activity affects another activity nor which is most important to complete the project on time. Analysis of the most important activities can be developed with more careful project analysis and a more complex color-coded bar chart. For most firms, either the milestone or the bar chart method will work very well.

For some very complex projects, a third method may be needed. The *critical path method (CPM)* is a scheduling method dependent upon the interrelationships of activities and the detailed tasks of each activity. Any one activity in a sequence cannot be completed unless the previous tasks and related activities have been completed. Due to its complex nature, only the larger interior design firms find CPM appropriate for project scheduling when they are involved in large projects. CMP is commonly used by architects and the construction industry to maintain control of the interrelated construction process.

Briefly, CPM scheduling starts by identifying the interrelationships of the tasks to be performed. This analysis shows the project manager which tasks must be done before the next or other tasks can be performed—thus establishing the critical path (see Figure 21-8). A simple critical path in an interior design project would be to obtain needs from the client, prepare floor plans, obtain client approval, order products, and install and/or deliver products. It is clear that it is impossible, as well as unwise, to try to do any of these tasks prior to completing the one directly preceding it. There are many computer programs that can help the interior designer utilize CPM for scheduling. Other computer software packages that can provide graphic charting using the other scheduling methodologies are also available.

Project: Weldone Residence						
Designer: Maryanne						
Task Name	Days	Earliest Start	Earliest Finish	Latest Start	Latest Finish	Actual Finish
Interview Client	3	9/23/86	9/26/86	10/3/86	10/8/86	9/23/86
Obtain Floor Plan	1	9/24/86	9/25/86	10/7/86	10/8/86	9/24/86
Inventory Existing Furniture	1	9/25/86	9/25/86	10/7/86	10/8/86	10/5/86
Sketch Preliminary Plan	7	9/26/86	10/7/86	10/8/86	10/17/86	10/6/86
Preliminary Selections	5	9/26/86	10/3/86	10/10/86	10/17/86	10/7/86
Prepare Preliminary Budget	2	10/6/86	10/7/86	10/15/86	10/20/86	10/8/86
Meet With Client	1	10/7/86	10/8/86	10/17/86	10/20/86	10/8/86
Revise Preliminary Plan	5	10/8/86	10/15/86	10/20/86	10/27/86	10/14/86
Revise Selections	3	10/7/86	10/20/86	10/27/86	10/30/86	10/17/86
Prepare Final Budget	1	10/20/86	10/20/86	10/29/86	11/3/86	10/23/86
Final Presentation to Client	2	10/20/86	10/22/86	10/30/86	11/3/86	10/24/86

Figure 21-6 A sample milestone chart. The chart indicates the activities to be performed, estimated days for completion, and target dates for starting and stopping each activity.

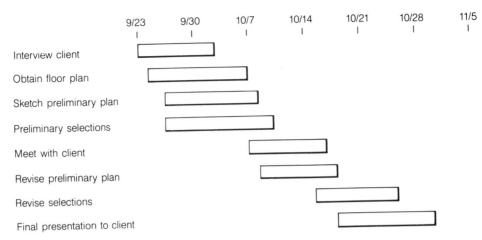

Figure 21–7 Bar chart that graphically shows the time span required to complete designated project activities.

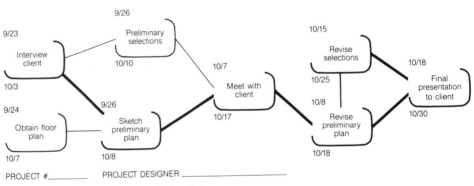

Figure 21–8 Critical path method chart. The heavy lines connecting the various boxes indicate the critical path of this project.

Product Budgeting

Did you know that specifying a project that comes in significantly over the client's budget could lead to a potential malpractice suit? That is not the only reason for designers to be concerned with understanding and staying within the client's budget. Few clients provide interior designers with a blank check for the budget. Often, the budget the client has in mind is smaller than can reasonably be accomplished. And many clients still do not tell the designer what the budget is. Perhaps those clients think that by revealing the budget, the designer will spend that much. If they keep it a secret maybe the project will come in below what the client thought he or she wanted to spend.

Many interior designers are hired after other budget decisions have already been made. The client, architect, and contractors have already made design decisions that affect what can be done and how much is left to be spent on the interior design and finishing of the project. It is never an easy task to convince the client to upgrade finishes, modify structural elements, or purchase higher quality furnishings. Being able quickly to determine an interiors budget helps the designer and the client explore possibilities rapidly.

One product budgeting technique utilizes quality ranges. Design firms can develop three or four quality ranges from among the manufacturers with which they commonly specify. In a way, it would be like using the grade ranges of fabric for upholstered goods. The lowest grade or group of manufacturers would be the budget lines. A second group would be those companies that provide medium quality goods—goods that will be serviceable and provide several years of satisfactory use. A third group could be many of the high-end manufacturers whose products are known for higher quality. The last or highest quality group might be the manufacturers who can supply custom goods or who are known for the very best quality items. Some design firms find it useful to develop a checklist that describes these quality ranges. These checklists can be shown to the client as a means of clarifying the differences in the product groups. The furniture representatives or the manufacturers' literature will be helpful sources of information to develop these quality ranges.

A second budgeting technique is the use of typicals. Office furnishings manufacturers like Herman Miller, Inc., Steelcase, Inc., and Haworth, Inc. have used typical office workstation layouts for project budgeting for years. At is simplest, this technique starts with an average or typical furniture arrangement for different kinds of interior spaces. Adding a quality group to the typical provides a budget idea to discuss with the client. This technique is especially useful in commercial projects where similar spaces are often involved. Residential designers also find it useful as a starting point in helping a client understand the potential overall cost of furnishing a portion of the home.

It is also possible to do product budgeting based on a square-foot factor.[1] Designers utilize historical data on a variety of project types and conditions to develop these factors. As preliminary discussions of project feasibility and budget are conducted, the designer can use these factors to clarify potential costs to the client. For example, a residential design firm can use this information to give a "ball-park" budget of architectural finishes for the average 2000-square-foot house. A commercial designer may use historical square-foot factors to provide information to a client considering furnishing a law partner's office. The designer could even show the client that a contemporary style office might cost X dollars a square foot, while a traditional style will cost some other factor a square foot.

There are, of course, a few built-in problems in using any of these techniques for budgeting. Clients may make decisions based on price over the quality required. This may back the designer into a corner of using products or design concepts that do not provide for the best finished project. The second problem is that client may assume these budgets are the designer's real price and go elsewhere trying to find a less expensive solution.

Project Files or Job Books

Another tool used by many designers to control the project is the project file or project job book. The *project file* usually consists of file folders or notebooks in which the designer keeps all the pertinent data and paperwork related to the project in progress. It serves as a complete record of all the designer's efforts to organize a project and can be used to create the installation manual.

Keeping a project file up to date and organized requires discipline—just as time management does. But it is immensely useful to the designer, the design firm, and the client. All the information the designer needs about the project is in one place. As questions arise or changes are made, the designer has a complete reference to use in talking to the client, vendors, or personnel in the design firm. The well-organized project file makes an impressive statement to the client about how the designer and the design firm keep control of projects.

---

[1]We are referring to furnishing the space, not design fees for services.

If the designer in charge of the project is absent for any reason, the project file allows other members of the firm to seek out answers to clients' and vendors' questions. Even if the lead designer leaves the firm, another designer should be able to pick up the project file and complete the project successfully.

Having all the information in one place saves valuable time when questions arise. There should be no need to look in separate files for information on ordering, delivery, or color number of the sofa.

The project file will also be invaluable as a future reference. Should the client want to duplicate or be in need of repairs or replacements of items specified, it will be easy to check the project file for exact product information. If legal problems arise during or after the project, the project file will serve as a thorough reference for the firm.

Although projects are all different, many have similar qualities. Project files help the firm with projects that are similar in many ways. For example, project files help determine:

1. Why the design time estimate was accurate or not.

2. Whether or not products performed as specified and if vendors were a problem.

3. If taking additional work from the same client would be inadvisable—perhaps because an inordinate number of changes were made by the client.

It can also be helpful as a sales tool in marketing efforts. Clients may wish to see how the firm expects to control their project and displaying a well-organized project file, with all its various parts, may be the answer.

In most cases, the project file should have the following categories of information: meeting notes, correspondence, samples, and floor plans.

Meeting Notes

Meeting notes are notes concerning the project taken by the designer or others in the firm. These would be the originals of any notes taken during the various meetings the designer might have with the client, contractors, manufacturers, subcontractors, and architect. Telephone notes to any of these parties would also be kept in this section.

Meeting notes should include the notes taken during the initial interview that are used to develop the design contract and all subsequent interview notes or forms obtained concerning client needs. These notes should contain the date and time of the meeting and the names of those in attendance. Many designers send transcribed copies of meeting notes back to the client or other interested parties to be sure there were no misunderstandings during the meeting. Preprinted forms especially designed for recording the meeting notes can be used. Preprinted forms do look a bit more professional. However, the idea is to take notes. Always take notes. Take a lot of notes. Do not trust your memory. Those notes may even be needed if a dispute arises in the future.

Correspondence

There are two broad categories of correspondence: general and project documents. General correspondence will include correspondence to and from client; to and from factories and representatives; and construction correspondence. Copies of all correspondence sent to or received from the client should be held in the project file. First among this group would be a copy of the signed design contract. Many firms find it best to retain the original, signed design contract in a separate file held by the design director or owner. Project designers utilize a copy that can be marked up while the original is protected from loss or damage. Insert any other letters or memos sent to or received from the client as well. Correspondence to and from factories and representatives might include letters concerning pricing, special treatments or fabrics, custom work, availability for shipping, freight charges, and so on. When the design project involves construction activities, the file will include correspondence to and from the general contractor or subcontractors.

A large number of original, or in some cases, photocopies of project documents should be in this section of the project file. Client interview forms, job-site analysis forms, employee work area summaries, existing inventories, furniture specification forms, architectural finishes and window treatment estimate forms, space programming questionnaires, and construction budgeting forms all relate to the predesign and design development stages of a project. Examples of some of these forms were presented earlier in this chapter. Another group of forms that may be filed in this section include those forms associated with contract administration or order processing states of a project. Contract documents, bid specifications or preliminary and final equipment lists, purchase orders, acknowledgments, invoices, shipping correspondence, change orders, punch lists, site inspection reports and certificates of payment are the kinds of forms that need to be kept in the file. In-depth discussion of these forms are contained in Chapters 24 and 25.

Everything that goes into the file should be fully dated. Do not throw away any of the preliminary work sheets, even when finalized sheets have replaced them. Murphy's law often clicks into effect just after something is thrown away. In addition, a client signature, pricing information, or brief comments might be on those preliminary sheets that did not get into the final documentation, but that are needed to clarify or defend some action or decision. Leave cleaning the files out until after the project is installed and all billings are collected.

Samples

Fabric samples for all items being specified should be included. These must be accompanied by a full description that would include manufacturer, product name and/or number, color name or number, and a code for determining to what furniture item (for upholstery) or room name/number (for window treatments, wall treatments, and floor finishes) the sample goes.

Samples may be done piece-by-piece using a control sheet—which has room for other specifications and information the designer would like—or room-by-room with all samples for one room going on one sheet. The former method works extremely well for contract projects, whereas the latter method would be more appropriate for residential projects. The control sheet, or some variation, would be ideal in setting up an installation manual to make the installation of furniture items go more smoothly. A form such as Figure 20–3 in the previous chapter can be used.

Floor Plans

The project file should have a copy of the final floor plan. This may be both the entire project plan or room-by-room plans for very complex projects. If the project is very large, it might be convenient to have the large floor plans reduced to smaller sheets. The copy of the signed, approved floor plans should also be in the file.

The design firm should develop a system of coding the plans to the control sheets, as previously discussed, and the written specifications. This will make it easy to identify specific items on the floor plan and will be a key in the development of installation manuals.

Other Items

Some projects will have additional items in the project file. Depending on the organization and size of the design firm, copies of many forms that normally would be in the bookkeeping area, in the warehouse, or in the hands of the managers might be in the project file. These items might include a copy of the formal bid specification, equipment lists, invoices from manufacturers, time records, and freight information. Follow-up notes, if done by management, concerning profitability, marketing information, problems, or successes may also be kept in the file.

Summary

Project management is a very important part of a satisfactory design experience. With so many firms vying for the few design dollars, customer service via good project management means the difference between a healthy firm and one that may go out of business.

It is vital for the interior designer to be able to manage his or her time and the time of the firm's employees. It is also important to keep the projects under control. For the individual, that means developing the discipline and skills of time management. For the firm, it is necessary to develop a satisfactory means of project management and of scheduling the various projects that come into the office. Project files are used to control the project itself.

In this chapter we have looked at the basic concepts of project management, time management, time records, different scheduling methods, and the value of the project file. All of these materials help the designer and the firm manage the projects.

References

Bliss, Edwin C. 1984. *Doing It Now.* New York: Bantam Books.

Burstein, David, and Frank Stasiowski. 1982. *Project Management for the Design Professional.* New York: Watson-Guptill.

Farren, Carol E. 1988. *Planning and Managing Interior Projects.* Kingston, Mass.: R. S. Means.

Karlen, Mark. 1993. *Space Planning Basics.* New York: Van Nostrand Reinhold.

Lakein, Alan. 1973. *How to Get Control of Your Time and Your Life.* New York: Signet–New American Library.

LeBoeuf, Michael. 1979. *Working Smart.* New York: Warner Books.

_____. 1983. *The Productivity Challenge.* New York: McGraw-Hill.

Loebelson, Andrew. 1983. *How to Profit in Contract Design.* New York: Interior Design Books.

Siegel, Harry, with Alan M. Siegel. 1982. *A Guide to Business Principles and Practices for Interior Designers,* rev. ed. New York: Watson-Guptill.

Stitt, Fred A., ed. 1986. *Design Office Management Handbook.* Santa Monica, Calif.: Arts and Architecture Press.

Chapter 22

Working with Trade Sources

Trade sources are the groups of manufacturers, suppliers, and tradespeople who provide the various goods and services a designer uses to complete a project. Designers work with many kinds of trade sources. The majority would be the manufacturers of different furniture and furnishings products. Others would be the suppliers and tradespeople who supply a custom product or install a product. The designer finds these trade sources in many locations. Trade sources provide valuable information and assistance to the designer beyond the actual products they offer.

Vendor, a term used often in this chapter and subsequent chapters, encompasses all the listed sources and even the interior designer. A *vendor* is someone who sells products or services either to the end-user or some middle person like the designer. Commercial clients are used to working with vendors, whom they classify as anyone from whom they purchase any product or service. Residential clients, on the other hand, are used to working with salespeople or designers and may not be familiar with the term *vendor*.

It is essential for the designer to find the sources that complement his or her business ideals. In this section we will look at the different kinds of trade sources utilized by the interior designer.

Manufacturers

Most of the goods that a designer will specify and/or sell to clients will be coming directly from the manufacturers. Designers obtain product catalogs, fabric samples, price books, tear sheets, and even sample products from the manufacturers to use in their design business. The manufacturers will also provide specification information, manufacturing criteria, maintenance information, and terms for how to obtain special products or semi-custom-designed products. Most of this information comes from the manufacturers sales representatives (discussed below), though some factories will deal directly with the designer. Unless you are dealing with a small manufacturer, discounts and special pricing decisions also filter to the designer through the representative.

The designer needs to be sure he or she understand the terms and conditions of ordering and selling of each manufacturer with which he or she deals. Although any size design firm needs to establish credit with a manufacturer, the smaller firm has a harder time and must be prepared to make substantial prepayments when ordering from many manufacturers for the first time. The catalog provides a lot of general information on how to order. And, of course, the representative can explain all the conditions required. Other information about working with sources and getting orders placed correctly is covered in Chapter 24.

Sales Reps

Representatives, or *reps,* are terms used to refer to the men and women who act as the informational source from the various manufacturers. Reps have authority to quote prices, give product information, make special product presentations, arrange for samples to be sent to the designer, provide the designer with information needed to write specifications, and distribute catalogs to designers and, in some cases, to the end-user.

Manufacturer's sales representatives may also have a role in generating sales independently of a designer or dealer. For products generally used in commercial design, reps are out making calls on potential clients. Leads are generally turned over to dealers or referred to designers. Sometimes, of course, the representatives sell directly to the client, bypassing the designer or vendor.

There are two kind of reps: independent representatives and factory representatives. Independent reps basically work for themselves or a sales-representing group. Many handle several manufacturer's products. These products may be related (all are from lighting manufacturers) or, as is more often the case, a combination of furniture and other products. Factory reps work for one particular manufacturer as employees of the company. They only represent that manufacturers' products or possibly only a segment of the manufacturers' product line. Both kinds of representatives are extremely helpful to the interior designer, and most small firms would not survive without their valuable assistance.

Market Centers, Marts, and Showrooms

Market centers are concentrations of trade sources in a city. *Market* is a term that many interior designers use to mean they are going to visit one of the annual shows held at the marts. A *mart* is a building in which many firms are located in separate showrooms or shared showroom space. Here, manufacturers and suppliers lease showroom space to display their products. This allows the designer the opportunity to see firsthand samples of the products he or she is specifying. Designers often bring clients to the mart so that the client can see the items to be specified.

The largest marts are located in the major urban areas of cities such as Chicago, New York, Los Angeles, and San Francisco. The Merchandise Mart in Chicago is still the largest single mart in the United States and holds the largest national contract market. Smaller regional contract markets are held in New York, Los Angeles, and San Francisco. Regional marts have opened in various parts of the United States and Canada. *Interior Design* magazine in its January, 1994, "Buyers Guide" lists 72 regional marts.[1] It is interesting to note that in the first edition of this book, *Contract* magazine listed only 45 regional marts in the United States.[2] These regional marts are, of course, much smaller than the large marts in Chicago, New York, Los Angeles, and San Francisco.

Traditionally, marts have had building-access policies, and in many cases admittance to

---

[1]"Interior Design Buyers Guide," January 1994, *Interior Design.*
[2]"Contract Furniture and Furnishings Mart Directory," December 1985, *Contract.*

the building and its many showrooms is to the trade only. Market centers that are open only to the trade require special passes to gain admittance. These passes are obtainable by trade members from the mart's leasing agent or other mart officials. Showrooms will generally admit those without passes if they have proper credentials identifying them as members of the trade. Student members of ASID and IBD and the other professional organizations will be able to get into most of the showrooms by showing their student membership card. Showrooms, however, have their own policies and some may not admit anyone unless he or she has official building passes. It should be noted that admittance to a showroom does not automatically allow the trade member to purchase products from the manufacturer. In recent years, many showrooms have begun to open their doors to the consumer with an Open House where one day a month the consumer could freely visit the otherwise closed showrooms. In the 1990s a heated debate began as more and more showrooms and trade marts made consumer access even more open.

Whether opening showrooms to the consumer is a good or a bad transformation for the interior design industry is beyond the scope of this book. But it is important to discuss briefly why this has happened. One of the key reasons for the opening of the showrooms was the sluggish economy in the early 1990s. Many manufacturers went bankrupt or were bought up by conglomerates, reducing the number of rentals in the marts. Smaller regional marts, many built during the construction boom of the 1980s, were particularly hurt by the closing of the showrooms of many of these suppliers. Another factor that contributed to increased access for consumers to trade marts was the closing of numerous retail furniture stores and the reduction of furniture departments in department stores. And, of course, the economy created a sales vacuum in which clients—whether residential or commercial—held off purchasing new products. Empty spaces and depressed rentals forced many mart owners to look at new ways to increase customer traffic. Inviting the retail consumer into the marts appeared to be one of the answers.

Design centers encouraged manufacturers to open showrooms to the consumer. Many did so, but without allowing the consumer to purchase goods directly. Some provide in-house designers to assist the consumer in reviewing potential products, and at the same time, educating the client as to the need and advantages of working with an interior designer. Other manufacturers have refused to allow the consumer into their showrooms, feeling that the design community is their customer. The argument continues and will probably continue after publication of this book.

Many designers feel that opening the doors of the design centers will turn interior designers into order-takers—if not irreparably harm the profession. Others feel that open access is just another opportunity for the interior design profession to educate clients in the necessity of design services.

Merchandise, if priced in the showroom, is often tagged with suggested retail prices or price codes. This is done to protect the designer's profit policies as he or she shows clients the products specified for the project. Occasionally, showrooms have display sales in which discontinued items or slightly damaged floor samples are sold to the trade at very good prices.

The larger marts have shows in which manufacturers introduce their new products. Probably the largest furniture show is held at the Neocon Market in Chicago's Merchandise Mart. Frequently more than 20,000 interior designers, architects, facility planners, and related professionals travel to Chicago in June to see the new product introductions. Although contract furniture is highlighted, many residential products as well as floor coverings, wall coverings, lighting, and accessories are shown. These shows often include seminars, workshops, and continuing education classes (CEU). The combination of educational programs with the opportunity to inspect a great deal of product is an important updating tool for designers.

Other large furniture shows are held in other parts of the country. The largest include Designer's Saturday in New York City (now called Inter-Plan Interior Planning and Design

Exposition) in September, the International Home Furnishings Market in April in High Point, North Carolina, and West Week held in Los Angeles in March. Shows are also held in San Francisco, Dallas, Atlanta, Miami, and other cities throughout the year. Specialty shows are also held at these same marts either just prior to the major market shows or at other times of the year. Actual dates and locations of furniture and specialty shows as well as the many conferences for interior designers are published in the trade magazines. The January "Buyer's Guide" issue from *Interior Design* magazine has an extensive calendar of industry events. Most of the smaller regional marts also have shows. These generally attract the local design community.

The first time a designer or student attends a major market show can be a mind-boggling and exciting experience. There is a tendency for first-timers to overload themselves with brochures and catalogs. If the designer remembers to bring an abundance of business cards, he or she should have no trouble getting materials mailed. Small design-firm owners who have had a problem in not getting mailings may want to bring their business license or resale license as well. This will clarify that small studio owners are serious business owners, not just a part-time individual sort of "doing" interior design. Students should also be cautioned not to grab for every sample, catalog, brochure, or gift lying around. It is true that some reps do not like to talk to students, but students who act professional, ask intelligent questions, and request information to be sent to them often earn respect and much information from representatives.

Even though everybody does it some, do not just go to a showroom during market for the food or the gifts. At least be courteous enough to listen to the sales pitch. Ask the rep questions and be attentive. Designers who attend market with serious intent find new product lines and helpful reps that can add immeasurably to the designer's business.

Small Local Showrooms

Although more and more of the larger urban areas have recently seen the emergence of centralized marts, many manufacturers have preferred to remain in freestanding trade showrooms. Most of these showrooms have similar policies for admittance, pricing, and purchasing as showrooms in the marts. These small local showrooms are usually restricted to fabrics, wall coverings, carpet, and flooring materials. However, there are some local showrooms that also display a limited amount of furniture and accessories. Designers can often buy directly from the small local showroom. The usual establishment of credit, prepayment, and other terms of sale will exist when working with the small local showrooms as with buying directly from the manufacturers.

Retail Specialty Shops

Another trade source for the designer is the retail specialty shop. These stores sell many products an interior designer might use. They are generally not owned or franchised by any of the manufacturers whose products are displayed. Retail specialty shops often give trade discounts to the interior designer. These trade discounts are reduced prices given to trade members so that the designer can then resell the products to his or her clients. The reader may wish to refer back to Chapter 13 for more information on trade discounts.

Specialty shops related to a particular manufacturer generally serve as retail outlets for the general public of the manufacturer's products and act as open showrooms for the design community. Notably are paint stores, some carpet and floor coverings stores, and many wall covering shops.

Manufacturer's Dealers

Manufacturer's dealers are usually retail furniture stores—as opposed to the specialty shops—that have made special arrangements with one or more manufacturers of furniture. These dealers feature those selected products in their showroom and frequently stock inventory of considerable size. Many retail furniture showrooms that are manufacturer's dealers also have interior designers available to assist clients. In some cases, these designers compete directly with independent interior designers for design business.

Tradespeople, Craftspeople

Tradespeople and craftspeople are individuals who provide goods and services to the design community—and often to the general public—such as drapery workrooms, carpet and floor-covering installers, painters, wallpaper hangers, and cabinetmakers, to name a few. Many, such as carpet installers, provide only the labor to complete the product construction or installation. Others, such as cabinetmakers, provide materials and labor for the finished goods.

It is important to work with quality craftspeople. New craftspeople and tradespeople should be investigated by the designer. This investigation should include obtaining references from their past clients and inspecting their work by visiting previous job sites.

It is also important, when hiring tradespeople, such as painters and carpet installers, to determine whether these individuals are licensed contractors. Individuals involved in structural work or installation of architectural finishes are often required to be licensed by their state registrar of contractors. Remember from our earlier discussion that hiring unlicensed contractors in states that require licensing can leave the designer open to lawsuits and possible criminal complaints.

When beginning to work with new tradespeople, the designer should be sure that he or she understands how the tradespeople work, not just what they make and the quality of their work. Will the cabinetmaker prepare working drawings of the custom furniture from just a plan and elevation, or is the designer expected to prepare all working drawings? If materials must be sent to the tradespeople—for example, fabric to an antique refinisher—how will freight charges be handled? Will the installer accept delivery of goods (such as carpet) in the designer's name or will the designer have to receive the goods and have the installer pick up the carpet from the designer? These are just a few questions that the designer must ask of potential tradespeople.

Construction Contractors

Design projects involving structural work will necessitate the use of one or more construction contractors. *General contractors* (often called the *GC*) are contractors that hold a license that allows them to contract and supervise all phases of a construction project. Commercial designers regularly work with general contractors or construction management companies that oversee the entire project. These general contractors hire *subcontractors* (also called *subs*) to do the specialized work. There are specialized subcontractors to do concrete work; plumbing; electrical; framing; sheet metal; heating, ventilation, air conditioning (HVAC); painting, roofing, carpet installation, ceramic tile, specialized trim work, landscaping, and many other specialized trades and crafts involved in the construction and finishing of commercial and residential buildings. Most residential and commercial work must be done by a licensed contractor.

There is a sort of etiquette in working with contractors and subs. The men and women who work in the trades will professionally do the work as it is drawn, specified, and contracted. That is to say, not how it is supposed to be or how someone tells them it is supposed to be, but how it was drawn, specified, and contracted. That is why working drawings have to be done right, or the work might be stopped as corrections are made. Making changes in a job after the contract is let (awarded) requires a change order. And change orders[3] usually result in higher prices to get something done than if they were called for in the original drawings and specifications.

Another important point about the etiquette of working with contractors. Even though the client is paying the bill, it is unwise to let him or her tell the subs how to do something on the job. Fights have been known to break out as the subs refused to make a change that was requested—demanded—by the client. Of course, in a residential project a client might be acting as his or her own general contractor, and then the subs must respond to the client's orders. But ordinarily any changes must be made through the general contractor with a change order. Designers must also be careful about giving instructions to subs on the job. Designers should always request changes through the supervisor of the tradespeople involved or through the general contractor. Again, subs might just ignore the request made by the designer. In some states, designers must hold either a contractor's license or a specialty license to give instructions and supervisory information to installers—even carpet and wallpaper installers. Be sure you known the law in your state.

Selecting Your Trade Sources

Working with trade sources is a two-way street. Vendors and suppliers are there to assist the interior designer by providing the goods and services the interior designer wishes to sell or specify. The trade sources are in business to make money when designers specify and sell their goods. In the highly competitive and economically recessive times, the street is not always smooth nor two-way. Many reps and suppliers have complained about designers demanding specification fees. And designers have complained about reps and suppliers being stingy with information or "buying" jobs. Both camps need each other and need to cooperate with each other.

Despite the round of bankruptcies and buyouts in the 1980s and 1990s, there are still thousands of sources of interiors products from which to choose. Designers receive mailings, phone calls, and drop-in visits from reps and suppliers constantly. Designer's libraries too often become clogged with sample books, catalogs, flyers, and price lists. "I still think they are like rabbits. You turn your back on your library, and it doubles," complained a small studio owner. Managing a firm's resources and selecting resources are important parts of the design firm's business practices.

The firm's business plan and annual plans have given management guidelines on what and who to keep as resources. If the firm is not doing residential design, there is little need for residential grade carpet. Design firms lucky enough to work with high-end clients will have little use for budget-furniture catalogs. But then these comments only state the obvious. How does a design firm really find and maintain the best sources? Some suggestions follow.

---

[3] *Change orders* are forms describing any modification in construction projects after the contract has been awarded. The concept is also applied to interiors furnishings projects.

Clarify the business plan. One should be prepared if no plan exists. This will show the firm who its client groups are, the kinds of design services the firm is prepared to offer, and will direct the firm to the kinds of trade sources needed.

Review current resource materials. Gradually clean out current library and resource materials. Catalogs with five-year-old price lists may need to be discarded, especially if no one in the office can remember buying from the source in the recent past. Besides, that old price list can get the firm in trouble should discontinued goods be specified. Request new tear sheets or even whole catalogs from manufacturers used frequently. Call the representative so that he or she can update the firm's catalogs and samples. It is, after all, part of the service that he or she provides. If existing employees do not have time to do the library work, hire an interior design student who, with direction, can pull out old items and purge sample books. The student will benefit from the opportunity to learn products and the firm will get an updated library. It is also a good idea to review project files and purchase order files to determine which major vendors have been the most successful for the design firm. Consider eliminating suppliers that have given the firm poor service, regardless of the products the supplier offers.

Carefully review new sources. Do not just file new catalogs, flyers, and sample books without looking them over. Keep those that fit the design firm's product and jobs profile. Return or discard those that do not add to the firm's library. Get to know the representatives or the craftspeople from the resources the firm maintains. Make an appointment to talk to the rep and get answers to questions on pricing, delivery schedules, exclusivity, custom work, warranties, quality, and manufacturing. The owner, design director, and lead designers should understand all the terms and conditions of sale from new sources.

Try to work with sources on the firm's terms. Small design firms need to find sources that will take lower prepayments with orders. Smaller firms might also have to work with firms that are closer to the design firm geographically, because the design firm may have to drop-ship goods directly to the client. This method will also reduce the cost of the project, because freight charges will be somewhat reduced as well. Unless designers enjoy constant interruptions, require reps to make appointments to show new items. Long ago, larger design firms began requiring the reps to meet with the design staff during lunch time, with the reps providing the meal. This works well and reps do not complain about the cost unless very few of the design staff show up. Firms that demand this of representatives, must be sure that all of the staff is available for these lunch meetings.

Summary

The sources the design firm uses or maintains information about are many and varied. Those chosen regularly by the design firm should complement the firm's work. Trips to market shows give designers a very good opportunity to review sources and talk to sales representatives or factory salespeople. Because of the wealth of products available to designers, it is important to carefully select the products, representatives, and other trade sources that fit into the firm's type of business.

The discussion of trade sources utilized by the interior designer in this chapter provides a brief reference for where to find the products and services the designer will use for his or her clients. The professional must become familiar with the sources available in the geographic areas in which he or she plans to conduct business. The student should investigate the many manufacturers of furniture and furnishings by visiting one of the market shows, looking at catalogs in the school's library, or by visiting local design offices.

References

"Buyers Guide." January 1993. *Interior Design.*

"Contract Furniture and Furnishings Mart Directory." December 1985. *Contract.*

Corlin, Len. December 1985. "Mart Fever Is Epidemic." *Contract.*

_____. December 1986. "Marts Accelerate Development." *Contract.*

"Open vs. Closed: The Results Are In." June 1992. *Interior Design.*

Veitch, Ronald M., Dianne R. Jackman, and Mary K. Dixon. 1990. *Professional Practice.* Winnipeg, Canada: Peguis Publishers.

Chapter 23

Contract Documents
and Specifications

The products specified for a small project, whether residential or commercial, are usually prepared as a simple "equipment list" of what the client is requested to purchase. But when the amount of the goods to be purchased is large or when construction of interior spaces is part of the project, then a simple list is not sufficient. Documents in both graphic and written form must be prepared in order for more than one contractor or vendor to provide a price to the client.

Contract documents and formal specifications are used when it is necessary for the client to obtain competitive bids—or prices—for the completion of an interiors project. Since it is not the purpose of this book to discuss the technical design aspects of the profession but rather the business aspects of the profession, this chapter will not describe how to prepare working drawings portion of the contract documents. The reader should refer to references on architectural drafting for this kind of information.

This chapter discusses construction documents, particularly the kinds of written specifications and documents required for an interiors project. Projects that have minimal or no construction work involved are often referred to as *FF&E* projects. That acronym stands for Furniture, Furnishings, and Equipment. Projects for any level of government agency are often called public projects. Utility companies, some health care organizations, and schools are often referred to as quasi public or public projects. Most other projects are called private projects since they involve work for private entities. Depending on whether a project is FF&E, construction and FF&E, public, quasi public, or private, certain processes in the preparation of construction documents and specifications will be different. It concludes with a brief discussion of the bidding process.

Construction Documents

Construction documents are "a set of legal contract documents of drawings and specifications that graphically and verbally describe what is required for a specific construction project."[1] A

---

[1]Wakita, Osamu A. and Linde, Richard M. *The Professional Practice of Architectural Detailing*, John Wiley and Sons, Inc., 1984, p. 549. Copyright by John Wiley and Sons, Inc.

complete set of construction documents would include architectural drawings, schedules, specifications, and modifications.

Construction Drawings

The drawings portion of construction documents typically consists of all plans, elevations, and details required to build the structure or the interior. For an interiors project, these documents might include dimensioned partition drawings, section drawings, mechanical drawings including electrical/telephone location plans, reflected ceiling plans, plumbing plans, HVAC plans, other mechanical plans (such as for sprinklers in a commercial building), interior construction elevations, and construction details. Additional specialized drawings such as plans from lighting designers, commercial kitchen and food service designers, health care systems designers, and others might also be included. Preparation of additional drawings would be by whoever designed the exterior structure.

Many interior and architectural firms also include equipment plans or furniture plans in the working drawings. Equipment plans show the location of, and identify by code, the movable equipment in the project. By movable equipment we mean furniture and other equipment, such as refrigerators, that can be easily moved and are not part of the structure. Movable equipment is rarely bid with the construction of the walls. In most projects, furniture and equipment drawings are provided to the general contractor for information only. They are, however, necessary for the furniture bid.

We will only describe how the equipment or furniture plan should be prepared as part of the construction documents and how this plan relates to written specifications. The equipment plan for bidding purposes must be very clear and understandable. When projects are to be bid, it is a helpful practice for interior designers to prepare a mylar or sepia intermediate of the furniture floor plan and add code information to the intermediate. Codes may be simple numbers or letters accompanied by a furniture schedule describing these items of furniture (see Figure 23–1) or more complicated multinumber codes that indicate generic types of furniture and furnishings—not specific product information. These codes then need to be further explained in the specifications. In Figure 23–2, the letter code refers to the kind of furniture piece (*CO* for chair, *SO* for sofa, *TA* for table, and so on); the next one to four numbers reference the item to the specification. The numbers after the slash (/)

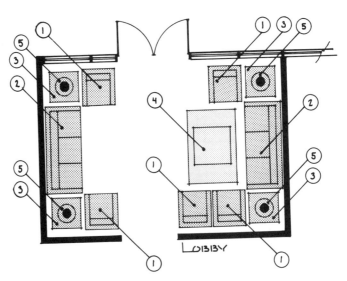

Figure 23–1 Simple furniture schedule as used in construction documents. (Drawing: Clayton E. Peterson)

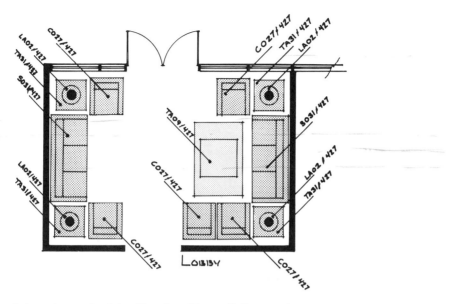

Figure 23–2 Coded furniture schedule. (Drawing: Clayton E. Peterson)

identify the location of the furniture item with the first number indicating the floor of the building and the last two to three numbers identifying the room number.

The exact format and coordination between plans and specifications must be clear enough for the vendor to know what he or she is bidding on, and easy enough for the design firm to produce and easily make required changes to the plans. However, formats should be individualized by the design firm.

Trade names and product numbers should not be used on the equipment plans since errors can occur. It is easy to transpose numbers, and if the designer must write product names and numbers many times, it would be easy to make this kind of error—resulting in an incorrect bid. Another example would be when substitutions have to be made. If it becomes necessary to change or substitute a different product, forgetting to make the changes in product numbers on the plans can cause incorrect bidding or the wrong product being ordered. Trade names and product numbers, if used, should be limited to the written specifications. All information in schedules or code keys should be generic descriptions.

Although it is better to use generic names for furniture, furnishings, and room names, generic descriptions can lead to misinterpretations if the terms used are not clarified. For example, *chair* can mean guest chair, arm chair, posture chair, club chair, dining chair, stool, occasional chair, and executive chair. *Table* can mean dining table, coffee table, end table, cocktail table, occasional table, conference table, table desk, and Parsons table. And *rest room* can mean ladies room, men's room, powder room, lavatory, bathroom, and lounge.

Many other examples of generic furniture, furnishings, and room terminology can be found. Although it is important to use generic terms, it is equally important for terms to be consistent, clear, and defined within the specifications. To aid in defining all genereic terms, a key needs to be placed either in the specifications or on one of the sheets of equipment plans.

Schedules

Schedules are used to clarify sizes, location finishes, and other information related to certain nonconstruction parts of an interior or structure. Schedules are commonly prepared for doors, windows, and interior room finishes. Interior room finish schedules include information for walls, floor treatments, and ceiling heights and treatments. Schedules for other specific items such as lighting fixtures and furniture are also used by designers.

Most schedules are prepared in tabular form. The format of these schedules varies greatly from office to office. The simplest form of a room finish schedule is shown in Figure 23–3. A design firm that has not used schedules before may wish to review examples in architectural drafting texts and then adopt or develop a format that works for the firm.

For the same reasons given for equipment plans, the information provided in the schedules should be generic. Trade or manufacturer's names are to be supplied in the written specifications. For interiors projects that are not very large or complicated, some designers use a materials key with the finish schedule. This materials key does name manufacturers. If it is used, it should be used in the specifications. It would not be appropriate to use a materials key if a performance or descriptive specification was used.

When the project includes unusual designs for doors, windows, or wall treatments, it is necessary to use a graphic schedule or elevation. This graphic schedule will help to clarify those items that do not easily fit into the regular tabular schedules.

Specifications

The *specifications* portion of the construction documents is the written instructions to the general contractors and vendors as to the materials and methods of construction of the structure or interior and the furniture and other movable equipment that is to be bid on. Specifications (simply referred to as "specs" by many in the industry) are written in technical terms and provide information about responsibilities of bidders, descriptions of the materials, qualities and workmanship, installation requirements, and the like. It is not uncommon for some designers also to provide the quantities of the goods required in the written specifica-

Finish Schedule

Room Name	Room #	Floors	Base	Walls					Ceiling		Notes
				N	E	S	W	Trim	Finish	Ht.	

© 1993, Christine Piotrowski

Figure 23–3 An example of a simple room schedule that can be used in a set of working drawings.

tions. Although this is very helpful to the vendors who are bidding, it is better and more common to require vendors to be responsible for the quantities. Specifications will be discussed in more detail later in this chapter.

Modifications

Modifications are changes in the construction documents. If the changes are made before the contract is awarded, they are called *addenda.* This type of modification may be in response to such things as requests of the owners, technical requirements, omissions, or errors. Addenda clarify the previously prepared documents. Addenda are discussed further later in the chapter.

Recall from the previous chapter that when changes are made in the project after the contract has been awarded, the documentation is commonly called a *change order. Change orders* are written permissions or instructions concerning any aspect of the project that modify design concepts, construction designs, or product specifications. Change orders happen for reasons similar to addenda.

General Conditions

Bid documents for projects involving any kind of construction will include a section of general conditions. These *general conditions* set forth the legal responsibilities, procedures, rights, and duties of each party to the contract. A standardized set of general conditions used by many designers and private business owners is the AIA form, AIA Document A201.[2] It is commonly used since it has stood the test of time and legal interpretation. However, many designers/clients find that the document does not meet their individual needs and modify the conditions of the document for their situation. ASID and IBD recommend either using the AIA document or having preprinted forms available that closely follow that document. Figure 23–4 shows but one page of the multipage AIA document.

Items covered in the AIA document include definitions of the contract document, the names of the architect (designer to be substituted) and owner, ownership of documents, and the kinds of activities for which the designer is responsible, the kinds of activities for which the owner is responsible, definitions and responsibilities of contractors and subcontractors, clauses concerning payments, time period of project, claims, insurance, change orders, and other definitions or statements related to the contractual relationship of the parties.

For bids that concern only furniture, AIA document A271, "General Conditions of the Contract for Furniture, Furnishings and Equipment," can be used. These general conditions are similar in scope to the A201 document but are related to interior furniture and furnishings rather than construction.

Since both of these forms are lengthy legal forms of a generalized nature, it is necessary for the designer to prepare supplemental conditions for the projects. The supplemental conditions spell out any conditions that are more related to the specific project. A supplemental condition that must be stated if the designer uses either of these forms is that *designer* or *interior designer* be substituted whereever the word *architect* is used. The AIA also has document A571, "Guide for Interiors Supplementary Conditions," available to help the designer prepare the supplemental conditions for the A271 document.

These documents have also been adopted by the ASID and IBD. Since the copyright of documents belongs to the AIA, it is necessary for the designer to obtain permission from the AIA to make copies or to modify the documents in any way. Should the designer/specifier wish to prepare his or her own set of general conditions, these should be reviewed by the

---

[2]Meier 1978, 18.

GENERAL CONDITIONS OF THE CONTRACT FOR CONSTRUCTION

ARTICLE 1
GENERAL PROVISIONS

1.1 BASIC DEFINITIONS

1.1.1 THE CONTRACT DOCUMENTS

The Contract Documents consist of the Agreement between Owner and Contractor (hereinafter the Agreement), Conditions of the Contract (General, Supplementary and other Conditions), Drawings, Specifications, addenda issued prior to execution of the Contract, other documents listed in the Agreement and Modifications issued after execution of the Contract. A Modification is (1) a written amendment to the Contract signed by both parties, (2) a Change Order, (3) a Construction Change Directive or (4) a written order for a minor change in the Work issued by the Architect. Unless specifically enumerated in the Agreement, the Contract Documents do not include other documents such as bidding requirements (advertisement or invitation to bid, Instructions to Bidders, sample forms, the Contractor's bid or portions of addenda relating to bidding requirements).

1.1.2 THE CONTRACT

The Contract Documents form the Contract for Construction. The Contract represents the entire and integrated agreement between the parties hereto and supersedes prior negotiations, representations or agreements, either written or oral. The Contract may be amended or modified only by a Modification. The Contract Documents shall not be construed to create a contractual relationship of any kind (1) between the Architect and Contractor, (2) between the Owner and a Subcontractor or Subsubcontractor or (3) between any persons or entities other than the Owner and Contractor. The Architect shall, however, be entitled to performance and enforcement of obligations under the Contract intended to facilitate performance of the Architect's duties.

1.1.3 THE WORK

The term "Work" means the construction and services required by the Contract Documents, whether completed or partially completed, and includes all other labor, materials, equipment and services provided or to be provided by the Contractor to fulfill the Contractor's obligations. The Work may constitute the whole or a part of the Project.

1.1.4 THE PROJECT

The Project is the total construction of which the Work performed under the Contract Documents may be the whole or a part and which may include construction by the Owner or by separate contractors.

1.1.5 THE DRAWINGS

The Drawings are the graphic and pictorial portions of the Contract Documents, wherever located and whenever issued, showing the design, location and dimensions of the Work, generally including plans, elevations, sections, details, schedules and diagrams.

1.1.6 THE SPECIFICATIONS

The Specifications are that portion of the Contract Documents consisting of the written requirements for materials, equip-

ment, construction systems, standards and workmanship for the Work, and performance of related services.

1.1.7 THE PROJECT MANUAL

The Project Manual is the volume usually assembled for the Work which may include the bidding requirements, sample forms, Conditions of the Contract and Specifications.

1.2 EXECUTION, CORRELATION AND INTENT

1.2.1 The Contract Documents shall be signed by the Owner and Contractor as provided in the Agreement. If either the Owner or Contractor or both do not sign all the Contract Documents, the Architect shall identify such unsigned Documents upon request.

1.2.2 Execution of the Contract by the Contractor is a representation that the Contractor has visited the site, become familiar with local conditions under which the Work is to be performed and correlated personal observations with requirements of the Contract Documents.

1.2.3 The intent of the Contract Documents is to include all items necessary for the proper execution and completion of the Work by the Contractor. The Contract Documents are complementary, and what is required by one shall be as binding as if required by all; performance by the Contractor shall be required only to the extent consistent with the Contract Documents and reasonably inferable from them as being necessary to produce the intended results.

1.2.4 Organization of the Specifications into divisions, sections and articles, and arrangement of Drawings shall not control the Contractor in dividing the Work among Subcontractors or in establishing the extent of Work to be performed by any trade.

1.2.5 Unless otherwise stated in the Contract Documents, words which have well-known technical or construction industry meanings are used in the Contract Documents in accordance with such recognized meanings.

1.3 OWNERSHIP AND USE OF ARCHITECT'S DRAWINGS, SPECIFICATIONS AND OTHER DOCUMENTS

1.3.1 The Drawings, Specifications and other documents prepared by the Architect are instruments of the Architect's service through which the Work to be executed by the Contractor is described. The Contractor may retain one contract record set. Neither the Contractor nor any Subcontractor, Subsubcontractor or material or equipment supplier shall own or claim a copyright in the Drawings, Specifications and other documents prepared by the Architect, and unless otherwise indicated the Architect shall be deemed the author of them and will retain all common law, statutory and other reserved rights, in addition to the copyright. All copies of them, except the Contractor's record set, shall be returned or suitably accounted for to the Architect, on request, upon completion of the Work. The Drawings, Specifications and other documents prepared by the Architect, and copies thereof furnished to the Contractor, are for use solely with respect to this Project. They are not to be used by the Contractor or any Subcontractor, Subsubcontractor or material or equipment supplier on other projects or for additions to this Project outside the scope of the

---

Figure 23–4 A page from "General Conditions of the Contract for Construction" (AIA document A201). (Reproduced with permission, American Institute of Architects)

design firm's attorney before being submitted to the client. Copies of these forms can be ordered from local AIA chapter offices or by contacting the AIA national office (see Appendix).

Specifications

Specifications, you will recall, are the written instructions as to what is to be provided by the contractor. They are prepared in a technical fashion and provide information as to the goods or materials required and workmanship expected. Since it is easier for people to interpret the written word than drawings when there are discrepancies between the two, the courts often base judgments on the specifications. It is therefore important for the designer to prepare the specifications clearly—without any ambiguity, errors, or omissions

The specifications should complement the drawings, not duplicate them. Specifications should primarily describe the type and quality of materials and goods, quality of workmanship, method of construction and installation, applicable testing methods, provisions for alternates, and requirements for warranties. Drawings should show locations, dimensions, quantities, sizes, generic identification of materials, and interrelationships of space, materials, and equipment. There are four customary kinds of formal specifications: proprietary, descriptive, performance, and reference. First, it is necessary to discuss briefly the differences between closed and open specifications.

Closed and Open Specifications

When a specification is written so that no other product can be substituted, it is commonly called a *closed specification.* Closed specifications require that only an exact match of the specification be provided by the vendor. Substitutions are not allowed. The proprietary specification base bid is a closed specification.

An *open specification* is one in which the owner is willing to consider substitutions to what was originally specified. This type of specification usually has the words "or equal" incorporated into the specifications. The "or equal" term means that products that are the same as or very closely similar to what was specified will be considered. The proprietary specification that allows substitutions, the descriptive specification, performance specification, and the reference specification are all considered open specifications because they allow the consideration of a multiple number of products for the item being specified.

Proprietary

A *proprietary specification* names the products and materials by manufacturer's name, model number, or part number. With the proprietary specification there is no doubt on what the designer and client wish to have bids (see Figure 23–5). If the specifications allow for no substitutions or do not have an "or equal" clause, then the proprietary bid might be called a base bid. "The term *base bid* means that all people who wish to provide materials for the project must base their bid on the product named in the specification."[3]

The advantages of the proprietary specification are:

1. It is the easiest to write. In many cases, the designer only needs to provide the basic descriptive information of manufacturer, product number, and finishes/fabrics to complete

---

[3]Reznikoff, S. C., *Specifications for Commercial Interiors,* p. 231. Copyright 1979 Whitney Library of Design, an imprint of Watson-Guptill Publications. Used by permission of publisher.

Reception Area

Item	Quantity	Description	Unit	Total
1	4	Knoll 50-125 Wassily Lounge Chair Leather: Black		
2	1	Knoll 705-1 Mercer Coffee Table Finish: Black Onyx		

Figure 23–5 Proprietary specification. (Reproduced with permission, Knoll International)

the specifications. When more detail is needed, manufacturers often provide information to the designer that can be reproduced into the specifications.

2. It is easier to prepare drawings. With known product sizes, drawings are more accurate. The designer does not have to allow in the drawings for possible larger or smaller sizes of product that might be bid.

3. The designer has maximum product control over the project. The carefully worked out design concept will be realized since the products used to develop the design concept will be the ones purchased.

4. The time element from invitation announcement to order entry is faster since alternates do not have to be evaluated by the client. Since everyone is bidding on the exact same products, the competitive bid concept is more fully realized.

There are some disadvantages, however. First, proprietary specifications can limit competition if there are not insufficient numbers of bidders that can provide the products. When there are insufficient numbers of bidders and the proprietary method is used, it is necessary to have an "or equal" clause in the specifications.

The *or equal* clause, commonly found in proprietary specifications, allows bidders to substitute what they believe to be products of equal quality to those that were specified. More time must be taken in the evaluation process to determine if equal goods are bid. Design control can be lost as the client may choose products that are similar in appearance but lower in price than the original specification. What is equal in this situation is open to subjective judgment—on the part of the client, the designer, and the bidders.

To protect all the parties concerned when having to deal with an "or equal" clause, definitions of what procedures will be followed concerning the submittal of alternates must be included in the specifications. A common practice recommended by the Construction Specifications Institute (CSI) is that requests related to substitutions be submitted prior to the close of bid. These requests might include detailed descriptions of the substituted product. In some cases, clients ask that a sample product be submitted prior to close of bid for evaluation.

Descriptive Specification

Descriptive specification does not use a manufacturer's or trade name for the goods being specified. Rather, it describes, often in elaborate detail, the materials, workmanship, fabrication methods, and installation of the required goods.

There are two advantages to the descriptive specification. First, it allows the designer to prescribe exactly what he or she wishes to specify for the project. When there are many similar products that have subtle differences, such as with floor coverings, a descriptive specification helps to ensure that what is bid is actually equal to what was specified—even if the goods come from different manufacturers. There are also situations when the client wants a certain product for the job, but may have a difficult time obtaining sufficient numbers of competitive bids on that product when using a proprietary specification. A descriptive specification helps to narrow the "or equal" alternates so that the client can get what he or she wants.

A second advantage is that the descriptive specification allows for some performance criteria to be used in the situations for which a complete performance specification would not be appropriate. With floor coverings, many manufacturers have carpets that can meet the simple descriptive specification of such things as fiber, pitch, stitches per inch, and pile height. This may not be enough to be sure that the carpet or carpet quality required of the project is bid. Performance criteria related to such factors as static electricity, delamination, and crocking can be included in the specification for these kinds of goods. Other goods, such as furniture, which may not have such stringent requirements, can be written as descriptive specifications (see Figure 23–6).

There are a number of disadvantages to the descriptive specification. First, it requires time to produce and it is also quite lengthy. It also requires more precise description of the products. The descriptive specification of an open office system work surface would have to read something like, "a cantilevered hanging work surface, 48 inches wide by 23 3/4 inches deep by 1 inch thick top with a total height of 8 3/4 inches. The finished top surface shall be white oak plastic laminate and the edge shall be dark charcoal gray rubber T-molding." The same description in the proprietary specification would read, "Herman Miller, AO 556 FF OLDT DT."

A third disadvantage is that the volume of information needed to prepare a descriptive specification can lead to errors and loopholes allowing for the bidding of products other than what was intended. In the previous example, if the designer did not write in "white oak

---

A. General
1. Systems products shall have work surface tops and storage units with equivalent hardware to suspend units from architectural walls or freestanding panels. Hanging components shall be removable by hand or with the use of a minimal of tools without disturbing adjacent components.
2. Vertical support elements (VSE 1–10) shall support hanging components on one-inch intervals and shall easily allow for vertical height adjustments.

B. Work Surface Tops
1. Work surface tops shall be manufactured of warp-resistant materials and will have radius corners and edges on all sides but the side that shall meet the wall or vertical support element(s).
2. Work surface tops shall be capable of having various undercounter drawers or storage units suspended below, installed with a minimal use of tools.
3. Work surface tops shall be finished with high-pressure laminates that are scratch and heat resistant (up to 250°) in a variety of colors, and top shall have a nominal dimension (without support member) of one inch.
4. Work surface tops shall be available in the following nominal sizes:
   WST-1:   30″ wide by 24″ deep
   WST-2:   36″ wide by 24″ deep
   WST-3:   48″ wide by 24″ deep
   WST-4:   60″ wide by 24″ deep
   WST-5:   72″ wide by 24″ deep
   WST-6:   30″ wide by 30″ deep
   WST-7:   36″ wide by 30″ deep
   WST-8:   48″ wide by 30″ deep
   WST-9:   60″ wide by 30″ deep
   WST-10:   72″ wide by 30″ deep

Figure 23–6 Descriptive specification for open office systems work surfaces.

plastic laminate" but only wrote "plastic laminate" the client would not be getting what was desired—the light oak finish—but would probably get a plain or neutral finish.

Finally, the descriptive specification, unless written very carefully, can result in a loss of the product and design concept control by the designer. As the example shows, an omission in the specification can result in the wrong finish being specified for the job. It would be within the right of the bidder to ask for additional moneys to change the product finish to the intended light oak. The omission and resulting cost to the client could also lead to the client's right to sue the designer.

Performance Specification

Another specification, the *performance specification,* is written without trade names. The performance specification establishes the product requirements based on exacting performance criteria. Any product that meets the performance criteria can qualify for use. The performance of the goods is based on the end product of the goods, and thus performance criteria are based on the accomplishment of that end result. For example, the performance criteria for the work surface discussed above is shown in Figure 23–7.

Performance specifications are based on qualitative or measurable statements. It is common for specifications to require certain tests and methods of testing and for bidders to submit test data with their bids. This information is available from the manufacturers both for the use of the designer to write the specification and for the bidders to submit the data to the client.

When data from the manufacturer is not available or appears inconclusive, it may be necessary for the bidder to supply a sample of the product for testing, as is often the case with

---

Performance Specification
Space Dividers

I. General
  A. Two basic types of panels will be required: hard surface and acoustical.
  B. All panels shall meet ASTM E-84 Steiner Tunnel Test.
    1. Maximum flame spread range of 0–25.
    2. Maximum smoke development below 450.
  C. All panels shall have support slots that allow component adjustability on one-inch (1″) increments.
  D. All panel connections shall be made with a minimum of hardware and special tools.

II. Acoustical
  A. Shall have a minimum NRC of .85 based on ASTM C-423-66.
  B. Shall have a minimum STC of 13 based on ASTM E-290-81.
  C. Above tests shall be based on the entire panel being tested. Both sides of the panel must be tested.
  D. Fabric covering panel must meet ASTM E-84 Tunnel Test.
    1. Maximum flame spread range of 0–25.
    2. Maximum smoke development below 450.

III. Hard Surface
  A. Panel frames shall be metal with factory-applied baked-on enamel.
  B. Panel face shall be metal with factory-applied baked-on enamel.
  C. Must meet ASTM E-84 Tunnel Test.
    1. Maximum flame spread range of 0–25.
    2. Maximum smoke development below 450.

Figure 23–7 Partial performance specification for a divider panel.

various textiles. For example, should the designer wish to use a carpet material on the wall, it would be necessary for the designer to specify some kind of performance criteria for that textile in this situation and the manufacturer to either supply data for this use or supply a sample that could be tested.

Advantages are the same as for the descriptive specification: full control when it is not appropriate to use proprietary specifications. Disadvantages are also the same: extra preparation and evaluation time, possible errors, possible loss of design concept and product control.

Reference Specification

A reference specification utilizes an established standard, such as the standards of the American Society for Testing and Materials (ASTM), rather than writing detailed descriptions or performance criteria for certain products. These established standards generally provide minimal acceptable standards of performance of various kinds of products.

The designer must check these standards to be sure that these minimums are satisfactory for the needs of the project. If the standard is too low, the reference specification cannot be used. It is also necessary for the designer to be fully familiar with the standards, because the standards sometimes provide options of materials or workmanship. The designer must be sure that he or she specifies the standard or level of standard required of the job. If this is not done, the bidder then has the option of using a lower standard than what the designer may have intended.

Although reference specifications are more widely used in construction, they may be utilized by the interior designer for such things as wall and floor products and installation.

The advantages are that there is a great time saving because only the standard must be stated; there is no need to write a long descriptive or performance specification. Reference specifications can also be used to help explain a complex performance or descriptive specification for specialized products or installations.

The disadvantage is that, if the designer is not fully aware of the complete, up-to-date standard, the designer may allow products and workmanship that do not meet the desired requirements.

Specification Organization

Because of the complexity and potential depth of the project, it is necessary to organize the specification in such a manner that it is easy to prepare and to locate information in an orderly fashion. As legal documents, specifications should not be written in obscure language or with information omitted. Even with the availability of computer applications in the preparation of specifications, this document requires a great deal of time, thought, and accuracy.

Following a standardized organization allows for greater speed and accuracy by the vendors who will be providing bids. The furniture vendor is only interested in what furniture and furnishing items are required. The framer, electrician, plumber, and all the other trades are likewise only interested in what they are being asked to provide.

The organizational format most used in the design and construction professions was developed by the Construction Specifications Institute (CSI). The Construction Specification Institute is a nonprofit organization whose purpose is to improve professional documentation, especially specifications. With its membership spanning the full range of the construction professions, CSI has been able to develop a common language of construction and a standardized format for the preparation of specifications.

Masterformat, published by CSI, is the most widely accepted method of organizing specifications (see Figure 23–8). The detailed numbering system and organization along materi-

BIDDING REQUIREMENTS, CONTRACT FORMS, AND CONDITIONS OF THE CONTRACT

00010 PRE-BID INFORMATION
00100 INSTRUCTIONS TO BIDDERS
00200 INFORMATION AVAILABLE TO BIDDERS
00300 BID FORMS
00400 SUPPLEMENTS TO BID FORMS
00500 AGREEMENT FORMS
00600 BONDS AND CERTIFICATES
00700 GENERAL CONDITIONS
00800 SUPPLEMENTARY CONDITIONS
00900 ADDENDA

Note: The items listed above are not specification sections and are referred to as "Documents" rather than "Sections" in the Master List of Section Titles, Numbers, and Broadscope Section Explanations.

SPECIFICATIONS

DIVISION 1 – GENERAL REQUIREMENTS

01010 SUMMARY OF WORK
01020 ALLOWANCES
01025 MEASUREMENT AND PAYMENT
01030 ALTERNATES/ALTERNATIVES
01035 MODIFICATION PROCEDURES
01040 COORDINATION
01050 FIELD ENGINEERING
01060 REGULATORY REQUIREMENTS
01070 IDENTIFICATION SYSTEMS
01090 REFERENCES
01100 SPECIAL PROJECT PROCEDURES
01200 PROJECT MEETINGS
01300 SUBMITTALS
01400 QUALITY CONTROL
01500 CONSTRUCTION FACILITIES AND TEMPORARY CONTROLS
01600 MATERIAL AND EQUIPMENT
01650 FACILITY STARTUP/COMMISSIONING
01700 CONTRACT CLOSEOUT
01800 MAINTENANCE

DIVISION 2 – SITEWORK

02010 SUBSURFACE INVESTIGATION
02050 DEMOLITION
02100 SITE PREPARATION
02140 DEWATERING
02150 SHORING AND UNDERPINNING
02160 EXCAVATION SUPPORT SYSTEMS
02170 COFFERDAMS
02200 EARTHWORK
02300 TUNNELING
02350 PILES AND CAISSONS
02450 RAILROAD WORK
02480 MARINE WORK
02500 PAVING AND SURFACING
02600 UTILITY PIPING MATERIALS
02660 WATER DISTRIBUTION
02680 FUEL AND STEAM DISTRIBUTION
02700 SEWERAGE AND DRAINAGE
02760 RESTORATION OF UNDERGROUND PIPE
02770 PONDS AND RESERVOIRS
02780 POWER AND COMMUNICATIONS
02800 SITE IMPROVEMENTS
02900 LANDSCAPING

DIVISION 3 – CONCRETE

03100 CONCRETE FORMWORK
03200 CONCRETE REINFORCEMENT
03250 CONCRETE ACCESSORIES
03300 CAST-IN-PLACE CONCRETE
03370 CONCRETE CURING
03400 PRECAST CONCRETE
03500 CEMENTITIOUS DECKS AND TOPPINGS
03600 GROUT
03700 CONCRETE RESTORATION AND CLEANING
03800 MASS CONCRETE

DIVISION 4 – MASONRY

04100 MORTAR AND MASONRY GROUT
04150 MASONRY ACCESSORIES
04200 UNIT MASONRY
04400 STONE
04500 MASONRY RESTORATION AND CLEANING
04550 REFRACTORIES
04600 CORROSION RESISTANT MASONRY
04700 SIMULATED MASONRY

DIVISION 5 – METALS

05010 METAL MATERIALS
05030 METAL COATINGS
05050 METAL FASTENING
05100 STRUCTURAL METAL FRAMING
05200 METAL JOISTS
05300 METAL DECKING
05400 COLD FORMED METAL FRAMING
05500 METAL FABRICATIONS
05580 SHEET METAL FABRICATIONS
05700 ORNAMENTAL METAL
05800 EXPANSION CONTROL
05900 HYDRAULIC STRUCTURES

DIVISION 6 – WOOD AND PLASTICS

06050 FASTENERS AND ADHESIVES
06100 ROUGH CARPENTRY
06130 HEAVY TIMBER CONSTRUCTION
06150 WOOD AND METAL SYSTEMS
06170 PREFABRICATED STRUCTURAL WOOD
06200 FINISH CARPENTRY
06300 WOOD TREATMENT
06400 ARCHITECTURAL WOODWORK
06500 STRUCTURAL PLASTICS
06600 PLASTIC FABRICATIONS
06650 SOLID POLYMER FABRICATIONS

DIVISION 7 – THERMAL AND MOISTURE PROTECTION

07100 WATERPROOFING
07150 DAMPPROOFING
07180 WATER REPELLENTS
07190 VAPOR RETARDERS
07195 AIR BARRIERS
07200 INSULATION
07240 EXTERIOR INSULATION AND FINISH SYSTEMS
07250 FIREPROOFING
07270 FIRESTOPPING
07300 SHINGLES AND ROOFING TILES
07400 MANUFACTURED ROOFING AND SIDING
07480 EXTERIOR WALL ASSEMBLIES
07500 MEMBRANE ROOFING
07570 TRAFFIC COATINGS
07600 FLASHING AND SHEET METAL
07700 ROOF SPECIALTIES AND ACCESSORIES
07800 SKYLIGHTS
07900 JOINT SEALERS

Figure 23–8 *Masterformat* Broadscope Section Titles from the Construction Specifications Institute. (Reprinted with permission, Construction Specifications Institute, 1988)

DIVISION 8 – DOORS AND WINDOWS

08100 METAL DOORS AND FRAMES
08200 WOOD AND PLASTIC DOORS
08250 DOOR OPENING ASSEMBLIES
08300 SPECIAL DOORS
08400 ENTRANCES AND STOREFRONTS
08500 METAL WINDOWS
08600 WOOD AND PLASTIC WINDOWS
08650 SPECIAL WINDOWS
08700 HARDWARE
08800 GLAZING
08900 GLAZED CURTAIN WALLS

DIVISION 9 – FINISHES

09100 METAL SUPPORT SYSTEMS
09200 LATH AND PLASTER
09250 GYPSUM BOARD
09300 TILE
09400 TERRAZZO
09450 STONE FACING
09500 ACOUSTICAL TREATMENT
09540 SPECIAL WALL SURFACES
09545 SPECIAL CEILING SURFACES
09550 WOOD FLOORING
09600 STONE FLOORING
09630 UNIT MASONRY FLOORING
09650 RESILIENT FLOORING
09680 CARPET
09700 SPECIAL FLOORING
09780 FLOOR TREATMENT
09800 SPECIAL COATINGS
09900 PAINTING
09950 WALL COVERINGS

DIVISION 10 – SPECIALTIES

10100 VISUAL DISPLAY BOARDS
10150 COMPARTMENTS AND CUBICLES
10200 LOUVERS AND VENTS
10240 GRILLES AND SCREENS
10250 SERVICE WALL SYSTEMS
10260 WALL AND CORNER GUARDS
10270 ACCESS FLOORING
10290 PEST CONTROL
10300 FIREPLACES AND STOVES
10340 MANUFACTURED EXTERIOR SPECIALTIES
10350 FLAGPOLES
10400 IDENTIFYING DEVICES
10450 PEDESTRIAN CONTROL DEVICES
10500 LOCKERS
10520 FIRE PROTECTION SPECIALTIES
10530 PROTECTIVE COVERS
10550 POSTAL SPECIALTIES
10600 PARTITIONS
10650 OPERABLE PARTITIONS
10670 STORAGE SHELVING
10700 EXTERIOR PROTECTION DEVICES FOR OPENINGS
10750 TELEPHONE SPECIALTIES
10800 TOILET AND BATH ACCESSORIES
10880 SCALES
10900 WARDROBE AND CLOSET SPECIALTIES

DIVISION 11 – EQUIPMENT

11010 MAINTENANCE EQUIPMENT
11020 SECURITY AND VAULT EQUIPMENT
11030 TELLER AND SERVICE EQUIPMENT
11040 ECCLESIASTICAL EQUIPMENT
11050 LIBRARY EQUIPMENT
11060 THEATER AND STAGE EQUIPMENT
11070 INSTRUMENTAL EQUIPMENT
11080 REGISTRATION EQUIPMENT
11090 CHECKROOM EQUIPMENT
11100 MERCANTILE EQUIPMENT
11110 COMMERCIAL LAUNDRY AND DRY CLEANING EQUIPMENT
11120 VENDING EQUIPMENT
11130 AUDIO-VISUAL EQUIPMENT
11140 VEHICLE SERVICE EQUIPMENT
11150 PARKING CONTROL EQUIPMENT
11160 LOADING DOCK EQUIPMENT
11170 SOLID WASTE HANDLING EQUIPMENT
11190 DETENTION EQUIPMENT
11200 WATER SUPPLY AND TREATMENT EQUIPMENT
11280 HYDRAULIC GATES AND VALVES
11300 FLUID WASTE TREATMENT AND DISPOSAL EQUIPMENT
11400 FOOD SERVICE EQUIPMENT
11450 RESIDENTIAL EQUIPMENT
11460 UNIT KITCHENS
11470 DARKROOM EQUIPMENT
11480 ATHLETIC, RECREATIONAL, AND THERAPEUTIC EQUIPMENT
11500 INDUSTRIAL AND PROCESS EQUIPMENT
11600 LABORATORY EQUIPMENT
11650 PLANETARIUM EQUIPMENT
11660 OBSERVATORY EQUIPMENT
11680 OFFICE EQUIPMENT
11700 MEDICAL EQUIPMENT
11780 MORTUARY EQUIPMENT
11850 NAVIGATION EQUIPMENT
11870 AGRICULTURAL EQUIPMENT

DIVISION 12 – FURNISHINGS

12050 FABRICS
12100 ARTWORK
12300 MANUFACTURED CASEWORK
12500 WINDOW TREATMENT
12600 FURNITURE AND ACCESSORIES
12670 RUGS AND MATS
12700 MULTIPLE SEATING
12800 INTERIOR PLANTS AND PLANTERS

Figure 23–8 (Continued)

```
DIVISION 13 – SPECIAL CONSTRUCTION          DIVISION 14 – CONVEYING SYSTEMS

13010 AIR SUPPORTED STRUCTURES              14100 DUMBWAITERS
13020 INTEGRATED ASSEMBLIES                 14200 ELEVATORS
13030 SPECIAL PURPOSE ROOMS                 14300 ESCALATORS AND MOVING WALKS
13080 SOUND, VIBRATION, AND SEISMIC CONTROL 14400 LIFTS
13090 RADIATION PROTECTION                  14500 MATERIAL HANDLING SYSTEMS
13100 NUCLEAR REACTORS                      14600 HOISTS AND CRANES
13120 PRE-ENGINEERED STRUCTURES             14700 TURNTABLES
13150 AQUATIC FACILITIES                    14800 SCAFFOLDING
13175 ICE RINKS                             14900 TRANSPORTATION SYSTEMS
13180 SITE CONSTRUCTED INCINERATORS
13185 KENNELS AND ANIMAL SHELTERS           DIVISION 15 – MECHANICAL
13200 LIQUID AND GAS STORAGE TANKS
13220 FILTER UNDERDRAINS AND MEDIA          15050 BASIC MECHANICAL MATERIALS AND METHODS
13230 DIGESTER COVERS AND APPURTENANCES     15250 MECHANICAL INSULATION
13240 OXYGENATION SYSTEMS                   15300 FIRE PROTECTION
13260 SLUDGE CONDITIONING SYSTEMS           15400 PLUMBING
13300 UTILITY CONTROL SYSTEMS               15500 HEATING, VENTILATING, AND AIR CONDITIONING
13400 INDUSTRIAL AND PROCESS CONTROL SYSTEMS 15550 HEAT GENERATION
13500 RECORDING INSTRUMENTATION             15650 REFRIGERATION
13550 TRANSPORTATION CONTROL INSTRUMENTATION 15750 HEAT TRANSFER
13600 SOLAR ENERGY SYSTEMS                  15850 AIR HANDLING
13700 WIND ENERGY SYSTEMS                   15880 AIR DISTRIBUTION
13750 COGENERATION SYSTEMS                  15950 CONTROLS
13800 BUILDING AUTOMATION SYSTEMS           15990 TESTING, ADJUSTING, AND BALANCING
13900 FIRE SUPPRESSION AND SUPERVISORY SYSTEMS
13950 SPECIAL SECURITY CONSTRUCTION         DIVISION 16 – ELECTRICAL

                                            16050 BASIC ELECTRICAL MATERIALS AND METHODS
                                            16200 POWER GENERATION - BUILT-UP SYSTEMS
                                            16300 MEDIUM VOLTAGE DISTRIBUTION
                                            16400 SERVICE AND DISTRIBUTION
                                            16500 LIGHTING
                                            16600 SPECIAL SYSTEMS
                                            16700 COMMUNICATIONS
                                            16850 ELECTRIC RESISTANCE HEATING
                                            16900 CONTROLS
                                            16950 TESTING
```

Figure 23–8 (Continued)

als, trades, functions, and space relationships reduces the chance of omission of important information. It also makes it much easier to make changes while the specs are being written.

With a word processor, the design firm can establish its own version of standardized specification language. All the popular word processing software products provide sufficient flexibility for the designer to develop template sections that will be needed in a furniture and finishes specification.

The larger design firm may be interested in obtaining a computerized version of one of the standardized text systems. Standardized text systems are available from trade associations, manufacturers, and some of the professional organizations. These standard text systems have a fill-in-the-blank format. However, these standardized text systems require the user to have a thorough understanding of the construction process in order to know what to leave in and what to take out of the specification.

Whatever format the firm chooses to use, remember to keep the language of the specifications clear and direct. For example, "The vendor shall remove all cartoning and packaging materials." It is also appropriate to omit words such as "shall" and "will." In the preceding example, the sentence would read, "Remove all cartoning and packaging materials."

A few other examples of the necessity of careful use of language that show that words can have a double meaning come from Reznikoff:

Shall and Will	Often used incorrectly. "Shall" is used to designate a command; "Will" implies a choice.
Any	"The Contractor shall assume the responsibility for any unacceptable work." This sentence implies that the contractor may select the work that is unacceptable.
All	"The Contractor shall assume the responsibility for all unacceptable work." This sentence leaves no doubt about the contractor's responsibility.[4]

Writing technical specifications and preparing the remaining documents needed for a bid are time-consuming activities. In truth, neither is an activity that many designers enjoy. Small firms that infrequently produce formal contract documents and bid specifications may wish to use specification writing consultants. Independent practitioners provide consulting services to design professionals who do not feel qualified nor have the time to prepare construction and/or interiors specification. Larger firms may have a staff member responsible for the preparation of all specifications issued by the firm. These specialists need to be experienced in interior design and/or architecture, have an eye for and interest in detail, and thorough knowledge of such things as materials, products, construction methods, and building codes. The Construction Specification Institute has developed a certification process for qualified specifiers who are entitled to refer to themselves as Certified Construction Specifiers (CCS).

Addenda

After the contract documents are in the hands of the contractors and vendors, changes or corrections can only be made by the use of addenda. *Addenda* are additions to the contract documents. Each addendum must be in writing and sent to all bidders. Corrections or clarifications should not be made or accepted orally.

According to Rosen, addenda are used to provide any of the following kinds of information to bidders:

1. Correct errors and omissions.
2. Clarify ambiguities.
3. Add to or reduce the scope of the work.
4. Provide additional information that can affect the bid prices.
5. Change the time and place for receipt of bids.
6. Change the quality of the work.
7. Issue additional names of qualified "or equal" products.[5]

---

[4]Reznikoff, S. C. *Specifications for Commercial Interiors*, rev. ed., p. 251. Copyright © 1989 Whitney Library of Design, an imprint of Watson-Guptill Publications.

[5]Rosen, Harold J., *Construction Specifications Writing*, 2d ed., John Wiley and Sons, Inc., 1981, p. 177. Copyright by John Wiley and Sons, Inc.

These clarifications may result from something that the client or designer sees in the documents, or from a question from one or more of the bidders. All addenda should be prepared as quickly and as clearly as possible. They should come from the person responsible for creating the documents. If an allied professional or other design team member finds a questionable item, it should be called to the attention of the specification writer, and that person should prepare and send the addendum. When addenda are mailed to bidders, there must be sufficient time for bidders to react to the addenda prior to the close of bid. Recall that notification begins upon receipt of the notification, not at the time of mailing.

Bid Process

Competitive bidding is a process whereby the client has the opportunity to obtain comparative prices from a number of contractors and/or vendors for the construction or supply of the project. Competitive bids are almost always required by law for projects involving federal, state, and local agencies as well as public businesses like utilities. Most private businesses also require competitive bids on construction projects and large furniture or equipment orders.

Governmental agencies often use forms called "requests for proposals" (RFP) or "request for bid or quote." These forms follow different procedures and ask for information in different ways than discussed in this chapter. Since bidding on government projects can be rather intricate, the reader is referred to Stasiowski, Stitt, or Jones for some introductory information on selling and bidding to government agencies. This chapter deals only in a general nature with the bidding process for governmental agencies.

The idea of the bid process is that it allows the client to purchase the products and services of the project at as low a price as possible while maintaining the quality and intentions of the original design concept. This assumption is valid as long as the goods or services being bid are either the same or can objectively be compared as equal. That, however, is not always possible. If a client is bidding an open office systems project, it must be possible for the client to objectively evaluate the differences—subtle or otherwise—in the various products bid so as to purchase the goods at the lowest price while maintaining the quality and/or design intentions of the specifications. When there are sufficient bidders of a like product, then competitive bids based on the original idea are possible. When a project is designed and/or specified in such a way that few bidders can supply the same product at a fair price, then the bid process is suspect.

Clients ready to purchase large quantities of product and required to use the bid process often are under pressure to accept the lowest bid. For the designer, this can mean the loss of the original design concept of the project since a different product that does not have the same aesthetic appearance as the original design might be purchased. For the client, it can mean ownership of product that does not meet the performance criteria of the original design.

Competitive bidding may also be more expensive than other purchasing methods. There is a greater amount of preparation time of complicated contract documents and specifications for the goods and services. Also, additional documentation related to the bid procedure, general conditions for performance of the bid contract, and other conditions related to the bid and subsequent work must be prepared. When similar but unequal products are bid or products are bid based on performance, the client and designer will be involved in time-consuming evaluations either before bid submittal or before the awarding of contracts. Additionally, there is a potential for claims and suits related to the bid award if one or more bidders feel that the award was improper.

Yet the bid process is likely to continue for most major commercial and governmental projects. The designer who will be involved in these kinds of projects will have to deal with the bid situation.

In addition to the contract documents, three bid documents must be produced in order to complete a bid. They are: the invitation to bid, instructions to bidders, and the bid form.

Invitation to Bid

The first step in the bid process is to prepare and conduct an invitation to bidders. The *invitation to bid* notifies potential bidders of the existence of a project. Government and public agencies will most likely advertise a bid in newspapers. This process is called *open competitive selection*. In this case, anyone interested in the project who meets qualifications spelled out in the invitation to bid may submit a bid. Private businesses rarely advertise a bid, though they may for a very large project. Some private organizations, through careful legal preparation, may have an acceptable "bid list" of potential designers/vendors who would receive the notifications. This selection process is called *closed competitive selection*. In this situation, the client will contact several designers/vendors to make them aware of the project. Only those invited to bid in this manner will be allowed to bid on the project.

The advantage of a bid list system is that bidders are prequalified by the client so that those bidders who have experience with the particular kind of project, proven personnel, capital to procure the goods, and so on, are the only designers/vendors with whom the client must deal. This also allows the client to maintain a reasonable number of bids rather than a very large number requiring careful evaluation to eliminate unqualified bidders.

One disadvantage is that too few bidders may be used with the potential of a higher price. There is also the probability that less experienced, yet qualified designers/vendors are prohibited from entering the market. Yet if it is possible to get a sufficient (by the client's estimation) number of qualified bidders through a prequalification bid list system, it is a satisfactory and legal method of obtaining competitive bids.

The invitation to bid provides a summary of the project, the bid process, and other brief pertinent procedures for the project. It informs potential bidders of the project, its scope, and ways to obtain further information. The invitation should also state whether a security bond is required, how much it will be and how long it will be held. The size or length of time the bond will be held may discourage some designers/vendors from bidding.

Instructions to Bidders

The *instructions to bidders* informs bidders how to prepare bids for submittal so that all submittals are in the same form. This helps to make the various bids easily comparable. Since some designers/vendors offer substitutions to what was specified or do not bid on portions of the project, called exclusions, it is not always easy to start with comparable bids anyway.

Information in the instructions should only relate how to prepare and submit the bids. The following represents what is commonly in the instructions: It will inform the bidders what form and format to use; information on how, where, and when bids are due; statements related to site visitations and familiarization responsibilities; statements related to resolution of interpretations of discrepancies in the documents; information on how bids can be withdrawn; the procedure for awarding the bid; conditions for rejecting bids; and any other pertinent instructions that may be required by the client (see Figure 23–9).

Important parts of the instructions are the portions of the bid documents usually referred to as the "drawings and specifications." These consist of working drawings and/or equipment plans and the written specifications related to products, materials, and construction methods. The instructions to bidders should only mention where and how these documents can be obtained, how they are to be used by the bidder, and—if substitutions or exclusions are allowed—how they are to be submitted. The actual drawings and specifications do not appear at this location in the documents.

AIA Document A771

Instructions to Interiors Bidders

1990 EDITION

TABLE OF ARTICLES

A771-1990   1

Figure 23–9 "Instructions to Bidders" (AIA document A771). (Reproduced with permission, American Institute of Architects)

INSTRUCTIONS TO INTERIORS BIDDERS

ARTICLE 1
DEFINITIONS

1.1 Bidding Documents include the Bidding Requirements and the proposed Contract Documents. The Bidding Requirements consist of the Advertisement or Invitation to Bid, Instructions to Bidders, Supplementary Instructions to Bidders, the bid form, and other sample bidding and contract forms. The proposed Contract Documents consist of the form of Agreement between the Owner and Contractor, Conditions of the Contract (General, Supplementary and other Conditions), Drawings, Specifications, and all Addenda issued prior to execution of the Contract.

1.2 Definitions set forth in the General Conditions of the Contract for Furniture, Furnishings and Equipment, AIA Document A271, or in other Contract Documents are applicable to the Bidding Documents.

1.3 Addenda are written or graphic instruments issued by the Architect prior to the execution of the Contract which modify or interpret the Bidding Documents by additions, deletions, clarifications or corrections.

1.4 A Bid is a complete and properly signed proposal to do the Work for the sums stipulated therein, submitted in accordance with the Bidding Documents.

1.5 The Base Bid is the sum stated in the Bid for which the Bidder offers to perform the Work described in the Bidding Documents as the base, to which Work may be added or from which Work may be deleted for sums stated in Alternate Bids.

1.6 An Alternate Bid (or Alternate) is an amount stated in the Bid to be added to or deducted from the amount of the Base Bid if the corresponding change in the Work, as described in the Bidding Documents, is accepted.

1.7 A Unit Price is an amount stated in the Bid as a price per unit for materials, furniture, furnishings, equipment or services or a portion of the Work as described in the Bidding Documents.

1.8 A Bidder is a person or entity who submits a Bid.

1.9 A Sub-bidder is a person or entity who submits a Bid to a Bidder for labor, materials, furniture, furnishings or equipment for a portion of the Work.

ARTICLE 2
BIDDER'S REPRESENTATIONS

2.1 The Bidder by making a Bid represents that:

2.1.1 The Bidder has read and understands the Bidding Documents and the Bid is made in accordance therewith.

2.1.2 The Bidder has read the bidding documents, contract documents or record drawings for other portions of the Project, if any, being bid concurrently or presently under contract and understands the extent that such documentation relates to the Work for which the Bid is submitted.

2.1.3 The Bidder has visited the Project premises, or, if not yet constructed, has reviewed the documents pertaining thereto, has become familiar with local conditions under which the Work is to be performed and has correlated the Bidder's personal observations with the requirements of the proposed Contract Documents.

2.1.4 The Bid is based upon the materials, furniture, furnishings, equipment and services required by the Bidding Documents without exception.

ARTICLE 3
BIDDING DOCUMENTS

3.1   COPIES

3.1.1 Bidders may obtain complete sets of the Bidding Documents from the issuing office designated in the Advertisement or Invitation to Bid in the number and for the deposit sum, if any, stated therein. The deposit will be refunded to Bidders who submit a bona fide Bid and return the Bidding Documents in good condition within ten days after receipt of Bids. The cost of replacement of missing or damaged documents will be deducted from the deposit. A Bidder receiving a Contract award may retain the Bidding Documents and the Bidder's deposit will be refunded.

3.1.2 Bidding Documents will not be issued directly to Sub-bidders or others unless specifically offered in the Advertisement or Invitation to Bid, or in supplementary instructions to bidders.

3.1.3 Bidders shall use complete sets of Bidding Documents in preparing Bids; neither the Owner nor Architect assumes responsibility for errors or misinterpretations resulting from the use of incomplete sets of Bidding Documents.

3.1.4 In making copies of the Bidding Documents available on the above terms, the Owner and the Architect do so only for the purpose of obtaining Bids on the Work and do not confer a license or grant permission for any other use of the Bidding Documents.

**3.2   INTERPRETATION OR CORRECTION
            OF BIDDING DOCUMENTS**

3.2.1 The Bidder shall carefully study and compare the Bidding Documents with each other, and with other work being bid concurrently or presently under contract to the extent that it relates to the Work for which the Bid is submitted, shall examine the Project premises and local conditions, and shall at once report to the Architect errors, inconsistencies or ambiguities discovered.

3.2.2 Bidders and Sub-bidders requiring clarification or interpretation of the Bidding Documents shall make a written request which shall reach the Architect at least seven days prior to the date for receipt of Bids.

Figure 23–9 (Continued)

3.2.3 Interpretations, corrections and changes of the Bidding Documents will be made by Addendum. Interpretations, corrections and changes of the Bidding Documents made in any other manner will not be binding, and Bidders shall not rely upon them.

3.3 SUBSTITUTIONS

3.3.1 The materials, products and equipment described in the Bidding Documents establish a standard of required function, dimension, appearance and quality to be met by any proposed substitution.

3.3.2 No substitution will be considered prior to receipt of Bids unless written request for approval has been received by the Architect at least ten days prior to the date for receipt of Bids. Such requests shall include the name of the material or equipment for which it is to be substituted and a complete description of the proposed substitution including drawings, product data, performance and test data, and other information necessary for an evaluation. A statement setting forth changes in other materials, equipment or other portions of the Work including changes in the work of other contracts that incorporation of the proposed substitution would require shall be included. The burden of proof of the merit of the proposed substitution is upon the proposer. The Architect's decision of approval or disapproval of a proposed substitution shall be final.

3.3.3 If the Architect approves a proposed substitution prior to receipt of Bids, such approval will be set forth in an Addendum. Bidders shall not rely upon approvals made in any other manner.

3.3.4 No substitutions will be considered after the Contract award unless specifically provided in the Contract Documents.

3.4 ADDENDA

3.4.1 Addenda will be mailed or delivered to all who are known by the issuing office to have received a complete set of Bidding Documents.

3.4.2 Copies of Addenda will be made available for inspection wherever Bidding Documents are on file for that purpose.

3.4.3 No Addenda will be issued later than four days prior to the date for receipt of Bids except an Addendum withdrawing the request for Bids or one which includes postponement of the date for receipt of Bids.

3.4.4 Each Bidder shall ascertain prior to submitting a Bid that the Bidder has received all Addenda issued, and the Bidder shall acknowledge their receipt in the Bid.

ARTICLE 4
BIDDING PROCEDURES

4.1 FORM AND STYLE OF BIDS

4.1.1 Bids shall be submitted on forms identical to the form included with the Bidding Documents.

4.1.2 All blanks on the bid form shall be filled in by typewriter or manually in ink.

4.1.3 Where so indicated by the makeup of the bid form, sums shall be expressed in both words and figures, and in case of discrepancy between the two, the amount written in words shall govern.

4.1.4 Interlineations, alterations and erasures must be initialed by the signer of the Bid.

4.1.5 All requested Alternates shall be bid. If no change in the Base Bid is required, enter "No Change."

4.1.6 Where two or more Bids for designated portions of the Work have been requested, the Bidder may, without forfeiture of the bid security, state the Bidder's refusal to accept award of less than the combination of Bids stipulated by the Bidder. The Bidder shall make no additional stipulations on the bid form nor qualify the Bid in any other manner.

4.1.7 Each copy of the Bid shall include the legal name of the Bidder and a statement that the Bidder is a sole proprietor, partnership, corporation or other legal entity. Each copy shall be signed by the person or persons legally authorized to bind the Bidder to a contract. A Bid by a corporation shall further give the state of incorporation and have the corporate seal affixed. A Bid submitted by an agent shall have a current power of attorney attached certifying the agent's authority to bind the Bidder.

4.2 BID SECURITY

4.2.1 If so stipulated in the Advertisement or Invitation to Bid, or supplementary instructions to bidders, each Bid shall be accompanied by a bid security in the form and amount required, pledging that the Bidder will enter into a Contract with the Owner on the terms stated in the Bid and will, if required, furnish bonds covering the faithful performance of the Contract and payment of all obligations arising thereunder. Should the Bidder refuse to enter into such Contract or fail to furnish such bonds if required, the amount of the bid security shall be forfeited to the Owner as liquidated damages, not as a penalty. The amount of the bid security shall not be forfeited to the Owner in the event the Owner fails to comply with Subparagraph 6.2.1.

4.2.2 If a surety bond is required, it shall be written on AIA Document A310, Bid Bond, unless otherwise provided in the Bidding Documents, and the attorney-in-fact who executes the bond on behalf of the surety shall affix to the bond a certified and current copy of the power of attorney.

4.2.3 The Owner will have the right to retain the bid security of Bidders to whom an award is being considered until either (a) the Contract has been executed and bonds, if required, have been furnished, or (b) the specified time has elapsed so that Bids may be withdrawn, or (c) all Bids have been rejected.

4.3 SUBMISSION OF BIDS

4.3.1 All copies of the Bid, the bid security, if any, and other documents required to be submitted with the Bid shall be enclosed in a sealed opaque envelope. The envelope shall be addressed to the party receiving the Bids and shall be identified with the Project name, the Bidder's name and address and, if applicable, the designated portion of the Work for which the Bid is submitted. If the Bid is sent by mail, the sealed envelope shall be enclosed in a separate mailing envelope with the notation "SEALED BID ENCLOSED" on the face thereof.

4.3.2 Bids shall be deposited at the designated location prior to the time and date for receipt of Bids. Bids received after the time and date for receipt of Bids will be returned unopened.

4.3.3 The Bidder shall assume full responsibility for timely delivery at the location designated for receipt of Bids.

Figure 23–9 (Continued)

4.3.4 Oral, telephonic or telegraphic Bids are invalid and will not receive consideration.

4.4 MODIFICATION OR WITHDRAWAL OF BID

4.4.1 A Bid may not be modified, withdrawn or canceled by the Bidder during the stipulated time period following the time and date designated for the receipt of Bids, and each Bidder so agrees in submitting a Bid.

4.4.2 Prior to the time and date designated for receipt of Bids, a Bid submitted may be modified or withdrawn by notice to the party receiving Bids at the place designated for receipt of Bids. Such notice shall be in writing over the signature of the Bidder or by telegram; if by telegram, written confirmation over the signature of the Bidder shall be mailed and postmarked on or before the date and time set for receipt of Bids. A change shall be so worded as not to reveal the amount of the original Bid.

4.4.3 Withdrawn Bids may be resubmitted up to the date and time designated for the receipt of Bids provided that they are then fully in conformance with these Instructions to Interiors Bidders.

4.4.4 Bid security, if required, shall be in an amount sufficient for the Bid as modified or resubmitted.

ARTICLE 5
CONSIDERATION OF BIDS

5.1 OPENING OF BIDS

5.1.1 Unless stated otherwise in the Advertisement or Invitation to Bid, the properly identified Bids received on time will be opened publicly and will be read aloud. An abstract of the Bids will be made available to Bidders. When it has been stated that Bids will be opened privately, an abstract of the same information may, at the discretion of the Owner, be made available to the Bidders within a reasonable time.

5.2 REJECTION OF BIDS

5.2.1 The Owner shall have the right to reject any or all Bids, reject a Bid not accompanied by a required bid security or by other data required by the Bidding Documents, or reject a Bid which is in any way incomplete or irregular.

5.3 ACCEPTANCE OF BID (AWARD)

5.3.1 It is the intent of the Owner to award a Contract to the lowest responsible Bidder provided the Bid has been submitted in accordance with the requirements of the Bidding Documents and does not exceed the funds available. The Owner shall have the right to waive informalities or irregularities in a Bid received and to accept the Bid which, in the Owner's judgment, is in the Owner's own best interests.

5.3.2 The Owner shall have the right to accept Alternates in any order or combination, unless otherwise specifically provided in the Bidding Documents, and to determine the low Bidder on the basis of the sum of the Base Bid and Alternates accepted.

ARTICLE 6
POST-BID INFORMATION

6.1 CONTRACTOR'S QUALIFICATION STATEMENT

6.1.1 Bidders to whom award of a Contract is under consideration shall submit to the Architect, upon request, a properly executed AIA Document A305, Contractor's Qualifica-

tion Statement, unless such a statement has been previously required and submitted as a prerequisite to the issuance of Bidding Documents.

6.2 OWNER'S FINANCIAL CAPABILITY

6.2.1 The Owner shall, at the request of the Bidder to whom award of a Contract is under consideration and no later than seven days prior to the expiration of the time for withdrawal of Bids, furnish to the Bidder reasonable evidence that financial arrangements have been made to fulfill the Owner's obligations under the Contract. Unless such reasonable evidence is furnished, the Bidder will not be required to execute the Agreement between the Owner and Contractor.

6.3 SUBMITTALS

6.3.1 The Bidder shall, as soon as practicable after notification of selection for the award of a Contract, furnish to the Owner through the Architect in writing:

   .1 a designation of the Work to be performed with the Bidder's own forces;

   .2 names of the manufacturers of furniture, furnishings, equipment and materials proposed for the Work; and

   .3 names of persons or entities (including those who are to furnish materials or equipment fabricated to a special design and those performing installation or assembly on the premises) proposed for the principal portions of the Work.

6.3.2 The Bidder will be required to establish to the satisfaction of the Owner and Architect the reliability and responsibility of the persons or entities proposed to furnish and perform the Work described in the Bidding Documents.

6.3.3 Prior to the award of the Contract, the Architect will notify the Bidder in writing if either the Owner or Architect, after due investigation, has reasonable objection to a person or entity proposed by the Bidder. If the Owner or Architect has reasonable objection to a proposed person or entity, the Bidder may, at the Bidder's option, (1) withdraw the Bid, or (2) submit an acceptable substitute person or entity with an adjustment in the Base Bid or Alternate Bid to cover the difference in cost occasioned by such substitution. The Owner may accept the adjusted bid price or disqualify the Bidder. In the event of either withdrawal or disqualification, bid security will not forfeited.

6.3.4 Persons and entities proposed by the Bidder and to whom the Owner and Architect have made no reasonable objection must be used on the Work for which they were proposed and shall not be changed except with the written consent of the Owner and Architect.

ARTICLE 7
PERFORMANCE BOND AND
PAYMENT BOND

7.1 BOND REQUIREMENTS

7.1.1 If stipulated in the Bidding Documents, the Bidder shall furnish bonds covering the faithful performance of the Contract and payment of all obligations arising thereunder. Bonds may be secured through the Bidder's usual sources.

7.1.2 If the furnishing of such bonds is stipulated in the Bidding Documents, the cost shall be included in the Bid. If the furnishing of such bonds is required after receipt of bids and before execution of the Contract, the cost of such bonds shall

A771-1990 **4**

Figure 23–9 (Continued)

be added to the Bid in determining the Contract Sum.

7.1.3 If the Owner requires that bonds be secured from other than the Bidder's usual sources, changes in cost will be adjusted as provided in the Contract Documents.

7.2   TIME OF DELIVERY AND FORM OF BONDS

7.2.1 The Bidder shall deliver the required bonds to the Owner not later than three days following the date of execution of the Contract. If the Work is to be commenced prior thereto in response to a letter of intent, the Bidder shall, prior to commencement of the Work, submit evidence satisfactory to the Owner that such bonds will be furnished and delivered in accordance with this Subparagraph 7.2.1.

7.2.2 Unless otherwise provided, the bonds shall be written on AIA Document A312, Performance Bond and Payment Bond. Both bonds shall be written in the amount of the Contract Sum.

7.2.3 The bonds shall be dated on or after the date of the Contract.

7.2.4 The Bidder shall require the attorney-in-fact who executes the required bonds on behalf of the surety to affix thereto a certified and current copy of the power of attorney.

ARTICLE 8
FORM OF AGREEMENT
BETWEEN OWNER AND CONTRACTOR

8.1   FORM TO BE USED

8.1.1 Unless otherwise required in the Bidding Documents, the Agreement for the Work will be written on AIA Document A171, Standard Form of Agreement Between Owner and Contractor for Furniture, Furnishings and Equipment Where the Basis of Payment is a Stipulated Sum.

Figure 23–9 (Continued)

Bid Forms

Bid forms are documents prepared by the designer or the client and provided to the bidders. The bid form is the document that the vendor uses to inform the client of the bid price. The format generally is set up as a form letter from the bidder to the client. The bid form has blanks in appropriate spaces to be filled in by the bidder. Figure 23–10 is a sample bid form. If no substitutions or exclusions are allowed in the instructions, a statement reinforcing disqualification of a bidder submitting a substitution or exclusion should be provided here.

Bond Forms

Bond forms are legal documents used to bind the designer or vendor to the contract as assurance that the designer/vendor will perform the requirements of the contract as agreed. There are three bond forms commonly used in the bidding process; bid bond, performance bond, and labor and materials payment bond.

The bid bond is required to assure that the designer or vendor awarded the contract will sign the contract. Most companies that submit a bid would expect to go through with the contract. However, some companies submit bids only to find out how the competition is pricing services or products. In another instance, if a company has made an error in its bid, the company may want to withdraw even after the bid is awarded. The bid bond thus acts as "earnest money" to be sure that all who bid are actually interested in going through with the contract. A bid bond in an amount of approximately 5 to 10 percent of the bid price is customary. The bid bond of the successful bidder is usually held by the client for some time after the contract is signed and other bid securities are obtained. For unsuccessful bidders, the bid bond is returned promptly.

The performance bond is required of the winning bidder as a guarantee that the designer or vendor will complete the work as specified and will protect the client from any loss up to the amount of the bond as a result of the failure of the designer or vendor to perform the contract. It is customary for the performance bond to be an amount equal to 100 percent of the value of the bid contract. The designer or vendor, however, pays a surety company a smaller percentage for the bond insurance. This actual amount would vary based on the actual project conditions and the surety company. The performance bond is returned after completion of the project.

A labor and materials payment bond is required by the winning bidder to guarantee that the designer or vendor will be responsible for paying for all the materials and labor that have been contracted for, in the event the designer or vendor defaults on the project. This is to prevent the client from being responsible to subcontractors for goods not delivered. This bond is also customarily in an amount equal to 100 percent of the contract price. It also is returned after the completion of the project.

A legal recourse related to the labor and materials payment bond is the mechanics lien. This lien is an action filed by the contractor, subcontractor, or possibly the designer with the county clerk to prevent the owner of the property from giving or conveying title or a Deed of Trust to the named property until the mechanic who filed the lien has been paid. In this situation, a "mechanic" is one who is an employee, subcontractor, or supplier who was hired to do work by the owner or a general contractor.

More simply stated, contractors, subcontractors, their suppliers, and in some states architects and interior designers, may find it necessary to file a lien against the property in order to insure that the owner or the property pays the contractor any moneys due. A properly filed lien prevents the owner of the property from selling or conveying title of the property until the lien has been settled. Not all states have provisions which fully allow for mechanics liens. The designer should check with the attorney general or registrar of contractors of his or her state to clarify how liens might affect the workings of the designer.

BID FORM
FOR
FURNISHINGS CONTRACT

CONTRACT NUMBER: _____

PROJECT: _____

BID OF _____
(name of bidder)
  ☐ a corporation organized under the laws of the State of _____
  ☐ a partnership, with the following individuals as partners:

_____
☐ a sole proprietor.

Present Bid To:

_____

$\left(\begin{array}{l}\text{Firm Name}\\\text{Firm Address}\end{array}\right)$

The Undersigned, acknowledges receipt and review of the Project Documents, consisting of _____ pages of drawings and _____ pages of written specifications, and addenda No. _____ through _____ , and hereby proposes to furnish all materials, labor, and miscellany necessary to provide and install the furniture and furnishings as specified in the aforementioned documents.

The Undersigned further agrees to hold his/her Bid open for thirty (30) days after the receipt of bids. Should the bidder be awarded the contract, he/she shall furnish a Performance Bond and a Labor and Materials Payment Bond in accordance to the General Conditions of the Bid, to the owner within ten days after award of bid.

No substitutions or exclusions to what was specified shall be allowed. Any bidder not bidding on all items as specified shall be disqualified.

##

The undersigned agrees to supply and perform, in accordance with the specifications, all the materials, labor, and miscellany as specified for

_____ Dollars

($ _____).

##

The Bid Bond and all other required documentation is attached by the undersigned bidder.

It is understood that the owner reserves the right to reject any or all bids, to withhold the award of bid for any reason, and reserves the right to hold all bids for thirty (30) days after the date of opening.

Date of Bid: _____

Name of Bidder: _____

Address of Bidder: _____

Authorized Officer: _____

Figure 23–10 Bid form used to obtain a vendor's price on a bid.

Bid Opening

Bid proposals are almost always required to be sent to the owner or designer in sealed envelopes. The exact labeling of the envelope, where it is to be delivered, to whom, and by what day and time are stated in the instructions to bidders. Any bid received that does not conform to the instructions can be rejected. It is also customary that bids cannot be withdrawn after the closing date and time for the receipt of bids even if the *bid opening* has not yet taken place.

Bids for governmental agencies or public companies such as utilities are required to have the bid opening at an open public meeting. The place and time will be noted in the invitation to bidders. At that meeting, the client or person charged with administering the bid will announce each bidder and his or her bid price. The client usually does not award the bid at that time. The invitation to bid should have informed bidders about the length of time the client would take to evaluate the bids and make the decision as to the award of the contract. Although most public agencies are most likely going to take the "lowest bid," they are not bound to do so if there are legitimate reasons to reject the lowest bid. Care must be taken by the client, therefore, to not announce that company X is the apparent lowest bidder at the bid opening since this announcement could later bind the agency even if they want to reject that bid.

For private companies, the bid opening is not required by law to be open to the public. This means that each bidder might not have the opportunity to know what the competition bid, to know if their own bid was low in comparison to the others, or that it may have been in error. According to Sweet, the courts are beginning to expect the closed bid opening client to act in good faith with the bidders if a bid comes in substantially lower than all other bids and thus not penalize the bidder who makes a legitimate mistake.[6]

Bid Award Notification

After the bids are evaluated and a decision is made as to the successful bidder, each bidder must be notified of the result. A simple form letter is usually sent to each of the unsuccessful bidders thanking them. It is not legally necessary to inform them as to who the successful bidder was or the amount of the bid. It is often a good idea to include a comment that the bids of the unsuccessful bidders will be held for a period of time as stated in the invitation to bid in the event that the successful bidder does withdraw. This means that the bids of unsuccessful bidders remain valid offers until the end of the holding period.

Summary

It is important for interior designers whose practices involve any structural design work or formal bid specifications to be familiar with the entire contract documents and specifications procedure. It is a common activity for commercial designers, but the residential designers must also understand how to prepare contract documents when they become involved in remodeling projects or custom manufacturing of products.

Floor plans and other working drawings, equipment plans keyed to equipment lists or formal specifications and various schedules are part of the contract documents. Most familiar to designers are the formal specifications needed when the client requires competitive bids. Four different kinds are discussed in this chapter: proprietary, descriptive, performance, and reference. For designers not commonly associated with the bid process, this chapter also briefly discusses how this important method for client purchasing operates.

---

[6]Sweet 1985.

References

Clough, Richard H. 1986. *Construction Contracting,* 5th ed. New York: Wiley.

Cushman, Robert F., James C. Dobbs, eds. 1991. *Design Professional's Handbook of Business and Law.* New York: Wiley.

Institute of Business Designers. 1981. *Forms and Documents Manual.* Chicago, Ill.: Institute of Business Designers.

Lohmann, William T. 1992. *Construction Specifications. Managing the Review Process.* Boston, Mass.: Butterworth Architecture.

Meier, Hans W. 1978. *Construction Specifications Handbook,* 2d ed. New York: Prentice-Hall.

Reznikoff, S. C. 1989. *Specifications for Commercial Interiors,* new rev. ed. New York: Watson-Guptill.

_____. 1979. *Specifications for Commercial Interiors.* New York: Watson-Guptill.

Rosen, Harold J. 1981. *Construction Specifications Writing,* 2d ed. New York: Wiley.

Simmons, H. Leslie. 1985. *The Specifications Writer's Handbook.* New York: Wiley.

Stasiowski, Frank. 1985. *Negotiating Higher Design Fees.* New York: Watson-Guptill.

Sweet, Justin. 1985. *Legal Aspects of Architecture, Engineering and the Construction Process,* 3d ed. St. Paul, Minn.: West Publishing.

Wakita, Osamu A., and Richard M. Linde. 1977. *The Professional Practice of Architectural Detailing.* New York: Wiley.

_____. 1984. *The Professional Practice of Architectural Working Drawings.* New York: Wiley.

Chapter 24

Order Processing

The client's acceptance of the equipment specification is the beginning of the next phase of the design project—paperwork management. The interior design firm or vendor responsible for purchasing and delivering merchandise will be required to order, track, and deliver perhaps several hundred—even thousands—of pieces of furniture and furnishings.

Many things can and often do go wrong when ordering merchandise. Product numbers can be transposed, the manufacturer puts the wrong item in the box, merchandise is damaged in transit, the ship date might be weeks after the move-in date, the client may not pay his or her bill, the client may claim that the merchandise delivered is not the merchandise agreed to, and many other problems can easily and commonly happen to designers that sell merchandise. It is therefore important for the design firm to develop clear policies on how to go about ordering merchandise and handling the paperwork involved in ordering. This is no place for sloppy handwriting, oral agreements, procrastination in reviewing paperwork, or even the lack of careful consideration of a client's credit worthiness. Profit margins on merchandise are too small and competition is too keen to allow any firm, large or small, to be careless in conducting order processing.

The ideal situation is to have an expediter—an individual familiar with the company's paperwork system and the requirements of the many manufacturers—be responsible for this order-processing function. However, in most firms, this function is the responsibility of the designer in charge of the project. In retail stores, some of this detail will be taken care of by others. Whatever the case, the designer should have a working knowledge of the paperwork system and terminology related to paperwork in the interior design office. This chapter will cover the kinds of forms generally used, including the purchase order, acknowledgment, and invoice. It will also provide additional information about shipping concerns and contract administration.

Credit Application

Interior designers specify and sell thousands of dollars of products to their residential and/or commercial clients. Unfortunately, some of these clients turn out to be bad credit risks. Management should establish a policy related to investigating the credit-worthiness of clients before the special order of merchandise or extensive design services begin. Firms that display items on a showroom floor or in inventory may find it impractical to require a credit check for all purchases. Management may decide, with the advice of the firm's accountant, that special-order purchases or design fees over some specific dollar amount require a credit application to be completed by the prospective client.

The form (see Figure 24–1) should be easy for the client to fill out. After it is completed, the form should be turned over to a financial institution or credit agency for review and recommendation. Although the opinion of the financial institution or credit agency should be taken very seriously, the final decision as to extending credit to the potential client should be that of the owner or appropriate manager.

A credit application will never provide 100 percent assurance as to the credit-worthiness or good intentions of a client. However, the procedure allows the design firm a greater opportunity to deal with clients who will honor their financial obligations.

Confirmation of Purchase/Purchase Agreement

Many firms will proceed with ordering merchandise on the basis of verbal agreement by the client. As the reader will recall from Chapter 16, a verbal "contract" for the sale of goods whose value is over $500 is not legally binding on the client. For this reason, many firms require a *confirmation of purchase*—also called a sales agreement, purchase agreement, or contract proposal—to be completed and signed by the client. This form legally requires the client to fulfill his or her financial responsibility to the designer. Company policy should be clear that no furniture or furnishings be ordered or begun until a signed Purchase Agreement has been obtained from the client.

A two-page or more form (see Figure 24–2), when signed by the client the confirmation becomes a legal contract for selling the described merchandise. The designer must sell the described merchandise at the prices quoted, and the client must pay for that same merchandise. The form must contain quantities, descriptions, and prices. It is impractical for a firm to type a series of these forms for a large volume of items. In those cases a statement such as "the undersigned agrees to purchase the items described per the attached list" will suffice.

The terms and conditions of the sale must be stated on the proposal agreement, and the client must be made aware of the terms (see Figure 24–3). Terms and conditions might relate to partial deliveries, changes in the job site, warehousing when the client is not ready to accept delivery, and warranties. These terms and conditions should be prepared with the advice of the firm's attorney.

Do not forget to have the client sign the confirmation. The client's signature is an important item in creating a legally enforceable contract for the sale of goods.

Purchase Orders

One of the most important forms of paperwork is the *purchase order*. The interior designer uses the purchase order to initiate orders for merchandise and services from factories, trades- and craftspeople, and other vendors. Additionally, many businesses use purchase orders of their own to initiate orders from the interior designer.

The purchase order must be designed so that all the information that the vendor or supplier needs quickly and correctly to complete the order is easily found. Considering the scope of projects and the number of different clients the design firm may deal with at any one time, it becomes apparent that the format must be standardized and complement the recording methods of the remaining paperwork and accounting systems used by the firm.

All firms, regardless of size, should have a policy prohibiting telephone orders. In any case, many manufacturers do not honor telephoned orders until the written order is re-

NEW ACCOUNT CREDIT INFORMATION
ALL INFORMATION MUST BE FILLED OUT COMPLETELY TO AVOID UNNECESSARY DELAY IN SHIPMENT.

PLEASE **PRINT** OR **TYPE**

Inital Order:
Purchase ☐
Lease ☐
Rent ☐

Salesperson: _____

Amount of credit requested $ _____

BUSINESS INFORMATION

NAME _____
(Give complete name as you are registered to do business)

ADDRESS _____ PHONE (____) _____

CITY _____ STATE _____ ZIP _____

PAYING OFFICE

NAME _____ PHONE (____) _____

ADDRESS _____ CONTACT PERSON _____

CITY _____ STATE _____ ZIP _____

Established: Mo. _____ Year _____
At present
location: Mo. _____ Year _____
Present
Ownership: Mo. _____ Year _____

☐ Sole Proprietor
☐ Partnership
☐ Corporation
☐ Other _____

Incorporation:
Date _____ State _____

Type of business: _____

PRINCIPLES

NAME	TITLE	ADDRESS	CITY	STATE	ZIP	DATE OF BIRTH	SOC. SEC. NO.

BANKING

BANK NAME _____ ACCOUNT OFFICER _____

BRANCH _____ PHONE (____) _____

CITY _____ STATE _____ ZIP _____

CHECKING ACCT. # _____ SAVINGS ACCT # _____ LOAN ACCT # _____

Purchase orders required _____
Authorized _____
Purchasers _____
_____
_____
_____

TRADE REFERENCES (SUPPLIERS)

(1)	(2)	(3)
NAME:	NAME:	NAME:
STREET:	STREET:	STREET:
CITY STATE, ZIP:	CITY STATE, ZIP:	CITY, STATE, ZIP:
PHONE:	PHONE:	PHONE:
CONTACT NAME:	CONTACT:	CONTACT:

I hereby certify that I hold valid sales tax permit # _____ issued pursuant to the sales and use tax laws of the state of _____ Type of permit _____

I hereby authorize Goodmans or its agents to make whatever investigative inquiries it deems necessary. In connection with my application or in the course of review and/or collection of any payments due. I further authorize all references and creditors, including banks, to release to Goodmans, or its agents, any and all information pertaining to my account(s).

I hereby agree to pay all invoices for purchases net 10 days subject to 2% per month service charge (Apr. 24%) on past due invoices. I further agree to **pay** all reasonable collection costs, attorney's fees, and court costs necessary to collect my account whether or not a suit is commenced. Goodman's Inc. retains and I grant a Purchase Money Security Interest in all goods purchased by me until paid.

I certify that the information contained herein is completed and correct, and given for the purpose of obtaining credit.

SIGNED _____ PRINT NAME _____ TITLE _____ DATE _____

PERSONAL GUARANTY

The undersigned, jointly and severally, unconditionally guaranty the payment when due of all present and future indebtedness of Customer to Goodmans, Inc. including but not limited to interest and attorney's fees.

_____   _____   _____   _____
PRINCIPLE'S SIGNATURE   DATE   SPOUSE'S SIGNATURE   DATE

Figure 24–1 Credit application used to obtain information about creditworthiness of clients. (Reproduced with permission, Goodmans Design-Interiors, Phoenix, AZ.)

SALES AGREEMENT

Date of Order_____19____   Delivery Date_____19____

Purchaser_____Phone_____

Address_____
       Street   City   State   Zip

Install at: Name_____Phone_____

Address_____
       Street   City   State   Zip

SPECIAL INSTRUCTIONS:_____

_____

_____

MATERIALS AND SPECIFICATIONS	Price Each	TOTAL

☐ Subject to final measurements

Read the back of this page before signing. The provisions on the back side of this page are part of this agreement.

Installer_____

Sales Representative_____

Purchaser_____

Satifactorily completed _____ Date _____

TOTAL MATERIALS $_____

Labor   _____

Sub Total   _____

Tax   _____

Total   _____

Deposit   _____

Balance Due $_____

Figure 24–2 The sales agreement (or confirmation of purchase) is used as the contract for the sale of merchandise. (Reproduced with permission, Cunninghams, Interiors, Flagstaff, AZ.)

TERMS AND CONDITIONS

TERMS

Terms of sale for all discounted items are Net 10 (ten) days from date of invoice. A monthly service charge of 1½% per month (18% per annum) will apply to all delinquent payments and will be added to the balance outstanding. Deliveries are to be paid for upon presentation of invoices covering each delivery. A deposit of 33% is required with all orders unless other terms have previously been established.

If for any reason the customer is unable to accept the merchandise as of the manufacturer's acknowledged shipping date, the customer (with Ball Stalker's assistance) will arrange for and pay for storage and handling. In this event, the Buyer hereby agrees to pay 90% of the invoice price for the merchandise within 10 days of the invoice date and pay the remaining 10% upon substantial completion of the installation. The final payment for all systems and furnishings is due upon substantial completion of installation. Substantial completion is the date when the work covered by this agreement is sufficiently complete so that the buyer can occupy or utilize the project work area or designated portion thereof for the use it is intended.

The security of all merchandise delivered to the project site is the responsibility of the buyer. The Owner shall be responsible for providing security against loss or damage for the materials, furniture, furnishings and equipment stored at the project premises between the dates of delivery and final acceptance by the Owner. Arrangements for such security shall be satisfactory to the Contractor.

This contract shall be governed by and construed in accordance with the laws of the State of Georgia.

This contract contains all the terms, provisions, conditions and warranties of the Sales Agreement and no extension, modification or amendment hereof shall be valid unless it is in writing signed by an Authorized Buyer and Seller.

CUSTOMER ORDER

A customer order is considered bonafide and Ball Stalker is obligated to perform to the order specifications when the customer confirms the order in writing by (1) issuing a purchase order, (2) authorizing letter, (3) signs and returns the Ball Stalker acknowledgment, or (4) signs a Ball Stalker Customer Agreement referencing a specific proposal or quotation.

It is incumbent upon the customer to confirm the order in one of the above mentioned methods within 10 calendar days from the date of the Ball Stalker order acknowledgment. The preceding conditions do not apply to QUICK SHIP orders.

CHANGES AND CANCELLATIONS

Changes by the customer cannot be accepted after 10 calendar days from the Ball Stalker acknowledgment date. The preceding conditions do not apply to QUICK SHIP orders. Changes in quantity or specification are subject to approval by Ball Stalker and manufacturer. Resultant charges from manufacturer would be paid by the customer. All requests for changes in quantity or specifications shall be delivered to Ball Stalker in writing.

Cancellation by the customer must be in writing and cannot be accepted after 10 calendar days from the Ball Stalker acknowledgment date. A restocking charge of 25% may be imposed for all approved cancellations at Ball Stalker's discretion. Changes at the job site must also be requested in writing and may be subject to additional charges.

MEANS OF SHIPMENT

The Ball Stalker responsibility regarding delivery, damage and freight inquiries and claims, etc. is conditioned upon the means of shipment specified in the original order. The following paragraphs identify the five means of shipment and the extent of Ball Stalker responsibility:

1. **LW-Delivered and Installed**—Ball Stalker will bear the full responsibility of delivering the merchandise in acceptable condition, obtaining written customer acceptance, and handling any difficulties regarding damage and freight inquiries and claims.

2. **DI-Direct**—The merchandise is shipped directly to the customer, but Ball Stalker personnel will meet the shipment and assume the full responsibility of "delivered and installed" terms.

3. **LD or DD-Delivery Only**—The merchandise is delivered to the customer's dock. Ball Stalker assumes the responsibility of damage and freight inquiry and claims but does not install the merchandise.

4. **DS-Drop Ship**—The merchandise is shipped and invoiced F.O.B. factory. The customer assumes all responsibility regarding damage and freight inquiries and claims.

5. **I/M-Inter-Market**—The goods are installed by another dealer as instructed by the manufacturer and the other "inter-market" dealer assumes full responsibility for delivery, damage and freight inquiries and claims.

TRANSPORTATION AND SPECIAL HANDLING CHARGES

Any transportation costs incurred in shipment of goods from the factory will be paid by the customer. Special handling charges, including special cartoning and crating, imposed by the manufacturer will be paid by the customer.

DELIVERY AND INSTALLATION

In the event that delivery and/or installation is required as a part of the proposal, the following provisions shall apply:

1. **Condition of Job Site**—The job site shall be clean, clear and free of debris prior to installation.

2. **Job Site Services**—Electric current, heat, hoisting and/or elevator service will be furnished without charge to Ball Stalker. Adequate facilities for off-loading, staging, moving and handling of merchandise shall be provided.

3. **Delivery During Normal Business Hours**—Delivery and installation will be made during normal working hours. Additional labor costs resulting from overtime work performed at the customer's request will be passed on to the customer.

4. **Installation and Assembly**—Ball Stalker's ability to install or assemble furniture shipped, knocked down or to permanently attach, affix, or bolt in place movable furniture is dependent on jurisdictional agreements between trade unions at the job site. If trade regulations enforced at the time of installation require on-site union tradesmen to complete the installation, the cost will be additional. Delivery of unusual items requiring special handling such as insulated files, marble, glass, etc., shall be charged to customer at applicable commercial rates for such handling.

5. **Delivered Goods**—Goods delivered and brought onto the job site as scheduled shall be inspected by the customer or his agent for damage and count verification. After delivery of merchandise by Seller to Buyer and acceptance of delivery by Buyer, pursuant to the provisions of the Georgia Uniform Commercial Code, all risk of loss or damage shall pass to Buyer, including, but not limited to, any loss or damage by weather, other trades such as painting or plastering, telephone installation, fire or other elements and Buyer agrees to hold Seller harmless from loss from such reasons.

6. **Receiving Documents**—Ball Stalker provides customer copies of receiving documents at the delivery point for all orders other than drop-shipments. It is the customer's obligation to process its internal receiving documents in such a way as to meet Ball Stalker's payment terms.

STATE AND LOCAL TAXES

The customer shall pay all taxes, levied or based upon the furniture and services invoiced by Ball Stalker, including state and local sales and use taxes. Customers who are exempt from the above taxes shall provide Ball Stalker with copies of exemption certificate upon confirmation of the order.

WARRANTY

All merchandise sold under this agreement is warranted by Ball Stalker Co. to be free from defects in materials or workmanship to the same extent as warranted by the merchandise manufacturers. Ball Stalker agrees to repair or replace at Ball Stalker's discretion defective merchandise covered by the above referenced warranty. This warranty agreement is contingent upon the Buyers promptly notifying Ball Stalker in writing of any claim with respect to the merchandise, and affording Ball Stalker a reasonable opportunity to examine the merchandise and investigate the claimed defect. Ball Stalker IN NO EVENT SHALL BE LIABLE FOR DAMAGES BEYOND THE PRICE PAID BY BUYER FOR SUCH DEFECTIVE MERCHANDISE. This warranty is in lieu of all other warranties express or implied, and it is agreed that there is no oral or implied additional warranties made in connection with the sale of the merchandise sold hereunder.

GENERAL LIABILITY

No liability will accrue against Ball Stalker as a result of any breach of these terms and conditions resulting from any work stoppage, accident, fire, civil disobedience, riots, rebellions, and Acts of God beyond Ball Stalker's control.

Figure 24–3 Typical terms and conditions on the back of a confirmation of purchase (reproduced with permission, Ball Stalker Co., Atlanta, GA.)

ceived. Telephone orders for any kind of product or service can lead to a duplication of orders and leave the design firm responsible for paying for two pink sofas with orange spots instead of the one requested by a client. It is a good idea to use the telephone to find out product availability or to request that yardages of fabrics be held pending a confirming purchase order. However, do not let the telephone substitute for proper paperwork. Critical orders can be faxed, but should always be followed by confirming original purchase orders.

Purchase orders play more than one role for the design firm. The first, of course, is the means of obtaining the needed goods and services in the client's interests. A second important role of the purchase order is to act as a record of all outstanding orders. This role plays a part in the financial accounting of the firm for income tax and loan application purposes. A third function of the purchase order is to act as a control mechanism for billings to clients. Many small firms with a very simple paperwork system will use the purchase order as a delivery ticket as well. What is shown as delivered on these forms will key the bookkeeper to send the necessary billing to clients. A fourth function can be for checking for correct pricing by the various suppliers. If the supplier acknowledges a price different from that on the purchase order, the designer should immediately find out what caused the discrepancy.

What the exact content and format of the purchase order is should be established by the needs of the individual firm and its accounting practices. Figure 24–4 is an example of a typical purchase order. The following information should be a part of the purchase order either as preprinted information, or blank spaces:

1. *Preprinted sequenced numbers.* Using numerically sequenced purchase orders allows the firm to keep track of each purchase order—whether used or thrown out.

2. *The firm's name and billing address, telephone number, and FAX number.* Preprinted forms look more professional, negate mailing or shipping errors resulting from illegible handwriting, and save time.

3. *Space for the supplier's/vendor's name and address.*

4. *Space for the "ship to" location.* This is very important when the design firm is not having the merchandise shipped to the design firm's office location. On occasion, designers *drop ship* orders. This means that the order is to be delivered to some location other than the designer's office. It usually means the shipment is made to the client's address or job site.

5. *Preprinted boxes or space for additional shipping instructions.* These instructions relate to expected ship date, preferred freight company, and collected or prepaid charges.

6. *Space for the "tag for" information.* The *tag for* information can be at the bottom or the top of the form. The client's name or a project number[1] is usually written in this space as a further means of identifying for whom this merchandise or service was ordered. Some firms also put other brief instructions to help the receiving party clearly identify for whom and how the materials are to be used or where the items are to be located on the job.

The body of the purchase order should have space for the following information:

1. *Quantity.* This is not only needed by the supplier, but it is required by the UCC to form a sales contract.

2. *Catalog number.* This should exactly reflect the sequence of numbers and/or letters

---

[1]Some design firms use project numbers rather than the client's name on all paperwork that goes outside the office. This is done for client confidentiality.

PURCHASE ORDER

PG	PGS
	OF

DIRECT INQUIRES REGARDING THIS ORDER
TO:
PHONE NUMBER:

VENDOR: SHIP TO:

VENDOR NO.

DATE

DELIVER:
☐ ASAP   ☐ NOT
          BEFORE

FREIGHT TO BE PAID BY:
☐ GOODMANS PHOENIX   ☐ SHIPPER   ☐ CONSIGNEE
SEND BILL OF LADING WITH INVOICE

NO C.O.D. SHIPMENTS

SHIP   COMPLETE ONLY ☐   PARTIAL ☐

NOTE: IF SHIPMENT IS MARKED ABOVE "COMPLETE ONLY" AND ITEMS ARE SHIPPED PARTIAL, THEN PAYMENT WILL BE WITHHELD UNTIL SHIPMENT IS COMPLETE.

UNLESS PRICES ARE SAME OR LOWER CALL OR MAIL CATALOGS WITH NEW PRICE LISTS

QUANTITY ORDERED	CATALOG NUMBER	DESCRIPTION	TAG LINE ITEM	NET COST EACH

PURCHASE ORDER PLEASE ACKNOWLEDGE

PLEASE COMPLY WITH INSTRUCTIONS BELOW:
IMPORTANT!!
1. Please mark all packages and papers with our Order No. and Line Item No. and Cust. Name.
2. Acknowledge receipt of this Purchase Order and confirm delivery date.
3. Submit all invoices in Duplicate.
4. Bill of Lading and name of carrier must be attached to invoices sent to Goodmans.

TAG FOR:
LINE ITEM NUMBERS AND CUSTOMER NAMES MUST APPEAR ON ALL INVOICES AND CARTONS.

P.O.

_____
AUTHORIZED SIGNATURE

VENDOR'S COPY

Figure 24–4 An example of a purchase order used by a commercial office furnishings dealer. (Reproduced with permission, Goodmans Design-Interiors, Phoenix, AZ.)

that the supplier uses to call out the products from his or her catalog. Reversing one number can lead to the wrong product being shipped.

3. *Description.* Maintain the method the supplier uses in the catalog. This helps prevent having the wrong item shipped. Remember, however, that many suppliers process orders by the catalog number on the purchase order, not the description. The description acts as a check against the catalog number. There is no guarantee that the supplier's order input desk will read the description.

4. Net price. Putting the expected net price on the purchase order works as a good pricing check. Net pricing on the purchase order can also help the firm attempting to utilize a cost accounting method for managerial control.

5. *Line item number.* Many firms use *line item numbers* as another method of controlling an order. Each item[2] on the sale order is given a line item number. This number is cross-referenced in the appropriate column on the purchase order. Problems and questions with orders can more easily be tracked with this number. Goods can also be tagged with the line item number.

At the bottom of the form should be space for the authorizing signature. This signature will be either the firm's owner or an authorized manager. Additional information about which the individual design firm wishes the supplier to be aware can be added in appropriate places. An example would be instructions asking the supplier to acknowledge receipt of the purchase order and to provide an expected shipping date. The bottom of Figure 24–4 shows some of the other kinds of instructions that might be useful.

Each supplier receives a separate purchase order. Multiple items to the same supplier for the same client can, of course, be sent on the same purchase order. If the designer is placing orders for multiple items to the same supplier but for two or more *different* clients, a different purchase order should be prepared for each client. Even though some firms place two or more customer orders to the same manufacturer on the same purchase order, better control is maintained by initiating separate purchase orders for each customer.

If two suppliers are involved in the completion of one finished product, such as a *customer's own material (COM)*[3] sofa, two different purchase orders must be prepared. One purchase order is written to the sofa supplier, referencing (according to the supplier's requirements printed in his or her catalog) the COM fabric. A second purchase order is written to the fabric supplier referencing the information required by the sofa supplier. This information is often written as an expanded "tag for" block of information in the body of the purchase order rather than in the normal "tag for" space. Most furniture manufacturers require that the fabric be shipped prepaid to the factory. The designer must be sure that the fabric supplier does this, and the designer must remember to add that estimated shipping charge to the cost of the sofa.

Number of Copies

For a small firm, a minimum of three copies of the purchase order would be required. To help in visually tracking the various copies, it is best if each sheet is a different color. The first sheet is always white. The other copies may be any color.

- The white or original copy is the copy mailed to the supplier.

- The second copy should go in the "open purchase order" file.

- The third copy should go in the client's active file to be used for reference.

---

[2]Multiples of the same item for the same order are considered one line item.
[3]*COM* indicates that the designer is not using a fabric available from the chair or sofa manufacturer. The desired fabric will have to be ordered from a different supplier and sent to the chair/sofa manufacturer.

The open purchase order file is a numerical sequence of all the purchase orders that have been mailed but against which merchandise or services have not yet been received. In a small firm, the bookkeeper may keep track of this file. When acknowledgments are received, they should be checked for accuracy against the information on the purchase order. Discrepancies should be dealt with immediately. When merchandise has been received and delivered, the bookkeeper can send the proper billing to the client. Orders not yet received can be tracked by checking the expected ship date on the order against the current date. If an order appears to be late, the designer responsible should contact the supplier to establish the reason for the delay.

Larger firms may have a use for one or more additional copies of the purchase order. The most common use for an additional copy is to send to a warehouse or warehouse service. This helps the warehouse effectively service the design firm, because the warehouse will know in advance the quantity and expected arrival dates of all the merchandise the firm has ordered. If, on occasion, the merchandise is shipped to the client's location rather than the warehouse, the warehouse is alerted to a responsibility to unload and inspect the merchandise as it comes off the truck.

Some firms use a copy of the purchase order as a delivery ticket. In this case, pricing is blocked out of the copy shown to the client. The client would sign or initial the items delivered. Any back orders or needed repairs can also be noted on the delivery ticket copy of the purchase order.

Office furnishings dealers and many large retailers of residential furnishings utilize computer ordering. In the most sophisticated arrangement, once the client has signed an order confirmation and provided a purchase order, the design firm can use their computer and a modem to order directly from the factory. This saves time in generating the design firm's purchase orders as well as preventing errors in the retyping of information. Design firms that do not have that ability use data base software programs to generate typed sales orders that then produce the purchase orders and any internal-use order control forms. At the appropriate time, the billing department can automatically produce the client's invoice or other needed paperwork.

Acknowledgments

Acknowledgments or confirmations are the forms that the supplier sends back to the designer to indicate what the supplier interpreted the designer's order to be (see Figure 24–5). Depending on the supplier, the designer should receive an acknowledgment in about ten days to three weeks.

Although acknowledgments will vary in format to suit the needs of specific suppliers, it is likely that the following kinds of information will be provided:

1. An order number assigned by the supplier.

2. The design firm's purchase order number.

3. Date the acknowledgment was prepared.

4. A scheduled shipping date. The order will be shipped some time during the week that day appears—not necessarily on that day.

5. What the expected shipping situation will be (for example: "Collect—Roadway" means that the design firm will have to pay the shipping charges and that the merchandise will come from the Roadway shipping company).

6. Notations as to who ordered the merchandise, the billing address, and the shipping address.

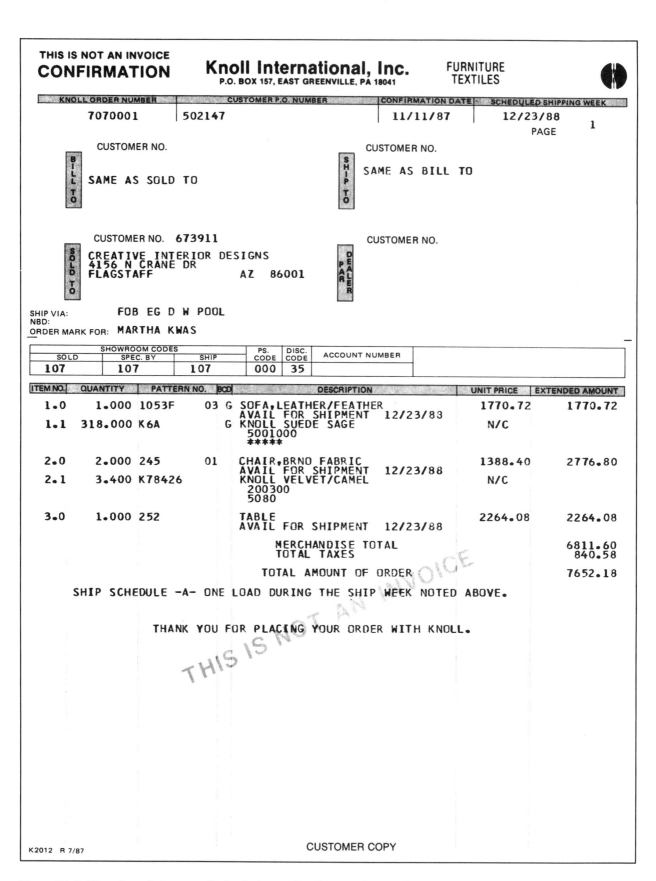

Figure 24–5 The acknowledgment tells the designer what the manufacturer believes to be the merchandise or service order. (Reproduced with permission, Knoll International)

7. What the "tag for" instructions are.

8. A restatement of quantity, catalog number, description, and pricing information. Many manufacturers will put the net price on the acknowledgment. However, others still quote retail prices. If the retail price has been quoted, the acknowledgment will often also quote the discount the designer is to receive for that order.

9. Other information related to billing and shipping.

Depending on the size of the firm and the organizational structure, someone must be responsible for checking the acknowledgment information against the purchase order. In smaller firms this will be the designer or perhaps the bookkeeper. Checking acknowledgments is a common responsibility of the expediter in larger firms. The expediting function will be discussed later in this chapter. Comparing the acknowledgment information against the purchase order should be done immediately in order to catch any discrepancies between the two forms. Any discrepancies in quantity, catalog number, description, and price should be discussed with the manufacturer. Delays in calling attention to errors often results in the design firm's receiving the wrong merchandise. This kind of delay can lead to an angry client and poor customer relations. Discrepancies regarding the expected shipping date or other shipping information should also be checked to see how they may affect project completion.

Speedy review of the acknowledgment against the purchase order is also necessary since there is generally very little time to make changes in the order. Major suppliers often give only ten days and certainly no more than three weeks "from receipt of order" to make any changes in the order. Time is of the essence.

The supplier will only send the firm an original copy of the acknowledgment. Again depending on the firm's size and paperwork structure, the original will probably be attached to the corresponding purchase order in the open purchase order file. A copy may be added to the active project file for reference.

Someone in the company must also be responsible for checking all outstanding orders. Many firms use a "tickler file" keyed to the days in the month. This file is checked daily (in very large operations) or weekly in smaller businesses to make sure that goods have been received within the expected ship dates. Checking can be done immediately on orders that are about to be shipped or that have not yet been received though the ship date has passed. Again, computer programs are useful in this situation.

Invoices

An *invoice* is simply a bill. The interior design firm sends out invoices to clients for services performed and/or goods purchased in the client's name. Suppliers send invoices to the designer for the goods or services that the interior design firm has ordered. Figure 24–6 is an invoice from the designer to the client. Figure 24–7 is an invoice from a supplier to a designer.

Invoices from suppliers are commonly sent at the same time that the merchandise is shipped. The invoice generally arrives at the office a few days before the merchandise. Many suppliers have invoices that look very similar to their acknowledgments. The only difference may be the label. Again, someone in the office must be responsible for checking the invoice to be sure that it corresponds to what was ordered. Since it often arrives a few days before the merchandise, it also should be checked against what was received.

It is important for the designer to check the invoice to determine if the manufacturer has extended any special pricing—especially related to prompt payment. The reader will recall the discussion on cash discounts in Chapter 13. These discounts can amount to substantial savings for the firm that can afford to pay the invoice within the specified prompt payment time. Not all suppliers offer this special discount to all designers.

Ball Stalker Co.
Office Furniture & Systems
151 Fourteenth Street, N.W.
Atlanta, GA 30318-7801 • (404) 876-8999

INVOICE

INVOICE DATE	INVOICE NO.	PAGE

CUSTOMER   SHIPPED TO

CUSTOMER ORDER NUMBER	SALESPERSON	BALL STALKER ORDER NUMBER

CASH TERMS

ITEM NO.		QUANTITY			DESCRIPTION	UNIT PRICE	TOTAL PRICE
OUR	CUST.	ORDERED	DELIVERED	B/O			

MAIL ALL REMITTANCES TO: 151 FOURTEENTH STREET, N.W.
ATLANTA, GEORGIA 30318-7801

NUMERICAL COPY

Figure 24–6 The invoice prepared by the design firm and sent to the client. (Reproduced with permission, Ball Stalker Co., Atlanta, GA.)

invoice

customer   date   invoice number

sold to

ship to

It is the orderer's responsibility to check this document for accuracy, correct fabric selections, etc. Report claims immediately. This order is subject to the terms and conditions on the face and reverse side. **Federal employer I.D. 38-0837640.**

order date	your purchase order number			terms	deposit	salesperson	territory	type	order number	ship date
contract number	ship to purchase order number			ship from	ship via					bill of lading number

item number	quantity this invoice	quantity remaining	quantity ordered	quantity previously invoiced	product number	product description		unit price	extended price

ZC21   R 3/87

customer original

•Remit to

Figure 24-7 An invoice from the manufacturer to the designer. (Reproduced with permission, Herman Miller, Inc.)

The designer should be sending out invoices to clients for services and/or goods as quickly as possible. Goods should be billed within ten days after the goods are delivered and accepted by the client. Services should be billed when services are completed (for short-duration projects), on a monthly basis for larger projects, or on whatever billing basis for services was agreed to in the contract. Delays in billing goods and services causes an increased amount of receivables and poor cash management. This is something that small and large design firms alike cannot afford. Delays in billing can also lead to a few unscrupulous clients into not paying for goods or services at all.

To help in having at least some legal basis for preventing late or no payment, the original contract for services or goods should contain language related to "billing upon delivery" or "payment due ten days after receipt of invoice." Some firms try to use item-by-item billing on large projects. This of course means that if the project has twenty items expected to be delivered, and two arrive, the firm delivers the two and bills for those two. The next time one or more items arrive, those are also delivered and billed. Although this may help somewhat with the firm's cash flow, it can cause many costs and headaches to the firm. It is suggested that whenever possible, deliveries be done in larger quantities of items or as a complete job. This will reduce the delivery costs and the bookkeeping costs of multiple deliveries and billings.

Freight Matters

Chapter 13 contains a discussion of how freight and delivery charges affect the price of the goods. And Chapter 16 reviewed freight concepts as regulated by the UCC. In this chapter we will look at the forms that are related to freight services.

There are various freight matters that result in additional paperwork management for the designer. The first is the bill of lading. The *bill of lading* is the form the supplier provides to the truck driver (see Figure 24–8). The driver carries this form with him or her in the truck; the contents of the truck must match what is on the form. Many times the bill of lading will not be a detailed list but rather a total quantity of items. The designer or the warehouse must check the number of items that are delivered to the firm with the number on the bill of lading. Discrepancies in quantity should be noted on the bill as well as any notations regarding damages to merchandise.

Another form that accompanies the delivery is a packing list. The *packing list* is commonly in a plastic envelope attached to the outside of one of the items being delivered. The packing list details by quantity and description what is being shipped to the warehouse at a specific time. The packing list should be checked against all items taken from the truck and against the number on the bill of lading. Again, discrepancies should be noted on the bill of lading.

The actual *freight bill* is another use of the invoice. It is usually sent a few days after the shipment leaves the manufacturer. This invoice comes from the shipping company, not the manufacturer, and is the bill for the shipping service.

It is important for the designer or a representative of the design firm (the warehousing service) to inspect all the items as they arrive at the designer's warehouse or job site. Many one-person design firms allow the merchandise to be delivered to the client without the designer being available at the time of delivery for inspection of the goods. This can be very costly when merchandise is damaged. Damaged cartons should be immediately opened and inspected. Whenever practical, all items should be unwrapped or uncartoned to inspect for *concealed damage*—damage that may exist even though the carton or wrapping appears intact. Concealed damage must be reported to the carrier as soon as possible. As the time from acceptance of shipment or the discovery of damages lengthens, successful claims become less probable.

Any damage to cartons, packing, and merchandise should be shown to the driver. Notations as to damaged merchandise must be made on the bill of lading in order to make suc-

UNIFORM STRAIGHT BILL OF LADING — Short Form — Original — Not Negotiable — Domestic

On Collect on Delivery shipments, the letters "COD" must appear before consignee's name or as otherwise provided in item 430, Sec. 1.

*If the shipment moves between two ports by a carrier by water, the law requires that the bill of lading shall state whether it is "carrier's or shipper's weight." NOTE—Where the rate is dependent on value, shippers are required to state specifically in writing the agreed or declared value of the property.

SHIPPER NO. | DATE

RECEIVED, subject to the classifications and tariffs in effect on the date of the issue of this Bill of Lading,

FROM

STREET AND NO.

CITY AND STATE | ZIP

CONSIGNED TO

STREET AND NO.

CITY AND STATE | ZIP

ROUTING

C. O. D. $

C. O. D. FEE TO BE PAID BY CONSIGNEE ☐ SHIPPER ☐

ADVANCE	C.O.D. FEE	T.L. REV.	C.L. REV.

the property described below, in apparent good order, except as noted (contents and condition of contents of packages unknown) marked, consigned, and destined as indicated below, which said carrier (the word carrier being understood throughout this contract as meaning any person or corporation in possession of the property under the contract) agrees to carry to its usual place of delivery at said destination, if on its route, otherwise to deliver to another carrier on the route to said destination. It is mutually agreed, as to each carrier of all or any of said property over all or any portion of said route to destination, and as to each party at any time interested in all or any of said property, that every service to be performed hereunder shall be subject to all the terms and conditions of the Uniform Domestic Straight Bill of Lading set forth (1) in Uniform Freight Classification in effect on the date hereof, if this is a rail or a rail-water shipment, or (2) in the applicable motor carrier classification or tariff if this is a motor carrier shipment.

Shipper hereby certifies that he is familiar with all the terms and conditions of the said bill of lading, including those on the back thereof, set forth in the classification or tariff which governs the transportation of this shipment, and the said terms and conditions are hereby agreed to by the shipper and accepted for himself and his assigns.

NO. PKG.	HM	DESCRIPTION OF ARTICLES, SPECIAL MARKS, AND EXCEPTIONS	*WEIGHT (Sub. to Cor.)	Class or Rate	Check Column

Subject to Section 7 of conditions of applicable bill of lading, if this shipment is to be delivered to the consignee without recourse on the consignor, the consignor shall sign the following statement:

The carrier shall not make delivery of this shipment without payment of freight and all other lawful charges.

(Signature of Consignor)

If charges are to be prepaid, write or stamp here, "To be Prepaid."

Received $______ to apply in prepayment of the charges on the property described hereon.

Agent or Cashier

Per______ (The signature here acknowledges only the amount prepaid.)

This is to certify that the above-named materials are properly classified, described, packaged, marked and labeled and are in proper condition for transportation according to the applicable regulations of the Dept. of Transportation.

THE AGREED OR DECLARED VALUE OF THE PROPERTY IS HEREBY SPECIFICALLY STATED BY THE SHIPPER TO BE NOT EXCEEDING ______ PER ______

1

IT IS HEREBY AGREED THAT THE DECLARED VALUATION ON HOUSEHOLD GOODS OR PERSONAL EFFECTS IS NOT EXCEEDING 10¢ PER POUND PER ARTICLE LOST OR DAMAGED UNLESS A HIGHER VALUE IS DECLARED.

______ SHIPPER

PER ______

______ Agent, Per ______

(This Bill of Lading is to be signed by the shipper and agent of the carrier issuing same.)

FORM 212-4 (11-77)
(TREAS-146)
ISSUED 9/82

Figure 24–8 The bill of lading provides information about the shipper, the receiver, and the merchandise being shipped. (Reproduced with permission, Transcon Lines)

cessful claims. Many firms also take pictures of damaged merchandise. This can greatly help in the filing of claims.

Since the filing of freight claims and disposition of the claim is very time consuming, many firms forgo filing claims on minor damage and make repairs themselves. These charges are costed as an overhead expense. Merchandise that has sustained substantial damage in transit should be refused.

Certain items are generally required when filing a freight claim.

1. The bill of lading.

2. The paid freight bill.

3. The manufacturer's invoice for the item.

4. The inspection report prepared by the freight carrier.

5. Documentation of repair costs.

6. Documentation of additional freight costs (if any) resulting from the damage.

7. Other written or photographic documentation that attests to the damage occurring before delivery to the job site or the designer's warehouse.

Most manufacturers will not accept merchandise for return once the design firm has accepted it. Therefore, the firm must get written permission to return damaged (or incorrectly shipped) merchandise. Each manufacturer has its own policy concerning returns, and these polices must be adhered to in order to receive proper credit.

When the design firm contacts the freight carrier concerning a shipping question, it should have the supplier's name and location, the date of shipment, the description and number of items shipped, and the delivery location. If the information needed is not on the manufacturer's invoice, this information, along with other needed information, can be obtained from the manufacturer.

Expediting

An *expediter* is an individual familiar with the design firm's paperwork system and the various ordering and shipping requirements of the manufacturers. In firms large enough to have this specific job function, the expediter is a person who will constantly monitor all orders *after* the purchase order has been sent and the acknowledgment has been received. He or she is responsible for the speedy processing of orders.

The first activity of the expediter would be to check the acknowledgment from the manufacturers against the purchase order. It is vital to be sure that all the information matches between the two forms to confirm that the correct products and/or services are being supplied. Discrepancies must be taken care of immediately.

Once all the product information has been checked, the expediter will look closely at the expected ship date. He or she must check to be sure that the products are going to ship within the time specified on the purchase order and that they will arrive when they were promised to the client. If the ship date is not when expected, the expediter should inform the designer so that proper actions can be taken. Merchandise shipped earlier than desired may have to be warehoused until the site is ready. If this is the case, the designer must negotiate with the client as to where and who will be responsible for the charges. At the time of order, it is relatively easy for the design firm to request that the merchandise not be shipped until a date beyond the normal shipping schedule. There may be an extra charge if the manufacturer must warehouse the finished goods when the designer requests the shipment to be delayed.

It is not uncommon for the ship date to be later than expected. The designer must contact the client to let him or her know about the delay. Short-term delays may be inconvenient but are seldom critical problems. Delays of three or more weeks may necessitate canceling the original order and finding alternate products.

The expediter would also be responsible for tracking shipments once they have left the manufacturer. He or she should alert the delivery people of the impending shipment and where it is to be delivered by the trucking company. If merchandise is to be *drop shipped* to a job site, meaning that the merchandise goes to the client's address rather than the firm's warehouse or warehouse service, someone representing the design firm must be on the scene to unload, inspect, and deliver the goods to the client. Truck drivers are not generally responsible for unloading the merchandise from the truck, unpacking it, and delivering it to the client. In some firms, the expediter may also be responsible for filing return permissions as well as freight claims. However, a warehouse service may be able to provide theses last two services for the design firm.

Once shipments leave the manufacturer, they are tracked by the bill of lading number, not the purchase order number. The firm receives from the freight company information as to what this number is. This number, along with the name and address of the design firm, the name and address of the delivery site, the name of the shipping company, the name and address of the original shipping location, a description and the number of pieces in the order, and the weight of the order must be available to track delayed shipments.

Contract Administration

In Chapter 21, we briefly discussed the activities of the contract administration phase of a project. In this phase occur those activities centered on the actual construction, placing of orders, and completion of the project. Most of this chapter is devoted to explaining the many different forms that are used to order and process the ordering of goods. However, something should be said about the administration or handling of the project in this phase.

With the exception of the installation of architectural finishes and delivery of furniture, most construction or remodeling done on either residential or commercial sites will require *building permits*. It is assumed that the plans have also been drawn so that the project will meet any applicable building, accessibility, or fire codes. But this does not automatically mean work can be started. Permits are obtained from the building or engineering departments of city, county, or other applicable local authority. For some projects such as restaurants and health care facilities, permits will also be required from the state health department. Although it is the owner's responsibility to obtain the permits, it might fall to the designer to fill out the applications and submit the drawings. Designers should also be available to go to the meetings with the building people as plans are reviewed. Interior designers must remember that construction projects over 3000 square feet for a home and over 20 occupants for a commercial project generally must be drawn—or, at least, the drawings be stamped—by an architect.

If a project involves any construction work, the designer will be working with the client in selecting contractors and initiating the construction contracts. The general contractor and the subcontractors should be required to work closely with the interior designer throughout the project. Errors or omission in the drawings need to be brought to the attention of the designer as well as the owner to be sure corrections are made that will not be detrimental to the aesthetic and functional goals of the project. Too often, the designer gets cut out of many of these decisions as the contractors and the owners rush to complete the project.

The designer needs to schedule regular meetings with the contractor as well as make regular visits to the construction site. In this way, the designer knows what is going on and can easily keep the client informed of the progress of the project. For out-of-town projects, the designer must include the expenses of traveling to the project site and have these visits approved by the client prior to the visit. Design decisions regarding any necessary changes in the plans or the orders that are being placed for goods are far more effectively made with this kind of coordination.

When the project is ready to begin, it is very important that the client understand the potential disruption in the family or work environment. Remodeling a home cannot be done without some mess and inconvenience to the family. And major remodeling or additions might make it necessary for the family to move to other quarters during the project. For commercial remodeling, few businesses can survive if they must totally shut down even to lay new carpet. Commercial projects must often be scheduled outside normal business hours with pricing considerations for overtime, or perhaps special permits for the construction. When a move is involved, additional scheduling must be planned so that employees can pack up the belongings that are in desks and file cabinets or inventory and mark items to be moved to the new location. Many times these moves are made on the weekends, with the start of the move at the end of business on Friday and the facility ready to have employees move back in on Monday morning. It can be a Herculean effort to schedule all that must be done, but it is an effort that is part of the responsibility of the interior designer.

When the designer has a minor role in the construction process, his or her energies will shift to the administration of the ordering of the goods. Clients become very nervous during a construction or remodeling project. They see the changes taking place, but those changes always seem to be coming too slowly. It is very important for the designer to spend time explaining how the project will proceed, prior to initiating orders and the construction process. The designer needs to go over the schedule at the very beginning, so that the client has a chance to question the designer and understand why the ceramic tile will not be installed until after the walls have been painted. Clients, especially it seems residential clients, become quite frustrated and stressed over the myriad decisions that must be made and made quickly during the course of the project. The designer needs to constantly assure the client that everything is under control and clarify where the project is on or off schedule. Weekly meetings with the client are not always necessary, but periodic meetings to show the client the schedule and what will be happening next are important to keeping the client comfortable with the progress of the project. Office furnishings dealers and many large design offices have found that a project manager, also called an installation supervisor, is a very good investment for the efficient project administration. The *project manager* takes care of many of the site visits and telephone calls that are needed to keep checking on the progress of the project. He or she then keeps the designer informed and suggests when the designer should visit the site or contact the client. This also provides the opportunity for the designer to be spending his or her time on fee-generating activities of higher value than on-site supervision. Of course, since the project is still the responsibility of the designer, the designer must make himself or herself available during the course of the project as might be required

If problems occur that affect the timely completion of the project, it is important to inform the client immediately. The concept of just taking care of things and "what they doesn't know won't hurt them" might sound good, but clients need to know when things are going awry. As long as the designer or the firm is working on a solution to the problem, the client will not become unduly nervous to hear, for example, that the truck with the furniture skidded on a slick road and rolled over so that all the items in the truck were damaged. Obviously, the client will be nervous to hear something like that, but if the designer has a solution prior to the call, the client will feel that the designer is taking care of things professionally.

Change orders are used to clarify anything on the job that digresses from the original contract. Moving a sofa from one office to another should be done with a change order. Moving a sofa from one side of the room to another should not. Instructing the framer to make the closet two feet bigger should only be done with a written change order—and only when verified that the change will not adversely affect some other part of the project. Contractors often bid projects very low, hoping that the client will want to make changes in the project during the course of the construction. These changes can be charged at far higher prices than the original bid. The designer must be very careful in the preparation of drawings, schedules, and specifications to prevent the necessity for change orders. And the designer must caution the client in what might be arbitrary changes on the job. "It sure would be nice to have a window on that wall of the bedroom," said the client to the contractor. "Yes, I suppose it would. But that window will now cost you about $600 since the wall is framed where it would have only been about $200 if you had thought of it sooner."

It is very important that the client understand the scheduling of a project. Spend a lot of time showing the client how each part of the construction and finishing of the project will be done and approximately when it will occur. There are reasons that projects often only have one or two trades working on the job at one time. The designer knows them and so do the trades, but the client often does not. For example, rough plumbing and rough wiring are done when the building is in the same condition. But it is not good to schedule both trades for the same day. The plumbers will need to be where the electricians are and vice versa. General contractors and job foremen have had to break up fights when electricians have unintentionally dropped wiring on the head of plumbers. Whole projects have been shut down because nonunion furniture installers have been on the job site while union workers are there to finish out a project.

Clients may require being kept informed of the progress of orders during the order processing phase. Here is where computer data base systems can save the designer time. Copies of the internal paperwork used by the designer or salesperson to track a client's order can be copied for the client. Designer/specifiers who are not actually selling the goods to the client may also wish to receive this information.

Just prior to the installation of the furnishings, the designer must schedule another detailed meeting with the client concerning the final work on the project. This time will be spent going over the floor plans to be sure the client has not changed his or her mind about the location of any of the items. If items are to be moved, revised plans need to be prepared so that the delivery and installation workers are not forced to place things more than once. Preinstallation plan reviews also become important during the walk-through (discussed in Chapter 25) to clarify that everything that was contracted for has (or has not) been delivered. Large commercial projects require closing parking lots or even parts of streets to allow the delivery trucks easy access to the building. If it is necessary to close a street, the client, designer, or contractor will have to arrange with the city police to obtain the proper permits for the closure. Projects in buildings with elevators will also have to arrange for perhaps continual access to freight elevators or one of the regular service elevators. Even the installation of furniture at a new home can cause neighbors to be upset about the number of delivery or tradespeople's trucks constantly in the neighborhood.

A smaller design firm will probably be using a warehouse service or subcontractors to deliver and install furnishings. One of the things the firm should look for in selecting a delivery service is whether the service is prepared for taking care of the little problems. For example, are they qualified to make simple repairs caused by box burns[4] on furniture?

Installation and delivery workers also need to be selected to project the kind of image the design firm is trying to convey to the client. Delivery people who are not dressed cleanly, or who allow dirty hands to soil fabric, will hurt the firm's reputation. Designers must insist on working with tradespeople and delivery people who will care for the firm's clients as the firm demands. Designers should not be hesitant to fire delivery and tradespeople who will not work to the firm's satisfaction. For example, it might not be possible to stop the plumbers

---

[4]*Box burns* occur on wood furniture or even fabric when the furniture item has shifted in the shipping box so that the box is rubbing against the furniture.

from smoking on the job during the course of the construction project. But, if it is important to the designer and his or her client, it is possible to insist that smoking not be done during the finishing of the project.

As was pointed out in Chapter 22, remember to caution the client about directly instructing workers on the job site. Construction workers in particular are not in the business of being diplomatic and responding to the instructions of clients. Be sure the client understands to direct questions and changes to the proper foreman or to the designer. On a residential construction project, the owner, being retired, spent most of every day on the site. He kept questioning and interrupting the workers until one day the framer said, "I was hired to do this job according to the plans. If you want to do the work, here's a hammer. I'll go home."

Summary

In this chapter we have looked at the various kinds of paperwork that must be managed in order to complete a sale of merchandise or the invoice of services. Design firms that function as "designer/specifiers" and do not sell merchandise to the end user save themselves a considerable amount of paperwork. Those that wish to sell merchandise as well as perform the design service must be prepared to understand and handle the multitude of forms and the paperwork involved.

We have described the credit application, confirmation proposal, purchase order, acknowledgment, and invoice. We have also looked at the paperwork involved in freight or shipping of merchandise to the delivery location and the delivery responsibility. The differences between the paperwork management for residential and commercial projects is very subtle. The forms themselves are the same. The delivery to the job site and other completion stages often require a bit more individualized attention in the residential practice.

Designers who are unable to manage the paperwork should hire someone skilled in that area. Not to do so could result in the firm's having serious or even disastrous cash flow and public relations problems that could lead to the dissolution of the firm.

The next chapter covers the activities involved in the delivery of merchandise to the job site as well as post-delivery activities.

References

Birnberg, Howard, ed. 1992. *New Directions in Architectural and Engineering Practice.* New York: McGraw-Hill.

Getz, Lowell. 1986. *Business Management in the Smaller Design Firm.* Newton, Mass.: Practice Management Associates.

Jentz, Gaylord A., Kenneth W. Clarkson, and Roger LeRoy Miller. 1987. *West's Business Law— Alternate UCC Comprehensive Edition,* 3d ed. St. Paul, Minn.: West Publishing.

Knackstedt, Mary. 1992. *The Interior Design Business Handbook,* 2d ed. New York: Van Nostrand Reinhold.

Loebelson, Andrew. 1983. *How to Profit in Contract Design.* New York: Interior Design Books.

Siegel, Harry, with Alan M. Siegel. 1982. *A Guide to Business Principles and Practices for Interior Designers,* rev. ed. New York: Watson-Guptill.

Chapter 25

Post-Ordering Considerations

Although the previous chapter dealt with the different kinds of paperwork involved in the handling of merchandise orders and billings, the project is not complete until all the merchandise is delivered and accepted by the client. In this chapter we will look at the activities that occur once the orders have been processed and are ready to be delivered to the client. These activities include delivery, installation, walking through, handling complaints, and following up.

In small design firms these activities are customarily administered by the designer, with assistance from others only in the delivery stage. In larger firms, many of these activities are handled by other employees whose specialized job responsibility revolves around the job completion aspects of the project.

Whether administered by the designer himself or herself or as part of the responsibility of others, the project designer always retains ultimate responsibility for the completion of the project. It is an important part of being a professional.

Delivery and Installation

Delivery includes the activities concerned with moving items such as chairs, case goods, accessories, and other furnishings from the showroom or warehouse to the job site and simply placing them in their correct locations. Delivery involves no special activities of assembly, construction, or physical attachment of the products to the building. *Installation* involves assembly, construction, or physical attachment of products to the building.

Delivery

When merchandise is delivered to the client, it is important for the client to sign documentation to indicate what he or she received. As we discussed in the chapter on the Uniform Commercial Code (Chapter 16), this signifies acceptance and transfer of title, thereby requiring the client to pay for what was delivered. If a copy of the purchase order was sent to the warehouse service or the designer's warehouse, the client can sign off on this form. Some firms have a separate delivery ticket that accompanies the merchandise. This ticket (Figure 25–1) is at least a three-part form:

1. The top or original copy goes to the client.

2. A second copy is sent to the billing office.

3. The third is retained by the warehouse whenever a back order, which is a partial shipment, occurs.

Any notations of damages or discrepancies between what is delivered and what was ordered should be noted on the delivery paperwork. This helps clarify which damages are the responsibility of the design firm and which damages are the responsibility of the client.

A delivery plan, showing locations for all the furniture and other items for the job, is prepared to let the delivery people know exactly where each piece is to be located. This is an essential aid to the smooth completion of the project. A floor plan keyed to the purchase order number and line item number is one way to do this if the project is small and does not involve many items. For larger projects, and especially in commercial design, other methods are used. Furniture items on the floor plan are keyed to the purchase order to facilitate delivery (refer to Figures 23–1 and 23–2).

Delivery service should include dusting and vacuuming of the merchandise as well as careful inspection for any scratches or other damage. It may also be the delivery team's responsibility to show the client how to operate certain items such as adjustable office chairs. However, this is often the responsibility of the designer or the salesperson.

A common responsibility of the delivery service is the removal of all cartoning and packaging materials. No matter how small the job, the empty cartons and paper padding materials should not be left to be disposed of by the client.

Clients often expect the designer to be present at all times during the delivery and installation of merchandise. This may seem to be an impractical use of the designer's time, but it can be key for maintaining good public relations. The designer at the job site during this crucial time can also reassure the client who is not so sure about the colors or patterns that are being installed in his or her home or office. Color variations and damaged goods may not be noticed until the wall covering or floor covering is about to be installed.

The designer who is present during the delivery and installation of merchandise can speed up the inspection process, assure the client and, when questions arise, help on the spot. How much time the designer spends at the job site during this time will depend on the client, the contract, the particular complexity of the job, and the designer's availability.

Installation

Installation is the part of the delivery process that also involves assembly, construction, or physical attachments to the building. Installation would be the attachment of wall-hung bookcases or other storage units, mirrors, and the assembly of open office furniture. Note that the installation of wall coverings, window treatments, and carpet and other floorings is often part of construction contracts and the responsibility of the general contractor. The installation of such items is usually done by someone other than the supplier of the goods, but not always. Installation service often depends on some other part of the project construction and delivery process being already completed, which requires careful scheduling of the construction and delivery/installation.

Where many items of furniture are to be assembled, specialized sets of drawings are necessary. With open office systems, for example, commercial firms prepare one or more sheets of drawings that aid in the assembly. Plans may be drawn to show panel configurations

Miles Treaster & Associates
3480 Industrial Boulevard
Suite 100
West Sacramento, CA 95691
916.373.1800
916.325.4877 Fax

Commercial Furnishings
Interior Design
Space Planning

DELIVERY/INSTALLATION

D/I FORM #   N⍛   6635

TODAY'S DATE   ____/____/____

SALESPERSON   _____

PRODUCT CT #   _____

INSTALL CT#   _____

MTA P.O.#'s   _____

_____

_____

_____

_____

_____

☐ Installation   ☐ Pickup

☐ Reconfigure   ☐ Punch List (see attached)

☐ Delivery   ☐ Other _____

Original D/I form # _____

Client Name _____ Proj. # _____

Site Address _____

_____

Client Contact _____ Phone # _____

Warehouse to call client to schedule   **Yes** ☐   **No** ☐

Estimated week of Installation _____

☐ Deliver/Install all P.O.'s at once

☐ Deliver/Install as arrives

☐ Keyed Alike

Detailed Instruction(s) of Service(s) to be Performed: _____

_____

_____

_____

_____

_____

_____

_____

Status of Installation:

☐ Installation Complete. No follow up required   ☐ Freight damage (see attached)

☐ Installation Incomplete. (see attached)   ☐ Additional items needed (see attached)

For Office Use Only

Charges:	TRAVEL TIME: (per man hour)	Installer Names:	Distribution
☐ Hourly		_____	**W** — Warehouse
$ _____ /man hour		_____	**B** — Operations
☐ Fixed Fee to Client	ON SITE TIME: (per man hour)	_____	**G** — Originator
$ _____		_____	**C** — Acct
☐ Inter dept to Project		_____	**P** — Client
☐ No Charge		_____	**Gold** — Originator

The products and services described above have been received/performed in a satisfactory manner except as noted.

Signed: _____   **Date:** _____ **Title:** _____

Figure 25–1 A form that is used to accompany merchandise for delivery and/or installation. (Reproduced with permission, Miles Treaster, Inc., Sacramento, CA.)

and finishes, electrical and telephone service, and either plans or elevations for the location of hanging components.

Routine architectural finish schedules, as part of the construction documents, provide the information needed to specify the locations of these finishes. Graphic schedules or interior elevations inform the contractor of the locations of such items as mirrors, complex wall treatments, and various wall-hung units.

Although it does take time to prepare delivery and installation drawings, it is the easiest and simplest way to help guarantee that all the specified goods are delivered and installed in their proper location. Success with these documents provides the designer the assurance that he or she is not needed on the job site at all times. Showing the client that these kinds of documents have helped on projects in the past also indicates to the client that the firm can deliver and install the products without the designer being there at all times.

It is also important for the installation crew to take care of dusting, vacuuming, and removal of trash. Since some companies do not perform such tasks as a routine part of their service, the design firm should be sure that these tasks are included in the contract with the installer. If they are not included, the designer or client will be charged for the extra work.

Flooring and wall covering manufacturers often provide maintenance instructions with their shipments. These should be carefully explained to the client by the designer. Most furniture manufacturers make this same kind of information available but may not include it with the shipment. The designer should explain maintenance requirements for all products specified and provide any brochures or maintenance guides available from the manufacturers. In addition, the designer needs to explain how to adjust seating, make simple adjustments to furniture items, and any other basic instructions in the use of the furniture.

Commercial clients frequently request the designer to prepare maintenance schedules. In general, maintenance schedules inform the physical plant workers how to clean, wax, vacuum, remove stains from, and otherwise maintain the furniture, fabrics, and architectural finishes. Such a schedule can be made up from the information provided by the manufacturers. The preparation of a formal maintenance schedule is often a separate design service, though it is sometimes included and charged for in the design contract.

Walk-Through

When all the furniture and furnishings have been delivered and installed, it is customary for the designer and client to have a *walk-through*. This is a final inspection of the job to be sure that everything that was ordered is present, and that any omissions or as yet unrepaired damages are noted. Some firms have a special form to record omissions and damages. This form is most commonly called a *punch list* and details everything that must still be taken care of in completing the project installation. A punch list should be carefully prepared by room or area so that it will be easier for the delivery and repair people to find and complete the omissions or repairs. A copy of the punch list should be given to the client. Another copy can be used by the design firm to prepare work orders, repair tickets, and memos to expedite missing goods. For firms charging design fees on a phased basis, the billing of the final part of the fee cannot be made until after the walk-through. Many clients will not make final payments until all the items on the punch list are taken care of. It is to the designer's benefit to take care of these items as quickly as possible

The walk-through is also a good time for the designer to "fine-tune" the project. Although this can involve some "free" design service, it also can result in some additional specification or sale of merchandise. Commercial clients especially have a hard time budgeting for accessories at the beginning of the project. But when the installation is winding down, they often see the need for wall hangings, desk accessories, plants, and other items that complete the project.

Complaints and Repairs

Complaints and repairs should be taken care of immediately. In addition, it is important for omissions and replacement of damaged items to be taken care of as soon as possible. Regrettably, this is the stage in which many designers lose total interest with the job. It is always more difficult to take care of nagging problems with a project than it is to be designing a new project. But unresolved problems cause bad feelings and poor recommendations from clients. Uncollected receivables, because of these small problems, can cause serious problems with the firm's cash flow. The design firm should have highly qualified furniture repair people, experienced with all kinds of wood and metal furniture, available to do repair work.

As much as possible, the firm's aim should be to handle complaints and repairs before the client is even aware of them. A competent warehouse service that inspects and repairs furniture eliminates minor damages before furniture is delivered to the client. Delivery personnel that handle the merchandise as if it were their own also avoid potential problems. The firm should hire only competent experienced installers. The delivery and installation people must be required to clean up the job site. And delivering all the goods at one time helps to solve a lot of complaints.

Postoccupancy Evaluations

About a month after the installation is completed, the designer should make an appointment with the client to discuss satisfaction with the project and the products. This site visit and project review is called a *postoccupancy evaluation* or *POE*. The POE is an opportunity to be sure that all problems have been resolved; and any leftover repairs, omissions, or other problems can be discussed and handled at this time. Commercial designers frequently use the POE, especially in large office projects. The POE is commonly handled with a questionnaire (see Figure 25–2) that gathers information on user satisfaction with the installation, aesthetics, functional planning, and other information that the individual client and designer may seek to obtain. A POE will help find any problems in the project and locate employees who might not be satisfied with their work areas. Oftentimes, these dissatisfied employees only require to be told how to adjust their chairs or need another file cabinet. However, left undiscovered, employees griping to other employees can give the impression of a totally ineffective project to the client. POEs often prevent the client from making changes in the interior that are a detriment to the aesthetics of the space or perhaps create code violations. In offices, the age-old lack of sufficient storage often leads to boxes being piled in corridors and near doors. A POE could discover the problem and lead to necessary fine-tuning or even new purchases by the client to eliminate the problem.

On large-sized or complex projects, it is also a good idea to have a second site visit with the client in another 30 to 60 days. It is a standard procedure for firms specifying and selling open office furniture to have these kinds of follow-up visits to help the client make the transition from conventional to open office products.

Follow-Up

It is a good practice for the designer and the design team to do an in-house evaluation of the project as soon after it is completed as possible. This evaluation should cover a time analysis to see if the project was completed within the time estimate. Review of any problems related to the project, the client, the manufacturers and suppliers, the delivery process, and so forth, should be included. The design director may also do a profitability analysis to evaluate

USABLE TOOLS

OCCUPANT SURVEY

We wish to conduct a post-occupancy evaluation of your building. The purpose of this evaluation is to assess how well the building performs for those who occupy it in terms of health, safety, security, functionality, and psychological comfort. The benefits of a post-occupancy evaluation include: identification of good and bad performance aspects of the building, better building utilization, and feedback on how to improve future, similar buildings.

Please respond only to those questions of the following survey that are applicable to you. Indicate your answers by marking the appropriate blanks with an "X".

1. In an average work week, how many hours do you spend in the following types of spaces (specify):

Space A _____
Space B _____
Space C _____
Space D _____
Space E _____

HOURS	A	B	C	D	E
0 - 5	( )	( )	( )	( )	( )
6 - 10	( )	( )	( )	( )	( )
11 - 15	( )	( )	( )	( )	( )
16 - 20	( )	( )	( )	( )	( )
21 - 25	( )	( )	( )	( )	( )
26 - 30	( )	( )	( )	( )	( )
31 - 35	( )	( )	( )	( )	( )
35 - 40	( )	( )	( )	( )	( )
40 +	( )	( )	( )	( )	( )

KEY FOR THE FOLLOWING
QUALITY RATINGS:

EX = Excellent quality
G = Good quality
F = Fair quality
P = Poor quality

2. Please rate the overall quality of the following areas in the building:

	EX	G	F	P
a) Space Category A	( )	( )	( )	( )
b) Space Category B	( )	( )	( )	( )
c) Space Category C	( )	( )	( )	( )
d) Space Category D	( )	( )	( )	( )
e) Space Category E	( )	( )	( )	( )
f) Restroom(s)	( )	( )	( )	( )
g) Storage	( )	( )	( )	( )
h) Elevator(s)	( )	( )	( )	( )
i) Stairs/Corridors	( )	( )	( )	( )
j) Parking	( )	( )	( )	( )
k) Other, specify _____	( )	( )	( )	( )

3. Please rate the overall quality of Space Category A in terms of the following:

	EX	G	F	P
a) Adequacy of Space	( )	( )	( )	( )
b) Lighting	( )	( )	( )	( )
c) Acoustics	( )	( )	( )	( )
d) Temperature	( )	( )	( )	( )
e) Odor	( )	( )	( )	( )
f) Esthetic Appeal	( )	( )	( )	( )
g) Security	( )	( )	( )	( )
h) Flexibility of Use	( )	( )	( )	( )
i) Other, specify _____	( )	( )	( )	( )

Figure 25–2 One of many different formats for a postoccupancy evaluation. (Reproduced with permission, *Post-Occupancy Evaluation*, 1988. Van Nostrand Reinhold, Inc.)

OCCUPANT SURVEY

4. Please rate the overall quality of Space Category B in terms of the following:

	EX	G	F	P
a) Adequacy of Space	( )	( )	( )	( )
b) Lighting	( )	( )	( )	( )
c) Acoustics	( )	( )	( )	( )
d) Temperature	( )	( )	( )	( )
e) Odor	( )	( )	( )	( )
f) Esthetic Appeal	( )	( )	( )	( )
g) Security	( )	( )	( )	( )
h) Flexibility of Use	( )	( )	( )	( )
i) Other, specify _____	( )	( )	( )	( )

5. Please rate the overall quality of Space Category C in terms of the following:

	EX	G	F	P
a) Adequacy of Space	( )	( )	( )	( )
b) Lighting	( )	( )	( )	( )
c) Acoustics	( )	( )	( )	( )
d) Temperature	( )	( )	( )	( )
e) Odor	( )	( )	( )	( )
f) Esthetic Appeal	( )	( )	( )	( )
g) Security	( )	( )	( )	( )
h) Flexibility of Use	( )	( )	( )	( )
i) Other, specify _____	( )	( )	( )	( )

6. Please rate the overall quality of Space Category D in terms of the following:

	EX	G	F	P
a) Adequacy of Space	( )	( )	( )	( )
b) Lighting	( )	( )	( )	( )
c) Acoustics	( )	( )	( )	( )
d) Temperature	( )	( )	( )	( )
e) Odor	( )	( )	( )	( )
f) Esthetic Appeal	( )	( )	( )	( )
g) Security	( )	( )	( )	( )
h) Flexibility of Use	( )	( )	( )	( )
i) Other, specify _____	( )	( )	( )	( )

7. Please rate the overall quality of Space Category E in terms of the following:

	EX	G	F	P
a) Adequacy of Space	( )	( )	( )	( )
b) Lighting	( )	( )	( )	( )
c) Acoustics	( )	( )	( )	( )
d) Temperature	( )	( )	( )	( )
e) Odor	( )	( )	( )	( )
f) Esthetic Appeal	( )	( )	( )	( )
g) Security	( )	( )	( )	( )
h) Flexibility of Use	( )	( )	( )	( )
i) Other, specify _____	( )	( )	( )	( )

Figure 25–2 (Continued)

OCCUPANT SURVEY

8. Please rate the overall quality of design in this building:

	EX	G	F	P
a) Esthetic quality of exterior........	( )	( )	( )	( )
b) Esthetic quality of interior........	( )	( )	( )	( )
c) Amount of space..........	( )	( )	( )	( )
d) Environmental quality (lighting, acoustics, temperature, etc.)......	( )	( )	( )	( )
e) Proximity to views..........	( )	( )	( )	( )
f) Adaptability to changing uses......	( )	( )	( )	( )
g) Security..........	( )	( )	( )	( )
h) Maintenance..........	( )	( )	( )	( )
i) Relationship of spaces/layout.......	( )	( )	( )	( )
j) Quality of building materials......	( )	( )	( )	( )
(1) Floors..........	( )	( )	( )	( )
(2) Walls..........	( )	( )	( )	( )
(3) Ceilings..........	( )	( )	( )	( )
k) Other, specify_____	( )	( )	( )	( )

9. Please select and rank in order of importance facilities which are currently lacking in your building:

10. Please make any other suggestion you wish for physical or managerial improvements in your building:

11. Demographic Information:

   a) Your Room #/Building area _____

   b) Your Position: _____

   c) Your Age: _____

   d) Your Sex: _____

   e) # of years with the present organization: _____

Figure 25–2 (Continued)

whether or not the project itself was a profit maker or a profit loser. This evaluation helps to determine if this kind of project should be sought by the firm in the future. A postoccupancy evaluation with the client also helps the design firm to evaluate whether or not to seek this kind of project or client in the future.

Within a week of the final delivery, it is important for maintaining good public relations to send a thank-you letter or postcard to the client. Such a note, often a form letter, shows an added measure of concern for the client and appreciation for his or her business. Although the main purpose of the letter is to thank the client for his or her business, it might also request comments on the handling of the project. At this stage, however, it is probably too early to ask about satisfaction with the products. Designers committed to excellent customer service carefully evaluate customer comments. They will use the in-house evaluation and the customer comments obtained from follow-up mailings to improve any phase of the service of the project determined to be substandard. Poor customer service is unacceptable in professional practice.

Summary

Many designers do not enjoy taking care of the paperwork or following up on the orders for the merchandise they specify. Still, this is a very important part of project management.

In this chapter we have looked at what the designer is responsible for after the merchandise has been ordered. We have also looked at some ways of making these final parts of the project easier to accomplish.

This chapter concludes the discussion on project management. The professional designer is constantly dealing with administrative activities and paperwork. These activities, along with the creative processes of the actual design projects, are the heart of the interior design profession.

In the last two chapters we will be looking at other issues of the profession—issues of interest to both the professional and the student of interior design.

References

Farren, Carol E. 1988. *Planning and Managing Interiors Projects*. Kingston, Mass.: R. S. Means.

Kaiser, Harvey H. 1989. *The Facilities Manager's Reference*. Kingston, Mass.: R. S. Means.

Preiser, Wolfgang, F. E., Harvey Z. Rabinowitz, and Edward T. White. 1988. *Post-Occupancy Evaluation*. New York: Van Nostrand Reinhold.

PART VI

Careers

Chapter 26

Career Options

Traditionally, people have viewed a career in the interior design profession to mean the designing of spaces and the selling of products related to the home. Some people are familiar with the work of interior designers and architects in the design of offices and other public buildings such as hotels, restaurants, medical offices, and so on and recognize this as another way to work in the profession. For the general public and to many potential students, the interior design profession represents selecting colors and fabrics, preparing floor plans, and selling furniture and furnishings such as draperies and carpet. Although these activities are very definitely an important part of the profession, the interior designer does much more.

Many students wonder, "What can someone who majors in interior design do after graduation?" Although most graduating students enter the profession as either a residential or commercial interior designer, there are other options for the graduate. No discussion of professional practice would be complete without viewing the options within the profession for either the student or the experienced professional.

In this chapter, we will first look at the two main options in the profession—that of being a residential interior designer or a commercial interior designer. Then we will discuss the various business aspects within those categories. The chapter will also explain other career options that the student or experienced professional may consider.

Residential Interior Design

Residential interior design primarily deals with private living spaces—most frequently, of course, the freestanding single-family home. Private living spaces have changed dramatically with fewer people being able to afford the single-family detached house. Residential designers also often design private living space variations such as townhouses, condominiums, and apartments. Although hotels, motels, and dormitories may also be considered private living spaces, they are actually part of commercial or nonresidential design.

Residential designers engage in a practice that frequently calls upon them to do smaller-sized projects than those done by commercial designers. The average single-family detached house today ranges in size from 1000 to 3000 square feet, whereas commercial interior designers may work on projects that can be 5000, 10,000, even over 100,000 square feet in size.

Once they have gained experience, residential designers are frequently engaged to design the entire house. However, in the early part of his or her career, the residential designer will do more project work with portions of the home. Perhaps single rooms within the residence or even consultations regarding individual items within a room.

The extent of the involvement of the designer will vary based, to a large degree, on what kind of firm the designer works for. If the designer is employed by a retail furnishings store, he or she may be more involved with smaller projects than an independent designer would be. Independent designers more frequently are involved in projects involving the entire house.

Another characteristic of residential design is the personal relationship that usually develops between the client and designer. Those engaging in residential design must have the ability to get along with people, be interested in their personal needs, and feel comfortable in becoming the client's "friend." This is due, in a large part, to the fact that residential clients are much more particular about what they buy and how it reflects their image when it concerns their home, than are those clients who purchase interior concepts and products for their businesses.

The residential designer must develop a sensitivity for questioning the client in such a way as to determine what the client really wants. The designer must also develop an empathy with the client so that expressed desires can be translated into a design concept with which the client can live. And the designer must develop tact and diplomacy in order to show the client the realities of good and bad design ideas.

A major difference between residential and commercial design is that the residential interior designer does far fewer drawings in his or her work. Detailed floor plans, working drawings, shop drawings, sketches, and other graphic presentations are day-to-day realities for the commercial designer. Most projects for private living spaces frequently require simple floor plans and perhaps color boards. Freehand sketches often suffice for even a floor plan. The amount of time "on the boards" preparing technical drawings is significantly less in residential design.

Although the amount of time spent drawing is less, product knowledge—especially with regard to availability of products—is crucial to successful residential designers. It is an unhappy fact that many clients put off redecorating their homes until just before the holidays or a big party. The designer who can quickly put his or her hands on just the right products needed will enjoy great success.

Commercial Interior Design

Commercial interior design involves the design and specification of public spaces such as offices, hotels, hospitals, restaurants, and so on. Figure 26–1 gives a partial list of these specialties. In this book we have labeled anyone working with these public spaces as a commercial interior designer. In some books, this branch of the profession may be referred to as nonresidential or contract interior design. Nonresidential is self-explanatory. Contract interior design, however, may have two meanings. Some refer to *contract design* as any kind of interior design for which the client signs a "contract" for services. In this case, contract could be for residential as well as "public spaces" interior design. *Contract* can also refer to public space or commercial design and the various kinds of business spaces.

Commercial design, which in this book refers to the design of public spaces, is often a more formal arrangement. This aspect of the profession very commonly, though not always, has a contract for services existing between the designer and the client. In many instances, this contract is for services only. However, part of the designer's responsibility would be to specify the products that are then often purchased by the client from other sources.

Projects are usually larger in size than those of the residential designer. A single office is always a possible project for the commercial interior designer. However, most projects in-

General Offices
Facility Planning
Corporate Executive Offices
Professional Offices
    Law
    Advertising / public relations
    Accounting
    Stock brokers and investment brokers
    Real estate and real estate development
    Financial institutions: banks, credit unions, and trading centers
    Architecture, engineering, and interior design
    Consultants of various kinds
Health Care
    Hospitals and health maintenance groups facilities
    Nursing homes and extended care facilities
    Medical and dental office suites
    Out-patient laboratories
    Psychiatric facilities
    Rehabilitation facilities
    Medical laboratories
Hospitality and Recreation
    Hotel, motels, and resorts
    Restaurants
    Recreational facilities
    Health clubs and spas
    Country clubs
    National and state park facilities
    Sports complexes
    Auditoriums and theaters
    Museums and restoration of historic sites
Retail Facilities
    Malls and shopping centers
    Department stores
    Specialized retail stores
    Gift shops in hotels, airports, and other facilities
    Visual merchandising and displays for trade shows
    Showrooms
Educational and Institutional
    Government offices and facilities (federal, state, and local)
    Colleges, universities, and community colleges
    Secondary and elementary schools
    Day-care centers and nursery schools
    Private schools
    Prisons
    Churches and other religious facilities
Industrial facilities
    Corporate offices
    Manufacturing facilities
    Training facilities
    Employee service areas such as lunchrooms and fitness centers
Transportation
    Airports, bus terminals, train depots, etc.
    Tour ship design
    Custom and commercial airplane interiors
    Recreational vehicles

Figure 26–1 A partial list of commercial interior design specialities.

volve greater amounts of space. A small suite of offices could commonly involve 5000 to 10,000 square feet. A large project could easily consist of hundreds of thousands of square feet.

As would be expected, the dollar amount of products specified would also be much greater for commercial projects. A product specification of $100,000 would not be unusual for a medium-sized office complex. Even the specification for a common single office could range from $5000 upward.

Because the designer is working with business people, the client expects the designer to be very organized, professional, and knowledgeable about what he or she is doing at all times. These, of course, are qualities that would be expected of today's professional designer, whether in residential or commercial design.

Although residential design deals with primarily satisfying the owners of the home, commercial designers must also consider how individuals other than the owners react to the design. The employees, although they may not be asked for input, must feel that the interior design of their spaces creates a pleasing place to work. The interior must also appeal in some way to the public or clientele of the business. A restaurant interior that pleases the owner but does not attract the public may be a beautifully designed interior, but may cause the business's failure.

Since much of what the commercial designer specifies into projects is special-ordered from catalogs or custom designed, the designer must have broad product knowledge and must be confident of visualizing product size and scale. The designer often does not have products available in stock at his or her company's warehouse. Thus, it is important to have up-to-date information concerning availability and delivery times on a wide range of products.

In general, in comparison to residential design, commercial design requires greater attention to details, since there are more details to be concerned with due to the size of projects; excellent scheduling and organizational skills; in-depth product knowledge; very good space planning and drafting skills; knowledge of building, safety, and handicapped-access codes; and knowledge of architectural and mechanical systems and their constraints.

Common Employment Options

In this section, we will look at the places where interior designers commonly obtain employment and what the working environment might be. It is important to understand that the descriptions of employment options are very general in nature. One persons' experience in a firm under any one heading might be rather different from someone else's experience in another, but similar, firm.

Residential Retail Furniture Store

In most residential retail furniture stores, the designer could be working with the client in either the store or the client's home. The working relationship is often a "sales" relationship where the interior designer is attempting to sell the client some selection of products. This selection could be for only one or two items or could involve items for the entire house. The designer is encouraged to sell what the store inventories, but is rarely limited to just those items. Most often, the design service is free to the client. For the business, the expense of the designer's service is covered through the sale of goods at retail (or a high markup), not the service itself. Designers most often are paid on a commission basis with a draw against that commission as a weekly salary. Entry-level individuals are more often paid a salary with a small commission. Depending on the philosophy of the store's management, it might take an entry-level person from two to four years to move up to a full designer's position.

Department Store

Many large department stores have significant interior design departments. Working for a department store is very similar to working for a retail furniture store. A designer could be selling one item or a whole house of products. Often, however, the designer is more limited to selling what the department store carries.

Other department stores have only an interior design studio with a limited range of services. Commonly housed in the drapery department, the designer mostly sells window treatments, floor coverings, and wall treatments. It is less common for the designer also to sell furniture, since this is often handled by furniture salespeople.

In both situations, the design service is offered free to the client. The designer is generally paid only commission on sales.

Retail Specialty Stores

A retail specialty store is one in which only a particular product other than furniture is sold (for example, lighting fixture stores, paint and wallpaper stores, and floor covering stores). These stores are open to the general public; their goods are almost always sold at retail. Many such stores offer trade discounts to designers and other members of the interiors and construction trade. Design services are most often offered free. These kinds of businesses represent excellent opportunities for the entry-level designer to gain sales experience and product knowledge. Designers are commonly paid a small salary plus a commission.

Office Furnishings Dealer

In many ways, the office furnishings dealer is similar to the residential retail showroom. There is a division of work between outside salespeople and the design department; the company has a showroom space and an inventory of furniture to back up what is displayed, and the company commonly has its own warehouse and delivery crews. The main difference is that office furnishings dealers rarely sell products at suggested retail. It is more common for them to sell products at a discount from suggested retail or to add a markup onto the cost to the designer.

As for the design employee, he or she may work in an in-house design department or in a subsidiary design company owned by the dealership. The designer works with the client either in the store or at the client's facility. Office furnishings dealers primarily design various office complexes. However, some also design other kinds of public spaces such as hospitals and hotels. Designers working in these organizations are often required to have substantial space planning skills and to be good draftspeople.

Depending on the exact nature of the firm, the client might be found by the design department or by a salesperson. Salespeople are usually not required to be designers, although many were at one time, and are often asked not to actually do any interior design. They are to sell the goods to the client while the interior designers space plan and specify the project. Products are often sold to the client through the firm, whether the project originated through the designer or the salesperson.

Many office furnishings dealers have certain exclusive products that they expect the designers to specify most often. Yet the designer can specify almost anything the client's project requires—whether or not it is carried by the firm. Larger dealers create an independent design firm so that they may function as designer/specifiers. In this case, the designers market the firm independently of the dealership and obtain contracts to design projects and prepare bid specifications for many vendors. In-house salespeople must prepare their competitive bids as would any other vendor.

Entry-level people do a wide variety of work for the more experienced designers. It often takes at least two years to advance to a position of project responsibility, although this time estimate may be less in smaller firms or in firms with more qualified entry-level designers. The pay is usually a salary for the designers and commission for the salespeople. Designers might be eligible for commission on certain items or for bonuses.

Architectural Office

More and more architectural offices are starting interior design groups. In the smaller firms, this group may consist of one person doing the interiors work for the architectural projects of the firm. In larger offices, it may be a separate design company that prepares interiors documents for both the building the architectural firm is working on and outside design projects. The work may involve residential or commercial projects or both, depending on the nature of the architectural practice. Architectural offices sometimes specialize in a type of facility, and so would, of course, their interiors department.

In larger firms, the designer will often be involved in team projects. In addition, this job opportunity requires the designer to have very good space planning and technical skills and to be more familiar with formal working drawings and formal bid specifications.

In the past, the company was compensated by charging a fee for the interiors service, since few architectural firms sold products to clients. Today, because some firms are discovering that income can be made by the selling of goods, the compensation method could come in many forms. Designers are most often paid a salary. However, some of the upper-level designers may be paid a commission if their job responsibilities also include marketing.

Independent Design Firm

An independent design firm is a company that has no affiliation with a particular product, unlike the residential retail store or the office furnishings dealer. Because these firms are "independent," they may specify any product for their clients that is available in the marketplace. The firm may specialize in residential or commercial work, but usually does a combination of both. It may be a small, one-person studio or a large firm with dozens of employees. Many independents are design/specify operations that do not sell products to the client. However, as with architectural firms, the independent design firm recognizes the added revenue potential of selling goods, and many are also offering this service.

Unless the firm also sells the goods, income is generated through the fees charged. Salaries, especially in the smaller firms, will generally be lower than in other situations. And often, the designers will be paid a salary only.

Specialized Independent Firm

A specialized independent firm is a firm that primarily designs a certain kind of commercial interior. This might be restaurants, hotels, or health care facilities (Refer to Figure 26–1 for additional specialties). The firm may deal with restoration work, or it may be very specialized, as in the case of lighting designers. These companies require the designer to do extensive traveling, since the firm's work would come from all over the country—if not the world. The specialized firm must either market itself very successfully or also engage in some other varieties of work to keep from being adversely affected by economic conditions that could limit its practice.

Because these companies do not usually sell goods to the client, they obtain all their revenues from design fees. The designers would be paid only a salary, with a possible bonus.

Manufacturer

An individual may work for a manufacturer in several ways. A designer could work in the manufacturer's showrooms. All the major manufacturers have showrooms in one or more cities. Designers would work with the interior designers and other allied professionals who come to the showroom. Usually, this is a sales position and the designer is paid on a small salary and/or commission.

A second way of working with the manufacturer is as a product designer. Depending on the product, the company may require the designer to have an industrial design background rather than an interior design background. A few manufacturers, notably those that produce open office furniture, have staff designers to aid designers and architects in planning and specifying the company's products. These last job opportunities are generally at a factory location rather than a showroom location.

Many manufacturers also hire interior designers who have a minimum of three years experience in the business to be sales representatives. Sales reps are almost always paid commission rather than salary. See the discussion of "Sales Representative" later in this chapter and in Chapter 22 for more information about sales representatives.

When working for a manufacturer, there is often the opportunity to travel around the United States and work outside the country. Many of the major manufacturers have showrooms in foreign countries: those doing design layout work with designers and architects also have the opportunity to travel within the United States.

Compensation would depend on the actual job. Showroom sales positions would be commission-based; product designer positions might be salary- or commission-based or paid by special compensation packages; and design layout work would generally be salary-based.

Industrial and Corporate Interior Designers

Many large corporations have in-house interior designers or facility planners. These individuals would either be in charge of the direct planning and design of all the spaces of the corporation or work with outside designers in the design of corporate facilities. Responsibility might involve the design of the chief executive officer's office or a collaboration with the architect on a new facility. Included in this career option are corporate designers who are responsible for specialized design types. Hotel chains such as Best Western, Inc., have in-house designers to work with architects and franchise owners in the new design or remodeling of their facility. In some situations, the designers might travel to various company locations. Designers working in this kind of situation would be paid a salary or possibly an hourly wage.

Facility Planners

Beginning in the early 1980s, many corporations experienced extensive growth in the numbers of employees. Many of these corporations realized the economic benefit of having their own planning and design departments as part of their facility management team. A new career option, today referred to as Corporate Facility Planners, emerged.

Generally speaking, facility planners are responsible for space planning for the corporation. This work is most frequently done at corporations that have extensively used open office systems products. These individuals are required to have experience with computer aided design (CAD) hardware and software. Specialized degrees in facility planning are available from a few universities, but most facility planners are interior designers or architects.

Designing solely for the corporation, facility planners often find traveling amongst the various plants and office buildings a necessity. These individuals are paid by salary only.

Facility manager, sometimes in the same department as facility planners, is a more specialized career and requires additional training in psychology, physical plant management, and engineering.

Federal Government

The federal government's General Services Administration (GSA) is responsible for employing interior designers. These designers prepare space plans and systems plans, design office facilities, and participate in other kinds of government agency interior design work. The designer is commonly limited to the products currently on the GSA purchasing schedule, although some projects allow additional flexibility in product specification. The GSA designer will design spaces in a certain geographic area of the country. He or she will be working on projects throughout that area, which may require some travel away from the main office. Salary, based on an individual's "GS" rating, is sometimes a bit higher than entry-level salary in the private sector, and the government, of course, offers excellent benefits.

State and City Governments

Some state and city governments have salaried interior designers and architects. This is rare, however. These professionals function much in the same way as designers for the federal government. Some state agencies, like the university system, have architectural or design personnel to either design or coordinate contracted work. Few state and city governments have designers preparing layouts and specifications for the state, since many states have laws forbidding state agencies from performing work that competes with the private sector. Compensation would be salary-based. States and cities also have very good benefits packages.

Universities

Many medium- and large-sized universities have a facilities planning office. This office would work with architects, interior designers, and the university staff to develop new building designs and remodel existing structures. As mentioned earlier, if the institution is part of the state system, the designer would only work to coordinate what is needed by the institution with private sector designers. Compensation would be by salary.

Universities and colleges also hire faculty members with experience in the interior design field. The minimal educational requirement for a full-time faculty position is a master's degree and some professional experience. Most universities expect faculty members to continue their education beyond a masters degree and/or remain active in the design profession. Many universities also hire practicing interior designers as adjunct or visiting instructors to teach part-time during a semester.

Alternative Career Options

The foregoing discussion shows many of the primary ways that interior designers may practice their profession. These typify the kinds of job opportunities that most students and the general public recognize as the career options in the interior design profession. However, there are many other ways that an interior designer, with certain specialized skills or experiences, may work in the field.

CAD Specialist

CAD has become a very important career option in the design field. Most large interior design and architectural offices have a CAD department. In some cases, these CAD specialists are called CAD technicians. These technicians may not be interior designers or architects, but individuals with specialized training concentrating on the use of CAD systems. In other situations, CAD designers are interior designers or architects who have received CAD training. Technicians rarely are responsible for design decisions. They input into the computer sketches from designers and produce the drawings required to finish a job. CAD designers use the computer as a design tool throughout the phases of the design project. CAD specialists are most likely to be salaried employees.

The work of CAD technicians and CAD designers has significantly replaced the hand drafting in larger firms. Even smaller design firms have added some CAD capability to the office service list.

Other Computer Specialists

Interior design firms also use the computer in other ways. One is for specification writing. The computer can speed up the production of complicated formal specification bid packages as well as of detailed equipment lists for open office systems projects. This use of the computer may be a specialized job or part of the everyday experience of the interior designer.

Computers are also used for project scheduling, word processing, order entry, and bookkeeping. Except in small firms, project scheduling would be the only use of the computer exclusively for the interior designer. Computers are becoming increasingly important in interior design and students and professionals alike must become computer literate.

Professional Renderer

The professional renderer is very skilled in perspective and various rendering media. He or she might be employed by a large interior design or architectural firm or may be self-employed as a free-lance renderer. If the individual works for a firm, he or she rarely would be expected to perform other interior design functions. The renderer would be compensated by a salary.

Those individuals who are self-employed work for many firms in the trade. They would charge their clients based on the rendering. Size and media used would be important criteria for determining the fee.

Model Builders

Allied to the professional renderer are model builders. These individuals might also be professional renderers or they may only produce architectural and interior models. A few large architectural firms have staff model builders, but this is not particularly common. In such a situation, the employee would be compensated by a salary. In the larger cities, there are firms that specialize in model building. Employees for such firms would also be compensated by salary. For the self-employed model builder, compensation would be based on the fee charged the architect or designer.

Model building requires an excellent sense of scale, knowledge of the kinds of material that can be used to produce a scale model, and a concern for detail and the patience inherent in model building.

ADA Compliance Consultants

The passage of the Americans with Disabilities Act in 1992 created a new career option for many designers. Those experienced or interested in health care or the design needs of the disabled have become consultants to interior designers, the architectural community, and business owners. Extensive knowledge and understanding of the ADA requirements allows these consultants to review plans for new or remodeled facilities to be sure the plans will meet the law prior to submittal for building permits. These consultants can also assist business owners when claims have been filed or prior to the beginning of design planning to review potential costs of meeting the ADA requirements.

Sales Representatives

Sales representatives could work in residential retail stores, office furnishings dealers, and specialized retail stores. Sales representatives can also work for manufacturers outside the showroom.

The reader will recall the discussion of the sales representative ("rep") in Chapter 22. The independent rep works for himself or herself, representing many products from a variety of manufacturers. The rep visits with all the interior design and architectural firms that might specify the products. The rep is compensated with a commission whenever the product is sold in his or her territory, whether or not the representative had anything directly to do with that sale.

A factory rep works for one manufacturer as an employee. He or she handles all or part of the product line of that manufacturer in a specified territory of the country. Much like the independent rep, the factory representative works with designers and architects who might specify his or her product line. Some factory reps also have specific obligations to dealers in his or her territory. A dealer might have an exclusive right to sell the product in a specific city or area of the country.

The factory representative would be paid a commission on all goods sold in his or her territory whether or not the rep had anything to do with that sale. Both kinds of reps can have large territories, especially in the western states, and must travel extensively. In most cases, individuals must have proven sales experience to obtain a position as a manufacturer's representative.

Architectural Photographers

An architectural photographer could be an interior designer who took several photography classes in college. However, most are photographers by trade. These individuals specialize in the photography of exteriors and interiors and are hired by the interior designer, the architect, or the owner of the building. It is rare that an architectural photographer would be on the staff of an architectural or interiors firm. Those working for an architectural photographer would be paid a salary. Those owning the business compensate themselves as any business owner would.

Product Designer

The independent product designer creates designs for furniture and interior products and then sells the designs to a manufacturer. Today, most product designers are industrial designers by training rather than interior designers. Compensation results from the royalties paid by the firm that buys the design.

Specification Writer

The larger firms have specialized individuals on staff to prepare the formal specification bid packages. These staff positions are often filled by trained interior designers or architects, but also by individuals with a general educational background who enjoy the detail of specification writing.

Installation Supervision or Contract Administrator

Installation supervisors (or contract administrators) are responsible for the on-site and in-office supervision of the installation and/or construction of the project. In an interiors firm, this individual would be out at the job site making sure the building and interior construction was not deviating from that on the original plans. When the furniture and furnishings were ready for installation, he or she would be on the job site ensuring that everything went where it was supposed to go and would take care of inspection for damages, omissions, and repairs. This vital function releases the designer to generate more design projects with his or her time. The position is not always filled by a trained interior designer. The individual with this responsibility must know how to read blueprints, understand the construction process, be familiar with the ordering process, and understand the installation process of a variety of products. Installation supervisors are most often salaried employees of the design firm, warehouse service, or installation service firm.

Interior Design Management

A position in interior design management requires extensive experience in the field or experience in general management. Most design directors are former designers who have worked their way up through the ranks. It is important for the design director to have knowledge of interior design and a good general business knowledge or experience related to the management of personnel, marketing, and general business principles. Design management personnel are most often paid on a salary basis, with some bonus or commission structure to supplement that salary.

Museum Work

Interior designers with experience or additional training in museum, restoration, or curatorial areas can work for the many historic site museums around the country. This can be very rewarding work for those individuals with a keen interest in history and restoration. Most of these job opportunities require advanced degree work in such areas as art history, history, and anthropology.

Journalism

It is possible for interior designers who are very good writers or who have had training in journalism to obtain employment with a city newspaper or a trade or shelter magazine.

With all these potential career options, the reader may be unsure which direction to go in the exciting and varied profession of interior design. If you looked at this chapter first, the author urges you to go back to the beginning of this book in order to gain an overview of the profession. Chapter 1 will give the reader a sense of the requirements of the profession in terms of educational preparation, and professional recognition status. Chapter 2, which discusses personal and professional goal setting, may help the reader who is confused as to which of these many career options he or she may be interested in pursuing.

Summary

One of the interesting, exciting aspects of the interior design profession is the variety of ways that one can work in the field. This chapter has reviewed many areas of interior design that one might find for an exciting, rewarding opportunity. Although some areas do require training or experience beyond the undergraduate level or the normal interior design program, many are positions that the trained interior designer can achieve with work experience in the field. It is not absolutely necessary for everyone to be a great salesperson, a great artist, or space planner to find a niche in interior design.

In the final chapter we will be looking at how to prepare for obtaining that first or next job by reviewing portfolios, résumés, and the job interview process.

References

Ball, Victoria. 1982. *Opportunities in Interior Design.* Skokie, Ill.: VGM Career Horizons.

Bolles, Richard Nelson. 1993. *The 1993 What Color Is Your Parachute?* Berkeley, Calif.: Ten Speed Press. (Revised annually.)

Knackstedt, Mary. 1992. *The Interior Design Business Handbook.* New York: Van Nostrand Reinhold.

Loebelson, Andrew. 1983. *How to Profit in Contract Design.* New York: Interior Design Books.

McLain-Kark, Joan H., and Ruey-Er Tang. Fall 1986. "Computer Usage and Attitudes Toward Computers in the Interior Design Field." *Journal of Interior Design Education and Research,* 12: 25–32.

Siegel, Harry, with Alan Siegel. 1982. *A Guide to Business Principles and Practices for Interior Designers,* rev. ed. New York: Watson-Guptill.

Veitch, Ronald M., Dianne R. Jackman, and Mary K. Dixon. 1990. *Professional Practice.* Winnipeg, Canada: Peguis Publishers.

Chapter 27

Getting the Next—or First—Job

Whether a designer is an experienced professional looking for more responsibility and different challenges, or the beginning professional getting ready to find that first job in interior design, the job search can be a time-consuming and stress-producing period. Going to a bookstore to look for a guide to aid in the job search can also be frustrating. There are a multitude of "how to write better résumés" and "how to interview" books on the market today.

This chapter will provide the professional and the student with some tips related to finding a job in interior design. All the examples are specifically based on the needs of the professional or beginning interior designer as he or she seeks a professional design position.

Portfolios

A *portfolio* is a visual presentation of what the individual can do as an interior designer. A person's portfolio is never "finished." It must be constantly updated and refined to meet current or expected needs in the job search process. For the experienced professional, the portfolio must show the complete range of present and past abilities. For the student seeking that all-important first job, the portfolio must exhibit the very best work that the student can do and also present the breadth of the student's abilities so as not to limit the prospective employee from any reasonable opportunity.

Whether the portfolio is for the professional seeking to change jobs or the student in search of the first job, the portfolio must be suited to the kind of job for which the individual is interviewing. A portfolio showing multiple examples of watercolor renderings when the company is looking for drafting skills wastes both the employer's and the job seeker's time. It also shows the prospective employer that the job seeker has not done any homework about the design firm or its needs.

In addition, portfolios should be self-explanatory. Many times it is necessary for the designer to send his or her portfolio to a prospective employer for a review before an interview will be granted. When the designer is not there to explain his or her involvement, the parameters of the project, and how the designer arrived at the solution, the prospective employer will expect the portfolio to be able to answer these questions. If it is not self-explanatory, all that can be reviewed is technical competence in the preparation of drawings and boards.

There is very little difference in what the portfolio will contain or even, to some extent, look like between the needs of the professional and the student. A professional's portfolio will be more extensive than a student's and will probably contain photo prints or slides of completed work. But the basic contents and even format will be very similar. For that reason, the remaining discussion of the portfolio will be a generalized discussion on what to include, the format, the media, and the written materials.

What to Include

It is important for the portfolio to include examples of all the skills of which the individual is capable. For the professional it is also necessary to show the breadth of project experiences that has been undertaken during professional practice. The portfolio should include as many of the following kinds of design documents as possible:

1. Freehand sketches.
   Perspectives, elevations, and/or isometric drawings.
   Sketch problems that show the decision making process.

2. Furniture floor plans.

3. Color boards.

4. Working drawings.

5. Examples of lettering skills.

6. Technical renderings in any media in which the designer is competent.

7. Examples of CAD work.

8. Slides, photographs, or publication reprints showing completed projects for which the designer was primarily responsible.

Although most of the examples are commonly parts of projects, it is important to show at least one complete project presentation. This complete project would include the verbal explanation of the design problem, floor plans, color boards, renderings, and any other written or graphic documents that were a part of the project requirements. A copy of the individual's résumé should be included in the portfolio. Having a neat copy of the résumé in the portfolio guarantees being able to present an unfolded copy to the prospective employer.

Format

A key decision in producing the portfolio is the format. It is important to remember that portfolios are hand-carried; laid out on conference tables and desks; possibly transported in taxi cabs, passenger cars, and airplanes; and may even be mailed across the country. A common format size for boards and drawings in the profession is 20 inches by 30 inches. Although this size format works well for the preparation of drawings and presentation boards, it makes for a very cumbersome package to carry. Format sizes that are easier to present and transport are 8 inches by 10 inches, 11 inches by 14 inches, 14 inches by 17 inches and 16 inches by 20 inches. The larger formats make it easy to present original work. Smaller formats are easier to handle.

Whatever format is decided upon, it is important for all the examples to be consistently presented in either a vertical or horizontal manner. This helps to show the designer as an organized professional. It also aids in reducing nervousness during the interview by avoiding having to keep flipping the portfolio around. If both horizontal and vertical presentation formats have been used, items may need to be eliminated from the final portfolio. However, if the item is particularly important to the overall story the designer is trying to tell, the item may be included by use of photo reproductions. It might also be appropriate to group horizontal items separately from vertical format items.

The pages of the portfolio will need to take a certain amount of abuse. Items that are not on mat boards might need to be mounted on a mat or similar backing materials. Sketches, renderings, and plans might also be mounted on colored paper or photographic paper and inserted into plastic notebook sleeves.

The physical binder itself should be of good quality and look very professional. Drawings rolled up in a tube may be convenient for carrying, but they do not communicate the right level of professionalism—nor do the cardboard portfolios that many students use during college. It is not, however, necessary to spend a lot of money on leather-bound books. Smaller formats can even be held in many common three-ring binders.

Media

Many examples of original work are done on paper and/or boards of 18 inches by 24 inches or 20 inches by 30 inches format. If the designer decides to present only originals, it would be necessary to use a large size portfolio. If it is decided to take advantage of the smaller sizes of formats, many items will need to be redone into other media. There are several different kinds of media that can be used to present the portfolio items.

Color-slide transparencies (35 mm) are a popular portfolio medium used by many designers. Slides are easy to transport, and are relatively inexpensive to produce. A disadvantage of using slides is the necessity of carrying a slide viewer. The job-seeking designer should not assume that the prospective employer will have a slide projector available to show slide-formatted work. Carrying and setting up a slide projector is also an extra headache the prospective employee may not want to add to the interview situation. A handheld viewer would be better than a projector, but these should be easy to operate and reliable.

Amateur photographers can take slides of flat work themselves with a small amount of equipment. All that is needed is a 35-mm camera, a tripod, and, if daylight film is used, an area where good consistent natural light can be available for the lighting of the design works. If natural light cannot be used, the proper combination of film and photoflood lights must be used. Using the camera's flash unit can produce glare, hot spots, and inconsistent results.

Photographic prints are easier to present but are more expensive than slides to produce. Photographic prints, whether color or black-and-white, should be at least 5 inches by 7 inches. Prints 8 inches by 10 inches are even better, yet each 8 by 10 print can cost several dollars to have made.

Many firms use the services of professional architectural photographers to take photos of high-quality or unusual projects. Designers involved in these projects should obtain duplicates of the slides or prints from the design firm or client through the photographer for their personal portfolio.

A common medium used by designers is the photo mechanical transfer (PMT). You will recall from Chapter 18 that PMT is a high-contrast positive print. This is an exceptionally good medium to use to reduce working drawings and floor plans to a manageable size. Design items to be produced as PMTs must be crisp, black-and-white technical work. Color work cannot be made into PMTs.

Written Materials

Each section of the portfolio should be labeled. Pieces that are not self-explanatory should have brief written descriptions of the problem or the piece. Since hand-lettering is considered an important skill by many design firms, written materials could be hand-lettered. However, it is also acceptable for written materials to be typed or done with transfer letters. Avoid using a large variety of typefaces and sizes. Different sizes of type will call attention to important identification items or statements, but too many type sizes will be confusing and may give an impression of disorganization.

Remember that the portfolio tells a visual story about the job seeker. If it is neat and well organized and contains design documents that show the range of skills for which the prospective employer is looking, the interviewer will have a favorable impression of the designer. If it is sloppy, has fabric samples falling off, and appears to have been thrown together, the sloppiness will likely lead to a short interview and a "don't call us, we'll call you," response.

The portfolio must show the job seeker's best work, provide a good impression, and supply an honest presentation of skills and abilities. It is acceptable to get a professional's help to photograph materials. It is not acceptable to use other peoples' work or have someone else do work on your portfolio submissions.

Résumés

A *résumé* is a summary of a person's qualifications. Yet, a résumé plays a significant part in whether an applicant will obtain an interview for a first or new job. In some companies, a résumé is also important in reviews for promotions. Presented on one or two pages (rarely more), the résumé must instantly communicate vital information related to work experience, education, personal information, special skills or experiences related to the desired position, and career objectives.

Content

Certain bodies of information will be expected in all resumes. This would include a limited amount of personal information, a career summary, educational accomplishments, and work experiences (see Figures 27–1 through 27–4). Some individuals also include professional memberships and information about community service and outside interests. Except for professional memberships, these are optional and should be deleted if they make the résumé too long or if they do not favorably add to the overall impression and qualifications.

The career summary, in a few brief sentences, provides a significant statement concerning the applicant's ability to handle the job for which he or she is applying. For example, "Fifteen years sales experience for office furnishings dealers, specializing in Herman Miller and Steelcase open office systems. Exceeded sales goals eleven out of fifteen years," might be a career summary for an individual now seeking a position as a representative with a manufacturer.

Educational accomplishments should begin first with the highest degree earned. Included would be the name of the institution and its location; the kind of degree and the year granted; major, minor, and any academic or career-related activities. Students should only list their grade point average if it was exceptionally high. About a year after graduation, the grade point average should be dropped from the résumé. Employers will not be quite as interested in how well a person did in school as they are in what the designer is currently able to do. Do not forget to also include professional continuing education units (CEU) and any other formal educational training in this section. Students do not need to list high school education. The author suggests listing high schools only if it was a prestigious school or a foreign educational institution.

Depending on which format is chosen for the résumé, the work experience portion will be written differently. Traditionally, the work experience section lists the name and location of the company, the years worked for each, and the title of the position held. One or more brief narrative statements as to skills developed or used and responsibilities in each position should also be provided. For example, to describe a job with a small specialty studio, the designer could write "Sales Associate. Sold drapery, wallcoverings and floorcoverings," or, to be more specific, "Sales Associate: Worked with clients in the store and in their homes. Re-

DIANE SMITH
606 W. Overlook
Kent, Ohio 44240
(216) 555-1912

OBJECTIVE:

Entry-level design position with office furnishings dealer or commercial interior design firm. Particularly interested in position combining client contact and design skills utilization.

EDUCATION:

(May, 1985)

Interior Design major. Marketing minor.
University of Cincinnati, Ohio.
Course work emphasized commercial space planning and design, architectural drafting, presentation techniques including marker rendering, mechanical systems, 2-D CADD and liberal studies courses. GPA 3.8/4.0.

EXPERIENCE:

Summer, 1985

Monroe's Interior Designs, Akron, Ohio.
Intern.
Student intern for commercial/residential independent design firm.
Was given responsibility for space planning and specification of two small offices. Became familiar with many commercial/residential products through attending presentations by sales representatives, visiting showrooms and product research for senior designers. Assisted senior designers by drafting working drawings and preparation of presentation boards.

Summer, 1984

DLW Construction Co., Kent, Ohio.
Draftsperson.
Assisted owner of small construction company in the preparation of various working drawings. Was responsible for completing all required drawings for five home remodeling projects.

Summers,
1983 & 84

J.C.'s Wallpaper, Toledo, Ohio.
Salesperson.
Estimated and sold wall coverings, paint and paneling. Developed sales skills and applied design skills in working with residential clients. Learned about the proper installation of wallcoverings by talking with installers and visiting installation sites.

HONORS/ACTIVITIES

American Society of Interior Designers
Student Chapter, 1983-1985

Phi Kappa Phi Honor Society

Arts Center, Kent, Ohio. Photography Exhibit
Two photos selected for exhibit, Spring, 1985.

PORTFOLIO AND REFERENCES AVAILABLE UPON REQUEST

Figure 27–1 Chronological résumé prepared by a student seeking a first job.

John P. Smith
3506 Prairie Drive
Bloomingdale, Illinois
(312) 555-0112

OBJECTIVE

Design management in progressive commercial interior design office.

SUMMARY

Eight years experience in commercial interior design. Thorough knowledge of building codes, several open office systems products, and all aspects of office design. Experience in contract negotiation and supervision of other designers for successful completion of projects.

DESIGN EXPERIENCE

Interiors Works, Inc. Chicago, Ill.
Project Designer (1984 to present)
Designer (1981 to 1984)
Space plan and design commercial facilities. As project designer, specialized in open office planning, primarily utilizing Haworth and Herman Miller systems. Also responsible for designing several branch bank facilities and medical office suites. Supervised designers and design assistants in completing assigned projects. Negotiated with clients to obtain design contracts. Responsible for obtaining contracts of over $55,000 in fees in past two years. Negotiated with vendors and tradesmen and supervised installations.

Professional Interiors. Chicago, Ill.
Design Assistant (1978-1981)
Space plan and design commercial facilities. Firm specialized in executive office design, law offices and banking facilities. First year assisted senior designers with drafting, product research and specification writing. Later given design responsibility for small to medium sized projects. Continued to assist senior designers on team projects. Assisted in space planning two open office systems projects of over 50,000 square feet each.

Associated Architects. Evanston, Ill.
Intern (Summer, 1978)
Student intern at architectural office. Worked in interior design department assisting project designers. Utilized drafting and rendering skills.

EDUCATION

Purdue University. Purdue, Indiana
1978 Bachelor of Fine Arts. Major: Contract Interior Design

AFFILIATIONS

Institute of Business Designers, Professional member.
American Institute of Architects, Affiliate member

Figure 27–2 Chronological résumé prepared by a professional seeking a change in employment responsibilities.

JOHN P. SMITH

3506 E. Prairie Drive,   Bloomingdale, Illinois   (312) 555-0112

SUMMARY

Eight years experience in commercial interior design. Experience in contract negotiation. Supervised other designers for successful completion of assigned projects. Thorough knowledge of building codes, several open office systems products, and all aspects of office design.

MAJOR WORK EXPERIENCES

1978 to present

Contract Negotiation

Responsible for making client contacts to negotiate design contracts. Provided draft of design contracts to Design Director for approval. Personally responsible for obtaining over $55,000 in fees in past two years (represents 22% of total fees obtained in those two years).

Employee Supervision

Supervised as many as three designers and five design assistants at one time for completion of various projects. Commonly supervised one designer and two design assistants.

Project Responsibilities

Designed projects during last four years of over 750,000 square feet with total design budgets of over 25 million dollars. Specialized in open office planning. Familiar with Haworth, Herman Miller and Knoll systems. Also experienced in designing banking facilities and medical office suites.

Most Recent Projects:
       Midwest Power Systems--25,000 square feet
       MicroChip, Inc.--14,000 square feet
       Sports Medicine Affiliates--35,000 square feet
       Harris Trust--approximately 15,000 square feet
       Chase, Harrigan and O'Neil--executive offices--5,500 square feet

Figure 27–3 The same professional's résumé as shown in Figure 27–2, but prepared as a functional résumé.

Mary Smyth
1223 Karen Drive
Phoenix, Arizona
(602) 555-0350

OBJECTIVE

Position with manufacturer as sales representative or working with
architectural/design community.

SUMMARY

Twelve years total experience in commercial and residential interior design
and sales. Includes seven years sales experience with office furnishings
dealers or as free-lance designer/sales.

SALES SKILLS

Maintained numerous commercial accounts with last employer. Developed
many new accounts. Generated over four million dollars in sales last year
(second highest total for twelve sales people). Equaled or exceeded sales goals
last four years.

SUPERVISION SKILLS

Hired, trained and supervised two sales assistants to help manage my
accounts. First sales assistant recently began working as sales
representative.

MARKETING SKILLS

Developed successful marketing strategies for three architectural firms, two
interior design firms and two contractors. Member of marketing committee
for present employer for last year.

DESIGN SKILLS

Experienced in residential and commercial space planning and interior design.
Familiar with open office systems products and various qualities of
commercial and residential furniture and furnishings products.

EXPERIENCE

Account Representative. Responsible for maintaining existing commercial
accounts and obtaining new commercial accounts. Territory is by client
rather than geographic limitation. Equaled or exceeded sales goals last four
years. Booked over four million dollars in sales last year (second highest of
twelve account representatives). Quality Office Furnishings and Products.
Phoenix, Arizona., 1982-present.

Figure 27–4 A combination résumé for a professional seeking new responsibilities in his or her career as a sales
representative.

sponsible for estimating, pricing, and installation supervision of custom window treatments, wallcoverings, and floor coverings. Obtained a 10 to 15 percent increase in sales last three quarters." The second example provides a prospective employer much more information as to what the designer could do at the new design firm. Students will want to place the internship first in the work experience section, followed by summaries of part-time jobs. Figure 27–5 provides a list of active verbs that can be used in résumés and cover letters.

A few words about personal information. What must be on the résumé are a current address and telephone number. Anything else is purely up to the individual. Applicants feel they must put down marital information, names of children, service records, height, weight, and health conditions. The employer cannot legally ask for any of this information, except within the bounds described in Chapter 10. Volunteering the information could prejudice a decision, and the applicant would not have any grounds for challenging the prejudiced decision.

Format

There are many formats for résumés. No one format works in all cases. Which of the three basic formats to use should depend on the audience the résumé is for and the purpose for the résumé. The experienced designer, attempting to make a career change from "on the boards designer" to salesperson, will need a different format than the technician trying to obtain a position of total project responsibility. The three basic formats are chronological, functional, and combination.

Chronological Résumé

The *chronological résumé* states educational and work experiences exactly when they occurred, in reverse order. It is easy to follow and clearly shows the work history of the individual. Many employers prefer to read this traditional format for résumés since it is familiar to most people in industry. It is not recommended, however, if the job seeker has a spotty work record, is seeking to make a significant change in his or her career, or has been out of the normal work force for some time (see Figures 27–1 and 27–2).

When using this format, experienced professionals should provide work history in reverse chronological order, followed by educational experience. For the professional, work history is more important than educational experience. Students should place educational experience first, since that is the most recent activity.

Accomplished	Executed
Achieved	Formalized
Arranged	Gathered
Assisted	Improved
Collected	Initiated
Communicated	Introduced
Composed	Managed
Conceptualized	Negotiated
Conducted	Organized
Contributed	Performed
Coordinated	Prepared
Created	Presented
Demonstrated	Reviewed
Designed	Scheduled
Developed	Selected
Directed	Supervised
Established	Trained
	Wrote

Figure 27–5 A partial list of active verbs that can be used in résumés and cover letters.

Functional Résumé

The *functional résumé* presents information to emphasize qualifications and skills, rather than the order in which they were obtained (see Figure 27–3). Many employers do not like the functional résumé since they are concerned with a prospective employee's work history. If a functional résumé is presented, it would not be uncommon for the prospective employer to ask for a chronological work history to be provided.

Combination Résumé

A *combination résumé* utilizes characteristics of both the chronological and functional résumé and combines them into one. Usually, this results in a résumé where functional skills are described as in the normal functional résumé, followed by a chronological listing of educational and work experiences. A combination résumé highlights skills related to the new job and de-emphasizes either a limited or spotty work history. This kind of format can work very well for students whose skills learned in school and internships will be of greater interest to a prospective employer than work history in a series of part-time jobs (see Figure 27–4).

References

Many employers check references or call previous employers. If there is any question that a previous employer will give a bad reference, ask that the employer not be contacted. It will be necessary to provide a brief explanation of the circumstances surrounding this request to the prospective employer, however. Remember that it is common courtesy to always ask individuals listed if they may be used as references.

Students can also use the services of college career placement offices to maintain references. This is a convenience for those who are asked to provide personal references since they only have to write the reference once and then it is kept on file at the placement office. Prospective employers then request a copy of the reference from the placement office.

Appearance

The appearance of the résumé can, by itself, make a good or bad impression. It must have perfect spelling and use good grammar. Headings should be bold so that they stand out and attract attention. Single-space the résumé with double-spacing between major sections. Do not forget to leave sufficient side margins so that the prospective employer may write notes in the margins. If at all possible, use only one page. However, if this means cramping all the information so that there are barely any margins, use two pages.

The original copy should be typed to produce a dark black image. If a good typewriter is not available, use a typing service. Word-processed résumés are acceptable, but be sure the final copy is printed on either a letter-quality printer or a laser printer. When a quantity of résumés at one time is required, have them offset printed on bond paper, not Xeroxed.

Interior designers tend to use a creative design or a creative method of printing or folding the résumé. It is rare that odd colors of paper, and creative designs on résumés really help to get an interview. Remember that the résumé will be filed in a standard letter size manila folder. If the résumé is a strange size or shape it might get lost or filed in the "round file." The content of the résumé and cover letter are what get the interview. Stick to white, buff, or maybe a light gray paper and minimal, if any, attention-getting designs.

Job Search

Professionals looking for new positions usually hear about openings by word of mouth. Others discreetly put out the word to allied associates that they are looking for a new position.

Sometimes it is necessary to start calling around to other firms in town to see if there is any interest in the job-seeking professional.

It is also common for professionals to use general or design-trade professional employment agencies. Professional designers often work with executive search companies when they seek management positions. Both of these organizations charge either the employee or the employer for the agency's aid. If the job seeker uses an agency to obtain leads, he or she should understand all the restrictions and fees involved.

Employed professionals looking for another position must be discreet. Understandably, employers do not like their employees looking for another job while still working. Yet, of course, not everyone can afford to quit the current job until a new job is found. And almost all job-search books advise readers to not quit the current job before a new job is obtained.

A few hints for the professional seeking a new job while presently employed follow. Do not use company time, company telephones, or company supplies for the job search. It is acceptable to schedule appointments over the lunch hour, but it is not acceptable to fake appointments to go on interviews. If it is necessary to take an extended period of time for the interview, use vacation time—do not call in sick. Remember, the employee owes a duty of loyalty to the employer as long as the employee is on the payroll. Abusing the employer by making interview appointments or long-distance phone calls at the present employer's expense is not only unprofessional, but it could be grounds for termination.

For the student, the job search begins long before graduation. The student must evaluate within himself or herself what part of the profession holds the most interest. Is it doing residential or commercial design? Is the student afraid to make presentations and therefore not a salesperson? Are technical working drawings boring, but working with colors exciting? These kinds of questions coupled with questions related to life-style choices, geographic preferences, and many others need to be asked to determine where and what kind of employment to seek. Sometimes using a book such as Richard Nelson Bolles' *What Color Is Your Parachute?* is a help in determining career goals more precisely.

The student should be seeking information about the various aspects of the field and potential employers from many sources. College advisers and career counselors are helpful sources of information regarding different design companies. The student should also be talking to relatives who might have worked with designers. He or she should also be asking for time to talk to working professionals. Who better to tell the student about what it is like to work in residential design than someone actively doing just that kind of work?

University career placement offices will have information about many corporate employers. Unfortunately, most interior design businesses are closed corporations and information about them will probably not be listed in the resources of the placement office. It is necessary to be more creative in employer research.

Students can review the Yellow Pages ads. This does not always provide the name of the owner or the manager, but it can give some information related to the company. Many firms list in their ads the product lines that the company carries. These product listings will help the student determine if the firm is primarily a residential or a commercial firm.

Many of the larger cities have home and garden magazines. These are filled with advertisements by many different interior designers. Also, some cities have a "promotional" magazine that covers cultural, home, business, and social events. Many design firms also advertise in these magazines.

The Sunday classified section is a likely place to find interior design and trade-related job notifications. These classified ads, however, often only provide the barest amount of information about the position. Sometimes the firm does not even publish its name, but asks the respondents to mail résumés to a box number. The job seeker should respond to anything that sounds remotely possible and interesting. A student should not be discouraged from applying if the ad states that only applicants with X years of experience apply.

Cover Letters

A good cover letter allows the job applicant the opportunity to personally introduce himself or herself to the prospective employer. In it, the applicant can point out significant skills that directly relate to the employment opportunity and express personal interest in the company. Each letter must sound as if it was written only for that firm, even if it contains primarily "stock" paragraphs used in many letters.

Content

The cover letter, as with most résumés, should only be one page in length. Longer letters, even from experienced professionals, may not get read by busy design directors or personnel managers. It is important for the letter to get the reader's attention and make him or her want to read your résumé as well as call you for an interview. This is done by using good business writing techniques.

It is generally recommended by business writing consultants and employment counselors that the cover letter contain about four paragraphs, each with a particular purpose (see Figure 27–6).

The first paragraph should attract attention by stating the purpose of the letter in concise words. If the letter is in response to an advertisement, this paragraph should give the name and date of the announcement. If it is a letter of inquiry, this should be clearly stated (see Figure 27–7).

The second and third paragraphs should contain specific information about the applicant's skills and interests in the position in order to keep the reader interested. These paragraphs would describe skills, previous work experience, or educational accomplishments specifically related to the position. Here, also would be statements as to personal goals and interests as related to the particular position and company. Although there is no set order in which this information should be presented, it is most frequently presented in the sequence of importance to the position as the applicant understands it. Professionals would not only describe skills but also other accomplishments, such as sales records and management experience (see Figure 27–8). For students, this section would deal primarily with course work, pointing out the skills in which they are particularly proficient. Students would also want to describe responsibilities during internships or other interior design or trade-related work accomplished while in school.

The last paragraph should seek action by the prospective employer. Ask for an interview, but do not just ask and then wait for the employer to respond. The paragraph should also state that the applicant will be calling the employer concerning a convenient time for an appointment. Many job seekers will only be in the city where the letter was sent for a few days. If this is the case, it should be mentioned in the closing paragraph so that the prospective employer knows when the applicant will be available. The last paragraph should also reference the enclosed résumé as well as the availability of the portfolio for review. It is also a good idea in the last paragraph to thank the reader for taking the time to review the letter and résumé.

Appearance

The appearance of the cover letter can quite easily attract more attention than the content. The author remembers receiving, in response to a newspaper advertisement for an experienced interior designer/space planners, a hand-written letter on ruled paper. Many interior designers try to make the letter as creative looking as possible, using fancy type styles, funny folds, logo-style designs, and pastel colors. These techniques do attract attention, but they also often get in the way of the content and businesslike attitude for which the employer

Applicants name
Address
Area code and phone number

Date

Name and title of employer
Name of company
Address
City, State, Zip Code

Dear Mr. (Mrs. or Ms.) Smith:

The first paragraph should state the reason for the letter. Give the employer information about the specific position for which you are applying. If you are responding to an advertisement or have gotten the contact through someone the employer will know, state that information.

The second paragraph is where you can provide some information about yourself, your skills, and why you are interested in working for the firm. Do not forget to explain how previous academic training or work experience qualifies you for the position. Do not simply repeat what the employer can read in the resume--expand or clarify upon what you have stated in your resume.

For professionals with several years of experience, a third paragraph will probably be necessary to complete the basic information you wish to tell the employer. A statement about willingness to move to the city in which the employer is located might also be part of a possible third paragraph.

A final paragraph thanks the reader for his or her time and indicates your desire for a personal interview. If you are going to be in the city at a particular time, mention that you will be calling to set up an interview at that time. This paragraph often concludes in such a way the you give the impression that you will be getting back to the employer rather than waiting for them to call you.

Add a closing greeting such as "Sincerely",

(leave four lines for your signature)

Your full name

Enclosure (or Enc.). Used to indicate you are sending something with the letter, in this case, your resume.

Figure 27–6 This sample cover letter is set up to explain what should go in each section of the letter.

may be looking. Use quality bond paper and business-size envelopes. Black ink on white, grey, or cream paper is the most businesslike combination. The exact job opening and the kind of design firm will dictate whether these creative techniques are a help or a hindrance to the effectiveness of the cover letter. It is very common to coordinate the paper, type face, and general style of the cover letter and the résumé.

Use letter-writing techniques that almost all personnel managers and owners will appreciate. Except when answering a blind ad, part of the research of the job seeker is to find out exactly to whom the letter should be sent, and the spelling of his or her name. This indicates to the prospective employer that the job seeker has made a serious effort to find out something about the company. Word processing makes perfect typing and absolutely perfect

Sally Jones
215 N. Ford Drive
Chicago, Illinois 60653
(312) 555-1278

August 18, 1986

Mr. Roger Smith, Director of Design
Myer's Interior Design
82 W. Willow Lane
Tucson, AZ.

Dear Mr. Smith:

I am writing in response to the classified advertisement for a position as a designer your company had in the Chicago Tribune of August 17. I would like to point out that I first heard of your firm while enrolled in the interior design program at the University of Arizona. Ms. Jane Johnson of your design department kindly helped me with product information for projects and told me quite a bit about the company. I was quite impressed.

At the University, I specialized in residential interior design. My training was quite complete, covering all phases of design development, production, presentation and business practices. From project evaluations, I can state that I have strong skills in space planning, color coordination, technical drafting, presentation skills and rendering.

My internship was completed at Beverly Miller's Interiors in Chicago. My responsibilities included color coordination, preparation of presentation boards, drafting, rendering and order processing. This experience has taught me the excitement and complexity of residential interior design.

I am anxious to begin my career and would like to meet you personally so as to present my portfolio to you. It is very exciting to me to find your organization has an opening as I have decided to return to the Tucson area permanently. I will be calling your office on August 27 to confirm an interview appointment. I have enclosed my current resume for your review.

Thank you for your time and I look forward to meeting you next month.

Sincerely,

Sally Jones

Enclosure

Figure 27-7 Cover letter prepared to respond to a newspaper advertisement for a design position.

Jennifer Woods
4436 Euclid Avenue
Kalamazoo, Michigan 49007
(616) 555-0809

November 15, 1985

Mr. Roger Brown, President
Design Associates, Ltd.
980 State Street
Erie, Pennsylvania

Dear Mr. Brown:

Over a nine year period, I have been promoted from Designer to Senior Project Designer at Environmental Interiors, a highly respected commercial design firm in Kalamazoo. During the last few years I have been personally responsible for obtaining and designing five of the eight largest projects ever undertaken at Environmental Interiors. As Senior Project Designer, I was also responsible for supervising up to six designers at a time on one or more projects.

At this point in my career, I seek an opportunity to apply my design and supervisory skills in a management position.

 It is not difficult to hear flattering comments about the quality design work produced at Design Associates. I believe the negotiation and design skills that I have refined at Environmental Interiors will further add to the success of your firm.

As you will see from the enclosed resume, I have broad commercial experience including open office planning for many types of facilities, professional offices, medical suites, banking facilities, university and college facilities and even restaurants.

Over the past four years, I have been preparing myself for management by enrolling in the local community college and the university with an aim of completing a second undergraduate degree in business.

I have considerable talent, enthusiasm and interest to offer as a design manager to Design Associates, Ltd. and would appreciate the opportunity to meet with you personally to discuss such a position. I will call you next week to confirm a convenient time for a personal interview.

Sincerely yours,

Jennifer Woods

Enc.

Figure 27–8 Cover letter inquiring about possible positions.

spelling simple for everyone to achieve. Utilize standard business letter format with the applicant's name and address at the top followed by the date. Next would be the company's address and a salutation followed by the body of the letter. The word *Enclosure* or the abbreviation *Enc.* should follow below the signature to indicate that something besides the letter is in the envelope. Figures 27–7 and 27–8 provide two complete letters of application to show content and format suggestions.

How Employers Review Résumés and Cover Letters

Potential employers receive dozens of résumés every week whether they have an opening or not. As they review each résumé and cover letter they are looking for several key items. Understanding these items may get your résumé on the "call back" pile rather than simply filed away.

1. *Neatness.* This is obvious, and enough has been said previously.

2. *Relevance to the design firm.* Employers are impressed when an applicant has done homework about the firm. For example, career objective and career summary statements that relate to the work done at the firm the designer is applying. Stating that the applicant wishes to do commercial design on a cover letter or résumé to a residential studio does not make a positive impression. Employers are also looking for any statement in the cover letter that has referred to the actual work of the firm or the advertised position.

3. *Clarity of employment history.* Employers want to know what a person did and where he or she worked prior to applying to them. Providing every single detail in the résumé is not necessary, but total vagueness gets the applicant nowhere.

4. *Good communication skills.* Designers do not just communicate in drawings. Writing skills and verbal skills are equally, if not more, important for some positions. The cover letter and résumé must use proper grammar. Students in particular constantly write paragraph-long sentences. Revise your letters and résumé. Have someone else make suggestions as well.

5. *"Creative writing."* Employers will get suspicious of résumés filled with more active verbs or claims of accomplishment than seem reasonable for the individual's apparent experience level. Out-and-out lying is easily discovered and absolutely should not be done.

6. *Broad interests.* Most employers want to hire individuals loyal and dedicated to the design profession, but they do not want one-dimensional employees. Applicants need to avoid going overboard with stating outside interests—he or she may sound too busy with hobbies to have time to work. Indicate involvement in professional associations, community groups, and other outside interests.

7. *Achievement.* Employers want to hire individuals with proven levels of accomplishment. They are looking for indications of successful project management, profit making, or anything else that indicates the applicant knows how to achieve goals.

8. *Care and thought.* Interior design is a profession that considers attention to detail as essential. Careful drafting, proofreading, and execution of a résumé and cover letter are no exceptions. Sloppy work, poor grammar, or minimizing statements related to the employer's potential needs will raise doubt as to the individual's concern for a client's project.

Interviews

Looking for a job is serious work. People spend an average of 1600 or more hours during the year at their job. It is important that any job be one that delivers fulfillment and rewards. The interview is the door to each job.

Preparation

Once an interview is obtained, it is necessary to do some preparation. First, find out exactly with whom you will be interviewing. It is not always the person who responded to your letter. Larger design firms will have a personnel manager who is in charge of interviewing prospective employees prior to the design director. Ask for the names and job titles of each interviewer. If more than one person will conduct the interview, ask if an itinerary will be provided so that you know how much time will be spent with each person.

Double-check the day and time of the interview. No matter how much time has passed from when you set up the interview, call the day before to confirm the time. If you have any question on how to get to the studio or office, or are not sure where to park, ask for directions at this time. In large cities, it is probably safer to take a cab than it is to drive, but check for suggestions on that also. If there is any reason why you cannot make the interview, call and personally talk to the interviewer to tell him or her. Most interviews will last from one to two hours. In either case, plan for about 20 minutes to show your portfolio and the rest of the time for questions.

There are many things to do the evening before the interview. Check the outfit you plan to wear. Make sure it is clean, well-pressed, and that it does not have loose buttons or threads. Be sure your shoes are shined. Go through your portfolio to familiarize yourself with what you are going to show and confirm in your mind the order in which you wish to show it. Place an extra unfolded copy of your résumé in the portfolio. Also check to be sure that a pen and pencil is in your portfolio, pocket, or handbag.

It is never permissible to be late unless it is due to something totally beyond your control. If you are held up in traffic, or miss your plane or connection, call the interviewer as soon as you can.

Make a point of arriving at the office or studio at least 10 to 15 minutes early. These few extra minutes give you a cushion in case of traffic jams or difficulty in finding the office. It also gives you a chance to try to relax and collect yourself before going into the interview. Before you check in with the receptionist, go to the restroom to check your overall appearance.

When you check in with the receptionist, be sure to smile and tell him or her who you are, with whom you have an appointment, and what time that appointment is for. Most likely you will be told to have a seat. Try to use this time to compose yourself. Read a magazine—don't fiddle with your portfolio, briefcase, or handbag.

What to Wear

What you wear to the job interview is a part of the overall impression you will leave with the interviewer. Many interior design professionals find it acceptable for everyday business apparel to be more trendy and flamboyant. However, most interviewers are expecting far more conservative apparel for the interview. If you have researched the company as well as you can, you will have some idea of what normal business attire is like at the design firm. This will be your guide as to how trendy or how conservative you must appear for the interview.

In general, however, more conservative apparel is the best bet. Wear apparel that is comfortable. Do not use the job interview to break in a new pair of shoes. Business suits with ties for men is standard. Conservative fabrics in solid colors are commonly accepted. Women should also choose conservative suits and dresses with jackets. Sun dresses, sleeveless dresses, or low-cut dresses do not project the kind of impression sought by business people.

Women should also be careful about what kind of accessories they add to the outfit. Refrain from wearing brightly colored or boldly patterned scarves, dangling, noisy bracelets, or oversized earrings—anything that attracts more attention to the accessories than to yourself.

Remember, many people begin forming their opinion within the first 15 to 30 seconds of the meeting. Although this impression will rarely make or break the interview in and of itself, it is often an important part of the overall decision-making process.

The Interview

The purpose of the interview is for the employer to get to know you personally, ask you questions, and try to evaluate whether you would be a good addition to the firm. The interview is also a time for you to evaluate whether this particular firm is really the kind of firm for which you wish to work. Just because a firm has a good reputation does not mean that everyone will want to work for it.

When the interviewer greets you, be prepared to shake hands. It is not necessary to use a bone-crushing hand shake. Just make it sincere. When you arrive at the conference room or office where the interview will be held, wait for some indication from the interviewer as to where to sit. If he or she does not make any indication as to where to sit, choose a chair either directly across from the interviewer or at a ninety-degree angle. These two positions make it easier to show your portfolio and to maintain eye contact.

Try not to use distracting habits. Don't play with a paper clip or pen, fuss with hair or accessories, and so on. No matter how much you might want a cigarette, don't smoke, even if the interviewer does. Smoking makes it difficult to talk and to show your portfolio.

Let your body language and visual "presentation" communicate the interested, complete professional. Be sure to listen to the questions. Do not think of what you want to say and then not hear what is being asked. Think before you speak, and do not interrupt the interviewer. Use eye contact, but do not try to stare the interviewer down. Use body language that is open and receptive to what is being discussed, not defensive. Smile, show interest. If you do not show interest in your work as you describe it, or in the company through the questions that are asked by the interviewer, you are guaranteed of not getting an offer.

Stress your qualifications and what you can do for the company. Be enthusiastic with your answers and stress your positive characteristics. But do not exaggerate your experience or abilities. It will not take much time to find out you are not an expert watercolor renderer if you are not. And do not try to pass off someone else's work for yours in your portfolio. That too will be found out very quickly, and will almost always lead to dismissal.

Graduating students, particularly, need to indicate a willingness to learn. Joe Allen didn't know much about computers, but when the interviewer asked about his computer experience, he was honest and said that he had a minimal knowledge but was definitely willing and interested in learning. When no one else expressed that willingness, he obtained the job offer.

Never bring up personal problems, argue, blame others, or beg for the job. Even if you left your previous job under difficult circumstances, do not blame anyone at the other company for the problems. It tags you as a difficult person and will probably influence the interviewer to pass you over. If you are asked if you were ever fired, you do have to be honest. But it is not necessary to go into a long, detailed discussion of what happened. Make some brief comments about what happened and hope the interviewer moves on.

If, during the interview, you determine you are not interested in working for that company, complete the interview, but inform the firm promptly that you are not interested in pursuing the position further. For students, do not accept an interview if you really have no interest in the company. Some students like to go to interviews to "practice" for the ones they want. This is bad business etiquette that can come back to haunt you later.

Unless the interviewer brings it up, do not ask about salary and benefits until the latter part of the interview. Be prepared with a salary range that you need to have. Employers, of course, want to hire you at as low a salary as is reasonable for the position. But, do not sell yourself short. If the salary offer is way below what you need to live on, or is way below what you understand the competition is paying, say so. Remember that benefits such as health insurance, reimbursement of professional association dues, and employee discounts are important parts of the compensation package. One company with an excellent health insurance program, a profit-sharing program, and a generous discount for personal purchases, but which offers a low salary might be a better opportunity than another company with a higher salary but weaker benefits (if all other things are equal). Interior design compensation is notoriously low in comparison to other professions. In 1993, junior designers were paid anywhere from $18,000 to a little over $30,000 depending on the size of the design firm and the location within the country.[1] Note that these are up from the salaries mentioned in the first edition of this book.

For the most part, if you are offered a position, be prepared either to accept or reject at that time. If you are offered a different position than what you expected or are being offered a lower salary than you were expecting, it is acceptable to ask for some time to consider the offer. If you really want the position, say so. If you have another interview that day, do not keep one employer dangling to see if someone else might have a better offer.

Should you not be made an offer, but you have no indication that you are being rejected, ask the interviewer when he or she will be ready with a decision. Ask if the design firm will be interviewing anyone else. Do not leave without knowing when he or she will make a decision and what the salary range is. These are important bits of information you need to make a decision.

The time of the offer or nonoffer is the best clue the interview is over. Watch for other clues such as the interviewer stacking the job application, your résumé, and his or her notes together, and the interviewer pushing his or her chair back in preparation for getting up. When the interview is over, get up and leave promptly. If an offer was made and you accepted it, many interviewers will take you on a brief tour of the office or studio and introduce you to some of the other employees. Be sure, at the end of this tour, that you understand what day you are to start, the time, and anything else that needs to be taken care of by you either prior to your first day or on your first day.

Typical Questions

There are many kinds of common questions that are asked in interviews. It is important to prepare yourself for these questions in advance. Any that are now considered illegal, will be discussed in the following section. In an interior design interview there are several questions that are commonly posed to prospective design staff employees. These questions are provided in Figure 27–9.

Illegal Questions

There are many questions that can no longer be asked in a job interview or appear on a job application. These questions relate to age, sex, religion, and ethnic origin (see Figure 27–10). Many questions that do not seem to indicate sexual discrimination actually do. Questions to women related to whether one is single or married, what one's husband does for a living, whether or not she plans to have children are all considered illegal. These discriminatory kinds of questions and responses must not form the basis for deciding to offer or not offer a job to an individual.

There are ways to ask certain "discriminatory" questions so as to make them legal. This is especially true if the question and response has a direct bearing on the ability of the individual to perform the job. Although it is illegal to ask you, "How old are you," it is legal to ask, "Are you between the ages of 25 and 45?"

When you are asked a question that you believe to be illegal or that you feel uncomfortable in answering, you must be prepared to say something. Many of the job-hunting books suggest that you either answer the question anyway, forget about it, or say something like, "I do not understand what that has to do with the requirements of the job or my qualifications

---

[1]Loebelson 1993.

Common Interview Questions

General Questions For Any Candidate

Why do you wish to work for _____ ?

How did you hear about _____ ?

How much compensation are you expecting?

Have you applied to any other companies?

Tell me about the qualifications you have for this position.

Are you willing to do the traveling out of town that is necessary for this position?

Tell me about yourself.

How long have you lived in this city?

Describe what you consider to be your weaknesses.

How do you plan to overcome those weaknesses?

Could you name a co-worker that we could contact that could tell us something about you?

For Entry Level Positions

Why did you select the college or school you attended?

Why did you select a major in interior design?

Did you have any leadership experience in college?

How do you think your colleagues in your major would describe you?

How do you view this job in relationship to your long-term goals?

Tell me about how you worked on design projects at school. Did you find it comfortable to
    work in the classroom studio?

For Candidates With Prior Professional Experience

Tell me about your previous experience and how those positions relate to this position.

How do you think you can best contribute to this firm?

Why are you looking for another position?

You appear to be over qualified for this position. Why are you applying for this position?

If you are offered a position with this company, tell me what you would do during the first
    month on the job.

How do you think your present boss would describe you?

May we contact your present employer?

Please tell me how many days of work you missed last year.

Figure 27–9 Commonly asked interview questions.

Interview Questions

Subject	Legal	Illegal
Age	Are you between 40 and 70 years of age? If not, state your age.	How old are you? What is your date of birth? Why did you decide to seek employment at your age?
Color		What is your skin coloring?
National Origin		What is you ancestry? What is your mother's native language? What is you spouse's nationality? What is your maiden name?
Citizenship	Are you a citizen of the U.S.? If not, do you intend to become one?	Of what country are you a citizen? Are your parents or spouse naturalized or native-born citizens? When did they acquire citizenship? Are you a native-born citizen?
Language	What languages do you speak and write fluently?	What is your native tongue? How did you acquire the ability to read, write and speak a foreign language?
Relatives	Do you have relatives already employed by this company?	Names, addresses, ages and other information concerning your spouse, children or relatives not employed by the company. What type of work does you mother/father do?
Marital Status		What is your marital status? Where does you spouse work? What does you spouse do? When do you plan to marry? Do you plan on having children? Who will care for the children while you work? What is you spouse's health insurance coverage? How much does your spouse earn? What are you views on the ERA? Are you a feminist? Do you advocate the use of birth control or family planning?
Arrest Record	Have you ever been convicted of a crime? Do you have a valid driver's license?	Have you ever been arrested?
Organizations	List all organizations in which your membership is relevant to this job.	List all clubs, societies and lodges to which you belong.
Religion		What is your religion? Are you available to work on the Sabbath? What religious holidays do you observe?

From *DON'T GET TAKEN* © 1985 by Steven Sack. Reprinted by permission of M^CGraw-Hill Book Company

Figure 27–10 This chart shows the questions that are illegal to be asked during a job interview. (From: *The Employee Rights Handbook* by Steven Mitchell Sack. Copyright (©) 1991 by Steven Mitchell Sack. Reprinted with permission by FACTS on File, Inc., New York).

to do the job." Many interviewers may not have hired anyone for some time and may not be aware that some questions cannot be legally asked anymore. Making a big issue of such questions, if you honestly feel the person is asking the question innocently, could mean not getting the job. If the interviewer asks too many of these kinds of questions or ignores your hesitancy to answer, you always have the right to terminate the interview and choose to obtain a job somewhere else.

The whole question of discrimination in hiring decisions is still in its infancy. Although

Judith Jones
5217 Prospect Street
Ft. Collins, Colorado 80525
(303) 555-0142

March 30, 1986

Mr. William Green, Director of Design
Practical Interiors
2300 S. College
Ft. Collins, Colorado 80526

Dear Mr. Green:

Thank you for giving me the opportunity to meet with you yesterday and learn about your design organization.

While you interview the other individuals you are considering, I hope you will take the time to examine my resume and will decide in my favor for the position of Project Designer. I feel confident in my ability to be a productive contributor to the on-going success of your firm.

I would like to review three important facts that show I am the most qualified candidate for the position of Project Designer. First, I have three years experience with a full-service independent design firm where my assignments required the utilization of all the traditional design skills in both residential and commercial design. Second, my proven sales skills affirm my ability to successfully work with clients. Third, my successful completion of the NCIDQ examination so recently after entering the profession confirms my dedication to my professional growth.

Should you need any further information I will be happy to provide it. I look forward to your positive response to my application at the end of the week when you conclude your remaining interviews.

Sincerely,

Judith Jones

Figure 27–11 Follow-up thank-you letter after a job interview.

legal cases are being heard, there is still a large gray area. You must decide whether or not you want to work at a firm that appears to discriminate.

Follow-Up

It is important that as soon after the interview as is practical, you make notes to yourself about what transpired. This is true whether you have accepted an offer, rejected an offer, or not even received an offer. Notes related to salary, benefits, expected performance levels, and general impressions of the firm will be important if you have not made a decision about the company or the company has not made a decision about you. If an offer was not made or you were rejected, these notes will help you understand what may have gone wrong so that you can correct the errors for future interviews. These same bits of information are necessary to be sure that agreed upon responsibilities are the responsibilities on which you will later be evaluated.

Good business etiquette also calls for you to send a thank-you letter to the interviewer immediately after the interview (see Figure 27–11). Thank the interviewer for his or her time, restate your interest in the position, if you are still interested, and follow through on any promised information you agreed to still supply.

If you were offered a position but asked for time to consider, it is best if you both call the interviewer promptly and follow with a refusal or acceptance letter. In this way, the company knows whether or not you are interested in the position and, in the case of a refusal, has a letter for company records.

If you are still interested in a position with the firm when you know that the firm will be interviewing others, it is necessary to keep the design firm interested in you. Be sure to add a short paragraph to summarize your qualifications and how you now see that you can contribute to the company.

Follow-up is a way of continuing the good impression of yourself to the employer. This short note, which should still be typed using good business-letter form, will indicate to the employer that you are a professional. Even if the firm does not have an opening for you now, you will be remembered later.

Summary

Each of us grows in our own way seeking fulfillment in our careers. As the professional gains experience in the field, he or she seeks greater levels of responsibility and challenges in the workplace. Often, it is necessary to seek new responsibility in other firms, even other cities. For the student, the first job is an important first step in a successful and satisfying career in the profession. Obtaining these positions does not come easily to most of us.

At one time or another, preparing portfolios and résumés, and embarking on the job search and the stressful interview process will affect all who read this book. It is hoped that the information in this chapter will help each level of professional make the search and achievement of the "right" position possible.

References

American Society of Interior Designers. April 1981. "Preparing Your Portfolio." *Report.*

Angel, Dr. Juvenal L. 1980. *The Complete Résumé Book and Job-Getter's Guide.* New York: Pocket Books.

Bolles, Richard Nelson. 1993. *1993 What Color Is Your Parachute?* Berkeley, Calif.: Ten Speed Press. (Note: a new edition of this book is published every year.)

Catalyst Publications. 1980. *Marketing Yourself.* New York: Bantam Books (Putnam).

Goodale, James G. 1992. *One to One.* New York: Prentice Hall.

Josefowitz, Natasha. 1980. *Paths to Power.* Reading, Mass.: Addison-Wesley Publishing.

Loebelson, Andrew. 1993. January and July. "The 100 Interior Design Giants." *Interior Design.*

MacMillan, Pat. 1992. *Hiring Excellence.* Colorado Springs, Col.: NavPress Publishing Group.

Marquand, Ed. 1981. *How to Prepare Your Portfolio.* rev. ed. New York: Art Direction.

McLaughlin, John E., and Stephen K. Merman. 1980. *Writing a Job-Winning Résumé.* Englewood Cliffs, N.J.: Prentice-Hall.

Piotrowski, Christine M. 1992. *Interior Design Management.* New York: Van Nostrand Reinhold.

Sack, Steven Mitchell. 1990. *The Employee Rights Handbook.* New York: Facts on File.

Stoltenber, John. April, 1987. "The Eight Laws of the Jungle." *Working Woman.*

Wilson, Robert F., and Adele Lewis. 1983. *Better Résumés for Executives and Professionals.* Woodbury, N.Y.: Barron's Educational Series.

Yate, Martin. 1990. *Hiring the Best,* 3d ed. Holbrook, Mass.: Bob Adams.

Glossary

Acceptance. Acceptance in contract law means that one person agrees exactly to the conditions in the contract set by the other party.

Accounts Payable. Claims from suppliers for goods or services ordered (and possibly delivered) but not yet paid for.

Accounts Receivable. The account that shows what others owe to the firm as a result of sales or billings for goods and services.

Accrual Accounting. An accounting method where revenues and expenses are recognized at the time they are earned (in the case of revenues) or incurred (in the case of expenses) whether the revenue has actually been collected or the expense actually paid.

Accrued Expenses. Expenses owed to others for the period, but not yet paid. Salary owed during an accounting period but not yet paid is an example.

Acknowledgments. The paperwork forms that the supplier sends to the designer to indicate what the supplier interpreted the designer's order to be.

Addenda. Corrections or changes are made to the contract documents by the issuance of addenda (*addendum* is the singular form). Addenda are written by the person or firm responsible for the original set of contract documents.

Advertising. Any kind of paid communication in media such as newspapers, magazines, television, or radio.

Agency Relationship. The common-law relationship in which one person or entity agrees to represent or do business for another person or entity. Today's employer-employee relationship is a reflection of the agency relationship.

Agreement. In contract law, a contract must be agreed to by both parties. Agreement must include an offer and an acceptance.

Allied Board of Trade. A national credit agency that specializes in the interior design industry.

Amortize. The accounting concept in which the value of intangible assets such as copyrights, patents, and trademarks are reduced. Similar to depreciation.

Annual Business Plan. A systematic investigation and written report of what the firm can do, what the client base of the firm demands, and what the firm then decides to try to accomplish for the year. The plan should contain information related to all areas of the business.

Arbitration. When a disinterested third party evaluates the arguments of two parties to a contract.

Assets. Any kind of resource—tangible or intangible—that the firm owns or controls and that can be measured in monetary terms.

Balance Sheet. An accounting form that shows the financial position of a firm as of a particular moment in time with a statement of its assets and equities.

Bar Charts. A scheduling method consisting of a description of tasks required in the left-hand margin, and horizontal bars on the right-hand side showing the time in days, weeks, or months required to complete the task.

Barrier-Free. Codes created and enforced to make public buildings more accessible to the handicapped.

Base Bid. Refers to a proprietary specification that contains an "or equal" substitution allowance. All bidders must base their bids on the goods specified by product name.

Basis of the Bargain. Information provided by a salesperson that is the primary influence on the buyer in the decision to buy.

Benefits Selling. A selling technique whereby the seller describes certain features of the product or service that relate to the needs of the client.

Bid. An offer for the amount one will pay to provide the specified goods and/or services required.

Bid Bond. Required of all bidders to assure that the designer/vendor awarded the contract will sign the contract.

Bid Form. Documents prepared by the designer or the client and provided to the bidders. The vendor (bidder's) price for the goods or services specified must be submitted on this form.

Bid Opening. The time that the owner of the project reveals who has bid on the project. In most situations, the bid opening is private and only the owners and designers responsible for creating the contract documents are present. Governmental agencies and many public utilities are required to have bid openings open to the public. In such a case, anyone may attend the bid opening and find out what others have bid for the project.

Bill of Lading. The form that the supplier provides to the truck driver to show what is being shipped and who has title to the goods.

Billing Rates. A rate combining salary, benefits, overhead, and profit that is used as the basis for charging clients for services.

Bond Forms. Legal documents used to oblige the designer/vendor to the contract as assurance that the designer/vendor will perform the requirements of the contract as agreed. Three common bond forms are the bid bond, performance bond, and the labor and materials payment bond.

Bonus Plans. Methods of paying extra compensation based on the employee's producing more than a specific personal quota.

Box Burns. Furniture damage caused when the shipping carton rubs against the fabric or frame materials.

Breach of Contract. *Breach* simply means "to break." A breach occurs when one of the parties of a contract does not perform his or her duties as spelled out in the terms of the agreement.

Breakeven Point. The point at which revenues equal expenses. At this point, the firm is neither making nor losing money.

Budgeting. Involves annual managerial goals expressed in specific quantitative terms, usually monetary terms. Budgeting encourages the manager to plan for the various events affecting the firm rather than reacting to them.

Building Codes. Regulations that primarily concern structural and mechanical features of buildings.

Building Permit. A permit granted by local governmental agencies that allows for the construction of a new building or major interior remodeling.

Buyer. A person who contracts to purchase or who purchases some good.

Cash Accounting. The accounting method whereby revenue and expense items are recognized in the period the firm actually receives the cash or actually pays the bills.

Cash Discount. An accounting term referring to an extra discount for paying the invoice promptly. A notation that commonly looks like "2/10 net 30" appears on the invoice to notify the designer of the cash discount.

Chain of Command. The organizational structure that helps everyone in the organization understand what the formal communication patterns are.

Change Order. Written permission or instructions concerning any aspect of the project that modify design concepts, construction designs, or product specifications.

Chronological Résumé. States educational and work experiences exactly when they occurred, in reverse chronological order.

Close Corporation. A corporation whose shares of stock are commonly held by only a few individuals. The stock is not sold on any of the public stock markets.

Closed Competitive Selection. An acceptable list of potential bidders who would receive notifications of impending bids.

Closed Specification. A specification that is written so that products cannot be substituted for what was specified.

Closing. The selling art of knowing when to ask for the sale.

Codes. Systematic bodies of law created by federal, state, and local jurisdictions to ensure safety.

Cold Calling. When the designer contacts potential clients that he or she has never met before.

COM (Customer's Own Material). When a designer uses a fabric on a special-ordered upholstered furniture item other than one of the fabrics available from the furniture manufacturer.

Combination Résumé. Utilizes qualities of both the chronological and functional résumé and combines them into one.

Commercial Interior Design. The branch of interior design concerned with the planning and specifying of interior materials and products used in public spaces such as offices, hotels, airports, and hospitals. It is sometimes called contract interior design because of the use of a "contract" for services.

Commission. A payment method for an agent acting on behalf of the employer. Commission relates to a percentage amount paid to the agent (interior designer) calculated on the sale of goods and/or services.

Compensation. The method of paying the employee for the work performed.

Compensatory Time. Time off during the normal work week to make up for the overtime hours worked by salaried employees.

Competitive Bidding. A process whereby the client has the opportunity to obtain comparative prices from a number of contractors and/or vendors for the construction or supply of the project.

Concealed Damage. Damage to goods that is not obvious since the original packaging is not damaged. Most often occurs when items are shipped in cartons.

Concept Selling. Explaining and obtaining approval from the client of the overall design idea. Concept selling is difficult since it involves selling intangibles.

Confirmation of Purchase. The business form that spells out what goods the designer has agreed to order or sell to the client. It is also called a purchase agreement or contract proposal.

Consideration. The "price" one pays to another party for fulfilling a contract.

Construction Documents. Legal documents consisting of working drawings, schedules, and specifications describing what is required for the completion of an architectural and/or interiors project.

Contract. A promise or agreement between two or more parties to perform or not perform some act. The performance or lack of performance of this act can be enforced by the courts.

Contract Administration Phase. The portion of the project that involves actual construction work as well as the placing of orders for all the items required. Also called the construction/installation phase.

Contract Documents Phase. Involves the final preparation of all construction or working drawings, schedules, and specifications required to build and install the design project.

Contractual Capacity. Each party to a contract must have legal competency to enter into a contract.

Copyright. The method of legally protecting, for a specified period of time, written materials and graphic designs.

Copyright Notification. In order to begin the legal protection of written materials and graphic designs, the following must appear in a conspicuous place on the work: (1) "Copyright," "COPR," or ©, (2) year of publication, and (3) the name of the copyright claimant.

Control Function. This management function requires the manager to monitor the activities of the firm and take any necessary steps to ensure that the plans, policies, and decisions of the manager and the firm are being carried out.

Corporation. An association of individuals created by statutory requirements creating a legal entity. The corporation has existence independent of its originators or any other member or stockholder. It can sue and be sued by others, can enter into contracts, commit crimes, and be punished. A corporation has powers and duties distinct from any of its members, and survives even after the death of any or all of its stockholders.

Cost-of-Living Increase. An across-the-board compensation increase meant to offset inflation.

Cost of Sales. Refers to the costs paid in the direct generation of revenues. In retail, it is called cost of goods sold; in this case, it refers to changes in inventory.

Cost Plus Percentage Mark-Up. A design fee method that allows the design firm to add a specific percentage to the net cost of the merchandise being purchased by the client.

Cost Price. The price that the designer must pay for the goods.

Credit. In accounting, this term means the right-hand side of an account.

Crime. When a person (or business, in the case of a corporation) commits a wrong against society that is regulated by statute.

Critical Path Method (CPM). A scheduling method that begins by identifying the interrelationships of the tasks to be performed. This analysis shows the designer which tasks must be done before the next or other tasks can be performed, thus establishing the critical path.

Debt Capital. Business loans that come from creditors such as commercial banks.

Debit. In accounting, this term means the left-hand side of an account.

Decision making. The activity of making reasonable choices between the alternatives available. An important part of the management function.

Deep Discounting. An extremely large discount from suggested retail price for very large orders.

Deferred Revenues. Revenues received for services or the future sale of goods, but the service or goods have not yet been delivered.

Delivery. Includes the activities concerned with moving tangible items from the showroom or warehouse to the job site and simply placing them in their correct locations.

Deposit. Money that is part of the purchase price prepaid by the buyer as security in contracts for the sale of goods or real estate.

Depreciation. Results from the concept that capital equipment has a limited useful life. It is intended to express the usage of a fixed asset in the firm's pursuit of revenue.

Design Development Phase. Involves the preparation of all final plans, presentation graphics, and specifications required to explain design concepts to the client.

Descriptive Specification. Describes, often in elaborate detail, the materials, workmanship, fabrication methods, and installation of the required goods.

Direct Labor. The time the various employees spend directly involved in the generation of the revenues of the firm.

Direct Personnel Expense (DPE). A number that includes, not only the salary of the employee, but also any cost of benefits such as unemployment taxes, medical insurance, and paid holidays.

Discount. A reduction, usually stated as a percentage, from the suggested retail price. A full or normal discount from suggested retail is 50 percent.

Doing Business as (DBA). A filing required when the name of the business is other than the names of the owners.

Domestic Corporation. A corporation formed in one state and doing business in that state only. Domestic corporations are also corporations formed within the United States.

Door-to-Door. The client is charged from the time the delivery truck (or others) leaves the designer's warehouse to the time it leaves the client's location.

Down Payment. A portion of the total selling price paid at the time goods are ordered.

Drawings. In accounting, drawings are the withdrawals from the profits of a business by owners in proprietorships and partnerships.

Drop-Ship. When the designer requests that the manufacturer ship goods to an address other than the designer's business location or warehouse.

Dun and Bradstreet (D & B). A national credit agency that gathers information on businesses.

Earnest Money. A sum of money paid by a buyer primarily when a contract for the purchase of goods or real estate has been created.

80/20 Rule. A business rule used in many situations. For example, from a list of ten items arranged in the order of importance, if one accomplishes only the two most important items, one achieves 80 percent of the total value of time spent.

Employment at Will. The doctrine that an employee, who is not bound by a written contract and who has no written terms of his or her employment spelled out, has the right to quit his or her job without notice and can also be fired by the employer at any time with no explanation.

Employee Handbook. A concise reference of company policies for all employees.

Entrepreneur. Someone who starts and manages his or her own business.

Equity Capital. Business funding that comes from investors such as stockholders.

Equities. Claims on a balance sheet by outsiders and/or owners against the total assets of the firm.

Ethical Standards. Define what is right and wrong in relation to the professional behavior of the members and even the practice of the profession.

Expediter. An individual familiar with the design firm's paperwork system and the various ordering and shipping requirements of manufacturers. The expediter is responsible for the speedy processing of orders.

Expenses. The amount of outflows of resources of a firm as a consequence of the efforts made by the firm to earn revenues.

Express Warranties. Promises, claims, descriptions, or affirmations made about a product's performance, quality, or condition that form the "basis of the bargain."

FF & E. (Furniture, Furnishings, and Equipment). Nickname for projects that have minimal or no construction work involved.

Feasibility Studies. In-depth estimates of the cost of planning and specification of a project undertaken prior to any actual planning.

Features. Descriptions of specific aspects or characteristics of a service or product. Used during selling.

Firm Offer. When a merchant makes an offer in writing, whether or not any consideration has been given by a buyer.

Financial Accounting. Concerned with reporting accounting information for use by individuals outside or inside the firm.

Financial Management Control. Concerned with the planning and analysis of all the financial aspects of the firm to help internal individuals manage and control the performance of the firm. Often called managerial accounting.

Fire and Life-Safety Codes. Regulations to provide a reasonable measure of safety in a building from fire, explosions, or other comparable emergencies.

Flat-Fee Method. The designer determines some dollar value to perform all the services required of a project. The client is then charged that amount whether the project takes a time shorter or longer than the estimate.

FOB (Free on Board). The shipper must assume the expense of loading the goods onto the truck as well as the expense and risk for shipping the goods to the FOB destination. Also referred to as "freight on board."

FOB, Destination. The manufacturer retains ownership of the goods, pays all shipping expense, and assumes all risks until the goods reach the delivery destination.

FOB, Factory. The buyer assumes ownership or title of the goods when they are loaded on the truck at the factory. The buyer assumes the transportation expenses and all risks.

Foreign Corporation. A corporation formed in one state but doing business in another state is referred to by the other state as a foreign corporation.

Freight Bill. The bill from the shipping company for moving the goods from the supplier to the designer or receiving location.

Fringe Benefits. Direct or indirect additional payments to the employee for the work performed. Benefits may include paid vacations, profit-sharing programs, and group health insurance.

Functional Résumé. Presents information to emphasize qualifications and skills, rather than the order in which they were obtained.

General Conditions. Documents that set forth the legal responsibilities, procedures, rights, and duties of each party to a construction project. A part of the bid documents.

General Contractors. Individuals or companies that hold licenses to contract and supervise all phases of a construction project.

General Partnership. Two or more people joining together for the purpose of forming a business. These people alone share in the profits and risks of the business.

Goals. Broad statements, without regard to any time limit, of what the firm wishes to achieve.

Goods. Tangible items have physical existence and can be moved.

Gross Margin. The difference between revenues and cost of sales. Represents the amount of revenue available to cover overhead (selling and administrative) expenses.

Gross Profit. Another term for *gross margin*. Does not represent profit.

Gross Revenue. All the revenue, prior to any deductions, generated by the firm for the accounting period.

Gross Salary. The amount of employee compensation before any deductions.

Hourly Fee. The most commonly charged fee. It is based on the firm's direct personnel expense. For each hour or portion of an hour that the designer works on the project, the client is charged some dollar amount.

Hourly Wage. A compensation method in which the employee is paid some amount per hour for every hour worked.

Implied Contract. Contracts formed by the actions of the parties rather than by express written agreement.

Incentive Compensation. Compensation payment over and above regular compensation.

Income Statement. An accounting report that formally reports all the revenues and expenses of the firm for a stated period of time. The result shows the net income (or loss) for the firm during the period.

Incorporate. To create a corporation.

Incorporation. The act or process of forming a corporation.

Independent Contractor. Someone who works for himself or herself and is not subject to the control of an employer.

Infringement. Any unauthorized use of copyrighted materials.

Installation. The specialized part of the delivery process that involves assembly, construction, or physical attachments of products to the building.

Instructions to Bidders. A document that informs bidders how to prepare bids for submittal so that all submittals are in the same form.

Inventory. Goods purchased and held by the business for resale to clients.

Invitation to Bid. Provides a summary of the project, the bid process, and other brief pertinent procedures for the project. It informs potential bidders of the project, its scope, and where to obtain further information.

Invoice. A bill that is sent from the manufacturer or supplier to the designer indicating how much the designer must pay. The designer also uses an invoice to bill the client for goods and/or services provided.

Job Descriptions. Communicates the qualifications, skills, and responsibilities of each job classification within a design firm.

Joint Venture. A temporary contractual association of two or more persons or firms who agree to share in the responsibilities, losses, and profits of a particular project or business venture.

Journal. In accounting, a chronological record of all accounting transactions for the firm.

Labor and Materials Payment Bond. Required of the winning bidder to guarantee that, should the designer/vendor default on the project, the designer/vendor will be responsible for paying for all the materials and labor that has been contracted for.

Ledger. In accounting, the ledger is a group of accounts. Sometimes called a general ledger.

Letter of Agreement. A simplified form of contract.

Liabilities. In accounting, amounts that the firm owes to others due to past transactions or events. Liabilities always have first claim on the firm's assets.

Lien. Someone other than the person who has ownership or possession of goods has a security interest in the goods.

Limited Partnership. A business formation created according to statutory requirements. A limited partnership is formed with at least one general partner and one or more partners designated as limited partners.

Line Item Number. On a sales order, items are identified in numerical order. This number helps to cross-reference merchandise to purchase orders and other documents.

Line of Credit. Short-term business loans that last for one year or less.

List Price. Generally accepted to be the same as suggested retail price—a price to the consumer.

Logo. A symbolic image of a company or organization.

Lyons Furniture Mercantile Agency. A credit agency used by retail furniture, accessories, and interior furnishings stores.

Markdown. A term used in retail to represent discounts taken from the normal selling price.

Market. In reference to designer resources, a term that many interior designers use to mean they are going to visit one of the annual shows held at the marts.

Markup. A term used in retail to represent percentage amounts (converted to dollars) added to the net or cost price to the designer.

Market Centers. Concentrations of trade sources in one area of a city.

Marketing. Includes all the activities of moving goods and services from producers to consumers.

Marketing Analysis. Involves gathering and analyzing data concerning such things as the abilities and interests of the staff, potential clients, the economy, and the competition in order to make better plans and decisions about the direction of the firm's business efforts.

Marts. Where many firms have located in one building.

Mechanics Lien. A legal recourse related to the labor and materials payment bond. It is an action that prevents the owner of the property of giving or selling the property to anyone until the lien is satisfied.

Merchant. Anyone who is involved with the buying and/or selling of the kinds of goods with which he or she is dealing. A person acting in a mercantile capacity.

Merit Pay. An amount added to an individual's basic annual compensation amount, often for the reward of quality work done in the past.

Milestone Charts. An easy scheduling method whereby the designer outlines the activities required by the project and establishes a target date for the completion of each task.

Misrepresentation. The altering of facts to deceive or use fraud in order to receive personal gain.

Mission Statement. A philosophical statement of what the firm sees as its role in the profession. It contains broad statements of what the company wishes to achieve during an unspecified time period.

Modifications. Changes in the construction documents. (see Addenda and Change Order).

Moonlight. When an individual holds or engages in work outside his or her main job.

Multiple Discounts. A series of discounts from the suggested retail price given by manufacturers to designers for very large orders.

Negligence. A failure by one party to use due care so that injury is sustained by another person or a person's property.

Negotiating. Where two parties are trying to reach agreement about some point of discussion.

Net Income (Loss). The amount of income or loss that results when all expenses are subtracted from revenues. If the result is positive, net income represents the dollar amount of profit the firm made for the period. If the result is negative, net loss indicates that expenses exceeded revenues for the period.

Net Price. A price representing a 50 percent discount from suggested retail.

Nonconforming Goods. Any goods that are not as described in a sales order or purchase order.

Objectives. Specific statements combined with time limits aimed toward accomplishing the firm's goals.

Offer. In contract law, one party makes an offer to provide something or do something for another party.

Open Competitive Selection. When clients such as government agencies advertise impending bids so that anyone interested in the project who meets qualifications may submit a bid.

Open Specification. A bid specification written in such a way as to allow multiple numbers of products for the item being required.

"Or equal." A term in a specification that allows bidders to substitute what they believe to be products of equal quality to that which was specified.

Overhead Expenses. Those expenses that are incurred whether the firm produces any revenues or not. Also called selling and administrative expenses.

Owner's Equity. The section on the balance sheet showing the amount the owners have invested in the firm.

Packing List. A detailed list of the quantities and descriptions of what is being shipped to the designer from a manufacturer or supplier. It is commonly in a plastic envelope attached to the outside of one of the items.

Percentage of Merchandise and Product Services. A fee method that allows the designer to negotiate a percentage of profit on the cost of the goods and installation what will be involved in the project.

Per Diem. A dollar amount that is charged to the client to cover hotel, meals, and transportation costs when it is necessary for the designer to travel out of town in the interests of the project.

Performance. In contract law, when each party does or provides what was agreed to in the contract, performance has occurred.

Performance Bond. Required of the winning bidder as a guarantee that the designer/vendor will complete the work as specified and will protect the client from any loss up to the amount of the bond as a result of the failure of the designer/vendor to perform the contract.

Performance Evaluation. Systematic evaluation of positive and negative work efforts of an employee. It is used to review past performance in relation to agreed-upon responsibilities to form the basis of salary increases, promotions, and/or retention.

Performance Reports. Managerial reports that consist primarily of financial or other numeric information and are used to evaluate the performance of many aspects of a business.

Performance Specification. A specification establishing product requirements based on exacting performance criteria. These criteria must be based on qualitative or measurable statements.

Personal Goals. Concrete ideas representing some kind of end that a person tries to achieve.

Photo Portfolio. A collection of photographs, slides, or other photographic media which represent projects for which the designer was responsible. Used as a promotional tool.

Planning. Involves research of capabilities and resources in order to provide a direction for the firm.

Portfolio. A visual presentation of what the individual can do as an interior designer.

Postoccupancy Evaluation (POE). Site visit and project review conducted to evaluate the existence of any problems in the design and installation of a project.

Practice Acts. Guidelines established by legislation as to what a person can or cannot do in the practice of a profession in a particular state. Individuals whose profession is guided by practice acts must register with a state board and meet exacting requirements.

Prepaid Expense. The early payment of expenses in a period prior to their being required. The prepaid expense is an asset since the value of the prepaid expense, not yet due, still has value to the owner.

Press Release. Information provided by the design firm or its representatives that might be of interest to news media.

Price. Any kind of payment from buyer to seller including money, goods, services, or real property.

Private Corporation. A special form of corporation created by persons in many professions. Its formation is regulated by state statutes.

Probing. A selling technique for asking questions in order to uncover the needs of the client.

Professional Corporation. A special corporation form created by individuals in professions such as law, architecture, and accounting.

Profit and Loss Statement. Another name for the income statement.

Pro Forma. Projected financial information such as the pro forma income statement.

Programming Phase. The information gathering portion of a design project.

Project Completion Phase. Last phase of a project that involves inspecting the job site to be sure that all work and merchandise required has been delivered and completed.

Project File. File folders or notebooks in which the designer keeps all the pertinent data and paperwork related to the project in progress.

Project Manager. Individual responsible for site visits and telephone calls to keep project on track. Also the job title for a designer who has overall responsibility for all phases of a design project.

Promotion. Providing information about services or products from the seller to the buyer. Includes publicity, publishing, advertising, and direct selling.

Proprietary Specification. Names the products and materials by manufacturer's name, model number, or part number.

Prospects. Potential clients in the firm's business area.

Prospecting. The process of locating new clients and obtaining appointments with them.

Publicity. A direct form of promotion that is unpaid.

Publication. When the creator of a copyrightable work has somehow distributed the work to others for review without restriction of use.

Public Relations. Refers to all the efforts of the firm to create an image in order to affect the public's positive opinion of a firm.

Puffing. Sales people's statements of opinion, not facts, about products

Punch List. A list prepared just prior to client move-in to record all omissions and/or damages at the job site.

Purchase Order. The business form that the designer uses to order goods and/or services for the client or to order supplies needed by the design firm.

Quantity Discount. A discount greater than the normal 50 percent discount allowed because a large quantity of merchandise is purchased at one time.

Realization Budgeting. A budget method that begins when the manager forecasts the potential revenue generation of each member of the firm.

Reference Specification. Utilizes an established standard such as the standards of the American Society for Testing and Materials (ASTM) rather than written detailed descriptions or performance criteria for required products.

Reimbursable Expenses. Those costs that are not part of the design contract but that are made in the interest of completing the project.

Representatives or "Reps." Refers to the men and women who act as the informational source to the interior designer about the various manufacturers' products. Independent reps work for themselves and are usually responsible for many different manufacturer's products. Factory reps work for only one manufacturer as an employee.

Residential Interior Design. Concerned with the planning and/or specifying of interior materials and products used in private residences.

Résumé. A summary of a designer's qualifications.

Restocking Charge. A fee charged by the designer for taking back merchandise the client ordered but does not want.

Restrictive Covenant. In an employment contract, a provision that would not allow, for example, an employee to work for a competitive employer.

Retail Method. A fee method in which the design fee is derived by charging the retail or suggested retail price for goods sold to clients.

Retail Price. Generally means the same thing as suggested retail. The price quoted to the consumer.

Retained Earnings. The claim on the assets arising from the cumulative undistributed earnings of the corporation for use in the business after dividends are paid to stockholders.

Retainer. Payments to a professional to cover future service or advice by that professional. In interior design, the retainer is customarily paid upon signing the contractual agreement.

Revenue. The amount of inflows from the sale of goods or rendering of services during an accounting period.

Sale. Occurs when the seller transfers title or ownership of the goods to a buyer and the buyer has provided some consideration to the seller.

Schedules. Used to clarify sizes, location, finishes, and other information related to certain nonconstruction parts of an interior or structure. Schedules are commonly prepared for doors, windows, and interior room finishes.

Schematic Design Phase. Involves preliminary design decisions for plans and specifications.

Secured Loan. A loan in which collateral is required as protection against nonpayment.

Seller. Any person who sells or contracts to sell goods to others.

Selling. Finding out what the client wants through the use of personal communication and providing it.

Selling and Administrative Expenses. Those expenses that are incurred whether or not the firm produces any revenues. They are often called overhead expenses and thought of as those expenses needed to keep the doors of the business open.

Selling Price. Refers to the actual price that is quoted to the client.

Sexual Harassment. Unwelcome sexual advances especially when one person supervises, hires or fires, or otherwise influences the other person's work performance or advancement.

Shop Right. Any creation or invention of tangible or intangible products that are not the result of the employee's normal working duties belong to the employee, not the employer, but can be used by the employer.

Sole Proprietorship. The simplest and least expensive form of business. The company and individual owner are one and the same.

Specific Performance. A type of remedy related to breach of contract that a court may require. The breaching party is ordered to perform the specific breached terms of the contract.

Specifications. The written instructions to the contractors and vendors concerning the materials and methods of construction or the interior products that are to be bid.

Statement of Cash Flows. An accounting statement reporting, for a specific period, the changes in cash flows from operating, investing, and financing activities.

Statute of Frauds. Statutory requirements that call for written contracts in certain circumstances. For the interior designer these include a contract for the sale of goods having a value of over $500, any contract that will take over one year to complete, and any sale of real estate.

Straight Salary. A fixed amount of salary to the employee no matter how many hours in the week he or she works.

Strategies. Specific actions as part of a business or marketing plan that have definite time limits within the year.

Strict Liability. When a person is held liable for injury to others regardless of fault.

Stocking Dealer. A vendor that stocks a certain inventory level of goods at all times. These sellers/designers often receive larger discounts because of the volume of product they carry.

S Corporation. A special form of corporation that may utilize many of the benefits of a corporation but that pays taxes as a partnership.

Subcontractor. An individual or company who is licensed to contract and perform specialized work on an interiors or construction project.

Suggested Retail Price. A term related to the price, to be used by the seller and suggested by the manufacturer.

SWOT. A marketing analysis technique. *SWOT* stands for strengths, weaknesses, opportunities, and threats.

Tag For. Information that the designer requests the manufacturer to affix to the goods and note on the invoice to help the designer deliver the goods to the correct client.

Tangible Personal Property. Any property that is movable, can be touched, or has physical existence.

Title. In sales law, title refers to the legal ownership of goods. The person who holds title to the goods, owns the goods.

Title Acts. Legislative measures concerned with limiting the use of certain titles to individuals who meet agreed-on qualifications and who have registered with a state board.

Tort. When a person commits a wrong against another and causes injury to the harmed party. Torts are civil matters and, therefore, are not legislated by statute.

Trade Discounts. Discounts given as a courtesy by some vendors to designers and others in the trade. These are usually a small percentage off retail.

Trade Sources. The groups of manufacturers, suppliers, and tradespeople who provide the various goods and services a designer uses to complete an interiors project.

Transaction Privilege Tax License. Allows the interior designer to pass on the state sales tax to the consumer. Issued by state and municipal taxing authorities.

Transmittal Letter. A form letter that can be used to send information to anyone involved with the project or from whom information is requested.

Uniform Commercial Code (UCC). The body of law that guides the relationships among the various levels of buyers and sellers in business transactions.

Use Tax. A tax on goods that a business purchases from a supplier in another state for use within the state that the purchasing business is located.

Unsecured Loan. Loans that do not require collateral as a guarantee.

Value-Oriented Fee Method. Uses the concept that the design firm prices services based on the value or quality of the services rather than the cost of doing those services.

Variance Analysis. A managerial technique in which one looks at financial and numerical data in relation to the differences between planned or budgeted amounts and actual amounts.

Vendor. Someone who sells products or services either to the end-user or to another merchant, such as the designer.

Vignette. A display of furniture and furnishings in a store or showroom that is done to simulate an actual room.

Walk-Through. A final inspection of the job to be sure that everything ordered is present, and that any omissions or damaged goods are noted.

Warranties. A statement or representation made by a seller concerning the goods. Warranties are related to quality, fitness of purpose, or title.

Wholesale Price. A special price to a merchant from a merchant at a value lower than what the good would cost the consumer.

Wrongful Discharge. Occurs when an employee is fired without good cause.

Appendix

Interior Design Professional Associations

American Society of Interior Designers (ASID)
608 Massachusetts Avenue N.E.
Washington, DC 20002
202–546–3480   FAX 202–546–3240

Association of Registered Interior Designers of Ontario (ARIDO)
717 Church Street
Toronto, ON M4W 2M5, Canada
416–921–2127

Association of University Interior Designers
University of Oklahoma
Architectural & Engineering Services
1652 Cross Center Drive
Norman, OK 73019
405–325–6006

Council of Federal Interior Designers (CFID)
P.O. Box 27565
Washington, DC 20038

Governing Board for Interior Design Standards
341 Merchandise Mart
Chicago, IL 60654
312–527–0517

Foundation for Interior Design Education Research (FIDER)
60 Monroe Center N. W.
Grand Rapids, MI 49503
616–458–0400   FAX (616) 458–0460

Institute of Business Designers (IBD)
341 Merchandise Mart
Chicago, IL 60654
312–467–1950   FAX (312) 467–0779

Interior Design Educators Council (IDEC)
14252 Culver Drive Suite A-331
Irvine, CA 92714
714–551–1622

Interior Designers of Canada (IDC)
Ontario Des. Ctr., 260 King St. East, #506
Toronto, Ontario, Canada M5A 1K3
416–964–0906

Interior Design Society (IDS)
P.O. Box 2396
High Point, NC 27261
919–883–1650

International Facility Management Association (IFMA)
1 E. Greenway Plaza, Floor 11
Houston, TX 77046
713–623–4362

International Furnishings and Design
  Association (IFDA)
107 World Trade Center
P.O. Box 58045
Dallas, TX 75258
214–747–2406

International Society of Interior
  Designers (ISID)
433 South Spring Street #1018
Los Angeles, CA 90013
213–744–1313   FAX(213)680–7704

Institute of Store Planners
25 North Broadway
Tarrytown, NY 10591
914–332–1806   FAX(914)332–1541

National Council for Interior Design
  Qualification (NCIDQ)
50 Main Street
White Plains, NY 10606
914–948–9100

National Legislative Coalition for Interior
  Design (NLCID)
202–675–2378

(Consultant to Unification Task Force)
Lawrence-Leiter and Company
427 W. 12th Street
Kansas City, MO 64105
816–474–8340

(Registry of Continuing Education Units)
American College Testing Registry
P.O. Box 1008
Iowa City, Iowa 52243
319–337–1329

Unified Voice
341 Merchandise Mart
Chicago, IL 60654
312–467–1950   FAX 312–467–0779

Allied Professional Organizations and Trade Associations

American Hospital Association
840 N. Lake Shore Drive
Chicago, IL 60611
312–280–6000

American Hotel and Motel Association
1201 New York Avenue, N. W., Suite 600
Washington, DC 20005–3931
202–289–3100

American Institute of Architects (AIA)
1735 New York Avenue N. W.
Washington, DC 20006
202–626–7300

American Society of Furniture Designers
  (ASFD)
P.O. Box 2688
521 Hamilton Street
High Point, NC 27261
919–884–4074

American Society of Landscape Architects
4401 Connecticut Avenue N. W., #500
Washington, DC 20008
202–686–2752

American Society for Testing and
  Materials (ASTM)
1916 Race Street
Philadelphia, PA 19103
215–299–5400

British Contract Furnishing Association
Suite 116, Business Design Center
52 Upper Street
London N1 OQH England
071–226–6641

Business and Institutional Furniture
  Manufacturers Association (BIFMA)
2335 Burton S. E.
Grand Rapids, MI 49506
616–243–1681

Construction Specifications Institute (CSI)
601 Madison Street
Alexandria, VA 22314–1791
703–684–0300

Contract Furnishings Council
1190 Merchandise Mart
Chicago, IL 60654
312–321–0563

Contract Furniture Dealer Div.,
National Office Products Association
301 N. Fairfax Street
Alexandria, VA 22314
703–549–9040

High Point Showroom Association
P.O. Box 175
High Point, NC 27261

Illuminating Engineering Society (IES)
345 East 47th Street
New York, NY 10017
212–705–7926

Industrial Designers Society of America
    (IDSA)
1142-E Walker Road
Great Falls, VA 22066
703–759–0100

International Association of Lighting
    Designers (IALD)
18 E. 16th Street
New York, NY 10003
212–206–1281

National Council of Acoustical
    Consultants
66 Morris Avenue,
P.O. Box 359
Springfield, NJ 07081
201–379–1100

National Fire Protection Association
    (NFPA)
Battery March Park
P.O. Box 9101
Quincy, MA 02269
617–770–3000

National Trust for Historic Preservation
1785 Massachusetts Ave. N. W.
Washington, DC 20036
202–673–4074

Ontario Ministry of Industry and
    Technology
900 Bay St. Hearst Block, 9th Floor
Queen's Park
Toronto, ON M7A 2E1 Canada
416–325–6666

Business Advisors

Allied Board of Trade, Inc.
550 Mamaroneck Avenue
Harrison, NY 10528
914–381–5200

American Bankers Association
1120 Connecticut Avenue N. W.
Washington, DC 20036
202–467–4180

American Management Association
135 West 50 Street
New York, NY 10020
212–586–8100

American Women's Economic
    Development Corporation
The Lincoln Building
60 E. 42nd Street
New York, NY 10165
212–692–9100

Ayer's Directory of Newspapers
    and Periodicals
IMS Press
426 Pennsylvania Avenue
Fort Washington, PA 19834
215–628–4920

Department of Justice (ADA inf.)
10th Street and Constitution Avenue, N.W.
Washington, DC 20530
202–724–2222

Department of Justice (Form I-9)
Immigration and Naturalization Service
425 I Street, NW
Washington, DC 20536
1–800–777–7700

Dun and Bradstreet Corp.
299 Park Avenue
New York, NY 10171
212–593–6728

Encyclopedia of Associations
Gale Research Company
Book Tower
Detroit, MI 48226
800–877–GALE
(Provides help in locating trade
    associations)

Equal Employment Opportunity
    Commission (EEOC)
1801 L Street, NW
Washington, DC 20507
800–669–3302

Minority Business Development Agency
US Department of Commerce
Washington, DC
202–377–1936

National Small Business Association
NSB Building
1604 K Street, N.W.
Washington, DC 20006
202–293–8830

Register of Copyrights
Copyright Office
Library of Congress
Washington, DC 20559
202–287–9100

Society for Marketing Professional Services
99 Canal Center Plaza Suite 320
Alexandria, VA 22314
703–549–6117

US Hispanic Chamber of Commerce
2000 M Street N. W., Suite 860
Washington, DC 20036
202–862–3939

U.S. Small Business Administration
1414 L. Street
Washington, DC 20416
800–827–5722

DEFINITION

SHORT DEFINITION The Professional Interior Designer is qualified by education, experience, and examination to enhance the function and quality of interior spaces.

For the purpose of improving the quality of life, increasing productivity, and protecting the health, safety, and welfare of the public, the Professional Interior Designer:
* analyzes the client's needs, goals, and life and safety requirements;
* integrates findings with knowledge of interior design;
* formulates preliminary design concepts that are appropriate, functional, and aesthetic;
* develops and presents final design recommendations through appropriate presentation media;
* prepares working drawings and specifications for non-load bearing interior construction, materials, finishes, space planning, furnishings, fixtures, and equipment;
* collaborates with licensed practitioners who offer professional services in the technical areas of mechanical, electrical, and load-bearing design as required for regulatory approval;
* prepares and administers bids and contract documents as the client's agent;
* reviews and evaluates design solutions during implementation and upon completion.

LONG DEFINITION (SCOPE OF SERVICES) The interior design profession provides services encompassing research, development, and implementation of plans and designs of interior environments to improve the quality of life, increase productivity, and protect the health, safety, and welfare of the public. The interior design process follows a systematic and coordinated methodology. Research, analysis, and integration of information into the creative process result in an appropriate interior environment. Practitioners may perform any or all of the following services:
Programming. Identify and analyze the client's needs and goals. Evaluate existing documentation and conditions. Assess project resources and limitations. Identify life, safety, and code requirements. Develop project schedules, work plans, and budgets. Analyze design objectives and spatial requirements. Integrate findings with their experience and knowledge of interior design. Determine the need, make recommendations, and coordinate with consultants and other specialists when required by professional practice or regulatory approval.
Conceptual Design. Formulate for client discussion and approval preliminary plans and design concepts that are appropriate and describe the character, function, and aesthetic of a project.
Design Development. Develop and present for client review and approval final design recommendations for: space planning and furnishings arrangements; wall, window, floor, and ceiling treatments; furnishings, fixtures, and millwork; color, finishes, and hardware; and lighting, electrical, and communications requirements. Develop art, accessory, and graphic/signage programs. Develop budgets. Presentation media can include drawings, sketches, perspectives, renderings, color and material boards, photographs, and models.
Contract Documents. Prepare working drawings and specifications for non-load bearing interior construction, materials, finishes, furnishings, fixtures, and equipment for client's approval. Collaborate with specialty consultants and licensed practitioners who offer professional services in the technical areas of mechanical, electrical, and load-bearing design as required by professional practice or regulatory approval. Identify qualified vendors. Prepare bid documentation. Collect and review bids. Assist clients in awarding contracts.
Contract Administration. Administer contract documents as the client's agent. Confirm required permits are obtained. Review and approve shop drawings and samples to assure they are consistent with design concepts. Conduct on-site visits and field inspections. Monitor contractors' and suppliers progress. Oversee on their clients' behalf the installation of furnishings, fixtures, and equipment. Prepare lists of deficiencies for the client's use.
Evaluation. Review and evaluate the implementation of projects while in progress and upon completion as representative of and on behalf of the client.

NATIONAL COUNCIL FOR INTERIOR DESIGN QUALIFICATION

Reprinted with permission, the National Council for Interior Design Qualification.

American Society of Interior Designers

ASID CODE OF ETHICS AND PROFESSIONAL CONDUCT

1.0   PREAMBLE

Members of the American Society of Interior Designers are required to conduct their professional practice in a manner that will command the respect of clients, suppliers of goods and services to the profession, and fellow professional designers, as well as the general public. It is the individual responsibility of every member of the Society to uphold this Code and the ByLaws of the Society.

2.0   RESPONSIBILITY TO THE PUBLIC

2.1   Members shall comply with all existing laws, regulations and codes governing business procedures and the practice of interior design as established by the state or other jurisdiction in which they practice.

2.2   Members shall not seal or sign drawings, specifications, or other interior design documents except where the member or the member's firm has prepared, supervised or professionally reviewed and approved such documents.

2.3   Members shall at all times consider the health, safety and welfare of the public in spaces they design. Members agree, whenever possible, to notify property managers, landlords, and/or public officials of conditions within a built environment that endanger the health, safety and/or welfare of occupants.

2.4   Members shall not engage in any form of false or misleading advertising or promotional activities and shall not imply through advertising or other means that staff members or employees of their firm are qualified interior designers unless such be the fact.

2.5   Members shall not take any action intended to influence the judgement of a public official for the purposes of any project.

2.6   Members shall not assist or abet improper or illegal conduct of anyone in connection with a project.

3.0   RESPONSIBILITY TO THE CLIENT

3.1   Members' contracts with a client shall clearly set forth the scope and nature of the project involved, the services to be performed and the method of compensation for those services.

3.2   Members may offer professional services to a client for any form of legal compensation.

CODE OF ETHICS, American Society of Interior Designers

3.3   Members shall not undertake any professional responsibility unless they are, by training and experience, competent to adequately perform the work required.

3.4   Members shall fully disclose to a client all compensation which the Member shall receive in connection with the project and shall not accept any form of undisclosed compensation from any person or firm with whom the member deals in connection with the project.

3.5   Members shall not divulge any confidential information about the client or the client's project, or utilize photographs or specifications of the project, without the express permission of the client, with an exception for those specifications or drawings over which the designer retains proprietary rights.

3.6   Members shall be candid and truthful in all their professional communications.

3.7   Members shall act with fiscal responsibility in the best interest of their clients and shall maintain sound business relationships with suppliers, industry and trades to insure the best service possible to the public.

4.0   RESPONSIBILITY TO OTHER INTERIOR DESIGNERS AND COLLEAGUES

4.1   Members shall not interfere with the performance of another interior designer's contractural or professional relationship with a client.

4.2   Members shall not initiate, or participate in, any discussion or activity which might result in an unjust injury to another interior designer's reputation or business relationships.

4.3   Members may, when requested and it does not present a conflict of interest, render a second opinion to a client, or serve as an expert witness in a judicial or arbitration proceeding.

4.4   Members shall not endorse the application for ASID membership and/or certification, registration or licensing of an individual known to be unqualified with respect to education, training, experience or character, nor shall a Member knowingly misrepresent the experience, professional expertise or moral character of that individual.

4.5   Members shall only take credit for work that has actually been created by that Member or the Member's firm, and under the Member's supervision.

5.0   RESPONSIBILITY TO THE PROFESSION

5.1   Members agree to maintain standards of professional and personal conduct that will reflect in a responsible manner on the Society and the profession.

5.2   Members shall seek to continually upgrade their professional knowledge and competency with respect to the interior design profession.

5.3   Members agree, whenever possible, to encourage and contribute to the sharing of knowledge and information between interior designers and other allied professional disciplines, industry and the public.

6.0   ENFORCEMENT

6.1   The Society shall follow standard procedures for the enforcement of this Code as approved by the Society's Board of Directors.

6.2   Members having a reasonable belief, based upon substantial information, that another member has acted in violation of this Code, shall report such information in accordance with accepted procedures.

6.3   Any deviation from this Code, or any action taken by a Member which is detrimental to the Society and the profession as a whole shall be deemed unprofessional conduct subject to discipline by the Society's Board of Directors.

CODE OF
PROFESSIONAL CONDUCT

OBJECT OF THE CODE

The object is to state the principles of ethical standards related to the practice of design which are accepted by all Members of IBD.

DEFINITIONS

For the purpose of the Code, the word "Designer"

A.   shall deem to include:
    I.   Designers concerned with graphics and visual communication.

    II.   Designers concerned with products and capital goods.

    III.   Interior architects/interior designers

B.   shall mean an individual, practicing design as a freelance or salaried designer, or group of designers, acting in partnership or within other forms of association.

OBLIGATION OF MEMBER

1.   The Designer's responsibility to the community

A.   A Designer accepts a professional obligation to further the social and aesthetic standards of the community.

B.   A Designer shall act in keeping with the honor and dignity of his profession.

C.   A Designer shall not consciously assume or accept a position in which his personal interests conflict with his professional duty.

2.   The Designer's responsibility to his client

A.   A Designer shall act in his client's interests within the limits of his professional duties.

B.   A Designer shall not work simultaneously on assignments which are in direct competition without informing the clients or employers concerned, except in specific cases where it is customary for the Designer to work at the same time for various competitors.

C.   A Designer shall treat all knowledge of his client's intentions, production methods and/or business organization as confidential and shall not, at any time divulge such information without the consent of his client. It is the designer's responsibility to ensure that all members of his staff are similarly bound to confidentiality.

Reprinted with permission, Institute of Business Designers.

3.   The Designer's responsibility to other designers

A.   A Designer must not attempt, directly or indirectly, to supplant another designer, nor must he compete with another designer by means of deliberate reduction of fee or by other unfair inducement. A Designer shall not knowingly accept any professional assignment upon which another designer has been acting without notifying the other designer.

B.   A Designer shall not accept instructions from his client which knowingly involve plagiarism, nor shall he consciously act in a manner involving plagiarism.

4.   Designer's remuneration

A.   A Designer shall not undertake any work at the initiation of a client without payment of an appropriate fee.

A Designer may, however, undertake work without fee or at a reduced rate for charitable or non-profit organizations.

B.   Before accepting an assignment the Designer shall define exactly and comprehensively to the client the basis on which his total remuneration is calculated.

C.   A Designer who is financially concerned with any company, firm or business which may benefit from any recommendations made by him in the course of his work shall notify his client or employer of this fact in advance.

D.   A Designer who is asked to advise on the selection of designers shall accept no payment in any form from the designer recommended.

5.   Publicity

A.   Any advertising or publicity material must contain only truthful factual statements. It must be fair to clients and other designers, and in accordance with the dignity of the profession.

B.   A Designer may allow his clients to use his name for the promotion of articles he has designed or services which he has provided but only in a manner which is appropriate to the status of the profession.

C.   A Designer shall not allow his name to be associated with the realization of a design which has been so changed by the client as no longer to be substantially the original work of the designer.

ACKNOWLEDGEMENT

The Model Code of Professional Conduct for Designers was adopted by the National Board in Chicago, June 11, 1989 and by the General Assembly of IFI in Hamburg, May 25, 1983.

INSTITUTE OF
BUSINESS DESIGNERS
NATIONAL OFFICE
341 MERCHANDISE MART
CHICAGO, ILLINOIS 60654-1104
312/467-1950
FAX 312/467-0779

Index